CYPRUS

Latakia
Banias
Hama
Homs

Tripoli
Jebel Tourbol

LEBANON

Baalbek
Rayak
Damascus

SYRIA

Beirut

Alexandretta
El Hamman
Afrine
Katma
Aleppo
edaine Ekbes
Azaz
Raju
Akterine

Tyre
Acre
Haifa

Amman

Tel Aviv
Jaffa

Jerusalem

Gaza
Rafah
El Arish

ISRAEL
(Palestine)

Maan

JORDAN

SEA

AN

Port Said

El Kantara

Ismailia

Suez

Alexandria
El Amirya
Ikingi Maryut
El Hamam
Damanhur
Zagazig
CAIRO

El Daba
El Alamein

October
1942

Qatara Depression

A.D.S. '83

DEDICATED
TO OUR TRADITION OF SERVICE

The Queen's Colours above the Regimental Colours
of the 17th Battalion – The North Sydney Regiment.

"WHAT WE HAVE WE HOLD!"

A HISTORY OF THE

2/17 Australian Infantry Battalion

1940-1945

BATTLE HONOURS
17TH INFANTRY BATTALION AMF

SUAKIN, 1885

The Honorary Distinction "SUAKIN, 1885" was granted in 1907 by King Edward VII to the Ist Australian Infantry Regiment, whose colonial predecessor, Ist Regiment of New South Wales Infantry, was represented in the New South Wales Contingent to the Sudan in 1885. Through its lineage and area association, this distinction was inherited by 17th Infantry Battalion in 1921. (Military Order 196/1907).

SOUTH AFRICA, 1899 - 1902

The Honorary Distinction "SOUTH AFRICA, 1899 – 1902" was granted by King Edward VII in 1908, to 1st Australian Infantry Regiment, whose colonial predecessor, 1st Regiment of New South Wales Infantry, provided drafts for service, firstly as infantry and latterly as mounted riflemen, for service in South Africa during the Second Boer War. This distinction was inherited by 17th Infantry Battalion in 1921 through its lineage and area association. (Military Order 123/1908).

WON BY THE 17TH BATTALION AIF IN THE GREAT WAR 1914-1918
Awarded to the 17th Battalion by Australian Army Order 112 of 1927.

THE GREAT WAR:
SOMME – 1916-18, POZIERES, BAPAUME – 1917, BULLECOURT, YPRES – 1917, MENIN ROAD, Polygon Wood, Broodseinde, Poelcappelle, Passchendaele, Hamel, AMIENS, Albert – 1918, MONTE ST QUENTIN, HINDENBURG LINE, Beaurevoir, France and Flanders – 1916-18, Suvla, GALLIPOLI – 1915, Egypt – 1915-16

WON BY THE 2/17 AUSTRALIAN INFANTRY BATTALION AIF IN THE SECOND WORLD WAR, 1939-1945
Awarded to the 17th Infantry Battalion (Australian Army Order 135 of 1961).

NORTH AFRICA – 1941-42, DEFENCE OF TOBRUK, EL ADEM ROAD, Alam El Halfa, EL ALAMEIN, South West Pacific – 1943-45, LAE-NADZAB, FINSCHHAFEN, SCARLET BEACH, Defence of Scarlet Beach, JIVENANENG* – KUMAWA, Liberation of Australian New Guinea, Sio, BORNEO, BRUNEI, Miri.

NOTES:

1. There is no limit to the number of honours that can be won. Only a controlled number can be emblazoned on the Colours. These are chosen by the participants as the most important. CAPITALS indicate the honours on the Colours of the 17th Battalion (The North Sydney Regiment) laid up in the Church of Saint Thomas, North Sydney, which overhang the Battalion's Memorial Area. Only a selection of Battle Honours is carried on the Colours of the present day linked serving unit, the 2nd/17th Battalion, Royal New South Wales Regiment.

* The Australian Army record has erred in the spelling of Jivevaneng.

First published by the 2/17 Battalion History Committee - 1990

This revised edition published in Australia - 1998
by AUSTRALIAN MILITARY HISTORY PUBLICATIONS:
13 Veronica Place, Loftus. 2232. Australia.
Phone/Fax: (02) 9521- 6515 or 015-284-760

Printed in Australia by Ligare Pty. Ltd. NSW

New artwork by Peninsular Grafics - Caringbah. NSW.

New typesetting by Typesmith - South Hurstville. NSW.

National Library of Australia

ISBN: 1-876439-36-X

THE COLOUR PATCHES OF AUSTRALIAN UNITS COMMANDED BY
9 DIVISION DURING THE SIEGE OF TOBRUK, 1941.

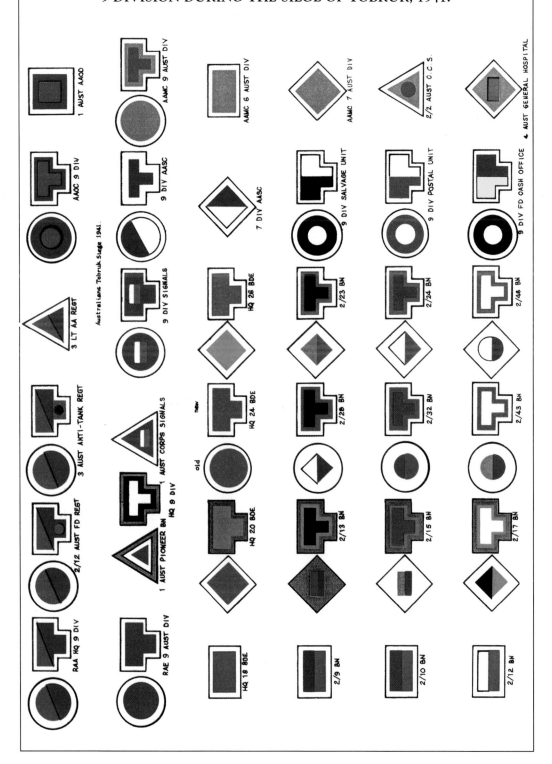

The 17th Battalion Memorial Area in the Church of Saint Thomas, North Sydney.
Dedicated on Remembrance Day, 1984. Battle Honours awarded before 1914 and selected Honours won by the
17th Battalion AIF, in the Great War of 1914-1918, are emblazened on the Regimental Colours of the
17th Battalion (The North Sydney Regiment).
Selected Honours won by the 2/17th Australian Infantry Battalion AIF
in the Second World War of 1939-1945, are emblazoned on the Queen's Colours.

The Pozieres Cross and Memorial Plaques.
Overhead are the King's and Regimental Colours of the 17th Battalion
(The North Sydney Regiment)

THE POZIERES CROSS

Situated on the northern wall of the Church of Saint Thomas, North Sydney, the Pozieres Memorial Cross is the focal point of both the Anzac Sunday and Remembrance Sunday Services attended each year by members of the Association of 17 Battalions.

The Cross was originally erected on the sector of the Pozieres battlefield held by the 17th Battalion during July and August 1916. In 1932 the Cross was brought to Australia and subsequently enshrined in the Church of St Thomas.

The erection of the Cross was suggested by Regimental Sergeant Major V J Sullivan MC, who secured the timber from the 5th Field Company Engineers, and co-opted the services of Pioneer Sergeant T Beer and Private Shipway to fashion it and write the inscription:-

IN THE PROUD AND LOVING MEMORY OF OFFICERS, NCOS AND MEN
OF THE 17TH BATTALION AIF WHO FELL IN ACTION AT
POZIERES JULY 25 TO AUGUST 5 AND AUGUST 21 TO 28,
THEN ARE THEY GLAD BECAUSE THEY ARE AT REST.

ERECTED BY THEIR COMRADES OF THE 17TH BATTALION – FEBRUARY 1917

Regimental Sergeant Major Sullivan had the distinction of being awarded the Military Cross as a Warrant Officer. He was later Commissioned and continued service in the 17th Battalion until the Armistice.

Some years ago, the 2/17 Battalion AIF Association, under the presidency of Major Colin Pitman, arranged with the Church Authorities for remedial treatment to the Cross to prevent further decay. The present Memorial Area in the Church was dedicated on Remembrance Day 1984 with a plaque, "To hallow the memory of all who in war and peace served the Infantry Tradition of 17 Battalion ".

Lieutenant Sullivan's medals are held by the Army Museum, Victoria Barracks, Paddington, having been donated during 1990 by his last surviving relatives, three nieces; Mrs G Freshwater, Mrs F Vale and Mrs M Vincin. Not until then were they aware of the existence of the Pozieres Cross and the role played by their uncle in its creation and dedication.

CONTENTS

SECTION 4   BORNEO CAMPAIGN

APPENDICES

LIST OF MAPS

COMMANDING OFFICERS
2/17 AUSTRALIAN INFANTRY BATTALION

LIEUTENANT COLONEL JOHN WILSON CRAWFORD DSO, ED, MID.
26 APRIL 1940 - 14 JANUARY 1942

LIEUTENANT COLONEL MAURICE ALFRED FERGUSSON DSO, MC, ED
15 JANUARY 1942 – 6 MARCH 1942

LIEUTENANT COLONEL NOEL WILLIAM SIMPSON DSO & Bar, MID.
7 MARCH 1942 – 27 FEBRUARY 1944

LIEUTENANT COLONEL JOHN RAYMOND BROADBENT DSO.
28 FEBRUARY 1944 – 8 FEBRUARY 1946

PREFACE

Time has denied 2/17 Battalion gracious written remarks from its senior wartime commanders but their actions showed their faith in the Unit. The first Victoria Cross in World War II, Corporal John Hurst Edmondson, was dying when his comrades carried him back. Yet the Battalion record shows analogy with his qualities. Calm, responsible, dependable, fundamentally Australian, co-operative, aware and ready to face duty with initiative, force, steadiness, endurance as occasion required or allowed, these were the attributes he showed before and in his gallantry.

Chance or allocation gave the Battalion prominent roles in critical and effective operations. The first assault on besieged Tobruk came where the famed German tank/infantry attack was given its first sustained defeat in World War II. Six months aggressive defence and patrolling gave the Unit soldiering maturity with desert know-how. This was called on again at El Alamein. There, in the attack that turned the tide of war, the Battalion broke in on the widest frontage. Without reprieve till the battle ended, through multiple attacks, it held ground vital to the offensive of Ninth Division, itself crucial to the Eighth Army success.

Returning to more proximate Australian defence the Battalion mastered conversion from desert to jungle. It prepared for its landings at Lae and Finschhafen, the first Australian landings after Anzac. It followed forceful breakout with spectacular achievements of skill and courage in jungle fighting.

Resilient through a year of national military indecision, it was reinforced with valuable officers and men and trained again to high individual and collective proficiency. Discipline and morale remained habit. When given the final call to land and release Brunei and its oil resources, the team worked with vigour and ability.

Through the years strong wishes to provide this story have never lapsed. Participation in the Battalion and its purposeful fighting produced good men to return to civilian life. There they have made small and not small contributions. With the calls on them reducing, there came scope to combine in this mingled report of achievement and reminiscence, made knowing that the Battalion did not fight alone.

My life among them from the first twenty to the last two, ensures comradeship and its dignity, but great pride must carry the endless sense of loss.

Maj Gen J R Broadbent CBE DSO ED.

ACKNOWLEDGEMENTS

The production of this History is a tribute mainly to two people — our late Association President Colin Pitman for his tenacity and inspiration, and Arthur Newton for his detailed, painstaking work in extracting the material from the Official records in Canberra, which has provided a framework for this publication.

Early in 1988, Colin Pitman formed a History Group consisting of John Broadbent, Bruce Trebeck, Alastair Urquhart, Ray Rudkin and Phil Pike. The task was subdivided into various sections and with tremendous support from the Advance Bank, particularly with typing facilities, the job got under way. Financial support came from funds of our Ladies' Comforts Fund, held in Trust, and donations from the History Committee. Later, Colin invited other members of the Battalion to assist and I am pleased to acknowledge donations from Bayne Geikie, Henry Zouch, Tony Nicholson, Jim Fletcher, Ken Gibb, Charlie Cutler, Jessel Silverstone and Reg Kennedy.

As work progressed, it was decided to purchase a word processor/printer unit and, once again, the Advance Bank provided accommodation, advice and support to set up our own production centre. This enabled us to complete the manuscript, maps and photographs for delivery to our Publisher at no cost to the Association, thus keeping the unit cost of the book to a minimum and within the range of our members.

Acknowledgement is made of the work done by previous History committees headed by Eric Blundell, Peter Bryant and others. A great deal of this material was collected from Dudley McCarthy's estate. However, with the passage of time, it was found impossible to use it other than for reference purposes.

Dudley McCarthy had hoped to write the history. He was eminently qualified as an original member of the Battalion and serving through Tobruk. Years ago he produced a draft for that period which with its clarity and turn of phrase provided a basis for this work.

A call for anecdotal material was well-supported and these personal observations are grouped under Platoons and Companies in the Appendix. It is regretted that all contributions could not be published, but volume and repetitions were a consideration. Extracts from our well known diarists, Bob Anson, Tom Fitzpatrick, Fred Camarsh, Jack O'Shea, Ces Greenwood, Pat Conti, Charlie Lemaire and others are scattered throughout the manuscript, and bring back many memories of the lighter side of soldiering and the mateship that exists within an Infantry Battalion.

The production of the maps drawn by the late Alex Crisdale was ably handled by my friend Paddy Fenton and the UBD mapping section of the Universal Press Pty Ltd, North Ryde. These and other maps obtained from the War Memorial Canberra will assist in following our narrative.

The Official Histories of World War II are basic sources. Tobruk and El Alamein are by Barton Maughan; South-West Pacific Area — First Year by Dudley McCarthy; The New Guinea Offensives by David Dexter and The Final Campaigns by Gavin Long. These references, together with the excellent co-operation by the staff of the War Memorial Canberra in the Research Mapping and Photographic Sections have made the task of our History Committee much more tolerable.

The committee is grateful for the generous support given by the Shell Company of Australia to the cost of this production. Our association with Shell is unusual as few Infantry Battalions had such a task as securing the Seria Oil Fields with about 40 high pressure wells blazing furiously. Thanks to Lt Burn Underwood, the Engineer Officer attached to the Battalion during the Borneo Campaign, for his excellent article, "Seria Oil Fires". The story rightly puts in perspective the work done by the Engineers and 2/17 Battalion in extinguishing the Fires and restoring this vast and valuable oilfield to commercial production. Burn Underwood was employed by the Shell Group of Companies after the War and worked in this area for a number of years and was awarded the MBE for his services. The field is still in full production and provides a staple income for the population of Brunei State.

Our choice of Mrs Linda Williams of Goanna Graphics as our Production Manager was fortunate and valuable. Linda, the daughter of our Treasurer, John Blockley, has given a personal commitment to this publication which is above and beyond the call of duty. The result is a quality book of which we can be proud. Thanks also to Bill Duffy, our Newsletter artist of long ago, for his helpful suggestions on the Dust Cover design.

Maj Pat Boland is thanked for his production of Chapter 23 "Postscript" linking the 2/17 Bn with the post war Army, in its many forms and the present day Army Reserve unit the 2/17 Royal New South Wales Regiment. This period covering more than 40 years highlights the awarding of Battle Honours,laying up of Colours and activities at our Garrison Church,St Thomas' North Sydney. Preservation of the traditions established in two World Wars by the Seventeenth Battalions is highly valued by the present day soldier.

Finally, I wish to record our thanks to the Advance Bank under the guidance of Mr Arthur Delbridge, who has for two years met our many requests for advice and assistance with alacrity and enthusiasm. To Rose Hay at the Computer Centre, Berry St North Sydney and Sue Porritt and the staff at St Leonard's Branch, many thanks for your assistance, co-operation and tolerance. To Mrs Dorothy Pantland, our Word Processor operator who has become an expert in Military writing and Staff Duties, our special thanks for your application and personal interest in our project.

In conclusion it must be recorded that contributions towards the compilation of this history have come from many sources.

The final editing, writing, and preparation of various chapters has been the responsibility of four editors as follows: —

Section 1   Formation of the Battalion to the end of Tobruk — Bruce Trebeck.
Section 2   Post Tobruk, Syria, Return to the Western Desert, Tel el Eisa — Phil Pike.
                 Rest and Rehearsal, Battle of Alamein, Post Alamein — John Broadbent.
Section 3   New Guinea
                 Lae, Finschhafen, Jivenaneng-Kumawa — Ray Rudkin.
                 Pursuit to Sio — Phil Pike.
Section 4   Borneo — Bruce Trebeck.

"The Editors"

EDITOR'S PREFACE TO THIS SECOND EDITION.

Minor changes have been made to the original text of the First Edition. Footnotes and Postscripts have been added. Corrections have been made to the Nominal Roll and casualty lists. Additions have been made to Honours and Awards. More abbreviations have listed as used in the original text. In Chapter 23, the Postscript regarding post war successors to the 2/17th Battalion, has been brought up to date; likewise Appendix 4, The 2/17 Battalion AIF Association. Some personal anecdotes have been added to Appendix 8. New Appendixes 9 to 14 are included as listed in the Contents.

With the exception of the late Bruce Trebeck, who is succeeded on the first " What We Have We Hold" Editorial Committee by Bob Pink, who completed the arduous task of the Index, the same committee members have worked on this Second Edition, namely; John Broadbent, Phil Pike, Alastair Urquhart and Ray Rudkin.

ACKNOWLEDGEMENTS

Completion of this work would not have been possible without the help of interested persons and the Editors thank them all for their support. Especially: Pat Boland, Regimental Historian, who brought up to date the original Chapter 23 on post war Units and researched the source and detailed accuracy of the Battle Honours; Ken Thompson for his research, knowledge and guidance emanating from his voluntary work over many years in the Historical Section of the Military Museum, Victoria Barracks, Paddington; Vince Ward, President of the Balgownie Heritage Museum, for his research of the Owen Gun and his knowledge of the Inventor, the late Evelyn Owen; Elizabeth Dracoulis and Fran Ballard, of the Australian War Memorial, Canberra, for the verification of information concerning our late members on the National Honour Roll and the provision of additional photographs, respectively; Robert Pink and Richard Rudkin in facilitating computer material for the Publisher, Clive Baker; Dawn Rudkin for proof reading; Bill Shaw for bringing Appendix 4 up to date: Paul Lavallee for his first-hand information concerning POWs; Arthur Newton, always available with his detailed knowledge of the Battalion's History; our Association members for their support and provision of additional photographs.

Ray Rudkin
For the Editors.

CHAPTER 1

A BATTALION IS FORMED

In February 1940 the Australian Government decided to raise a second division of the 2nd AIF, but it was not until some two months later that the tangible signs of formation of 7th Division became visible. In this new division was 20 Brigade, which included 2/13 Battalion and 2/17 Battalion (to be formed in New South Wales) and 2/15 Battalion (to be formed in Queensland).

Lt Col J W Crawford was appointed to command 2/17 Bn on 26 April 1940. John Crawford was a Sydney Solicitor who had been just too young for the 1914/18 war. His long Militia service had culminated in command of the Sydney University Regt and then of 4 Bn Militia. He was rather dapper and punctilious, and in training the battalion he sought particularly to develop the responsibility of his Coy Comds and Junior Officers. For some weeks before this, he had interviewed many Officers and Senior NCOs in various Militia units in the process of selecting his initial Officers and NCOs for the Battalion when it was officially formed.

1 May 1940 was the day on which 2/17 Bn began its embryo existence with Bn HQ at Room 37 Coronation Stand RAS Showground comprising a small nucleus of the CO plus 9 Offrs, NCOs and Ors. These included Maj J M (John) Williams, an Engr from 4 Bn; Capt J (Jessel) Silverstone, an Electrician also from 4 Bn; Capt L C (Claude) Brien, ex Vacuum Oil Company from 56 Bn; Capt D (Duncan) McNab, Regular Soldier from the Australian Instructional Corps; WO R A (Bob) Halloway, also from AIC Sgt H D McLucas, admitting to having been in the Royal Irish Constabulary; Sgt I P K (Snow) Vidler, ex State Parliamentary Staff.

On that day most of the original Officers — many of whom were in various militia camps — received their advice of appointment to the Battalion.

18 Bde had recently marched out of Ingleburn and embarked for overseas. On 4 May 1940, an instruction was received from HQ 20 Bde covering the administrative arrangements for the Nucleus Camp, the essentials of which were:—

LOCATION: Ingleburn Camp HQ E Block and F as from 7 May.

OFFICERS: The nucleus of Officers will assemble at Engrs' Depot Moore Park, at 0900 hours 7 May for final medical examination, photographs etc, which will be completed prior to moving to Ingleburn.

WOS AND NCOs and essential personnel to be advised by their respective units to report to Engineers Depot, Moore Park, for completion of final medical examination prior to moving to Ingleburn.

20 Bde will be established at Ingleburn from 1400 hours 6 May.

Main call up to commence 20 May.

Signed: Major N W Simpson
Acting Bde Maj, 20 Brigade

(Noel Simpson was later to become CO of 2/17 Bn)

On 7 May 1940 at 1300 hrs the Battalion proceeded to Ingleburn with temporary quarters occupied in F Block. Next day, Maj Ogle, Acting 2 i/c was allocated G Block as 2/17 quarters, and gradually Offrs, NCOs and essential Ors began to arrive. There were no Mess facilities functioning in the 2/17 Bn quarters as yet, so everyone went across to Bde HQ where a skeleton staff provided food for all those in camp.

During the period up to 16 May 1940, the gradual build-up of the Battalion to the "first hundred" mark was achieved, and on that day a photo of the first hundred was taken.

In fact the photo contained 102 made up of 17 Offrs and 85 Ors. The Officers in this first hundred were:—

Lt Col Crawford	Capt Balfe	Capt Wilson	Lt Blundell	Lt Mackell
Maj Ogle	Capt Silverstone	Lt Pitman	Lt Mc Cullock	Lt Trebeck
Maj Williams	Capt Brien	Lt Pike	Lt Bjelke-Petersen	
Capt Moffatt	Capt Grant	Lt Geikie		

In addition to these Officers in the photo, four others had marched in but were temporarily seconded to 20 Bde — Capt Magno, Lt Broadbent, Lt Windeyer, Lt McNab.

On 14 May, the Officers had drill instructions from RSM WO1 Bird — obviously known as Dicky Bird. Troops in camp received their initial issue of boots and working dress. That afternoon, Lt Gen Sturdee, GOC Eastern Command, delivered a lecture to all Officers in Ingleburn Camp, the important information being:—

(a) He stressed the gravity of the war situation, and he thought that an early departure from Australia of 7 Div would have an excellent effect on morale in the community.

(b) Lack of equipment made it advisable for 7 Div to be transferred overseas for training. As soon as 7 Div was equipped and organised it would be sent abroad.

(c) For these reasons he directed that the initial training should be subordinate to administration and organisation.

New enlistments arriving at camp

The First Hundred

It must be remembered that, following the Depression Years the citizen forces (Militia) and the permanent forces were hard hit and severely reduced in numbers, while political views regarding Australia's approach to defence requirements and expenditure were vastly diverse. The world events of 1938 saw a great increase in Militia numbers but, when war came in 1939, Australia was gravely deficient in equipment and warlike stores of all kinds. At the same time Britain was deplorably short of the necessary arms and equipment for its own needs, with little to divert to Commonwealth troops.

On 20 May, Lt Hipkins reported for duty as Adjt, and on 21 May Capt J F Sullivan reported for duty as RMO, and WO1 A J C Newton as RSM replacing Dicky Bird who had been commissioned. It is important to remember that, other than Officers and members of the Permanent Military Forces, all enlisted as Privates in the AIF, irrespective of the rank they may have held in the Militia. Therefore in these early days there were many promotions to Sergeant and Corporal.

As advised in the original Bde instruction, 20 May saw the start of the main recruiting for the units of 7 Div. This involved various Offrs of the Bn being present each day at the main enlistment centre at Moore Park where, in competition with Officers from other units they tried to influence likely looking recruits to apply for 2/17 Bn. At the end of each day they escorted the day's new enlistments to Central Station then onto a train for Ingleburn and into the Bn Camp.

Many of these new recruits were from Militia units, and many had no previous training — a fairly rough guess is that 35 to 40 percent of the original battalion had no previous training.

The early weeks of June and July were spent in equipping the troops and gradually turning a group of civilians into soldiers. The training consisted of basic training and discipline, physical fitness, marching and arms drill. First and second TAB inoculations were necessary for everyone and, because of the prevalence of respiratory infections, instructions were issued for personnel to sleep "Head to Foot", and each man to gargle twice daily.

Basic training centred initially round the "bull ring" system under which squads moved from point to point with each instructor repeating the same lesson throughout the day to successive squads. On 1 July, the bull ring gave way to the more advanced requirements of section and platoon training, with an increasing emphasis on the long "toughening" process which was to send the men finally into action with hard bodies and clear eyes. Necessarily the foundation of this was route marching to give these foot soldiers that self-contained mobility and endurance which was the basis of their stock-in-trade.

There appeared no immediate war to rush to. No urgency was required by politicians or the Army. Supply was poor. Sizes for working dress, khaki drill blouse, slacks and hat, were extraordinarily ill-matched to demand. The description, "Giggle suits", showed the lack of scope for military deportment. There was scope for the soldier to learn about his rifle and bayonet, the same as had been used for winning War I, and it was to serve effectively again. The issue of Lewis guns as the automatic weapon meant time spent in dead-end knowledge, and fortunately the same was to apply to gas masks.

Within the Battalion at Ingleburn automatic weapons were not limited to the Lewis gun. Pte Owen, one of three brothers in the Bn, showed a small automatic weapon that he had invented. His working model fired .22 rounds. Lt Col Crawford was impressed with its simple and effective action and supported Owen. Owen was to leave the Bn to assist in the development of the famous Australian Owen Sub-Machine Gun. It was later valued in the Bn for more than the historical association.

The issue of War I webbing equipment was no surprise as Militia infantry knew no other.

Soldiers knew its role and learned to carry pack and haversack. Slowness in development cannot be attributed to weapons or equipment nor to Offrs and NCOs of the Bn. Two years before the huge expansion of the volunteer Militia had, with like deficiencies, led to the production of some highly motivated Junior Offrs and NCOs who were at home teaching proficiency with what was supplied. By the end of the War a very large proportion of Offrs, including to the rank of Major, had come from this class.

Camp life was not, however, simply a smooth process of ordered training. About the end of June a slight epidemic of German measles developed. In some cases the effects of smallpox vaccinations and anti-typhoid inoculations were severe. For several weeks the sound of hollow coughing could be heard in every hut during the quiet night hours as the so-called "Ingleburn Throat" (medically, Upper Respiratory Tract Infection — URTI) set in with its characteristic high temperatures and general strength-reducing effects.

But, sick or well, training or resting, the Bn depended on the quiet work of men of whom little was heard, such as Ration Sgt V A (Vic) Dunn and his offsider R B (Bob) Askew; the Bn Butcher, C W (Butch) Holland, who used to scrub even the ceiling of his store; there was grey haired George Farrar-Pugh, the Medical Sgt, old soldier of 1914-1918 who was making his Stretcher Bearers also into Bandsmen — and Sgt J S Brown who was actually training the Bandsmen and hid them among the trees during their early struggles, where they could be heard if not seen!

Quickly the small but significant occasions of a new group life developed. With the passing of each, a little more firmness, something more enduring, had been added to "the thing" that was shaping; a "thing" for which there was no name, for it would mean that to each of the 900-odd men who might make up the battalion at any given moment, that battalion would become something which would be forever part of them and of which each and every one of them himself would be forever a part.

At the end of July each coy in turn marched to Anzac Rifle Range for musketry practice. In actual fact another range shoot at Bathurst and a third at Jaffa in February 1941 were the full extent of the unit's range practices. The beginning of August recorded the first mention of the unit's march to Bathurst.

On Friday 9 Aug, there was a combined Sergeants' Ball at the Trocadero before departure for Bathurst. The Trocadero had also become quite a regular visiting venue for many of the eligible young Subalterns as so many Debutante Balls were being held, and there were frequent requests for a number of Officers to do escort duties for the presentation of the Debs.

On the next day, a unit Sports Meeting was conducted, followed that night by a Regimental Dance at Liverpool Town Hall.

11 Aug, saw the first Battalion Ceremonial Parade during which the Mayor of North Sydney presented band instruments. There was a presentation of the Regimental Flag by members of the original 17th Battalion. The Bn marched past the Bde Comd, Brig J J Murray, in close column of platoons.

At 0830 hrs 14 Aug, the Bn (33 Offrs, 978 Men) marched out of Ingleburn en route to Bathurst, the 2/13 Bn having marched out on 12 Aug. First day covered 17 miles to Wallacia. As a pattern for the remainder of the march, the unit was billeted in halls, private houses and guest houses. Second day to Penrith, third day to Springwood, fourth day to Hazlebrook and Lawson, fifth day to Katoomba. At 1500 hrs the Bn marched through Katoomba. Next day was spent at Katoomba and the Governor General, Lord Gowrie, inspected the Bn.

All the way across the Blue Mountains and on to Bathurst the people were really wonderful in the warmth of welcome they gave to the troops. It was also rather marvellous how so many were prepared to offer accommodation in their homes to billet troops in the various overnight stops. No doubt lots of friendships were made and no doubt a few hearts broken as well. There was one rather macabre twist though — somewhere, possibly at Springwood, one young girl was most diligent in collecting many autographs and names; when someone asked why she was so keen to collect so many, her reply was that she wanted to be able to see how many of the names she collected appeared later in casualty lists.

The Bn departed from Katoomba 20 Aug to Mt Victoria, then to Lithgow, to Wallerawang, to Meadow Flat, to Walang and finally arrived Bathurst Camp 1200 hours 25 Aug, where 2/13 Bn joined them for the last mile, and Brig Murray greeted the troops at the Camp Entrance, and the Bn occupied their new home in Blocks 3 and 6.

On 30 Aug, 20 Bde marched through Bathurst and the Governor General took the salute. The march to Bathurst, having been done in easy stages, was not hard but did a lot of good to generally toughen up a batch of new soldiers. Possibly more important was the training exercise and organisation necessary to move the Bn.

During September, basic training continued with more emphasis on Pl and Coy exercises, and a second range practice was conducted for all coys. Then came the news — final leave before embarkation. Leave started 27/28 Sept and troops returned 6 Oct.

The Bn entrained at Kelso Station 19 Oct at about 1600 hrs. Despite the movement being "Secret", along the route to Darling Harbour it was farewelled at all stations and by groups along the track.

The Battalion's first Ceremonial Parade at Ingleburn.

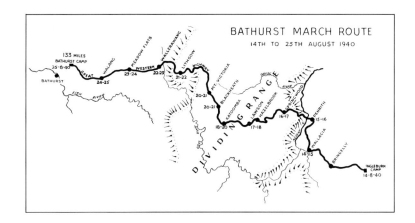

left: Marching through Katoomba
below: Marching through Bathurst

Having arrived at Darling Harbour at approximately 2100 hrs, troops embarked on ferries for transfer to the *Queen Mary* between 2200 hrs and midnight.

A small advance party had departed from Bathurst a couple of days earlier and were already aboard *Queen Mary* to help guide coys to their allotted quarters for the trip. This was very necessary because there were some 6,500 troops aboard, consisting of:

20 Brigade Headquarters	20 Anti-Tank Company
2/13 Battalion	7 Division Provost Company
2/17 Battalion	7 Division Mobile Bath Unit
2/5 Field Regiment	52 LAD
2/5 Australian General Hospital	58 LAD
2/1 Field Hygiene Unit	7 Division Signals
7 Division Mobile Laundry	56 LAD
2 Anti-Tank Regiment	7 Division Supply Company
54 LAD	7 Division Ammunition Company
2/5 Field Company RAE	7 Division Field Cash Office
2/6 Field Company RAE	YMCA
7 Division Intelligence Corps	Salvation Army

And so on Sunday 20 Oct 1940, the *Queen Mary* and *Aquitania* began moving down the Harbour at 1000 hrs, being fondly farewelled by dozens of small craft on the Harbour and thousands of spectators crowding Bradleys Head, North Head, The Gap, and any other available viewing point. It was a lovely day and *Queen Mary* cleared the heads at 1030 hrs, the first time that most of the 6500 aboard had headed away from Australia and destination still unknown.

Departing on Queen Mary

CHAPTER 2
OVERSEAS TO PALESTINE

When the *Queen Mary* and the *Aquitania* cleared Sydney Heads (incidentally sailing by a Japanese merchantman hove to just outside the Heads) and later were joined off Wilson Promontory by the *Mauretania* carrying troops from Victoria, it was by no means impossible that the convoy could meet interference either from enemy ships or mines. The escorting Australian light cruiser *Perth* was not there simply as a matter of form.

But apprehensions regarding attack were generally far from the minds of the 2/17 Bn as they settled down to life on the *Queen Mary*. On boarding her they had discovered a maze of corridors stretching for great distances, huge dining rooms, and a swimming pool. Capt Blue Allan, Ship's QM for the voyage, had looked after the Bn Offrs and some NCOs, allocated to A deck, were quartered in luxury, for most of the peace-time trappings of this great passenger liner still remained. Similarly, the food in the dining rooms was of the standard and diversity normal for first-class passengers travelling in their peacetime occasions. However, most of the troops' messing arrangements were necessarily more in the general Army style. Though these arrangements presented few problems of organisation, confusion at first marked the daily beer issue; each man was allowed two containers but at first the size was not specified. One soldier lined up with a new rubbish bin to be filled, a few had buckets, and so supplies for the less fortunate late comers ran short before the issue was standardised to two mess tins per man.

Waiting in the queue one evening on an open deck in heavy rain, water streaming off him, Pte T E Fitzpatrick, formerly a senior official in the Queensland Farmers' and Graziers' Association, gloomily contemplated his lot. A young Subaltern from another unit whom he recognised as a very junior clerk in the same Association, approached him and said, "Excuse me, aren't you Mr Fitzpatrick?" Tom regarded him thoughtfully and then, taking his pipe from his mouth, admitted sadly, "I *was* lad, I *was*".

Soon however, the initial difficulties of settling the battalion down to shipboard life were overcome. Forms of training which lent themselves to shipboard life were developed (physical training; lectures on such subjects as security, gas warfare, conduct of prisoners of war, health and hygiene, elementary weapon training). There were duties to be carried out — galley and mess fatigue; piquets. So the days were spent and the evenings were comfortable and pleasant.

The convoy ran far south to the bitter fringes of the Antarctic approaches (to avoid, it was said, possible enemy encounters) before turning westward. But at night the interior of the closely sealed and blacked-out *Queen Mary* had a warmth and cosiness that was in pleasant contrast to the bitter darkness outside lying over the bitter sea. There was the beer to loosen the tongues of the talkers and add a touch of recklessness to the forbidden gambling games that went on. As the ship crossed the Great Australian Bight there was a short and sudden storm which blew out of the north just before dark one day. Sheets of rain drove with it and even the huge bulk of the Mary moved uneasily; to the watchers from her decks the *Perth* seemed at times to be quite hidden in the troughs of the great waves. But the storm quickly passed and the rest of the run was calm until, on 25 Oct, the *Perth* delivered the three great ships safely to their anchorages at Fremantle.

To the troops on board the *Queen Mary*, however, this was a frustrating occasion for the ship was too big to berth and lay well offshore while the *Mauretania* and the *Aquitania* landed their complements for leave. The disappointment was probably a contributing cause of a fracas in the wet canteen the following day when troops there clashed with the piquets and, as a result, several men were admitted to the ship's hospital. (In this the 2/17 Bn was *not* involved.) The disappointment was not long drawn out, however, for, having taken on board the Western Australian members of the units in them, the ships sailed from Fremantle early on the morning of 27 Oct.

After Fremantle, the Bn really settled to the routine of shipboard training. Probably the burden fell heaviest on the Pl Comds who had to attend a multiplicity of Officers' classes and cloth model exercises as well as working hard with their own Pls. But sports meetings of various kinds relieved the training routine with boxing contests evoking the greatest interest. Excitement was high in 2/17 Bn as Ptes Moore and F J Hudson fought their way to the titles in the middle-weight and lightweight divisions respectively and particularly as Pte F Snelson battered his way into the light-heavy-weight finals. The ship's paper ("Published by the AIF for the AIF" *Wouldn't it…?*) reported:

> "Sitting on boat davits and clinging to the rigging, several hundred troops yesterday saw great fights in the concluding semi-finals of the boxing tournament. They roared approval as Ptes Snelson and Carruthers fought desperately in one of the best bouts yet seen. Snelson won by a single point".

By that time the ships were well on their way into the Indian Ocean. On 30 Oct, off the Cocos Islands, HMAS *Perth* handed over her escort duties to HMAS *Canberra*. At midday she went racing down the convoy line in farewell. The blue water danced about her in the sunlight; her ensigns were spread; all in white the sailors lined her decks; white bow waves folded away in a perfect symmetry of lazy foam; a boiling white wake spread behind her like a fan. In her there was all the gallantry of the sea — and not a single watching soldier but felt this. The soldiers cheered the sailors as they went racing past; the sailors cheered in reply. And then the *Perth* wheeled on her course and set off back for Australia signalling "Goodbye", and the *Queen Mary* replied "Thank you; goodbye. Success against the enemy".

The convoy headed on through calm seas. Only one incident disrupted its progress. The night it left Cocos behind, it halted suddenly for half an hour; a man had been reported overboard from the *Aquitania*. Though this was a mistake, strict warnings to the men of the *Queen Mary* followed; if any man went overboard the ship would not stop to pick him up; one life could not be allowed to imperil all the lives on board. Everyone took the warning seriously; even the most unimaginative could picture himself struggling alone and left in the vastness of that sea.

But serious moments were rare. There would be enough to be serious about later. The voyage continued through hot flat seas; flying fish scuttled and skidded away from the *Queen Mary*'s bows; phosphorescent lights swirled in the water at night. On the morning of 4 Nov, many gathered on deck about 0600 hrs but still no sign of land although they were cruising along at reduced speed. As the sun rose like a great fireball, they could see that it was cradled between two mountains which had previously been hidden in the morning haze. They had their first view of India rising from the lazy mists and the coast appeared very rugged and mountainous. By the time they could see the buildings of Bombay ahead, the *Queen Mary* started slowing down to a complete stop while the other ships proceeded slowly into the harbour, leaving them some 7 miles out which was as close as the *Queen Mary* could reasonably approach in the shallow waters off the harbour.

At 0830 hrs, the *Queen Mary* anchored, her propellers spinning to a stop and discolouring the seas with mud. At once, the heat rose in waves which quivered over the sea and seemed to lick round the ship. A great clutter of shipping lay ahead.

Searing heat about them, excitement moved within them all. To some this was the land of the Khyber Pass, the nursery of great soldiers; to some it was "the East", full of mystery; to some it was merely a foreign city offering relief from the monotony of shipboard life; to all it was in some sense the beginning of that for which they had enlisted.

They stayed at anchor for two unpleasant days and nights — very hot and humid and a strict blackout at night. On the morning of the third day orders were received to move and Tim McCulloch and Bruce Trebeck went ashore early by launch with the mail, hoping that they could complete their task at the GPO and still have some time to look at the city before the rest of the Battalion disembarked. Unfortunately this was frustrated because, on leaving Australia, they had been given wrong rates for both letters and cables. With something over 6,500 aboard there was a great mass of both letters and cables and so, having talked with Bombay's Postmaster General, he brought about 30 boys to sit around his large office and lick stamps and place them on the mass of letters. While this was going on, McCulloch and Trebeck went through the cables and crossed out any apparently unnecessary words that would not detract from the meaning so they could save sufficient on the cables to subsidise the additional postage on the letters. This exercise took so long that they had only half an hour before being due to report at the wharf and rejoin the Bn.

It was not until 1430 hrs on the 6th that the 2/17 Bn began to transfer to a smaller vessel (the *Rohna*) of the British India line which ferried them to the docks. At midnight they entrained for Deolali. The train was comfortable, specially designed to carry troops for long distances. At 0630 hrs on the 7th it pulled in at Deolali. The soldiers, burdened like pack animals, then set out on a 2-mile march to a camp which had been planned and used originally as a rest camp for troops from the North-West Frontier. It was comfortable and well appointed, the tents in which the men were quartered spacious and well furnished. To each tent there was an Indian servant (and others to be had almost for the asking) and the Australians revelled in their unaccustomed attentions.

Life was pleasant at Deolali. The camp was in a basin surrounded by rugged hills. The air was fresh and bracing. The British troops there were friendly and helpful. Training in the form of squad drill and route marches was not arduous. The unaccustomed sights and sounds were a pleasure and constant interest to the newcomers. There was the bazaar and nearby temples; there were cobras swaying before the music of the snake charmer's reed pipes; there were interesting souvenirs to be bought; there were fortune tellers and magicians; there was the whole atmosphere of India and the East. But beneath the surface of all this, there were strange and violent currents. A group of the 2/17 Bn men discovered this for themselves when they visited the nearby village of Narsik, where feeling against the British was strong, and where potential trouble quickly developed.

Reveille sounded at 0200 hrs on 10 November. At 0630 hrs the long troop train pulled out of Deolali on its way back to Bombay. By midday the battalion was once more in the city and moved straight on board the *Rohna*. The men spent the rest of the day settling themselves on what seemed, after the *Queen Mary*, a very small ship which accommodated only the 2/17 Bn itself and a few others. They would sleep in hammocks, between decks. The transfer of their baggage and equipment from the *Queen Mary* was almost complete. While they had been at Deolali Capt McNab and Lt Newton (the latter had by then been commissioned) with a hard working baggage party had been sweating at Victoria Dock to unload the Bn's possessions from the *Queen Mary* and load them onto the *Rohna*. The baggage party's greatest difficulty was the Indian wharf labourers who smashed and cluttered the stores into almost hopeless confusion. But somehow the strewn goods were collected from the dockside, the shattered cases repacked and rewired, the loading completed.

Next day 11 Nov, there was general leave in Bombay. To most of the men the city was rich in interest and evidence of ancient civilisation; they visited the Towers of Silence, and the Burning Ghats where the city's dead were being cremated; they realised for the first time in such cities there were homeless thousands (perhaps hundreds of thousands) who ate, slept, and lived their lives in the streets. Although it had been carefully and strictly placed out of bounds, they went down Grant Road where, on either side of the narrow street, prostitutes were displayed in cages, offering themselves for a shilling or two. This was an introduction to a human degradation which few of the soldiers had considered up to that time could be possible; to some it was an aspect of the realities of living in a country where life itself is the cheapest thing and where, at the same time, a human could be almost rich with little more than life itself in his possession.

On 17 Nov the *Rohna*, in convoy with 13 other troop ships and two armed merchantmen, left Bombay. Capt Murphy, a native of Wollongong, was pleased to have his own countrymen on board his ship and determined to do everything possible to make their voyage pleasant. At first however, they found some causes for complaint. It was difficult for them to forget the spaciousness and luxury of the *Queen Mary* and settle into hammocks in cramped quarters. They thought the food was meagre, provided on the British Army rations and to Australians the light evening meal was particularly unsatisfying. But such difficulties as lack of space soon came to be accepted and Maj Williams (2 i/c of the Bn and therefore responsible for its administration) found his own way through the ration situation — so that probably to this day the 2/17 Bn still owes about 200 pounds to the British Government.

There was the incident of the goat. This animal belonged to the Indian crew and became firmly fixed in the soldiers' affections so that they fitted him out with a life jacket and took him with them to boat drill. But their feelings changed when the goat began to eat the chin straps of sleeping soldiers and then piddle on them. Some of them were planning to throw the goat overboard and were only restrained from doing so for fear of outraging the religious feelings of the crew.

Apart from such incidents the voyage was uneventful enough until the ship approached the African coast — except that (though this was not generally known) some cases of venereal disease developed, presumably in soldiers who had found that the attractions and bargain prices of Grant Road had outweighed the warnings which the MO had sounded loudly and constantly.

Offr postings at this stage were as follows:

BN HQ

CO	Lt Col J W Crawford	Int Offr	Lt D McCarthy
2 i/c	Maj J M Williams	RMO	Capt J F Sullivan
Adjt	Capt J G S Moffatt	Chaplain	Chap B H Watson
		1st Rein	Lt J G Ochiltree

Lt Col J.W. Crawford

HQ COY

OC	Maj H T Allan
1 Pl	Lt P H Pike
2 Pl	Lt E M McCulloch
3 Pl	Lt E T Chapman
4 Pl	Lt H F Windeyer
5 Pl	Lt G G Limn
6 Pl	Lt A Lewis-Mathias
QM	Capt D McNab
1st Rein	Lt H L Malthouse
2nd Rein	Lt R V Burgess

A COY

OC	Capt L C Brien
2i/c	Capt C H Wilson
7 Pl	Lt P E O'Brien
8 Pl	Lt J B Blundell
9 Pl	Lt C R Bird
Rein Pl	Lt A E Tuckwell

B COY

OC	Maj J Silverstone
2i/c	Capt J D Grant
10 Pl	Lt J M Owen
11 Pl	Lt W B A Geikie
12 Pl	Lt C G Pitman
Rein Pl	Lt A J Wright

C COY

OC	Capt C K M Magno
2 i/c	Capt E H C Hipkins
13 Pl	Lt A J C Newton
14 Pl	Lt L C Maclarn
15 Pl	Lt G S Le Couteur
Rein Pl	Lt G T Reid

D COY

OC	Capt J W Balfe
2i/c	Capt J R Broadbent
16 Pl	Lt F A Mackell
17 Pl	Lt N B Trebeck
18 Pl	Lt J H Dinning
Rein Pl	Lt G D Vincent

At 2100 hrs on 16 Nov, land was sighted, part of the coast of Italian Somaliland. The ship was moving into the Gulf of Aden. On 18 Nov, increases in the number of escorting war ships reminded the men on board the *Rohna* that they were now in actual battle area. At 1100 hrs an aeroplane was sighted; the ship moved to action stations in anticipation of air attack but the aircraft was British. About the middle of the afternoon a convoy of about 15 ships passed. Land was sighted to starboard, then to port. The convoy was approaching the Straits of Bab el Mandeb. The following day, training was interrupted at 0900 hrs by the sound of firing from the escorting war ship *Carlisle*. The men took up their air raid stations but were reluctant to go below for fear of missing something. Hard after the firing a sentry reported a submarine 1,000 yds to

Lt Col R.W. Ogle 2/15 Bn   *Lt Col J.M. Williams 2/2 Pnr Bn*

Lt Col C.K.M. Magno 2/15 Bn   *Lt Col J.W. Balfe 2/32 Bn*

Four original Coy Comds promoted to command units

port (a report subsequently confirmed by HMS *Cumberland*) but at 0945 hrs the all-clear was sounded as a British aeroplane flew over the ship. At 1400 hrs a sudden burst of flame and a thick column of smoke rose from the sea some 10 miles east of the *Rohna*: it was said that an Italian reconnaissance plane had been shot down.

On the morning of 23 Nov, at 0600 hrs the *Rohna* anchored off Suez. The land was harsh and forbidding; sandstone cliffs, parched and barren towered high near the ship and stretched away. Small boats flocked round the convoy, native hucksters in them shouting their wares and "gully gully" men displaying their magic. Ships travelling through the Canal stretched northward through the sand; they seemed to be sailing over the desert's very face. The next day the *Rohna* herself entered the Canal and moved slowly up that famous waterway; on the right the Biblical sands of the Sinai Desert, on the left a panorama of cultivated fields. Then the ship berthed at El Kantara.

This was Egypt — its coastline forming the southern shores of the Eastern Mediterranean. With Palestine, Syria, Turkey and the other countries adjacent to the Eastern shores of that ancient sea, it made up the Middle East.

For the men of the 2/17 Bn, now in Egypt, Reveille sounded at 0100 hrs on the 25th. Three hours later the battalion had disembarked. There was hot breakfast at the British canteen (the NAAFI) — sausages and mashed potatoes (a meal with which they were to become very familiar and which they never ceased to appreciate). By this time the picture was building up in a little more detail, particularly as many of the men had friends, brothers (or other relatives) in the 6 Div and they anxiously inquired the whereabouts of these men.

Immediately after the entry of Italy into the war, Wavell, his planning in the forward areas based on Mersa Matruh (about half way between Port Said and the western border of Egypt) at once began harrying the Italians in the border area. By the end of July the situation had temporarily stabilized. In preparation for an Offensive there, however, Wavell had begun building up an attacking force at Alexandria and westward. So, in September, the 6 Div (less one Bde) had moved to Helwan near Cairo to complete its training and equipment. By 6 Oct it was concentrated at Amirya (about 12 miles west of Alexandria) where 19 Bde joined it on 14 Nov.

2/17 Bn at 0930 hrs on the 25th, bound for Palestine, boarded a waiting train at Kantara. Around them clustered hordes of small Arab children asking for money and food, ragged urchins, noisy, dirty, half naked, chattering like starlings and in their importunity at times using the most frightful language they had picked up from the thousands of other soldiers who had passed through Kantara. But as the train moved off at about 0930 hrs already thickly coated with dust, it left them far behind as it moved through and into a strange land for these Australians. They were travelling along the eastern corner of the southern Mediterranean coast, across the Sinai Desert, and about 100 miles further on would pass into Palestine. The Sinai Peninsula is a rugged roughly triangular wedge hemmed in between Palestine on the east and the main part of Egypt on the west. Since time immemorial the Sinai Peninsula and its grim deserts has been a highway for merchants and soldiers. In every age great armies have marched across its grim wilderness, going down into Egypt, or up to Syria and beyond. Sinai, and the Palestine for which they were bound, were lands of acquired memories for the Australians who had arrived from their own far-distant country.

The railway on which they travelled had been built by the British as part of the operations in the 1914-1918 War when the Australian Light Horse had formed the cream of the British Forces in that part of the world. Romani, where the railway first touched the coast after striking across the north-west corner of Sinai from Kantara, was the place where Gen Chauvel's

Australian Light Horse had taken the brunt of the attack of 28,000 Turks in 1916. The turks had been beaten with great loss and fallen back on El Arish.

Vividly, to a few of the soldiers of the new war, to nearly all, dimly, such things were known as they travelled from Kantara to Gaza, Sometimes they saw the sea but were particularly conscious of the desert stretching away on their right. They passed occasional oases of date palms and a few gum trees which brought vivid memories of home.

The train let them down a mile or so beyond Gaza. Heavily burdened they marched a similar distance and came to a place called Kilo 89 at 1500 hrs in the afternoon and moved into an area where the 2/8 Bn of 6 Div had been training before it left for Egypt.

This was a tented camp. The men would sleep 10 to a tent on Indian beds made of Bamboo approx 2'6" wide by 6'6" long. The beds had to be securely staked to the ground or they would roll over as the sleeper turned. Securely fastened to the centre pole of each tent were racks into which rifles would be locked while the men slept. Palestine had been (and still was despite a temporary and uneasy truce) a troubled land where an Arab would give almost anything for a rifle and where, moving like a shadow, he would slide into a darkened tent and steal the weapons almost from beneath the hands of the owners.

Colonel Crawford was settling his Bn to elementary training once more to get them fit after the long voyage. The days were filled with route marching, trench digging, weapon and Pl training. Although torrents of rain swamped the Bn during its first few days in camp the weather soon cleared to the bright days and cold crisp mornings which were typical of that time of the year in Palestine. There were few complaints; it was accepted that the token weapons which were used in some phases of the training would soon be replaced by real weapons as War Establishment entitlements arrived. More serious for the moment was the unending diet of baked beans which, day after day, appeared three times in the messes, either because nothing else was available or because the army was indulging in one of its periodic attempts to "turn over" supplies of tinned food. Leave parties got off to Jerusalem and other ancient places. Thus the Bn was building up a pleasant pattern of work and leisure when it received orders to move.

On 11 Dec, Colonel Crawford and the IO, Lt McCarthy, left for Port Said in Egypt, followed that afternoon by an advance party Comd by Lt Ochiltree. 2/17 Bn would relieve 2 Bn of the Highland Light Infantry at Port Said Garrison. It left Kilo 89 by train on 15 Dec and arrived at Port Said next morning. Soon after it took over from the Highlanders, and found its Coys and Pls spread from Kantara to various vulnerable areas throughout the Port Said area. They were so scattered and so occupied with guard duties that there was little opportunity for training. Nevertheless the men welcomed the opportunity of sampling life in an Egyptian city and their period in Port Said rapidly became one which none would ever quite forget. It was full of humorous incident and interest and stories which those who survived would tell again and again in the years to come.

Colonel Crawford figured in the first of them — the night he and McCarthy arrived in the city. They went to dinner at the Continental Hotel with the British Security Officer for Port Said — an Australian named Griffin who had been there since the 1914-1918 War and knew everybody. Griffin was talking at another table, the CO was about to have a word with some other Officers nearby and McCarthy said casually that he thought he would dance. The CO followed his gaze, brightened visibly at the sight of the dark-haired, beautiful girl who sat opposite with only an elderly man for company. He commanded his disconcerted Subaltern: "Then bring her back here for coffee", and went off jauntily stroking his moustache.

Griffin came back and McCarthy asked him "Do you know the girl in blue?" Griffin said quietly "Yes! She is the most active and successful enemy agent operating in Egypt at the present time". As he digested this information, McCarthy was considering the curious state of affairs in the Middle East where, Egypt not being at war, the British could do nothing about such a situation. His CO returned and inquired sharply why he was still sitting there alone. McCarthy informed him of the lady's status, Colonel Crawford wilted and then announced that it was time they returned to camp.

Other ladies of different interest engaged some of the attention of the 2/17 Bn at Port Said. The Australian soldier, compared with most others of his kind, cared little for women other than his own in any absorbing way; as a diversion, yes, to be taken lightly and briefly by some, usually with much amusement, and quickly cast aside when more serious things were afoot. And it is probably true to say that more Australian soldiers deliberately kept themselves aloof from women who sought them out. There were a variety of reasons; faithfulness to their own; a genuine preference for beer and the company of men; fear of venereal disease.

It was partly this fear of disease (stimulated by the experience of a few of his men in Bombay) which caused Crawford to take a decision which must have been difficult for him (fastidious and idealist as he was). While he placed all other brothels strictly out of bounds for his Bn, he ordered that the Constantinople and the Golden House were within bounds each alternate night. He directed "Slam" Sullivan to have a medical detachment on duty each night at whichever of these places was in bounds to provide compulsory phrophylaxis for the 2/17 Bn men who might patronise the place. So in 6 weeks of Garrison duty at Port Said only one case of venereal disease occurred in the Bn — and this in an overlusty soldier who after 8 successive nights at the Constantinople and the Golden House wandered illegally into the Arab quarter seeking something different — and found it.

For the most part, however, the battalion sought its nightly diversions in the clubs and cafes which were open to all ranks throughout the city. High in favour with them were the Hotel de la Poste and the night club La Cigale with its orthodox entertainment and its friendly staff. There indeed some fleeting romances bloomed. Memories of these more exotic places of entertainment were to blend in the men's minds with most grateful memories of hospitality by the British residents of Port Said in their own homes, and in their own particular haunts. Most of them at this time were employees of the oil companies.

So their leisure was made pleasant with such friends in such places, and with plenty of sport. But there was also much work. Thus their days and nights were very full, and the sights and sounds of this eastern city quickly became a familiar scene to them; the gully gully men with their magic; the vendors of "feelthy postcards" who, more often than not, they drove away with a shouted "Imshi"; the shoe shine boys who would sometimes spit on the soldiers' boots when they said they did not need cleaning; the beggars; the shops with their unusual wares.

Christmas came and, with it, plenty of bottled beer. But trouble came with this abundance. It seemed that many cases of beer had disappeared from the dump of canteen supplies at Cherrif Quay, and official investigations began. It was said that a British guard on the dump had been relieved by a "new guard" with a Sgt in charge; but that the "new guard" was not in fact a guard at all and the "sergeant" was a private soldier from 2/17 Bn. There were inquiries and some searches but the story generally was officially discredited because none of the missing beer was found. It was buried beneath the sandy floors of the tents in HQ Coy lines; the relieving "guard" had been from the Sig Pl.

This first Christmas abroad was nevertheless a solemn and nostalgic time for many of these soldiers. While probably few would admit to it, perhaps the remarkable orderliness throughout the city was proof of it on this Christmas Eve. On Christmas Day special dinners were provided for all and every man received an Australian Comforts Fund parcel. The contents (sweets, tobacco and cigarettes, tinned fruit, plum puddings, a bottle of beer) were much appreciated but probably not a man who didn't get his greatest satisfaction from the quiet knowledge that in this way, as best they could, the people of his own country were reaching out to him.

After Christmas the days passed quickly, with guard duties — and training that began to be concentrated in part on the Bren light machine guns, the first of which were then arriving on issue to the Bn. On 30 and 31 Dec, however, there were reminders that the War was not simply a Middle East affair. On those two days almost 5,000 troops were disembarked at Port Said — some Indian some British. The Bn assisted the disembarkation. So far they had seen little of the British Army but, while most counted themselves in no way inferior to those British troops, nevertheless they regarded them with a curious respect. A feeling of personal fellowship very rapidly grew with these men and, listening to some of their stories of the bombing which England was suffering, and the circumstances of living in that little island in the midst of conflict, many of the Australians felt a new and even stronger resolve to stand by the British to the bitter end.

With December, news had come to the Garrison at Port Said of battle in the desert. To the ordinary soldier, security precautions so shrouded the details that the impact of this news was muffled. Then came the news that the first Australians would soon be going into battle in the desert — and with reports in early January that the 6 Div was actually heavily engaged. The news and some of the evidence, was however sufficiently real to cause impatience with their static role to grow in the 2/17 Bn. This increased when the first of the Italian prisoners taken in the desert arrived in Port Said on 3 Jan on their way to India. The guards from the 2/17 Bn found them quiet and orderly, poor physical types but intelligent looking — apprehensive, however, of Australians of whom many believed "They do NOT take prisoners".

The 2/17 Bn men were excited when they learned they were soon to move again, but it quickly became disappointingly clear that they were returning to Palestine. At 0815 hrs on 10 Jan they moved out from Port Said by train and arrived at Kantara about 2 hrs later. They had some 5 hrs there in a setting which was already becoming very familiar; the Canal and the desert stretching into the distance; a meal at the NAAFI; ragged and foul-mouthed Arab urchins; and then the train pulling out once more along the familiar and historical route. Eight and a half hours after they left Kantara they were back at Kilo 89.

They lived 10 or 12 men to a tent in conditions of some discomfort. They settled to hardening exercises to get the softness of the Garrison city out of them; to weapon training once more; to Pl and Coy training; to special exercises by day and by night. For the first week or two after their return, the weather was dull and cold and they worked in rain with the ground heavy beneath their feet. Then the fine clear Palestine weather set in once more. There were alarms of various kinds; in late January warning of the possibility of organised raids on the Kilo 89 camps by Arab rifle thieves, and so all security measures were rechecked, extra guards and patrols provided; air raid warnings were not infrequent.

They went on leave to Jerusalem and wandered through the labyrinth of little ways in the Old City. They wondered at the unchanging nature of it all and saw the people with downcast eyes and their donkeys as beings from another world; they saw the holy places; they rested their foreheads on the Wailing Wall. They drank and danced in the New Jerusalem which wrapped round and enclosed the Old (already wrapped around by its ancient walls). They went off on leave to the modern Jewish City of Tel Aviv and contrasted its newness and its bright fever with the old Jaffa from which and beside which it had grown. A few went to the farms and the fields where Jewish communities — men, women and children — were at disciplined and minutely organised work building new lives and a new country from the ashes of their pain-filled pasts.

Some went as guests to Arab villages and marked the contrasts with the Jewish settlements and purposes. They fostered in 2/15 Bn at the beginning of February. (It had been on Garrison duty in Darwin when the rest of the Bde left Australia).

On 4 Feb they paraded at Deir Suneid for mysterious "Mr A " — to find that they were being reviewed with the rest of the 7 Div by their own Prime Minister, Mr Menzies, who told them "Australia is proud of you; we on the home front will work 24 hours a day to give you the backing you need".

They grumbled at the lateness and slowness of the mails. Rumours of movement and possible action rippled through them like wind through wheat fields and, passing left them feeling cheated and bored. They became hard and fit and noticeably better trained.

On the morning of 19 Feb they moved out towards Beersheba on their first battalion exercise; they advanced on, attacked, occupied, and defended old 1914-1918 positions. They withdrew from these, they moved in the night as well as the day. They arrived back at Kilo 89 in the mid afternoon of 22 Feb, comfortable and well within themselves after 14 miles on foot through very hot, dry country in very hot, dry weather.

Then rumours of impending movement began to sweep through the camp with a strength that no previous rumours had had. Excitement grew and continued to grow. There were wild guesses at the destination, but many said confidently, "Greece".

It was nearly midnight on 27 Feb when 2/17 Bn began the 2-mile march to the railway station at Gaza, burdened as only foot soldiers and pack animals can be burdened. But they moved through the darkness with an ease and practised discipline which promised well for their future operations. This time rumour had not lied; another Inf Bn of the AIF was moving up into battle.

Postscript

While in Australia soldiers had constantly asked, "When are we going away?" The Army had not answered with a time or a standard to be attained. Many felt that the Army was just filling in time, not unpleasantly, but without purpose. It had taken 10 months for 2/17 Bn to move to an operational area. This was not an unusual delay for AIF Battalions in War II but barely a gratifying military performance.

Kilo 89 Camp in Palestine, November 1940

CHAPTER 3
INTO THE DESERT

When 2/17 Bn left Gaza early on the morning of 28 Feb 1941, many of them still thought they were going to Greece. But they were headed for Libya, beyond the western borders of Egypt.

The River Nile is the life blood of Egypt. Rising far to the south in the centre of Africa, it is already a great river by the time it enters Egypt, becoming greater as it flows through the fertile delta parallel with the Red Sea. Then it parallels the Suez Canal and reaches the Mediterranean through several mouths which extend from Port Said westward to Alexandria. But west of the Nile is no other life-giving river. Between the delta and the Libyan border stretches what the British call the Western Desert; a desert which continues then across the whole breadth of Libya.

By February 1941 Gen Wavell's forces, including 6 Div, had defeated the Italians at Bardia, Tobruk, Derna and Benghazi, while south of Benghazi the 7 Armd Div which had struck across the desert to Beda Fomm, finally defeated the Italian armoured troops desperately trying to escape along the road to Tripoli.

Meanwhile, other Australians had pushed on to the south of Benghazi to help the British in the Beda Fomm fighting — but they did not get there in time to take part.

Then developed what may possibly have been one of the most costly mistakes of the war for British arms. Mr Churchill and the Chiefs of Staff in London had consistently regarded the advance through Libya as basically a defensive operation with the purpose of achieving "a safe flank for Egypt", perhaps at Tobruk, perhaps at Benghazi.

Thereafter, all operations in the Middle East were to be subordinated to sending forces to a threatened Greece. Early Greek refusals to accept aid had led to the decision to extend the flank past Tobruk to Benghazi. Reconsideration of these refusals now led the British virtually to abandon their sweeping successes in Libya as they re-assembled their forces for an expedition to Greece. From 20 Feb onwards only one Bn (of 17 Bde) remained in the forward area, where the line had been established at Marsa Brega (over 100 miles south of Benghazi), together with an Armd Car Regt of the Kings Dragoon Guards, a little artillery and some ancillary troops. From that date these troops were brushing with questing German forces and subject to daily and increasing air attack. But even then there appeared little, if any, appreciation on the part of the higher formations responsible that the war in Libya might be entering a new phase and that an enemy of a far different calibre from the Italians was beginning to measure his opponents. This lack of appreciation was soon to prove to be a very costly mistake.

If this enemy came forward in strength it was likely to meet opposition which, brave though it might be, seemed doomed in advance to be largely ineffective. Not only would it lack strength (the main forces having been drained away to Greece) but it would be offered by troops who were far from fully trained, were at the very best only about half equipped, and were only then gathered for the first time into a completely new formation — the 9th Australian Division.

It should be recalled that the decision to form this Div had been taken in September 1940.

Before that, however, (following the formation of the 6 Div) the 7 and 8 Divs had been forming and training and their development greatly affected the plans which had originally been made for the formation of the 9th.

By the end of 1940, the 7 Div was in the Middle East and planning was advanced to send part at least of the 8 Div to Malaya. There were other AIF troops abroad, however, whom Army re-organisations and the chances of war had so far excluded from actual integration with any of these divisions.

Not only had the 18 Bde been diverted round the Cape of Good Hope to England but various other units had been diverted in the same convoy. In England these units had been reorganised into the 25 Bde. In October it was decided that these two Bdes would form the nucleus of the 9 Div with Maj Gen Wynter (possibly the most profound military thinker in the Australian Regular Army and then commanding the troops in England) in command. The third Bde would be formed in Australia, together with additional artillery and ancillary units which would be required. But Gen Blamey insisted that 18 and 25 Bdes should be linked with units of a standard of training as similar as possible and not with new untrained units. It was decided, therefore, to divert 24 Bde, the 2/3 A/Tk Regt, and the Fd Coys from the 8 Div and send them to the 9th in the Middle East.

Wynter sailed from England in November with 18 Bde, left the convoy at Cape Town to fly to Cairo, and then opened the HQ of the 9 Div at Julis in Palestine on 24 Dec. About one third of his Div (including 18 Bde) would arrive from England at the end of the month; on 3 Jan 1941, 25 Bde and the other troops still left in England would sail for the Middle East and on the same day 24 Bde and other troops raised in Australia would leave Fremantle. But Wynter would never command a concentrated 9 Div for he fell seriously ill soon after his arrival in Palestine and Brig Morshead was promoted to succeed him in Comd of the Div.

Maj Gen L. Morshead

At that time Morshead had his Bde at Ikingi Maryut (just south and west of Alexandria) preparing for operations in a detached role against Giarabub (oasis about 150 miles south of Bardia where some 2,000 Italian and Libyan troops had been bypassed and isolated). Lt Col Wootten was promoted to succeed him in Comd of 18 Bde. Morshead then reported at Julis to take over his new Comd on 5 Feb. But the composition of this Comd was to change even before he had a chance to get the feel of it.

Towards the end of February a final decision was made to send an expeditionary force to Greece. Blamey, who considered the projected enterprise a most hazardous one, wanted his best trained and most experienced troops to make up the Australian component. He decided, therefore, that the 6 Div should be brought back from the desert (although Wavell had planned that they should stay there) and that the 7 Div (which it was thought would follow the 6th to Greece) should be re-organised to include 18 and 25 Bdes which would be replaced in the 9 Div by the 20 and 26 Bdes "as a temporary expedient only". The reconstituted 9 Div would then relieve the 6 Div forward of Benghazi.

In his new Comd, Morshead was going to need all his great qualities; the strength of his forceful personality; his incisive imperturbability; his determination; and the knowledge of soldiering he had developed from experience and built by military study and reflection.

Of his three Bdes, the 20th was the oldest, the best trained, and had been longest in Palestine (although it had not reached the point of carrying out its first battalion exercise until the second half of February); 24 Bde had been formed in July and had only recently arrived in the Middle East (less its 2/25 Bn which was on Garrison duty at Darwin). The 26th had also been formed in July and had arrived in Palestine about a month before the 24th. All these Bdes were far below their authorised scale of weapons and equipment and greatly deficient in transport. The Div's artillery (2/7, 2/8 and 2/12 Fd Regts and 2/3 A/Tk) were similarly deficient in training and equipment — perhaps more so.

Deficiencies in the training and equipment of his formations were only part of Morshead's difficulties. He had to build a new staff around him which would need experience to weld it into an efficient team (although he was fortunate in having as his chief Staff Officer, Col C E M Lloyd, a brilliant and highly trained Duntroon graduate, direct, impatient of humbug, but friendly and patient with those who had something to offer). And just as this Staff could not be a team for some time to come, neither could their Div, not only because the formations had not worked together but because two at least of them (20 and 26 Bdes) would be bitterly resentful of being transferred out of the 7 Div. They saw themselves proudly as members of one of the two earliest AIF Divs; they had no wish to belong to a Div which was numbered 4th among the Divs in order of creation (an important point to proud volunteers to whom their early enlistment and all the outward signs of it were a matter of great pride); at this time they knew little or nothing of the story behind the 9 Div's development, cared less, and regarded it as an upstart formation.

Orders for the transfer reached Brig Murray on 26 Feb but some time was to elapse before the news seeped down through the ranks of the Bn. With the other two Bns the 2/17th was getting ready for the move for which they had waited so impatiently. As it dawned on them that this move was towards Libya, and not Greece, there was some disappointment among them; they feared that the fighting in the desert had been finished off by 6 Div — and the one thing they now wanted to do was fight.

To most of the soldiers it mattered little that they had had little or no experience in the higher levels of military activity (at the Battalion, Brigade and Divisional level). Many of them were not even aware that their Officers particularly needed this form of training before they could be regarded as being really trained and competent. There was in this Bn an individual confidence which events were more than to justify. Each man felt himself to be hard and fit; he knew his weapons; he fitted well into an integrated place in his platoon or company and could move confidently in that place by day or by night; he knew and trusted his comrades; he was proud of his Bn and knew enough of what the first 17th Battalion had done to have a standard below which he was determined not to fall. He was very proud of the success of the 6 Div in the desert but was getting very tired of hearing about it while he himself had done no fighting and burned to prove that he could do as well or better.

The 2/17 Bn men were packed closely in the train as it left Gaza on the night of 27/28 Feb. The journey to Kantara had now become very familiar to them, but they were on new ground as they crossed the delta by the desert railway, skirted Alexandria and headed for Mersa Matruh where the railway ended. Many of them lay on the floors and it was difficult to move about the crowded train among these tightly packed bodies and soldiers' equipment and weapons which had to be fitted in. As they approached Ikingi Maryut towards 1500 hrs on the 28th they had their first taste of the true desert; a violent windstorm blew up, driving such masses of dust and sand before it that many put on their respirators so that they could breathe better in the closely packed compartments which they were now almost choking with the swirling dust. At Ikingi Maryut itself there was a hot stew waiting — but the dust ruined it. They got cakes, cigarettes and tobacco from the Comforts Fund. After about half an hour, they were on their way again and soon the darkness of their first desert night closed heavily around them.

It was 0130 hrs on the morning of 1 Mar when they arrived at Mersa Matruh. The darkness was bleak with bitterly cold wind and rain, a strange introduction to soldiering in the desert. They could see nothing of this place at which they had arrived with an anticipation born of the feelings that here the real desert began — and here, they felt, they would begin their first real experience of war. This anticipation became numb as they stood and waited in the cold, wind-driven, dust-streaked rain for some order to be developed out of the chaos of their arrival, for the trucks which would take them to the old barracks about 4 miles west of the port. The last of them reached the barracks well after dawn. In that broken and war-scarred place, the excitement of the first part of their journey over, weary, hungry and numbed by the wet and cold, shrill wind, not knowing what lay ahead, their spirits drooped a little. But they quickly got fires going and before these they sheltered from the wind and the rain, became warm and comfortable, and their first issue of rum added the final touch. By unpractised hands, however, the demijohns were issued with such liberality that they ran to about a pannikin per man of the fiery, overproof spirit. Soon the excitement of their journey, fatigue and the rum catching up with them, most of the men slept where they were in the ruined barracks, while the desert sun climbed high.

They awoke in their usual high spirits. For the first time they felt that they were in a battle area. They could see where bombs and machine gun fire from the raids had shattered and scarred the buildings and pocked the ground. In some places there was a great clutter of salvaged and captured material which had been brought back from further up in the desert. As Gen Wavell had initially made this place his most forward base it had become the centre of widespread defences and the minefields which had been part of these added a sense of danger — particularly as occasional mines were detonated during the day.

These mines were an irresistible attraction to some of the men like Neville West who had inquiring, mechanical minds and who welcomed the chance to pull these dangerous playthings to pieces and re-assemble them. To such men the possibility of being blown to bits as they worked added the ultimate fascination.

To others in the Bn, Mersa Matruh offered different interests, to everybody at this time it offered *something*. To such men as "Blue" Allan (who had just taken over from John Williams as 2 i/c of the Bn) and Duncan McNab (who had just arrived by road and whose QM's duties were endless) there was the opportunity to scrounge from the military paraphernalia which was all about; items which would add to the Bn's too scanty warlike stores and its efficiency — even motorcycles. Other men sought out soldiers of the 6 Div who were on their way back to Egypt to learn first-hand from them of the fighting which had been taking place in the desert and perhaps to get news of friends and relatives in that Div.

On 3 Mar, a long convoy of motor vehicles carrying the whole of the 20 Bde, with the 2/13 Bn in the leading vehicles and the 2/15th at the tail of the column, took the long desert road westward.

At Mersa Matruh they left behind groups of men who watched them go with heavy hearts. These men would return to Palestine to staff the 20 Inf Training Bn. To this training Bn would

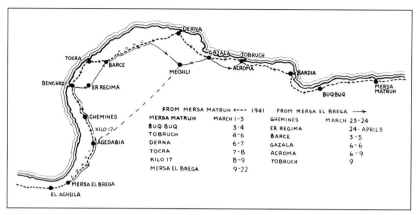

Libyan Desert

come reinforcements for the 3 Bns of the Bde; through this training Bn would pass "X List" men (who because of wounds, illness or for various other reasons, had been temporarily away from the Bns in the field and were on their way back to those units). Within the 20 ITB there would be 3 Coys, made up of men belonging to, destined for, or on their way back to 2/13, 2/15 and 2/17 Bns respectively. To form and work their Coy, 2/17 left behind Maj John Williams, Capt John Broadbent, Capt P E O'Brien and Lt A J Wright; 9 Sgts; 5 Cpls and L/Cpls; 13 Pte Soldiers. This group of Offrs and Men would carry a heavy responsibility for ensuring that soldiers going up to the Bn in action were sufficiently hard and well trained to be effective as soon as they arrived, and at the same time have themselves that greater chance of survival in battle which the trained man has. John Williams and his group were specially chosen; most of them would rejoin the Bn after a few months and several would distinguish themselves greatly. But this was poor consolation as they watched the long convoys go forward out along the desert road while they prepared to turn back. On return to Australia, the system was discontinued. A Branch apparently found it better to handle reinforcements en masse.[1]

Also watching the Bn leave was Jessel Silverstone (now a Major). He was going to a Corps HQ posting in which the chances of war would take him later to Greece. He would be marked for his courage and efficiency there before being taken by the Germans as a snapping and unwilling prisoner.

So, followed by the gaze of these comrades, 2/17 Bn disappeared into the desert haze and dust. For 2 days they travelled through it, 17 to 20 men packed tightly in the back of lurching trucks. As they travelled into and through Bardia the debris and waste of war became thicker. Thousands of weapons of all kinds, from field pieces to rifles and bayonets, lay about or had been stacked in great heaps. There were hundreds of broken cars and trucks, smashed or burnt out tanks by the score, sometimes crashed and gutted aircraft.

On 5 Mar, they were bivouaced 4 miles west of Tobruk. The wind was blowing great clouds of dust over the town so they could not see much. They did note, however, the white and broken buildings; the great masses of captured material on all sides; the wrecks in the harbour among which friendly ships were moving or at anchor; thousands of Italian prisoners at work repairing the port installations. They kept a sharp lookout for anything they might "pick up" to help along the way or in the fighting to come and particularly made good their lack of light machine guns by helping themselves to Bredas and Fiats. Some optimists peered into buildings or recesses here

1
   See Postscript – page 34

and there, hoping that 6 Div might have overlooked some small store of Chianti. But it was a vain hope.

When they took the roads onwards the next day, the head of the Bde convoy was straffed by 5 aeroplanes. Two of 2/13 Bn were killed. As the column moved on again after these attacks it spread to a greater space between each of the vehicles and a greater alertness marked its movement. Towards the end of the day it climbed sharply and steeply over and down the great escarpment into Derna, white-walled, compact and attractive, not much touched by war. Next day it wound a toilsome way round the steep bends and turnsof the road which led out of Derna again across the escarpment. As it approached Giovanni Berta the fertile beauty and cultivated land of the Jebel Achdar spread out before and around the amazed soldiers. Italian settlers (who had already learned that they had little to fear from Australians) greeted them and were given friendly greetings in return. The locals gave or sold fresh farm food to the travellers and waved them on their way as they moved towards the thriving town of Barce (on the high lands of the escarpment as it now spread widely eastward.

After Barce the Convoy moved slowly down the western slopes of the escarpment and halted for the night at Tocra by the sea. They were approaching their journey's end as they headed south next day, moved out of the Jebel Achdar into semi-desert country and travelled towards Benghazi. The convoy approached that busy town by way of Er Regima and Benina (where many broken and burnt out aircraft lay on and about an airfield) then wound steeply once more down the western slope of the escarpment but turned sharply south just before they reached Benghazi. The road then took them through Beda Fomm and there, almost as it was when the desperate fighting ended, was the field of battle where the tanks of 7th British Armd Div (after their swift, outflanking dash across the desert road) had flung themselves upon the Italian armour and foot which were seeking safety on the long road which led to Tripoli. The Italians had fought bravely and skilfully so that the outcome of the battle was for some time in doubt. But now, some three weeks later, there was silence at Beda Fomm. All about was the waste of war, and over the desert the wind was gently moving many thousands of letters and other items of mail which had never reached the men to whom they were addressed and now never would. Silently through this sad litter 2/17 Bn moved on into darkness and camped that night about 2200 hrs near Agedabia. It was the night of 8 Mar.

Ahead some 30 miles lay a natural defensive area which they were to occupy. Spreading inland from the little town of Marsa Brega on the coast was an area of salt marshes which enclosed sand dunes and rolling stretches of firmer going. Occupation of this area could deny the road from Tripoli which approached Marsa Brega by way of El Agheila some 20 miles to the south-west. The position could, however, be outflanked on the east by an approach from the south.

2/15 and 2/17 Bns relieved 17 Bde of 6 Div on 9 Mar. On the right, just north-east of Marsa Brega, 2/15th took over the positions astride the main road leading in from Agheila; on the left of the road, and some 10 miles further back, 2/17th took over from the main body of 2/7 Bn. 2/13th (less one coy) remained in the Beda Fomm area as Bde reserve. As soon as the relief was completed 17 Bde set out on the road back to Egypt. 20 Bde was then left as the main Inf component of the force which would face any advance from Tripoli. The other two Bdes of 9 Div were still in Palestine.

With 20 Bde was an attenuated British force. 7 Armd Div, worn out, had been withdrawn to Egypt. Half of Wavell's only other available armour, the recently arrived 2 Armd Div, was to go to Greece, and the half in Cyrenaica was not only incomplete in its tank strength but most of its vehicles already needed repair. The main component of this half was 3 Armd Bde; on the vulnerable eastern flank for which they were responsible they had only 3rd Hussars with about 25 light tanks and two Coys of 1st Free French Motorised Bn. Patrolling forward to Agheila and the south they had 1st King's Dragoon Guards, a Reconnaissance Bn equipped with armd cars. 1 Tower Hamlet Rifles, a motorised Inf Bn, was guarding prisoners of war at Benghazi, with 1st Royal Northumberland Fusiliers. As far back as the approaches to Tobruk were most of 5th and 6th Royal Tank Regts (the main tank strength of 3 Armd Bde) equipped with worn out Cruiser tanks or re-equipping with captured Italian tanks. The force was, however, pretty well set up with artillery 1st and 104th Royal Horse Artillery and the 51 Fd Regt.

The top command in Cyrenaica had been taken over by Lt Gen Sir Phillip Neame VC, KBE, CB, DSO, on 26 Feb. He was a most gallant and highly trained British regular who had been Deputy Chief of the General Staff of the British Expeditionary Forces in France in 1939 and early 1940. But he had had no experience in operational command in this war and none at a high level in the previous war.

Neame apparently shared the delusion which was so common to British generals that Australian forces were not only undisciplined but could operate effectively only when broken up and placed under British commanders. He told Morshead when the latter arrived at the HQ of Cyrenaica Command on 7 Mar, that shortly 20 Bde would come under the command of the 2 Armd Div while Morshead himself would supervise the training of the rest of his Div much further back towards Tobruk. Very coldly Morshead replied that he was "not impressed with this arrangement".

About 3 weeks after that Neame was complaining bitterly to Morshead about the conduct of Australian troops in Cyrenaica. The latter was very angry believing that, although *some* of Neame's criticisms were no doubt justified the general picture which he drew was gross exaggeration. He believed also that the use of such terms as "Australian drunkenness" revealed an obvious anti-Australian bias on Neame's part. He made his feelings very clear to his superior.

Meanwhile, however, events were moving so swiftly to a climax in the field that there was little time for brooding on such matters.

In the most forward area at Marsa Brega, after taking over from 2/7 Bn in the darkness, 2/17th spent the rest of the night undisturbed while they dug in their new positions. With the dawn they continued their digging in flying sand and dust which was driven by a strong wind. About 0915 hrs a single German aircraft flew fast and low over them with AA shells bursting behind it from positions further back. This was the day's only incident. Just after dark, a hot meal was brought forward from their own maintenance area further back, and this put them in good heart.

They settled cheerfully enough to the discomfort of their new positions. They worked on the holes in which they lived and from which they prepared to fight. As they worked the winds blew dust and sand over them in clouds; sometimes it seemed to advance before the wind as a solid wall; as they slept it buried them. They covered these holes and camouflaged them. Sometimes at night, getting his first experience of moving about that featureless desert in the darkness and, lost for a little while within his own lines, someone would fall into someone else's hole (or even his own).

Quite often aeroplanes attacked them with machine gun fire (usually Heinkels or Dorniers), sometimes circling and studying them carefully and then coming in low out of the sun. They took these on with light machine guns, rifles, and sometimes A/Tk rifles. They suffered no casualties in these attacks and began to learn at first hand that troops dug in on the ground had little to fear from air attack (knowledge which was to stand them in good stead later).

Constantly watchful of air attack, and, more importantly, anxious not to betray the extent of their positions and their strength to reconnoitring aircraft, they had to keep close to their holes.

Nevertheless they did not merely sit and wait. They patrolled all round their positions. The first patrols to the south (on 11 Mar) went through Marsa Brega and found no life there, only bomb scars, broken houses and all the desolation of a deserted village. On the 14th, Capt Curly Wilson took his B Coy to an outpost position at Cemetary Hill, forward to 2/15th positions and west of Marsa Brega. The following day John Balfe had patrols from his D Coy reconnoitering to the north of the Bn positions. On the night of the 19/20th, Lt "Kanga" Maclarn took a patrol from his Bren Gun Carrier Pl, 8 or 10 miles west of Agheila but without any contact.

In general however, the period in the Marsa Brega positions was dull and uneventful, except for the air attacks. Water was scarce. The food was generally dry and monotonous. Sand flies were a pest. Some men who had salvaged small bits of furniture from abandoned Italian houses found that they had imported bugs into their holes; the bugs tormented them at night. The changing winds blew the sand backwards and forwards. A type of sandfly fever and influenza appeared in the Bn. Many of the men (with the average Australian soldier's ability to assess any situation in which he found himself) found their military senses sharpened by their static conditions and, as their knowledge of the general area in which they were sited built up, asked themselves why they were not further forward.

Already Gen Morshead had been asking that question. He visited them on 16 Mar, surveyed their positions, and said that they were too far from the enemy. The next day, summoned unexpectedly to meet the Chief of the Imperial General Staff, Gen Dill, and Gen Wavell near Beda Fomm at Neame's HQ, he enlarged this view saying that the forward line should be based on the salt marsh country just forward of Agheila and should consist of mobile forces; that, despite the existing orders, his 20 Bde could not avoid becoming seriously committed in their present positions. Dill and Wavell accepted this view, told Neame to arrange the relief of 20 Bde by mobile troops and ordered that, if an attack came (and they then accepted that one on a limited scale was building up), Neame should fight a delaying action to the escarpment east of Benghazi. Dill said to Neame:

> "You are going to get a bloody nose here Phillip, and it is not the only place we shall get bloody noses".

In accordance with this revised planning (although knowing nothing of it) 20 Bde began the move back on the night of 22 Mar, over a road which straffing German aeroplanes made most hazardous by day. By 1930 hrs, 2/17 had assembled on the road, packed into trucks and started a long, cold journey. There was no moon and the night was very dark. The lightly clothed men shivered as they huddled uncomfortably in the backs of the jolting trucks. On the dark narrow road, with no lights, the laden vehicles felt their way in a long fumbling line. Occasionally one of them lurched heavily and plunged off the road, hung on the very edge of overturning but, its motor roaring and straining, clawed a way back again. Soon even such misadventures began to lose their meaning to the numb soldiers who could only sit in the cold and inky darkness and hope vaguely that their own truck would keep to the road. Time and distance lost much of its meaning to them. It was the dawn of another day when they halted about 4 miles south of Ghemines (between Beda Fomm and Benghazi). They dug their holes quickly and then got in them and slept.

About 1100 hrs heavy bombing nearby roused them and they watched a column of smoke rise and billow into a spreading black pall at nearby Ghemines where the bombs had fired 32,000 gallons of petrol. Except for that smoke the day was bright and clear with no wind or dust. For the first half of the night the Bn waited in its bivouac area. The men rested or smoked and talked in the quiet darkness. At 0200 hrs they climbed back into the trucks and took to the road once more. The journey was rather different from that of the previous night for, although there was the same bitter cold, the night was still and bright with stars.

Early the following morning the convoy was climbing the escarpment east of Benghazi. It passed through Benina where the airfield was marked by the wrecks of many aircraft. Australian airmen silently watched it pass. Shortly afterwards, at 0900 hrs it lumbered to a halt at Er Regima. There was green grass there and trees, soft and pleasing to eyes which had quickly become used to peering through flying dust and over the barrenness of salt marsh and desert. There was plenty of water to drink and for washing. Below, forming an avenue leading into Benghazi, were Australian gum trees and wattles. The town itself, with its white buildings in ordered squares, looked inviting and far from war. In fact, however, it was so much part of the war that systematic and daily bombing had denied the use of its fine harbour to the invaders so that all their needs had to be carried from Tobruk over some hundreds of miles of desert road.

The next morning Colonel Crawford was off to an early start with the Adjt, Capt J G S Moffatt. The two went off to reconnoitre the positions which the Bn would occupy along the escarpment, looking west across the coastal plain to the sea and down on Benghazi from the heights above. By this time it was fairly well known through the Bn that the higher planning envisaged an advancing enemy being shepherded into the coastal plain with the sea on one side and on the other the escarpment. Attempts to break out across the escarpment were to be destroyed by 9 Div troops sited along that bold feature.

The following day, Crawford issued his orders for the occupation of the escarpment position to his Coy Comds: Claude Brien, A Coy; "Curly" Wilson, B Coy; Keith Magno, C Coy; John Balfe, D Coy. Brien's, Wilson's and Balfe's Coys would be forward, covering about 20 miles of front, with Magno's C Coy in reserve. On the right Brien would have a common boundary with

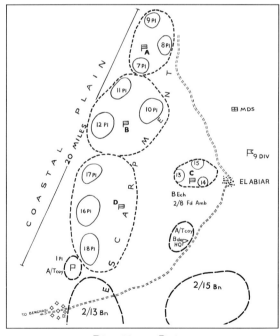

Dispositions at Regima

26 Bde which would begin moving into the Barce-Tocra area the following day, although Brig Tovell could assemble only his 2/23 and 2/24 Bns (2/48 being forced to wait at Gazala, not far forward from Tobruk, for transport to become available to move it). On the left Balfe would have a common boundary with 2/13 Bn which had the task of holding the pass over the escarpment at Er Regima. 2/15th would cover the southern flank of 20 Bde. These dispositions called for the line of the escarpment from Tocra to Er Regima, a distance of 62 miles, to be held by 3 Bns — 2/24th (2/23rd was at Barce), 2/17 and 2/13. To their positions on this line 2/17 Bn set out on foot at 1400 hrs on the afternoon of 26 Mar.

The going proved to be very tough and the maps lacked detail and were unreliable. The country was scrub covered, mountainous and scored through with difficult ravines. The struggle by the heavily burdened troops to get into position continued during the 27th but, by the end of that day, Wilson's men and Balfe's were in the areas which had been allotted to them. From Brien's A Coy, however, on the right flank, there was no word. On the 28th, Wilson and Balfe were siting their positions on a wide and wild front, reconnoitring tracks, and seeking to cover the routes by which armoured fighting vehicles might climb the escarpment. But by the end of the day there was still no word from Brien. On the 30th, Crawford himself went looking for his missing Coy but the tracks running north from El Abiar towards the edge of the escarpment at first proved impassible to vehicles. He persisted, and about the end of the day, he (McCarthy with him) located Brien and his men about 17 miles north of El Abiar. The Coy had had a rough time; lost on occasions (or at best, most uncertain of their way); the country rugged and tangled, with few tracks; their only food the hard rations which they carried with them since they had had to leave their Coy truck behind; clad only in light clothes and with few blankets in the bitter cold. But they were getting vigorously on with the preparation of their defences when Crawford found them.

Strangely enough, this period on the escarpment above Benghazi was peaceful and pleasant for 2/17 Bn. Although the nights were sharp and cold (so cold that buckets of water left standing would freeze solid during the night), the days were sunlit and calm. To be among trees and grass again after the desert was a delight. From cleared spaces in the bush, quail would whirr away before the soldiers' approach; and there were pheasants to rocket unexpectedly through the sunlight, plumage streaming. There had been Roman towns all along this coast and indeed, further north-east, Cirene (between Barce and Derna) had once been a city of about a million people — the largest Roman city after Rome itself.

The peace of this pleasant place was, however, not to last for long. Each day stories of a strong German advance became more numerous. To the men of the Bn they lacked detail but none doubted their general truth — partly because of the scraps of official news which filtered down; partly because the instinct of these soldiers was a true one.

The prospect of fighting the Germans excited them greatly, despite their lack of adequate weapons, despite that they were spread over a 20-mile front and despite that they were quite sure in their own minds that the tactical plan, of which they formed a part, had no chance of working. Despite all this, they dearly wanted to "have a go".

The climax came even more quickly than the leaders had expected:

After the withdrawal of 20 Bde from the positions there, Neame still had his main forward line in the Marsa Brega area. Although (as Morshead had pointed out) it was the positions just forward of Agheila which completely controlled any approach by the road which led from Tripoli, Neame felt that he could not maintain a force there. So patrols of the King's Dragoon Guards simply operated forward daily to Agheila from the Marsa Brega positions. They clashed with advancing Germans and Italians on 24 Mar and then had to retire, leaving open the gateway to Cyrenaica. Through that gateway a German and Italian advance in force began on 31 Mar. There was determined fighting before Marsa Brega in which the most forward British troops did all that their orders required and more before falling back and leaving the way to Benghazi open.

By that time, Neame had most of his 2 Armd Div forward of Benghazi. The Div was deficient in tanks and all other types of equipment from signals gear to transport. The air force in Cyrenaica could do little to help. It was distressingly weak both in aircraft numbers and types.

Against the threadbare force represented by these few aeroplanes, the woefully thin Armd Div, and the willing but extraordinary widespread 9 Aust Div, a most formidable force was advancing — under a most formidable leader. The poor British strategy was to be exposed.

Lt Gen Erwin Rommel, as a young infantry officer in 1914-1918, had proved so brave and able in the front line that he was one of only 4,000 German Officers permitted by the peace treaties to be retained in the Army after the German defeat. He led one of the armd divs in the smashing German advance through France in 1940. He proved himself a master of the "blitzkrieg", brave, vital and colourful in the forefront of battle.

In the desert this man would show that from the moment he came under fire he stood out as the perfect fighting animal, cold, cunning, quick of decision, incredibly brave. The Afrika Korp knew that Rommel was the last man to spare Rommel. They, and the men they fought, would never know him by any other name except simply "Rommel".

Such was the man who was leading the Afrika Korp — the name which Hitler announced on 19 Feb would be applied to the German forces in Africa.

At first the withdrawal of the 3 Armd Bde on Neame's right flank was orderly and well-managed as they began a planned pivoting movement north of Agedabia designed to shepherd the advancing Germans into the coastal plain near Benghazi. They lost some tanks through breakdowns (but had expected this) and fought strongly in a few small and isolated actions. By 2 Apr the situation of 3 Armd Bde was serious but by no means out of control. On the morning of 3 Apr, they were told to cover the left flank of 9 Div and hold the escarpment south for some 30 miles. Meanwhile, Neame had directed that all stores and supplies in Benghazi should be destroyed (preparations for this by British and Australian engrs had been going on for some time) and that the town should be abandoned.

20 Bde was now in danger of becoming the centre of a whirling mass of movement, destruction, battle and disorder spinning in upon them. But they were not particularly perturbed by what they could sense of this. Perched ready and waiting along the escarpment, 2/17 Bn had watched the beginnings of the destruction in Benghazi. On 2 and 3 Apr it seemed to them that Benghazi was on fire below them; they heard the heavy sound of many explosions and watched the rolling smoke from burning dumps. Along the road out of the city they saw flowing a stream of troops and vehicles leaving for the enemy the place so brilliantly taken such a little while before.

About 1600 hrs on the 3rd they had definite news that the Germans were much closer than had been thought and that they must prepare for desparate fighting soon. At midnight the CO was called hastily to a conference at Brig Murray's HQ. Burrows of 2/13th was there, and Lt Col Marlan of 2/15th. Murray (anxious and regretful) told them that the Bde was to get out as quickly as possible but that there was only enough transport to move one Bn at a time. 2/13th was to hold the Regima Pass and cover the movement of the others. 2/15th would move first with the help of the vehicles of 2/17th which would wait for the vehicles to return and then follow the road back to Barce. When they were clear, 2/13th could leave.

Colonel Crawford at once began to move his Bn in from the edge of the escarpment to an assembly area near El Abiar — in darkness, through rugged bush country. By dawn of the 4th the move was well under way. But it was difficult to get word to Brien's A Coy. By mid afternoon however, the whole unit was gathered and waiting near El Abiar. That shaded green area was a pleasant place on that hot and brittle day but the Bn was in an uncomfortable military situation. It had no transport. It was clearly in the path of a determined enemy advance and of a retreat which was already disordered and milling round El Abiar. It was not in a defensive position nor deployed for action. Crawford's anxiety for his men, though concealed from them, was acute. Early in the afternoon Morshead visited him briefly and told him that the German advance was not rapid enough to threaten him that day and that he might, if he wished, wait for nightfall (when there would be no danger from attacking aircraft) to take to the road. By about 1600 hrs however a convoy of captured Italian lorries (which the divisional staff had assembled only as a result of frantic day-long efforts) had pulled in. Crawford decided to move his Bn at once and they were quickly under way.

It was a wise decision. It became known later, but lack of communication and general confusion ensured that 2/17 Bn did not know of this at the time. Already the 2/13 Bn (a few British guns supporting them) was heavily engaged at nearby Er Regima by large numbers of skilful and determined German infantry and tanks. They had sighted the first of these on the road between Benghazi and Benina about 1400 hrs and by 1530 hrs some 2,000 lorried infantry were reported to be approaching the escarpment with tanks and armd cars. The British gunners' Howitzers, and 2/13 Mortarmen with 2 salvaged long-range Italian mortars took them on. About half an hour later 16 tanks, 30 or 40 lorries carrying troops just behind them, approached the pass and the main fighting developed. This was still going on when darkness fell about 2000 hrs. The Germans then paused to consolidate and did not press their advance further in the night. About 2300 hrs the transport arrived to take the Bn out and 2/13th followed in the wake of the rest of 20 Bde. They were tired; they were discouraged with the knowledge that they were retreating. But their hard-fighting stand, which cost them the best part of 100 men killed, wounded and missing (many of the last-named becoming prisoners) probably saved havoc being created among the great mass of men and materials clearing through El Abiar as the fighting went on.

Thus started the mass withdrawal that became known as "The Benghazi Handicap".

Confusion really began to develop at El Abiar by the time 2/17 Bn gathered there on the 4th. When late in the day it began to move back to Barce, the 50 miles of road which lay ahead were choked with vehicles. There was no dispersion and the fleeing vehicles, filled with men, were helpless targets for any aircraft which cared to attack them; nothing mattered but to get back; the dust rose in choking clouds.

When night came this dust made more dense a blackness which itself was almost opaque. In that dust filled darkness there were the blundering lorries filled with quiet patient soldiers; motor cycles trying to weave their way in and out of the densely packed lines; staff cars trying to pass through and hurry on; armoured cars grinding a heavy and dispirited way from confusion, through confusion, to further confusion; sometimes field guns, jolting and bouncing behind their prime movers, muzzles pointed backwards as though reluctant to leave.

When speed was all that mattered the best that could be achieved in that crush was 10 miles per hour — a crush so great that when Ptes Widerberg and Gilmour of D Coy were jolted from the back of their truck they were killed beneath the wheels of the vehicle following. But in spite of the many hundreds of vehicles, and the many men who were in them, as the retreat went on through the darkness the road seemed very lonely and each lorry load seemed almost to move in an isolated and very lonely world of its own.

In the darkness, 2/17 Bn scrambled out of their vehicles in the early hours of 5 Apr on the escarpment 4 or 5 miles east of Barce. 2/15 Bn was forward of them; a little to their rear, 2/13th. By this time also 26 Bde was in position around Barce. Below them Barce seemed to be on fire — there was the roar of exploding dumps and flames leaping high in the night. The local Arab Senussi were looting the town. As the men of 2/17 Bn made their burdened way to their new positions, the uncertainty of the night fell from them; they were going to dig in and fight, a compact and efficient force once more and no longer a loose and wandering band being hurried through the night to an unknown destination.

The confusion of the night was followed during the day by a different kind of confusion.

Word was coming to the commanders of enemy movements which showed that Rommel was moving fast and by several different routes. But the details were often contradictory.

There was some confusion too with regard to command. On the 3rd, Wavell had sent Gen O'Connor hastily forward from Cairo to relieve Neame. But the relief did not actually take place; O'Connor said that Neame was doing well and that he would constitute himself liaison between Neame's HQ and subordinate formations. But to Gen Morshead at least, the higher command situation remained perplexing. Neame told him as reports of large-scale German movements in the desert to the east came in, that these movements threatened to cut their communications in the rear and that he should get his Div out that night to positions near Derna. Orders for the move went out. Then it appeared that the forces which had been reported to the east were the British armd troops. The orders were cancelled. Scarcely, however, was this done than the original orders were renewed by Neame's HQ.

Like the rest of the force 2/17 Bn scarcely knew what to make of this welter of orders and counter-orders. They had a quiet day. As they looked down the valley ahead of them they could see no sign of any enemy advance. Near them huge dumps of food remained intact and they helped themselves freely from these so that each man had all the food, cigarettes and tobacco that he could carry.

At the end of the day they got the latest of the day's conflicting orders and moved down to the waiting vehicles. Just as they were ready to go, however, these orders were again cancelled. In the darkness they made their way back to their positions. They were savage and critical and made no secret of their feeling that they were being badly "buggered about". Their own wishes were very simple — to fight anyone who wanted to force a way along the road. They were more fortunate than some other units, however, which had actually taken to the road and had to put movements already well begun into most difficult reverse on the choked road. Nearby food, petrol and ammunition dumps had been fired and the heavy smoke of waste and destruction was rising high.

By the morning of the 6th, it was clear that what had been considered the false reports of the previous day were indeed true regarding rapid German movements through the desert to the east of the Jebel Achdar. The closure on Mechili was well under way, and there were other reports which all combined to give a pattern of the whole movement of Rommel's troops. Far to the east, one column, which had launched straight into the desert from Agheila, was striking in an almost direct north-easterly line towards Tobruk. Further west (but still in the desert and east of the Jebel) a second column had driven from Agedabia through Maus and to Mechili and, if it maintained its line, would strike the coast in the Tmimi-Derna region. A third force had driven up the coastal plain and would pass through Barce as it followed the main coast road.

When this pattern (still much blurred around the edges but becoming clear enough in outline) emerged about 1100 hrs, O'Connor told Morshead to get the move back to Derna under way. Morshead suggested that defensive positions at Gazala would give more security to the lines of communication. But with Neame away trying to get in touch with his Armd Comds, it was difficult to take a firm decision. Later, however, O'Connor agreed that the Australians should go to Gazala and, although reluctant to have them on the dangerous roads by day, agreed that they should begin their move that afternoon. To cover his retreat through the danger points where the two tracks from Mechili joined the main road Morshead arranged for 2/13 and 2/48 Bns to move first and take up positions in the Martuba-Tmimi area.

Just after Lt Col W J V Windeyer had actually given his men their orders to withdraw, Germans in lorries, escorted by a tank and armoured cars appeared in the 2/48 Bn positions. Quickly the Germans sprang out of their vehicles and engaged Windeyer's men and a detachment of the Northumberland Fusiliers who were supporting them with machine guns. The sharp resistance by the British and Australians stopped the German advance and the Australians got clear without casualties though the machine gunners were not so fortunate and lost a few men.

None of this, however, was known to 2/17th men as they smouldered with bitter disappointment and shame that once more they were drawing back without fighting. Once more the road was choked with fleeing vehicles of all kinds. Once more the dust rose round them in choking clouds. Once more the dark, cold night covered them as they rode in a numb silence which was the expression of their weariness, the misery of their packed bodies, their ignorance of everything that was going on except knowing that they were being pulled back and back against their own wills. Now they were beginning to wonder if this senseless flight could have any other end than their own destruction to no purpose. And as they travelled this bitter road the confusion and sense of defeat deepened about them, the terrible chaos in which they found themselves became almost impossible to describe as tanks and other vehicles of 3 Armd Bde debouched from the desert track onto the main road in their ill-timed and ill-advised attempt to get to Mechili by detouring along the coastal road instead of following the desert route which had led direct from their positions to that now hard pressed outpost.

D Coy was the last of the Bn to leave Barce, and it was about 1600 hrs after the demolition engrs had left, that D Coy finally set off. Following them were Dudley McCarthy, Bn IO, and Tim McCulloch, Bn Transport Offr, who were responsible to make sure the whole Bn was clear of Barce. Being at the tail end of this exodus the road was clear and so good progress made. The orders were not to follow the main road down the escarpment into Derna, but turn off at Giovanni Berta onto a desert track which led to Martuba and, as darkness fell, and was added to by the powdered dust churned up by thousands of wheels, this last group of the Bn soon caught up with the main struggling mass.

It was now indescribable chaos and confusion, there was no defined track, let alone a road to follow through the dark night and the all encompassing pall of finely powdered dust. Some trucks were getting bogged in the sandy dust, many were losing contact with the remainder of their units, while some groups stopped for the night — possibly despairing of the chaos — while others, including 2/17 Bn, kept going, where necessary detouring around halted vehicles. In this strange night the Bn moved through the confusion and many hazards almost untouched, indeed having little or no knowledge of the events occurring not far from them. (McCarthy and McCulloch stopped and dozed for a couple of hours).

Shortly after dawn McCarthy and McCulloch came upon Lt Col Marlan and part of his 2/15 Bn who had stopped for a breakfast break on the side of the road near Derna airfield. Both D Coy earlier and then a bit later McCarthy and McCulloch declined an invitation to share some breakfast but pushed on to rejoin the rest of their Bn. Unknown until much later, within a very short time Lt Col Marlan and his men were fighting desperately against swift moving Germans who took them unawares and completely surrounded them. The CO and his HQ staff as well as many of 2/15 Bn were taken prisoners.

2/13 and 2/48 Bn were astride the road near Tmimi settling into what positions they could behind stone sangars. 2/17 Bn continued their move back, during the morning there was some artillery action on their right as guns engaged the advance elements of a German armd column. Moving through 26 Bde positions at Gazala, 2/17 Bn pressed on to Acroma where they took up holding positions, with the rest of 20 Bde, to cover the final withdrawal into the Tobruk defensive perimeter. Weary and frustrated they set about digging themselves in once more. They found the area littered with Italian thermos bombs (so called because of their resemblance to the ordinary silver Thermos flask). Full daylight and the realisation of the hopelessness of the position they were holding, engendered a sullen rage in these men, exhausted and angry at continually withdrawing without fighting. D Coy had the heartbreaking task of clearing stones and rocks, mostly by hand to make a withdrawal road down the escarpment for the inevitable time when it came.

As the dusty day wore on, German tanks could occasionally be seen in the distance. Then, out of a cloud emerged a group of vehicles packed with Indians. Their British Officer leapt from his truck, saluted Lt Col Crawford and said "From Mechili Sir. What are your orders?". In short time these Indians were dug in and waiting with 2/17th men. Towards evening a lone Hurricane aircraft dropped a message reporting tanks approaching the position and Lt Bruce Trebeck was sent out on a patrol to try and locate them. The patrol consisted of two 15 cwt utility trucks with three men in each, armed with Boys A/Tk rifles, grenades and Bren guns; fortunately for the patrol it failed to find any trace of the reported tanks.

Once again as the desert night closed in, the orders came to leave. Once more the long lines of trucks filled with quiet soldiers made their way back along the desert road. The last of the retreating and exhausted troops entered the fortress of Tobruk in the early morning hours of 10 Apr 1941. The Bn was met by Maj Ogle near Pilastrino and directed into areas to camp for the rest of the night. A sandstorm was blowing and the exhausted men climbed from their trucks fell to the ground and slept, not caring if the drifting sand covered them as they lay. Not long after daylight they started moving to the perimeter, still under cover of the sandstorm, to take up their positions in the original Italian fortification posts that now offered good defensive positions. They were now cut off in Tobruk; there would be no more retreating and every man had a fierce determination that now he would be able to give a full account of himself.

INFANTRY TRAINING BATTALION

The AIF Battalions in Palestine constituted a significant presence in the areas north and south of Gaza. The function of the training battalions seemed realistic. The fighting unit provided its own staff to greet and care for its own 'x' list returning from convalescence or duty and to greet, equip and train the reinforcements who later, would be serving in the Battalion. The success in each case depended on the personnel sent by the fighting unit to the Infantry Training Battalion (ITB). The first CO, Maj John Williams, was an intent and capable officer with good administrative ability and human understanding. He warned his Company Commanders of the substantial administrative work necessary for each man arriving in a draft of reinforcements. A mildly competitive mood was introduced and helped to improve the proficiency of each battalion team.

Before the first intake, 20 ITB team had time to study the problems they might face. There was a requirement for detailed planning and training of all staff members for their particular duties. There was also a need for a flexible procedure capable of handling day or night intakes with a minimum of queues and bottle necks.

Then there was a requirement for a training and fitness syllabus using instructors that were prepared for their task. The system had to be capable of drastic modification to "cram" knowledge into those men who were urgently required in the front-line units. The reinforcement HQ was later to produce a standardised program for training those men where a longer stay was anticipated. The little program publication with its pink cover was known as the "Pink Pusher". Staff posted to the training unit, later came to accept that spending some time in the ITB was inevitable – however, the value of the unit was acknowledged.

When the Battalion returned to Australia, the system was discontinued. A Branch apparently found it better to handle reinforcements en masse.

CHAPTER 4
EASTER BATTLE OF TOBRUK

Tobruk, as mentioned in the previous chapter, was a town of mostly white buildings, now mostly battle scarred and some broken, nestling beside a fairly narrow but safe and deep harbour. It was partly blocked with the wrecks of ships, some awash and only partly above the level of the sea.

Inland from the town and harbour the desert rose gently southwards, with three slight escarpments until, some distance away, was the pronounced El Adem escarpment. The ground was arid, rocky and bare, except for occasional patches of low camel-thorn scrub.

The perimeter defences built by the Italians — and which in late January 1941, the 6th Australian Division had breached and defeated the Italians — ran in a rough semicircle with a radius of some 9 miles from the town, covering approx 28 miles in all. To the west (towards Derna) the outer perimeter started along the rough and rugged Wadi Es Sehel, then circled southwards to Ras el Medauuar and Hill 209 (which was the dominant feature nearly 700 feet above sea level), then eastwards across relatively flat ground some 500 feet above sea level, finally swinging north to the sea again (on the Bardia side) along the deep and rugged Wadi Es Zeitun.

This outer perimeter consisted of 128 concreted posts arranged in two rows, the outer posts being 600 to 800 yards apart with the inner posts some 500 yards behind and sited roughly midway between two outer posts. Outside the posts were barbed wire entanglements about 5 feet high beyond which was an uncompleted a/tk ditch about 12 feet wide, but in places very shallow and no obstacle to tanks.

Each post was circular in design and the outer posts surrounded by its own small a/tk ditch, in some posts this ditch being covered by timber slabs. In each post was a large shallow pit, designed to accommodate an a/tk gun and two "fighting pits" all connected to each other by trenches and an underground shelter roughly in the centre of the post. Each post was numbered starting from Ras el Medauuar — S1 to S45 on the western, or Derna side, and R1 to 101 on the eastern, or Bardia side (on the original Italian maps, posts numbered above 80 were prefixed Z, being in the Wadi Es Zeitun region). The outer posts bore odd numbers and the inner posts even numbers.

Outside the major part of the perimeter the desert rose slightly more or less as far as the eye could see. Visibility was good in early morning and late evening but, during the heat of the day, subject to often weird mirages and, of course, often obscured by the swept dust of sandstorms.

On the morning of 10 April, the main troops making up the defence force were the three Bdes of 9 Aust Division, plus 18 Bde (which arrived on 7 April), 2/1 Pnr Bn, four British arty regts, a British MG regt, two a/tk regts (one British one Australian) and three Australian a/tk coys, four Australian Engr Fd coys, 18 Indian Cav Regt, British Tk units and British AA regts, plus ancillary troops.

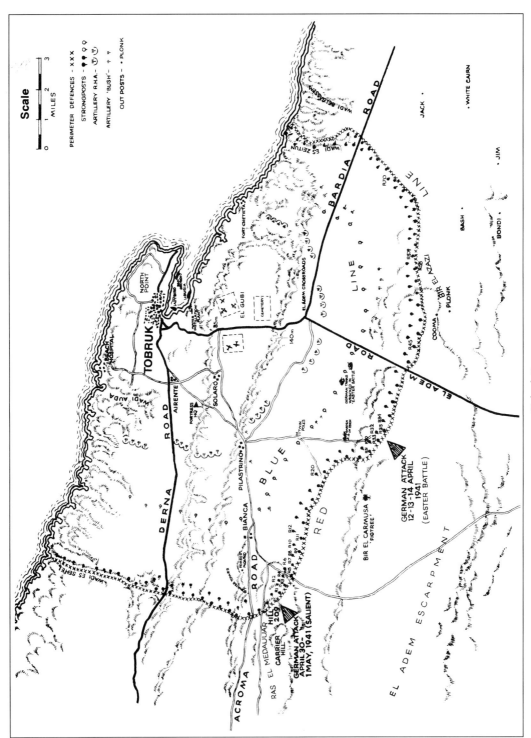

Tobruk Fortress

Gen Lavarack's instructions were: —

> "Your main task will be to hold the enemy's advance at Tobruk, in order to give time for the assembly of reinforcements, especially of armoured troops for the defence of Egypt. To gain time for the assembly of the required reinforcements it may be necessary to hold Tobruk for about two months. Your defence will be as mobile as possible and you will take any opportunity of hindering the enemy's concentrations by offensive action."

And so the deployment of the Tobruk defence force began on the morning of 10 April, with 2/17 Bn occupying a central position. In the western sector, the 18 Indian Cav Regt occupied the posts from the coast, then 26 Bde occupied posts from the Derna Road entry to Hill 209 with 2/48 Bn on their left flank adjoining 2/17 Bn which was on the right of 20 Bde, then 2/13 Bn on the left extending eastwards and covering the entry of El Adem Road, with 24 Bde covering from the left of 20 Bde to the coast and astride the main coast road from Bardia.

Waking from their short sleep of utter exhaustion the 2/17 men shook the sand off as best they could, tended to their weapons and moved off to occupy the perimeter posts which had been allotted to them — posts R11 to R35. On the right was Claude Brien with his A Coy; then Keith Magno's C Coy; on C Coy's left was HQ Coy organised as a rifle coy; then on the left flank of the Bn was John Balfe's D Coy in posts R31 to R35, with two sections of B Coy attached to D Coy while the remainder of Curly Wilson's B Coy formed the battalion reserve. D Coy was deployed with 17 Pl in R31, 16 Pl in R33, 18 Pl in R35 with HQ Coy in R32 just to the right rear of R33. Post R35 occupied by 18 Pl had been partly demolished during the January capture of Tobruk. There was much to be done and time was a pressing element. Partly exhilarated by the prospect of action, knowing this time that they were in positions, after their long and frustrating retreat, from which they would stay and fight. Tough and fit as they were, quickly refreshed by their short sleep, Crawford's men cast aside their exhaustion like a forgotten cloak and prepared for battle.

Quite an amount of filth and debris left by the Italians had to be cleared from the posts.

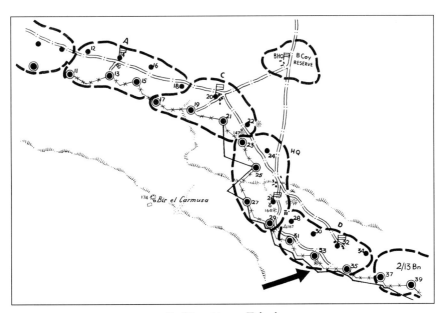

Bn Dispositions – Tobruk

Food, water and ammunition reserves had to be laid in. The Italian posts were not well designed from which to fight and they were not well sited in relation to the terrain. They were too far apart, so digging intermediate posts was an urgent necessity that must be quickly got under way, and sappers were at work arming and laying mines.

German aircraft roared in from time to time during the day, diving on, or bombing from a high level, the installations around the Harbour. Towards the end of the day, three aircraft screaming downwards with bombs and machine guns firing onto the 2/4 AGH near the Harbour, killed 35 of the staff and patients.

To most of the men the situation seemed somewhat confused and it was difficult to realise where they were and where the rest of the Battalion were, let alone the rest of the Brigade. However, in the perimeter posts it was a relatively peaceful night after the last six or seven days and nights with extremely little sleep or rest.

How little time there was to spare became clear very rapidly. On 10 April, while still moving into their positions, 26 Bde had to fight against a German column coming along the Derna Road. Elsewhere on their front they had to hold back German elements probing out of the desert and then digging in towards nightfall. Late that same afternoon, tanks were observed in the El Adem area, while aircraft reported three German columns, each of about 200 vehicles, approaching El Adem from the direction of Mechili.

The morning of Good Friday, 11 April, was bright and clear after the swirling dust of the previous day, which was fortunate for the garrison as it permitted them to observe in some measure what was building up against them. Enemy columns were skirting the perimeter western and southern defences as they moved eastward through the desert. Accurate arty fire dispersed some of these tanks and vehicles but, inevitably, the enemy movement continued round the perimeter. Unknown to virtually all the defenders, except Fortress HQ staff, a mobile force of various British elements was operating outside Tobruk under Brig 'Strafer' Gott and he was able to give some details of the enemy encirclement. Soon after midday, the Bardia Road was cut and the siege had begun. At 1330 hrs, Gott ordered his mobile force back to the Egyptian border.

Rommel was quick to strike. He would remove this irritation in Tobruk from his path and press on to Egypt. Somewhat over confident from his previous experiences, he saw no need to plan a set-piece attack. His tanks and men would simply walk in and take these defences — and this is precisely what they set out to do at about 1600 hrs on the afternoon of Good Friday, 11 April. A combination of tanks and then infantry made a move against D Coy 2/17 Bn in what was half demonstration and half attack. About 70 tanks in three waves of 20 and one of about 10 came right up to the tank ditch in front of the wire and the 75mm guns of the German tanks plus the fire from the Italian and light tanks poured fire into the forward posts. With no a/tk guns forward, the men in the posts fired all they had, but these were only Bren guns, rifles and a few Boy's a/tk rifles. Over most of the D Coy front the a/tk ditch was no real obstacle to the tanks, and the minefield had only been hastily rearmed. However, the tanks did not attempt to come on, apparently thinking a demonstration would be sufficient, so they blazed away and then sheered off east. As the tanks turned away they came against a freshly laid minefield on the El Adem Road, four Italian and one German medium tank were destroyed by British tanks and arty fire for the loss of two British medium tanks.

As the tanks moved off, Inf came on in three rows, one behind the other. In each row they seemed to be almost shoulder to shoulder and there were some 700 of them. Arty fire from 1 RHA (directed by Maj G W Goschen) fell among them but still they came on. When they were about 500 yards away, D Coy opened fire on them with Brens and rifles. This was their first actual action and it was uncanny to see these lines of enemy troops continuing to advance through what seemed, and was, accurate arty shelling, and yet their Bren gun fire put them to ground.

Gradually, the Germans came forward in bounds under cover of their machine guns. In this way, they advanced right up to the a/tk ditch and from there, put down heavy mortar and MG fire on D Coy posts. Unfortunately, D Coy had no mortars which could reply and the arty could not fire on the ditch without risking hitting the forward posts. By then, darkness was falling fast.

Crawford ordered the Bn mortars up and Sgt Lance O'Dea brought them forward, although he had been slightly wounded during the day. Two platoons of B Coy, moving behind a timed mortar shoot, patrolled along the ditch, but found no Germans either alive or dead. Other patrols throughout the night ensured that the enemy did not establish themselves in the ditch. About 2300 hrs, Colin Pitman took out a fighting patrol with the objective of locating exactly where the Germans were. He located them in strength some 200 yards or more south of Post R33 and his patrol was engaged by very heavy fire. The strength of the enemy positions and the concentration of their fire resulted in L/Cpl A Wilkinson and Pte A B Gifford being killed, and Sgt E Mudie being wounded. Pitman was forced to withdraw his patrol and return to the perimeter. These were the first battle killed in the Battalion.

Easter Saturday, 12 April, saw German aircraft busily attacking the garrison and three were shot down as they went after the ships in the Harbour. German arty shells and mortar fire fell within the perimeter at various times.

The garrison was ready and waiting for a dawn attack but none came. Daylight revealed enemy dug in about 400 yards in front of D Coy and these enemy brought down heavy fire on the forward posts and this continued throughout the day. There were clear signs of preparations for an attack with dust clouds betraying the German movements to concentration points. Bombers attacked one of these concentrations, and the gunners shelled others heavily, possibly delaying an attack from developing. During the day, Cpl F A Benson took out a party of 18 Pl from R35 and repaired a gap in the wire, while Pte E McKee swept the nearest enemy positions with Bren gun fire. In the late afternoon twelve tanks came up to the ditch along D Coy front, but were driven off by a/tk guns which had been brought up during the night.

At about 1430 hrs, under cover of a heavy dust storm that was developing large numbers of Inf were seen through gaps in the dust immediately south of posts R33 and R35 at a distance of 500 yards and over approx 1200 yard front. At 1530 hrs, the enemy advance commenced and was engaged by arty. Through gaps in the dust, it was seen that the shelling was very effective and heavy casualties must have been inflicted. No attack developed, but some parties of enemy succeeded in advancing close to R33. L/Cpl Dunbar had a section here of reinforcements which had been sent into the line immediately on their arrival on 11 April. L/Cpl Dunbar, with reckless disregard of danger, so stimulated his men that they went into action with a will, and the enemy broke and withdrew.

That evening, the moon rose early and clear moonlight made observation easy. Around 2200 hrs, two groups of enemy vehicles were observed by John Balfe from Post R32, consisting of 29 large troop carrying vehicles and 12 vehicles apparently towing guns. A moonlight shoot followed with John Balfe acting as OP Officer, and the vehicles ultimately moved off after a number of direct hits had been scored.

On Easter Sunday morning, 13 April, there was a lot of movement. Staff cars were seen and motorcycles, standing apparently near a battle HQ being established. At this extreme range of 2000 yards a/tk guns engaged the staff cars and motorcycles, hitting one staff car and two motorcycles. Arty engaged the HQ but in spite of the heavy shelling, this movement and preparation continued all day. An enemy reconnaissance Heinkel plane came flying west to east

along the posts during the morning. All this activity made 2/17 quite sure that a major attack
would come soon. At about 1600 hours, Crawford moved his reserve, B Coy, up to the rear of
D Coy position and told Curly Wilson to be ready for a counter attack at dawn. He also
borrowed Capt Peek's coy of 2/15 Bn as additional reserve for the area. At 1700 hours enemy arty
fire concentrated on D Coy posts, but made no attempt to use arty fire to cut the perimeter wire.

By 1730 hrs there was seen much movement on a 1200 yard front about 500 yards out, and
then small arms and MG fire became heavy on the forward posts.

Once it became dark, Crawford sent out a patrol. Colin Pitman went out to bring back news
of what the Germans were doing and just exactly where they were. Then about 0200 hrs Bayne
Geike on another patrol went out to establish the position of the enemy left flank, going out
from HQ Coy lines. Both patrols duly returned with useful information and a German prisoner
each. Early in the evening, Lt George Vincent, who was one of the original members of the Bn,
had been to the Cairo Officer Cadet Training Unit, and rejoined the Bn on 11 April, came
forward and joined 16 Pl in post R33, destined to take over the platoon from Austin Mackell.
However, such was not to be. During the early hours of the battle, he saw a German aiming at
him from not far away and tried to beat the German to the shot but lost. He was hit in the head,
probably should have died, but survived. Within a couple of hours of moving to the forward
post, he was critically wounded and would serve no further part in the War.

By 2300 hrs after an hour's heavy mortar and MG fire on D Coy forward posts, the Germans
succeeded in getting through the wire, a party of about 40 Inf men with 8 MGs, a mortar and 2
small fd guns and established themselves inside the perimeter wire just east of post R33. 16 Pl
fired on them but the Germans replied with their heavier fire from mortar, fd guns and MGs,
clearly intent on taking out R33 preliminary to preparation of a crossing of the tank ditch. As
platoon fire from R33 was unable to silence them, Lt Austin Mackell organised a fighting patrol
of himself and Cpl Jack Edmondson's section which consisted of Ron Keogh, Splinter Williams,
Ted Smith, Doug Foster and Ron Grant, with the object of eliminating this enemy strong point,
or driving them out by a bayonet charge. Each member had rifle with fixed bayonet plus
grenades and, while the rest of the platoon concentrated all the fire they could on the enemy
position, the patrol left from the back of the post and swung around in a semicircle to take the
Germans from the flank. On the way around they had a couple of spells and went to ground for
the last time about 30 yards from the Germans. At first there was spasmodic MG fire but once
the patrol was sighted they came under considerable fire. On the second run to their last spell
before the bayonet charge, unknown to the others, Jack Edmondson was hit twice. At this last
resting spell, they pulled pins from the grenades and, at the arranged zero hour of 1145 hrs, firing
from R33 stopped. Austin Mackell yelled, "Into them, boys". They hurled their grenades and
ran full steam forward. As the grenades burst, the German fire temporarily stopped and, before
they could open up again, the patrol, yelling like wild men, were into them with bayonets, Jack
Edmondson included, in spite of his fatal wounds. In Mackell's words afterwards, Jack Edmondson was magnificent, killing at least two Germans, by which time Mackell was in
difficulties wrestling with one German on the ground while another was coming straight for him
with a pistol. He called, "Jack", and Edmondson ran to help him and bayoneted at least one
more. He only stopped fighting when he could no longer stand. When Austin Mackell got back
on his feet he bayoneted one German, breaking his bayonet in the process and then used his
rifle as a club on the other. By this time at least twelve Germans were dead, one taken a prisoner
and the rest turned and fled as fast as they could back outside the wire, leaving their weapons
littering the ground behind them. While Mackell and Ron Grant gathered up as many weapons

as they could, the rest of the patrol moved Jack Edmondson back to R33, but he died in the early hours of the morning.

After this successful encounter, the first couple of hours of Easter Monday, 14 April, did not see much enemy movement until about 0215 hrs. Then German troops once again started pouring through the gap near post R33, and a couple of hundred got through and established a bridgehead while their engrs prepared a way for the tanks.

John Balfe had gone to Bde HQ shortly after midnight and the successful fighting patrol from 16 Pl had completed their mission. At 0230 hrs he returned to his Coy HQ in post R32, two Bde Liaison Offrs, Capt Greg Keirath and Lt Doug Cubitt, accompanying him with orders to visit the forward posts so as to be able to give the Brig a firsthand account of just how things were in the forward posts. Unfortunately, they ran into fire from the newly established bridgehead before they reached post R33 and were both killed. L/Cpl Dunbar confirmed to John Balfe the situation of the new bridgehead and John Balfe put up the SDF Signal (for defensive fire). Down came the arty fire but it did not dislodge the Germans from their position inside the wire. All through the night an intense fire fight continued as the forward soldiers poured fire at the bridgehead area and the Germans tried to silence the forward posts.

Shortly after 0400 hrs, in fairly clear desert moonlight, tanks were assembling west of the El Adem Road. Gun fire was now drenching the defence, vivid among these being flaming explosions of 88mm air bursts from AA guns being used as fd arty. The tanks had to spend valuable time looking for their point of entry and, at 0520 hrs, the first tanks moved in through the gap which their engrs had prepared near the point from which Mackell's patrol had earlier driven out the first German bridgehead party. The tanks passed by the forward perimeter posts and assembled almost on top of Balfe's HQ in post R32. With orders not to worry about the tanks but to let them pass through if necessary and wait for the following Inf, post R32 lay low so as not to attract attention. The leading tanks moved up to within 30 yards of R32 with another 12 tanks behind them. They moved up in extended line and then swung away to their right and headed for the town some 9 miles away. Behind, or riding on, each tank were 15 to 20 Inf with MGs and, as the tanks went on, post R32 opened up on the Inf who they put to ground.

Meanwhile, more tanks came through the perimeter gap racing straight on and not waiting for their following Inf. While the tanks were coming through, Balfe had the arty firing on them even though it meant landing shells on and around their own post. As soon as the tanks were gone, the men in the various posts opened up with everything they had on the German Inf. Some had got through in the half light with the tanks, of course, and moved beyond post R32. Mostly the Inf were now pinned down where they spread out inside the wire, or while still outside the wire.

By 0600 hrs all the tanks had gone through but, as the light improved, Balfe saw three German a/tk guns being hauled up. He allowed them to come within 50 yards of post R32 and then ordered his men to snipe the crews. Although the Germans continued firing back, eventually all were killed. The Germans started bringing up three 105mm fd guns and, a little later, a 75mm gun. The forward posts let them come as far as the a/tk ditch and then, with deliberate fire, shot up the crews before they could open fire. As a result, nothing more got through the perimeter posts.

By 0630 hrs a strong party of Germans, who had moved with the tanks, was establishing themselves in a ruined house behind Balfe's HQ — in fact, in the house that Maj Goschen of the 1 RHA had been using as his observation post — and some surrounding stone sangers. There were some 100-150 Germans in this party and, had they become properly established, could have brought fire to bear on the forward posts from the rear. They had a mortar and some 10 MGs.

B Coy went into action against this enemy post. Lt Paddy Owen was wounded, having a hand badly shattered. Sgt Brady was deceived into thinking a group were friendly and, on approaching, was shot dead. Some time after 0700 hrs, Sgt McElroy lead an attack against the house. With other sections giving covering fire, he was able to move up to within 50 yards of the enemy, moving to dead ground. From this point, he gave the order to charge and they went in with bayonets, pitching hand grenades ahead as they ran. As the grenades burst the Germans came running out, crying for mercy. As McElroy and his men came down on them, the Germans hardly fired a shot. Some had remained in the house, and another section went right in and got them with the bayonet. Most of the German casualties were caused by hand grenades and supporting fire. They took eighteen German prisoners and there were nearly as many dead found later in the day, while many had turned in headlong flight back towards the wire.

Meanwhile, the tanks had gone on towards their goal, but soon found themselves committed to slug it out with the British fd arty and with a/tk guns. In the half-light of early dawn, the gunners saw 20 or 30 tanks about 1000 yards from them and opened fire, only to receive immediate reply from 75mm shells and MG fire. An RHA Sgt-Maj described it thus, "The air was lit with tracer bullets and shells until it looked like Blackpool Illuminations". The gunners only had HE shells which didn't stop the tanks because they were well spread out.

The tanks continued firing their machine guns on the move, but would stop to fire their 75mm, then move on again. Eventually, with the tanks only some 600 yards away, the gunners engaged them over open sights and knocked out at least seven tanks with many more damaged and thus relatively easy targets for the 2-pdr a/tk guns as they limped back to the wire. At 0715 hrs, the tanks wheeled to their right and made for the perimeter gap through which they had come. A/tk guns and five British tanks took further toll as the Germans tried to escape.

As the sun rose so that its rays lightened the new day, the whole desert seemed full of battle. Above the battlefield, aeroplanes screamed into a similarly swirling mass and one or more would come down. From their crash would rise first a cloud of dust, then a column of heavy smoke and, through the smoke a flicker of flame. The planes still in the air would twist and turn, and the same thing would happen again. The sky was full of bursting AA shells, and the gunners, listening on their instruments, heard the approach of many bombers. Forty Stuka dive-bombers came diving at the guns and Harbour installations in an attack timed to coincide with the arrival of the German tanks — which never arrived. The gunners shot down four Stukas as they dived, and the Hurricanes accounted for two more.

The German exit was an amazing sight to behold. There was only one gap in the perimeter wire and terrible confusion as tanks and Inf pushed their way through, with the tanks raising clouds of dust, smoke from two tanks blazing just outside the wire and the garrison firing a/tk weapons, Bren guns, rifles and 25-pdr shells into this cloud of dust and smoke. A lot of the German Inf was shot up in trying to get out and many took refuge in the a/tk ditch and were later taken prisoner.

But the crews of three of the retreating tanks kept their heads and made a last dangerous challenge. Taking advantage of the partly demolished condition of post R35 they overran John Dinning's 18 Pl position and proceeded to demand that they were all prisoners and should get into the tanks. During the scuffle that following, John Dinning and most of his platoon fought free, but seven of his men, who were covered at point-blank range and had no chance to escape, were taken prisoner. Outside the ditch, these tanks then hitched behind them the 105mm guns whose crews had earlier been knocked out. When they had dragged the guns about 1000 yards, the arty had their range and the guns were unhitched and the tanks fled back into the desert.

By 0830 hrs, the battle was clearly over but some isolated and dangerous pockets of Germans, who had not been able to get away, had to be mopped up and mostly taken prisoner. This lasted until mid-morning. Also, dead and wounded had to be attended to, as well as the many prisoners who had been taken.

The statistical records show that 38 German tanks penetrated the outer perimeter of which 17 were destroyed and several that eventually escaped had been damaged. The number of casualties that Rommel's forces suffered is not really known. How many were wounded, killed or died outside the perimeter must have been high. Inside, mostly in 2/17 Bn positions, at least 150 dead were counted and 250 prisoners taken. Amongst the garrison troops total casualties were surprisingly small — 26 killed, 64 wounded and 13 taken prisoner.

As the morning wore on, B Coy (less one Pl) were moved back into Bn reserve, while Capt Peek's Coy of 2/15 Bn moved up to take over from Balfe's D Coy. Late in the afternoon, D Coy 2/17 Bn moved out and went into reserve position.

Late that day, 14 April, Gen Lavarack handed over the defence of Tobruk to Gen Morshead. Before he left, he sent the following message:

"I wish to congratulate all ranks of the garrison of Tobruk Fortress on the stern and determined resistance offered to the enemy's attacks with tanks, infantry and aircraft today.

Refusal by all infantry posts to give up this ground, a prompt counter-attack by reserves of the 20th Bde, skilful shooting by our arty and a/tk guns combined with a rapid counter-stroke by our tanks, stopped the enemy's advance and drove him from the perimeter in disorder. At the same time the RAF and our AA defences dealt severely with the enemy in the air.

Everyone can feel justly proud of the way the enemy has been dealt with. Well done TOBRUK!"

It is easy enough now to tell the story as all the pieces fall into place, but none of this could happen at the time for "battle is confusion, worse confounded". No man in Tobruk that Easter could be sure at any time just what was happening in the overall picture. In such battles as this, once the issue is joined, there is comparatively little that generals can do to affect the issue — it is in the hands of the men on the battleground. It is a question of whether they stand or flee; whether they trust in their comrades and whether they are prepared to fight or die, with or for them; whether they have confidence in their leaders. These are the issues which decide the battle. And these were issues in which the men of 2/17 Bn on whom so much depended that day, were not found wanting.

Tuesday, 15 April, was a fine and relatively quiet day on the ground but aerial activity was intense. The many German dead were collected and buried and the enemy apparently remained quiet to lick his wounds. The Easter Battle of Tobruk had ended.

There were some well deserved decorations earned during this Easter Battle, and the citations on the following pages are appropriate to reproduce.

VICTORIA CROSS   (Posthumous Award)
Corporal John Hurst Edmondson
2/17 Australian Infantry Battalion A.I.F.

"On the night of April 13/14, 1941 a party of German infantry broke through the wire defences at Tobruk and established themselves with at least six machine guns, mortars, and two small field pieces. It was decided to attack them with bayonets and a party consisting of one officer, Corporal Edmondson and five privates, took part in the charge. During the counter-attack Corporal Edmondson was wounded in the neck and stomach but continued to advance under heavy fire and killed one enemy with his bayonet. Later his officer had his bayonet in one of the enemy and was grasped about the legs by him when another attacked him from behind. He called for help and Corporal Edmondson who was some yards away, immediately came to his assistance and in spite of his wounds killed both of the enemy. This action undoubtedly saved his officer's life. Shortly after returning from this successful counter-attack Corporal Edmondson died of wounds. His actions throughout the operations were outstanding for resolution, leadership, and conspicuous bravery."

MILITARY CROSS   NX 12329 Captain John Walter Balfe   2/17 Battalion A.I.F.

"Action at Tobruk. This officer was in command of one section of the perimeter defences which was attacked by enemy infantry and army fighting vehicles including medium tanks, on the night of April 13/14. All his posts were attacked and his company H.Q. overrun by tanks.

He continually carried out detailed and difficult observations of enemy movements from the vicinity of his post under heavy fire, reporting the result with accuracy, and continually keeping his command in touch with the situation as it developed.

He kept his company in action during a most difficult engagement, and inspired confidence in his officers and men to a high degree by his own coolness and devotion to duty."

MILITARY CROSS   NX 12231 Lieut Frederick Austin Mackell   2/17 Battalion A.I.F.

"Action at Tobruk. On April 13 Lieut Mackell was commander of a patrol which counter-attacked a body of enemy which attacked post 33.

During this attack with a small party of one corporal and five men, he showed remarkable gallantry and brilliant leadership which enabled his small force to rout the enemy who were armed with two field pieces, machine guns and two-inch and three-inch mortars.

He killed one enemy with the bayonet clubbed his rifle and smashed it on the head of another.

By his dash and vigour he inspired his small force to overcome the heavy odds against them.

From April 11 to 13 Lieut Mackell distinguished himself by his active and brilliant leadership and care of his men."

MILITARY MEDAL
NX 23052 Sergeant Robert McLean McElroy, 2/17 Battalion A.I.F.

"Action Tobruk. For bravery in the field on the night of April 13-14. This soldier in the absence of his platoon commander, led his platoon in a counter-attack upon an enemy post containing eight machine guns, with such skill and disregard of personal danger that the post was overcome.

This action made the resultant counter-attack so successful that the enemy were completely demoralised and driven from their positions in disorder.

Sergeant McElroy's leadership was such that only one life was lost in the attack upon this strong post."

MILITARY MEDAL
NX 16216 Lance Corporal Alfred Edward Dunbar, 2/17 Battalion A.I.F.

"At 6 pm on April 11, when the enemy first attacked Lance Corporal Dunbar was in command of a section of reinforcements who had only just joined the unit. They were very nervous and did not at first expose themselves sufficiently to engage the enemy with fire.

Lance Corporal Dunbar himself and the machine guns engaged the enemy alone. As a result of this example all the men attached to him were very soon engaging the enemy with great determination.

On the afternoon of April 13, under heavy small arms fire, Lance Corporal Dunbar left post 33 and proceeded to Company HQ at post 32, a distance of some 500 yards, being exposed to the enemy the whole time, with the information that the enemy were attacking his platoon post. Having given the information he returned to post 33, still under heavy fire and resumed command of his section.

On the early morning of April 14, Dunbar again manned the machine gun and supported by the rifle fire of his section, knocked out six enemy machine guns.

These reinforcements were led and inspired by Dunbar in such a manner as to make their efforts invaluable to their post. His excellent shooting, his willingness to take risks enabled the platoon to engage the infantry with a far greater degree of safety than had been the case before he silenced the enemy machine guns which had been considerably harassing the posts.

His coolness and determination to win are worthy of the highest praise."

Cpl John Edmondson was the first Australian to be awarded the V.C. in WW2 and 2/17 Bn men were justly proud that the highest bravery award went to one of their members.

Lieutenant R M McElroy   *L/Corporal A E Dunbar   (later Lt)*

CHAPTER 5
PATROLS AND ACTIVE DEFENCE

With the Easter Battle over, the first round of the battle for Tobruk had gone to the garrison defenders — but it was only the first round. There was no possibility of resting on their laurels and taking things easy; it was clearly going to be a grim and protracted business.

The forward posts around the perimeter wire were known as the Red Line — the main line of defence. Some two to two and a half miles behind this Red Line was another line of strong posts, which had never been properly completed, and this was known as the Blue Line. Whenever not committed on other specified tasks, troops such as the garrison reserve brigade, the 2/1 Pioneer Bn, Engr Fd Coys and so on, were engaged in completing and strengthening the Blue Line so as to add greater depth to defensive positions. The British Arty positions were behind the Blue Line again, although at times a detached troop of guns would be moved forward close behind the Red Line in order to engage some specific targets. An important addition to the defence was the "bush artillery", made up of captured Italian weapons, mainly 40mm a/tk guns, but also some fd guns as well. Ample supplies of ammunition for these guns had been captured when Tobruk fell in January. These guns were manned by various infantrymen given

*"Bush Artillery" manned by Privates, **L-R:** ———,*
R Reading, R L Stanton, "Butch" Bryant, G W Kearney.

46

Bush Artillery

brief training and when in action many of the orders were in rather unscientific terms such as "Cock 'er up a bit" or "Swing the spout a bit more to the left".

As told earlier, the instruction to the Commander of Tobruk Garrison included, "Your defence will be as mobile as possible and you will take any opportunity of hindering the enemy's concentration by offensive action". Thus patrol activity outside the perimeter became virtually synonymous with Tobruk. The general edict regarding active and aggressive patrolling was fully accepted by the garrison and — perhaps irrationally — the troops developed a frame of mind that said, "Be damned if we are going to remain hemmed in by the perimeter wire and merely wait to respond when the Germans do something. At least by night we'll make that territory outside the wire more ours than theirs so they will be more scared to move about it than we are".

Patrolling was essentially divided into two categories — daylight patrols were either fighting patrols or raiding patrols. The fighting patrols, consisting of possibly a half Pl to full Pl size, would often go out during the frequent duststorms. In the intolerable conditions they were frequently able to take advantage of surprise. They would come upon a disconsolate post or group, strike suddenly, create alarm and havoc, as well as casualties, and be able to withdraw under cover of the sandstorm before adequate opposition was organised. Raiding parties were usually up to a coy in strength and often supported by Bren Carriers and/or tanks and artillery.

Night patrolling was organised on a three-tier basis. The normal pattern was for a Bn to have three coys in the forward posts and one in reserve. Each forward coy was responsible for a wire patrol just outside the a/tk ditch. Then the Bn usually had two shallow patrols up to about 500 yds out on their front. Finally, the reserve coy provided a deep patrol which would have some specific task and go out 1500 to 3000 yds or more. Night patrols went out as lightly laden as possible, carried more automatic weapons than normal, each member with grenades, being

L-R: Lt C.G. Pitman, Lt Col J.W. Crawford, Capt C.H. Wilson, Capt L.C. Brien,
Capt H.F. Windeyer, Maj J.W. Balfe, Capt J.D. Grant, Capt A.M. Alison   (AWM 20791)

sure not to take personal letters or such things that would help the enemy identify units if they happened to be taken prisoner. The deep patrols were sometimes fighting patrols, sometimes reconnaissance patrols, basically seeking information. The two essentials, when proceeding substantial distances outside the wire, were navigation (or direction) and distance travelled. Quickly they learnt to use the stars to navigate and check their direction and various features in this No Man's Land became familiar and could be recognised at night.

The night of 21/22 Apr saw the first of the major raids carried out by the garrison. About 1,000 yds outside the perimeter from Ras el Medauuar, was a smaller feature known as Carrier Hill. Behind this hill, attacking forces could form up in concealment. 2/48 Bn would attack this position, destroy or capture the enemy dug in there and their guns. Co-ordinated with this would be an attack by 2/23 Bn on the western side against strong positions there, and an assault by 2/17 Bn against enemy field guns and troops facing the southern perimeter. B Coy, under Capt Curly Wilson, moved out through post R26 at 0300 and proceeded to the appointed position where they lay in the open desert in the dark waiting for the zero hour of 0640 hrs to synchronise with the other raids away to their right, and supporting tanks and artillery. Unfortunately, the timing was not as good as it could have been, being probably at least 15 minutes too late for zero hour. As daylight of the early dawn came, and still waiting for zero hour to creep around, Curly Wilson observed some enemy lined up apparently in a breakfast parade or drawing their day's rations.

In Wilson's opinion, had he been able to attack at that time, B Coy may have had some success and got away with it without arty support — but having to wait to synchronise with the 2/48 Bn raid meant that the opportunity was lost. The element of surprise had gone when 0640 hrs arrived and the arty opened fire. One gun was off-line and some shells fell amongst B Coy. The enemy troops opened up with heavy fire from three sides and put down an arty barrage using 75mm guns. Having tried probing right then left, at 0715 hrs Wilson realised that it was impossible to continue any further with the raid, and decided to withdraw. 10 Pl was operating in a detached role on the flank and were able to engage targets with relatively light fire in retaliation, but as soon as they started to withdraw they encountered heavy arty fire, and were eventually picked up by the battalion Bren carriers and brought back to the wire.

Meanwhile, 2/48 Bn was highly successful and they destroyed the Italian positions behind

Post 32 – OP pole in the left middle distance

Carrier Hill, took 368 prisoners, and brought back anti-aircraft guns, machine guns and some motor transport. The 2/23 Bn spent nearly 4 hours of fighting in rough country in routing the enemy and taking 87 prisoners, as well as bringing back anti-aircraft and machine guns and mortars, but the cost was heavy in killed and wounded.

During the night of 23/24 Apr, 2/17 Bn was relieved by 2/15 Bn and moved into Bde reserve occupying a section of the Blue Line. The new morning was a perfect day and the Bn mostly enjoyed a well earned day of comparative rest. The next day was also fine, but this weather was not to last for long. 26 Apr dawned with wind of gale force and almost solid dust, reducing visibility to nil, and bringing everything to a standstill. The only compensation was that the vile day spared Tobruk from its daily air raids.

No longer stimulated by actually standing face to face with the enemy, the men of the 2/17 Bn, while a little to the rear of the firing line, were still in some constant danger from air attack and arty fire. To many, appreciation was growing each day they were there, that sheer physical discomfort and monotony might be their worst enemies. They were committed now to a programme which would not vary much in outline all the time they were in Tobruk — one in which only two phases would regularly alternate — being on the perimeter or back from it only a short distance, in reserve or "resting". Wherever they were, harsh environment and conditions weighed equally upon them.

Vital though it was to their survival, there was only a very precarious supply of water in this desert outpost. The two main but meagre sources were always in danger of destruction, as was the only other source, which lay outside the western perimeter in land which no man held and on which, therefore, there could be no continuing dependence, even while it lasted. Before the fighting had first begun in these areas, the main water supply to Tobruk was by means of a pipeline from Derna. But Rommel now held Derna and the whole area between, and the pipeline was cut. Therefore the entire garrison had to depend for water on two distillation plants which the Italians had installed on the southern shore of the harbour and on two pumps which drew sub-artesian water up through the dry bed of Wadi Auda, two miles west of the town's centre.

From these two sources came 40,000 gallons per day of a harsh and chlorinated, but potable liquid. This was rationed out initially on the basis of half a gallon (i.e. about 8 cups) per man per day for all purposes.

The constant dust and sand made water even more precious than it would otherwise have been. Sometimes the desert wind would blow dust and sand for days on end so that one might not see more than about 20 yds, if that. It covered the skin with a deep coating, parched the throat, clogged eyes, ears, and nose, matted the hair and seeped into the moving parts of weapons despite everything that could be done to protect them. It buried men as they slept so that when they awoke they rose from beneath mounds of sand which had concealed them completely, and then beat at themselves to loosen the dust and shook themselves like dogs. The very sound of the wind, moaning and shrilling over that desolate place became an almost unbearable thing.

On cloudless days when the dust storms were not blowing, each day's first light etched the desert scene in clear outline but, as the summer day warmed, a mirage would subtly transform it. The change was scarcely apparent at a casual glance — the colour and broad masses were unaltered — but a more intent examination would fail to reveal the detailed configuration of remembered features, which tantalisingly shimmered in eddies of sun-scorched air, as though through a watery glaze. The mirages soon imposed a degree of regularity on siege arty program-mes, for only in the early mornings or late evenings could guns be ranged onto targets by observation, or the effectiveness of their fire be gauged. As each new day dawned, the guns of both sides saluted it and, as it departed before the oncoming night, they saluted it again.

In the front line or out of it, the soldiers lived in holes in the ground. Each "dingus", was made by those who shared it a degree or two less uncomfortable, or a degree safer, as their ingenuity might suggest. Those on the perimeter who occupied the strong concreted positions which the Italians had made, counted themselves fortunate despite the fleas and lice — the fleas at least were common to every place. As the siege progressed though, more and more of the men found themselves occupying positions they had dug for themselves.

The old Italian positions were too far away from each other and their fields of fire, although mostly good, emanated from too few points. So, from the beginning, when the men in the front line were not fighting or patrolling or sleeping, Morshead had them hard at work digging new positions, some of them with intercommunicating trenches, to thicken the old line and from which they could give one another mutual support and meet an attacking enemy more effectively.

Always by night (and sometimes by day) they must dominate No Man's Land. Each night, not less than half of the men in each of the perimeter battalions were out beyond the perimeter, sometimes far out, at some time or another. As soon as darkness threw its friendly cloak around them they slid through the wire on their dark and often dangerous patrols, moving stealthily on quiet feet. Whatever the particular purpose, they never lost sight of one common and pervasive purpose behind whatever they did at night out there in No Man's Land — to strike terror out of the darkness into the hearts of the Germans and Italians and give them no rest, nor allow them ever to feel secure.

When out of the Red Line, there was generally respite from fighting and patrolling. There was little respite from digging. Most of the besieged area was soon pounded to a thick, grey powder, many inches deep, by the shells and bombs and the countless turnings of endlessly crushing wheels except, perhaps, about the centre of the town immediately around the harbour, and in the ground raised and cleft by nature where the Red Line joined the sea in the east and the west. This powder drifted and blew on the winds and crept and settled in a way even the natural dust and sand of the desert, with which it mingled, had never achieved, blow as the desert winds might have done through all the ages.

Besieged in such circumstances, there is no way men can hold out for long without food, however stout their hearts. They cannot fight without weapons and the ammunition for them, nor can their fighting and transport vehicles operate without petrol, oil and spares. Everything the garrison needed to maintain the three months' supplies that were there when they arrived, and to build up those supplies for the period more than twice as long that they were destined to remain; everything to enable them to go on fighting and digging and building; everything to treat them when they were ill or wounded, even to bury them decently when they were killed; everything had to be brought in by sea from the moment the Bardia Road was cut on 11 Apr and the siege began.

This would have been hazardous enough even when there was some degree of air cover for the ships. But there was none at all for some time onwards from 25 Apr. On that day the last few fighters left Tobruk (one or two Hurricanes only remaining there in underground hangars from which they could sally forth from time to time on brief reconnaissances — just to "take a quick look"). In the previous three weeks the RAF in Tobruk lost 27 of its 32 Hurricanes, fighting against great odds, although they had taken toll of the enemy aircraft in doing so. Now, in the whole area from Alexandria to Tobruk, there were only 13 fighters. Wretched as this situation was for the garrison, it was probably even more awkward for the Navy. Now their task of supporting Tobruk was to be intensified. In the last days of April a very critical test was looming for the garrison. The Commanders knew this. They knew that Rommel had received instructions from the German High Command on 20 April directing the early reduction of Tobruk. They knew that his preparations were in hand for a large scale attack, using all of his available formations simultaneously along the whole front, as soon as he was reinforced by the arrival of the main body of the 15th Armoured Division. They knew that elements of this Division had already been identified on the frontier. They knew that Churchill had responded to a desperate plea from Wavell on 20 April for more tanks, by diverting through the Mediterranean, from its projected route around the Cape of Good Hope, a convoy carrying 295 tanks. However, they knew also that, even if this most hazardous Operation Tiger succeeded, there was no way the tanks could arrive before Rommel struck again.

Fortunately, they also knew where the main weight of this strike would be directed. Their own tactical appreciations had been confirmed by a marked map recovered from the wreckage of a German aircraft shot down by the last of the Hurricanes on its last day in Tobruk.

Despite the current doctrine that all relevant information must be made known to the humblest soldier, there was no way that the men who would face the attacker could know much of what was pending. But they could see what was happening around them, and with that instinct which the intelligent fighting man develops, they could feel from that and from what information did get to them, the shape of what was to come. During the last three weeks of April, the German aeroplanes were there for all to see as they made 677 separate attacks against the harbour installations and the anti-aircraft positions. The Hurricanes shot down about 30 and the guns brought down about 40 more. From their forward positions, the men of 2/17 Bn and the others watched the mounting scale, first of the struggle in the air between the vastly outnumbered Hurricanes and their attackers and then, after the last of the Hurricanes left, between the guns around the harbour and any ships caught there, on the one side, and the swarming aircraft on the other side.

Of these aircraft, the Stuka dive-bombers (JU87s) were the most spectacular and the most frightening until the men on the ground discovered their vulnerability. The fighters came and went so quickly, storming and shooting; the big bombers droned lazily across and, when they were not so high, one could see their bomb doors open and count the bombs as they fell away, and make a good guess where these were going to hit. However, the Stukas first circled like eagles spotting their prey, then, one after another, would bank and, in the one electrifying movement, hurtle down like thunderbolts diving at an angle of about 70°. The roar of their engines rose to a crescendo as they dived, mingled with the screaming sound of the passage of the machine itself through the air and sometimes the wild shrieking of noise devices which some had attached to them. The wheels thrust out below them like the outstretched talons of a plummeting eagle.

The fury from the air could not deny the use of the harbour to the intrepid ships, nor put the guns out of action. Except for very small craft, the ships took to racing in under cover of darkness, discharging their cargo in an avalanche of activity, and then racing out again to be as far as possible from Tobruk before the light of the new day came. The gunners stood to their guns beneath the bombs and continued to fight the Stukas all the way down.

As the violent month of April edged towards its finish, the raging aeroplanes wheeled to include in their attacks the field gun positions in the centre of the besieged area and the infantry in their perimeter posts and reserve areas.

On the 29th there was continual movement westward of troops and armour across the front of 20 Bde, still centrally sited on the perimeter where 2/13 and 2/15 Bns were holding the line, with 2/17 backing them in reserve. Shells fell exploding among these Australians all morning and then about 45 aircraft came bombing and straffing 2/17 Bn. In those open areas, and among the holes where the soldiers waited, they did no damage. Soon it became evident that the focus of their main attention was to the right of the 20 Bde — the high ground at Ras el Medauuar (Hill 209) where 26 Bde was holding.

Bombs and shells fell heavily there on the afternoon of 30 Apr. With the coming darkness through dust and smoke, the Germans began their advance, disarming mines, and blowing gaps in the wire. They moved through the gaps into a welter of confused fighting that went on through the night and into the mist of the following morning — a deathly white mist hanging over all the land, in which no man could see where the enemy held or moved, or where were his friends.

When the mist rose it could be seen that the Germans were in 7 of the perimeter posts and 40 tanks were around the hill. These tanks began to move with the rising of the mist, and visible battle was once more joined with tanks fighting tanks, the shattering burst of many shells, aeroplanes diving and shooting, bombs exploding and soldiers pouring fire into opposing groups or closing in the shock of separate encounters. By dark the attacking Germans had taken fifteen of the defending posts, along a 5,000 yd front but were halted with the darkness, their dead and wounded scattered wide. The defenders counter attacked early in the night and, although beaten off with heavy losses, they forced the intruders onto the defensive. The Germans stayed there the following day, swept and blinded by wind-driven dust through which shells rained on them. They still stayed there on 3 May and made no move forward out of the salient they had driven into the defences — about 3 miles wide and 3 miles deep. When the night came again they still held — for the loss of only one post — against a counter-attack by 18 Bde.

In the 3 days of that fighting the Germans and Italians lost some 950 men and the Australians about 800. But this was not the importance of it. For Rommel, the maintenance of this salient would constantly immobilise some of his best troops, arresting them from striking at the frontier of Egypt. For the defenders the attack marked the end of a phase. Henceforth, for some time, they could concentrate on strengthening the line around the salient and on general reorganisation.

During those critical days, there was little that the three Bns of 20 Bde could do, except stand and wait, in constant readiness to join the fighting whenever they might be called upon to do so. With the coming of night on 1 May, smart patrol work by one of the 2/13 Bn patrols, against about 1,000 Germans, foiled an attempt to lever another opening for tanks to come through.

At the back of the 2/13 Bn, the 2/17 watched the little they could see of the battle unfold by day and by night were bathed in the glare from the bursting shells, the questing searchlights, the flares rising high and hanging in the surrounding darkness through which curved the long, lazy, bright lines that the tracers made. They heard the continuous roar made by artillery and tanks and many thousands of shells churning up the desert to billow in great clouds around Hill 209. A 2/13 Bn soldier might have written for them as well as for himself and his own unit:

"We watched, speculating, the continuous action in the Medauuar sector. It was a maelstrom of dust, noise, gun flashes, Stukas and, through it all, the distinctive ripping double-drum of the German Spandau machine gun. We saw a Stuka deliver his bombs, complete with his aircraft, into the side of the much scarred Hill 209, and in the evening, for the first and only time, the searing flare of the flame-thrower used against the counter-attacking troops of the 18 Bde".

Battalion Officers at Tobruk - see page 487 for a full list of names

The 2/13 and 2/17 Bns changed places again during the night of 4/5 May. They followed a procedure which had rapidly become standard. The 2/13 simply moved out, leaving for their relief their ammunition, their rations and the chattels that were common for the fighting to be done. Such a drill, although not unproductive of some individual irritations, made for smoothness, speed and quiet there in the darkness on such occasions which are always edgy. Any soldier then feels himself exposed and off-balance, vulnerable to sudden alarms and excursions, until he gets himself firmly fixed once more into his fighting posture.

Morning came on 5 May with a dust-storm which was almost unbelievably intense even for that accursed desert place, The 2/17 Bn was holding the area where the road from El Adem came due north out of the desert and passed through the perimeter. That was the road which had formed the planned axis of Rommel's Easter attack upon them. However, they could see nothing of it now, nor of the Germans, through the opaqueness of the flying dust and sand which shut out the sun and all else there was of the world. They could scarcely see their comrades beside them. Breathing was difficult. They could not eat. To guard against the possibility of any German movement upon them under the cloak of this furious obscurity they sent patrols out beyond the wire to wait on guard. But the Germans must have been suffering equally and it was scarcely likely that they could mount any threat in those conditions.

The following day was clearer. Perhaps it would have been better if it had not been. From the perimeter posts, high flying aeroplanes could be seen in a clear sky and then followed the explosion of bombs. A column of smoke rose from somewhere back in the base area to become a great swirling pillar, climbing majestically thousands of feet into the air. A large petrol dump had been hit, with the flames spreading voraciously to a nearby diesel oil dump. This loss compounded a very serious supply problem which was to become worse a little later in the month.

There were no special highlights during the three weeks that the Bn spent in the El Adem positions. But then the highlights of any period of war are fairly well spread out for fighting soldiers.

Deep night patrols were out every night and a degree of competition developed between those doing the patrols. On the night of 12 May, Bruce Trebeck, with Peter Bryant's 6 Section, did a reconnaissance patrol of some 8 miles outside the wire which they claimed as a record distance at that stage. On the Italian maps were marked a couple of huts or houses east of El Adem Road just over 3 miles from the road block. The patrol went out from post R51 and firstly moved to Bir el Azazi (later known as 'PLONK') and from there turned south of west and headed towards the huts shown on the maps. As they approached the area, they could see several objects — many more than the Italian maps had indicated. When within about 100 yds of the first of these dark objects they realised it was a German tank, and they had virtually walked into the outskirts of a tank laager, counting at least a dozen with most of the crews sleeping on the ground beside their tanks. Being only 8 in the patrol against probably 50 at least plus a dozen tanks, the odds were against a successful attack, so they circled around the tanks towards the El Adem Road, hoping there were no very alert sentries at the laager, before starting the long trek back to the wire. When still about a mile from the perimeter, they began to relax a little when, suddenly, they were challenged with, "Halt who goes there?", and immediately hit the ground. Fortunately, Trebeck recognised Swede Weldon's voice so reponded to the challenge with, "Swede, you bastard, what are you doing out here?" Weldon had a wire patrol that night, but decided to wander out about a mile to see what he could find! At the patrol debriefing, an accurate position of the laager was given and a troop of 25-pdrs did a predicted shoot on the area before dawn.

German tanks, some of them estimated to be up to 50 tons, prowled the open spaces beyond the perimeter, usually carefully just beyond the effective range of the garrison's guns, but occasionally coming close enough to patrol the perimeter while they swept it with systematic fire. In the moonlight, soon after midnight on 16 May, one such tank came fairly close in front of Capt Brien's coy on the left of the Bn's front. It moved methodically westward to engage Capt Wilson's men at the road block itself and then took on Maj Magno's coy on Wilson's right. The frustrated fd and a/tk gunners had to hold their fire because several of the Bn's patrols were at work out there in the night where the German tanks were cruising. Soon after dawn 3 more tanks could be seen coasting along the Bn's front — but too far out for the infantry to waste ammunition on them. This was not the case later in the night though, when Brien's men hotly engaged another tank which shelled and machine-gunned them from a distance of only about 300 yds.

There were waves and eddies washing around the front from heavy fighting which had developed in and around the salient and, on17 May, 3 tanks began to close in on Wilson's coy. One of the Bn's bush artillery crews joined in the fight from a little further back, sighting their captured and sightless Italian a/tk guns by peering through the barrels to fix on the target. They scored a direct hit on one of the tanks, killing one of the crew and seriously wounding two others. The remaining 2 tanks made off, leaving to their fate the wounded men, and one other who could be seen cleverly dodging the shells bursting around him.

Sgt F G Clark, as intrepid in this war as he had been in the previous one where he was awarded the DCM and MM., was quickly out through the perimeter and hard behind them with a small patrol, intent on examining the damaged tank and capturing the survivors. The other tanks halted their flight long enough to engage his patrol and shoot one of his men.

Clark could not find the unwounded German but, in one of those bizarre occasions with which war is studded, Pte F Fields did. He was a stretcher bearer who had followed behind Clark's patrol. The German rose suddenly from a slit trench where he had been hiding. The startled Fields, unarmed but carrying a shovel, stiffened in the "on guard" position with that awkward instrument. There in the wide desert the Australian and the German stood motionless regarding one another.

Suddenly, the German (obviously a man with a most unteutonic sense of humour) started laughing at the incongruity of it all. Fields, a brave and cheerful fellow, stood stiff and still for a second or two more in front of his laughing enemy. Then he too began to laugh. The German went amicably with him as his prisoner, to be greeted without rancour by the men he had just been trying to kill and who had been trying to kill him.

The Australians in the salient were determined to advance their positions and shorten their line. As the situation boiled up, both sides used tanks, lavish arty fire and medium machine guns to support their infantry in savage local attacks and counter-attacks. The toll taken of all the troops engaged was a heavy one.

As had happend at the beginning of May, 20 Bde was only on the fringes of that fighting. What they could do, however, they did with a will; that was mainly to goad and harass their enemies by even more agressive patrolling in front of, and even right up to, their forward positions. To this end they add a new element on 14 May.

6 of the 2/17 Bn Bren Gun Carriers set out into the open desert to try to trap some of the German tanks lurking out there. They sallied out through Magno's coy to harass one tank which was squatted down in a good observation position due south of the road block which closed off the El Adem Road, and three others further to the east. They took with them a forward Observation Officer for some of the British guns which were waiting to have a crack at those tanks if they could be lured in close enough.

Lt Kanga Maclarn was in charge of the carriers; the task was one after his own heart. Since Bren Gun Carriers were open vehicles, with only lightly armoured sides, designed primarily for the quick transport of troops over bullet-swept ground, there was no question of the carriers slugging it out with the tanks. Their task was to goad and tempt the tanks. This they did, firing

Carrier Patrol – **L-R:** *Pte W A G Stewart, Lt R S Rudkin, Pte D Y Nesbitt, Pte V J Fitzpatrick*

Various scenes in Tobruk

as they wheeled and twisted at speed among their own dust, until the tanks battened down and went after them. The carriers beat them back to the perimeter where Wilson's men covered them in with fire. The frustrated tanks shelled the coy positions there, and then as though trying to drive a lesson home, turned on Magno's coy. By that time, however, the guns which had been waiting were making it so hot for the tanks that they did not linger.

The next day, the carriers repeated the performance, vastly to the entertainment of the rest of the Bn, watching from their perimeter posts like a Roman holiday crowd at a gladiatorial contest.

After the abortive mid-May fighting, the last days of May simmered and bubbled away in the salient in violent and dangerous discomfort. Elsewhere around the perimeter the danger, though ever-present, was rather less acute but the main elements making for danger and discomfort were common.

In 2/17 Bn, the patrolling never slackened. The thermos bombs, which they had first encountered at Acroma during the retreat from Benghazi, were dropped thickly on all the ground around them by bombers on 12 May and added their own separate hazard to any movement. The food was monotonous and always heavily laced with sand. Bully beef was the most constant constituent of all their meals. It was supplemented by vitamin pills and meat extract. Each man was ordered to take half a teaspoon of the extract a day and reminded that "It also makes a pleasant soup". So it did for a time — but soon the stage was reached when it took exceptional strength of character to look a jar of meat extract in the face without a shudder.

Above: A Blue Line Post. ***Below:*** *BnHQ Salient Area*

They accepted the foul taste of the water but its scarcity was always worrying. Early in the siege, they had grumbled when Lt Col Crawford ordered that, water shortage or not, each man in his Bn would shave — preferably each day, but most certainly every second day. "Another of the Cake Eater's bright, bloody ideas", they muttered. (This was Lt Col Crawford's nickname.) Despite this, shaving made them feel good and marked them out — like the guards coming back from Dunkirk. Anyway, they had quickly found that very little water could be made to go a very long way. With less than half a cup of water, a man can clean his teeth thoroughly, shave his face smooth and clean. Then he can swab free of sweat and dirt the feet on which, with his weapon, rests the main dependence of an infantry soldier.

They had muttered similarly when Crawford announced that every enemy aeroplane which came within their range would be engaged by every available man with every available weapon. They felt that the chances of this damaging enemy aircraft did not justify the risks of betraying their positions and calling down a storm of avenging fire on their heads. However, it soon became a source of great satisfaction to them to see any aeroplane that came over regularly giving them a wide berth. This was particularly noticeable with the reconnoitring Henschel which they cursed every day as "Schmidt der spy". It patrolled the perimeter assiduously, but quickly learned to swing wide as it approached the 2/17 Bn, resuming the line of its steady flight again only when it was well past them.

The Bn was relieved on the night of 24 May and, with the rest of the Bde, went into Divisional reserve in "the Dust Bowl" near the centre of the garrison area. However, the food went on being just as monotonous and the water as evil-tasting but even more precious. Every second day, each of the coys set out at dawn for the Blue Line, the road being heavily shelled as often as not as they passed over it, to work on the most urgent sections — immediately behind the salient. The heat mounted in intensity as the day advanced so that, with the toil, the heat and the dust combined, they were hard put to make their miserable water ration last out at all.

At the site of each new post which had been marked for digging, they struck rock so solid beneath the few inches of topsoil that often their picks bent almost like putty. Drilling to site explosive charges was no less arduous. The place was too exposed for the engineers to bring up many of their pneumatic drills during the daylight hours.

For a short time, however, everything seemed different when the trucks returned in the afternoon and took the working parties to a little cove east of the harbour. Its salt water was deep and very clear and cool. They could relax there and catch up with the news from men of other units. They could relax, that is, until the Stukas came screaming down through the thick anti-aircraft barrage, or went skimming back low overhead in their attempt to escape from the quick-firing Bofors guns.

By this time, the two months which Wavell had originally thought the Garrison in Tobruk would have to hold out were already almost gone. There was a steady whittling away of the fighting men. 2/17 Bn had been watching this happen to themselves, and the process accelerated when, with the rest of 20 Bde, they moved into the salient on the night of 4 June. In that damned place they would experience the nearest approximation to conditions at Gallipoli in such areas as Lone Pine and Quinn's Post, as Australian troops were to know in this war.

The Bn moved to the Bianca area as the left forward Bn. The Germans had been engaged in laying a wide, heavily infested booby trap minefield of "S" type mines (jumping-jack mines). As a result of the constant aggressive activities of the Bn, both by fire power and patrols, work on this minefield ceased the night after taking over the Bianca positions. After about a week, the enemy had withdrawn from their original positions only 100 yds in front of the Bn to new positions about 1,000 yds further back.

Watching posts were established very well forward of the Bn positions. From these, there was a good view of practically the whole salient area, and I Section did good work in plotting and mapping the enemy defences, so that specific weapon pits could be engaged by arty and mortar fire.

One night a patrol, under Cpl Peter Bryant, managed to get through to an enemy dump, and brought back a wooden crate containing what proved to be 2 Teller mines. These were the first to come into the possession of the garrison and were very valuable — they enabled the engrs to issue detailed instructions on how to handle and delouse them, possibly saving many lives.

At its maximum, the salient established by Rommel's forced over nearly a 3-mile width of the perimeter, being almost equal distance either side of Hill 209 (or Ras el Medauuar) and pushed in a semicircle almost 3 miles deep in a north-east direction directly towards the town and harbour. In the counter-attacks carried out by 18 Bde, 2/9 Bn had regained a strip of the desert on the eastern side of the salient on 3 and 4 May, while 2/10 Bn regained an area of the salient on the north and west side on 15 and 16 May. Now that 20 Bde were in the salient, one of their major objectives was to continually push out patrols and endeavour to win back and regain more of the salient area. During the period 11 to 16 June, they succeeded in regaining something in the order of 1,000 yds in the centre of the salient area. This overall reduction of the bulge that the salient made into the fortress area eventually enabled the Garrison to employ one less Bn to man the Red Line front positions.

Life in the salient was really terrible — opposing positions varied from about 70 yds to 300 yds apart; they lived in shallow holes scratched in the desert, often not much more than 2 feet deep before striking solid rock, and a ground sheet stretched over part of it to provide some shade during the day. It was impossible to move during daylight hours without bringing down a hail of machine gun fire and mortar shells. It was midsummer and hundreds of dead bodies, either in shallow scraped graves or unburied, attracted myriads of flies. There was nowhere for adequate toilet facilities and an increasing number of cases of dysentery were inevitable. With no possibility of any form of cooking in the forward areas, nightfall became a relief when a few could crawl back behind the forward positions and bring some food and water that had been brought as far forward as possible by the tireless B Echelon Drivers and Quartermaster Staffs.

14 June recorded the first Officer of the Bn killed in action — Lt Alf Tuckwell trod on a mine whilst on patrol and, in addition, two of his patrol were wounded. That same day, Keith Magno and John Balfe were promoted to Major, their original recommendations having been put in by Lt Col Crawford on 15 Mar, but possibly lost or gone astray somewhere on the run back from Marsa Brega. The Bn was called to "stand to" at 2025 hrs when there was enemy movement in the salient and rather heavy artillery, but nothing developed and the stand down order came at 2325 hrs. During this period, the enemy was using a 'spotter' recce aircraft to fly over the Garrison positions and direct their artillery fire. There was generally heavy shelling during this time, sometimes on the forward positions but possibly even more on the slightly rear areas.

After a short time back in the Blue Line reserve position, 2/17 Bn again went forward and relieved 2/13 Bn at Forbes Mound on the right flank of the Ras el Medauuar sector on the night of 25/26 June. There were many anti-personnel mines and booby traps which could cause heavy casualties unless great caution was exercised, particularly by patrols. When attempting to improve a weapon pit on the second night, 6 Sec of 17 Pl suffered 4 casualties. It transpired that the Pl position had actually been dug in on the edge of the booby trap field and, while digging, a pick struck an "S" mine, wounding Peter Bryant, Jeff Moncrieff, Jim Taylor and Reg Tait.

The patrols and night carrying parties had reason to become thankful for the methodical attitude of the Germans who had many machine guns operating on fixed lines of fire — as they used tracer bullets, it was possible to accurately pin-point these lines of fire to the extent that men would move to a certain point then go down and crawl under the fixed line of fire, then get up on the other side and happily move on.

On 6 July, the British arty were finding it difficult to continue supplying forward Observation Officers, so Trebeck, from his hole in the ground at the head of the salient, acted as Observer in liaison with the arty and a shoot on enemy mortar and machine guns was carried out. At least 1 machine gun and 1 mortar were knocked out.

A further shoot against mortar positions was carried out on 9 July. On the night of 10/11 July, 2/17 Bn was relieved by 2/32 Bn and 20 Bde became Divisional reserve, with the Bn in the Ariente area. Here they enjoyed the rest after the salient, and a good canteen issue, including a bottle of beer for each man, proved very acceptable. During the 14 days in reserve over 50 reinforcements and 5 Officers joined the unit but, on the night of 26/27 July, they were on the move again and took over from 2/9 Bn as the left forward battalion in the El Adem sector again.

CHAPTER 6
THE FINAL STRETCH

By this time the Siege of Tobruk had existed for three and a half months and a routine had been established that now had some elements of monotony and even almost boredom. But it was not really possible for monotony and boredom to be conscious feelings when at any minute of day or night the completely unexpected could strike like a thunderbolt regardless of where or what was being done. Lord Haw-Haw (a renegade Englishman who was broadcasting propaganda for Nazi Germany) had given the garrison troops the title of "desert rats". But, instead of being disturbed by a description which was meant to be insulting, the troops were proud of it, and, in fact, retained it after the conflict was over by forming the "Rats of Tobruk" association.

From this time onwards, the Battalion war diary increasingly refers to "a normal day or night" — but normality for a besieged garrison — living in constant threat of sudden death, appalling living conditions with frequent dust storms, the same uninteresting rations and little water — is a relative concept. To any individual soldier it was possible that any day could be his worst day; it made no difference what part of the routine cycle he was in — the few weeks at a time as one of the forward battalions in the Red Line or the odd week in the Blue Line as Brigade reserve, or the even rarer few days as Divisional reserve. He could be part of a working party in the harbour area and be caught there in a particularly heavy air raid; he could be out on a regular night patrol and be suddenly under fierce fire from an enemy strongpost, when the patrol was within a minefield; he could be peacefully minding his own business either in a forward post or in a reserve position when a sudden hail of artillery shells or mortar bombs started exploding on the one little piece of desert he happened to be occupying.

The only thing that was really normal was the inevitable pattern when a forward battalion — daytime vigilance on clear days or dust filled days, night-time patrols outside the wire, either shallow or deep patrols, and either reconnaissance or fighting patrols. When in reserve, perhaps a day of comparative rest, then digging to improve existing positions or to prepare new positions. And at all times wherever he was, the same rations and the same few days of reasonable weather interspersed with the days when the fine dust blown by hated winds obscured everything and even made breathing a problem.

Back again in the El Adem sector with D, B and C coys forward and A Coy in reserve, the Battalion found conditions different. The enemy positions were now much closer to the perimeter, and dug into sangars astride the El Adem road about 3000 yards out from the road block. As a result, patrols on company fronts were not to move further than 2000 yards from the wire, and all deep patrols would be fighting patrols. Also the enemy was using a mobile searchlight west of El Adem road to hamper the battalion patrol operations. However various patrols were successful in locating and plotting the enemy minefields laid in front of all company fronts.

Late in the afternoon a couple of days after occupying these positions, C Coy suffered the heaviest shelling received since the battalion moved into the El Adem sector. A considerable amount of vehicle movement was observed on the El Adem escarpment and road as well as occasionally troop carrying vehicles across both 2/17 and 2/13 Bn fronts.

As a typical example of nightly patrols, on the night of 30/31 July there were 8 patrols listed as follows:—

Series 1 1 NCO 2 Ors out R41 at 0130 hrs in R41 at 0530 hrs

Series 2 1 NCO 2 Ors out Rd Block 1915 hrs in Rd Block 2120 hrs

Series 3 1 Offr 3 NCO 5 Ors out R43 2330 hrs in R45 0320 hrs

Series 4 1 Offr 10 Ors out R45 2230 hrs in R43 0410 hrs

Series 5 1 Offr 10 Ors out R47 2130 hrs in R47 0310 hrs

Series 6 1 Offr 10 Ors out R39 2200 hrs in R39 0245 hrs

Series 7 1 Offr 10 Ors out R53 2145 hrs in R49 0330 hrs

Series 8 2 Offrs 4 Ors out R53 2330 hrs in R53 0500 hrs

So that is an example of a "normal night", 65 Offrs, NCOs, and Ors out in No-Man's Land on patrols.

On 30 July, Colin Pitman took over as Adjt from Tim McCulloch.

It was decided that a fighting patrol should attack the positions astride the El Adem road, and that this raid should be supported by a diversion supplied by C Coy. Thus on the night of 31 July/1 Aug occurred one of the mysteries of War that has never really been solved. Keith Sabine commanded the raiding patrol from A Coy which was to carry out a quick raid from the flank at 0100 hrs. Some 45 minutes before this the enemy brought down a great deal of defensive fire which severely held up the raiding party and, after an hour of continual heavy fire, the raid was abandoned as the patrol was quite unable to reach their objective.

Meanwhile the diversion patrol from C Coy was commanded by Capt Ted Chapman, Coy 2 i/c, with Lt John Downing plus Sgt Rand and 7 Ors. The patrol split into two with Ted Chapman and 4 Ors on the west of the road, and John Downing with Sgt Rand and 3 Ors on the east of the road.

They reached the 9 Kilo peg along the road and then found a minefield of Italian type mines across the road. Having moved a further 150 yards on, two Verey lights were fired and the patrol was fired on from their front, as well as the searchlight going on as soon as the Verey lights were fired. They were being fired on from positions astride the road, as well as there being one a/tk gun each side of the road. The patrol went to ground and commenced to retire, and Ted Chapman ordered the men to withdraw to, and rendezvous at, the 7 kilo peg as had been previously arranged. Sgt Rand remained with John Downing and he believed Lt Downing was behind him as he crossed the minefield when a mortar bomb exploded and the party again went to ground. On resuming the retirement Sgt Rand found that the man behind him was not John Downing but another member of the patrol. Sgt Rand and the 7 Ors waited at the RV for 45 minutes for the two officers to turn up but when they did not, Rand sent the others back to report while he remained at the RV.

At 0400 hrs another patrol from C Coy, under Lt George Reid with 8 Ors and two stretchers, was sent out to try and find the two missing officers. With Sgt Rand, it proceeded to the area, where the two officers had last been seen. An hour and a half search of the area both east and west of the road failed to find a trace. George Reid proceeded across the minefield where he found a mine with the top blown out, and 250 yards away found part of the lining of a steel helmet marked "J Downing" which appeared to have been torn out by hand; no blood stains or remains were seen. During this patrol no enemy was seen nor was the patrol engaged by fire, and

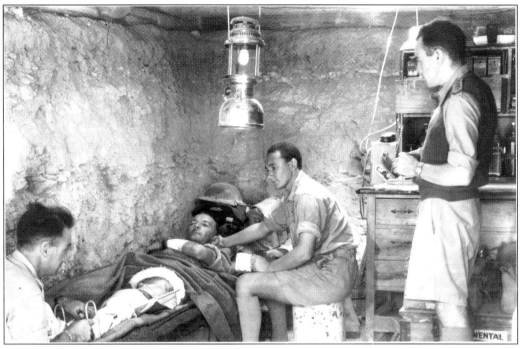

An Underground RAP at Tobruk. Captain J F Sullivan, the RMO, is at right, holding a hypodermic needle.
(AWM 021019)

George Reid only returned at 0700 hrs when daylight had come. At 1300 hrs that afternoon when the heat haze set in, a patrol of three Bren Carriers went out and, under fire, carried out a complete search of the area without result.

It was believed that Ted Chapman and John Downing were missing, believed Prisoners of War, but at a much later date it was confirmed they were both dead — but never were the circumstances known. Only a day or two before this patrol, Ted Chapman had received a letter from his lass at home accepting his proposal of marriage and Ted was as happy as a sandboy.

On the night of 4/5 Aug normal patrols were out but this night succeeded in quite a "mine delousing" evening — A Coy (who had replaced D Coy as a forward Coy) deloused 27 Anti-personnel mines while B Coy patrols lifted 134 mines.

On the night of 7/8 Aug 2/15 Bn relieved 2/17 Bn who moved back to Bde reserve in the Blue Line for a brief well earned rest after very active patrolling which mostly occupied about 50 percent of the forward companies' strength each night. For the next 9 days the weather was mostly fine, and from their Blue Line positions they were in a good position to watch air attacks on the Tobruk area and corresponding AA fire on the enemy planes. On a couple of occasions the battalion area was straffed by JU87's (Stukas) flying low after having delivered their bombs in the town and harbour area.

On the night of 18/19 Aug the battalion changed over with 2/13 Bn as right forward battalion of 20 Bde and were now once more occupying the area they had originally moved into on 10 Apl when the "Benghazi Handicap" ended.

On 22 Aug Colonel Crawford issued a "Fighting Memorandum" for the information of all ranks which pointed out that it was over three months since the last enemy attack so a further attack must be considered overdue, and a state of constant readiness must therefore be maintained at all times.

All weapons especially captured enemy weapons, were to be thoroughly checked, all mortars allotted a fire position and provided with range cards. He was seeking approval to carry out test manning and fire exercises when all weapons would be fired simultaneously for a period of two minutes. All perimeter wire requiring repair was to be strengthened at once. Careless movement, particularly in late afternoon or evening, around posts should be avoided. All men were warned not to take orders from unknown officers.

Approval for this fire exercise was obtained for 0630 hrs on 26 Aug. Some interesting information was obtained and, contrary to some thoughts, there was no retaliation from the enemy. On 27 Aug an enemy working party was observed and a hastily organised fighting patrol of B Coy under Capt Austin Mackell went out from post R31 and R33 at 1600 hrs. As soon as the patrol was observed, the enemy at once started to withdraw and were engaged by the main part of the patrol which expended all its ammunition. The other (covering) part came under enemy fire and was not able to engage the enemy.

On 29 Aug the advance party of 2nd Bn Polish Brigade arrived to get a thorough knowledge of the sector and fortress routine. This Polish Bde arrived to replace 18 Aust Bde in the garrison and the 2nd Bn would in due course, take over from 2/17 Bn when the Polish Brigade relieved 20 Bde between 3 and 6 Sept. Patrolling continued each night, now including a Pole in each patrol as the battalion did their utmost to pass on every bit of useful information they could to their new friends before being relieved.

On the night of 31 Aug/1 Sept an unfortunate incident occurred in which two D Coy patrols clashed resulting in 5 being wounded one of whom was a Pole. The conclusion reached following all statements after the clash was that loss of direction had resulted in the protective patrol going beyond its limit, and coming into direct collision with the fighting patrol. In reporting all the circumstances to Bde HQ, Lt Col Crawford concluded, "The night was an extremely dark one and such a collision is likely to occur at any time unless adequate numbers of prismatic compasses are available".

On the night of 3/4 Sept the Poles took over from 2/17 Bn, with the CO and coy rear parties remaining with the

Brig Murray with three Bn Commanders: L-R Lt Cols: J W Crawford (2/17Bn), R W G Ogle (2/15 Bn), F A Burrows (2/13 Bn).

Battalion Officers at Tobruk – see page 487 for a full list of names.

Polish Bn for 48 hours to assist them in settling into their new role. The remainder of the battalion settled in their new areas and spent the rest of the day at comparative rest in a very dusty area. Then the battalion supplied large working parties to the ammunition point, the Hospital, and West Pilastrino Blue Line defences where they were required to complete digging strong defensive positions which must be completed by the battalion before leaving their present position. The CO and rear parties returned. Three companies worked each day on digging while one company had a rest. Maj Keith Magno was evacuated with jaundice and the duties of 2 i/c were taken over by Maj John Balfe.

The arrival of the Polish Brigade, and their relief of 18 Aust Bde who were evacuated back to Alexandria and Palestine, was the first phase of the relief of the original Tobruk garrison. To follow the Polish Brigade was 70 British Division including British 14, 16 and 23 Bdes, and also 32 Army Tank Brigade and British AA regiments.

During the period of 8 to 18 Sept the main occupation was digging and more digging, interspersed with a couple of more enjoyable events. Chester Wilmot of the Australian Broadcasting Commission's Field Unit arrived in Tobruk early in September and, to coincide with this, 20 Bde HQ had organised a Brigade concert party of talent from within the Brigade. This concert party entertained the battalion on the nights of 10 and 11 Sept and the concert was recorded live by Chester Wilmot's unit and later played back in Australia — the concert was greatly enjoyed by the battalion. On the night of 11 Sept, the Officers of the battalion held their first formal mess dinner for many months, and the little liquor available went a long way after so many months in the desert. A good time was had by all present, even if the striking of the tent resulted in some being on top and some underneath when it finally subsided.

On 18 Sept Lt Wright and 21 reinforcements arrived and joined the battalion strength while 20 Bde prepared to relieve 24 Bde in the Sidi Daud area — the Eastern sector. Coy comds made a recce of their new positions where 2/17 Bn was to relieve 2/28 Bn as the left forward battalion. This relief was completed by midnight on 19 Sept, and during the night of the change over, one of 2/28 Bn Bren Carriers was blown up on our own minefield near post Z81, and Bayne Geike was slightly wounded by one of the booby traps set in the wire.

This was the first time the battalion had been in this Eastern sector covering the Bardia road entry through the perimeter. AASC were holding the posts over the rugged Wadi Es Zeiting to the coast on the left of the battalion. The next couple of days were basically spent in becoming familiar with the new area. D Coy ration truck was blown up on our own mines near the forward wire — lateral mines laid around the forward posts proved difficult to tape, and engineers were laying new rows of mines each night and company personnel had great difficulty in keeping check of them.

On 22 Sept Maj John Williams, Capt John Broadbent and Capt Peter O'Brien arrived from 20 ITB and resumed duty with the battalion. John Williams was detached to 2/15 Bn to become 2 i/c to Lt Col Ogle, John Broadbent was to take over as OC B Coy while Peter O'Brien was to become 2 i/c C Coy. Next day Capt Curly Wilson relinquished command of B Coy to John Broadbent and, with 5 NCOs and 4 Ors set out to go back and take up duty at 20 ITB.

That day, 23 Sept, an advance party of 2nd Leicester Battalion — part of 16 Bde (British) — arrived prior to their taking over the Sidi Daud Sector; also a number of Officers of 16 Bde and Leicester Battalion visited Bn HQ while on a recce tour of the area. 16 Bde (British) was the first brigade of 70 Division to arrive in Tobruk and relieved 24 Aust Bde. Next day the CO 2nd Leicesters arrived to stay with the 2/17 Bn until they took over. On 25 Sept the operational order was issued relating to the relief of 2/17 Bn by 2nd Leicesters on the night of 26/27 Sep. The battalion would move back — as part of 20 Bde in Divisional Reserve — to the Ariente area. That day an A Coy truck was blown up on our forward minefields and one soldier badly injured. At 1400 hrs, 26 Sept, Capt Austin Mackell left the battalion on a special mission to Middle East HQ relative to a/tk ammunition after which he took up duties at 20 ITB. That evening the relief by 2nd Leicesters was completed and the battalion settled into the Ariente area. The CO issued orders that every man would have at least one swim before the battalion once again took over the El Adem sector on the night of 29/30 Sept, this time from the 3rd Polish Bn.

The battalion took over from posts R35 to R55, with C Coy right forward D Coy centre forward, A Coy left forward and B Coy as reserve. When the relief was completed before midnight 29 Sept the battalion was holding the El Adem Sector for the third time. During the night there were three casualties from our booby traps in the a/tk ditch. This was always a major difficulty as succeeding troops tried to make their positions more secure but relieving troops were not fully conversant with new booby traps that had been set up, or moved out on patrol on slightly the wrong track.

Part of the job of the battalion was now to maintain an outpost at Bir El Azazi, known as PLONK, while the battalion adjoining the left flank — 2 Bn Queens Regt — maintained an outpost at BONDI, also known as the walled village. BONDI was some 3500 yards south of the perimeter while PLONK was some 1750 yards south of post R49 or R51, and both these outposts were used as observation posts.

During the early days of October, heavy traffic movement was observed on the El Adem escarpment and about the El Adem road, particularly in the early daylight hours and late in the afternoons. There was also activity by working parties digging at night, and tanks moving across battalion front at night — including three tanks passing 500 yards south of PLONK. On the night of 6/7 Oct, the tank movement, particularly on A Coy front on the battalion left flank, was sufficient to make the battalion "stand to" from just before midnight until 0100 hrs, and Brig Murray visited Bn HQ to assess the situation, staying about 40 minutes before returning to his own HQ. Meanwhile a patrol led by Dal Cartledge contacted a working party of approximately a coy strength and, from a range of 100 yards, opened fire on them creating casualties and disorder until their ammunition was almost exhausted. An enemy protective party engaged them from the flank, but the patrol was able to withdraw without casualties.

The increased enemy transport and tank movement south of the El Adem sector, together with much activity of working parties discovered by the battalion's various patrols, especially in the vicinity of the outposts PLONK and BONDI, made it very apparent that the enemy was building up to attack and eliminate these outposts. As a result the battalion organised Tank Hunting Patrols, increased minefields (in conjunction with the engineers), and a/tk guns positions were dug-in at the outpost PLONK. Also proposals were developed for tanks to be available to operate outside the perimeter to engage enemy tanks and cut off their line of withdrawal when they ventured to harass PLONK and BONDI.

Lt Col Crawford made a special report to 20 Bde on PLONK operations of the night of 7/8 Oct and the day of 8 Oct, which included the following observations:—

1. PLONK is a detached OP comprising three alternative observation posts, one or other of which is normally manned by 1 NCO and 6 Ors.

2. Signal cables are laid from PLONK to the coy exchange at post R50 and the artillery OP.

3. As PLONK is an OP and not a defended post, the orders of the observation group are to withdraw in face of threatened attack.

4. Reports from PLONK on the night of 7/8 Oct included (a) 0025 hrs five enemy tanks approx 1200 yards SE of PLONK, (b) 0030 hrs five enemy tanks moving north along same route as on the night 6/7 Oct, (c) 0120 hrs the tank hunting platoon had engaged tanks near PLONK — heavy machine gun fire, (d) 0130 hrs tank hunting patrol reported in at listening post 3 — tanks engaged and leading tank stopped, (e) 0430 hrs listening post 3 informed that PLONK was clear of our troops and artillery now at liberty to carry out predicted shoot of PLONK area, (f) 1110 hrs PLONK heavily shelled.

5. During day of 8 Oct, in anticipation of heavy shelling and other enemy reprisals, PLONK not re-occupied.

6. Engineer party plus a covering party moved out at last light on 8 Oct to the vicinity of PLONK to mine the route followed by enemy tanks on the previous two nights.

7. No special party was detailed for PLONK up to the time of the arrival of Brigade Commander at 1800 hrs when the position was fully discussed and a request made for one section of Portee a/tk guns for use in the vicinity of PLONK during moonlight hours.

Meanwhile, an advance party of the 1st Bn Durham Light Infantry Regiment, which had arrived a few days earlier to observe forward battalion routine, had left the battalion area. This was part of the familiarisation program for the newly arrived British Bde which was to relieve 26 Aust Bde.

On 9 Oct planning was carried out for a tank operation on the night of 9/10 Oct. During the late afternoon 16 Matilda tanks were to move up to the rear of A Coy area in preparation for a move out through the gap at post R53 and then out to the vicinity of PLONK with the intention of engaging and defeating any enemy tanks met in that area. A patrol, with engineers, took up all mines in the PLONK area before moonrise. During the day PLONK was heavily shelled by the enemy throughout the day, with something like 200 shells around PLONK and between the OP and the perimeter wire. Normal protective patrols that night were ordered to withdraw to 500 yards from the perimeter at moonrise so that they would not conflict with the tank operation and resume their normal patrol beats after 0200 hrs.

At 2130 hrs the tanks moved out from R53 with Capt Ian McMaster guiding them, and were moving slowly so that they would not be heard. However, shortly after 2200 hrs, there was noise of tank movement from the area of BONDI towards PLONK and the Matilda tanks moved at full speed to PLONK where they found C Coy standing patrol, still intact though they had been heavily shelled, with one wounded. Also with them were two men from the 2nd Bn Queens Royal Regt, who had escaped from BONDI and it was learnt that this outpost had been taken by a strong enemy party of infantry and tanks.

The rumble of tanks coming from the direction of BONDI gave warning of the enemy intentions, and our British tanks disappeared into the night in a south east direction to meet them. One tank returned almost immediately with engine trouble and took up a hull down position within the PLONK area as four enemy tanks approached from the southwest. Capt Ian McMaster and the C Coy standing patrol started withdrawing as they had no a/tk weapons, and they were only just clear of the position when the German tanks opened fire. The hull down Matilda tank returned fire, scoring a hit with an armour piercing shell on one of the German tanks which managed to pull out of the fight and was followed by the others. Meanwhile the other Matildas, roaring across the desert to the East in search of the German tanks, eventually sighted them when they were only about 150 yards apart, and immediately engaged the enemy. The Germans scattered and used their greater speed to disappear in the dark, but at least some hits were scored judging by the sparks that flew. By 0115 hrs all British tanks had returned to R53 gap, and the standing patrol at PLONK had been re-established. The sound of tank engines and heavy transport movement was heard throughout the night, but by 0500 hrs the front was quiet, while the resumption of normal activities proceeded in the early hours of the morning.

10 Oct was a rather grim day for 2/17 Bn as they received an Operation Order from 20 Bde which stated:—

"GOC 9 Aust Div has directed that PLONK area will be held and defended by 2/17 Aust Inf Bn.

9 Aust Div has stated that protection by tanks will be provided, but the occupation of this area is not dependent upon this support. The area will be defended at all costs.

It is left to the discretion of the Comd 2/17 Bn as to whether he provides extra protection in the nature of fighting patrols or any other methods to ensure that this area is denied to the enemy. Comd 2/17 Bn will arrange allocation of a/tk guns and crews direct with OC 20 Aust A/Tk Coy".

This order from 9 Aust Div completely changed the original concept of occupying PLONK as an observation post, not a defended area. Both Lt Col Crawford and Brig Murray were opposed to the plan as they both felt that PLONK could not be defended by so small a garrison and that Tobruk could not afford to place a force strong enough to hold out against enemy tanks in such an exposed position. However, General Morshead was always determined not to allow the enemy to occupy any ground the garrison had once held, and he was very conscious of the importance of delaying in every way possible the closing-in activities that Rommel had begun.

So the battalion proceeded with the necessary planning. and Capt Frank Windeyer and 20 other ranks of his C Coy prepared to established a defensive locality as ordered, with occupation to commence at 1900 hrs on the night of 10/11 Oct. C Coy to provide a covering party of one platoon for standing piquets and fighting patrols 300 yards south of PLONK, and they were to carry a/tk bombs and grenades. Both A Coy and D Coy were to provide a section of 1 NCO and seven men each as working parties in conjunction with the fd engrs to lay mines, wire the posts with trip wires fill sandbags and build gun pits. Two 30 cwt trucks were to carry tools, engineer stores and mines, rations and water— the PLONK garrison was to take 3 days reserve rations and water, and the plan was to relieve the PLONK garrison every 48 hours.

During the morning enemy tanks were seen in the PLONK area and these were dispersed at various times throughout the morning by artillery fire. When night fell the operation got under way and, shortly after 1900 hrs, the covering party arrived at PLONK with the occupation party arriving there about 45 minutes later closely followed by the working parties and stores trucks. At about 2030 hrs enemy artillery shelling started on PLONK and also A Coy perimeter areas. By 2050 hrs the occupation party reported that the place was untenable and Frank Windeyer had been badly hit. The main post withdrew out of the area being heavily shelled and PLONK was now out of communication. Lt George Reid was then ordered to take over command of PLONK.

There was a lot of activity with enemy armoured fighting vehicles pushing in 2 Bn Queens Patrols, on left of 2/17 Bn. As small parties of men reached the forward posts, they were under heavy shell fire, while deep patrols reported digging activity of new enemy defences and tank movements. Shortly before 2200 hrs the CO ordered George Reid to proceed with all available men to PLONK in order to provide local protection for the a/tk section, and ordered Capt Kanga Maclarn to get back the trucks with A/tk guns and reorganise as a fighting patrol to go out and re-occupy PLONK, with a covering party 1000 yards south of the occupying party. 20 minutes later Capt Maclarn reports PLONK absolutely untenable and the trucks carrying A/tk guns had been hit by shells and were unserviceable, so the only course was to place the guns in open ground. At 2245 hrs George Reid reported that tanks appeared to be using smoke and so it was impossible to count their number but tanks were now moving between PLONK and the perimeter and enemy artillery was following returning parties with fire almost to their own lines.

In spite of his wounds, Capt Frank Windeyer was still trying to control the occupying party for PLONK and had George Reid again moving out towards PLONK. Towards midnight Frank Windeyer reported that the area in the vicinity of PLONK was particularly hard and stony and digging was difficult. He attempted to organise the working parties under shell fire to continue the work but visibility was reduced to 15 feet by the dust of bursting shells. At midnight 9 Div HQ advised that there were no further instructions for the CO of 2/17 Bn. Accordingly 20 Bde instructed Lt Col Crawford to establish an OP at PLONK at dawn, if it was not occupied by the enemy. By 0400 hrs the two trucks carrying a/tk guns had been salvaged and were back inside the forward posts. Brig Murray informed 2/17 Bn that our own artillery could shell PLONK in daylight and, at 0520 hrs, they opened fire. Following this there were sounds of motor transport and picks and shovels being loaded onto trucks. At 0600 hrs the artillery again engaged PLONK until visibility became nil owing to the dust from bursting shells. In reply the enemy brought down heavy artillery fire particularly on A and D Coy positions.

Frank Windeyer was evacuated to hospital at Tobruk, and a couple of days later to 2/11 AGH in Alexandria, where sadly he died of wounds.

Following this night of intense, but rather abortive, activity Gen Morshead again ordered 20 Bde to attack and recapture PLONK and to establish a new outpost in the general area but not at the site of the old outpost because it was appreciated that the previously held positions were registered by the enemy artillery. The site chosen for the new post which was to be called COOMA was some 800 yards north west of PLONK. During the day enemy shelling was particularly heavy on forward posts and between the wire and PLONK, as well as in C Coy reserve company area where Col Mills and Ted Barnett were slightly wounded and Ron Fyffe killed. Tank movement and men were seen during the day about PLONK — between 0930 hrs and 1000 hrs, 30 tanks were visible well out from the wire and these were heavily engaged by our artillery which succeeded in forcing all but 12 to return to the south out of range.

The arrangements for the operation on the night of 11/12 Oct were 1 Squadron 4 RTR, with a C Coy party of 33 under Lt George Reid, to move in after artillery concentrations on PLONK, to capture the post and annihilate all occupants. Meanwhile a party from D Coy under Ted Howard was to dig in and establish the COOMA observation post which was to be connected to D Coy HQ by cable line and telephone. Timing for the PLONK attack set zero hour at 2220 hrs with artillery slow rate of fire, commencing 30 minutes before zero hour, but changing to fast rate from zero for 40 minutes after which time the tanks and George Reid's party should be ready to launch their attack.

However everything did not work according to clockwork plan. George Reid took his party out half way to PLONK, waiting for the tanks to open fire, but nothing happened. He sent a runner back to post R49 to report that he intended to attack PLONK without the tanks. The runner returned to say he had seen the tank commander so George Reid went back himself. The tank commander told him that, having missed his time (the first tank clearing the wire 10 minutes late), he was waiting for further instructions. George Reid reported to Lt Col Crawford who arranged a new timing with zero from the opening of artillery fire at 15 minutes after midnight. Having returned to his party, they waited and the artillery opened up at 25 minutes past midnight. While waiting, Reid heard digging and voices from the direction of PLONK which continued after several rounds of artillery but ceased when the artillery fire became heavier. Then the enemy replied with defensive fire, and Reid moved his party to approximately 300 yards from the northwest corner of PLONK to wait for the fire from the tanks to open. The tanks opened fire as arranged and the battle developed, with tanks slowly moving east and enemy defensive fire redoubling. Cec Greenwood's diary reports:

> "The barrage put down by our artillery was an insult to a man's intelligence; we could practically count the shells, but the German barrage was something I'll remember all my life. It was terrific, the place was full of flying metal and bullets and it was impossible to see more than a yard or so.

> The I tanks (Matildas) went right up through it and plastered PLONK. It's marvellous how they can stand up to such concussion".

The enemy heavy defensive fire was brought to bear on the PLONK position, and as tanks moved away the enemy heavy artillery fire became so intense that George Reid considered that if he took his party into PLONK nothing would be gained and he would lose his whole patrol. He sent back one section with one casualty and made a sweep due east with the rest of his party for about 150 yards but found nothing. He sent his party moving back towards the wire while he remained behind to fire a prearranged white over red over white verey signal. He rejoined his party at the a/tk ditch and reported to post R49, while the tanks also withdrew to the gap. Reid believed the enemy vacated PLONK when the tanks arrived, and a Sgt of the RTR told him that the enemy were cut off whilst attempting to withdraw.

This was the culmination of the PLONK operations. The defensive artillery fire put down in front of PLONK and 2/17 Bn positions was so intense that when the bombardment was heard at Brig Tovell's distant 26 Bde HQ he ordered two battalions to be ready to move at call to assist 20 Bde. (26 Bde was ready to be relieved from Tobruk.)

With the coming of a new day observations from COOMA reported visibility good, and tank movements still reported. With PLONK again in possession of the enemy, observations were mainly concerned with movement in that area, and a new line of sangars soon appeared behind PLONK. On 13 and 14 Oct enemy artillery activity dropped to a relatively light level but tank activity continued with 9 tanks moving in close to COOMA position, one approaching to within 70 yards. On the night of 13/14 Oct a special patrol from A Coy of 1 Sgt and 2 Ors went out to investigate and locate definite enemy position in the PLONK area. When moving in from the west towards Bir El Azazi, at least six machine guns as well as mortars opened up on the party, and they were given the order to withdraw. After about 250 yards the patrol leader noticed Pte Hill was missing — sending the other man back, the leader went back to search but found nothing although he heard a tank start up. He returned to his post at 0600 hrs, with Pte Hill still missing — it was to transpire that Pte Hill became a POW.

By now they knew it would soon be their turn to leave.

On 15 Oct the Advance Party was nominated to 20 Bde for movement from Tobruk, a total of 25 with Lt Allan Wright as OC. This party left the Bn area at 0930 hrs on 17 Oct for the staging camp and then on to Palestine, going out that night. At 1400 hrs that afternoon the advance party from 2nd Bn Essex Regt temporarily left the Bn area but returned again on 19 Oct. Also on 19 Oct the operation order was issued covering the relief of 2/17 Bn on the night of 21/22 Oct. On 20 Oct Brig Murray issued an Order of The Day in which he congratulated all the Brigade for the honour of being the last Brigade to leave Tobruk, and assuring them that every effort would be made to ensure all had a well earned rest with the fullest possible amenities.

By 2300 hrs 21 Oct, the change over with 2 Bn Essex Regt was completed, and the Bn was now in the Sidi Mahmud area at the junction of Bardia and El Adem roads, D Coy being the last coy of the Bn to occupy forward positions in Tobruk. With the battalion out of the line for the last time in Tobruk, the men felt a certain relief as if a long sought goal had been reached. At 1930 hrs on 22 Oct, 180 men of A Coy and C Coy marched out for embarkation with Maj John Balfe acting Bn 2 i/c in charge of the party and they duly embarked on HMS *Encounter*. Next day two coys of 1st Bn Bedfordshire and Hertfordshire Regt arrived in the area, and at 1830 hrs on 24 Oct the Bn embussed for their point of embarkation. Bn HQ, B Coy and HQ Coy — less Carrier Platoon — moved out to the wreck of the Liquria. HMS *Kingston* drew alongside and quickly all were embarked. D Coy and Carrier Pl embarked from No. 6 jetty on the north side of the harbour on to the destroyer HMS *Griffin*. At 1500 hrs 25 Oct, the destroyers arrived at Alexandria after an uneventful trip and the troops embussed for Amiriya staging camp where a hot meal and certain comforts, including one bottle of beer per man, was provided. Then at 2000 hrs the Bn entrained for Kantara on the way back to Palestine. They arrived at Kantara at 0745 hrs on 26 Oct and after breakfast entrained for Beit Jirja where they arrived at 1830 hrs. Next day, 27 Oct, they moved to Hill 69 where A and C Coys, who had arrived earlier, had the camp in order.

Over the period the Battalion fought in the 9 Div's Libyan Desert campaign, casualties were; KIA or DOW, 39; accident, 2; missing, presumed dead, 1; WIA, 127 and POW, 14. Fatal were:

NX21783	Pte Allsop L P 4/7/41	NX22739	Pte Hill V H 14/10/41
NX17784	Pte Beazley A J 11/4/41	NX13729	Cpl Jaggers M G 13/6/41
NX17458	Pte Bell C S 15/6/41	NX47743	Pte Larkin E 11/10/41
NX21205	Pte Bird K R 10/7/41	NX16416	Pte Law J W G 30/6/41
NX14388	Sgt Brady H M 14/4/41	*NX16597	Pte Laws J E POW 15/6/43
N21773	Pte Brinkley W H 10/10/41	NX22643	Pte Legge F G 2/5/41
NX14837	Pte Brock B E 21/7/41	NX17847	Pte Maher H T 14/4/41

NX12420	Capt Chapman E T 31/7/41	NX16457	Pte Mason G R 3/5/41
NX17124	Sgt Clark F G 7/6/41	NX23111	Pte Mathews A E 12/6/41
NX21237	Pte Conlon R T 11/10/41	NX23057	Pte Musgrave J D'A 13/7/41
NX34136	Pte Crute N 14/4/41	NX14494	Pte McHenry M 14/4/41
NX17417	Pte Dillon L H 14/4/41	NX17338	Pte McRae G 11/6/41
NX47176	Pte Donohoe M 1/10/41	NX60246	Cpl Roberts F 0 27/9/41
NX15076	Lt Downing J N 31/7/41	NX58529	Pte Rowell C J J 10/6/41
QX1628	Pte Dunn R C 2/7/41	NX16141	Cpl Sheehan F C 3/7/41
NX15705	Cpl Edmondson J H 14/4/41	NX23134	Pte Smith V 12/10/41
NX60291	Pte Flemming D C 15/6/41	NX14997	Lt Tuckwell A E 13/6/41
NX23055	Pte Fyffe R M 10/10/41	NX21760	Pte Widerberg J C 4/4/41
NX21406	Pte Geary E C 12/6/41	NX13902	L/Cpl Wilkinson A 11/4/41
NX17051	Pte Gifford A B 11/4/41	NX12224	Capt Windeyer H F 17/10/41
NX22099	Pte Gilmour J L 4/4/41	NX18166	Pte Young G T 14/4/41
NX28404	Pte Harrison C G 13/8/41		

LEST WE FORGET   * DOW in Italy.

Top Left: *Captain ET Chapman*
Bottom Left: *Lieutenant JN Downing*
Above: *The Tobruk Memorial built by 9 Div Engineers.*

CHAPTER 7
RETURN TO THE PROMISED LAND

The 2/17 Bn left Gaza on 28 Feb 1941 bound for the Western Desert and returned to the camp at Hill 69 in Palestine on 27 Oct 1941. This was our first "Active Service", dependent solely on the Army Supply System, no leave, little recreation, sporadic mail or comfort parcels and the knowledge that we were soon to test ourselves in battle. It is interesting to reflect on this period as it certainly had a marked effect on our future.

We were fortunate to have a sprinkling of World War I veterans serving in the Unit, "Blue" Allan, Matt Higgins, Arthur Hellman to name but a few. These men were great educators in what was to lie ahead and I am sure that their influence was widespread.

During this period our sense of values, our attitudes and our reliance on each other developed to a marked degree. The true sense of comradeship became a reality and few would argue that the 2/17 Bn came of age.

Shortage of equipment, weapons and vehicles was overcome in many ways and it was not long before many deficiencies in all categories were solved by the capture and repair of enemy equipment. The ability of the Australian soldier to acquire and adapt equipment for his comfort and survival never ceased to amaze some of our Allies. However the technique of "scrounging" which was highly developed had to be restrained at all times to ensure that it did not react against the needs of all.

Rationing and feeding was an area where it was difficult to provide variety and attraction, but when "Section" cooking (groups of 6-10 men) became a necessity it was surprising the number of "chefs" that were discovered. Using the basic issue of Bully Beef, M & V, Herrings and Biscuits plus the additives of curry powder, Marmite, rice and other goodies, many culinary delights were produced.

Our Bn Sgt Cook, A J McKean, had a "Cookery Book" published which gave many recipes and hints using "iron" or "hard" rations. This publication, widely circulated, proved particularly useful throughout the War whenever cooking in small groups became necessary.

Few of us took kindly to the average water issue of 2 water bottles per man per day (one bottle stayed in the kitchen). The personal water bottle was for drinking, cleaning of teeth, shaving, ablution and washing of clothes. With ablutions, unless you were near to a brackish or salt water source, one used a cloth or sponge to wash up as far as possible, down as far as possible and every third day you washed "possible".

The forced abstinence of alcohol was a matter of adjustment for some but with an uncertain canteen supply of one bottle of beer per man per month or a half bottle of spirits per officer, few problems of excess arose. When the weather turned cold an issue of OP rum (1/8 of a pint per man) became available for medical purposes. It was effective but not generally popular.

On reflection I think our greatest problem was boredom as there was little escape from the monotonous routine of survival and existence. Little in the way of entertainment, sport, recreation, library, music, news or female companionship had its effects on morale. The arrival of mail or parcels from home became a major event in our lives and any interruption to this routine was felt by us all. For some who felt the stress of the campaign from loss of a comrade or bad news from home, the presence of our Padres provided support for those who turned to their religion for comfort.

One joyous thing that resulted from the period of our being besieged was the healthy increase in the balance in our pay books. Many of us had more money in credit than ever before and the desire for leave and recreation was very attractive.

As a Unit we enjoyed a collective pride in knowing that the 2/17 Bn had performed well and had stopped the enemy in his tracks in our first encounter. We were of course saddened by the loss of so many of our gallant comrades and anxious to learn of the condition of those wounded and evacuated to base hospitals. Nevertheless this was part of the World at War and we had all grown up a little.

Before continuing it is appropriate to make mention of the conflict between the British and Australian Governments regarding the relief of Australian troops from the Tobruk Garrison. It appears that a medical report received by General Blamey towards the end of June 1941 indicated that, "due to the strain of continuous operations there was a decline in the physical condition of the Tobruk Garrison — definite decline in the health resistance of many troops, recovery from minor wounds and sickness is markedly slower". Gen Blamey informed our Prime Minister, Mr Menzies that he concurred with this report and also he desired to concentrate all Australian troops into one Corps in accordance with the policy agreed with the British Government for the employment of Australian troops. He therefore recommended that strong action be taken by the Australian Government to expedite the relief of the Garrison.

Mr Menzies contacted Winston Churchill who consulted with Gen Auchinleck and the matter was deferred, delayed and postponed for many months. Finally in September, Mr Arthur Fadden succeeded Mr Robert Menzies as Prime Minister and, despite further opposition from Mr Churchill, he insisted that the Australian Government's request for relief be executed. On 15 Sep 1941, Churchill telegraphed Fadden "Orders will at once be given in accordance with your decision". (Relief could not be completed until the end of October.)

This brief explanation may help to explain some of the unusual activities of rest and recreation which were the format during the first few months of our return to Palestine. An opportunity was given to record oral messages for families in Australia. It gave a greater sense of contact and was great for morale in Australia as messages were broadcast.

On 2 Nov 1941 the effective strength of the Bn was 32 Offrs and 717 Ors which included 96 marched in from 20 ITB.

Lt Col Crawford became Acting Comd 20 Bde and Maj Keith Magno took over as Bn CO. During November the main concern was to rest the men as much as possible. Large numbers were sent on leave and organised sport, cricket, football (all codes) and hockey were encouraged. This first month of training was described as "building up" after 8 months of desert warfare.

In the Routine Orders some sporting fixtures and results were shown. For example, 2/17 Bn Hockey Team beat 2/8 Fd Amb with 5 goals to 2, Corps Ammunition Park 14 goals to 1 and RAMLE RAK Station 9 goals to nil. In this latter game, Farrelly scored 3 goals, Percival 2, R Smith 1, Moon 1, Roper 1, Frew 1. I believe the Bn Hockey Team was in fact undefeated from the time it was formed at Bathurst until the end of the War. There were some very fine players — Ron Percival, Chris Moon, "Toc" Reid, "Kanga" Maclarn are some that come to mind.

In one cricket match we won by 16 runs, top scorer being Perkins 87, Thorley 26, Conway 29. Conway also took 4 wickets for 67 runs and Kidd took 3 wickets for 32. At Australian Rules

Back row: *left to right –*
Fred Dryley, Jim Sutherland
(Diamond Jim), Rex Auckett,
Blondie Wilcox, Ernie Drew,
E— Lambert, Bruce Culey.
Front row: *left to right –*
Ray Rudkin, Ron Smith,
Herb Chapman, Steve Lowry,
"Daisy" Utting, Ken Pratt

Left: *Crew on pontoons*

Below: *Crew afloat*

we were less successful being defeated by 9 Div AASC with 7 goals 6 behinds to 2 goals 6 behinds and by 2/32 Bn 5 goals 12 behinds to 2 goals 4 behinds. We make no excuses but 2/17th was really a Rugby Bn and it was mainly because we had Riverina players like Tasker, Bill and Hal Pearce and the odd Victorian like Arthur Newton that we were able to field an Aussie Rules team. We were always scratching to make up the team.

During this period the Bn was requested to supply a Rowing Eight to compete in a Regatta held in Tel Aviv. The following crew was chosen: Jerry O'Donnell, Bruce Wight, Col O'-Donnell, Oki O'Connor, George Reid, Bob McElroy, Phil Barnett, Rodney Robinson, Ross Jamieson (Coxswain) and coached by the charismatic Capt Barry "Joe" Blundell (Qualification Unknown). Despite training difficulties they performed creditably but they are not recorded as "Head of the River".

On 23 Nov 1941 a contingent of 200 members of the VAD (ME) arrived in Palestine and were initially attached to the 1 AGH to assist in the care of the sick and wounded. One of these young ladies, Miss Kathleen Rudkin, was the sister of Lt Ray Rudkin and it is known that Ray was under great pressure to invite his sister and her friends to visit the Unit and meet some of his comrades. This was a highly successful exercise as during the course of the War, Miss Kathleen Rudkin married Capt Austin Mackell MC, Miss Marie Robinson married Capt John Dinning MC and Miss Nancy Liston married Capt Hugh Main MC. This only proves that the Army will go to great lengths to look after the morale and welfare of the troops.

Also in November the Bn was ordered to provide a Rifle Coy for guard duties at British 9th Army HQ at Broumana in Lebanon.

A Coy under command of Capt Claude Brien was chosen for this task and Pat Conti a member of the Company gives an account of their activites during this detachment from the Bn.

"The morning of 19 Nov 1941 was fine, clear and chilly when A Coy was seconded from the Bn and left Hill 69 Camp. After leaving Tobruk we had been told that all troops would be granted extended leave but apart from a 3-day leave here we were again on the move leaving the rest of the Bn to enjoy that precious commodity. Claude Brien had informed us we had been chosen over all the Div and given the sinecure job of guarding 9th Army HQ. There was a lot of muttering among the boys about 'That'll be the day'. So he gave a further reason that it was because we had endured a battering at our last forward post in Tobruk, the number escapes me but it was either R51 or R52. It was from here that Capt Frank Windeyer took his assault troops from C Coy from which he returned mortally wounded. I still recall him on a stretcher asking continually about his men, quite unconcerned about his own desperate plight.

So there we were on the road to our new posting, oblivious of the delights which lay ahead. The route was long, dusty, uncomfortable and very rough, but to those of us who could remember a smattering of Biblical history, most interesting as we passed through such localities as Sidon and Tyre. On reaching the outskirts of Beirut we headed east and commenced climbing what looked to be a range of mountains 3 to 4 thousand feet high. To the ex-farmers in our ranks it was amazing how the natives had tackled farming by literally terracing an entire mountain side with innumerable little farming ventures; vines, vegetables, fruit trees etc. The road itself was not unlike the old Bulli Pass Road, rough and full of "S" bends; one moment we would be looking at the terraces, next Beirut and the Mediterranean, the views were even more spectacular than from the top of Bulli Pass. Some 7 miles from Beirut we came upon Broumana which was to be our home for 7 weeks. Harold

MacLachlan who had been on the advance party with Ned Kellie and Dal Cartledge and his batman, Rooster Fenn, had this to say:

'The town was situated on a ridge some 2 miles long, a narrow strip of flat ground at top with terraces on both sides. We were housed in 4 stone houses, the largest a two-storeyed building on the main road and three smaller cottages reached by paths down the western side. Coy HQ plus Offrs and Sergeants in you know what: a platoon to each of remaining cottages. A Coy was to man two check points, one at each end of the one and only street, to provide a roving piquet on the General's residence as well as a formal guard at his Admin HQ — the General was Sir Henry Maitland Wilson, well nicknamed 'Jumbo'. Saluting, always a problem with Australian troops, was an even greater one here where there were so many high ranking officers. He remembers well my playing the piano and our lusty voices carrying well into the village.'

Leave was plentiful both in Broumana and to Beirut. French was the second language and at cafés French cooking was favoured. I remember a group of us trying snails for the first and only time. Bernie Gilfeather looked at the plate with horror and disbelief and refused point blank. Goff Schrader tried one and spat it out, almost in one motion. I had one, thought I must have had a bad one, tried again and decided they were not for me. Peter Pollock on the other hand, made out as though he had lived on them all his life and manfully ate the rest. Years later I asked Peter to tell me truthfully what he really felt, to be told he thought they were dreadful.

To keep in reasonable condition route marches down the one and only road were regularly held. Because of the many "S" bends, the file near side had less distance to travel than his opposite number. One NCO who claimed he was unfairly given the outside running, despite urging from Dal Cartledge, got further and further behind. On approaching one "S" bend which the other file had already rounded, he gave the order to "disperse and hide". Mystified, Dal halted the file he was with and went back looking for his vanished file. Was it the Mystery of Hanging Rock all over again? Joke over, the troops got to their feet, reassembled, received a dressing down and then made to run to catch up with the others.

There was also a memorable guard. On one occasion one of our more rugged types was on guard — Wagga Joe. He was not the most handsome of men and less so when he smiled as he was almost devoid of his front teeth. As luck would have it, the General decided on his first (also his last) inspection of the guard. Hurriedly the guard was fallen in with Joe as right marker.

The General was led to Joe, who was examined by a practised eye head to toe and back again. It was when he reached Joe's face for the second time Joe had decided that the General was not a bad sort of a b—— and gave him his toothless grin. the General blanched, shuddered uncontrollably and hurriedly made for his car and was gone in a flash. No doubt if ever the General was asked his opinion of 9 Aust Div he would recall and graphically recount his unnerving experience.

Our 7 weeks passed all too quickly. A Coy, after its most enjoyable period of the entire War, returned to Hill 69 on 4 Jan 1942, after handing over duties to a coy of the 2/3 MG Bn."

In Dec 1941 the second phase of training was carried out by the Bn to culminate in a Bn exercise. This programme had to be curtailed owing to inclement weather. Heavy rain commenced on 21 Dec and continued until the end of the month. Training was difficult and Bn manoeuvres had to be postponed. Organised sport was encouraged and matches were arranged with other units. Several members of the Bn toured Palestine with a hockey team selected from

20 Bde. On Christmas Day, despite inclement weather the Bn was in good spirits. Every man received a parcel from the Australian Comforts Fund containing a plum pudding, cake, tinned fruit and toilet requisites. A real Christmas spirit prevailed. In the soldiers' mess the duties were carried out by the Officers and Sergeants and good fellowship pervaded the whole proceedings.

The souvenir menu read as follows: (A strong Tobruk flavour)

Savoury:	Hurricane Rarebit
Soup:	Soup a la Bird Cage
Poultry:	Medauuar Pigeon
Meat:	Roast Bianca Beef
Vegetables:	El Adem Cauliflower and White House Sauce
	Cooma Cabbage and Roast Salient Spuds
Sweets:	Aussie Plum Pudding and Plonk Sauce —
	BSD Fruit Salad and Junkers Jelly
Confections:	Colonel's Cake — Stuka Nuts
Beverages:	Beer — Tea (?)

During November and December patrols were made to various villages in the area. Axis agents were said to be attempting to provoke rebellion in Palestine and to be disseminating rumours that British forces there were at low strength. The British Comd instituted patrols to villages and 9 Div was made responsible for them in the Gaza area. Comds and soldiers taking part were briefed on behaviour required and certain talking points listed. In December, B Coy were required to visit two Arab villages, Beit Daras and Barqa whilst D Coy visited a Jewish village, Gan Yaune. Details of one such visit reads:

"REPORT ON PATROL TO BEIT DARAS — DECEMBER 9, 1941

By:	Capt J R Broadbent — 2/17 Aust Inf Bn
Map Ref:	Tel Aviv Sheet 1200 1260
Strength:	One Pl of B Coy, one Sgt, one OR '1' Sect Med Cpl and an interpreter attached.
Weapons:	# Brens, rifles, bayonets and one Carrier.
Type:	Formal visit and efficiency display.
Procedure of Patrol:	The platoon arrived at village square at 1000 hrs immediately followed by the 'Q' truck with EPIP and RD tents. One Section mounted guard over the area, another Section erected tents whilst the third gave display of bayonet training. Whilst this was proceeding, Int Sgt with interpreter had gone to warn the Mukhtar (Mahmoud Ismail Baraud). Capt Broadbent arrived in a Bren Carrier and guard turned out and presented arms as he entered his tent.
	At 1050 Mukhtar and one Headman arrived and were received in EPIP tent. Later another Mufti-Mukhtar (Abdullah Salah) who had been absent on our arrival presented himself to Capt Broadbent. Conversation ran through general channels. Invitation to feast with Mukhtar was refused but an invitation to coffee was accepted. At 1140 hrs after coffee had been served in the tent we adjourned to the Mukhtar's house and

partook of more coffee with him. In the meantime, tents were taken down and troops continued their training displays. At 1230 hrs we excused ourselves and were escorted back to the village square where troops marched past with fixed bayonets, Capt Broadbent taking the salute."

Jan 1942 opened with wet weather and training was greatly hampered On 6 Jan, orders were received from Bde that the Bn must be ready to move to Syria. The advance party was selected and told to pack immediately. At 1330 hrs on 7 Jan, the advance party left by MT for Aleppo under Maj Keith Magno. Maj Balfe acted as Admin Comd of the Bn. For the next few days everyone was preparing for the move, getting kits in order etc. 2 Offrs and 18 Ors (reinforcements) joined the Bn and a further 29 "X" list men re-joined.

At 0930 hrs on 11 Jan, verbal orders were received from Bde: "The Bn moves at dawn on 12 Jan for Syria. HQ Coy, D Coy and Bn HQ to move by MT whilst A, B and C Coys to go by train to Haifa, MT to Tripoli and then by train to their respective destinations.

At 0600hrs on 12 Jan 1942 the road convoy left Hill 69 with Maj "Blue" Allan administrating Comd of the Bn. The advance party of the convoy arrived at Acre transit camp at 1200 hrs and the main convoy at 1500 hrs. We are to sleep in the open. At 2000 hrs, A, B, and C Coys left Hill 69 for El Madjal to entrain for Haifa. On 13 Jan the advance party of the convoy left Acre at 0545 hrs for Tripoli and the main convoy left at 0620 hrs. The convoy arrived at Le Gault barracks Tripoli at 1530 hrs and after a hot meal served at 1700 hrs most of the troops were given leave to Tripoli until 2230 hrs. At 2300 hrs the train party arrived at Tripoli having come from Haifa by motor transport. These companies then entrained for Aleppo.

14 Jan was very cold and wet — the road convoy left Tripoli at 0630 hrs and arrived at Afrine camp at 2130 hrs. Huts were available but the diary records — "Many slept in the open".

On the following day — 15 Jan — the Bn took over from 2/12 Bn of 18 Bde. A and B Coys with part of HQ Coy were guarding tunnels and a bridge on the railway between Radjou and Meidan Ekbes where two Secs of A Coy were on station patrol and frontier duty.

Pat Conti of A Coy gives a further account of this period on the Turkish/Syrian border:

"A Coy's tour of duty was not a very happy one for two-thirds of us. It was one of the worst winters for many years, snow everywhere, and when we arrived in jumping off the train I badly sprained my ankle and spent two weeks in an Italian Hospital at Aleppo. What bad luck — fancy missing all that snow, the cold walks through the tunnel, the scrounging for firewood and the deadly boredom. Evidently someone up there liked me. What happened at Radjou and the Saddle I have not the slightest idea nor was I even the least bit curious. I did get back to the Tunnel, where there was a guard placed at each end to stop sabotage. Harold MacLachlan says, "We made a toboggan out of galvanised iron and it was reasonably successful down the hillsides. It was no fun in the tents trying to find enough wood to keep a fuel stove going sufficiently to thaw the snow on the roof". At Medaine Ekbes it was far more interesting. A piquet had to be provided to accompany a Security Sgt of English/Greek extraction for all trains in and out of that station which was on the actual border between Syria and Turkey. On occasions odd numbers of troops (English and Australians) who had escaped from Greece would come through, one of whom, "Doctor" Ross, was very well known to our ex-17 CMF Bn personnel. It was a very lawless area inhabited mainly by Kurdish tribesmen and several murders took place while we were there, but not in our presence. There was a swift flowing river — the Kara Su — from which 7 Pl gained a great deal of fish by expert use of hand grenades. On our second visit it was midsummer and a complete change in the temperature which at times was well over 100 in the shade. The river was now a series of water holes, some of which yielded a great number of fish to a stick of gelignite. Harold told me how greatly affected he was when a train load of Greek refugees, including young pregnant girls and children arrived in a shocking state of malnutrition, literally starving and who were so grateful to our boys who supplied them with food out of their own meagre rations, that they kissed them in gratitude. The chief of the village was known as the Mukhtar and on some nights he used to play cards against some of our better players such as Goff Schrader and give our chaps a hiding. Goff swore the Security Officer, who didn't play but walked around the tables, was telling the Mukhtar in their language what Goff's cards were. Meanwhile the Bn had lately commenced training under the new CO Lt Col Ferguson. A Coy, because of its guard duties, was unaffected. Little did we know how that was soon to alter when we joined the Bn at Latakia."

Two Pls of D Coy were on frontier duty at El Hammam while C Coy HQ was at Azaz — one Pl at Katma tunnel, one Pl at Akterine on frontier duty and one Sec guarding the road at Soudjou. Because of some mistake in convoy arrangements 2/15 Bn advance party became temporarily attached to our unit until our advance party returned from Idlib where they had been attached to 2/15 Bn.

On 18 Jan 1942 the last Routine Orders were issued by Lt Col J W Crawford as CO 2/17 Bn. In fact he had been away from the unit for some time but a replacement had not been appointed.

On 19 Jan Lt Col M A Fergusson assumed Comd of 2/17 Bn. Maurice Alfred Fergusson was born on 5 Dec 1895 and served in the 1st AIF. He was a Lt in the Fd Arty on 15 Dec 1916 and served with the 4th Div Arty until the end of the War. He served between Wars as a captain and major in the Royal Aust Arty Militia and joined 8 Lt Horse Regt in Feb 1939 and was appointed Lt Col in that Regt on 10 Jun 1939. He was appointed CO of 6 Aust Div Cav Regt on 13 Oct 1939 and relinquished that appointment on 26 May 1941. Later in the War he became a Brig commanding 2 Aust Armd Bde and 8 Aust Inf Bde and was decorated with the DSO and ED.

He was not long in the Bn before he was known as the "Ant Eater" — no doubt because of a longish nose, and as a suitable replacement to the "Cake Eater". However, though he was only with us until 28 Feb, there are several documents with the War Diary and 20 Bde which indicate he was fully employed during that time. In January a new type of War Diary was introduced into the AIF which included a CO's report. The one for January signed by Lt Col Fergusson is of interest. Relevant extracts are:

"On the 15th the Bn took over from 2/12 Bn in the Afrine, Radjou, Azaz, El Hammam area. Their duties comprise firstly the guarding of certain demolitions in the event of a state of tension arising on the Turkish Syrian frontier; secondly, general security duties.

The weather during the first days of our arrival was cold and very wet. On 25 Jan snow fell generally on the whole Bn area but cleared quickly except at Radjou. Troops are billeted in tin huts and quickly established friendly relations with the local inhabitants. Tactical recce by Commanders of all grades has been carried out and route recce etc is proceeding as rapidly as weather conditions permit. Liaison has also been established with the Free French and civil authorities.

Despite very severe conditions, cold snow, rain and wind the morale of the men improved. On one night several huts were destroyed by wind and considerable damage was done. The men in the more isolated posts had extreme difficulty in ensuring a supply of dry clothing and the temporary shortage of boots caused considerable discomfort. The living conditions of Radjou HQ, Meidane Ekbes and Akterine were reminiscent of the Somme in 1916.

The poverty of the natives at Meidane Ekbes is worse than has been seen anywhere else in the world. The quality of the ploughing by the natives, often using a cow and a donkey in the team is remarkable. Nine out of ten would win a ploughing contest anywhere in Australia and the agricultural practice is high above that of the natives of Palestine."

In the Feb COs report of the War Diary, Maj Keith Magno made the following comment:

"On 28 Feb, Lt Col Fergusson relinquished Comd of the Bn. Although he had only been with the unit for a month his loss was felt strongly by those who had had an opportunity of seeing him at work."

The following Int Summary based on reports up until 0900 hrs 18 Jan 1942 helps to explain Syria and our presence there:

General

a. Syria is a feudal country. Each village has a Mukhtar. Districts of which there are eleven, have a Kyma Khan. Groups of districts have a Sheik.

b. The country is not administered by us but by Free France and it is a definite responsibility for all ranks to maintain friendly relations with all French officials and officers regardless of personal opinion in the matter.

c. The police force consists of a Surete-Generale, Gendarmerie (town police), Guarde Mobile (country police) and Duanne (Customs).

Our relations with Turkey are friendly and fraternization is encouraged. It is the duty of all ranks to carry this out where possible.

Points of interest from recent reports are as follows:

a. It is considered that the Germans are in no position at the moment even to threaten Turkey.

b. Despite recent successes, Russia has lost very important industrial areas and Germany is likely to be the stronger nation in the Spring.

c. German Naval personnel at Burgas and Varna (the Black Sea ports where concrete vessels are being built) may have amounted to some 20,000 about mid-December. Although administrative preparations for the reception of large numbers of troops in Bulgaria continues there has been no reliable report of any such troop movement. Germans are now reported to be building concrete vessels in Greece also.

d. It is thought that a further ten divisions will be ready in Japan for service within two months. This will increase the total strength of the Jap army to its estimated ceiling of 72 divisions plus 20 independent mixed brigades, 4 cavalry brigades and 14 tank regiments.

e. Germany was estimated by the Air Ministry 12 Oct 1941 to have approx 2400 troop carrying gliders available for operations. The types ranged from those capable of carrying only 8 men in full equipment to those able to carry 50 men or alternatively for transport of field guns or small tanks.

Enemy Methods

a. It is well known that the German sabotage unit Lehrregiment Brandenburg — z.b. V800 has been operating from Greece. A group from 1 Bn of the unit known as "P" Group is thought to be composed of Arabic speaking personnel.

b. It is reported that 400 Arab refugees are being trained mostly in Athens in modern weapons,

200 of these have already qualified as parachutists and will act as guides for German troops in the Middle East.

Frontier Information

The following information has been received from D Coy at El Hammam. "The sergeant of the Gendarmerie informed Lt Waterhouse that the Turkish troops manning the El Hammam post had been doubled. The strength is now roughly 40 men. They apparently have not increased their weapon strength.

He also stated that the French Special Police had questioned a man crossing into Syria and that he states that the Turkish forces in the Alexandretta and Antioche areas are being, or about to be, trebled. He said formerly the troops in those areas numbered roughly about 15,000. This had been estimated from the number of Mosques, Inns and other large buildings that have been evacuated by the Turkish Government as billets.

Radjou Area

Position normal. The roads are all very frozen and impassable between the Fort and Meidan Ekbes. Snow fell on the higher peaks yesterday and last night.

El Hammam Area

Position normal. Usual contraband traffic continues from the Turkish side. On 16 January an Arab train passenger was detained by the Surete and escorted to Aleppo. The road between Azaz and Akterin is very bad at present.

During January and February there was plenty of activity in the Bn areas. Generally the weather remained cold and wet for the first few weeks. By 7 Feb the war Diary comment was "fine and warm weather". However, by 20 Feb the weather was "cold with heavy rain and hail".

On 2 Feb, a showery day, Maj Gen Sir Leslie Morshead, accompanied by Brig Windeyer and Col Wells (GS01 9 Div), inspected the Bn area. The CO's report for the month of February in part read as follows:

General: The initial period of settling in being over a thorough review of all tactical problems affecting the Bn, together with the necessary recces was carried out. In particular demolitions came under review and certain important modifications in the plan were suggested by Lt Col Fergusson (CO) in an appreciation. Commanders of all grades were given an opportunity to express their opinions on their own problems and the resulting appreciations were carefully studied by the CO.

On 8 Feb intensive training for each coy was begun commencing with C and D Coys. C Coy remained at Azaz, D Coy moved to Afrine. Syllabus included 4 tactical exercises, 2 at night and involving high physical demands as they took place over rugged and hilly country, route marches, weapon training and range work.

At the end of the month field firing was commenced. When C and D Coy finished, HQ and B Coy commenced their training. Several films shown by the mobile cinema unit during the month. A YMCA hut filled out and much appreciated as are the 2-day leave parties to Aleppo which are continuing twice each week.

(Sgd)   C K M Magno, Maj.

The end of February was marked by windy, showery weather. The Bn was still occupying the positions in Northern Syria from Meidan Ekbes on the Turkish border to Afrine with many places in between or thereabouts.

February 27: Effective strength 34 Offrs, 757 Ors. 0330 hrs: A gendarme was shot at Houlilo by bandits. Troops at Radjou post "stood by" but the Gendarmes eventually arrested 11 men without further loss.

(Note by Arthur Newton: The assault was led by a Capt Francois of the FFL (Force Francais Libre) on a white horse. The arrested men were brought back via Afrine to Azaz shuffling along on foot to keep up with their mounted captors. Later it was rumoured at least one of the men had been shot attempting to escape.)

February 28: At 0430 hrs Lt Col Fergusson relinquished command of the Bn and left for the Canal Zone to embark. Maj J W Balfe takes the administrative command of the Bn in the absence of Maj C K M Magno detached on special duties. B Coy do tactical exercise No 3 and HQ Coy commence their 10 days' training.

March 3: Weather fine and cloudy. Sitnor all posts. Advance party of 2 Offrs and 13 Ors leave Bn area for unknown destination. NAAFI English concert party gave two concerts in recreation hut — excellent show.

March 6: Weather: low cloud and rain. HQ Coy continue field training exercises under adverse conditions. Advance party of 24 NZ Bn (2 Offrs and 26 Ors) arrive. A deputation of 50—60 villagers waited on Capt Brien at Radjou asking for a distribution of food to alleviate their conditions, saying that scarcity of food was so great they were forced to eat grass. Capt Brien promised to pass their request on to a higher authority and they then dispersed quietly. Subsequently the matter was discussed by Maj Magno and the Bde Comd.

March 12: Weather fine and warm. Brig Windeyer and Brig G H Clifton, Comd 6 NZ Bde, visited the Bn area. 5,000lbs of flour arrived from the American Red Cross Society for distribution under Army supervision to the poor of the district.

March 13: A conference consisting of the following personnel met to decide the disposal of the flour:

Maj C K Magno The Khymer Khan	Capt Renault, Afrine, French SS
Capt Yah Yah — The Gendarme	Capt Carroll — 24 NZ Bn and the IO

(The name Capt Yah Yah recalls an incident which occurred when he invited some of the Bn Officers to his home to dinner. I was speaking to him through the interpreter and for want of anything better to say, asked him if he had ever met Australians before they arrived in Syria. His eyes lit up and he replied rapidly in Arabic translated his reply went something like this: "Oh yes, I met Australians in the First War when I was an officer in the Turkish Army, in fact I was captured by them at Gaza. They were very good to me. Good old Aussies!")

March 14: Weather fine and warm. The Bn has been moving small detachments to new area during week and another detachment goes today. The remainder of the Bn move tomorrow. In fact the Movement Order signed by our indefatigable Adjutant, Colin Pitman contained the following relevant information.

1. 2/17 Aust Inf Bn will be relieved by 24 NZ Bn commencing night 14/15 Mar 42.

4. Relief will be carried out in two separate groups:

    Group A — comprising Radjou, Saddle, Fort, North Tunnel and Medaine Ekbes.

    Group B — comprising Soudjou, Azaz, Katma, Afrine and El Hammam.

    Capt Brien will be Officer I/C Relief Group A.

    Capt Maclarn will be Officer I/C Relief Soudjou, Azaz, Katma, El Hammam.

10. Group A will detrain Aleppo night 15/16 Mar and will be quartered at Quatre Vinque

Barracks. This group complete with baggage will move at 0900 hrs 16 Mar direct to new area. Tpt for above movt. will be provided by Bde.

17. Group B — C Coy 2/17 Bn plus Sec D Coy and attached personnel at El Hammam will move direct to new Bn area on completion of relief on 15 Mar 42. Personnel not required at Afrine will also move with this party. Capt Maclarn to issue orders for concentration and timing. Remainder of Gp B will move with Bn HQ on 16 Mar 42.

20. The following Officers will remain in their respective areas until 20 Mar. Lts Garnsey, Holtsbaum Waterhouse, Thompson, Halloway. Lt Garnsey will arrange for one interpreter to remain in Afrine camp. Transport will be sent to HQ 24 NZ Bn to collect rear party on morning 21 Mar.

Communications

23. 2/17 Aust Inf Bn Sig Offr will make mutual arrangements with 24 NZ Bn Sig Offr for handover. Sig Offr will move with Bn HQ on 16 Mar 42.

March 15: (Afrine) Quarter guard of 24 NZ Bn changes duties with 2/17 Bn. 0930 hrs: Bn HQ leave for new area. CO, Adjt and IO stay to finalise the changeover. Weather fine and warm.

March 16: (Latakia) Weather fine and warm. Bn settling in new area. MT arriving at periods during the afternoon with personnel from various coys.

March 17: Effective strength 26 Offrs and 730 Ors. Weather fine and warm. Lt Col Simpson assumes Comd Bn starting training in new area.

Our new CO arrived in the Bn on St Patrick's Day may be thought as an Irish joke by irreverent members of the Bn but the "Red Fox" was no joke.

(Note by Arthur Newton: Noel William Simpson was born on Feb 22, 1907. He was commissioned in 17 Bn on 29 Mar 26 then joined 25/33 Bn on 1 Sept 29, became a Captain in that unit on 18 Aug 30 and was transferred to the Unattached List on 10 Jun 32. On 16 Oct 34 he joined 34 Bn and then moved to 45 Bn on 5 Aug 37. He became a Temporary Major on 1 May 40 being allotted to 2/13 Bn. He left that Bn on 7 Jan 41 when seconded as DAAG (Staff learner) HQ 7 Div. He was appointed DAAG HQ 7 Div on 2 Mar 41 and remained in that appointment until 27 Dec 41 when he ceased to be seconded and resumed regimental duties with 2/13 Bn on 3 Jan 42. On 7 Mar 42 he was appointed CO of the 2/17 Bn and remained as CO until 28 Feb 44 when he was appointed to Comd the 2/43 Bn. He remained as CO 2/43 Bn until appointed to Comd 29 Inf Bde. On 15 May 46 he was transferred to the Reserve of Officers (Gen List) 2 Military District. On 8 Mar 50 he was appointed ADC (Hon) to the Governor General of Australia. From 15 May 50 to 1 Jul 53 he served on the Staff Gp of the CMF in E Comd (NSW) and later in Victoria and then on 1 Jul 53 was appointed to Comd 6 Inf Bde in Victoria. He remained in this appointment until 30 Jun 58 when he was again transferred to the Reserve of Officers. On 1 Jul 59 he was appointed as Comd 3 Inf Div and promoted T/Maj Gen — this rank was substantiated on 1 Jul 60. On 30 Nov 60 he relinquished this appointment and on 1 Jul 60 was appointed the CMF Offr on the Military Board (the highest position for a CMF Offr). He relinquished this position on 30 Nov 62 and was transferred to the Reserve of Officers until 23 Feb 64 when he was placed on the Retired List having reached the age of 57 years, the compulsory retiring age for this rank. On 18 Nov 71 Noel Simpson died.

During his service he was awarded the DSO after the El Alamein Campaign, a Bar to the DSO after the New Guinea Campaign. The ED (Efficiency Decoration) early in 1946. Mentioned in Despatches in 1946. Awarded the CBE on 30 Dec 55 and the CB (Military Division) in the Queen's Birthday Honours 1963. Maj Gen Noel Simpson CB CBE DSO and Bar ED never married. His twin brother was killed in action in Italy when commanding a British

Infantry Bn. Both brothers were bank officers in civilian life. Australia owes a lot to officers like Noel Simpson. He served as a dedicated officer in the Army during many years when there was little kudos in serving the Armed Forces, particularly the Citizen Military Forces or the Militia. Battalions particularly in the early '30s after the cessation of compulsory service were undermanned. Camps were irregular and pay and allowances were poor by any standard. It was fortunate for the 2nd AIF that such officers as Noel Simpson and others had prepared themselves for war often by some sacrifice to their civilian careers. All who served in the Bn during the period that he commanded it, will have some story or other about the "Red Fox". There is no doubt he left his mark on 2/17th. When I was Staff Capt of HQ 24 Bde later in the War, I witnessed the influence of the "Red Fox" on 2/43 Bn and although he left it before the Borneo Campaign, I am sure that 2/43 Bn's fine record in Borneo can be directly attributed to Noel Simpson's training methods. When news of his appointment as Comd 29 Bde was announced at a Mess Dinner by Mervyn Jeanes, 2 i/c 2/43 Bn, a young Lt remarked quite loudly, "Never heard of it!" at which the Fox in incisive tones stated: "You will gentlemen, you will.")

(Note by John Broadbent: Noel Simpson had held latent his awareness of training methods but was immediately in form to develop 2/17 Bn after its scattering and disruption beyond Afrine. There was a sudden co-ordination. A strictness was demanded that produced uniformity of dress, equipment and procedures. Talked about but not unwelcome because of the sudden feeling of re-integration. Welcome also was to be the application to tactical exercises on the Bn level and the fitness from the efforts required.

That there was a CO and the "Red Fox" was it became evident immediately. Respect for his ability quickly arrived. His operational orders to his O Gp on exercises soon were showing his ability for immaculate form and sequence, expression of authority and clarity.

Those who worked near him realised here was a thoughtful and responsible man contributing a full effort. Exacting in general requirements he made purposeful analysis of individuals, but with scrupulous fairness. Offending soldiers before him suffered such powerful but correctly spoken comments that escorts shuddered and found that duty unwelcome.

Compassion was available and understanding of stress and strain including in battle were to be shown. Operations were to show his own calmness and unflinching perseverance in duty.)

March 18/23: Dull weather, light rain. 1400 hrs: Brig Windeyer and Brig Tovell (acting 9 Div Comd) visited the Bn area. 2000 hrs: Bn carries out night approach march exercise in Jinnata area returning to camp at 2300 hrs. Weather: raining steadily throughout the day. At 0830 hrs the Bn moves out for a Bn exercise in Damsarko-Bisnado areas. Heavy rain night 19/20 Mar. Bn exercise in Damsarko area. Weather dull and raining. Bn carried out exercise in deployment and attack. (Sunday) Weather dull and overcast. Bn resting in camp. Draft of 27 soldiers arrive from ITB. Weather fine and clear — remainder of draft, 1 Offr and 8 Ors arrive from ITB.

March 26 to March 31: Marked by fine and warm weather. Coy Trg, a Bn exercise in the Kanjara area, embussing and debussing exercises formed part of the training. In the medical report for March, Capt J F Sullivan, the RMO included the following:

> "Health was generally good. 31 cases were evacuated to medical units during the period. In the second and third weeks 9 cases of urti, 7 tonsillitis, 2 peritonsillar abscesses were evacuated.

> At the end of the month after the unit moved to Latakia and began intensive training, the number of foot troubles increased rapidly. Most predominant feature was the number of men

who suffered from tenosynovitis of the tendo-archilles, or of the peroneal muscles. This was considered due to gaiters becoming wet and constricting the muscles at the back of the heels.

Difficulties were experienced in making incinerators for the area but eventually empty 44 gal drums were fitted with fine bars and used successfully.

Malaria Control: From the beginning of March mosquito nets were issued to personnel at Meidan Ekbes and El Hammam where spleen rates were high. These villages were sprayed by unit personnel in association with 2/8 Fd Amb and 2/4 Hygiene Sect. Mosquito nets for the Bn became available at the end of the month and all troops began to use them from the 25th." (End of RMO's report.)

During March there were several interesting paragraphs in Routine Orders such as:

Drugs — possession of: The possession of hashish, cocaine, morphia, morphine, marihuana, heroin and other similar drugs by personnel of the MEF is strictly forbidden.

German type returnable container: 20 litre captured German petrol containers of the pressed and welded type with hinged quick-acting cap, will in future be referred to for the sake of brevity as Jerricans.

Up to the beginning of April many changes occurred to the list of officers on the Bn strength. Many of the original officers who had embarked on Oct 19 1940 were no longer with the Bn or the staff of 20 ITB. Jim Moffatt who had been an officer in 17 Bn before joining 2/17th and Adjutant until some time after we arrived in Tobruk had left us before the siege ended. Dudley McCarthy, the IO in the early stages of Tobruk and later a Pl Comd, after attending a staff course, was seconded to HQ 6 Div on Nov 21 1941. Bruce Trebeck also from 17 Bn CMF and who was a Pl Comd in D Coy for most of the siege, completed a staff course a Sarafand and was posted as IO HQ 19 Bde and returned to Australia with 6 Div. Years later he returned to the Bn and was OC D Coy when the war ended. Austin Mackell, who had joined the staff of 20 ITB in Sept 41, also returned during this period. With him, I believe, some NCO's left also but unfortunately the War Diary is not specific in this regard. On 1 Mar 42 Capt Joe Blundell and Lt Bayne Geikie were detached from the Bn for return to Australia. Major "Blue" Allan, or more correctly, Herbert Trangmar Allan MC, who had served in 17 Bn 1st AIF winning the MC, was in and out of the Bn. Originally A Coy Comd he had become BM 20 Bde in Tobruk then returned to the Bn and acted as CO during John Crawford's detachment to 20 Bde. Somewhere about this time he left us, this time permanently. I remember him at Afrine knocking on the door of a hut which Slam Sullivan and I were valiantly trying to close during a blizzard saying "Let me in Sirs!" All officers, junior or senior, were always addressed by "Blue" as "Sir". He never lost interest in 2/17th and appeared in the most unlikely places, as many of the Bn will testify. As at the end of March 1942, Tony Nicholson, appearing on the list before Keith Beard and Hugh Main, was the junior sulbatern having been commissioned after graduating from the Middle East OCTU in Cairo. If memory serves me correctly, Hugh was a cadet at OCTU when as Barton Maughan, the Official Historian states — "The cadets found themselves, in addition to undergoing the prescribed course of indoctrination for their future responsibilities, participating in activities not included in the syllabus — the staging of a coup d'etat." This came about on 4 Feb 42 when Sir Miles Lampson, British Ambassador, delivered an ultimatum to King Farouk to the effect that he required action to appoint Nahas Pasha, Prime Minister of Egypt. The cadets formed a column of light tanks and artillery and deployed in the courtyard of the King's palace. Nahas Pasha formed a government. Perhaps Hugh may be entitled to an "Egyptian Star". Besides the officers mentioned, attached to the Bn from 20 ITB were the following: Lts J F McKinley, N E McDonald, S M Williams, R J Bennie, S H Yeend, A P Craik, T E Swan.

Further changes were to occur before we left Syria. I should add that the reason for the return to Australia of Joe Blundell and Bayne Geikie was because of a scheme to provide battle experienced officers for the Militia units which had been called up for service when Japan had entered the War. Later Bob Halloway was in this category but I believe these officers were not always welcomed in their new units, such is human nature. It would have been value had they stayed in their Bn.

From 1 to 15 Apr 1942 the Bn trained hard at Latakia. The weather was generally fine and warm, in fact by 4 April swimming parades were being held. In this period a variety of exercises including: 1) deployment for attack from MT; 2) Night exercises — approach march, dawn attacks; 3) Occupation of defensive positions. By 11 April it is recorded a Bde exercise in attack is carried out and a considerable improvement is noted. The Bde Comd, Brig Windeyer was frequently in attendance at Bn training and of course at the Bde exercises. April 14 showed effective strength at 39 Offrs, 762 Ors. Bde exercise No 2 is carried out at Nahr El Kandil area and moves smoothly, speed attained being most noticeable. As the Official Historian states of 20 Bde — "This was the first occasion on which it had undergone field training, the first occasion in the 22 months since its formation that it had been given an opportunity to conduct exercises in the field with troops."

April 15/16: Weather fine and warm. Advance party of 2 Offrs and 18 Ors move to Tripoli to relieve 2/24 Aust Inf Bn. Coys check boots and prepare for move in addition to normal training. Final preparation for move and camp struck. All ranks bivouac for night.

April 17: (on the march) Weather fine and warm. Bn moves at 0800 hrs. A 23-mile stage is carried out with a halt for lunch and a swim. A speed of 3 miles in the hour was maintained. Troops in good condition. Rear party arrives Tripoli.

April 18: 0800 hrs Bn on move. A 17-mile stage completed and bivouac area is near sea. Troops in good condition but some trouble with boots. A bootmaker follows the column to carry out minor repairs.

April 19: Weather fine and warm. 0800 hrs: Bn on move — a 22-mile stage carried out.

As on previous days "Q" arrangements function very smoothly.

(Note by Arthur Newton: As QM at this period I took the liberty of underlining the above statement, for rarely in the War Diary does the Q work of the Bn get a mention. Bert Oliver, the RQMS, Stan Scott, the Tech Stores Sgt, Sgs Alan McKean, Vic Dunn, in charge of Cooks and Rations and Keith Sabine, the Transport Offr with Sgt Gordon Newman his "side-kick" together with the many others including the splendid CQMSs gave the Bn fine service here and in every other area. QMs like myself came and went, but most of the Q staff were with the Bn from "go to whoa".)

In the last 2 miles the Bn passed through Tartous where compliments were exchanged with a Free French Guard of Honour. The standard of marching to attention by the Bn is high.

April 20: Effective strength 39 Offrs x 754 Ors. Fine weather. 0800 hrs: Bn on move. A 20—mile stage covered. Speed remains a steady 3 MIH.

April 21: 0800 hrs: Bn on move. Marched 10 miles to luncheon area from where Bn is lifted by MT to its new area. The move is completed by 1630 hrs.

April 22/23: Bn now in Tourbol sector of Tripoli defences. The day is spent in settling in. Coy Comds commence recce of area and CO carries out a general recce on the whole Bn area. Training syllabuses are drawn up.

April 24: Training mainly in weapons commences. The Bn sector is situated on a rocky mountain to the NE of Tripoli and commands the approaches from the north and the foothills between the main range and the sea. It is approx 2000 ft high and though some roads have been constructed, it is still only possible to ration the left forward coy by mule. The defences are all sited and some posts are already completed as is some wiring and the A/tk ditches.

April 25: Weather fine and warm. 1 Offr and 52 Ors detached as security guard to El Mina port and drawn from A Coy under Comd Lt J K Thompson.

April 26 and 27: Cool day — Coy training. CO i/c. Adjt and Offrs representing Fd Regt, A Coy 2/2 MG Bn, 2/3 A/Tk Regt and 2/3 Fd Coy carry out recce of area allotted to the Bn as beach defence responsibility. Lt Col Bob Turner, Comd 2/13 Bn visited us whilst on recce.

April 29: CO takes Coy Comds on recce of beaches during morning. Detailed recce is made by Coy Comds and Sec posts decided on during afternoon. The Bde Comd visits Bn area.

April 30: Weather fine. Coy trg continues. Pl Comds of certain Coys proceed on recce of beach areas.

In the War Diary was a report by the QM which showed deficiencies in weapons and transport, eg, we only held 26 LMGs instead of 50, 12x2" mortars instead of 16, 10x15cwt trucks, not the 38 on establishment. Clothing was in reasonable supply and an earlier shortage of boots had been overcome. During April, NZ frozen beef and mutton were a welcome change to local meat. Potatoes, pumpkins and cabbages were brought through the Supplementary Ration A/C. Our entitlement for April was Syrian Pounds 1318 but our expenditure was Syrian Pounds 1631. The RMO reported on the "march from Latakia". On the first day 17 April he treated 107 cases, mainly for blisters and other foot or leg problems. About 10 could not march on 18 April. On the 18th he treated 187 cases of whom 38 could not march on the 19th, and on the 19th 207 were treated, 57 unable to march on the following day. On the 20th, 134 cases treated of which 82 were considered unfit to march on 21 April. Capt Sullivan considered the new type of boots with toe caps appeared to be less satisfactory than the old type of boot — the toe caps causing pressure and irritation.

In his summary of the April 1942 War Diary, Lt Col N W Simpson stated:

1. The month falls into two periods. Of these the first is from 1st to 16th April when the Bde trg period was completed. This left all ranks in good physical condition and raised the standard of tactical training in the unit appreciably.

2. The second period from 17 to 21 April covers the march from Latakia to Mt Tourbol. All available personnel including Coy Orderly staffs etc marched.

3. The third period covers the occupation of the Mt Tourbol sector of Tripoli fortress and the preparation of a beach defence plan in the El Mina port area.

4. Leave, sport and amenities received attention where possible — eg Inter-Coy cricket, picture and town leave to Tripoli, leave parties to Beirut, a Coy Canteen in each Coy area."

May 1: The Bn stationed on Mt Tourbol sector of the Tripoli Box. Effective strength is 37 Offrs and 784 Ors. The weather was fine and warm. The diary entry noted that it was the second anniversary of the formation of the Bn.

The events of May are covered in the following summary of the War Diary signed by Maj C K Magno.

"During the month Coys have continued with the field works of the sector where work on alternative weapon pits, crawl trenches and sleeping bays is well on the way to being completed. Two Pls of one Coy have been on security piquet duties at El Mina docks and airport for the period under review, and from 16 to 30 May the Coy each night has manned emergency stations in the area. All Coys have carried out extensive training exercises as

Front row— *Capt P O'Brien, Capt L C Brien, Maj J W Balfe, Capt C G Pitman (Adjt),*
Lt Col N W Simpson (Comd Offr), Maj G K M Magno (2i/c), Capt J R Broadbent, Capt A M Alison,
Capt I F McMaster, Capt J F Sullivan. **Centre Row**—*Lts R C Garnsey, J M Owen, S G Waterhouse,*
A L Mathias, Capt P H Pike, Lts T E Swan, H H Main, Chaplain W L Byrne, Lts G F Holtsbaum, R S Rudkin,
K B Sabine, R V Burgess, Capt A J C Newton. **Back row** — *Lts S M Williams, S H Yeend, D J Cartledge,*
J W Bray, R J Dick, A E Nicholson, A P Craik, R J Bennie, A H Till, K E Beard, N F McDonald, R A Holloway.

NCOs of HQ Coy
Front row — *Sgt A J Quick, WOII D C Dunbar, Sgt A L Hellman, Sgt E J Blundell.*
Back row — *Cpl J W McVey, LCpl R G Edwards, Sgt H Dobie, Sgt G A Farrar-Pugh,*
Cpl F W Field, Cpl W P Gleeson.

Top: The NCOs of D Company.

Bottom The NCOs of C Company.
L - R Front row: *Sgt H J A Whittaker, Sgt A J Vincent, LCpl W K Bartlett, LCpl C W Mears, Cpl B G Dawes, Cpl T P Brightwell.* **Centre row:** *LCpl R Jenkins, Cpl A J Conway, LCpl G Ranson, WOII R A Hannaford, Cpl E Tasker, Cpl W B Pearce.* **Back row:** *Cpl T W Holland, Sgt J McLaren, LCpl A Cook, Cpl H W Pearce, Sgt C B Cutler, Cpl G R Morgan.*

NCOs of A Coy
Front row — *Sgt H P Conti, WOII N D F Kelly, Sgt P I Pollock.*
Back row — *LCpl J H Littlewood, Cpl D Kidd, Cpl J A Ahern, Cpl G W Stoyles, LCpl P J Acres.*

well as their field works program. Training is designed to fit the unit for Bde exercises during July. Field firing range at Znabile was used by the Bn on 7 to 9 May inclusive and all Coys through the handling and loading of mule teams after which each Coy will do a 2-day bivouac using mule teams.

On 16 May all Officers did a TEWT (tactical exercise without troops) in the Nahr Sene area south of Banias. On 3 May, Gen Sir Leslie Morshead and Staff with Sir Bertram S B Stevens attended the unit Church Service. On 19 May HRH the Duke of Gloucester visited the Div and this Bn was represented on the general parade in his honour. (6 Offrs, 1 WO, 3 Sgts and 198 Ors was our strength on this parade).

Two drafts arrived from the ITB, one on 6 May and 5 NCOs and 10 Ors and the other on 23 May of 2 Offrs and 40 Ors. During the month the weekly 2-day leave parties to Beirut were discontinued pending the completion of 7-day leave camp. Three 1-day tours were arranged using unit transport on 10 May to Beirut, 24 May to Krak des Chevaliers, and on 31 May to Becharre.

The mobile cinema visited the area on 14 May. All Coys established canteens within their areas, original stock being supplied out of Regimental Funds. Three tents have been erected in HQ Coy area as a recreation hut whilst purchase and distribution of wireless sets are mentioned in QM's report attached."

On 17 May 1942 a new posting of Offrs within the unit occurred:
Capt C G Pitman from Adjt to 2 i/c of B Coy
Capt A J C Newton from QM to Adjt
Capt P E O'Brien from OC D Coy to QM
Capt I F McMaster from 2 i/c A Coy to OC D Coy
Capt P H Pike from 2 i/c B Coy to 2 i/c A Coy.

Signed: C K M MAGNO, Maj

The report of the QM for May included the following relevant information:
Weapon position improved, the following were received:
10 LMGs, 2 Mortars 2", 2 Rifles A/Tk
9 Pistols signalling
This made the deficiencies 14 LMGs, 19 Rifles A/Tk, 2 Mortars 2" and 18 Pistols signalling.

Three carriers were received leaving 11 still required to bring us up to the establishment of 21. The vehicle position was fair, but 20x15 cwt GS trucks were deficient and although there was a deficiency of 8—3 ton GS trucks we held 5x30 cwt GS trucks and 3x2 ton dual wheeled vehicles in lieu. All items of summer dress have been received but some difficulty was experienced in obtaining large size shirts. Two boot repairers were operating and a fairly good stock of boots was held. 5 wireless sets (one to each Coy) and 5 typewriters (one to each Coy) were purchased from Bn funds.

Capt J F Sullivan's Medical report for May disclosed among other matters that the total personnel sick was 486 and that there were 89 evacuations to hospital, the most prevalent complaints were dermatitis in the early part of the month and PUO (Pyrexia of unknown origin) at the end of the month — only those cases needing evacuation are considered.

Two drafts of reinforcements were examined and the physical standard was generally fair. One doubtfully fit man was found. This man stated he had had 5 months in hospital suffering from a duodenal ulcer.

Malaria and malaria control: No cases noted. Villages in area sprayed weekly. Wells in village treated with kerosene.

Medical Training: Pte Bade, AAMC attd passed the school for unit orderlies at 3 Fd Amb with 75%. Unit stretcher bearers divided into two sections. 8 employed as medical orderlies with Coys. Remainder trained in First Aid and evacuation of casualties in mountain areas. "Slam" also suggested the use of trained mules for the evacuation of casualties, forward of the RAP.

Routine orders for May included the result of a Court Martial in which one of our soldiers was sentenced to 60 days' detention. Two of the four charges were: "Conduct to the prejudice etc; that whilst in detention was in possession of liquor – one bottle of whiskey." and "Conduct to the prejudice etc. . . improperly broke a bottle which was to be used in evidence against him". He was found guilty of three charges but NOT guilty of breaking the bottle.

From the Australian Comfort Funds, 817 pkts of razor blades, 817 face washers, 817 cakes of toilet soap and 100 pairs of socks were received and distributed.

A cricket match between our Bn and 20 Bde resulted in a win for 2/17th. 7 wickets for 310 whilst Bde's total was all out for 221.

Pte Hardiman scored 80 runs, Cpl Culey 58, Pte Ferguson 43 and Pte Conway 39 not out. Bowlers were Pte Hardiman 2 for 32, Pte Coventry 2 for 51, Cpl Culey 2 for 13.

During May, Lt George Reid was evacuated to 6 AGH — he had broken his leg in an accident. Lt A H Urquhart joined the Bn on 23 May after being commissioned from the OCTU Middle East. Alastair was an original enlistment who had served in the Sig Pl.

(Note by Arthur Newton: Whilst 2/17 Bn carried on with their role in Syria, action was occurring in the Western Desert to quote Barton Maughan's Official History. "Meanwhile in the desert west of Tobruk where the opposing armies had been sparring with each other around Gazala from static defence lines for more than 4 months, intense fighting had broken out and 8 Army appeared to be in danger of being thrust from its ground. The possibility was in the minds of the planning staff and of every soldier of the Div, that the day might not be far distant when 9 Div, which had seen no action for 7 months, might be required to fight again. To fit it

Pte E E Bell of A Coy who was aged 17yrs when mentioned in dispatches for bravery at Tobruk.

for such a role, training in motorised battle deployment in a desert terrain, in which the Div had never had an opportunity to practise, was an urgent need. A program for training each Bde in turn was arranged.")

The area in which these exercises were to be held was at Fourgloss, east of Homs but in fact only 24 Bde Gp completed the training during June.

The happenings of June 1942 are contained in the CO's Summary which reads:

The Bn was still stationed in Mt Tourbol sector of the Tripoli Box at the beginning of the month. Coys were continuing with intensive training and improvement of defensive positions. Additional training with pack transport in conjunction with both Cypriot and Indian Mule Coys of the RASC was carried out. Cadres for NCOs and potential NCOs and unarmed combat schools were held at Tourbol. During the period under review a Bn Offrs TEWT was held in Mercherfeh area and a 3-day Bde TEWT at Nahr Litani including Offrs of all supporting arms. On 12 June CO and Coy Comds attended lecture and demonstration by 57 Bty 2/7 Fld Regt. The classification range at El Abde was used freely during the month by all Coys. D Coy was still supplying the security guard at the El Mina docks area and for the second time the Port Comd congratulated 20 Bde on the manner in which these duties were being done. C Coy took over these duties from D Coy on 14 June.

(Note by Arthur Newton: One evening Keith Magno drove the CO, Lt Col Simpson, and I down to inspect the El Mina guard and straddled the railway line which ran parallel to the road near the wharf area, The car was a new Chev, and the wheels spun on the track ballast. In the distance a train appeared and gradually drew nearer. I sprinted up the track and called in poor Arabic for the driver to stop. The CO debussed, or "de-carred" and poor Keith was trying desperately to drive the car off the rails. When about 50 yards from the car I called for Keith to get out, and at the same time the engine driver became aware of the car so he pulled levers and turned wheels but too late, and the engine buffers hit each car door on the right side and pushed the car about 20 yards along the track. The CO instructed me to take the number of the engine. Later when we drove back to the transport lines and turned the car over to Keith Sabine (the Transport Offr) and said that we would drive up Mt Tourbol in a jeep, he was quite happy — until I showed him what had befallen his pride and joy.)

On 4 Jun B Coy moved to supply dump area between Bechemezzine and Kfar Hazar on security duties. All duties were subsequently handed over to 2/24 Bn on 16 Jun.

On 11 and 20 Jun small drafts of 14 and 31 Ors arrived from the Training Bn. On 17 Jun the main body of the Bn left the Tripoli Box having been relieved by elements of 2/48 Bn and moved to our old and well known Coy areas at Afrine district north of Aleppo and relieved 24 NZ Bn.

Owing to the malarial nature of the areas the majority of our troops were withdrawn under Bde orders, from Meidan Ekbes and Hammam. Radjou post was closed. On 22 Jun D Coy began special training at Azaz whilst the other line Coys carried on with normal post duties. On 25 Jun D Coy carried out attack exercises at Azaz in co-operation with carriers used as InfTanks.

On 26 Jun Brig Windeyer, CO and 2 i/c attended D Coy exercise. Meantime, on the amenities side, already four Bn parties totalling 13 Offrs and 310 Ors had enjoyed or were enjoying the 7-day Beirut leave camp.

(Note: It is interesting to read in Barton Maugham's History that: "The War Office had authorised the granting of 28 days' leave during the summer to all officers and men serving under British Command in the Middle east, with free travel to and from an approved leave centre. Troops stationed in Syria or the Lebanon were not permitted to take their leave in Palestine or Egypt. 9 Army HQ stipulated that the leave be taken in two periods of 14 days. Gen Morshead authorised leave for the AIF on the prescribed scale but directed that it be taken in 7-day periods in order that as many troops as possible should have some leave before anything could occur to interrupt the program.)

It proved a wise decision, the scheme had been in operation for only 4 weeks when the Div moved to Egypt. Leave camps were established at Beirut and Damascus, but Beirut was preferred, Damascus being extremely hot and, after a few days of sightseeing, having little to offer. At Beirut the camps were near the city and close to the sea. Cool breezes, bathing and complete freedom from duties made the stay very enjoyable. Accommodation at the camps was free, but other ranks were allowed a choice of accommodation at reasonable cost at hotels or "pensions" controlled by the Australian Comforts Fund. 10% of each unit went on leave weekly, approximately 1500 from the Div.

On the evening of 26 Jun, Afrine personnel were entertained by NAAFI (Navy, Army, Air Force Institute) Concert Party.

On 29 Jun all surplus gear and heavy kit was sent to the AIF Kit Store. The Western Desert situation was becoming increasingly serious and the Bn was awaiting orders.

On 30 Jun the Bn had packed and was standing ready to move. Its effective strength was 29 Offrs and 825 Ors. (End of CO's summary).

The Bn Intelligence Summary of Jun 27 continued this report on Meidan Ekbes.

21 Jun — Ahmed Agha a wealthy and influential resident of Bul Bul, was shot dead by bandits near the Greek ruins, between 0600 and 0700 hrs. Later two arrests were made but suspects subsequently released. The two suspects were carrying Mauser rifles and Turkish, German and Italian small arms ammunition. Bandits are reported to be crossing the Turkish frontier and burning crops. According to a message from Sgt Baker, Field Security Services, bandits are planning to raid Meidane Ekbes and trouble is expected to begin in the very near future.

Capt Sullivan's Medical Report for June stated that 87 evacuations occurred. these included 38 cases of PUO (Pyrexia of unknown origin), 10 cases of gastroenteritis, 3 cases of appendicitis, 1 self-inflicted gun shot wound. In addition, because of shortage of accommodation in the Main Dressing Station, 31 other cases had to be detained in the RAP at Afrine.

QM, Peter O'Brien, reported that very little change had occurred during the month and with few exceptions our war equipment was as at the end of May. Considerable difficulty was experienced in procuring "curtains sandfly" and there were not sufficient to issue one to each man. Rations continued to be of good standard and supplies of fresh vegetables were maintained. On a few occasions local meat did not keep overnight due to hot weather. Ice then became a regular issue.

After the units move to Afrine area, demands on motor transport were not as heavy as at Tripoli so full advantage was taken of the lull in activity and all vehicles were overhauled and serviced.

(Note by Phil Pike: In closing the account of this "post Tobruk" period, it is appropriate to acknowledge the work and research done by Lt Col A J C Newton MBE. His dedication to the task of providing a chronological record of the Bn Service in World War II has been prodigious and an inspiration to others to complete this History.

Arthur Newton was born in Geelong, Victoria on 7 Oct 1910, he joined the Permanent Army in 1936 and at the outbreak of War he was an Instructor at RMC Duntroon. He was posted as Regimental Sgt Maj of the 2/17 Inf Bn on 19 May 1940. He was commissioned on 28 Sept 1940 and appointed as a Rifle Pl Comd of 13 Pl C Coy. In April 1941 he took over as Bn QM and tended our needs in this department through Tobruk, back to Palestine and up to the Syrian border. After the Unit moved to Mt Tourbol near Tripoli he took over from Colin Pitman as Bn Adjt on 19 May 1942. He filled this posting with distinction through the Battle of Alamein and finally brought us back to Australia.

Few members of the Bn had the opportunity to serve in such a variety of appointments and few people attained the respect and affection that was bestowed on Arthur Newton by all ranks of the Unit.

On return to Australia he was moved to Advanced Land HQ in Brisbane and in 1944 he returned to 9 Aust Div as Staff Capt 24 Inf Bde. For these services he was awarded the MBE.

He retired from the Australian Army on 7 Oct 1972 with the rank of Lt Col and now lives in happy retirement in Dickson ACT.)

Lt Col N W Simpson appointed to
Comd of 2/17 Bn — 7 Mar 42

CHAPTER 8
RETURN TO THE WESTERN DESERT

The Battalion Commander's Summary for July begins with:

"On 1 Jul with an effective strength of 28 Offrs and 777 Ors the unit moved south from its various stations on the Turkish border. Some 228, all ranks from the Bn, moved by MT whilst the majority moved by rail via Rayak, Damascus, Haifa and Kantara. Conjecture was high amongst the troops. The general opinion was that our destination was the Western Desert and the task, the Battle of Egypt. Others held that homeward bound ships were assuredly waiting in the canal. The MT party reached Egypt without major incident. The rail party had the unusual experience of having to dismount and push the train over a substantial hill some 20 miles east of Haifa when coal ran out. The humour of this reversed method of travelling to war was lost neither on our troops nor on the local inhabitants."

At 0500 hrs on 4 Jul, MT party left Canal area for EL Deir, approx 15 miles west of Alexandria, where Bn took up defensive position.

At 1700 hrs on 5 Jul, the first rail group arrived in Bn area after having staged at Sidi Bishr. On 6 Jul a Bde Op Order foreshadowed a move 26 miles west and with the arrival of the second rail party, the Bn was again united with an effective strength of 30 Offrs and 762 Ors. On the 7th, the following day, there was much heartburning when LOB personnel were selected. This group included Maj Magno (the 2 i/c). On 8 Jul, LOB personnel left the unit and 35 troop carrying RASC vehicles reported to implement the Bde Op Order. To quote Barton Maughan's 'History': "In future each unit was to leave out of battle a certain number of officers and men of all ranks, who were to remain in the 'B' Echelon area when the unit went into battle; thus if a unit had very heavy losses there would be a nucleus round which it could be reformed. In an Inf Bn, eg the Bn 2 i/c, 6 other Offrs and 61 others of specified ranks or qualifications were left behind; this was a minimum as it was also laid down that an Inf Bn was not to go into action with its rifle sections of greater strength than 1 NCO and 7 men." Our LOB party remained in the Alexandria area as did, I believe, all other 9 Div LOB parties.)

At 0200 hrs on 9 Jul we received the first of a long series of warning orders. The Bn was placed on one hour's notice to move as from 0500 hrs.

At 0900 hrs (9 Jul) the Bn moves by vehicle together with a Pl of 2/2 MG Bn. Detachment of 11 Bty 4 Lt AA Regt, one detachment of 2/3 Fd Coy (RAE), one mobile Sec of 2/8 Fd Amb and 58 Aust LAD, 70 vehicles of 10 Coy AASC, approx 150 vehicles in all.

Route is via Amiriya and by 1400 hrs reaches destination by desert track and takes up defensive position Imayid area. Night uneventful. Slight enemy air activity. Continual flights of RAF heard.

Diary entry for 10 Jul 1942 records a fine hot day with light sea breeze. Many flights of RAF fighters and bomber planes seen. One tactical reconnaissance Hurricane, SAAF (South African Air Force) makes forced landing near Bn HQ. 1200 hrs: Bde Comd, Brig W.J.V. Windeyer visits Bn HQ. Men are anxious to "get into it".

Jul 12: Effective strength 24 Offrs and 623 Ors. Nothing operational to report. During past 7 days approx 100 men of the unit have been evacuated with "sandfly" fever. RAF maintains local superiority.

Jul 13: Heavy fog at "stand to" does not rise until 0900 hrs. We hear of the success of Maj Day's column. 26 Bde stands firm on new line (Tel el Eisa area).

Jul 14/15: Bn on 4 hours' notice to move. 0700 hrs: CO and IO attend Bde Conference. 0800 hrs: Bn on 1 hours' notice to move. 1200 hrs: Bn arrives and takes up defensive position at Map Ref El Hammam Sheet 44558861. D and B Coys forward, A and C in reserve — men cheerful and hope for attack rather than defence.

Jul 16: Effective strength 24 Offrs and 594 Ors. 0530 hrs: CO attends Bde Conference. 0630 hrs: Warning order — we move at this hour — personal order from the C-in-C (Auchinleck) stating that no conditions of fatigue or any other disability can permit withdrawal from our new position.

CO and IO go forward to recce. Bn moves forward and disperses in Area TRIG 79 (89132780) by 0900 hrs. Bde Comd commends Bn on administration and speed of movement. We take up defensive positions on ridge 88952790. South of our positions a flank of forward troops has been turned by enemy forces. Considerable air activity, light shelling of our Coy areas during afternoon. 3 casualties. 1600 hrs: Bde Conference attended by CO and IO. Warning order to move to coastal area. Coy recce groups sent forward with Capt Maclarn in carriers to new position. El Shammama sector of El Alamein defences (map reference 48129015). 1830 hrs: Cancellation of movement order brought by LO. We must await relief by British Bde. Coys debus and return to their areas. During night ridge to west of our positions attacked by enemy tanks and inf. Arty continues all night. Protective patrols sent out by us. Attack successfully resisted by 5 Indian Bde.

Jul 17: Effective strength 24 Offrs, 585 Ors. We are to move today without being relieved. 1030 hrs: Zero hour for Bde convoy. Bn moves at zero plus 130 (1240 hrs) by road and desert track "C" to El Shammama. 1600 hrs: Bn in position. Men are glad to be by the sea. Coy parties given leave to go swimming and do washing. Fine and warm by day and night.

(Note by Arthur Newton: This 3-day excursion south into the desert by 20 Bde Gp was quite an odd affair. Barton Maughan in the Official History describes it as follows: "Meanwhile 20 Bde Gp (Brig Windeyer) had moved on the afternoon of the 15th to the defensive positions close to Gen Auchinleck's tactical HQ. Late that night a LO from 8 Army was sent to Windeyer's HQ with orders that the Bde was to move at 0520 hrs next morning in three Bn groups, each in mobile box formation to a position (Mubarik Tomb) behind 5 Indian Div, against which a counter-attack was expected. There the Bde formed next morning a hastily improvised and dangerously exposed defence line. These orders were given without Morshead's knowledge. When Morshead learnt what had occurred, he telephoned Gen Auchinleck and said he was dumbfounded that Auchinleck should have done this; it was opposed to their agreement, he said, and opposed to Morshead's charter. Auchinleck agreed to return the Bde but soon afterwards sent news that he was being attacked heavily, whereupon Morshead agreed that the return of the Bde should be deferred, but asked to have it back as soon as possible. The Bde was released and returned to 9 Div on 17 Jul.)

John Moore in his biography of Morshead refers to Gen Morshead's earlier "strained interview" with Gen Auchinleck concerning the "dismemberment of the Division" in which Auchinleck finished up by saying: "So you are being like Blamey. You are wearing his mantle." And then Moore referring to 20 Bde's scamper states: "On 15 Jul, Auchinleck exacerbated an already tenuous relationship with Morshead when, without advising him, he ordered Brig

Windeyer to place his 20 Bde in rear of 5 Indian Div. Morshead was livid when told and at once phoned Auchinleck to criticise his 'theft'. Auchinleck agreed at once to return the Bde, though when this was not immediately propitious, Morshead sensibly agreed until the situation eased."

The following are extracts from 20 Bde War Diary covering the period 15-17 Jul 1942.

"15 July — After receiving a map reference from 30 Corps HQ, Brig Windeyer and Lt Gemmell-Smith arrived at 8 Army HQ at 0810 hrs. Gen Auchinleck had a few words with the Brig, who received instructions from the BGS (the principal staff officer) to move the Bde to occupy positions around Trig 132 and Trig 104 as well as to be able to provide a mobile column of one Bn plus one Fd bty with supporting arms. The O Gp was picked up and the party proceeded to Trig 104 when the Brig was informed by the CCRE 30 Corps that a NZ Bn was in occupation of Trig 112, the Brig decided to occupy Trig 104 with 2/15 Bn and Trig 112 (446886) with 2/13 and 2/17 Bns. The CCRE liaised with the BGS about alteration to plans. The orders for the Bde move were verbal. Move commenced at 1200hrs. 2/17 Bn Gp moved across country via El Imayid station (443899). The remainder of the Bde Gp went via El Hamman thence across country to the destination. A mine field around the Trig 112 position made the movement into the dispersal area more difficult. The position around Trig 112 was wired in. The last elements moved in at approx 2000 hrs 16 July (Bde War Diary) — At 0335 hrs a message was received from 8 Army for the Bde Gp to be ready to move at 0530 hrs to vicinity Mubarik Tomb, 890280 and to place light out for an LO. The LO arrived at approx 0445 hrs with further instructions that a Fd Regt would come under command and that a 20 Bde Offr was to meet a representative of 11 Fd Regt at Mubarik Tomb at 0600 hrs. A further written message stated that an attack was expected by the combined German forces along Ruweisat Ridge and that the present positions held by NZ and Indian forces must not be overrun. The Bde Gp could not move on time due to the late arrival of the message and the bad state of communications to sub-units then existing. The Bns were ordered to move as soon as ready direct by dead reckoning to the Tomb. Capt Hamer (later Premier of Victoria) left at 0545 hrs to meet 11 Fd Regt Offr, Brig Windeyer, and Lt Gemmell-Smith left at 0615 hrs to make a recce arriving at destination at 0900 hrs. The move of 2/17 Bn was very good as they selected a firm route throughout, the other units went direct and had much trouble due to bogging in the sand. The remainder of the Bde HQ left after 2/13 Bn and arrived at 1230 hrs. Bns went into positions along the ridge about 1500 yds apart with the right forward Bn, 2/17 Bn behind a minefield from 88802795 to 89002800 right near 2/15 Bn from 89052800 to 42408905 and the left forward 2/13 Bn from 88902775 to Trig 79891278. 2/7 Fd Regt were in three battery positions to south and south-east, Trig 79 with primary task of covering Bde front with DF fire and secondary task an A/tk role. The remaining supporting arms were distributed amongst the Bns equally. The gunfire in the forward area was intense during the morning but quietened down about 1130 hrs after the forward troops had succeeded in beating off a strong attack by German armour. At 1430 hrs the Brig commanding 69 British Bde arrived and informed Brig Windeyer that 69 Bde was along the road waiting to relieve 20 Aust Inf Bde.

This was the first intimation of a relief except a rather cryptic message from 8 Army by R/T (radio telephone) via a LO that on relief the 260 Bty was to pass to the command of the incoming brigade. Our brigade had experienced much difficulty moving in due to loose sand and the area was very congested with MT. Commander 69 Bde required 20 Bde to move out before the 69 Bde would move in. Arrangements were made immediately for the move to commence. Zero for the move was 1730 hrs. 10 Coy AASC moved on time but were halted by Capt Elliott, 20 Bde AASC Offr. 8 Army was contacted by R/T by an Army LO and orders were received that the relief was to be made on the ground. Lt Sheldon, LO was sent to contact Comd 69 Bde but could not find him. This was made more difficult as the message received named the Comd of 69 Bde as Brig Hassel who was not the Comd and whose name was never discovered.

It was then decided that the brigade would remain in position until dawn 17 July at least. In the late evening when a further heavy attack developed to the west along Ruweisat Ridge, Brig Windeyer ordered the return of 10 Coy AASC which had stopped 10 miles to the east. It was considered the ammunition may be required. By dark the attack had been beaten off and a quiet night followed except when arty and medium machine guns of 5 Indian Bde engaged a party of Germans employed in recovering damaged trucks.

July 17: By 0800 hrs there was still no sign of 69 Bde so Brig Windeyer called on 5 Indian Div HQ where he was informed that 69 Bde was not occupying our positions but had moved into others further to the west. No attempt had been made to notify this Bde (20th) of the change in places. After notifying 8 Army of the situation the Bde commenced to move at 1030 hrs. It had been decided to send a tactical HQ forward early on future moves so that it could be established and working when the main body arrived. Maj Wilson (BM) took forward the Tac HQ consisting of the IO command vehicle and a detachment of Signallers. Brig Windeyer and the IO left at 1045 hrs and proceeded direct to Tac HQ 9 Div where Brig Windeyer conferred with Lt Gen Sir Leslie Morshead and Colonel Wells (GSO 1). The Bde was to occupy positions recently vacated by 24 Aust Inf Bde and be in 9 Div Reserve."

(End of relevant 20 Bde War Diary entries.)

(Arthur Newton's personal comments are: "I recall these three days as rather a bewildering experience. Eric Blundell, then the Int Sgt was responsible for the navigation of the Bn across the desert and did a magnificent job. Part of the Bn group vehicles on the journey of 15 July (the first day) bogged down close to 8 Army HQ and Gen Auchinleck, a fine looking soldier figure, came over to speak to Maj John Balfe who was OC of the main body (as the CO had gone forward), Phil Pike and myself. He made the comment that he often got bogged in the sand himself and after stating he hoped to have us in action shortly, sent one of his Aides, a Sudan Defence Force British Offr, to show us the route to take to move on better. I also recall the LO staggering into 2/17 Bn lines (on the night 15/16 July) somewhere about 0430 hrs and asking the whereabouts of HQ 20 Bde. He stated he had been wandering about the desert for hours. He said he had a personal despatch from the C-in-C. Dal Cartledge, the IO, was not to be 'hoodwinked' by a possible German spy and insisted the British Offr produce identification papers. The poor fellow was most distraught and after satisfying Dal, was guided to HQ 20 Bde and the story unfolded as told in the Bde War Diary. Also on 16 July Maj Keith Magno who was OC LOB personnel, drove into the area. He had driven up from near Alexandria unaware that we had been committed to this desert scamper. We virtually pushed the cheerful 2 i/c out of the area before he was embroiled in the battle which luckily did not eventuate."

July 18: Effective strength 24 Offrs and 584 Ors (still dropping). Administration and improvement of dug positions. 1730 hrs: CO attends a Bde Conference — the Bn on 2 hour's notice to move. We are quickly getting used to this. CO and IO leave on forward recce to El Alamein with Bde Offrs.

July 19: Weather hot. 0900 hrs: CO and Coy Comds recce day and night debussing areas forward to El Alamein. 1200 hrs: CO and IO with Bde Comd and Bde O Gp recce FDLs of 26 Bde. 1600 hrs: Bn O Gps go forward and see 2/24 Bn positions at Trig 33 feature. The Adj was sniped at and Bn O Gps retire in good order from Trig 33 under 88mm shellfire — mostly duds (?). Local air superiority maintained.

July 20: Waiting — weather hot with light north breeze. 1200 hrs: Hurricane shot down by ME109 south-east of Bn area. 1600 hrs: Lt Col Clark and Coy Comds 28 Gurkha Regt visit Bn area and recce our positions. His regiment is at 50% strength and he will move in with us on night 20/21 July and complete El Shammama defences. Lt Williams returns from A/Tk school.

July 21: Effective strength 24 Offrs and 567 Ors. Administration — waiting — general rest — good swimming. 1100 hrs: CO and IO leave for Bde Conference. Bn again on 4 hours' notice. 1630 hrs: 67 reinforcements arrive, 45 "X" men, 22 others (including 9 from 3 Aust A/Tk Regt). 2000 hrs: Coy Comd Conference at Bn HQ.

July 22: A/Tk Pl in process of formation. Two A/Tk Portee, 2-pdr guns to be increased later to six. Pl under command Lt Stuart Williams.

July 23: Fine and warm. Heavy night and morning dews. Quiet night. 1600 hrs: CO and IO recce 26 Bde Area. Observation of enemy positions carried out from Pt 17 and 33.

July 24: 1730 hrs: CO and Lt Col Ogle 2/15 Bn, BM and Asst BM and IO recce 2/24 Bn area. CO, Major Balfe and IO recce 2/13 Bn area and go forward to new 2/28 Bn positions along Qattara Rd. Quiet day, coy training and administration.

July 25: Effective strength 24 Offrs and 648 Ors. Shoot carried out by A/Tk Pl with 2-pdr guns of which we have three. Hot and windy.

July 26: Weather hot — flies becoming a problem in spite of hygiene efforts. 4 Offrs, Lts S Yeend, T Swan, A P Craik and G Wray join the unit from ITB

July 27: Effective strength — 28 Offrs and 639 Ors. 1300 hrs: For the first time ME109 recce aircraft flew over the Bn area. Bofors and our light AA engaged.

July 28: 1900 hrs: MEs ground straffed area, no casualties. At 2300 hrs repeat performance of ground straffing by moonlight. Draft of 33 Ors arrive from ITB.

July 29: 0900 hrs: CO calls meeting of Offrs and NCO's to discuss Bn policy. Enemy air activity over area, apparently recce only.

July 30: CO makes recce of 2/13 Bn area. Fine and cool. Lt McKinley was accidentally injured by a mine and lost the sight of an eye.

The RMO, Capt John Sullivan's report for July referred to the number of Pyrexia cases which occurred during the month most of which were later notified as Malaria cases. The total number evacuated with PUO was 163. The last suspected case of Malaria occurred on 23 July 1942, which suggested the maximum incubation period of Malaria is not over 23 days, thus confirming previous estimates. Capt Sullivan's theory was that despite malarial precautions in Syria the breakdown appears to be in one or two suspected loopholes. (a) The majority of men who became infected had numerous bites confined to forearms and knees. It is now considered probable that these were mosquito bites. The peculiar distribution being due to the fact that these parts were more likely to come in contact with nets during sleep. It is felt the type of net provided, i.e. barrack room pattern, is not suitable when men sleep on the ground in tents or huts, as the average bed, even with mattress, is not wide enough to spread the net sufficiently to prevent any part of the body coming in contact with the net during sleep. (b) A less probable factor but worthy of consideration is that the majority of those infected were used as guards in dark tunnels by day when no anti-malarial precautions were taken.

There were three battle casualties evacuated with wounds to elbow, knee and thigh respectively. Most reinforcements appeared fit. There was a larger number than usual over 35 years of age. The QM, Capt Peter O'Brien, in his report made several interesting references to changes in the War Equipment Table.

"(a) Boys A/Tk Rifles were no longer on issue (25 to a Bn) but it was not intended to recall the six (6) still held by the Bn.

(b) Although the unit held 14x2" Mortars against an establishment of 16, enquiries disclosed that further issues could not be expected as the establishment had been reduced to 8 for an Inf Bn. The Bn had acquired its share of enemy and salvaged weapons and those recorded by the QM were: 3 Spandau LMGs, 1 Breda LMG, 1 Browning (7.92mm), 12 Browning .303. One of the major problems was lack of sufficient vehicles of the right type. That the move from Afrine to the desert was accomplished so quickly and successfully was mainly due to the service of the units LAD."

Actually, the unit did not have a light aid detachment, this was located at Bde HQ but we did have fitters, etc, attached and from my experience, many of our drivers had mechanical ability. The Bde LAD Offr was also of great assistance.

"The majority of the vehicles are not desert worthy and for many of these sand trays were not at first available. Deficiencies appeared to be 7 carriers, 15 motor-cycles, 31x15cwt GS trucks and 8x3-ton GS lorries although we did have 3x2-ton dual wheeled lorries in lieu. Rations for part of the month were 'hard' but later bread and Australian beef came in, vegetables later in the month became almost a daily issue. Potatoes, beans, marrows, beetroot and tomatoes were generally received. By the end of the month rations were better than for quite some time past."

(End of QM's report for July.)

The Coy Comds at the end of July were:

Maj J W Balfe, OC HQ Coy (but acting as Bn 2 i/c as Maj C K Magno was LOB)

Capt L C Brien, OC A Coy, (he was evacuated to 2/8 Fd Amb on 30 July and Capt P H Pike administered command during his absence.)

Capt J R Broadbent, OC B Coy

Maj A M Alison, OC C Coy (he was promoted to Maj during July)

Capt I F McMaster, OC D Coy

Capt L C Maclarn was OC Carrier Pl

Lt R J Burgess was Sig Offr

Lt R S Rudkin was Mortar Offr

Lt A E Nicholson was Pioneer Offr

Although July 1942 was relatively quiet for 20 Bde, 24 and 26 Bdes has been in the "thick" of fighting. The first action was a raid by a coy of 2/43 Bn in the Ruweisat Ridge area, this was roughly in the area where we were on 15/17 July. To quote the Official History: "The task was given to Capt Jeanes' Coy of 2/43 Bn (Lt Col W J Wain) with 4 Offrs and 64 Ors, plus 20 Sappers and 6 Stretcher Bearers. By 2230 hrs on 7 July the raiders had formed up at Pt 71 whence they moved off at 2300 hrs. After 1400 yds the leading Pl (Lt Grant) reported the presence of enemy troops about 800 yds to the north-west and promptly attacked; the other Pls fanned out to right and left and joined in.

Under fire from a variety of weapons, Lance Sgt Curren's Pl thrust forward for about 700 yds destroying guns and vehicles and taking prisoners. Grant's Pl moved a similar distance and its sappers destroyed 3 disabled British tanks. Lt Combe's Pl destroyed a gun and a tractor. Pte Franklin in Curren's Pl, who acted with great dash throughout the attack, recaptured a British carrier, killing 2 Germans and drove it back to his own lines. By 0300 hrs the Coy was back at Point 71.

Throughout the raid the enemy fired wildly and sent up many flares. Soon flares, blasting guns and blazing tractors illuminated the area. When it was over, 1 Australian was missing and 7 had been wounded, 4 A/tk guns, 1 field gun, 3 damaged British tanks and 6 tractors had been destroyed, and at least 15 enemy troops had been killed and 9 prisoners taken — all German of an A/tk unit. The raid had an inspiring effect on the Div and on neighbouring troops."

On 10/11 July, 26 Bde attacked in the Tel el Eisa area and much bloody fighting occurred. "In all, the Bde knocked out 18 tanks and took 1,150 prisoners." By the end of July the Tel el Eisa area had been consolidated.

On the 26/27 July, the Div suffered a cruel loss when 2/28 Bn, after an attack at Ruin Ridge, was forced to surrender on the morning of 27 July, although as stated in the History of the 2/28 Bn: "The final opposition did not cease until early afternoon. One platoon from C Coy comd by Lt John Draper, was occupying a position on the forward slope of the ridge and well out on the right flank. Unaware of the surrender and believing that the Bn had withdrawn to safety, this Pl fought until it was finally over-run by the tanks of the Briehl group." 69 British Bde which had not made contact with 20 Bde on 16 July was also in 30 Corps attack on the night of 26/27 July. It was to attack further south of 2/28 Bn but westward. Brig Philip Masel, who wrote the History of 2/28 Bn and who was OC of the Carriers of the Bn in July 1942 had this to say of 69 Bde's attack: "It was obvious that everything now depended on 69 Bde which was operating on the left of the Qattara track. Tired from weeks of heavy fighting, it put in its attack with its Bns at less than half strength. 500 of its men were reinforcements who had arrived in the Middle East three weeks previously and who were so poorly acclimatised that 5 died from heat exhaustion." (It must be remembered that the threat to Egypt was so acute that acclimatisation had to be regarded as a luxury.) Forward of the Bde start line was a protective minefield laid by the South Africans. Two large gaps were cleared. The darkness caused confusion and the two assaulting Bns tried to use the one gap at the same time. The Section leaders did not know their men, the men did not know their NCOs. The confusion doomed the operation to failure. Only two coys reached their objectives."

They fought desperately but were quickly over-run. 2/28 Bn's left flank was wide open, but even up until 1000 hrs on 27 July, the Australians had only a vague realisation of what had happened to 69 Bde.

According to Barton Maughan's Official History:

"2 Offrs and 63 Ors of 2/28 Bn were known to have been killed or wounded, and 20 Offs and 469 men were missing. 69 Bde lost about 600 men. So ended Gen Auchinleck's last attempt to dislodge Rommel's army from the El Alamein line. Auchinleck's efforts to exhaust the enemy forces had succeeded in exhausting his own. For more than a month afterwards neither of the opposing armies launched a major attack. Neither was strong enough. Rommel commenting later said of the situation, after the failure of the attack by 30 Corps: 'It was now certain that we could continue to hold our front, and that, after the crisis we had been through, was at least something. Although the British losses in this Alamein fighting had been higher than ours, yet the price to Auchinleck had not been excessive, for the one thing that had mattered to him was to halt our advance and that unfortunately, he had done."

Of this period at Alamein, General Morshead recorded this entry in his diary. "No stability, a wealth of plans and appreciations resulting in continual TEWTS. Fighting always in bits and pieces and so defeat in detail. Formations being broken up automatically — it has been difficult and unpleasant keeping 9th Division intact.'"

CHAPTER 9
TEL EL EISA

So ended July 1942. August was to give 2/17 Bn a more positive role and new personalities were to join the Higher command.

A phone message from 9 Div to 20 Bde HQ at 1100 hrs on Friday 31 July 1942 was to result in a change of scenery for 2/17 Bn. The message stated that 20 Bde would relieve 26 Bde. At 1400 hrs the same day, Brig Windeyer with his Staff Offr, Capt Hamer went to 9 Div HQ where they received more specific instructions and then on to HQ 26 Bde and 2/23 and 2/24 Bn HQ to make arrangements for the relief

Most of the area of the El Alamein fighting by 9 Div can, in good conditions, be seen from the south-west slopes of Point 33 captured in July by 26 Bde and held for a long defensive and patrolling period by 20 Bde. The area is marked on the north by the low ridge on which the road runs west to Sidi Abd el Rahman with its village mosque and minaret seeming to give surveillance over all to the east. North of the road, salt flats stretched to the sand hills on the coastline where nothing critical transpired. South are the twin points 24 more evident on the map than on the ground marked Tel el Eisa. This, on the south, sloped down a few metres to the area of the start lines of 23 Oct. Further to the south the desert ran away in flatness while, to the west, it rose very gradually over miles to the enemy's north-south Rahman supply track. Here and there the map showed a spot height barely discernible as a feature. The surface often just hard, flat, baked, shallow earth on white stone. In other places, low desert tussocks marked small mounds of sand and dust. Tough and urgent digging was necessary for the soldier to get any protection. Critical was the time taken to dig an A/tk gun pit.

Except for a few metres rise north to the road from the nearby railway line, there was no sharp rise and the maximum height variation of about 10 metres was spread over miles. In such flatness visibility for the man on the ground is necessarily limited except as to men, tanks and vehicles approaching. There were occasional desert dust storms. The usual haze build up its protective value through the middle of the day, distorting or obscuring things at a distance. When there, add in dust from shellfire, bombs, moving vehicles and smoke from those burning, and the view even while standing is limited.

August 1: Location map reference[1] 4339901El Qasaba Sheet 1:50,000 effective strength 26 Offrs and 666 Ors. Weather still warm, surfing the order of the day. 1000 hrs: CO calls a Coys Comds conference and at 1100 hrs CO and Coy Comds move forward to recce 2/48 and 2/23 Bn areas on the Div FDLs.

August 2: 1000 hrs: Recce of new battalion positions made by all specialist Offrs prior to change-over tonight. 1600 hrs: CO's Conference of all officers. At 2030 hrs Bn convoy moves

---

[1]
 Patrol activities and dispositions may be followed by reference to El Alamein gridded map on pages 154, 155, 156, 157.

out to take over forward coys from 2/23 and 2/48 Bns. Everyone in high spirits at prospect of real action again.

August 3: The change over with 2/48 and 2/23 Bns completed without incident at 0030 hrs. The Bn is now in a front line position after 9 months spell. The Bn area centres around Tel el Eisa, now well known to everyone as "Hill of Jesus" and it was the pivot point of the attack by 9 Div on 10 July. Our dispositions are as follows: A Coy to occupy the railway cutting, B Coy astride the railway close to Tel el Eisa Station, C Coy east of B Coy near the railway line and D Coy on eastern 24 feature. 0700 hrs: situation normal. Our patrols made no contact —an uneventful night. A quiet day — everyone employed in settling in cleaning up the area. There is much evidence of the previous encounters in the area — many dead, still unburied in forward areas. Flies abound everywhere and drastic measures initiated to combat the pests. 1600 hrs: Bde Comd Brig Windeyer visits the area to inspect site of new Bn HQ. He approves of new site over the ridge from present position. At 2000 hrs Bde Comd again visits the area accompanied by Maj Copeland 2/3 A/tk Regt (Officer for co-ordination of A/tk defences) and discussed A/tk defence with our CO.

Far left:
Tel el Eisa station.
Left:: *The cutting*

August 5: A draft of 16 "X" men rejoined the unit. During the night patrols still make no contact. Some artillery and machine gun fire reported on 2/15 front (right flank). Nothing comes of it. During the day increased enemy movement was observed forward of A and D Coys. This observation culminated in an artillery shoot about 1900 hrs on a dump forward of enemy lines, directed by Capt McMaster (OC D Coy). Shoot was successful — men were dispersed and at least one dump destroyed. The increased MT movement throughout the day may be the result of a changeover of enemy units on our front. During the day several requests made of CO.

(i) 2 Offrs of 245 General Transport Coy sought permission to recover 2 Bedford trucks north of A Coy area. This was granted and recovery took place during the hours of darkness.

(ii) Approval was given to OC 58 LAD (Capt Morrisby) to recce forward coy areas during the day.

CO 2/2 MG Bn (Lt Col Macarthur Onslow) visited this HQ. Subject of visit was the siting of MG Pl in Bn area and also the probable use of Bn carriers with MMGs in a small mobile operation.

Maj Copeland called and gave an assurance that the a/tk guns (2/3 A/Tk Regt) were sited in left forward coy of 2/15 Bn that gave protection to our A Coy FDLs. All regimental guns of 2-pdr calibre within the area would be changed during the night to guns of 6-pdr calibre. He would also give early consideration to the siting of a/tk guns further south in B and C Coy areas. 1600 hrs: Bde Comd called and visited forward coy areas.

August 6: Nothing to report from patrols and other activity. Between 0600—0700 hrs another arty shoot was conducted on dump area previously engaged last night. Good results this time — troops reported "running like hell" and heavy black smoke seen rising from the area. Again at 1100 hrs and 1400 hrs troops were dispersed in this area by our arty. Between last light and 2100 hrs Bn HQ moved to new forward Bn HQ on SW slopes of ridge at 87733004 (El Alamein Sheet 1: 50000). 1100 hrs:

Visitors.

(i) Lt Col Cairns and his 2 i/c visit this HQ and inform CO that 2 tanks, 1 Matilda and 1 Valentine will be available tomorrow in the Bn area for inspection and instruction of troops 1230 hrs.

(ii) Lt Stevens (2/13 Fld Coy) calls and gives details of minefields between A Coy and 2/15 Bn area.

August 7: Patrols still fail to make any contact. Movement forward of our wire is hampered after midnight by bright moonlight. Enemy FDLs must have moved as patrols by B and C Coys now cover the first 2000 yds by MT, 60 cases of mines salvaged by D Coy during the night. More are still to be recovered and this will be done as soon as practicable.

During the afternoon men and vehicles are sighted around West Pt 24 — much ado and after frantic enquiries they turn out to be an unauthorised "scrounging" party from a flanking unit. 1815 hrs: Two waves of aircraft (ME 110s) bomb the ridge about 2 miles SW of this HQ. There were 2 sticks of bombs and at least one air burst amongst them. These air bursts are devilish weapons and every precaution is taken against them. During the first half of night, many coloured flares are reported by forward coys coming from enemy lines. To the old patrollers these flares have no terrors. They seem to indicate increased working activity on the part of the enemy. Even in Tobruk we found him very partial to the use of flares.

Visitors 1000 hrs. Capt Nicholson (2/3 Fd Wkshops Recovery Sec) and Capt Morrisby (58 LAD) called to discuss salvage of vehicles in Bn area. They will salvage any worthwhile material tonight. 1500 hrs: Maj Francis, Lt Eales and Lt Butlerwith and 8 soldiers of 7th (British) Rifle Bde arrived to spend a few days with the Bn to study our methods.

(Visits such as this became a regular feature during the next couple of months; in retrospect, many units from British Divs and the Highland Div should be grateful for the help received from units of 9 Aust Div).

August 8: Effective strength 32 Offrs and 687 Ors. (a sharp rise) as a draft of 6 Offrs and 30 "X" list men and reinforcements join the unit. Many enemy documents have been found in the Bn area and just forward of our wire. These have been forwarded on and much useful information gleaned therefrom. A quiet night with nothing of interest from the patrols who for the past few nights have attempted to contact enemy wire. Very little has been accomplished in this direction so far. Enemy shelling increased especially in cutting area. Even Bn HQ receives some attention but from *our own* arty — 2 unexploded 25-pdr shells falling near this HQ.

August 9: Nothing to report from patrols. Despite this it was not for the want of trying, as on the night 8/9 Aug the following patrols operated:

C Coy:	1 Offr	1 Sgt	10 Ors from 2100 to 0330 hrs
A Coy:	1 Offr	1 NCO	8 Ors from 2100 to 0200 hrs

| C Coy: | 1 Offr | 1 NCO | 6 Ors from 2100 to 0230 hrs |
| B Coy: | 1 Offr | 1 NCO | 4 Ors from 2100 to 0130 hrs |

1210 hrs: Lt Dewhurst and 4 Ors from Rifle Bde arrive to stay 48 hrs with the Bn.

August 10: Patrols make some progress positioning enemy FDLs in Square 871299 (El Alamein Sheet). 0715 hrs: D Coy report heavy enemy shelling forward of their FDLs — nothing falling in the coy area. 0845 hrs: Bde Comd phones and is pleased that our patrols had made contact during the night. 1100 hrs: Lt Col R Turner CO 2/13 Bn and Lt Barton Maughan, his IO call and discuss patrol boundaries on respective fronts.

(*Note*: At this period 2/13 Bn was the reserve Bn of 20 Bde but was also pushing out patrols through our (the 2/17th) front in a south-westerly direction.)

August 11: D Coy patrol encounters enemy wire and disturbs a listening post which hastily withdraws.

(*Note*: On night of 10/11 Aug, D Coy's patrol, consisting of 1 Offr, 1 NCO and 8 Ors, went out at 2045 hrs and returned at 2355 hrs. This fighting patrol found no opportunity target but confirmed existence of enemy FDL in Square 871299 striking the triple dannert fence at approx 87142999. At 87243001 a Mark 75 mine was laid in a north-south track recently used.)

1650 hrs: GOC 9 Aust Div accompanied by Bde Comd visits Bn area. No shelling in this area today.

August 12: Draft of 29 "X" list men rejoin unit. A patrol from C Coy saw an enemy patrol but were unable to intercept them. A quiet day. The patrol which consisted of 1 Offr, 1 NCO and 8 Ors plus 1 Offr of D Coy, were at 87183010 — after flares fired, enemy patrol of 8 men seen making for their wire; could not intercept. A standing patrol will use gap on night of 12/13 Aug to intercept enemy.

August 13: Quiet night. Two deep patrols reported no movement seen but constant sounds of enemy working parties were heard behind his FDLs. Our arty and aircraft continue to harass the enemy on our front. 0900 hrs: Bde Comd visit this HQ.

August 14: One deep patrol made contact with an enemy post at 86932995 after penetrating an apparent gap in his wire, while another left the railway cutting and went for nearly 6000 yds along the general direction of the railway line and just south of it without contacting enemy. This patrol crossed numerous dannert fences and inspected unoccupied posts. The recce information later proved valuable. A daylight OP at 87313003 was able to direct several arty shoots before the midday haze and at about 1900 hrs, phone being relayed from OP to coy then Bn Command Post and then Arty Bty Offr. 1057 hrs: A plane was shot down near B Echelon and at 1353 hrs ME 109s bombed the echelon area — one casualty resulting.

(Note by A Newton: At this stage it may be appropriate to enlarge on the patrol situation. First, according to the Official History, on 3 August, the day on which 20 Bde took over the front, Brig Windeyer laid down a policy of aggression. The enemy, he ordered, was to be fired on whenever seen and harassed by patrols and raids. Second, 2/15 Bn, which was on our right, patrolled between the railway and the coast. The enemy appeared to be closer in here than on 2/17 Bn front with the result that on the night of 4/5 Aug a patrol led by Capt Bill Cobb and 12 others of 2/15 Bn found themselves in the midst of a German position when they reached their objective some 1500 yds north of Point 25 (Baillieu's Bluff). In the resulting fire fight Cobb was wounded, Cpl R C Cooper was killed and another soldier wounded. A prisoner from 125th Regt was killed during the withdrawal. On the night 10/11 Aug, Capt "Bull" Angus of 2/15 Bn led a patrol 17 strong, some 2400 yds ahead of the forward coys, surprised a party of 25 Germans and killed or wounded all of them. One Australian was missing and one wounded. Third, our patrols, sometimes 4 each night, whilst gathering valuable knowledge, did not always clash with the enemy during his period. However, because of the sheer distances covered, deserve more detailed mention. Unfortunately the War Diary does not list the names of those who comprised the patrols.)

Examples are:

(a) On night 12/13 Aug, B Coy sent out a patrol of 1 Offr, 1 NCO and 8 Ors — it went out at 2130 hrs, returned at 0400 hrs. D Coy on the same night sent out a patrol of 1 Offr, 1 NCO and 8 Ors to take up an ambush position — as planned the previous night — at 87203004 with a covering party at 87283000 but no movement seen.

(b) On night 13/14 Aug, B Coy again sent out a patrol of 1 Offr, 1 NCO and 10 Ors which went out at 87483002 on a bearing approx 310 on general line of track parallel to railway line for 5000 yds then west 900 yds, then 127 to start point. The patrol went out at 2100 hrs and came in at 0400 hrs — 7 hours in all.

At approx 87273020 single dannert which extended at least 300 yds south-west. Patrol went through in extended line and found further single dannert 250 yds further on. At approx 87233023 camouflaged unoccupied a/tk gun position — net over it. Sounds of working activity coming continuously from northern side of railway line in 2/15 Bn patrolling area. At 4000 yds sent left flank man to locate strong post wire which was found at 87183024. Patrol continued on its course and passed road heavily used by both wheeled and track vehicles at 87183028 at 4700 yds from start point, continued 300 yds past track and then turned due west for 900 yds. No movement seen or heard in this area. Appeared to be moving away from the enemy. At the end of leg, patrol came to ground with hard flat surface — patrol leader thought momentarily that he had reached a small aerodrome. Third leg 127 brought patrol as intended to strong post wire (single dannert) at approx 87143025. Patrol moved over wire in extended order and searched strong post. Two dug positions were found with ammunition pits in rear. No ammunition. No sign of recent occupation, broken sandbags, fallen sandbags and general rubbish. Patrol commander suggests that positions might be occupied by day by very careless and untidy troops. 50/100 yds between dug positions and first line of dannert. Area thoroughly investigated. Unusual system of wiring with 3 separate single dannert fences surrounding strong post on northern and eastern sides and yet apparently open to the south. No mines seen although commander picked up pins from mines near outer fence — believes that it was formerly mined. After completing investigation, patrol moved back to our lines without incident. This patrol, the deepest yet sent out by any unit in this sector had established that the enemy do NOT at least occupy by night the positions investigated.

(c) The same night (13/14 August) another patrol from C Coy went out at 2100 hrs and returned at 0330 hrs. This was led by Lt E O Norton and with him were 1 NCO and 10 Ors. The route out was from 87432998 due west for 5478 yds, returned due east to start point. At approx 3200 yds patrol commander without having struck enemy's wire, heard distant sounds of working activity in his general line of march. Therefore continued due west with the object of finding it. At 4090 yds he was fired on by a Spandau on a bearing of 320 — the burst flying high. At 4311 yds patrol passed trip wire and subsequently within the next 600 yds two more trip wires were encountered. A breast high wire on long pickets was struck at 5478 yds (map ref approx 86932995). The scout did not see this wire and hit it — a warning rattle was given by tins suspended on it. Patrol was immediately challenged at a distance of 70—100 yds. The language was uncertain but the sentry subsequently said "Ullo — Ullo". The direction of the challenge could not be immediately determined and the patrol went to ground. There was no sign of the sentry who was apparently in a trench. Patrol commander waited some minutes and moving forward again 30 to 50 yds was again challenged. He gave the order to charge and was immediately met by heavy sub-machine gun and rifle fire from trenches. Patrol replied with grenades, 3 Thompson sub-machine guns and rifles. The engagement lasted approx 2 minutes. The enemy's fire remained intense all coming from a trench system but there was some slight enemy movement above ground and at this time one man screamed as though hit. Patrol commander decided to withdraw to east and as he did so came under mortar fire and subsequently, fire from a single Spandau but completed withdrawal without casualty. Before the mortar came down the enemy fired a series of red tracers. Patrol then returned to our lines without further incident. The patrol penetrated further west than has up to this time been done in this sector and there is reason to believe that at least one casualty was caused to the enemy.

(Note by Arthur Newton: A resume of this patrol and two others the following night are contained in the Official History in which Lt Norton is referred to as a "particularly accurate and reliable officer." "Wimpy" as he was affectionately known to many in the Bn had joined us in Tobruk. For some reason, possibly a slightly swashbuckling air, he did not immediately please the CO, John Crawford. However, he soon became a very worthy member of the unit as the above patrol report indicates. Like so many of our comrades he was killed in action with the Bn at Finschhafen on 25 Sept 1943).

(d) On night 14/15 Aug a patrol from A Coy of 1 Offr, 1 NCO and 10 Ors went out at 2100 hrs and returned at 0530 hrs. The route out was from 87433002 on 310 on line of track parallel to railway line for 6000 yds then on 225 for 1400 yds and then 118 for 6300 yds to start point. The Comd, was Lt J K Thompson, whilst the NCO was Cpl S C H Monaghan. The first leg to 87083037 was completed without incident — details given in yesterday's patrol report concerning first 5000 yds were confirmed. There was the customary enemy working party on north side of railway line. Well used track at 87173018 was crossed and during the last 1000 yds of the leg sound of chopping could be heard on the north side of line. Just north-west of ring contour feature at 87173028 on which there is an oil barrel and which is believed to be an enemy OP, a narrow but well worn motor track was found running generally north-west of this point but subsequently swinging almost due south and was crossed during the third leg. After 1570 yds on third leg, the wide motor track was crossed at approx 87123020 and at 870 yds further on at approx 87203017 — after passing through a DA and single dannert fence, patrol found itself inside a strong post. On quick investiga-tion the post appeared to be most extensive having at least one position designed as a pill box and with a series of connecting trenches. Patrol was NOT challenged and patrol leader was in the course of investigating the pill box when a large body of enemy, probably not less than 50 approached from the south and west. They apparently did not see our patrol and were completely surprised when the patrol opened up on them with 5 Thompson sub-machine guns and rifles at 20 yds range, the signal being grenades thrown by the Offr and NCO. The enemy did not return fire but as one party of them began to outflank our patrol, the patrol commander withdrew north to the railway line passing through the post wire in doing so. There was still no reply from the enemy who must have been completely surprised. Flares were sent up but by this time our patrol had made good its withdrawal. At least one of the enemy is believed killed by our grenades and further casualties are expected but unknown. Patrol leader, who was himself hit by a grenade splinter, believes that the area in which the engagement took place was at least a platoon and possibly a coy area. This fighting patrol which was the deepest yet sent out by this unit (and perhaps the Bde) in the Western Desert has apart from successfully engaging the enemy established the existence of a strongly held locality around Pt 87203017.

(Note by Arthur Newton: Several interesting aspects are revealed in reference to this patrol report. Though not mentioned in the report above, in the Official History, it is stated that Lt John Thompson was stunned and that Cpl Monaghan coolly and skilfully extricated the patrol.

From the patrol by A Coy the position they had reached and investigated was named Thompson's Post — "A destination that was not apt to describe a defended area of considerable extent.)

(e) The same night 14/15 Aug D Coy had a patrol of 1 Offr, 1 NCO and 10 Ors out from 2100 hrs to 0300 hrs. Route out 87432998 on 280 for 3300 yds thence generally south for 800 yds then due west 100 yds return to start point generally east for 3500 yds. Patrol struck triple dannert wire at approx 87133004 and moved generally south with the right flank maintaining contact with the wire. This contact was maintained for 800 yds and the wire took a sharp due west turn for about 100 yds and then continued running generally south east. It was apparent that a gap along the 871 Grid Line between approx 87083002 and 87132998 had been closed during the past 24 hrs, probably as a result of Lt Norton's successful penetration of the gap and engagement of the enemy at 86932995. Considerable enemy working activity, compressors, sounds of picks and shovels could be heard well in the rear of the wire. At one point where our patrol went to ground adjacent to the wire, enemy patrol of 6 men were seen to move and go to ground again several hundred yards inside their wire and too far away to engage by fire. Moving south along wire patrol noted three enemy positions which had the appearance of squat rock and concrete pill boxes well camouflaged with bushes about 25 yds in rear of the dannert fence. Enemy MT could be heard continuously about 1000 yds away. The patrol has established a closure of the gap — a continuance of working activity and the existence of certain pill box-like positions, exact location of which will be determined by further recce.

(f) The Carrier Pl was not idle. At 1520 hrs on the afternoon of 14 Aug, 4 carriers went out on patrol and returned at 1810 hrs. The route was 87592989 — gap in the minefields in B Coy to western Pt 24 by carrier, thence to 87173002 on foot — 1 Offr, 1 Sgt, 1 Cpl. Returned by same route. Enemy position located at ring contour feature 87133009. Position wired. The wire was easily picked up by small triangular pieces of shiny tin. The wire was picked up coming over the ridge at 87353024 running south-west to the railway line. The wire was lost at this point and again picked up at 87173015 running south-east approx 600 yds then turning due west. Patrol then endeavoured to pick up the wire south of this area but was unable to locate any sign of wire. In this wire enclosure were 5 stationary vehicles and a small number of men were seen moving about. There was considerable MT movement both north-south and south-north and the main supply route seemed to be Sidi Abd el Rahman — south to 25 contour line and following that line around escarpment past Trig 29 at 86833008. There was also a slight MT movement in square 871302 and square 869298. Patrol on returning from OP located small minefield running east-west approx 50 yds in length and 4 rows in depth of EP Mk II mines all primed and well concealed in area 87183002. Foot patrol returned to carriers and returned to start point without incident. This report was signed by Capt Les Maclarn as Carrier Offr but whether he led the patrol is not clear.

August 15: The effective strength — 36 Offrs and 737 Ors. 39 "X list men arrive on draft. 1000 hrs: A British Pte was found wandering about some diggings near our HQ apparently suffering from loss of memory. He was taken to Bde HQ for handing over to Fd Security Sec. 1150 hrs: Maj Magno and Lt Wright report in from LOB. 1520 hrs Bde Comd visited forward coys. 1630 hrs: Majors Green and Ralph call to examine some of the 6 unexploded 25-pdr shells which have fallen in this area lately.

August 16: A quiet night regarding patrols. Deep patrols continue the good work of recce along enemy wire and FDLs. Carrier Pl established an OP at 87243002 to remain during daylight each day. Considerable enemy movement seen along his FDLs and several arty shoots were directed from the OP. Enemy shelling on our forward coys was light (12 shells — this is unusual for our sector. 1150 hrs GOC 9 Div and the Bde Comd inspect D Coy area. 1345 hrs Pilot Offr Buchanan RAF and Maj Hodgman G2 learner spend the afternoon and inspect our forward area.

August 17: Lts Ross, Male, Coulton and Murphy march out to the Training Bn. A patrol from B Coy consisting of 1 Offr, 1 NCO and 10 Ors — while reconnoitring DA type wire around an empty post some 4000 yds forward were challenged and a grenade thrown at them causing 3 slight casualties. Our patrol with 2 Brens and 4 TSMGs engaged the enemy through the wire and reported at least 2 enemy hits. Other patrols reported no movement seen. Carrier OP at west Pt 24 took ranges with rangefinder to various enemy posts. A quiet day — enemy shelling nil — our arty continue harassing enemy positions. Visitors — 8 Army Comd, Lt Gen Montgomery, GOC AIF ME, GSO I and Bde Comd inspect the Bn area. (Interesting to note that Monty had only arrived in Cairo from England on 12 Aug.)

August 18: A patrol from C Coy observed an enemy patrol and gave chase but lost sight of them in the darkness. Patrol continued towards enemy FDLs and eventually were challenged from an enemy post. Patrol leader threw a grenade at an MG and saw a man fall over the gun. Our patrol withdrew under heavy small arms fire without casualty. After a 10-day lull of practically no shelling D Coy and A Coy shared 68 shells for the day. Visitors — 3 Offrs, 3 Sgts from 1st and 5th Black Watch and 2nd Seaforth Highlanders arrive to stay a few days with forward coys to study our methods in desert warfare.

(Strangely there was no mention in our War Diary entry nor in the patrol report referred to above of the patrol clash which occurred on the night of 17/18 Aug 1942. However in 20 Bde War Diary is a letter from our Bn which refers to the matter. It reads as follows:

HQ 2/17 Bn
20/5/1632

REPORT ON PATROLS 2/17 BATTALION NIGHT 17/8/42

20 Aust Inf Bde:

2 patrols of this unit clashed at 87303000 at about 2220 hrs 17/18 Aug 41. The following casualties occurred:

NX44504   Pte Tink I M   KIA
NX15891   Lt Burgess R V   Wounded
NX17871   Pte Anson R J   Wounded

The facts concerning the incident appear to be as follows:

Two deep patrols were detailed in accordance with instructions contained in this unit's proposed patrol report of 17 Aug 1942.

Capt L C Maclarn together with Lt R V Burgess and a party of 4 Ors set out from D Coy area at 2120 hrs to establish an OP at 87242996. Full precautions appear to have been taken by Capt Maclarn to ensure that the presence of his party and his intention was made known to both patrol commanders concerned before the OP party moved out. The action taken by Lt J W Bray was as stated by him because of his knowledge of the location of Capt Maclarn's party. I do not consider that negligence can be attributed to any person or persons.

N W SIMPSON Lt Col
COMD 2/17 BN.

9TH DIV.
REPORT ON PATROLS — 2/17 AUS INF BN

1. The attd reports are forwarded.
2. It seem that the clash between the patrols was an unfortunate misadventure and that there was no failure to give the usual prior notification of patrols to all persons concerned.
3. Lt Bray's party opened fire without previous challenge in the belief that the other party was definitely enemy.
4. Lt Bray after the incident continued his patrol as ordered and engaged an enemy post later in the night.

SGD: W J V WINDEYER
CMD 20 Aust Inf BDE

Statements by Capt L C Maclarn, Lt Bray, Lt Burgess and Sgt K S Robertson were also attached to the above letters.

Sgt K S Robertson of D Coy with 10 Ors commanded the second deep patrol on the night of 17/18 Aug. His patrol went out from 87432998 at 2030 hrs and came in at 0200 hrs. This patrol located a strong point some 3300 yds out on a bearing of 270. Lt Bray's patrol went out from the same point at the same time but on a bearing of 297 and returned at 0330 hrs. In the brief patrol report of Sgt Robertson is the remark — "extremely dark".

August 19: Our patrols had a quiet night — one patrol from A Coy found that the enemy had put extensive wire in a gap that we were using just south of the railway about 3000 yds from our FDLs — evidently our sharp raids on his posts during the past week have had some effect. The patrol was led by Lt Till with 1 NCO and 10 Ors plus a detachment of Sappers from 2/13 Fld Coy. Other patrols reported — no movement seen. A very quiet day. Our activity has decreased very considerably of late. Enemy shelling was normal except for the fact that a large proportion of shells are 25-pdrs. This is the first indication we have had that he is using these weapons on our front — 2 casualties for the day. Visitors: Bde Comd, Capt Hamer and Capt Evans G3 visited the Bn area during the day.

August 20: Only protective patrols — arty had a night of continuous harassing fire on enemy FDLs. 23 Armd Bde salvaged one Valentine tank on our front during night 19/20 Aug. An early morning shoot by our Mortar Pl using a Italian 81mm mortar silenced the enemy mortar which was firing on 2/15 Bn on our right flank. CO states that salient in our FDLs on left flank is to be strengthened. Recce made today by CO, Bde Maj and Majs Magno and Balfe. C Coy will take up new position. Visitors — Corps Comd, Lt Gen Ramsden, GOC 9 Div and Bde Comd visit coy areas. 2300 hrs: Advice is received from Bde Comd that new C in C, M.E. (Gen Alexander) will pay us a visit tomorrow.

August 21: Bde order. Priority for patrol information to be (1) Enemy minefields, (2) PW and identification One patrol on night 20/21 Aug found and lifted one small enemy minefield at 87283009. This patrol was from B Coy and was led by Lt Jim Dick with 1 Sgt and 8 Ors plus 2 Sappers and an NCO from A Coy. The patrol was out from 2200 hrs until 0430 hrs. Other patrols have little to report. Shelling was light, only 54 shells in the Bn area. 1000 hrs: C in C, M.E. (Gen Alexander) accompanied by staff, GOC AIF ME and the Bde Comd inspected a representative group of Offrs and Ors at Tel el Eisa station. The C in C was very interested in a German 20 mm Flak gun "scrounged" and mounted for action at B Coy HQ. CO made a recce of new C Coy position between Pimple 87592982 and Barrel Hill 87552974. Rest of the day uneventful except for the dropping of propaganda leaflets by the enemy in our lines after dark. These were in great demand as souvenirs.

August 22: As arty conducted harassing fire on enemy FDLs in our sector, patrols were of a protective nature only. RTR salvaged two Valentine tanks from in front of D Coy position during the night. Shelling of our FDLs occurred as usual before 0900 hrs and after 1800 hrs and was a little heavier than usual — 154 shells in all. 0930 hrs: a Sec from C Coy moving out to continue diggings in their proposed new area captured 2 German prisoners at 87592982. Both were from 125 Inf Regt. They said they got lost whilst out on a recce patrol. They were sent to

Bn HQ. (Actually if my memory is correct they came back to Bn HQ literally escorted by the CO, Lt Col Simpson — in fact I'm not sure they did not travel with him in the same jeep. The CO had gone off to see how C Coy's efforts were proceeding. I also think this was one of the rare occasions when the Red Fox displayed a certain amount of self satisfaction as if he had literally "collared" the prisoners personally). C Coy occupied their new positions and move was completed by 2359 hrs. C Coy HQ at 87592974 and a coy front of 2000 yds. This move closes the gap between this Bn and 2/43 Bn who occupy area to north of Trig 22 (87672950). Visitors to this HQ during the day included Bde Comd, Col Falkiner and Lt Col Ogle, 2/15 Bn. 2100 hrs C Coy ration truck blown up on own minefield. Drivers Nicholls and Vick injured.

August 23: Effective strength 28 Offrs and 748 Ors. Bright moonlight is making it increasingly difficult for our patrols to recce inside enemy working areas. There is little to report from our patrols of night 22/23 Aug. The two deep patrols were one from A Coy consisting of Lt J K Thompson, 1 NCO and 8 Ors and the other from D Coy commanded by Sgt McGrath, 1 Cpl and 10 Ors which went out on a bearing of 260 for 2300 yds then to another point where they laid up for some time awaiting an opportunity target but without luck. This patrol went out at 2145 hrs and returned at 0440 hrs.

The CO visited Brig Godfrey, Comd 24 Bde regarding dispositions of 2/43 Bn, our left neighbour. Agreement reached whereby the right elements of 2/43 Bn would be adjusted to close the gap between C Coy 2/43 Bn and left Pl of C Coy 2/17 Bn and Barrel Hill. Bde Comd had made it clear to 9 Aust Div that 2/17 Bn could not move further left than its present position on Barrel Hill. Shelling for the day was normal — 132 shells.

August 24: Our patrols on night 23/24 Aug were confined to only one deep besides usual protective. This was a special patrol requested by its 2 members Sgt I V West and Pte R Jamieson who at an S.R. school had learnt silent night assassination of enemy maybe coming out to urinate. The C O had required a preliminary daylight recce with Capt Broadbent to report on plausability. Restricted hours of darkness reduced their chances. They went out at 0100 hrs and returned at 0600 hrs. First to gap at 87572990 then to small enemy OP which had been discovered by daylight recce at 87262994. Laid up to watch and at 0313 hrs moved forward. When they reached 87172991 series of bright flares forced them to move right and enemy wire was reached at approx 87152997. Patrol crossed wire and about 10 yds inside found an Italian cotton reel booby trap, one cord attached to wires and one to each side at 90 angles — laterals anchored to bushes — cords about 10 yds long and about 8 yds between the anchors and the cords. While waiting in hope a careful search within a radius of 50 yds was made and other booby traps were found. With coming daylight the patrol withdrew to our lines.

Enemy aircraft seem to be unusually active especially recce planes. Shelling was fairly heavy especially before 0830 hrs when D Coy was pasted by some 168 shells mostly 25-pdrs. Day's total was 254 shells. 1950 hrs: A message was received from 9 Div to the effect that 8 Army expected the enemy to attack. All units to be prepared. The attack never developed.

August 25: Effective strength 28 Offrs and 750 Ors. 10 Engrs from 2/13 Fd Coy with protective patrol of 1 Offr, 1 NCO and 10 Ors of this Bn search area west of C Coy for 7 hours during darkness clearing scattered mines in preparation for 2/15 Bn "Bulimba' operation. Altogether 112 British MK V and 23 Teller mines were lifted and stacked in weapon pit. A quiet day. Light shelling in the area, there being only 67 shells reported. Enemy air activity was on a reduced scale.

August 26: Arty harassing fire on our front curtailed our patrol activities to protective duties only. Shelling during the day was normal. C Coy received most attention. Day's total — 203 shells with one casualty. Movement on enemy FDLs very slight otherwise nothing to report.

August 27: Again no deep patrols. 2/15 Bn operated on our front making recce before Bulimba. All quiet — no movement seen. Shelling was of a harassing nature — enemy has been using mobile troops (arty) which came close in, then changed position rapidly. Shells land almost as soon as reports are heard. One casualty in A Coy. The Bde Comd visited the area during the day and we also had a visit from Mr William Munday, an Aust War Correspondent. 2 Vickers MGs are delivered to the Bn for the newly formed MG Pl.

August 28: Both deep patrols on night of 27/28 Aug took up vantage positions and lay up hoping to ambush enemy patrols which have been operating to a small extent on our front but without success. No movement seen or heard. (Both patrols consisted of 1 Offr, 1 NCO and 6 Ors and were from A and D Coys — they moved out at 0030 hrs and returned at 0530 hrs. The A Coy patrol was led by Lt A P Craik, the D Coy patrol by Lt H Main.) A quiet day. Our arty caused the enemy to hastily withdraw two troops of guns brought well forward to harass our FDLs. At 2330 hrs one of our planes was shot down by AA in enemy lines and crashed in flames. Only 23 shells from enemy guns in our area and 4 premature bursts from our own arty. 3 British, 4 Indian Offrs with 3 NCOs of Punjabi Regt march in and are attached for desert experience and exchange of ideas.

August 1942 was an important month in the Western Desert. First, there had been changes in Command. Churchill, dissatisfied with Gen Auchinlech's apparent slowness in mounting an offensive operation, had replaced him with Gen Alexander as CIC, Middle East. Lt Gen "Strafer" Gott, an old Desert hand, had been selected to command 8th Army but on 7 Aug when flying to Cairo his plane was shot down and he was killed. As a result General Montgomery was hastily summoned from England arriving in Cairo on August 11 as Gott's replacement. General Montgomery was quick in imposing his methods and personality on 8 Army and in the words of Barton Maughan, the Historian: "giving it revived hope, a better tone and new confidence." It is appropriate to consider the opinion of the officers of those days as some historians have belittled Monty's efforts. Gen Morshead told Brig Windeyer – "This man (Monty) is really a breath of fresh air." Capt Geoffrey Keating of the Army Film and Photographic Unit, and who had served in Norway, France, Dunkirk, France again, the desert, Tobruk, Greece, Crete, Syria, Iraq, Persia and in the retreat to Alamein stated: "Monty knew all the rules of the conduct of war and the fighting of battles, I had personally experienced endless defeats, I'd been wounded 5 times; and here I was sure that this was the man who had victory, and you ask me to explain why I was sure — it was something he exuded, it was professionalism."

An IO of HQ 8 Army, Maj "Bill" Williams (later Brig Sir Edward T. Williams) almost 40 years later stated of Monty's first address to his staff: "I think the interesting thing was the astonishing removal of dubiety, the feeling that, well, thank God this chap has got a grip. He talks the most astonishing sort of stuff, but he has the meat of the gospel as it were — there was very much a feeling of — well, we'll give it a go."

At this time, 9 Div was a mature battle and desert-experienced, well-trained infantry division of high morale. Its commanders through all levels were proficient, established and respected. Discipline had already become team work and orders were awaited as the arrangements for a job to be done. The disappointment at being left behind had merged in the realisation that the Division was there to represent Australia and help the Empire finish the Middle East task. Montgomery's call for aggressive eagerness came to listening ears, and with his plans, came the sense of purpose which was welcomed, even exhilarating.

9 Div did not need his orders for it to stand and fight, to know there would be no withdrawal. From its rebuff of the first German attack at Tobruk, such an operation played no part in the service of 2/17 Bn. Now, a more positive role was to emerge.

Monty's first test was the Battle of Alam el Halfa. In this he was successful and on 5 Sept, he issued his own special message to his troops. "The battle has now lasted 6 days and the enemy has slowly but surely been driven from 8 Army Area. Tonight, 5 Sept, his rearguards are being driven west, through the mine field area north of Himeimat. All formations and units, both armoured and unarmoured, have contributed towards this striking victory and have been magnificently supported by the RAF. I congratulate all ranks of 8 Army on the devotion to duty and good fighting qualities which have resulted in such a heavy defeat of the enemy and which have far reaching results." In his memoirs Rommel in referring to this battle stated: "There is no doubt that the British commander's handling of this action had been absolutely right and well suited to the occasion, for it had enabled him to inflict very heavy damage on us in relation to his own losses and to retain the striking power of his own force."

August 29: Effective strength 27 Offrs and 761 Ors. Deep patrols were mainly of a recce nature but strong enough to deal with any enemy patrols which might be encountered. The front was very quiet and patrols reported no movement seen. Our arty put down a regimental concentration on enemy positions between 1530 and 1545 hrs. Enemy shelling normal — 156 shells causing 1 casualty. On the night 28/29 Aug, Lt Bennie and 1 NCO and 6 Ors of B Coy plus 1 Offr and 1 Cpl of the Punjabis were out on patrol from 2100 hrs to 0210 hrs. They travelled 3200 yds on a bearing of 285 then due south for 500 yds then back on a bearing of 98 to the start point. They reported finding 3 British mines, hearing digging behind enemy FDLs — saw what appeared to be a British aircraft brought down in flames about square 872304. A four-way power cable drum was found and sent to 20 Bde. Sgt C. Cutler with 4 Ors plus 4 Engrs went out at 2345 hrs and returned at 0445 hrs. The route was on a bearing of 285 to 87402985 then due west 1100 yds, due south 500 yds, then due east 2700 yds back to the start point. Same route as followed by mine lifting patrol of night 24/25 but no mines seen. Sappers failed to located their previous small mine dump. An old Sidi Barrani map was found in Italian trenches. This was forwarded to 20 Bde. No movement seen.

August 30: An artillery HF (harassing fire) night — no deep patrols — a recce patrol of 2 Offrs and 2 Ors went out before first light to vicinity Pt 17 (87233002). Returned at 0900 hrs and gained much valuable information. Lts Dal Cartledge and Ray Rudkin were the Offrs but the names of the 2 Ors (one a photographer, the other a field sketcher) are not shown. The route out was from 87483002 — 285 for 1800 yds then due north for 200 yds. Returned via railway line at 87433007 to start point. They went out at 0500 hrs and returned at 0900 hrs. The object was a general daylight recce of enemy positions — photographing of enemy positions and a panorama sketch. The report stated visibility was excellent about 1 hour after first light and enemy posts, wire and personnel were clearly seen. Considerable progress has been made with wiring on the side sector observed (from Trig 33 area to Pt 87353025) thence south-west to ring feature at 87133010. Along the ridge is a maze of single and triple dannert and another type of fence on long pickets probably apron. These fences stretch from a skylined dannert continuous along the ridge from 87453020 to 87303025 down the southern slopes of the ridge across the flat towards the railway line in a weaving pattern. Areas, probably mine fields, clearly without diggings are completely wired in. Dannert wire running parallel from the ridge was seen as far back as approx 87263030. There appears to be a wired strong post at 87273025. We could not see wire crossing railway line or adjacent to it on the northern side. From the railway line to approx 87303016 to ring feature point 87133010 dannert wire was seen to be continuous not straight but could not judge its shape accurately. Appeared to run at right angles to railway track for approx 1000 yds — turn at right angles again — distance difficult to estimate. Behind this primary dannert ground open plain for 2000 yds and appears to rise very gradually. Immediately behind primary dannert appears circular post wiring at approx 87203016 and 87123019. Several further rows of wire in middle distance at right angles to our line of sight. (One row picked up by apparently shining tin triangles suspended on it.) Building adjacent to railway line at approx 87133033 flying flag from north-east corner. 2 vehicles parked on northside — one driven away at 0750 hrs over the ridge. At 0805 hrs 2 heavy trucks drove up very slowly in rear of wire in square 870302 and drivers dismounted.

Personnel — Shortly after first light movement of enemy personnel seen. In no section post were more than 5 men visible. Mostly 1 or 2 men only. Dressed in greatcoats — surprising in view of climate.

Habits — At first light enemy tested its weapons. Registered with 81 mm mortars on dummy OP pole at 87333005. He opened with a tp of 25-pdrs, his first shot almost falling on our panorama sec at 87383007.

At 0120 hrs Pte Augus Evans of the 1st Bn Sherwood Foresters was picked up by one of our sentries on the minefield. He had escaped from Tobruk and had taken 2 months to get back to our lines. The Report on his interrogation is as follows:

30 August 1942

Time 0330 hrs.

1. This soldier was found by 2 sentries of A Coy at 87443000 at 0120 hrs this morning and duly escorted to Bn HQ. He was questioned by us and the following is a summary of his statement.

    "I escaped from Tobruk on the day the fortress fell along with 12 other members of my regiment. My Sgt Major had informed us that the fortress had capitulated and we were told it was a case of every man for himself. I was MT driver on HQ Coy attached to C Coy and at the time the town fell I was at rear B Echelon. Our party made its way out of the perimeter via deep wadies and hills along Bardia Road. We moved on foot veering inland and by the time we reached Sollum there were only myself and my mate left. We were pursued by a party of enemy and whilst hiding in adjoining holes my mate was taken. I continued on following generally the line of the road but south of it as most enemy traffic was moving along or dispersed north of the road. I did not see great numbers of the enemy. I lived by stealing scraps of food and by searching old dugouts — sometimes I found water in tins. I noted that on the Sollum pass the enemy was working hard using concrete mixers and building posts. Nobody took any notice of me although on one occasion I went by mistake into a German camp but as I had an Italian water bottle and made a movement with my hands that I had seen Italians make they did not stop me. At various places I met Arabs who treated me well. I talked to them in "pidgin" Arabic and English. They gave me food. They said they liked the Germans and the British but *not* the Italians. I knew Matruh had fallen and skirted it keeping south of the railway line. I struck no fixed line of defences until the last place I stopped, which is where I came from tonight. About a fortnight ago I reached this place and found some old diggings in which I slept. There was some stale Italian bread in the diggings and a drum with some rusty water in it. I did not know in what direction our lines were or how far until the area near me was shelled. I then realised I was pretty close. I tried several times to move along south of the railway line but each time I was stopped by the wire and large enemy working parties who were laying mines — black boxes with sig wire attached about the size of a 12 volt battery. I stayed in my dugout most of the time and the area was shelled frequently. I think that the shells were falling about 400 yds short of a place where the enemy were. I kept trying to move on but each time the enemy got in my way. Tonight I tried again and passed through the enemy's wire and after walking for some distance, I saw your wire near a big gun. I was not certain they were British lines and I came on cautiously when the clouds were covering the moon. I heard voices directing a vehicle and, as the men were swearing I knew they were Australians. The moon gave me away and two sentries challenged me. I could not speak and they took me."

2. Pte Evans was obviously tired, unshaven and his face was swollen but he answered the questions clearly and intelligently although he was still under great strain. We fed him before interrogation and he was duly sent under escort to 20 Bde.

When Pte Evans spoke of the barrel hills that he used as landmarks on his last leg he was referring to ring feature at approx 87183028 and Pt 17 87233003. The former was referred to as enemy barrel and the latter as "your barrel hill". Analysing his statement relative to 14 days which he spent just behind enemy FDLs we are of the opinion that he was living in deserted diggings at approx 87143025 investigated some time ago by a patrol of this unit. He spoke of diggings being dilapidated, disused and that sandbags in some cases had been taken away from the pits. The working parties laying mines (probably Teller from the description of booby trap wires) were apparently working in the gap between strong post at 87203017 and railway line. Pte Evans also spoke of 2 roads near but west of the wide road at 87183028 being used more frequently than the wide road. This accords generally with information brought back by our patrols.

(SIGNED) D J CARTLEDGE LT
INT OFFICER

When Pte Evans reached HQ 20 Bde he retold his story and on this occasion Lt Col Bob Ogle — CO 2/15th Bn — and a Maj A E McIntyre of 9 Div Cav Regt. were present as these officers were to take active parts in 9 Div's diversionary attack — Operation Bulimba. Evans had spent 2 weeks in the vicinity of west Pt 23 where Bulimba would take place.

August 31: No deep patrols by the Bn. 2/15 Bn to do some recce for Bulimba raid which comes off on night 31 Aug/1 Sept. Shelling which started at 2330 hrs 30 Aug continued till 0520 hrs. The attack which we expected turned out to be merely a diversion mainly on the 2/13 Bn front.

The Intelligence Report to 0500 hrs 31 Aug contains more details:— 2343 hrs (30 Aug). Report from A and D Coys that mortar and SAA fire was falling in their areas (A Coy "cutting", D Coy on their left on 24 feature). Shelling had started and was becoming heavier.

0122 hrs — A Coy patrol reported a jeep type car came in close to A Coy and then moved towards west Pt 24.

0147 hrs — D Coy 2/43 Bn reported having seen enemy in extended line on their front and on our left flank.

0210 hrs — MG and mortar reported to be firing from near big gun 87402995 — was engaged by our mortars and enemy party ceased fire.

0215 hrs — 2 tks were reported on A Coy's front south of main road but by 0340 hrs a patrol reported no signs of any tanks on our front.

0250 hrs — Men reported to be in vicinity of Pimple 8758529813. Patrol failed to locate but at first light about 20 freshly scratched slit trenches were found 250 yds west of the Pimple.

0455 hrs — A machine gun was firing from Sandy Knoll 8743829770 — engaged and silenced by our mortars.

0588 hrs — A Coy protective patrol which had been out since 0200 hrs reported NMS 1400 yds from our FDLs west of A and D Coys.

Shelling — 6 Shells had fallen in A Coy up to 1900 hrs. 26 shells in D Coy. Our FDLs were shelled from 2320 hrs till 0515 hrs with a slight lull from 0400 hrs to 0430 hrs. Rough estimates of extent of shelling:

A Coy	1000 – 1500 shells	B Coy	500
C Coy	500 – 1000	D Coy	500 – 1000
Bn HQ	100 with a radius of 500 yds.		

Large percentage 75mm some 25-pdr and some larger calibre. D Coy reported large dud probably 150mm near their HQ. From 0430—0442 hrs 26 enemy heavily mortared area in front of FDLs in square 873299. (End of Int. Report).

Personnel of Punjabi Regt — Royal Sussex — leave our area. Bde Comd visited our CO. Our mortar detachments which take part in Bulimba prepare for the raid which will take place at daylight on 1 Sept. Our C Coy is also assisting with the passing of POWs to the collecting point near our Bn HQ. Enemy aircraft very active and several dog fights took place during the day with varied results.

(Note by Arthur Newton: Before we finish with Aug 1942 — Rommel on 30 Aug announced to his troops: "Today our Army sets out once more to attack and destroy the enemy, this time for keeps. I expect every soldier in my army to do his utmost in these decisive days." Rommel's main force moved east on night of 30/31 Aug to the south of Alam Nayil but became tied down in British mine fields. At 0240 on 31 Aug the first of British air bombing occurred and the scene was lit up by parachute flares. The activity on the 2/17 Bn front or rather the 20 Bde front as 2/13 Bn was also involved, was in the nature of a raid with the aim of capturing prisoners. In fact there were several diversionary attacks this night (30/31 Aug) from the coast to Ruweisat Ridge.

HQ 20 Bde diary of 31 Aug states: "The enemy was successfully repulsed by 0100 hrs and some prisoners captured. At 0435 hrs it appeared as if another attack would develop to the south-west of Trig 33. This was prevented by our arty fire." This night was thus the beginning of the Battle of Alam el Halfa. I remember this night as I was Adjutant and it was really Lt Col Noel Simpson's first test as Comd Offr. He spend most of the night pacing up and down near the Command Post receiving coy reports as they came in — he appeared quite calm.

In the late 1950's I discussed this particular period with Gen H Wells who in 1942 was Colonel Wells GSO 1, 9 Div. He stated that at Div HQ the staff were impressed by the fact that 2/17 Bn was the only forward Aust Bn which had not called down defensive arty fire and considered this a tribute to the CO. This no doubt enhanced their opinion of the Red Fox but I do believe the forward Coy Comds, Mac Alison, Claude Brien, John Broadbent and Ian McMaster do deserve credit as my recollections are that they felt they were quite capable of dealing with the situations and besides they had patrols operating which if defensive fire had been called down may have suffered casualties.)

Capt John (Slam) Sullivan's medical report for August stated that gastro-intestinal complaints were most prevalent and that when we took over the FDLs around Tel el Eisa station and the "cutting", the area had not been cleared since the battle. Many unburied dead outside the wire and flies present in swarms. Vigorous measures taken and numbers of flies lessened. Deep trench latrines were dug and flyproof superstructures were made. Fly traps were made by

Above: *German flags captured.* **Below left:** *German tank destroyed.* **Below right:** *Few fellows in Section post*

unit pioneers. Sodium arsenate was supplied as fly poison at end of month. Total battle casualties were 1 killed in action, 23 wounded of whom 19 were evacuated and 4 remained on duty — evacuations because of illness were 110.

Capt Peter O'Brien, the QM, reported that in Aug the Coy Q trucks went forward each night with rations and water and right throughout the month not one hitch occurred. Restrictions on water were removed and unlimited supplies were available. Two more 2-pounder a/tk guns were received, the total now 5. Enemy-type weapons held were — Breda LMG 12 (7 for A/Tk Pl) Breda MMG 2, Breda DP 27mm 1, a/tk 47mm 1, Browning LMG 1, Spandau 4, Fiat MMG 3, Mortar 81mm 1. In addition a number of weapons were salvaged and made serviceable including 5 Brens. Weapon and vehicle spares were in short supply so maintenance was difficult. Wear and tear on clothing was heavy and, as no new stocks were being received, position at end of August was acute. Rations were of high standard. About 10 days reserves were held and all Sec Posts held at least 3 days' reserves at the posts. End of QM Report. Routine Orders for August contained some interesting items, eg. hospital patients were still arriving without steel helmets and respirators, indiscriminate firing of weapons must cease, jerricans were NOT for water, may be used for petrol but restricted to 3 per lorry, 2 for Lt vehs and cars. 745 pkts of tobacco papers, razor blades and cakes of soap were received from the Aust Comforts Fund and issued to all. Later the ban on indiscriminate firing was lifted and troops were encouraged to practice in fwd areas. One of our soldiers was sentenced to 60 days field punishment and forfeiture of 60 days pay for being AWL in Syria in June.

On 29 Aug a concert party "Between Ourselves" consisting of 3 men and 2 girls arrived in Bde area about 1100 hrs and 3 concerts were held at 1200 hrs, 1500 hrs and 1700 hrs. During the midday session 4 enemy shells landed in the area bracketing the party. The least disturbed was the girl singing. The visit of this concert party was the result of a directive by Gen Montgomery which stated that front line troops were to have what amenities were available and that concert parties with girls should visit the forward areas. George Holtsbaum, who was Bde Amenities Officer, travelled from Alexandria with the party and was embarrassed at first when the girls in the party seemed interested in troops bathing in the sea when the road passed close to the shoreline. The original intention was that the party perform in the Bn area but Brig Windeyer would not permit this and 2/17 Bn sent parties from each coy back to the Bde area to attend the concerts.

September 1: Effective strength 31 Offrs and 778 Ors. A quiet patrolling night with no ambitious deep patrols. Shelling was back to normal and evenly distributed over all coy areas — days total 222 which was a respite after the intense harassing fire of 31 Aug. 2/15 Bn attack on enemy FDLs west of C Coy area took place at first light. The Bn passed through our C Coy area at approx 0430 hrs. 2/13 Fd Coy had cleared several gaps in the mine field forward of B and C Coys for the passage of all A Echelon vehicles and those of supporting arms. By 0915 hrs the raid was complete and all arms had returned to our FDLs. 2 bombing raids by ME 109s at 1130 and 1340 hrs behind C Coy positions — evidently retaliation for 2/15 Bn raid. No casualties in C Coy area. 3 requests were made to the CO during the day.

1. Maj Copeland — 2/3 A/Tk Regt requested Lt S Williams liaise with him re changes in a/tk defence in our area.

2. Capt Robinson of 40 RTR wishes to salvage a tank forward of C Coy's FDLs and asks for a protective party from C Coy — Maj Alison will send patrol as requested.

3. Maj Dawson — 2/2 MG Bn requests that he be given permission to salvage a W/T set and MG ammunition about 1200 yds forward of D Coy. All requests were granted. Lt Watson of 2/13 Fd Coy will check mine field on B and C Coy's FDLs on 2 Sept to make sure that everything is secure after 2/15 Bn's raid.

(Note by Phil Pike: The raid referred to was, of course, the action known as "Bulimba" in which 2/15 Bn commanded by Lt Col Bob Ogle played the main role.

This action was planned as a diversionary attack following the appreciation by Auchinleck and Montgomery that Rommel would mount a major attack in the southern sector of the main defensive line. The British staff expected that the offensive would be launched in the moonlight period between 25 Aug and 1 Sept. It was planned that a counter-stroke would be mounted against the enemy's vulnerable supply routes in the North as soon as his attack commenced.

The battle of Alam el Halfa commenced early in the night of 30/31 Aug and the costly but successful defence by the British forces was later described by a German writer as "the turning point of the desert war".

The task of 2/15 Bn was to make a breach in the enemy lines to enable a mobile exploiting force to pass through and harass the enemy supply routes to the main battle area.

Zero hour for "Bulimba" was fixed at 0535 hrs on 1 Sept and the Bn passed through our C Coy area at 0430 hrs and moved with two coys forward to a taped startline approx 2000 yds from the enemy FDLs.

The advance from the start line went smoothly and quietly until our arty support fire opened up at Z plus 15. The leading inf reached the enemy mine field before our arty fire lifted then crossed the mine field into the enemy position before they came under the enemy defensive fire.

By 0630 hrs all the attacking inf had reached the enemy's position and Bn HQ had been established. Unfortunately shortly after 0600 hrs Lt Col Bob Ogle was badly wounded when his Bren carrier ran on to a mine. He remained conscious and gave orders to Maj Copeland of 2/3 A/Tk Regt to get the tanks through the mine field as soon as possible and to summon Maj Grace, the Bn 2 i/c.

When Maj Grace arrived at approx 0705 hrs, the situation was uncertain — the left forward coy was not on the objective, casualties were heavy and the supporting tanks had not arrived.

Meantime, the engineers who had accompanied the leading coys had made and marked gaps in the mine fields as planned, despite heavy casualties. Unfortunately the passage of the tanks through the gaps was not very successful. 2 tanks ran onto mines by turning abruptly while in the gap.

By 0740 hrs enemy appeared to be forming up for a counter attack and were engaged by our arty. Maj Grace, was informed by the Bde Comd that our exploiting force must not be committed until the position was stable. By 0845 hrs, Maj Grace, influenced very largely by the reports from one coy of its casualties and by the absence of his Bn mortars (believed lost), and after consultation with Maj Johnston, Arty LO who supported him, decided to break off the engagement.

Orders were given for the withdrawal of the coys in a specified order to commence at 0900 hrs covered by machine guns from 2/2 MG Bn and the support of the 5 remaining tanks.

The behaviour of troops during the withdrawal was very commendable and they came out in an orderly, unhurried manner well under control.

In the operation 140 German prisoners were taken and it was estimated that at least 150 were killed. 2/15 Bn lost 39 killed, 109 wounded and 25 missing.

Valuable lessons in co-operation with other arms, detailed planning, breaching of mine fields and other matters were well absorbed and used to advantage in future operations.

The events of the 1 Sept were closely monitored by our Bn as so many members of 2/15 Bn were known and highly regarded by us all.)

September 2: Effective strength 31 Offrs and 774 Ors. Lts Ross Coulton and Murphy marched in from ITB. Patrols found the enemy's front very quiet and one part of their FDLs had been set with AP mines since our patrols visited the particular area some days previously. Usual enemy harassing fire during the day — 290 shells in all and resulting in one casualty (shell shock). The Valentine tank was salvaged by 40 RTR from forward of C Coy's FDLs during the early hours of the morning. 2030 hrs 2/2 MG Bn salvage party returned to C Coy with 27 MG belts. MT movement both north and south on enemy supply route has been heavy all day.

September 3: Arty programme of harassing fire curtailed our patrolling activity. All standing patrols and listening posts reported NMS. Enemy seen to be adopting nuisance tactics with periodical airbursts. Shelling was heavier with 440 shells which included 12 airbursts. 1255 hrs an ME 109 dropped 2 bombs on our mortar platoon HQ. It is thought that they were intended for the dummy arty position 200 yds south of the mortars. Generally enemy aircraft passing westward over our FDLs on a reduced scale. News of the tank battle of the south is very meagre and information very difficult to obtain.

The Battle of Alam el Halfa was finished by 7 Sept. That is the day Field-Marshal Montgomery officially called off the battle. The New Zealand Div and 132 British Bde on the night of 3/4 Sept attacked to close the gap that Rommel had made in the British defences. This action, code-named "Beresford" was at best only partially successful. The New Zealanders suffered 275 casualties and the raw 132 Brigade, 697. Nigel Hamilton in his biography of Monty states "A debacle ensued". He also wrote that: "No less than 1140 men were killed, wounded or captured on the 36 hours of the operation; without it 8 Army would have finished the battle with fewer than 500 casualties." However, there is no doubt the battle of Alam el Halfa was a British success. As Barton Maughan states in the Official History: "Montgomery's conduct of the Alam el Halfa battle differed from earlier defensive battles in that the Army was kept compact and armoured formations were stationed alongside inf divs with benefit of some support from their guns."

"Alam el Halfa" (wrote Gen Alexander in his despatch) "was the last throw of the German forces in Africa, their last chance of a victory before, as they calculated, our increasing strength would make victory for them impossible. . . To me at the time the great features of the battle were the immediate improvement in the morale of our own troops, and the confidence I felt in Gen Montgomery, who had handled his first battle in the desert with great ability. The valuable part played by the RAF during the battle was a good omen for future air support. I now felt sure that we should be able to defeat the enemy when we were ready to take the offensive."

September 4: A small raiding party from A Coy were unable to penetrate additions to wire at Thompson's Post (87203017) without being detected and therefore withdrew as patrol commander realised that loss of surprise meant a failure of the raid. A small protective patrol from D Coy was fired on by a large enemy party on west Pt 24. A stronger patrol was sent forward but the enemy could not be located. Only light shelling of cutting and east Pt 24 area (176 shells). A very quiet day on our front. We hear some news of the engagement in the south. We appear to have the situation in hand and the enemy's main force is retiring. The Int Summary for 5 Sept stated: "A marked increase in shelling reported from 27 Aug to 3 Sept inclusive — approx 5000 shells falling in Bn area compared with 1212 shells up to that period (3—26 Aug). C Coy since taking up its new position, has been shelled consistently — possibly a repercussion from "Bulimba" whilst the cutting continues to receive the enemy's closest attention. It has also been noticed that the enemy is now using larger calibre guns. Individual shelling for whole period is as follows:

| A Coy | 2085 | B Coy | 659 |
| C Coy | 1061 | D Coy | 2344 |

September 5: 13 reinforcements arrive from ITB. Patrols made no contact but reported that the enemy is constantly working behind his FDLs. Digging and stake driving was heard by all patrols. Daylight recce patrol by Lts Wright, Cartledge and Thompson with view to a raid on enemy posts at 87203017. Patrol got within 700 yards of enemy FDLs before an enemy patrol was sent to intercept them. Our patrol made a hurried but dignified retreat to Pt 17. Scanty news is now coming through from the south and seems to be in our favour. At 0900 and 1200 hrs area was recce-ed by enemy ME109. At least once a day we get attention of this sort. 2 Spigot Mortars are an addition to the Bn fire power. C Coy has been given both weapons. Shelling — light — only 111 shells in cutting area.

September 6: Further recce patrol to post at 87203017 was detected and subjected to heavy SAA fire — no casualties. Other patrols NMS. Day quiet — enemy shelling in D Coy area between 1900 — 2000 hrs caused 3 casualties. Sig Commins killed, Cpl Moncrieff and Pte Donovan wounded. Total for day (304) was heavier than usual.

Our sixth a/tk gun (2-pdr) which arrived yesterday was mechanically unsound and cannot be sited. Arrangements being made for its repair. Enemy MT unusually active in both directions on the Sidi Rahman Supply route. This probably has something to do with the recent engagement in the south.

September 7: One Offr and 10 reinforcements arrived from ITB. Carrier Pl and C Coy patrols made valuable recce in area south of Northing 299 which has been patrolled by 2/13 and 2/15 Bns and B Coy patrol salvaged a Ford V8 truck from an enemy mine field well forward of our FDLs. Enemy arty had an off day and only sent over 15 shells in our area. Our sixth a/tk gun is now in good condition and will be sited in B Coy area during night 7/8 Sept.

September 8: Recce and standing patrols only — nothing of an outstanding nature to report shelling normal — 228 shells in battalion area. Bde have arranged for 2/13 Fd Coy to instruct all sections of the Bn in the handling of all types of mines.

September 9: Patrols report a very quiet night. No shelling except between 1815 and 1835 hrs when 137 shells landed in the cutting and east 24 areas (A and D Coys). During the night 8/9 Sept the enemy salvaged a Crusader tank left near their FDLs after "Bulimba". Maj C K M Magno, our 2 i/c and Maj J W Balfe, have both been appointed Lt Cols and posted to command 2/15 and 2/32 Bns respectively. The Bn is sorry to lose such keen and popular officers.

(Note by Arthur Newton: Charles Keith Massy Magno was born on 6 Sept 1910. He was commissioned in 17 Bn on 3 Aug 1931 and promoted to Capt on 18 July 1938. In the records his promotion to T/Lt Col is dated 9 Sept 1942. He took over as CO 2/15 Bn replacing another ex-2/17 Bn offr, Bob Ogle, who was badly wounded in the "Bulimba" battle. John Walter Balfe was born on 18 July 1912 and commissioned in 45 Bn on 3 April 1934. He was promoted to Capt on 7 Nov 1939. In the records his promotion to T/Lt Col is dated 10 Sept 1942. However, as Adjutant, I recall receiving a message relating to Keith's promotion. Shortly afterwards another call came from

Two new COs Keith Magno and John Balfe

Bde in which the caller referred to John's promotion. I suggested that they meant Keith's promotion but to my great joy I was told both officers were to be promoted. I believe that having two officers promoted to Command from the same unit in the one day could be unique in the 2nd AIF annals. John Balfe became CO of 2/32 Bn replacing Lt Col D A Whitehead who was promoted to Brig and Comd of 26 Bde. Both Keith Magno and John Balfe had great influence on the development of 2/17 Bn which by September 1942 was equal to any battalion in 9 Div. Sadly neither remained in their new postings for very long, Keith was killed in the first few days of the Battle of Alamein whilst John was seriously wounded twice on the night of 30/31 Oct 1942. He later served in Staff appointments until the end of the War.)

Visitors: Lt Col Arthur Noten, ADOS visited the CO during the day and stated that urgently needed shorts and shirts would be available within a few days.

Patrols on the night of 8/9 Sept were from B Coy: 1 Offr; 1 NCO, 10 Ptes, a dismounted patrol from the Carrier Pl of 1 Sgt, 1 NCO and 8 Ors and a C Coy patrol of 1 Offr, 1 NCO and 10 Ors. The latter patrol considered the enemy showed signs of nervousness firing intermittent flares without cause. Otherwise, it was a quiet night.

September 10: Effective strength 33 Offrs, 765 Ors. Enemy working parties continued to be very active behind the FDLs. Our patrols made no contact. A scattered mine field was taken up and blown by a time pencil. Ineffective harassing fire during the day — 244 shells — one slight casualty. 11 drop shorts from our own arty fell in the Tel el Eisa station area. During the midday heat haze a small enemy patrol of 6 men was seen to approach BOB OP (West Pt 24). They were engaged by arty and a patrol was sent out from D Coy. Later 2 men were seen to carry another towards their FDLs. Nothing was seen of the rest of the party.

During the night 9/10 Sept, Lt A. Urquhart led a patrol of 1 NCO and 10 Ors of D Coy on a bearing of 243 for 3200 yards to enemy wire. The time out was 2015 hrs and the time in 0330 hrs. The main body put to ground at 87192985 and recce party went forward 150 yards to the single dannert wire and one "strong arm party" of 3 men including a NCO moved through the wire for approx 30 yards to lay up. Another "strong arm party" of 3 men including patrol comd remained at the gap. It was anticipated that a wire patrol seen on the night 7/8 Sept would pass between the two parties on its beat. (Lt Urquhart on 7/8 Sept had led a patrol of 2 NCOs, 10 Ors and 2 Sappers which had made a detailed recce of the area and studied the activities and routine of the enemy working parties in the area.) This time no working party on the left flank and he found by recce that the working party on the right flank was far in the rear of the tactical wire. 100 to 150 yards on the immediate front could be seen the breast feature reported on the night 7/8 and several times, figures could be seen skylined. German voices were identified in this area. Identification of the working party as Italian was confirmed. Ambush party remained inside the wire for 2 hours from 2250 to 0105 hrs. During this time they had given no indication of their presence and although flares were continuously being sent up from rear posts on both flanks none were fired from Urquhart's Post on the breast feature 87152984. At 0105 hrs gap in wire was closed and patrol returned towards mine dump in vicinity 87222986. Mines were found already laid — British MK V — scattered without pattern or marking. Appeared to run generally north and south. A few mines were gathered together and the time pencil and explosives inserted. These mines will explode at approx 0700 hrs today. Patrol returned to our lines without incident.

Barton Maughan refers to patrols of this nature in his History, stating of this period: "The 2/17th, who had been longer in the line also maintained their policy of rigorous patrolling, which was carried out in greater depth. Capt Hamer of 20 Bde HQ made a brilliant analysis of the reports of the two Bns (2/13 and 2/17) and information derived from air photographs and built up a composite picture of the order-of-battle and defensive lay-out in front of the Bde which was later published in the Int Summaries of the higher formations."

On 10 Sept Capt E M (Tim) McCulloch at his own request returned from HQ 9 Div where he was T/Maj. He became OC A/Tk Pl, Maj A M Alison became 2 i/c and Capt John Dinning OC C Coy.

September 11: Our patrols swept a wide area to enemy FDLs without finding anything unusual. Enemy arty unusually quiet — 41 shells including 12 airbursts was the day's total. Enemy aircraft was active during the day. Recce planes flew over arty positions to our rear before and after 12 Stukas with fighter escort had bombed their positions. 1 truck set on fire and 2 casualties to arty personnel was the result. 2 patrols were out on night 10/11th. Sgt A. Roberts led a patrol of 1 NCO and 10 Ors from B Coy and were out from 2015 hrs until 0250 hrs but no incidents occurred. Lt Norton led a patrol of similar strength from C Coy and were out from 2030 to 0245 hrs but NMS.

September 12: 3 deep patrols out but enemy FDLs very quiet. These were from B Coy led by Lt A. Wright, out from 2000 hrs to 0230 hrs. D Coy led by Sgt K. Robertson out from 2030 to 0200 hrs and the Carrier Pl (dismounted) led by Sgt Bruce Culey. This patrol was out from 1945 hrs to 0230 hrs and hoped to ambush any enemy patrols moving to our lines but no sight or sound of enemy. Shelling was heavier with a total of 305 shells during daylight hours. An enemy daylight patrol advanced to within 900 yards of BOB OP (West Pt 24) 2400 yards from our FDLs. This, the second time this week that enemy parties have moved in daylight from their FDLs. It is usual for our troops to move around in small groups at will forward of the FDLs but the enemy has not made this daylight recce before.

The HQ 20 Bde diary of 12 Sept contained the statement that Brig Windeyer was evacuated at 1400 hrs to 7 AGH with jaundice. It was not until 27 Oct that he resumed command, during a crucial period of the Alamein Battle.

September 13: A patrol from D Coy was lucky enough to see an enemy patrol passing through their mine field and after a brisk engagement took 1 Italian POW. Other patrols made valuable recces.

Lt Bennie of B Coy led a patrol of 1 NCO and 10 Ors which was out from 2000 hrs to 0310 hrs. At 87152999 movement was heard on the immediate front including 1 vehicle, outline of which was visible through glasses — moving to right and stopping occasionally. 50 yds further on patrol found newly dug pits 4 ft long and 2 ft deep, sited amongst tall bushes and patrol lay up at this point. Comd and 2 men made forward recce. 25 yds west of the pits north-south track crossed showing recent signs of use. At 4000 yards Comd met a single dannert 3 ft high. Good condition but no pickets. A man was seen to approach within 50 yds of the wire and disappear into a trench. As it was entirely open ground Comd withdrew 15 yds and observed. After 15 minutes 6 men approached wire from inside and after checking with man in the trench withdrew a short distance. Nearby there were large numbers of safety collars for mine fuses and it is considered mines have been laid along the wire. About half an hour without fresh movement inside the enemy FDLs patrol Comd withdrew to his patrol and moved due north, a barbed trip wire taut on short iron pickets was crossed running in an arc to the left. Patrol moved 1050 yards to 87133007 and lay up. Recce group moved 100 yd west and found new diggings and a number of crates. One was forwarded for inspection. Movement again heard and the sound of a truck being unloaded to the west. After lying up for 3/4 hrs patrol returned to our lines.

Sgt Ken Gibb of C Coy also took out a patrol of 11 men from 2000 hrs to 0300 hrs, located knocked-out tanks and vehicles. Identified 1 tank as a Crusader and 1 truck with radiator blown off as a British vehicle. It was flying a dark coloured flag and loaded with 2" mortar bombs. NMS.

September 14: Effective strength 31 Offrs, 757 Ors, quiet night. D Coy patrol under Lt G. Wray after making contact with enemy in area 87102985 returned with a POW.

PATROL REPORT NIGHT 13/14 SEPT, 1942:

D Coy, Comd Lt G. Wray. Strength 1 Offr, 1 NCO and 10 Ors. Out 2030 hrs. In 0400 hrs, route out 87432997 to approx 87192983 and then 200 yds to south. Returned to start pt.

REPORT:

At approx 87252986 Patrol Comd became aware of sounds and movements on his front. Patrol continued on its course and found a group of unoccupied roofless sangars. There were still sounds on the front and on both flanks and patrol continued on its course to 87192983. Italian voices identified on the direct front and what sounded like German voices about 100 yds right bearing 235. These voices certainly came from the vicinity of Urquhart's Post as the breast shaped feature could be seen clearly through glasses. Patrol Comd moved forward on recce for 90 yds. 4 aerial flares were dropped to the west and it became necessary to lie low. At this point about 150 yds on left front there were sounds of men walking and climbing through wire. Comd saw a patrol of 13 men move past about 150 yds to his left and move due east. He moved back to his patrol and attempted by moving south to gain contact with the enemy. At approx 200 yds Patrol Comd struck dannert wire, was challenged by a sentry from inside the wire and the challenge was repeated by other sentries to the east and west. A grenade was thrown by first sentry and Patrol Comd fearing a cul-de-sac turned the patrol due north-east with the object of fighting its way out. The enemy patrol of 13 men had meantime established itself deployed with its left flank in the sangar area and the right flank astride the patrol's course. As patrol moved forward Comd and Pte Griffiths simultaneously saw a man between them in a trench and together they seized him. The enemy were now firing bursts at our patrol with 3 automatic weapons. The automatic fire coming from the sangar area. Carrying the prisoner along with him the Comd reorganised the patrol and now gave orders to open fire which hitherto had been held. Patrols opened with Bren and TSMG on the sources of enemy fire. Our shots were heard to hit the stones of the sangars and after about one minute of quite fierce engagement, the enemy automatic ceased fire. Casualties among the enemy could not be estimated but shouts and cries were heard. It is probable that either guns or gunners were put out of action. The enemy began to withdraw in confusion and our patrol with prisoner moved back to our lines in good order. No casualties were sustained by us.

The prisoner was an Italian Infantryman of 62 Fanteria 1 Bn 3 Coy Trento Div. He was one of a special patrol of 13 led by an Offr and has given us valuable information. After his capture and whilst being led along by Patrol Comd the patrol was challenged — our prisoner replied: "Italiano" — and we passed without question. His one regret was that his friend who was fiercely firing a Breda was not a POW too. The POW confirms the destruction of Sabratha Div which he states no longer exists.

(Lt George Wray, who was born in Napier, NZ on 19 June 1906 joined the Bn in July 1942. He was a very big, placid man, very quietly spoken. At one time he was "sweep oar" on the Manly Life Savers boat.) Attached to the September 1942 War Diary is a note written on Australian Comforts Fund (Queensland Div) note paper and dated 14 Sept 1942. It reads: "Received with thanks 1 bottle of Whisky from Col Simpson. Sgd: George R. Wray, Lt. Receipt in respect to a wager made by Bn Comd with Lt Wray, D Coy and is payment for first POW captured by Bn Patrol in Tel el Eisa sector."

To the reader of extracted patrol reports as above many questions can occur. Often initiatives have to be controlled because of orders giving the purpose of the patrol and general patrol policy. Performance more than requirements are reported.

In the Int Summary of 9 Sept appeared the following not mentioned in the main portion of the War Diary.

"1900 hrs 2 planes, a JU52 flying at about 100 ft escorted by a fighter, passed over station area, circled and flew back to enemy lines. It appeared as if it was going to land and then realised it had overshot its own lines. Landing wheels were down. Engaged by SA and 20mm Breda and at least one hit from Breda observed. Both planes returned the fire. One man in the Tel el Eisa station area was wounded by a spent bullet fired at this plane."

(Note by Arthur Newton: I remember this incident clearly. The plane flew over Bn HQ. At that time Squadron Leader Bob Gibbes Commanding 3 Squadron RAAF (which had a magnificent reputation) and a Pilot Offr, Glen Dinning, were visiting our Bn and dined at the little mess near our HQ. Keith Magno, John Balfe, Ian McMaster and Tim McCulloch and myself were there when the JU52 flew over. The airmen reckoned the plane had flown in from Italy and had made a wrong landfall. They had driven up to the forward areas mainly to see on the ground the results of the RAF and RAAF sorties against Rommel's ill fated attack at Alam el Halfa. Squadron Leader Gibbes had met George Reid in hospital at Gaza and the latter had suggested that when the opportunity offered Bob Gibbes should visit our Bn. On this occasion George Reid had not rejoined the battalion. The RAAF offrs travelled in a staff car "acquired" from the French in Syria as 3 Squadron had supported 7 Div in that campaign.)

Other patrols on night 13/14 Sept were from A Coy led by Lt B. Ross with 1 NCO and 10 Ors. This was out from 2030 hrs to 0330 hrs and operated in the Thompson's Post area. The enemy was alert and put up flares, fired 2 mortar rounds and fired several Spandau bursts. Important information on enemy defences was obtained. A patrol from C coy, 1 NCO and 6 Ors, was out from 0400 hrs to 0530 hrs. They were out over 1750 yds and drew fire from MGs and Mortars.

Bn protective patrolling system is changed to a series of listening posts with lateral connecting links. It is thought that this system will be better than the constant patrolling system used previously. The day was quiet except for the fact that Bn HQ area was heavily shelled — 234 shells landed within a radius of 600 yds from this HQ. Our mine and explosive dump was hit — a terrific explosion resulting — no casualties. Our arty kept up a heavy harassing fire on enemy FDLs. A Coy were able to observe some casualties being carried out of an enemy position. One ME109 dropped 3 bombs near our Bn HQ — slight damage to a DR motor cycle resulting.

September 15: Nothing to report from patrols. An extremely quiet period with only 36 enemy shells directed out our area. Most of MT on "skyline track" has been very heavy during the day but does not seem to be for any operational purpose that directly concerns the Bn.

Visitors: Lt Col Campbell and Lt Hewitt of Argyle Sutherland Highland Bn (51 Highland Div) visited this HQ and discussed arrangments whereby members of their unit live with our Bn over 4-day periods in order they may see at first hand just how our troops live and work in the desert. F/O Morgan of RAF visited this HQ and went forward to C Coy area.

As stated in Barton Maughan's Official History:

> "On 12 Sept Morshead met Gen Wimberley of the recently arrived 51st Highland Div which was to be "affiliated" with 9 Div to enable it to gain desert and battle experience as quickly as possible. Each inf, cav, arty and engr unit of the 51st was linked with the corresponding unit of 9 Div. The Association was welcomed most warmly by all."

September 16: Effective strength 31 Offrs and 751 Ors. Engrs are to begin a systematic check of enemy mine fields and our patrols must provide protection each night. Nothing occurred last night to disturb the work and our patrols reported enemy working activity in rear of his FDLs. Coys were harassed by enemy shelling from 1100 hrs onwards, 529 shells falling in our area. No doubt this was a reprisal for the intensive shelling our arty directed against enemy FDLs at first light this morning. One slight casualty in B Coy resulted. 1 Offr and 16 Ors constitute the first Bn leave party for Alexandria and Cairo which starts today. A similar number will leave every 3rd day until further notice.

Visitors: Lt Gen Sir Oliver Leese, the new Comd of 30 Corps visited our FDLs with the Comd of the Highland Div. A detachment of Offrs and Ors of the Argyle and Sutherland Highlanders arrived at Bn and groups were sent forward to the coys on the night 15/16 Sept.

A Coy had a patrol comd by Lt J K Thompson with 1 Cpl, 8 Ors and 3 Sappers. This was out from 2000 hrs to 0245 hrs — 9 "S' mines were found spacing being from 20 yds to over 100 yds — 6 British MK IV mines were also located. Thompson's post has at least a percentage of Italians as their voices were quite clear. Patrol returned without incident. D Coy had a patrol of 1 Sgt, 1 Cpl and 6 Ors out from 0100 hrs to 0545 hrs. This patrol after searching the area in vicinity of 87332986 took up a position in sangars and waited until almost first light anticipating that it may be used by enemy daylight observers who would probably approach the sangars before first light. Patrol returned with nothing to report. C Coy also had a patrol comd by Lt Paul Mendham who had with him 1 Cpl and 8 Ors. While approaching Pt 87302972 patrol could hear our HF landed behind Pt 23 at 87302970, patrol could hear digging on bearing 235 about 600 to 800 yds away. At this point a LMG firing after the report of our arty fire drew hilarious applause in what sounded like Italian from a position in vicinity of Pt 23. Patrol completed its second leg but no movement seen or heard. No wire encountered throughout the course of the patrol.

September 17: Engineers continue with mine field check — B Coy to provide the protection. The B Coy patrol was comd by Sgt A. Roberts who had 1 NCO, 6 Ors and 3 Sappers with him. A field of mines running 140— 320 scattered from 4 yds to 40 yds apart was discovered. Patrol followed field to the right for about 400 yds after which no more mines were seen. Width of field approx 50 yds. Patrol returned at 0210 hrs after leaving at 2000 hrs. Only 44 shells, which was a relief after yesterday's intensive period. The Bn is to change over with 2/15 Bn tonight and go into the Bde reserve position. We are responsible for patrols until daylight 18 Sept. Changeover complete by 2245 hrs. C Coy are in their old position east of Tel el Eisa Station whilst A and D Coys are on southern slopes of coastal ridge near Pt 26 (87913001) B Coy is at 87823007 and Bn HQ at 87913002. The Bn's role in this position was defence in depth and counter attack.

(Note by Arthur Newton: As Adjutant I have some memories of this changeover. First I was to meet Keith Magno as CO 2/15 Bn. In his hearty manner he suggested that the changeover be celebrated by the outgoing and incoming COs having a "short snort" — we lesser lights (the Adjutants) also had a nip. After leaving our old HQ and travelling for a mile or two the Red Fox suggested that we might be travelling in the wrong direction. I assured him that we were on the right track but had to prove my point by showing him the position we were leaving, after departing from the Comd Post at night he would frequently have difficulty locating his "dingus". Generally the duty offr walked with him until he was sure he had reached his bunk. I'm sure Eric Blundell would agree with me. The second point was that the changeover was arranged by a brief signal being sent to all coys informing them of times of changeover and stating "normal procedure" or words to that effect. The Adjutant of the Argyle and Sutherland Highlanders with us, was non-plussed that several pages of orders had not been issued. What he was not aware of was the fact that the Bn had nearly 2 years' experience of such handovers and was a highly skilled and well trained unit with a wealth of experience by this time. No doubt the Argyles learnt quickly and must have been similarly adept in a year's time.)

SUMMATION

In the period covered by this chapter the Bn occupied the Forward Defended Localities (FDLs) at Tel el Eisa from 3 Aug to 17 Sept a period of 46 days. This was the longest time during the War that our Unit was in constant contact with the enemy. Shelling reports disclose that 8640 shells fell in the Bn area during that time (Average 188 per day) — fortunately with comparatively few casualties.

Every day and night, patrols of all types, reconnaissance fighting, protective or standing were provided. Our Int personnel were able to collate vital information gained about enemy dispositions and mine fields which proved to be of tremendous value in later operations.

The value of our operational experience in Tobruk and the intensive training in Syria became apparent during this period. New Comds and many reinforcements were assimilated into the Bn and it soon became an effective fighting force capable of any tasks allotted. We also enjoyed many visits by members of the 51st Highland Div and other British Units for observation and training. This was a compliment to the reputation and high standard reached by all ranks of the Bn in most aspects of desert warfare.

CHAPTER 10
RELIEF & REHEARSAL

The changeover with the 2/15 Bn in the Tel el Eisa sector was completed without incident on the night 17/18 Sep. The operation "Relief in the Line" is normally a detailed and complicated affair but was executed with the minimum of orders, made possible because of Tobruk service and the close affinity and liaison with 2/15 Bn. As Bde reserve situated 2 miles from the FDLs, we were there only 4 days, then moved 18 miles to the rear sector of the Divisional reserve position at Shammama where the next 30 days was not all Rest and Recreation.

Sept 18: One Offr and 28 Ors arrive from 20 ITB. Two engineer parties out on the night 17/18 with A and C Coy patrols. The A Coy patrol was led by Lt B Ross and 3 Ors and 3 Sappers made up the strength. The patrol was out from 2000 hrs to 0300 hrs and sighted a large working party of an estimated strength of two Coys working on a frontage of approx 800 yds. Principal work seemed to be hammering of iron pickets and wiring. German voices identified. The C Coy patrol was comd by Cpl Cyril Mears with 1 NCO and 2 Ors plus 2 Sappers. It was out from 2000 hrs to 0300 hrs. After passing by three burnt out vehicles at 87402970 a small knoll was reached at 87312968 with a single dannert wire running due south. A large working party heard on direct front including sounds of digging. Sappers moved through wire and found four empty British MK IV or MK V mine boxes. Patrol moved south along the wire and at 87312967 crossed a well-defined road running east-west through gap in the wire. At 87312965 another large working party was heard to the south, estimated distance 400 yds from patrol. At 87322966 pile of circular boxes containing shell cases was found. A label from one was attached to the patrol report. The precision and details illustrate the level of patrol efficiency.

A standing patrol comd by Sgt Peter Bryant from D Coy and consisting of 6 Ors was also out from 2000 hrs to 0300 hrs. This patrol took up position at 87212992 before moonset. No sound from enemy lines. At moonset enemy showed considerable nervousness putting up repeated flares without cause. In general the Bn spent a quiet day in their new area and the troops enjoy a good swim and rest. The period at Tel el Eisa had become a strain. The Div Comd visits the CO during the afternoon.

Sept 19: No patrols, a quiet day. Engineers blew up a bomb.

Sept 20: Coy Comds' conference at 1030 hrs to discuss our present role of Bde counter-attack force.

Sept 21: An A Coy patrol was fired on by an enemy listening post on railway line — no casualties. This was our last patrol before coming into Div Reserve. This was a composite patrol, Comd by Lt R J Bennie with 1 NCO of B Coy plus 1 Offr and 10 Ors of 2/15 Bn. This patrol was out from 2000 hrs to 0200 hrs night 20/21 Sept — the route was from 87453001 to 87303017 then due south to 87303008 and return to start point. The patrol went to ground at 87303016. Considerable noise was heard to north of railway line — men talking — scraping of shovels. The patrol comd saw four men move through north of railway line and disappear SE into dead ground, although visibility good in moonlight, enemy group may have been larger —

others may have reached dead ground before. Nobody was seen to cross the railway line. After 10 minutes, working party on hillside north of railway line increased to approx 40 men. A truck arrived — men moved across to it — it appeared to be unloading mines. Comd and 1 Or moved towards railway track to get better observation, when within a few yards of the embankment, a low voiced order was heard followed by great noise of scrambling up far side of embankment. Comd withdrew being called to halt twice in German. Enemy opened with tracer straight into air followed immediately by Spandau and machine pistol fire directed generally around the patrol. Grenade was thrown in the direction of the patrol Comd who reorganised his patrol facing the embankment. Another Spandau opened fire from Thompson's Post but quite contrary to habit, no tracer.

Enemy fire was not accurate; by this time no satisfactory target was visible — our patrol did not return fire but continued on leg two, noting when crossing the pipe line that all water pipe lengths had been separated. Our patrol sustained no casualties.

This patrol of Bob Bennie is significant as it may be considered the last deep patrol of our Bn in the Western Desert.

At 1500 hrs 21 Sept the CO and Adjt attend a Bde conference. We are to change over with 26 Bde on night 22/23 Sept. 2130 hrs advance party of 2/24 Bn arrive at this HQ.

Sept 22: Effective strength 28 Offrs and 727 Ors. Nothing to report during the day. Bn packs and prepares for move to Shammama area. All Coys move out by 2330 hrs.

Sept 23: 0200 hrs move complete. Bn HQ now at 43209022 El Qasaba — Sheet 1:50,000. This is familiar ground as the Bn was in this area before moving to Tel el Eisa Sector. The whole Bde is close together and some solid training is contemplated. 2030 hrs B Coy practise drill of moving to assembly area and FUP in attack. The exercise is carried out in the Coy area.

Sept 24/25: A dull, misty day. C and A Coys practise attack drill with start lines. 33 "X" men from ITB.

Sept 26: 1400 hrs: CO and all Coy Comds go to Bde training area for general recce. 2359 hrs: 8 bombs dropped near C Coy area — one unexploded.

Sept 27: A tank demo by A Squadron 40 RTR at Pt 17 (42568992) is attended by all ranks. Lt Col Finigan lectured on Infantry co-operation with tanks and answered many questions.

Visit by
Winston Churchill with
Lt Gen Sir Leslie Morshead
at 9 Div HQ , El Alamein.

1400 hrs: CO issues preliminary orders to Coy Comds and all supporting arms for exercise on night 28/29 Sept.

Sept 28: 0710 hrs: Bde exercise No 1 ended and troops marched back to camp. Rest of day spent sleeping. The exercise according to Op. Order No 1, dated 26 Sept 42, has as its intention: "2/17 Aust Inf Bn will capture Point 25 and the high ground to the south of Point 19 and exploit NOT beyond the general line shown on the trace."

Troops in support were 40 RTR less two squadrons, 1 Pl MMG, 2 troops ATK Regt Detachment RAE Reps of Artillery both Field and Lt AA. The Bn frontage was 600 yds — the forward Coys were A right, B left with C Coy right reserve and D Coy left reserve. Zero was NOT before 0200 hrs.

The reference to Zero was slightly out of date as on 21 Sept the 9 Div informed all its formations that the Zero hour for an attack would henceforth be known as H hour, the day on which operations started would be referred to as D Day, the day before, D minus 1 and subsequent days D plus 1, D plus 2 and so on.

Significant changes in military terminology were introduced in the 8th Army in late September when it was decided to bring into immediate use a common vocabulary for British and U S forces. Uniformity was obtained by adopting American terms. Words and phrases, that had become the everyday speech of soldiers were removed with a stroke of the pen from a time-honoured military vocabulary but orders and reports show detailed application of changes was slow.

Sept 30: Was a quiet day. The September Report on Medical Services by the RMO, Capt J F Sullivan, showed some interesting information.

Sick treated at RAP in weekly periods were: —

1 to 5 Sept	99	6 to 12 Sept	139
13 to 19 Sept	164	19 to 26 Sept	191
27 to 30 Sept	93		

The peak in the latter weeks represents the period when troops came to reserve positions and various minor illnesses — notably desert sores, which had previously been treated by stretcher bearers reported to the RAP for treatment. Despite the heavy shelling of our positions, battle casualties were NOT high. Capt Sullivan's figures are:—

KIA	1	
BW thigh (remaining on duty)	1	
BW shoulder	2	
BW legs, face	1	
SW concussion	1	
SW shoulder etc	1	(DOW)
SW scalp, wrist, severe head injury	1	
SW R knee	1	
SW face	2	
SW thigh	1	
SW elbow	1	
SW shoulder	1	
TOTAL:	14	

Of which 11 were evacuated.

In addition there were 9 accidental wounds including three cases of 2nd degree burns to hands and feet. There were 27 cases of sickness under "elimentary" including 11 gastro-enteritis and 8 dysentry cases. Hygiene was satisfactory, latrines, fly traps and fly poisons were provided in all areas, rubbish was burnt in open pits and buried. Stretcher bearers did refresher courses in first aid after coming out of the line. Of 33 Offrs shown on the Field Return of 26 Sept 1942, 3 were not with the unit. These were Lts R J Dick, H H Main and S H Yeend, all attending various training courses.

By 30 Sept Lts L C Simpson and P K Murphy arrived; Capt C H Wilson also with Lt R J Dick. Lts R S Rudkin, E O Norton and T E Swan left on 27 Sept for 20 ITB. Back at Nuseirat in Palestine, Cec Greenwood noted in his diary: "29 September — we are erecting tents all day and a large number of re-os due in on Thursday." On 30 Sept he noted: "Crowd of Offrs and sergeants arrived this morning from Bn. Percy Brightwell and Dutchie Holland from C Coy. Still working on tents."

Routine Orders issued during Sept included the following items: ACF issues 828 handkerchiefs, 207 ozs pipe tobacco, 621 ozs cigarette tobacco, 207 tubes toothpaste, 621 shaving soap. In the customarily published list of punishments by Court Martial, there were (not 2/17 men) nine cases in all, from a Lt striking a soldier and using obscene language, a staff sergeant leaving a vehicle unattended in Alex., a pte soldier on 3 charges of AWL and another for misapplying rations. Punishments ranged from 2 years imprisonment with hard labour to severe reprimands, forfeiture of 28 days pay and loss of 12 months seniority. There was a letter from the AA & QMG 9 Div, Col E W Woodward — later Lt Gen Sir Eric, who became Governor of NSW which read:

"Salvage:

1. Since arrival in the El Alamein area the salvage work done by 2/17 Aust Inf Bn has been an example of what can be done in this regard by a unit, both when in contact with the enemy and during training. It is considered that the very valuable results obtained indicate a high standard of administration and appreciation of unit responsibility in an isolated theatre of war such as the Middle East.

2. If a similar standard was reached by all units, the effort required to maintain the MEF would be enormously relieved."

Credit for a lot of our results was due to the efforts of Sgt Owen Windeyer who was temporarily placed in charge of salvage operations and was Mentioned in Despatches for this work.

A list of salvage returned from 11 Aug to 19 Sept contained such items as 434 cwts of brass scrap, 3 tons of tank track, 53 rubber tyres, 50x44 gallon drums, 20 rounds of 25 pdr, 1 meat safe, 1x7lb hammer, a washing tub. These are just a few of the items.

There was a plaintive paragraph which read: "Loss of dentures — too many being lost in last three months during swimming. There is no excuse for free replacement. Dental Offrs unable to maintain supplies."

So Sept closed and as Lt Col Noel Simpson stated in his summary of the War Diary describing the exercise of 28/29 Sept:

"This was a forerunner to other exercises early in October planned on the lines of our anticipated attack when the 8th Army offensive began. Coys were marched from our bivouac area to the assembly area and at the end of the exercise marched home travelling in all 16 miles during the night. It was a severe and instructive exercise, the worth of which was proved in operations later."

Men of the I Sec at work

Within the Bn there were many things which, for security and other reasons, were not known, but steadily a wide spread mood of preparation had become evident in 8th Army. More particularly, 2/17 Bn realised the new Comd saw that training for the imminent job was the way to success. The Bn already knew it that way — as you train, so you fight — was an accepted maxim. Individually also, all knew as the clue to survival — there are only the quick and the dead. Lt Col Simpson's style in Syria had seen to that. The sense of deliberative approach and exact preparation became strong as the Bn developed the unit night attack. Composure and physical fitness grew with marching out at dusk, some to have covered almost 20 miles on returning to beach living areas after daylight. With each night techniques evolved. Wide experience of patrolling, keeping direction and counting distance by night are no more than a valuable basis on which to train for co-ordinated Bn approach and attack on a wide front. Now it had to perfect how a Pl, and with it a Coy, can spread on a frontage and keep control. Secs had to move in two files a few yards apart and at an interval from the adjoining sec at the limit of night visibility. At the same time was developed the skill of planting a line of rearward-showing lights to lead from the assembly area to start lines (FUP).

Finally, the specific requirement for the Bn to have a frontage of 1200 yds was faced by rehearsal and everyone took confidence in the control achieved. The ultimate was for three coys forward, each on a separate start line facing the axis of attack, but staggered back to the left, to provide contemporary arrival at the enemy's forward positions. Their line ran somewhat north-west to south-east across this front. So much for the first phase of how the attack was expected. It is to be noted that enough information had to be leaked from the final secret plans to allow this exact training.

For the second phase for the Bn attack the reserve coy trained to come through to advance with whichever of the three forward coys was to be at that time in the battle best fitted to move ahead. Alternatives were practised at night with maximum silence. Teamwork and know-how were perfected. An orderly showing himself was enough to say that his pl was in place. The field

*Above: Meal time at 16 Pl,
D Coy.*

*Pte Gordon Kibby of D Coy at
housekeeping chores*

signal for acknowledgement, rather like our Brigadier's parade ground salute, told the silent orderly that his message was understood. Daylight adjustments before standing down illustrated lessons on spacing and location to be applied before digging in the darkness. Something of the detailed build up can be seen in the following days.

Oct 1: Still at 43209022 El Qasaba Sheet 1 — 50,000. Strength 30 Offrs and 721 Ors. 1 Offr and 5 Ors marched in.

Oct 2: Coy Comds Conference regarding training and administration.

*Relaxation between
Rehearsals:
Doug Fraser (L)
and Leon Marcus*

Below: *Meal preparation at a
private kitchen*

Oct 3: Normal coy training — route marching in the morning. A severe electrical storm, some rain and then a dust storm breaks the fine spell. The Field Return for Ors this date showed that the Bn was deficient 2 WO II. Surplus 1 Sgt and deficient 1 Cpl. The Pte Soldier strength was 644 which meant there was a deficiency of 106 Pte Soldiers. NX60279 Cpl G Throsby then in 7 AGH was shown as a soldier whose return was "particularly requested". Lt S H Yeend marched in from attending 9 Div MG School.

Oct 4: A quiet day with nothing to report (NTR). Eleven reinforcements marched in.

Oct 5: A two-coy attack (exercise) was done by A and D Coys with C Coy taking the part of the enemy in the area near Cairn 24 (42648969). Tps crossed the Start Line at 0430 hrs and finished consolidation at 0645 hrs. 0945 hrs all Offrs and senior NCOs attended a demonstration of tanks using 2 inch mortar smoke in the attack by 40 Royal Tank Regt (RTR). 1430 hrs CO attends conference at Bde to discuss details of Bde exercise being done on 6/7 Oct.

Oct 6: Administration in preparation for Bde exercise. Coy Comds Conference at 1000 hrs and Adj and IO go forward to recce assembly area and start line. 1400 hrs: CO issues orders. Coys begin their long march to assembly area and then to FUP (forming up place) — over 10 miles in all and then a 2 mile trek to the objective. 1800 hrs: A Glen Martin plane crashed in 17 Pl area and burst into flames — none of the crew survived.

Oct 7: Coys took objectives and started to dig in by 0130 hrs. System of lighting axis of advance proved a great success and help to A Echelon vehicles. Carriers with trailers seem to be the answer in desert warfare for carrying up consolidation stores. Very few vehicles were bogged considering the bad ground. The morning was very cold and troops shivered in the mist until "exercise ends" signal was given at approx 0730 hrs. Coys marched back to camp and spent the rest of the day sleeping.

Oct 8: Dull and Cloudy. For the past few days the weather has been unsettled and it looks as if the Bn will experience some wet weather in the desert this year. At 1030 hrs it rained heavily for about 15 minutes. Coys have a day of rest and sport. C Coy has a surf carnival during the afternoon.

Oct 9: A fine clear day. Surf Carnival B Coy versus C Coy during the afternoon. The 9 Div Concert Party gave a series of performances during the day in Coy Areas.

Oct 10: B Coy use Rifle, TSMC and Bren on beach range and other Coys swim and play cricket.

Oct 11: 0800 hrs, all rifle Coys leave Bn area and repeat our exercise of night 6/7 Oct to give all Comds an opportunity to see night formation during daylight. Lunch in the field and march home. A/Tk Pl have practice shoot on Bde range.

Oct 12: Bn continues intensive training. C Coy use the beachrange and Mortar Pl train with their new carriers. Bn MG Pl now has four guns. 1800 hrs: CO attends Bde conference.

Oct 13: A hot, clear day. The whole Bn moves at 0815 hrs for the 2nd daylight practice of Div Exercise No 2. Exercise ends at 1600 hrs.

Oct 14: A quiet day, fine and warm. HQ Coy use the beach range. CO attends a Bde conference. 1800 hrs, all Offrs and Sec Leaders move out for practice of night exercise in square 431897. Coys form up on start line and use navigation parties for guidance to objectives. Exercise ends at 2230 hrs.

Oct 15: Quiet day — nothing to report. The CO, Lt Col Simpson, and Maj Broadbent visit Alexandria on leave with Lt Col Magno, 2/15 Bn.

Oct 16: During the afternoon a terrific dust storm developed and, while it was at its height, the Bn moved out for second night practice of Div Exercise No 2 in area 429896. The wind was terrific and it rained heavily at 2000 hrs while the Bn was on the start line. Exercise was completed by 0115 hrs on 17 Oct when the troops marched back to camp area wet and cold but in good cheer.

Oct 17: Effective strength 30 Offs 731 Ors. The day is very cold and squally — a real touch of winter. It seems as if the change of season is here to stay. Tps spend the day resting. CO attends conference during afternoon. The Offrs Field Return of 17 Oct shows that Lts R A Hannaford and R M McElroy joined the Bn on 13 Oct. These Offrs had recently been commissioned after attendance at the ME OCTU. Both had been original members of the Bn and had distinguished themselves as magnificent Sgts at Tobruk. Lt J R Bray and Lt H H Main rejoined the Bn on 16 Oct, the latter after attendance at an Army School. The return of Capt C G Pitman was particularly requested. The return also showed we were 2 Capts deficient on establishment. The Ors Field Return for the same date showed the Bn deficient one WO2 but surplus 5 sgts and 1 cpl. Also there was a deficiency of 108 pte soldiers.

(Until now there is no mention in the Diary of the impending battle but, according to Field-Marshal Montgomery's "Memoirs", Unit Comds were given all information on 10 Oct and Coy Comds on 17 Oct. From now on, events will move rapidly.)

As the Battle of El Alamein is about to begin, it may be desirable to list the names of senior Offrs commanding in the Western Desert at this time together with Offrs of 9 Aust Div with particular reference to 2/17 Aust Inf Bn Regt List.

Comd-in-Chief, Middle East, Gen The Hon Sir Harold Alexander: Eight Army Comd, Lt-Gen B L Montgomery: 30th Corps, G O C Lt-Gen Sir Oliver Leese: 2nd New Zealand Div G O C Lt-Gen B C Freyberg, V.C.: 51st Highland Div G O C Maj-Gen D N Wimberley: 4th Indian Div G O C Maj-Gen F E S Tuker: 1st South African Div G O C Maj-Gen D H Pienaar: 9th Aust Div, Lt-Gen L J Morshead. The 13 Corps was Comd by Lt-Gen B G Horrocks and consisted of 7 Armd Div, 44 Inf Div and 50 Div (which contained a Greek Inf Bde Group) and 10 Corps by Lt-Gen H Lumsden and consisted of 1 Armd Div, 10 Armd Div and a nucleus of 8 Armd Div. The Western Desert Air Force was Comd by Air Vice-Marshal A Coningham. On the enemy side the Panzergruppe Afrika was comd by Panzer-Gen Georg Stumme who had taken over from Field Marshal Rommel on 22 Sept. (Rommel was to return to Africa on 25 Oct 1942. The German Afrika Korps ("D A K ") was Comd by Lt-Gen Von Thoma. So much for the more senior Comds. In 9 Aust Div, Gen Morshead had as his senior Staff Offr Col H Wells GSO 1 and Col E W Woodward AA & QMG. 20 Bde was commd by Brig H Wrigley (Brig Windeyer was still recovering from a severe illness). 24 Bde was Comd by Brig A Godfrey. 26 Bde by Brig D A Whitehead. The Bde Maj of 20 Bde was Maj B V Wilson, the BM (Learner) was Capt R J Hamer (in more recent years, Premier of Victoria), the Staff Capt was Capt T W Young and Capt Murray Hamilton was Staff Capt Learner. Lt-Col R W N (Bob) Turner was CO 2/13 Bn whilst Lt-Col C K M (Keith) Magno was CO 2/15 Bn.

And now to our list:

CO 2/17 Bn, Lt-Col N W (Noel) Simpson	2 i/c Maj J R Broadbent
OC HQ Coy, Capt L C (Kanga) Maclarn	OC A Coy, Maj L C (Claude) Brien
OC B Coy, Capt E M (Tim) McCulloch	OC C Coy, Capt J H (John) Dinning
OC D Coy, Capt I F (Ian) McMaster	Adjutant, T/Capt A J C Newton
QM Capt P E (Peter) O'Brien	IO, Lt D J (Dal) Cartledge
Transport Offr, Lt K B (Keith) Sabine	Sig Offr, Lt S R Coulton
OC A/Tk Pl, Capt C H (Curly) Wilson	Pnr Offr, Lt A E (Tony) Nicholson
RMO, Capt J F (Slam) Sullivan	Chaplain W L (Willie) Byrne.

The following Offrs were with the Bn on 23 Oct 42 but some (not always indicated) were LOB (left out of battle). T/Capt G T (George) Reid, LOB; T/Capt A J (Alan) Wright Lts; J K (John) Thompson; J R B (John) Norris; J W (John) Bray; H H (Hugh) Main; A H (Al) Urquhart; N E (Norm) McDonald; S M (Stuart) Williams; R J (Bob) Bennie; S H (Stan) Yeend; G R (George) Wray; L C (Les) Simpson: P K (Paul) Murphy; R A (Ocker) Hannaford; R McL (Bob) McElroy.

Capt C G (Col) Pitman returned to the Bn during the battle and took over as OC B Coy.

Oct 18: In view of our deficiencies of transport and in order to gain some surprise on the night of the attack, it was envisaged that the troops would be brought forward on night 23rd and lie in covered slit trenches until night 22/23.

Relaxation prior to the battle. L-R: Doug Barnard, Les Giles, Bob Painter, "Bluey" Powell.

0930 hrs, CO and Maj J R Broadbent recce position near Pt 26 which is to be our A Echelon vehicle park and the lying up area east of the Pimple. Coy Comds inspect their areas in the afternoon. CO attended a Bde Conference during the afternoon. The men know that something is on and there are many rumours about the Bn.

Oct 19: A quiet day for the troops. CO accompanied Bde Comd to 30 Corps HQ for a conference. A and B Coys dig slit trenches in our proposed assembly area for the troops to lie in on D Day.

Oct 20: Effective strength 32 Offrs and 726 Ors. All Comds are given permission to divulge information to the troops as regards "Lightfoot" (the code name for the operation). Everyone is pleased to know definitely what is to happen and to have some facts disclosed to them. Coy Comds conference at 1100 hrs. C and D Coys dig their positions in assembly areas after dark.

Oct 21: Bn Operation Order No 4 is issued and CO issues his orders at Bde sandtable model. The Bn rests while administrative details are finalised.

(The following is a full reproduction of Bn OO No 4 and Bn ADM Order No 1.)

SECRET
COPY NO . . . . . .
20 Oct 42

2/17 AUST INF BN OO NO 4
"LIGHTFOOT"

Ref Maps :   EL ALAMEIN 1 in 50,000
                    GHAZAL 1 in 50,000
                    EL HIQEIF 1 in 50,000

INFORMATION

1. Enemy

    (a) Enemy fwd posns are sited on gradually rising ground which is itself dominated by the secondary line just fwd of the 25 metre contour.

    (b) The ground is hard and in places bare and stony. There are many mounds — on the reverse side of which enemy diggings will frequently be located.

    (c) For latest dispositions see map EL WISHKA overprint 1 in 25000.

(d) On the DIV front we are aware of elements of two hostile DIVS 164 German DIV and TRENTO ITALIAN DIV.

(i) 164 GERMAN DIV — 9,000 men, 180 ATK guns, 24 Fd guns 18 75mm Inf Guns, 200 MT. A bn of this DIV consists of approx 500 men, 16 5cm ATK guns, 6 hy Mortars, 9 Lt Mortars, 12 hy MGs, 35 LMGs also possibly from regt 2 75mm Inf guns and 4 ATK guns.

(ii) TRENTO DIV — 4,600 men, 40/48 fd guns, 70 ATK guns minimum MT. A bn of this DIV consists of approx 500 men, 12 hy Mortars from regt (these figures represent present holdings rather than WE).

(e) Armd Res: The 15 PZ Div and LITTORIO Armed Div each about 120 tanks at 860297 TEL EL AQQAQIR — will probably be used in mixed battle gps. Tanks of these Divs can be seen along the 860 Easting between the 300 and 290 Northings.

(f) Intercomn: PW have stated that intercomn in both 164 and TRENTO Divs is by runner to coy, L/T coy to bn, L/T and radio above bn. During "BULIMBA" no reports were received of telephones in fwd inf posns. Light sigs are extensively used by the enemy during ops but no recent infm is available on the actual sigs in use.

(g) Minefds : Attention is drawn to overprint EL WISHKA for infm re minefds as interpreted from air photographs. Minefds located as a result of patrolling are covered by special trace X issued separately. It should not however be assumed that where mines do not appear on the map they do not exist on the ground. Mines should be expected anywhere in the vicinity of the fwd wire as working parties have been reported covering at various times almost his entire FDL. Interior minefds were met during "BULIMBA" and must be expected. Not all minefds are marked. The general arrangement seems to be minefds laid fwd of all defensive posns marked by wire on the enemy side and this wire fitted with AP mines and booby traps. Scattered unmarked fds are laid fwd of this outpost line. It is also considered that area A (see trace X) is a mined area. PW has stated that some rear minefds are laid in blocks and fired electrically — in between these blocks are aerial bombs exploded by sympathetic detonation. The statement by a BRITISH escapee who spent some days in general area of WEST Pt 23 may have some bearing on this. He reported having seen what he took to be accumulators wired together and a connecting wire running away to the rear. Another possible explanation for these objects is prepared smoke generators, a similar type having been used at GAZALA earlier this year. Another PW speaks of observation mines fwd of foremost posns and fired by a type of instantaneous fuse or electrical current. Patrols report having seen mines in a fwd fd wired together and the wire leading back to the enemy posns. If this practice is in operation it is anticipated that the enemy would fire the mines when tps are seen in the vicinity. It is not known however whether these observation mines are explosive or illum.

2. Own Tps

(a) EIGHTH ARMY is attacking with the object of destroying the enemy forces in their present posn.

(b) On capture of 30 Corps objectives as a bridgehead 10 ARMD CORPS is to debouch through 30 CORPS to continue the battle to the WEST and SW.

(c) 9 AUST DIV is to:

(i) Capture and hold the area incl the enemy locations at 87122991 — Pt 23 872296 — 8670296 — Pt 867298.

(ii) Facilitate the passage of 10 CORPS through the bridgehead.

(iii) Exploit.

(d)26 Aust Inf Bde less 2/23 Aust Inf Bn and the 20 Aust Inf Bde are to be fwd, 26 Aust Inf Bde on the right.

(e) 26 Aust Inf Bde less 2/23 Aust Inf Bn with under comd 12 Aust ATK Bty, A Coy 2/2 Aust MG Bn and 1 sec 9 Aust Div Pro Coy and in sp 2/7 Aust Fd Coy with under comd 1 scorpion.

TASKS

(i) Capture and hold NORTHERN 800 yds of the DIV area.

(ii) Protection on the NORTHERN flank. For this task, a composite force to hold this flank present FDL and enemy locality 87142993 is under comd 26 Aust Inf Bde.

(iii) Exploitation NORTHWARDS to trig 29 868300.

(f)24 Aust Inf Bde with under comd 66 Mortar Coy (18 4.2 in mortars) and det SL (2).

TASKS

(i) Hold the present FDL in the Coastal Sector.

(ii) Carry out a diversionary op commencing at Zero designed to draw enemy arty fire on to 24 Aust Inf Bde area.

(iii) Maintain 1 bn at call as DIV res.

(g) Composite Force : Comd Lt-Col Macarthur-Onslow, 2/2 Aust MG Bn. Tps C Sqn 9 Aust Div Cav Regt, 2 Tps 11 Aust ATK Bty, D Coy 2/2 Aust MG Bn, A Coy 2/3 Aust Pnr Bn and one ATK Pl 2/3 Aust Pnr Bn (4 47/32mm).

TASK

(i) Secure NORTHERN flank from our FDL area EASTERN 24 to excl enemy FDL area 87142993.

(h) Air : TacR and air Sp are under control EIGHTH ARMY and are being provided as follows :—

Fighters — D day	: F cover over 30 Corps not continuous.
Night D/D plus 1 day	: Night F patrols over NORTHERN routes in 30 Corps area.
D plus 1 day	: F cover over NORTHERN area after first light.
Bombers —	
night D/D plus1 day	: Hy B attack on enemy posns from Zero onwards.
D plus 1 day	: Hy B attack on NORTHERN flank 9 Aust Div after first light to assist east of defensive flank.
TacR — D day	: Extensive TacR particularly last light.
D plus 1 day	: TacR at first light on NORTHERN sector.

Air Sp: Normal air sp tasks are being accepted to the extent that available aircraft allow.

(i) Additional Tps :

(a) Under comd 20 Aust Inf Bde :

40 RTR
9 Aust ATK Bty
B Coy 2/2 Aust MG Bn
One sec 9 Aust Div Pro Coy

(b) In Sp :   2/13 Aust Fd Coy with under comd:

                   B Coy 2/3 Aust Pnr Bn

                   One Tp scorpions(less one scorpion)

Of the foregoing additional tps the following are under comd 2/17 Aust Inf Bn —

                   C Tp 9 Aust ATK Bty

                   3 Pl B Coy 2/2 Aust MG Bn

and in sp 3 Sec 2/13 Fd Coy.

(j)The attack by 20 Aust Inf Bde will be carried out in two phases:

Phase 1 — capture of 1st objective by two bns.

Phase 2 — " " 2nd " " one bn with Tk sp

(i) Tps : 2/13 Aust Inf Bn with in sp

                   40 RTR

                   9 Aust ATK Bty less two tps

                   1 Sec 2/13 Aust Fd Coy

                   2 Pl B Coy 2/2 Aust MG Bn

(ii) Objectives and Boundaries : See Appx "A"

(iii) FUP : See Appx "A"

(iv) Centre Line : from Pt where 2/13 Aust Inf Bn leaves 2/17 Aust Inf Bn centre line route will be marked by green lights.

(v) Zero : There will be a pause of one hr between Phase 1 and beginning of Phase 2

INTENTION

3.   2/17 Aust Inf Bn will :—

     (a) capture and hold objective as shown on Appx "A".

     (b) facilitate the passage of 2/13 Aust Inf Bn and 40 RTR through the objective.

METHOD

4.   Dispositions

     (a) Fwd Coys —   Right   A Coy

                         Centre   B Coy

                         Left   C Coy

     (b) Res Coy —   D Coy

       See Appx "E"

5.   Objectives and Bndys : See Appx "A" to 20 Aust Inf Bde OO 23 issued separately to Coy Comds.

6.   FUP

     (a) Will be laid in accordance with Appx "B"

     (b) Pts 87322992, 87342984 and 87432965 are to be marked by CRE 9 Aust DIV by D minus 3 day

7.   Bearing of attack : 268 deg grid

8.   Rate of Adv

     (a) From FUP to enemy wire 75 yds in 1 min

     (b) From enemy wire onwards — 100 yds in 3 mins

9.   Assembly Posns and Route to FUP : As shown on appx "A"

10. Unit Centre Lines

(a) Markings : Unit centre lines will be marked by lights from FUP to objective —
  2/17 Bn — WHITE
  2/15 Bn — RED
  2/13 Bn — GREEN where axis diverges from 2/17 Bn centre line.

(b) Unit vehs will move as follows —
  2/17 Bn — RIGHT of centre line
  2/13 Bn)— LEFT of centre line
  2/15 Bn)

(c) A TCP will be est 500 yds EAST of enemy minefd. TCP to be marked by lighted tin TCP with serial number 52

11. Timings : As shown on Appx "C"

12. Distances :

(a) From Coy centre to enemy wire :—
  A Coy 1760 yds, B Coy 1700 yds, C Coy 1540 yds, D Coy 2250 yds.

(b) From Coy centre to First Pause :—
  A Coy 2530 yds, B Coy 2500 yds, C Coy 2460 yds, D Coy 3100 yds.

(c)From Coy centre to objective :—
  A Coy 3640 yds, B Coy 3700 yds, C Coy 3760 yds D Coy 4320 yds.

13. Junc Pts2/17 Bn with 2/24 Bn 87342984, 87112983, 87012983.

14. Report Centres

  20 Inf Bde report centre — 87402973
  2/17 Bn report centre — 87372987
  IO will report to bde at 87402973 when 2/17 Bn has formed up at FUP.

15. Liaison with 2/13 Bn

  On capture of objective Maj J R BROADBENT will report to comd 2/13 Bn on centre line and inform him of the situation.

16. Zero Hour

(a) Zero hour and D day will be notified separately.

(b) Will be time at which fwd Coys of 2/15 and 2/17 Bns cross their FUP.

17. Adv to First Pause

(a)Fwd Coys will halt at Zero plus 55 on First pause to permit D Coy to pass through either one of B or C Coy. The decision as to which Coy will form the Bn Res will be given on the ground.

(b)At Zero plus 70 the adv to the objective will be continued.

18. Adv to the Objective

(a)At 3100 yds A Coy willstop its adv and reorganise facing NW.

19. Action on Capture of Objective

(a)Reorganise to defeat counter-attack.

(b)Fwd Coys to send protective fighting patrols to attack enemy posns not beyond 300 yds of objective.

(c)Assist the passage of 2/13 Bn and 40 RTR through the FDLs.

20. Traffic Control

    (a) Traffic Pts will be est as follows :—

TP 1 — Rd junc.	88732942
TP 2 — Main rd and track junc	87912984
TP 3 — Track turning	87702974
TP 4 — Control (X tracks)	87622973
TP 5 — Main rd and track junc	87812992
TP 6 — Track turning	87732980
TP 7 — Control (X tracks)	87632979

    (b)All TPs will be marked by ONE BLUE LIGHT and numbered signs.

    (c)Bde TO will est Control Pt at TP 1 and supervise traffic as laid down in Appx.

21. Unit A Ech Veh Parks

    Until such time as the first enemy minefd is opened unit "A" Ech vehs and vehs of sp arms will park as follows under unit arrangements.

2/17 Aust Inf Bn Gp	—	Outside own FDLs on right of centre line.
		No movement through own FDLs before Z.
2/15 Aust Inf Bn Gp	—	Outside own FDLs on left of centre line.
		No movement through FDLs before Z.
2/13 Aust Inf Bn Gp	—	Inside own FDLs in 2/17 Aust Inf Bn Assembly area.

22. RAC

    On completion of Phase 2 40 RTR will move to fwd rally 869297 coming under comd 26 Aust Inf Bde for employment with either 20 or 26 Aust Inf Bde.

23. Arty

    (a) From Z minus 20 to Z minus 5 CB programme.

    (b) Arty sp will be timed concentrations under control 30 Corps.

    (c) Timings are in accordance with rate of adv of attacking inf as laid down.

    (d) Arty concentrations are to comply with life line issued separately.

    (e) Trace showing arty concentrations will be issued separately.

24. (a) Arty AA defence is under control 30 Corps.

    (b) AA defence is being provided for minefd gap defence.

25. ATK

    (a) 9 Aust ATK Bty. C Tp will sp the attack and protect the right flank from counter-attack by tanks from posns on right of right fwd Coy and in area 87032983.

    (b) 2/17 Bn ATK. Both pls will sp the attack and on reorganisation one will add depth to and assist ATK defence of right flank from the area right Res Coy and in vicinity 87082983; the other will protect the left and front from posns in area left Fwd Coy and in vicinity 87052973.

26. RAE : 3 Sec 2/13 Coy will —

    (i) supply 2 men with each Fwd Coy, 1 man with Res Coy. Duties will incl:

        (a) location and disarming AP mines.

        (b) firing of Bangalore torpedoes.

        (c) carrying of mine signs to be placed in area of mines located by Coys during adv.

(d) after capture of objective to report Bn HQ with Coy orderlies and on way recce for mines a route to Coy areas from Bn axis suitable for MT.

(e) to guide ATK guns from axis by such routes to respective Coy areas.

(ii) provide 3 Bangalore torpedoes per Coy and personnel to fire them. Carrying parties provided by Bns.

(iii) make and mark gaps in enemy minefd, each gap to be initially 8 yds wide.

(iv) widen one minefd gap to LEFT 24 yds on each Bn front on centre line.

(v) further widen and increase number of minefd gaps as possible for the employment of our Tks.

(vi) provide RE stores for, and assist Bn in, reorganisation on objective.

(vii) minefd recce party (6 men) will move with Bn Pnr Offr (Lt NICHOLSON) at head of axis lighting party. Duties will incl (a) recce and reporting minefds on axis of adv to 3 Sec 2/13 Fd Coy. (b) advising minor detours for axis to avoid minefds.

(viii) All RAE personnel to move with Bn will report at Bn assembly area by 2015 hrs.

27. MMGs

(a) Comd B Coy 2/2 MG Bn will coordinate Bde MMG defence.

(b) 2/17 Bn MG pl will move to area 87062984 on right flank on capture of objective.

TASKS

    1. DF on front of 2/17 and 2/15 Bns

    2. Right flank protection 2/17 Bn and 2/13 Bn

(c) 2/2 MG Bn No 3 Pl will sp the attack and is to move to area 87052974 on capture of objective.

TASKS

    1. DF on 2/17 Bn front

    2. Right flank protection.

    Every opportunity will be taken by these guns to shoot on observed targets on the right flank of the bde.

28. Carrier Pl

    1 sec allotted to Mortar pl for carriage of mortars fwd.

    1 carrier to each rifle coy for consolidation stores.

    1 sec for mopping up bn area.

    1 sec for patrolling bn right flank at first light.

    1 sec for patrolling bn front at first light.

    1 sec res, Carriers allotted for carriage of consolidation stores and mortars will rally in area 87122981.

29. Mortar Pl

    Two mortars under comd to each fwd coy.

    1 mortar under comd A coy.

    1 mortar in mob res at HQ Coy area 87122980.

30. Pioneer Pl

OC Pioneer Pl will be responsible for:—

(a) marking with lights centre line of adv.

(b) marking of Bn HQ and route thereto from centre line of adv.

(c) maintaining in serviceable condition all lights.

(d) providing det to move with RSM for digging of Comd post, Int office, Sig office.

On completion of tasks Pioneer Pl will move to HQ Coy area about 87122980.

31. A A Pl

Will be located in Bn HQ area about PITS in area 87102980 for the protection of Bn HQ. RSM is responsible for siting of A/A Pl and allocation of tasks.

ADMINISTRATION

32. Adm O issued separately.

33. INTERCOMN   Passing of Infm

(a) The capture of objectives down to and incl coy objectives will be reported and repeated by every means available.

(b) Reports will be furnished when each coy objective is secured or, on the event of delay, at the time at which it was planned to secure the objective. In the latter case progress reports will be furnished at short intervals until the objective is gained.

34. Code Words for Objectives

(a) Code-words given in Appx "D" is issued by coy comds will be used for reporting capture of objectives.

(b) They will be used as follows e.g.:—

(i) BITTERS left captured.

(ii) Am held up 500 yds short of FIG.

(iii) Am held up 500 yds short of BRIEN B.

(iv) COBB captured.

35. MAP REFS System of lettered squares as issued separately.

36. Success Sigs

(a) Success signal to be used by bns on 1st Objective and 2nd Objective will be signal rocket yellow.

This signal will be repeated twice at intervals of one min to ensure recognition.

This rocket shows a large number of yellow stars.

Signal rockets yellow will not be used for any other purpose than shown in this area.

(b) In addition, the following sigs will be fired: —

2/17 Bn — THREE REDS rptd after 5 secs.

2/15 Bn — THREE GREENS rptd after 5 secs.

2/13 Bn — RED—GREEN—RED rptd after 5 secs.

37. L/T

(a) Lines will be laid to coys *after* A Ech tpt has moved to coys and *after* 2/13 Bn and 40 RTR have passed through objective.

(b) Lines will be laid to coys in assembly area on night D MINUS ONE.

38. W/T and R/T

(a) W/T gps will be provided within the Bde as follows:—

(i) Bde HQ working to:—   Comd

2/13 Aust Inf Bn

2/15 Aust Inf Bn

2/17 Aust Inf Bn

Bde "B" Ech (101 sets)

Res 101 sets for each Bn will be provided. Will be supplied to 9 Aust ATk Bty for intercept purposes.

(ii) Arty LOs set working to Fd Regt.

(iii) LOs from 23 Armd Bde at Bde and Bn HQs working to 23 Armd Bde.

(iv) 2/13 Bn gp (incl MG Pl) 18 sets Trig 8250 k/cs

(v) 2/15 Bn gp (incl MG Pl) 18 sets Trig 8500 k/cs

(vi) 2/17 Bn gp (incl MG Pl) 18 sets Trig 8750 k/cs

(b) Call signs for Bde Gp (down to Coys) and flanking units will be issued separately.

(c) Call signs within Bns will NOT change after D Day until ordered by this HQ. Unit Comds may either continue to use call signs allotted for D Day or may allot numbers to each sta. These will not be used before D Day.

(d) Distribution of 18 and 108 sets

18 sets —	A Coy	1	HQ Coy	1	
	B Coy	1	COs Jeep	1	and res 101 set
	C Coy	1	COs Carrier	1	and 101 set
	D Coy	1	Carrier pl	1	Reserve 1
108 sets —	Mortar pl	1			
	A/Tk pl	1			

39. Pigeons

(a) One pigeon will be provided to each Bn and will be released on capture of Bn Objective, or later as required.

(b) Message will notify by Code-word capture of objective.

(c) Mob Homing loft is situated at MAIN HQ 9 Aust Div.

40. Wireless Deception

(a) Complete Wireless Silence will be maintained from 1000 hrs on D Minus 1 until ZERO.

(b) All wireless sets within the Bde will operate on normal schedules from present locations until 1000 hrs D minus 1.

(c) 2/13 Aust Inf Bn will NOT use W/T after move on night D minus 3/D minus 2.

(d) All frequencies will change at 0300 hrs D minus 1.

41. AFV Recognition: will be notified by signal later.

42. SOS

(a) SOS will be called for by:— light signals and through sigs.(b) SOS light signal will be "signal rocket three star with trailer Mk I TP".

This rocket shows three white stars with a very pronounced trail.

(c) SOS will be answsered only by div concerned.

(d) On capture of objectives def fire plan will be co-ord by CRA.

43. Ground to Air Recognition:

(a) Ground to Air Recognition : —

Blue Smoke

Aldis Lamp letter "G"

(b) Target Landmark : —

Red Smoke

Aldis Lamp letter "V".

44. Location of HQ

(a) 20 Aust Inf Bde

Main HQ 87642977

Rear HQ "B" Ech area

(b) On capture final objective Tac HQ moves new location on 2/15 Bn centre line.

Bde HQ marked by two blue lights.

(c) Bn HQ : Assembly area until Zero minus 88.

(d) From Zero minus 88 until capture of final objective — centre line of bn on right flank of res coy.

(e) On capture of objective Bn HQ will move to new location in PITS about 87102980.

(f) Bn HQ to be marked by lighted tin showing serial No 52

(g) Lighted tin showing 52 with arrow pointed in direction will be placed on centre line to indicate route to Bn HQ.

(h) On capture of objective by coys two orderlies will report to Bn HQ, one orderly returning to coy HQ.

45. Synchronisation : — Through Bde Sigs at 2000 hrs.

ACK   (A.J C Newton) Capt

(Signed)   Adjt 2/17 Aust Inf Bn

Signed at 1400 hrs

Issued by Orderly and D/R

DISTRIBUTION

	Copy No		Copy No
HQ Coy	1–3	2M	13
A Coy	4	C Tp 9 ATK Bty	14
B Coy	5	3 Sec 2/13 Fd Coy	15
C Coy	6	3 Pl 2/2 MG Bn	16
D Coy	7	20 Aust Inf Bde	17
Comd	8	2/13 Aust Inf Bn	18
2 i/c	9	2/15 Aust Inf Bn	19
Adjt	10	War Diary	20–21
IO	11	File	22-23
TO	12	Spare	24-30

2/17 AUST INF BN ADM ORDER NO. 1
(Issued in conjunction with 2/17 Aust Inf Bn OO No. 4)

Ref Map : —   EL ALAMEIN 1/50000
EL QASABA 1/50000
EL HAMMAM 1/100000

SECURITY

1. Information of operation "LIGHTFOOT" must NOT reach the enemy. There must be the minimum apparent change of adm installations and methods as observed from ground or air or by enemy agents in rear areas until after zero.

2. The contents of this order will be disclosed only to those required to act upon it, and then only in sufficient detail and in time to enable them to act efficiently.

AMN

3. Coys will ensure that 1st line amn holdings for all weapons are complete before 1200 hrs on D Minus 3. Tps will carry 100 rds SAA plus two grenades incl 1 — ST.

4. RSM will arrange that the two Bn reserve trucks are loaded with balanced loads of all amn. One third of Bn reserve amn will be loaded as a balanced load on one veh and will be pooled with vehs from other units to form a mobile Bde Res. This veh will be under comd B.S.M. and will report to "overflow" veh RV by 2330 hrs D MINUS 1. This reserve will move on night of Day and will establish in vicinity Main Bde HQ. Report centre will be at Pro post at Main HQ.

5. RSM will arrange to deliver contents of one veh to fwd coys as soon as re-organization commences and replenish from Bde Res and NOT from Res AP at 88102975. In addition all carriers and portees carry a supply of SAA and tps will be informed so that they can contact them if supplies are short.

6. Careful control must be exercised by all tps to prevent excessive expenditure of amn.

STORES

7. A minimum of 1 pick 1 shovel will be carried by each sect,and 3 sandbags by each man. HQ Coy pls will carry picks, shovels, sandbags with their weapons.

SUPS

8. Tps will carry one days ration for D PLUS 1 and mid-day meal for D Day. Emergency rations will be carried by all tps. Breakfast for D Day will be taken fwd by tpt with tps and must be consumed by 0500 hrs. Vehs will then move back to B Ech area dropping hot-boxes at kitchens. Evening meal will be cooked in 2/32 Bn Area at kitchens selected by QM and delivered by three trucks made available by 2/32 Bn. Every effort will be made to supply a hot evening meal from B Ech on D PLUS 1.

POL

9. All vehs will have full tanks plus 100 miles POL on Veh. In addition unit petrol veh will be fully loaded.

10. A reserve PP will be established at 88062976 but POL will not be drawn until veh and unit reserves have been used.

WATER

11. Scale: One gall per man per day for all purposes.

12. QM will arrange that half gall per man in containers is taken fwd on night D MINUS 1/D DAY. The containers will be stacked in coy lots by 1900 hrs D DAY. QM will arrange collection.

13. Tps will be encouraged to drink freely on D DAY as this has a beneficial effect if wounded. Water bottles will be filled.

ORD

14. Loss of weapons, compasses, binoculars, will be notified to Bn HQ as soon as possible. Bn in turn will notify Main Bde HQ.

PW

15. Coys will be responsible for getting PWs back to a collecting post on the line of advance as quickly as possible and by all available means. The Bn is also responsible for PWs sent back through the area by 2/13 Bn. Coys will be expected to co-operate.

   A collecting post will be established by Sgt Cameron, who will arrange quick evac to Bde PWCP at 87642977. A minimum number of guards will be used, and they will be instructed to take determined action in the event of trouble.

MEDICAL

16. RAP at FUP until capture of objective. On capture of objective RAP will move to 87172979.

17. 2/8   Fd Amb ADS at 88272981

   2/11 Fd Amb ADS at 88022980

18. Walking wounded move back along lighted axis of advance to RAP.

19. Vehs returning from coys will be used to take back lying and sitting wounded to RAP.

20. To enable our medical organization to concentrate on our own rather than enemy casualties, coys will ensure that

   (a) Enemy medical personnel are allowed to continue work.

   (b) Enemy medical equip is NOT touched except by medical personnel, and that it is returned to RAP as soon as possible.

   (c) Enemy med vehs are not used other than for medical purposes.

DRESS

21. Battle Order with trousers KD, gaiters or puttees, shirts, sweaters. Gas cape and pr of eyeshield will be carried in Haversack.

BLANKETS

22. One blanket per man will be taken fwd on D MINUS 1 and used in slit trenches. After 1900 hrs D DAY they will be rolled in bundles of ten in coy areas and picked up under arrangement by QM.

23. On D MINUS 1 two blankets per man will be dumped at B Ech and carried to new B Ech area under arrangements by QM.

24. On night D PLUS 1 two blankets per man will be taken fwd in Q trucks and delivered to tps in fwd area.

PACKS

25. Packs and Gt coats will be dumped at B Ech on D MINUS 1 and held until required.

LOB

26. Personnel LOB will report to B Ech at 1800 hrs D MINUS 1 and move fwd to a new area under arrangements by QM and TO.

BURIALS

27. Coys will do their utmost to avoid burials in scattered graves. No burial will take place without prior knowledge by Bn. A Bde cemetery in which all possible burials will be effected is to be selected.

(Signed) A J NEWTON Adjt.

Oct 22: Quiet day — Coy administration etc. All Coy Comds took their NCOs down to Sec leaders to Bde sandtable made to see the area in which we are to attack. GOC 9 Aust Div was there while C Coy was in attendance and the whole scheme was explained by GOC himself. 2300 hrs. Bn moved by MT to lying up area behind Pimple in Square 876298.

Tom Fitzpatrick noted in his diary at 2200 hrs on 22 Oct: "All ready at last to move up to assembly area behind the front line at Tel El Eisa where we will wait for the big attack on Friday night. Last four days have been very busy getting the carrier in first class order, checking ammunition, guns, water stores and 1001 other details. We have been told the time and date of the coming offensive. The Bde has practised the first attack four times and we all know our jobs. This evening at mess, Capt Maclarn called us together and gave us a few final instructions re small details such as giving morphia to wounded."

During the period the Battalion was engaged in operations at Tel El Eisa and the build-up to the Battle of El Alamein, battle casualties were: KIA and DOW, 3: accident, 1: WIA, 37. Fatalities were:

NX52185	Pte Commins F 6/9/42	NX44504	Pte Tink I M 17/8/42
NX19225	Cpl Moncrieff J A 6/9/42	NX16224	Pte Fell J 4/10/42

LEST WE FORGET

Left: *A dummy truck built as part of the deception for the El Alamein attack.*
Right: *The wreck of a Messerschmidt – Tel El Eisa.*

CHAPTER 11
THE BATTLE OF EL ALAMEIN

Montgomery used deceptive engineering works to suggest that he was going to attack in the south later than the October moonlight. An operation there would have repeated the open desert warfare escapades in which there had been frequent failures by British armour. Destruction of the enemy where they were located was his purpose.

In the north, the enemy had built up extensive positions in depth with minefields and wiring. He had proved sensitive to westward thrust there which could offer the use of rail and road. It was expected he would stand and fight if attacked there getting his armour massed for counter-attacks and so available for destruction.

Direct infantry frontal attack by night was the solution getting surprise and hiding from the daylight visibility. Montgomery had the Infantry to do it. They could go through wire and minefields, fight in the dark and hand to hand. The depth of minefields and the night fighting contemplated precluded close support from tanks until more mine-free areas were reached. A lot of artillery and ammunition was available. There was space for gun positions to be dispersed. The co-ordination achieved through artillery command and liaison allowed huge concentrations of fire against enemy counter-attack. Pre-planned defensive fire strips were practicable and were planned to produce from every gun within range defensive fire across the front of the planned infantry objectives. Each 1,000 yds was given its code name to be called on when the fire was needed. Air photos and patrol information and normal artillery skills allowed effective fire to be produced with surprise for the opening attack.

Engineers were to be relied on to get a vehicle gap through minefields so that, on reaching an objective, a Bn could call forward its supporting vehicles with a/tk guns and machine guns and mortars in time to be prepared for enemy counter-attack with the tanks by daylight.

Start time for any attack had to be calculated back from first light. Go back, first the time needed to dig in and camouflage a/tk guns. Add the time to reach and capture the objective plus the delay in arrival of vehicles, itself the subject of contingency time to get a gap through any minefields. Adjust for the slowing period of no moonlight and you come back to an hour of night after which attack is unsound.

In brief, infantry with planned artillery support would move through minefields and wire, fighting to its objective measured in yards from its start line. There it would dig such holes as possible and, with the a/tk guns there, dug in and camouflagedand the planned artillery defence, it could face the day with confidence and hope.

In concept, this could be repeated through a dog-fight with the enemy, a bashing of his counter-attacks and ultimately a break-out by armoured forces to cut off and destroy his remnants.

Montgomery had established a special Armoured Corps (X Corps with 1st, 10th and some 8th Armd Divs) with the concept that, on its own, it would break out from the infantry penetration, through remaining enemy positions and end up fighting on ground of its own choosing to annihilate enemy armour. It is now clear that his armoured commander gave indications before the battle that it was not the role of armour to break out as envisaged and that role would not be performed. At stages in the battle, Montgomery gave insistent orders for this to occur, but it did not happen. The dog-fight stage extended with the bulk of the burden cast on 9 Aust Div earning ultimate thanks, acknowledgement and congratulations from Churchill and the President of the United States and all the senior military commanders.

From its initial break-in to the west, 9 Div was turned to fight to the north to the line of the railway-road ultimately inwards and to the east with the invidious consequence of Bns attacking into the face of their own artillery support fire. At that stage the enemy were proving even more resilient perhaps because of morale elevated by their belief that, on the initial night, this German division had lost no ground. It had not realised that the "attack" on their ground was a deliberate deception using limited raids, a heavy mortar fire plan and artificial figures of attackers to sustain the idea that it was a full attack

It is not the role of a unit History to trace each step even within the Division. First reference for the Divisional story is to read Barton Maughan: *Tobruk and El Alamein* Series 1, Army Volume 3 of the Official Publication *Australia in the War of 1939-45*.

On 23 Oct the 9 Div break-in was by two Bdes — 26 Bde led by 2/24 Bn on the right with 2/48 Bn to follow through, each having also a right flank protective role.

The left two-thirds of the front was covered on the right by 2/17 Bn with a frontage of 1,200 yds and on the left 2/15 Bn, reduced in strength after its Bulimba raid, with 800 yds frontage. From the Bde's first objectives 2/13 Bn with tank support was expected to reach the final objective for the night, the Oxalic line from which X Corps could break out.

To cover its front, it will be seen from the orders that 2/17 needed three Coys forward for the first phase with the Reserve Coy and B or C to move on after the pause to the Bn objective.

Thanks to detailed training and rehearsals this geometry was achieved. The start line, in fact, consisted of three parallel coy start lines as prepared in training. From the right of A Coy through B Coy and to the left of C Coy the 1,200 yds was covered. Beyond to the south was 51 Highland Division.

Oct 23: Effective strength 26 Offrs and 610 Ors. 0100: All tps settled in Coy areas and occupy slit trenches. By midday the men were getting restless in cramped positions.

The slit trenches were covered by sand-coloured mats to conceal from air observation. There was no enemy ground observation. From midday on, Bn was harassed by calls from Bde officers to stop soldiers emerging. This was an impossible task and, generally speaking, the bulk of the men kept under cover.

Tom Fitzpatrick, who was in the vehicle assembly area, noted at noon on this day: "Splendid trip up last night. Arrived here 0100 hrs. Busy morning checking and cleaning guns. My carrier has 1 Vickers, 1 Bren, 1 Browning, also 1 dozen hand grenades, 3 rifles and 10,000 rds. Must have a spell this afternoon as it will be a long time before I get another chance. During the trip up last night we saw plenty of evidence of the huge amount of preparation going on. Passed Division HQ on the way. Morshead turned out to watch us pass." As the Official History states:

> "The 9th Division developed in its summer fighting at El Alamein a unity of spirit it had not entirely achieved before. The men were developing confidence in Morshead as their Commander and an affection for him they never had in Tobruk."

Engineers parties arrived and began the work of opening our minefield. Detachments reported to Coys for the attack.

1930 hrs, 23 Oct: FUP party leaves assembly area.

El Alamein Opening Barage – 2140hrs, 23 Oct 42

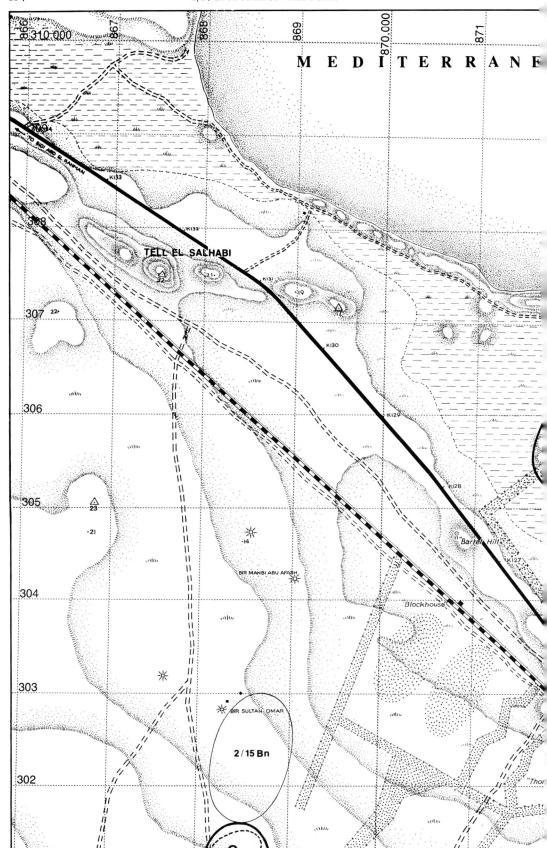

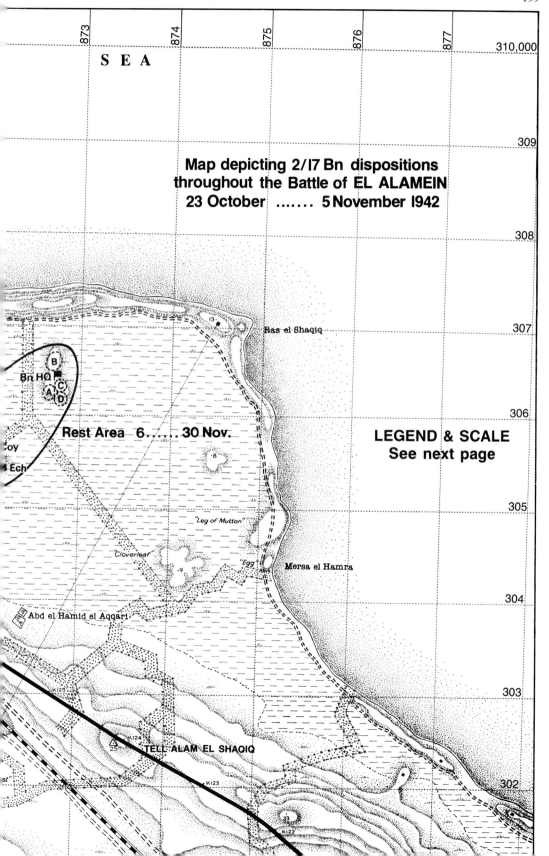

Map depicting 2/17 Bn dispositions throughout the Battle of EL ALAMEIN 23 October .... 5 November 1942

S E A

Ras el Shaqiq

B
Bn HQ
A C
D

Rest Area 6 ..... 30 Nov.

LEGEND & SCALE See next page

.8

"Leg of Mutton"

"Cloverleaf"
.9

"Egg"   Mersa el Hamra

Abd el Hamid el Aqqari

K123

K124
25   TELL ALAM EL SHAQIQ

K123

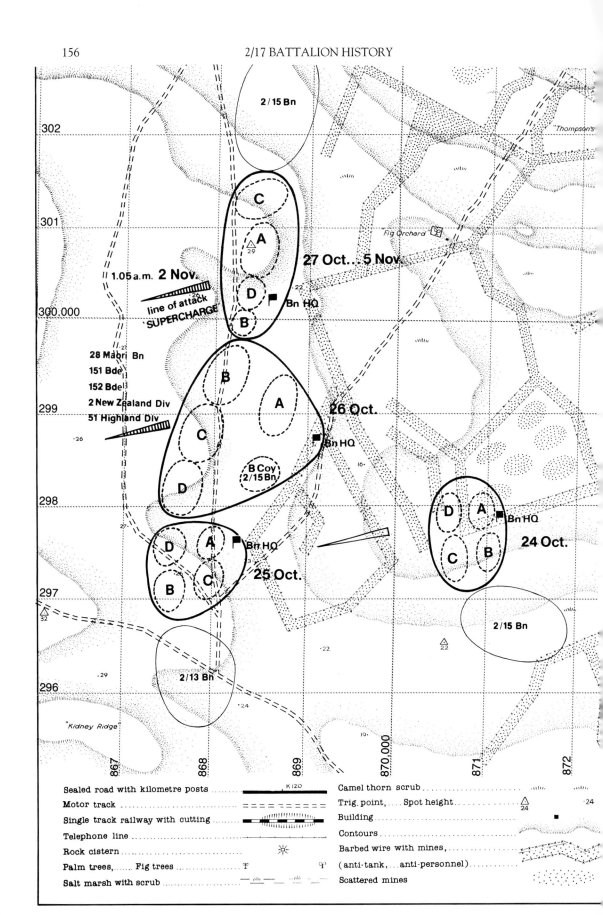

2/15 Bn

302

"Thompson's

301

C

A
29

Fig Orchard

27 Oct... 5 Nov.

1.05 a.m. 2 Nov.

D
Bn HQ

300.000

line of attack
'SUPERCHARGE'

B

28 Maori Bn
151 Bde
152 Bde
2 New Zealand Div
51 Highland Div

B

A

26 Oct.

299

C

Bn HQ

·26

D

B Coy
2/15 Bn

298

D   A

D   A
Bn HQ

B

24 Oct.

C   B

Bn HQ

D

A
Bn HQ

25 Oct.

297

B   C

32

2/15 Bn
22

·22

·29

2/13 Bn

296

·24

"Kidney Ridge"

867   868   869   870.000   871   872

Sealed road with kilometre posts ....   K 120   Camel thorn scrub ....
Motor track .... ========   Trig. point, ... Spot height .... △   ·24
                                                                                                      24
Single track railway with cutting ......   Building .... ■
Telephone line ....   Contours ....
Rock cistern ....   ☀   Barbed wire with mines, ...
Palm trees, ... Fig trees ....   Ŷ   ℗   (anti-tank, ... anti-personnel) ....
Salt marsh with scrub ....   Scattered mines

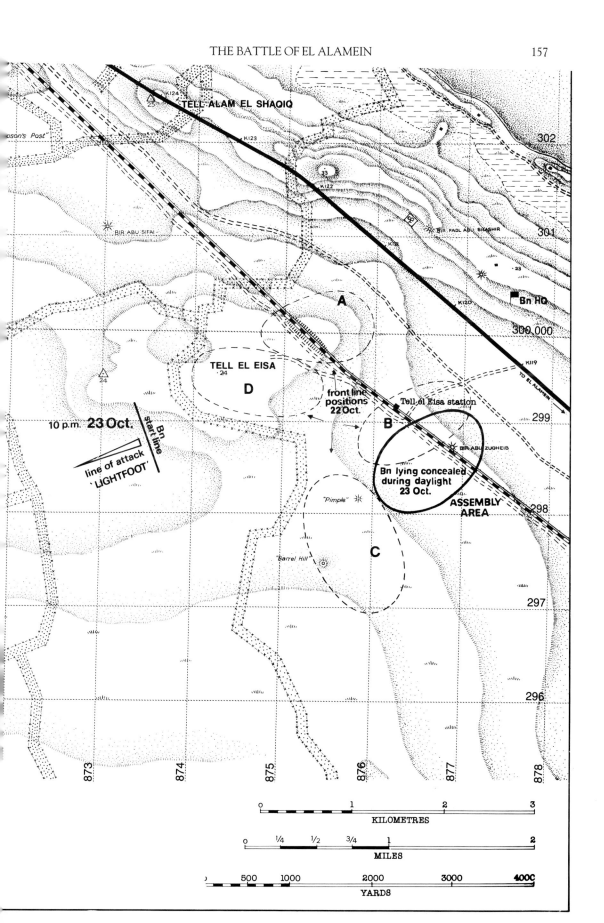

TELL ALAM EL SHAQIQ

son's Post

BIR ABU SIFAI

BIR FADL ABU SHASHIR

Bn HQ

A

300,000

TELL EL EISA
·24

D

front line
positions
22 Oct.

Tell el Eisa station

B

299

BIR ABU ZUGHEIB

10 p.m. 23 Oct.

Bn
start line

line of attack
'LIGHTFOOT'

Bn lying concealed
during daylight
23 Oct.

ASSEMBLY
AREA

298

"Pimple"

C

297

"Barrel Hill"

296

873   874   875   876   877   878

0   1   2   3
KILOMETRES

0   ¼   ½   ¾   1   2
MILES

500   1000   2000   3000   4000
YARDS

The daytime of 23 Oct lying hidden in holes did nobody any good, but confidence quickly built up with a hot meal, and talk and checking among ourselves. Moving out at 2030 hrs in column of route to the start lines was like another rehearsal. "There was no doubt we knew how to do what we had to do, and we knew we would do it." (Broadbent).

There was the extraordinary silence of the desert at night. 2140 hrs and the eastern skyline was marked with the unbelievable flashing line of the opening of gunfire. Then came the whistling swish as the first shells went overhead, to some, exhilarating, to all, confidence inspiring. Then in seconds came the gun sound and the shell explosions. A pause in the gun fire showed start time was near. At 2200 hrs the lines moved forward. It was the first Bn attack. The Lt AA horizontal tracer went overhead showing the axis for advance. The clear moonlight dulled with dust and smoke from artillery support as the enemy positions were approached.

Arthur Newton's recollection of the evening of 23 Oct was moving out with a small party of about five to meet up with the IO of 2/15Bn and his party and the Bde IO with two signallers from 20 Bde HQ. These tape-laying parties were to locate the centre of the Bde start line with 2/17 Bn operating to the right of that point and 2/15 to the left.

"Some delays occurred and, worried about the time aspect, we moved off. We identified ourselves the centre for the start line. The main tape-laying parties moved up with coy guides etc. Eric Blundell, then Int Sgt, was in charge of this party and he and his men did an excellent job but we did not have much time to spare before the Bn arrived. A platoon commanded by Lt Hugh Main was out in front of this area in a protective role and as Hugh and I had served in C Coy together, I knew his worth, and had no cause for anxiety. When I joined the CO for the advance at 2200 hrs, besides Dal Cartledge, with us was also Lt Cuthbert Shelden, then a Bde LO, who, after we had advanced perhaps 100 yds, whipped off the CO's cap and hurled it into the darkness and clapped a steel helmet on the Red Fox's head. Colonel Simpson, in his inimitable fashion, had worn his cap perhaps as his badge of office but just as likely because he may not have liked wearing a steel helmet."

A Coy, our right forward company, struck the strongest opposition and suffered many casualties including the OC, Maj L C Brien, who was badly wounded. The Bn successfully achieved the objective.

Casualties sustained up till midnight 23/24 Oct were:— Killed: nil Offrs, 15 Ors; wounded: 2 Offrs, 45 Ors and missing: 14 Ors.

In this first phase the magnitude of our arty concentration seemed to dwarf the enemy's DF which was quite heavy. A Coy suffered most of their casualties in silencing two strongly defended enemy positions. Lt Hannaford took command of the coy when Maj Brien was wounded and the coy went on to reach its objective on scheduled time.

Few POWs were taken by the Bn in this first advance. Bn success signal was fired at 2357 hrs. Communications were effectively maintained by '18' sets, old and heavy packs, but both Bn HQ and A Coy were off the air for a time owing to damage by enemy action. The CO passed messages through the reserve Coy set as the Comd Gp (CO, Adjt and IO) moved just forward of Coy HQ. The Bofors gun tracer was of great assistance in keeping direction in the smoke and haze of arty. In crossing the maze of enemy defensive fire, it was a most difficult task to keep on the correct bearing.

Cpl Ellison described how A Coy fared:

"As our terrific artillery barrage was switched from the enemy gun positions on to his FDLs, A Coy cross the start line with a strength of 80 men. This included only 2 Offrs, the OC, Maj Brien, and Lt Hannaford, who had just recently gained his commission.

Casualties began to mount up immediately as the enemy unleashed a strong defensive barrage, and by the time the German wire was reached the coy had suffered heavily. 7 Pl, on the left flank, had run into trouble and was being subjected to harassing fire from German positions behind a thick protection of barbed wire. This called for the use of a Bangalore torpedo which had proved so effective in previous operations of this type. The Bangalore torpedo is a hollow iron tube packed with high explosive and is used to clear a path through barbed wire entanglements. Torpedomen Graham Hardie and Roy Barker performed an excellent job in edging the long torpedo under the wire and blowing a wide gap through which the platoon went straight on to overwhelm the German resistance and take prisoners.

Over on the right flank, 8 Pl and Coy HQ faced a very nasty situation. The wire was riddled with booby traps, and an enemy mortar lined on this section of the front claimed a heavy toll of the attackers. Pl Comds, Sgt Chilvers and Sgt McHenry, had become casualties, as had the two engineers attached to the coy, and in a direct exchange of shots with a German officer, Maj Brien was badly wounded.

A conspicuous act of gallantry was performed by Sgt-Maj Cliff Polson who was killed when he dashed forward in an attempt to close with a powerful German post.

The position of A Coy had now become desperate, and 9 Pl, which was brought forward out of reserve to assist the attack, also suffered casualties. Over this bloody scene a great fire had somehow started and the whole area was illuminated by a pulsating, unnatural glare.

The turning point in a very serious situation was, perhaps, an act of outstanding bravery by L/Cpl T Harris, who was later awarded the DCM. He stormed a German mortar and MG post and, although wounded, he insisted on carrying on until the following morning. Although still facing heavy fire, A Coy maintained the pressure and finally overran the German positions and pushed on to its objectives.

A check on casualties revealed that Coy HQ had practically ceased to exist, only the Sigs being left. 7 Pl had fared relatively lightly, but 8 and 9 Pls had both lost more than two-thirds of their men. The Coy was now commanded by Lt Hannaford.

Despite heavy losses, A Coy stuck to its task magnificently. The steadiness of its officers and men prevented a costly mopping-up operation which would have had to be undertaken if the Germans had been allowed to hold these positions."

Bob Anson of Sig Pl kept a diary and noted for this day, 23 Oct:

"B Coy HQ with Capt Tim McCulloch, Duty Sigs Eric Vincent, George Henderson and myself. Hot day, confined, black flies a nuisance — made a fly veil. George in 2/4 Bn tells me of his escape from Crete. At night emerge from our burrows like rabbits in the sand country of far west NSW. I start quoting 'Rabbits' to Eric and George — 'stuck in me dugout 'ere, down in a hole, I'm feeling like I've grown a rabbit's soul'. We check our phones, the cable layer and telephone lines. Check out wireless code. Join Tim and Co. I see two long search light beams draw together overhead (a signal for H Hour) then fairly jump out of my hide as the guns open up. Skirl of bagpipes away on left. I think of my grandfather — he was a good piper and my blood thrills. A big flash and bang and 'R over T' goes Eric, two others and me. Eric is badly wounded, the others look dead. Stretcher bearer arrives. Take phones from Eric, catch up to the fighting, Germans shot. Tim shoos me off to RAP. Many wounded. Dr Sullivan pulls out shrapnel from right arm and neck. Vic Rae bandages. On way back run into Blue Morrison laying lines. D Coy Capt McMaster and Sig Joe Murray pass by us. Spend a noisy, painful night. I wonder about my young brother, somewhere near us."

Tom Fitzpatrick, in his diary, noted at 2105 hrs:

> "We are waiting just behind FUP, excitement intense. Arty will open barrage in 15 minutes. It will be the heaviest ever known. All hands in good spirits. If anyone is nervous, he is now showing it. Just before we left last position Gordon Newman and I received a bottle of Scotch from Frank Bryant. We argued who should carry it, but have now decided that both will carry it — inside us. Heard some bagpipes playing as we were moving up. What a war! 2120 hrs: Apart from the noise of our own vehicles there isn't a sound. 2139 hrs: Just heard an Arty Offr behind us call out: 'One minute to go'. . . A few seconds later there was a great sheet of flame extending as far as could be seen to north and south, followed immediately by a terrific roar. We heard the first salvo go screaming over our heads.
>
> 2210 hrs: We are on the way. Enemy arty opened up for a few minutes during a slight lull in our barrage. As soon as our guns resumed, his stopped. My crew comprises Don Osborne, Derek Cunningham and Bill Friend. 2230 hrs: We are halted about half-way to his forward line. It is a magnificent sight. 2245 hrs: Met first of prisoners coming back, also some of our wounded. They don't know what is happening ahead of us.

It is interesting to note that, earlier in the evening, the German Comd, Gen Stumme, radioed his routine report to Hitler's HQ in Germany. "Enemy situation unchanged."

Under date 24 Oct, Sgt Cec Greenwood wrote:

> "The show started last night — 9 Divisions going in. . . Our arty put up a marvellous barrage and we followed it in. 13 Pl had some bad luck, the gun we were following was dropped short, one shell got Bill Inglis, Joe Wilson, the engineer, Dead Eye and Bob McElroy. Dead Eye and Bob came on. Well the arty gave the enemy such a pasting that there weren't any there to fight — couple of 'Ities surrendered to the stretcher bearers. Reached our objective and dug in and got tons of ammunition."

Oct 24: Place 87082979 El Whiska Sheet. Effective strength, 24 Offrs and 540 Ors. 0010 hrs: Bn HQ was in dummy minefield with D and C Coys forward on a line from 87022981 to 87032973. Contact was immediately made with 2/24 Bn on our right and 2/15 Bn on our left. The engineers soon completed their difficult task of cleaning and marking a lane in the intensely mined areas within enemy FDLs and A Echelon vehicles were brought up. Coys immediately set about consolidation tasks. At 0100 hrs, 2/13 Bn passed through just south of our Bn HQ and went forward towards the Bde's second objective. No tanks came up for them.

Enemy shelling during the remainder of the night and during daylight hours was not excessive even though casualties from 0001 hrs until last light on 24 Oct were 2 Ors killed and 1 Offr and 50 Ors wounded.

1600 hrs: A movement order was delivered by a LO. 2/13 Bn were not on objective and 2/17 Bn and 2/13 Bn were to push forward by attack to the 867 grid line due to have been reached the night before.

Broadbent was sent across to co-ordinate arrangements. He was a longtime friend of Lt Col Turner (both had served together in Sydney University Regiment for years). Prompt agreement on a simple plan was expected. On arrival he found that Turner had been mortally wounded and evacuated with his Adjutant. Major Colvin had not yet arrived to take over. Some of 40 Royal Tank Regt were in the area after late arrival for support of 2/13 Bn the preceding night. Their CO had been talking to Turner when he was wounded but he was not then available and no tank support could be arranged for 2/17 Bn. There appeared a possibility that no enemy would be encountered. No officer was present from Bde HQ and communications with it were inadequate for instructions. There was no artillery plan and no artillery officer was available for discussion. Co-ordination of start lines could not be agreed and in the ultimate, Broadbent designated the start line for 2/17 Bn with an 800yd frontage, accepting that 2/13 Bn would probably put their start line in rear to the left. Indications were that 2/13 Bn could not meet the suggested start time of 0100 hrs and a loss of 1 hr digging in time might have to be accepted. 2/13, by starting at minus H Hr, could catch up to the alignment of 2/17.

On return, Broadbent found the CO more seriously sick and barely able to speak. He whispered that Broadbent was to give the orders and control the advance. He accepted he would have to wrap up in a blanket and come up in his jeep. He knew from the completeness of rehearsal training that there need be no concern about the coys forming up and going on this job.

McCulloch from B Coy left forward had patrolled and found Germans. British tanks had moved forward in what must be considered a break-out gesture, but withdrew, leaving 2 Sherman tanks blazing in the area. In the flatness and restricted visibility specific German positions had not been located.

At 2200 hrs B and C Coys relieved two coys of 2/13 Bn occupying the prospective area of the Bn start line. The illumination of the burning tank may have invited bombing which hit B Coy, killing two and wounding three.

Sig Bob Anson's Diary describes thus:

> "Long periods of battle noise. I can see heavy shellfire going across C Coy, on our left and in front, explosions around D Coy. Looking to the right, A Coy is copping plenty.
>
> Some tanks crawling around. Shellfire and sniping from posts as George and I take turns to maintain lines. We crawl by posts with enemy dead. Tank battle to south-west. At night, as I go back to Sig Office a flare from overhead bomber, I pass East's section, then a bomb lands, dive into a hole with dead Germans. East's section lost."

The Bn O Group was assembled for Broadbent's oral orders. B and D Coys forward distributed across the frontage distance corresponding with rehearsals and as used the previous night. The distance for advance was designated so that the so-called Oxalic line on Grid 867 would be reached and held, the vague possibility of armour exploitation was ignored. Reserve Coys A and C would move in rear with Bn HQ Group in the centre. Transport would come forward in the dark to pick up Bn and other supporting weapons in the area to form up in A Echelon to come forward after capture of the objective, rejoining in new localities with the same coys.

It was to be a silent night-attack which meant the normal no lights, smoking or talking discipline of night movement without the benefit of supporting fire. No artillery fire plan could be called in on contingency, nor was there any artillery officer to move forward with the Bn.

Barton Maughan's Official History states that the silent attack was agreed between Colvin and Simpson but it is not now known how contact for such agreement was achieved. Bn tradition is that Simpson would not have agreed to such a gap and blame was attributed to lack of co-ordination and support from Bde HQ which, in turn, was attributed to the acting Brigadier whose status had not been established in the unit.

The Bn formed up with the white start line tape glaring in the light of the burning tanks. The start time of 0200 had been accepted and was observed. Nothing was seen of 2/13 Bn coming up on the left. Distance to the objective had been indicated but, subject to contingencies, it was planned to keep spacing co-ordinated and for Bn HQ to break wireless silence and give the code word for "Halt". The map showed a line of cairns would be crossed in the advance and this was seen. Later Broadbent was nudged to show pace counting indicated the objective was reached. He waited a while before ordering "Halt". It was better to be sure the line had been reached this time. If exceeded, then, a little nearer to the planned line for artillery defensive fire could be gratifying. It was 0250 hrs 25 Oct.

The advance had been without contact. The silent moonlight was bright. The Coy's distances had been kept and, subject to usual local adjustment, digging in could begin. Soldiers would take their lightened picks and shovels with shortened handles carried down their backs between the haversack, and set to work with the vigour and urgency upon which life might depend.

Suddenly, across the front the fast rip of Spandau MGs broke out being fired from positions on the ground shortly ahead. Their tracers showed lines of fire no distance above the very flat desert which, with its small tussocks, added to the eccentricity of the ricoches.

Unbelieving, Broadbent heard his Sig report the code words for "B Coy Comd killed". Sigs say he kept demanding checks about his friend until ultimately it was passed in clear, "Capt McCulloch killed". On the objective completing his orders for consolidation, a bullet had gone through his forehead. The other Coy Offr, Lt Bennie, had been wounded. Sgt Eric Williams had to take command.

Sig Anson notes:

> "With wireless on my back, a burst of machine gun kills Tim. I go to ground alongside, relay news. Eric Williams keeps control. Truck explodes and burns near us. Lt Bob Bennie takes over, a German sniper plants a bullet in his arm and he moves out for RAP. Terrible day as George and I crawl back repairing lines. A badly wounded German from a scout car knocked out by Frank McGrath is sheltered with George and me. We look after him till nightfall when he is taken back to Bn HQ."

In this situation, coys have to retaliate with their own weapons. A Echelon, with support weapons, was not due to move forward until a signal from Bn HQ so that by the time they got up coy guides would have arrived to help dispersion. It is to be remembered that the CO was in his jeep with A Echelon and hearing the sounds of fire and not accepting delay, he had ordered the vehicles forward. A chance aeroplane overhead may, perhaps in the moonlight, have seen the unlighted vehicles as they arrived. More probably by a chance of war it dropped its bombs in the region of the Bn HQ at 86802978. Some were killed and Lt D J Cartledge, the IO, gravely wounded also the Sig Offr, Lt Coulton. Bill Waters, the loyal soldier and cheery batman to the Adjutant was noted for his care of the wounded. In this disturbance, a British tank arrived with a Lt offering a/tk guns. He did not seem interested about fulfilling his offer, closed down the tank and drove off, running over our dead.

First job given a Section of mortars was to put down a baseplate and get bombs the short distance ahead to the enemy fire source. A carrier patrol went to give covering fire for the dig-in. On the left the MMG vehicle was set on fire and men hit. With great coolness, Sgt John Cortis got out a Vickers and brought a subsection into action, silencing Spandau posts. Elsewhere, Lt George Wray walked calmly around his Pl delivering ammunition and encouragement. Somehow, the enemy fire abated. It is probable with our controlled objective so close and threatening they decided to be gone. In any event, they had moved by daylight. Within this time, all possible digging-in had been done and a/tk guns were in position under their nets.

Early light showed signs of enemy appearing to form up for a counter-attack. Their 88mm guns were firing low overhead, aimed at, and hitting, vehicles to the near rear, including the mortar ammunition truck driven by Pte R B Williams. With spectacular calmness and bravery, Williams patched up his truck three times in the battle and each night delivered bombs to all baseplates.

Tom Fitzpatrick noted:

"0930 hrs. It was a hell of a night. Our attack was held up by one strong post. Three carriers, including mine, were sent to try to attack it! We reach D Coy after passing through heavy fire. Lt Murphy contacted Capt McMaster who said that the Germans had too many a/tk guns and that it would be useless to go any further forward. Murphy then returned to Bn HQ, leaving Bill Stewart and self. After waiting half an hour, I walked over to where D Coy was digging in to ask McMaster just what the position was. Told him we would not last two minutes once daylight came. McMaster told me to give him covering fire until his men were dug in, then he would send word for us to go back. While walking back to the carrier, I heard bombs falling and ran for it. Managed to dive under the carrier just as they hit the ground. Two more attacks in the next few minutes. Learned afterwards that Ron Avery had been killed in one of these. About this time an ammunition truck behind us was hit and blew up. Shortly afterwards, word came from Capt McMaster telling us to go back, so we went to platoon area just near Bn HQ and had to work like hell to dig in before daylight. Derek Cunningham, after digging his own hole helped me with mine – very decent of him. I deepened my hole between shells later on. Also mounted the Vickers. Ken Pratt did a good job when some bags in the back of a truck caught fire. He got the fire out somehow before it got to some petrol tins in the back. Since daylight we have been heavily shelled, mainly air burst very well placed. Twelve more of the platoon wounded and Hank Farrelly killed in the hole next to mine. Who next?"

A mortar carrier had been crippled and left standing. From training times in Syria, friendships had been developed with 57 Bty of 7 Fd Regt, allotted as the primary liaison and support source for artillery to the Bn. Lt Tim Rodriguez from that Bty had joined the Bn on its objective on the first night but with orders to stay there as a fixed observation post in depth. He was unhappy that 2/17 Bn set off without a gunner. He resolved early on 25 Oct to come forward and join us. He reached the disabled mortar carrier and halted alongside. Having to stand to see anything the two vehicles gave some shelter. The protection was limited. Flying shell pieces tore holes in his sweater. His impact was immediate and enemy pressure greatly reduced. Many in the Bn were to write in about this bravery and the feeling of teamwork and confidence it gave. Rodriguez received a MC. Later in the morning desert haze was rising and the Acting Bde Comd arrived. He expressed strong views to Rodriguez about his indiscipline in concentrating two vehicles and inviting enemy fire. Next criticism was the shallow diggings done at Bn HQ and that dead still lay there. Rodriguez got on with the job as enemy tanks began their approach.

There had been a torrid time since arrival at the objective at 0250 hrs. When it stops, it's over and you press on with what is left. If you are not near the line of Spandau tracer, you can dig, but shallow holes onto rock with no chance of overhead cover suggested problems when the 88mm fire began and enemy tanks could be seen. Already there was justification for the day to be called "Black Sunday".

At 0650 hrs Bn reported to 20 Bde: "12 enemy tanks and lorried infantry forming up on our right." The attack developed and the relevant pre-planned artillery SOS defensive fire strip "Waterford" was called down. A/tk guns watched patiently concealed. No firing until within positive killing range. This first display of the SOS fire was very encouraging. It foreshadowed how artillery concentrations were to be a major factor in the battle success. At 0745 hrs Bn told Bde, "Artillery fire now right on target. Attack not developing very well". It did not reach our FDLs and appeared to move back without quite going away. Tanks stood off and watched from 600yds and fired at occasional targets.

Later through the haze, tanks could be seen about a mile off the left front of the Bn and to the south in front of 2/13 Bn. The movement became more purposeful. Tanks appeared in irregular waves with infantry vehicles in rear. The strange straight line silhouette of the top of the turrets of German Mark III and Mark IV became apparent. The protruding heads of tank Comds could be seen. True to training, forward infantry posts fired. The effects of their bullets could be seen. The heads disappeared and the straight line silhouette merged into the turret as the lid flaps were folded in. Shells landed amongst them but the advance continued steadily. Thoughts turned to their ultimate arrival with hopes for survival until a hand-held a/tk sticky bomb could be placed! But suddenly that was over. Simultaneous long flashes of flame and clouds of rising dust showed the discipline of the 6-pdr gunners of 2/3 A/Tk Regt waiting till the killing range. Rear tanks caught fire, then forward tanks. The advance broke down. Smoking tanks turned aside and sought to go back. Vehicles in rear, plastered by field artillery, turned away. The mood of impending crisis had built up watching tanks or some of the 8th Army's new self-propelled a/tk guns ("Priests") firing head on, but without seen effect, and withdrawing to bait the enemy forward. We had heard that this had been part of the earlier success at Alam Alfa.

The German attack operation had lasted about 2 hours. Exposed to fire and suffering casualties in their forward positions, the Bn's a/tk 2-pdrs did not fire a shot as the attack was stopped before reaching their accepted close range limitation. To fire beyond that would have disclosed a position otherwise not readily seen through the camouflage nets. Disclosure invited annihilation from a tank's gun of greater range and the end to a proper fulfillment of their role in the defence. During this stage, Lt Stuart Williams took over the Bn a/tk guns. For the rest of the battle, he did a consistent and courageous job re-siting and co-ordinating on moves, visiting and supporting, always forward. Hit once on the head, he acknowledged a day plus later he still had a headache. He continued to wear what surely must have been the most rent-open tin hat in the 8th Army.

In the afternoon, an attack on the Bn included M13 Italian tanks. It went on from about 1400 to 1630 hrs involving for a lesser period 2/48 Bn on the right and more intensively, 2/13 Bn on the left. Field artillery pounded the enemy. 6-pdrs shot. Again our 2-pdrs remained watching. Enemy fire was landing everywhere, without evident co-ordination or target. Finally forward movements broke up. Vehicles turned back or away. No distant infantry could be seen forming up. There was no renewal of smoke screen to cover a new surge. The attack was over.

Orders had come to move right and relieve 2/48 Bn. It was to attack north to Point 29 while 2/24 Bn was to attack north-east from its first-night objective.

Getting wounded back during daylight, including wounded enemy was pressing and dangerous. Arthur Newton has commented:

"Carriers picked up some. I recall Skipper Mendham driving a jeep to various positions to pick up wounded. Among killed were Sgt Darby Green who, at his own request, had moved from being the Bn Orderly Room Sgt to the Mortar Pl. A wonderful man who was killed, as he had foretold in a poem he once wrote, by a Spandau burst. Uki Cameron was another fine man and soldier who died by an airburst shell. Lt Coulton, the Sig Offr, also was badly wounded losing a leg. Stepper Stephens, who had been a quartermaster in C Coy, and then transferred to the Carriers, was also wounded. I recall him walking back to the RAP."

Just after last light, as on every subsequent night, Keith Sabine, the Transport Offr, arrived with vehicles, hurriedly getting around with a hot meal, rations, clothing, equipment, any needs for the following day, including water. Other vehicles evened out and/or replaced ammunition supplies. (They had also to take back the dead to be buried next day. They are to be found today in the same groups of graves.) This loyal and reliable support, the conversations, the spattering of news gave relief and stability to those who had been forward all day. They were sustained and grateful. That night and, on subsequent reliefs, Sabine was a great help in the detailed control and directions needed to meet, bring in, identify and re-direct troops coming for the relief. The relevant Coy Orderly would be waiting to take them on to his coy area. There the Pl guide or orderly would get them to relevant section positions. Whatever could be said about positions and possibilities was explained. The relieved coy would move back in turn to get its directions.

During the afternoon for the relief, this night and the same for the next relief, Broadbent moved across to liaise with Lt Col "Tack" Hamer, a great CO, to hear from him how he was winning the War and get a briefing from his IO about their localities. On the first time, Hamer was having a desert bath with a sponge, very gleeful. His patrols had captured the German officers acting respectively as regimental and Bn commanders and with German speakers on his South Australian HQ, they got useful minefield and occupation information. Hamer planned to exploit this with a carrier rush and troops on vehicles for the second phase of his attack. It happened accordingly.

Shortly after dark, the Bn advance party moved across, Sigs and I Sec people to start in the Bn HQ, Coy Orderlies to glean information from their counterparts if to be found. Suddenly something hit a vehicle which exploded. Flames jumped from vehicle to vehicle with huge increasing blasts, hurling pieces of tyres, vehicles and goods with unknown noises in all directions. Despite this, 2/17 Bn, less D Coy which held its position, moved in, sheltering in any holes while seeking true positions. By 2200 hrs relief was completed. The fire plan began at midnight and 2/48 Bn completed a brilliant attack. By first light they had laid out 2,000 Hawkins mines, occupied positions and made contact with 2/17 holding their old positions.

Point 29 was no great prominence, but significant in the battlefield flatness. The ground near it ran away slightly more to the south than the east and north, and not in any evident way to the west. The locality offered a few feet better height for viewing but the Germans thought it vital ground. At this time it was almost the westernmost point occupied by 8th Army. It suffered 25 German attacks mostly on 2/17 Bn.

Moves to the north from the original break-in had been in contemplation and Point 29 was an obvious mark. On 26 Oct, Montgomery was holding important conferences. Progress in the south had held German forces there, but no break-out through the Highland Division had been achieved by X Corps. Elements had come forward up different mine-cleared tracks and had some engagements. Rear congestion had been terrible but, at the front, reconstituted enemy positions and the depth and range of 88mm guns were not mastered. From such disbursed commitment, the Army commander's concept of a stage-managed break-out thrust by X Corps could not be achieved. He had to regroup to form a new strike force, directing that 9 Div should continue the crumbling attacks and dog fight towards the north. Meanwhile, plans for, and the location of the break-out operation "Supercharge" would be decided.

To those committed on the battlefield, little of these matters could then be known. The rest of the night of 26 Oct required settling down in the shelling and developing the positions occupied. First light seemed reasonably calm when Broadbent and Blundell, casually carrying their rifles, began a circuit for a visual check and passing shouts with coy positions. The MG on one of the tanks standing off at about 500yds put them to ground behind old earthworks. They could feel the rounds hitting. They seized an opportunity to get away, but the tanks stood off and continued threatening. It was an extended feature of the battle. The War Diary noted:

"It was a hectic night which finally ended with 12 enemy tanks sitting on the ridge in Square

866299 harassing and annoying us with a/tk and small arms fire. They remained there throughout the day to our discomfort. Their bag for the day included 1 carrier, a scout car of 46 Royal Tank Regt, an ambulance and the back wheel of our Bde LO's jeep."

On 25 Oct, Rommel had returned from Germany to resume control.

For a while on 26 Oct, the Bn was out of the range of 2/7 Fd Regt's guns but during the day, they occupied new gun positions and the nearby FOO had a phone to Bn HQ. Shellfire was causing Sig lines to be cut. Every day, every night Sigs with courage bolstered by duty and tradition would run sig line in hand until the break was located, mended, tested both ways and the run back or forward resumed. Skilled coy orderlies running in to give a fuller picture, faced the same risks. Ross Jamieson of B Coy HQ was killed by small arms fire on this duty. John Carter of C Coy arrived at Bn HQ with a bullet sear across his rifle butt.

Sig Anson noted:

> "Sitting ducks we exposed linemen. Run and claw my way back as dawn breaks. Shelter at wrecked gun. German tanks sitting on ridge. Terrible day, as we cop all sorts of fire. One 88 airburst wrecks our set, useless bloody thing. Every time we put the aerial up we get shot at and then if we lay out the ground aerial no contact can be made. Ross Jamieson is dead — Bren carrier with consolidation gear arrives out of the smoke. A shot goes through the carrier and Merve Williams and Harold Cremin dive for cover. Really bad day for nerves. Cable lines are frustrating communications."

Brig W J V Windeyer resumed command 20 Bde on 27 Oct.

On that night, 2/17 Bn, itself relieved by the Seaforths, relieved 2/48 Bn on and around Point 29 as it was counter-attacked. B Coy of 2/15 Bn had been placed under command to add depth to the defense. From the start Point 29 was plastered. Enemy shells came in from all directions and even 25-pdr from SE, eventually traced to an unaligned Scottish gun. By 0300 hrs 28 Oct, the changeover was complete, but close fire continued. At dawn mortars, MMG and C and D Coys firing got the position in hand. Strength was 17 Offrs, 416 Ors.

Practically all communications had broken down. At Bn HQ the two carrier pidgeons given for such a case were looked out. Their basket had been hit but immediate duty was delayed. A few days later, they were released with a note saying, "Herewith two bomb-happy pigeons".

Attack developing from the north-west had been repulsed, Bn mortars joining in with artillery defensive fire. Throughout the day, Capt John Dinning crouched with his I-man, Vic Walshe, in holes in the torn up dirt that constituted Point 29, managed to give directions for artillery fire and get in information. Dinning was awarded a MC and Walshe sustained his reputation for courage and calm, valuable service.

The night had involved counter-attacks and the day continued the same. The fighting continued endlessly. Morale beat fatigue. Despite the drain of casualties, the closeness of threats and the lack of information, nobody had doubts that 2/17 Bn would hold, and on the ground it was felt that somehow, ultimately, it would be over and won.

Vic Walshe was the I Sec representative with C Coy throughout the battle and recalled its takeover at Pt 29 on the night 27/28 Oct with Dinning and Bill McLennan. They had got some sleep in dugouts that seem solidly constructed with sandbag roofs. The Germans knew its exact location, having previously been in occupation and woke the party with shellfire. Sandbags burst in on them. Getting a look around when things got quieter about 1100 hrs, two people were located he thought were British, who claimed they were waiting for a jeep to take them back from their Arty OP duties. Dinning's pressure could not get them to do anything. There was a good view of the coy area and of D Coy.

Captured Breda Gun AA Defence at B Ech

Result of good Anti-Tank support

Walshe's account continued:

> "Spotted a Jerry mortar dropping shells on D Coy. Enterprising bloke had a weapon pit and at rear ammunition pit, was running from ammo pit to mortar, drop one in and scurry back to pit at rear. Had a crack at him with rifles but range too far, or he ran too fast. John got on to D Coy and observed the firing of their mortars and put him out of action in fast time. Our lines of Bn HQ out of action. . . Place seemed deserted but one of our arty OPOs came crawling along a slit trench to find his Sigs. Seemed badly dazed, had been in a forward OP of Pt 29 which had received a direct hit. Went forward to look for his Sigs — what a bloody mess, his 2 Sigs, youngsters, and hanging grotesquely from the beams, went back, shocked with the thought of telling him. He wouldn't believe and pleaded that I go back and make sure. I couldn't refuse. Went back and found his field glasses which saved further explanation . . . Saw a Sig mending line, had his back to me and for a moment thought it was another repair job to own line. Suddenly noticed he was not moving, went closer and found it was Bruce Weary — no apparent mark on him, sitting upright but he was dead."

Walshe described the attack of motorised infantry coming on until halted by small arms fire and debussing to start infiltrating. Dinning was getting back messages directing artillery. Ted Rand was wounded by a mortar blast and stretcher-bearers with a white flag managed to recover him. He waved his hand in reply to Dinning's greeting but Frank Fields, the rear bearer, shook his head. "Relieved that night by A Coy and move forward down the track to position north of Pt 29 with 2/15 Bn across track and on our right." He quoted the true story of the capture of the Volkswagon and the capture of a fair-headed athletic English-speaking German Captain and the unreal calmness with which he and Dinning discussed their comparable ages and rank. There were some quaint little quiet interludes in the battle.

On 28 Oct the broad story was that 2/17 Bn after its break-in and the second night attack to the Oxalic line, had side-stepped to the north and on the second take-over from 2/48 Bn assumed the defence of Pt 29. It was to hold there against all attacks until the end of the battle.

Montgomery's order for 9 Div to go north was to lead to very complicated plans for night operations. The multi-phase attacks depended on prior phase success, timely relief in line, hopeful arrival of tanks and support weapons, all to be achieved in reduced moonlight and confused battlefield conditions.

For the night 28/29 Oct, the first phase was for two Bn attacks at 2200 hrs.

On the right from the north facing FDLs east of Pt 29 2/13 Bn was to close up south of Thompson's post. The Bn was depleted by casualties and fatigued from prior operations, having completed only at dawn that day its takeover from 2/24 Bn. It advanced some way, overran posts and captured enemy. At dawn, it was in an exposed position. Its Comd, Colvin, wounded and other casualties led to problems locating officers in the chain of command.

On the left 2/15 Bn was to extend to the north the Div's western face.

The status of Pt 29 was such that, at night it was inevitably bombarded if the enemy thought attack was likely anywhere, which seemed to be every night. It started as 2/15 Bn came up to its SL north of Pt 29. Broadbent greeted CO Magno (an ex-2/17 Bn original) with information and an offer of shelter. Magno chose to move forward to be among his soldiers on the SL. He suffered wounds from shellfire. He was evacuated for forward surgery, but he died. His Bn's attack succeeded and, encountering no mines its A Echelon vehicles got forward promptly for effective consolidation. C Coy 2/17 was moved north to block the gap between 2/15 and Pt 29. B Coy 2/15 Bn remained under command 2/17 Bn to give depth.

In the centre, later on night 28/29, 2/23 Bn of 26 Bde was to attack with 46 Royal Tank

Regt and get through to the low ridge of the railway line-road. These two units had trained together and it was planned that the forward troops would be carried on tanks and others on Bn carriers. Tanks missed the gap made in our minefields and moved about searching. Confusion ensued. Regrouping under fire from six a/tk guns they lost their infantry. Ultimately, the CO gathered some 60 or 70 men and advanced to capture the enemy post with its a/tk guns. They had to dig in short of the objective.

The Div plan had intended (1) 2/23 Bn to reach the road, (2) 2/48 Bn to come up there and attack east, (3) 2/24 Bn to follow and then attack south to capure Thompson's Post and (4) 24 Bde to attack west from the old defensive positions and capture the original German FDLs facing them. The much respected commander of 26 Bde, Brig "Torpy" Whitehead (a War I soldier and original CO of 2/2 MG Bn and then CO 2/32 Bn) learning the difficulties of 2/23 Bn planned an alternative course to launch 2/48 Bn followed by 2/24 Bn from the new 2/15 Bn position. It was certainly appropriate that 9 Div cancelled this desperate effort to fulfill its orders.

C Coy's Trophy

Not surprisingly the enemy was uncertain locating the new positions. Vehicles drove in and were captured. C Coy got a small military model Volkswagon, then reporting its possible capture sought Bn HQ approval to retain it on success. Approved.

In the morning and the afternoon, enemy tanks and infantry formed up for attacks and again, about 1700 hrs a further attack was made at C Coy and 2/15 Bn. Between times, tanks stood off menacing and sniping. 6-Pdr crews relaxed enough to fire some long-range shots which occasionally succeeded. Dinning's fire direction and information were again commended.

At this time the westward Bns had encountered the 90th Light Div hurriedly brought forward from El Daba to the west of the battlefield. The German 15 Armoured Div was brought up from the south to join the efforts against 9 Div but had few tanks left.

While confidence, but uncertainties existed in the battlefield, uneasiness was developing in London. Alexander protected Montgomery from some pressures while the latter developed his plans for a breakout. He stated it was the morning of 29 Oct he decided on "Supercharge". A composite force under the New Zealand General Freyburg, consisting of one British Brigade and a Highland Division Brigade, helped by the Maori Bn were to make the initial infantry attack towards the west. It was expected the north flank would go through Pt 29 and strike Italians but Germans were in front of 2/17 Bn.

Meanwhile, 9 Div was to continue attracting German attention and counter attacks in the north. The Germans had already prepared to fulfill their part in this future. Rommel had appointed his 90th Light Division commander to take charge in the north and establish a new German line including Pt 29, the 2/15 Bn position and then north-east to the coast.

At dawn 29 Oct, 9 Div FDLs, beginning at Pt 29 with 2/17 Bn faced west, then went north to 2/15 which faced west and north. From there FDLs ran east and a bit south to 2/23 Bn which faced north with 2/13 Bn on its right. To the east again 2/13 Bn linked on its right with the Divisional composite force designed to cover any gap between the break-in points and the old defences still held by 24 Bde in a line going north to the sea. During the night 29 Oct, 2/23 Bn was moved forward about 1,000 yds to match the east-west alignment between 2/15 and 2/13 Bns.

On 29 Oct, the effective battle strength was 16 Offrs and 377 Ors. A dust storm reduced visibility to a few hundred yards. Lt Hannaford, an original and recently commissioned from the Middle East OCTU, was killed by a sniper's bullet. Lt Nicholson took over.

Bn HQ just south of Pt 29 had its share of casualties and others were struggling in. The RAP was quite close. Again Bill Waters and Bob Bevan, the Bn Clerk, went wide-ranging to bring in wounded. Padre Byrne also helped carry. The RAP consisted of an inherited hole with a wide ramp leading down a few feet to what had been made a room by earthworks on the side of the initial digging and covered with overhead protection. The RMO, John "Slam" Sullivan, despite the traffic, had by no means been stuck in the RAP, but ranging about with normal calm and brave attention to his duties. He earned a MC. Born 1915, he was an early identity. Having been a L/Sgt in S.U.R. he threatened subalterns with a demonstration of how to be Comd of a guard. Post-War he was a GP in Newcastle and served in CMF as a CO of a Fd Amb and later as Colonel, Senior Medical Officer in NSW. From our supporting 8 Fd Amb, vehicles would arrive to take back wounded. On 31 Oct, Sullivan himself was to be wounded and evacuated. That day an ambulance had been accompanied forward by another MO, Capt H L (Bill) Hughes, who stayed on as RMO, a bright and, in some ways, extrovert personality, who helped sustain Bn welfare in body and spirit until after the New Guinea Campaign. He was to acquire the nickname, "Snow", priviledged only to 2/17 Bn users. In Queensland, a disgruntled soldier had returned from the RAP, complained to his tent mates, "Its no use going to see him, he will only give you an Aspro". Quickly someone noticed, "Snow 'ughes going to see him".

9 Div plans became more complicated. Within 2/17 Bn, little was known. Not much could be seen by day and reliable information was not available during the nights. Daytime traffic just east of 29 was considerable and added to the occasions for bombardment.

To draw more attention self propelled (SP) 25-pdrs had moved up at one stage very close behind Bn HQ and fired on enemy positions and concentrations all day. Their equipment was known as "Bishop" being a standard 25-pdr gun mounted on the chassis of a Valentine tank. Another SP gun was "Priest" which was a properly designed American weapon with a 105mm gun in a Grant tank chassis. "Deacons" were 6-pdrs mounted on lightly armoured chassis self-propelled.

On Montgomery's general task to the Division, Gen Morshead seemed to fix some more specific purposes. (1) to cut the road/railway running along the east/west spur on the north of the battlefield. (2) to drive back eastward and open the road. (3) to branch north and south and clear Thompson's Post and the rest of the original forward positions occupied by the German 164th Division and (4) to break north from the road/railway to the sea and cut off German remnants to the east.

Revised plans for these purposes were prepared for the night 30/31 Oct. 2/32 Bn to attack northwards from rear of Pt 29 to breach the road/railway line. 2/24 and 2/48 Bns on right and left respectively to form up and attack east and then turn south and north respectively and clear enemy positions. 2/3 Pioneer Bn, in its alternative infantry role was given contingency tasks. 2/32 Bn breached the road/railway line near Barrel Hill (ref.87093046). They had severe casualties, including a badly wounded CO, Lt Col John Balfe. 2/24 and 2/48 Bn formed up and attacked east into the face of the artillery support and, after heavy casualties, and some confusion and misunderstandings separately withdrew to join 2/32 Bn. 2/3 Pnrs were launched in the pre-dawn hour to go north from 2/32 Bn trying to reach the coast. In the ultimate, two of its companies were gravely exposed and lacking in support and supply. They were fired on by the enemy from three sides. They suffered bad casualties. With ammunition expended some were captured after desperately holding on against the enemy's furies. Some regrouped with 2/32 Bn. British tanks and Rhodesian a/tk guns were got forward to support this Barrel Hill locality.

During 31 Oct fire on the Bn area reduced. That night, while traffic abounded our guns seemed quiet. No attack was being made but a silent and effective relief. The joint remnants of 2/24 and 2/48 Bns, totalling probably less than 100 all ranks, were relieved by 2/28 and 2/43 Bns, moving up by wide detour from the original Pt 33 Tel el Eisa defences. 24 Bde, now together, made a terrific success of the night-time revision and co-ordination of defences about Barrel Hill. Soon they faced fierce German fire and counter-attacks with tanks and infantry, the fire and threats extended south to the 2/15 and 2/17 positions. Heavy casualties continued and included 24 Bde Comd, Brig Godfrey and several senior officers at his HQ. They got the benefit of the 18 British bomber flights successfully bombing the German attackers.

Montgomery's plan for 9 Div to attract and occupy the German forces in the Divisional area was thoroughly served. On the night 1/2 Nov, "Supercharge" went in with huge artillery support and heavy bombing in rear areas and pressure on 9 Div reduced.

With major attacks beaten off, there frequently remained near the Bn, or had somehow penetrated, relatively small groups. For example, enemy voices could be heard in a slight hollow near C Coy and were engaged with a platoon 2" mortar. 3" mortars were continually in use. Some 3,000 rounds were fired in a 3-day stretch. Targets were as near as 150yds and out to a concentration at 1,500yds.

About this time, Cec Greenwood in C Coy, as a Pl Sgt, recorded:

"Had a few hot moments yesterday. The enemy started to advance and the boys got stuck into them. I got a couple of hits with the 2" mortar. During the early part of the night a Hun truck, which I think was lost, had got pretty close to our Section and we fired on it and sent up a Verey light. Huns were yelling and running everywhere. We killed one and took two prisoners, one wounded. It was a ration truck loaded with bread. Unluckily, we moved last night, came some thousand yards forward and dug in — had a good sleep all day. Bob McElroy died. Ted Rand badly wounded."

Cpl Tom Fitzpatrick even recorded a quieter day with enemy air activity striking in rear.

The Bn did not suffer much during the battle from enemy air attack. A substantial degree of air superiority had been established and scattered forward infantry could expect a lower priority than congested vehicles, obviously thought to be waiting to make a break-out. Some thought earlier bombing on night 24 Oct had been by our own planes. After long periods of no air support in Tobruk, there was gratifying change. The sight of 18 bombers flying undisturbed in formation to pattern bomb the enemy was gratifying and would produce cheers as an area of dust cloud arose from striking bombs. The planes were not to finish the battle immune from enemy action, nor Allied criticism when demarcation smoke lines were not effective. Gratifying also to see raiding Stukas shot down by Spitfires.

Through to the end of October the battle continued for 2/17 Bn with enemy fire from tanks and artillery. Between what seemed serious attacks, occasional enemy groups formed up for dispersal by our mortar fire. A special bombardment was suffered when some signal flares were fired by order or request to establish a location. Lt A.H Urquhart, a Pl Comd was wounded in

the back. Originally a Sig, he had been commissioned at ME OCTU. The wound lost him a
kidney. In WWI, his father had been wounded with the same result.

31 Oct, effective battle strength, 17 Offrs, 379 Ors. By night and by day just to the east,
there was a lot of traffic moving to the Bns in the north. News of the operations was very vague.
The plans, as far as known, seemed involved. Subsequent knowledge of the intensive fighting
and the struggle with uncertainties leaves no doubt as to why news reaching the Bn was sparse
and conflicting. Special interest was in 2/32 Bn, Comd by Lt Col J W Balfe, an original Coy
Comd in 2/17th he was twice wounded and evacuated.

The continuing problem of 88mm airburst was brought home with the fatal wounding early
on 1 Nov of Capt Ian McMaster, OC D Coy. Pre-war he had trained with Light Horse and like
many suffered adjustment with the arrival of Lt Col Simpson to command the Bn. He had
managed D Coy well through its diverse roles in the battle. It was found he had been awarded
a MC and his control of the Coy appropriately marked. Arthur Newton confirmed Maughan's
description that McMaster was: "An outstanding OC and an excellent manager who got the
best out of his soldiers. A studmaster and grazier of Dalkeith, Cassilis, he had been commissioned
in 12 Light Horse in February 1939. He was in his 35th year when he died. His calmness and
clarity in describing a situation and dry sense of humour remains firmly in my memory." Lt Hugh
Main took over Comd of D Coy.

Other visitors were COs and Offrs about to do the attack for "Supercharge". Groups of
officers with map boards illustrated perfectly the, "What not to do", the subject of repeated
criticisms in training exercises — at least in the Australian Army. But the Maori CO gave the
impression of a tall, handsome, quiet, intelligent man.

On the first night of "Supercharge" and another later, at least part of the Bn had to withdraw
from positions against the contingency that Bns on "Supercharge" formed up in rear might, on
reaching the Bn's position, fire before realising that they had not run into enemy. On the
evening of 1 Nov, their SLs were laid out a few hundred yards east of Bn HQ. Bn guides moved
forward with them from their SLs. Bn withdrawal was not popular and some men got wounded
on the exposed return through enemy shelling. B Coy found some DLI sheltering in their holes
and sent them on their way, 2 Germans had hidden and gave themselves up to A Coy at dawn.

Events following "Supercharge" involved uncertainty and enquiries were addressed to the
Bn to determine where was the Maori Bn and what had happened to it. The small, friendly
groups of Maoris walking back as company for a wounded comrade could give no information.
It fell to Broadbent to follow their advance and analyse the situation. Our own forward Section
posts had no information, but L/Cpl Jack Wilson gave him a friendly warning about MG fire
that could be expected. A little better news was obtained when the Maoris got thicker and with
greater semblance of operational function. Their CO had been wounded and the command
function had lapsed. The omission of information sent back did not appear to have been
noticed then. Nevertheless, the Bn was on the ground in a relevant area.

2 Nov was to be quiet except for two periods of heavy shelling.

It is noted that at 0800 hrs, Bn HQ was treated to an amusing incident. Some 16 German
POWs had been doubled in for about 400 yds by an escort of two and halted, exhausted and
frightened. Broadbent was questioning them, surrounded by the usual interested spectators
when some enemy shells landed more or less nearby but suitably disregarded by the locals,
disregarded except that the Germans cowered and went to ground. Maj Broadbent gave vent to
a typical Broadbent yell: "Get up". The startled expressions of the POWs and their swiftness in
obeying the order is something that everyone who witnessed the incident will never forget.

Through the day, away to the south-west there seemed to be hundreds of vehicles and tanks moving forward through dust and smoke as some were hit and burned. In the afternoon they were seen subjected to two Stuka parades. Nothing was heard of the tactical situation, but it was again evident that no breakout had been achieved.

About this time the Bn got a rum issue!

3 Nov, effective battle strength was 16 Offrs and 359 Ors. The diary recorded this as the first day of the battle that the Bn area had not been shelled. Many tanks and vehicles could be seen away to the south-west. Troops could move about without danger and almost everyman went forward to view the areas of the battlefield and search for souvenirs and seeing a/tk guns dug in tanks, a new type of enemy mortar and other interesting items. Carrier patrols sent to search for enemy towards Sidi Adl Rahman brought an Austrian OPO who claimed he had been on the eastern front but the last 10 days were by far the worst he had ever experienced. Other carriers towed in a long-barrelled Russian a/tk gun and 4x50mm guns rid of beach blocks and sights. It was clear that the previous night the enemy had abandoned his positions in front of the Bn.

Brig Windeyer visited during the afternoon to indicate that 2/15 Bn were to extend to their left front to contact the Maoris. Subsequently, Capt Pitman as OC B Coy was directed to reconnoitre a new coy position to give depth. Frequent flights of 18 bombers passed overhead to unload their bombs on enemy targets.

Later in the afternoon, Lt Col Simpson submitted to the sustained medical pressure for evacuation and rest for the intense throat infection that had been heavily affecting him from the second day of the battle. Broadbent took over administering command.

Bob Anson recorded how he and fellow Sig, Fred Camarsh, had moved out and seen the wastage of knocked-out tanks and guns, helped some Maoris bury their dead and collected a complete German eating kit as a souvenir embossed with the German Swastika. "Back at B Coy, I ponder on how could one survive as I, and yet never fired a shot, except wave his cable pliers in moments of despair and frustration."

Most of the Sig Pl had been so concentrated on their specialist duties, but not all. On the first night, Farrell had joined with his Coy Comd, Claude Brien, in a successful assault on an

B Coy Survivors — Cpl C O'Donnel, Capt C Pitman, WO Snow Vidler, WO C Iken, G Perry

enemy post and their CSM Polson killed. Steve Champion had acted in that role. Frontline communication was very important, but in defence it relied on Sig wire which was very vulnerable to the intense and extensive enemy shelling. Many Sigs had been killed on line duties. Spinks killed in bombing and Cpl Ife blasted in the 2/48 Bn truck inferno. The Sig Offr, Lt S R Coulton had been wounded on night two and Sgt Pincham who was older than most, had carried the strain for some days before relief by Cpl Macmillan (the Woolly Pup) whose bravery and application was notorious, and confirmed, in his later service.

The B Coy move was cancelled. Capt Murphy was ordered out with a series of carrier patrols. Enemy were seen in the distance and remote shots exchanged. On one Tom Fitzpatrick commented:

> "0600 hrs: 4 Nov on patrol again three carriers expected to contact the Germans. From where we are, we can see them a long way off. They are sending a few shells over. Had a look at some of the recently evacuated positions. Plenty of dead lying around, but no worthwhile loot. 1600 hrs: after waiting some distance out this morning we decided to go further and attack the enemy we could see in the distance near El Rahman mosque. Paul Murphy in one of the other carriers lead us to about 500 yds of them . . . fired about 3 belts of ammunition. We stayed until an 88mm shell came over and then, much to my relief, Murphy signalled for us to get back. On the way in, an a/tk shell just missed the front of my carrier. It would have been my fault if we had been hit as I had got out of the dead ground without realising it and it was running along a ridge — very careless."

On the same day, Greenwood wrote:

> "Well, I think our part of the stoush is over. We have been in this same spot for close on a week now and everything is quiet. I can see at present a long line of prisoners marching down the road a mile away. Went scrounging, got some water, had a good wash, can see the road from here and there are thousands of our trucks going up the line."

On 5 Nov, things were quieter still. Bn transport brought in extraordinary quanties of salvaged weapons, including 25-pdrs, captured by the enemy in earlier campaigns.

The Battle was over!

*El Alamein -1942 **(L)**: A captured German 88 mm gun. **(R)**: A German grave with its ornate headstone.*

Battle casualties at the Battle of El Alamein were KIA and DOW, 62; WIA, 203 and PW, 4.
The foremost are listed below:

NX14503	L/Cpl Ahearn J A 26/10/42	NX21348	Cpl Kidd D 23/10/42
QX22538	Pte Alexander L E 25/10/42	NX23136	Pte Lane C 24/10/42
NX23135	Sgt Avery R 25/10/42	NX14594	Pte Lee N 1/11/42
NX21463	Pte Burns F 23/10/42	NX59927	Cpl Lloyd J T 27/10/42
NX23059	Pte Cameron E A 25/10/42	NX22101	Pte Marcus L J 28/10/42
NX18165	L/Cpl Connor F 28/10/42	NX17195	Cpl Minehan A W 23/10/42
NX20615	Pte Crane N C 25/10/42	NX21689	Cpl Monaghan S C H 24/10/42
NX18440	Pte Dawson L T 23/10/42	*NX21758	Pte Murray A 27/10/42
NX21757	L/Cpl Dodd G W 27/10/42	NX14631	L/Cpl McAndrew J R 28/10/42
NX51675	L/Cpl Dreghorn A D 31/10/42	NX12408	Capt McCulloch E M 25/10/42
NX17220	Cpl East P S 25/10/42	NX37780	Pte McCully J R 25/10/42
NX60664	Pte Eccleston H J R 27/10/42	NX39870	Pte McDonald H E 23/10/42
NX38225	Pte Eccleston W L 30/10/42	NX23052	Lt McElroy R McL 27/10/42
NX36997	Pte Eyre P W E 23/10/42	NX12510	Capt McMaster I F 2/11/42
NX60325	Pte Farrelly W H 25/10/42	NX16313	Pte McMullen A W 29/10/42
NX60295	Cpl Franklin E S 28/10/42	NX60187	Pte Neus D M 30/10/42
NX36915	Pte Friend L G 25/10/42	NX53626	Pte Norris W T 26/10/42
NX21399	Pte Gash E A 25/10/42	NX54997	Cpl O'Connor J M P 12/11/45
NX33215	Pte Gersback J 23/10/42	NX20773	WO2 Polson C B 23/10/42
NX14617	Sgt Green N R N 27/10/42	NX24709	Sgt Rand E J 31/10/42
NX20774	Lt Hannaford R A 29/10/42	NX24694	Pte Reading R 26/10/42
NX24589	Pte Hawkins A J 25/10/42	NX22614	Pte Sharp C N 28/10/42
NX11557	Pte Henderson W G 15/11/42	NX16279	Cpl Shields S J 30/10/42
NX21791	Pte Hermon J C 24/10/42	NX39036	Pte Soorley J F 23/10/42
NX28867	Pte Hinds F A 25/10/42	NX26453	Pte Spinks R H 25/10/42
NX17783	Pte Hollingsworth F J 25/10/42	NX60548	Pte Sterling R S 29/10/42
NX24477	Pte Holmes W 1/11/42	NX56487	Pte Taylor R C 24/10/42
NX22425	Cpl Ife N R 25/10/42	NX16015	Pte Trevena J A 25/10/42
NX68744	Pte Jamieson J R 26/10/42	NX60524	Pte Venables W H 24/10/42
NX50419	Pte Johnson W 27/10/42	NX47936	Pte Weary B 29/10/42
NX16221	L/Cpl Jordon W A 26/10/42	NX66583	L/ Cpl Weston H L 28/10/42

*True name, Burrows F W

LEST WE FORGET

A stick of bombs falling on a 9 Div convoy with three vehicles damaged.

CHAPTER 12
POST ALAMEIN AND RETURN TO AUSTRALIA

It is still a matter of pride and waning dignity to have taken part in the great and important military achievement at El Alamein. The time gap has allowed calmer review.

It has yet to be shown that the Battle was unnecessary. That information was available to some from the British code breaking ULTRA, and otherwise, about the enemy's huge logistic problems does not establish that they should have been left to wither. The international scene called for action. The Russians were calling for another front and the Americans demanding a successful distraction before their North African landing. Churchill's build-up of resources in Egypt, his aggressive philosophy, and the orders and opportunity for Montgomery to show his military ability and the spirit of many soldiers in 8th Army overwhelmingly called for action.

The control and weak performance on the final break-out, and the rain, did not allow a complete annihilation but the defeat was total. Allied morale, particularly British was raised spectacularly and a new confidence felt in the Army. The Battle is truly spoken of as the turning of the tide of the War. It was a battle of achievement.

For interest or purpose, the conduct of the Battle is still examined. It has to be looked at with the resources at that time and place, although imagination can play with the use of technical advances. Infra red, heat detection, night vision, radar and other ranging and location, night and day exact position determination by satellite, transformed close radio and other developments separately would have saved much death and bravery. Together, without atomics, they would have transformed the whole scene, but they were not there.

Looking at the past as it was, the 9 Div preparation still seems excellent, the plan for the battle sound, the opening tactics inevitable, the objectives achieveable and the time frame reasonable. Yet there came no break-outs, the duration extended and the tasks within the Div more sudden and exacting. Why? Firstly, before the Italians became irrelevant, the German strength had been selected for destruction. Its minefields, motivation, morale, military efficiency, resilience and desperation proved very tough and the 88mm guns were not neutralised. Secondly, the potential of the break-out forces was over-estimated and the battlefield problems of getting them forward under-estimated. With new tanks and equipment, many new persons and teams superimposed on old desert practices and commanders, it is easy to guess that they were inadequately trained for such tasks as the break-out. Perhaps Montgomery knew the weakness and sought to remedy it with his frequent yet ineffectual insistence they fight their way out. Much armour did fight valiantly and valuably, but mainly within or close beyond the infantry localities which restricted the German fluidity that had devastated British armour in the desert before. Getting up to or back from such localities through narrow gapped minefields forfeited flexibility and failed to get concentration of effort. Reserves got committed but not involved, not manoeuvred but replaced by regrouping which takes time. The concept and use of X Corps is challenged.

In the more integrated fighting, tank/inf set piece co-operation with 9 Div did not succeed

*Alamein Railway Station. Now a
more famous name.*

on any occasion. Timely night movement near minefields with narrow gaps are not for tanks. Such realities cannot be matched in co-operative training, and flexible infantry have to control their expectations. But daylight defensive support is valued.

Within the Div, commanders and staffs seem to have been mesmerised by the success of the training and initial break-in, into believing there was no end to the involved geometry to which Bns could be committed. In fact, every unit ordered for a second or later phase which proceeded got to their FUP. Every relief planned was carried out. But distress followed committing weak or disrupted battalions or over-reaching without strength and support on the objective. Eastward attacks were unfair. Opening the road not essential and a divergence from the dogfight aim. Equal enemy aggression could have been provoked with greater security by a full 24 Bde attack on Barrell Hill to hold, maybe with daylight Bn exploitation with tanks to the coast. No jumbled and mistaken use of Pioneers was needed.

The achievement in drawing the German forces to frustration in the north showed their fighting power. It raises doubts about the possible success of the theoretic alternative of an early repeat of the break-in inf night attack to the west, using 9 and 51 Divs to penetrate the 88mm areas, make wide gaps in lesser minefields and push through an armoured div. Certainly, heavy enemy attacks would have been provoked yet there were the same resources of arty and sp armour to defeat them, the rest of 8th Army in reserve and some armour maybe broken out to harass. Hitler would not have let them run away too soon.

Years influenced by the dignity of participation and the tradition of military respect, often mellow subordinates into understanding and comradeship with commanders. By then, age adjusts the inclination or ability to question or analyse. When the battle concluded, 2/17 Bn had no questions to its commanders and received their visits and congratulations with pride.

The Div generally was ordered to bivouac away from the immediate battle areas. 2/17 Bn was to move to Squares 871308 and 862306 where there were slightly raised areas shown by single contour lines, one outlining the shape of Italy. At 1600 hrs, the Bn moved off cross-country in column of route from Pt 29 to reach the road with its continuous stream of two-way traffic. It was morale boosting and seemed to suggest a great administrative preparation for the exploitation of the battle success. As far as could be seen to the east or the west, the traffic was moving in a fast and steady flow. Broadbent marched the Bn into a line facing the road. A quick rush over would then be the least hold-up. With difficult intrusion the traffic was stopped each way and the Bn crossed. It reached and dispersed on Little Italy and the adjacent feature. A mood of quiet comradeship prevailed. The sense of relief was there, varying with the individual. A gnawing, deep sadness affected everyone as they reluctantly considered the reality. It took at least months for these feelings to adjust.

The battle had been fought in khaki drill shirts and slacks with sweaters mostly in haversacks, but everything was needed on night of 6/7 Nov when the desert was struck with very heavy rain and wind through the night. Further west British armour had been very slow to move and now got bogged in mud. Next morning, Col Simpson returned, restored to health by the short rest and medical treatment. He held a conference of all Offrs and NCOs Pl leaders and read several congratulatory messages from Senior HQ.

Comd 9 Div had repeated a message from the Comd of the 8th Army: "I want to congratulate you on the magnificent work your division has done on the right of the line. Your men are absolutely splendid and the part they have played in the battle is beyond all praise. Please tell the Division that I am delighted with the way it was fought.

Leese, the XXX Corps Comd had written to Morshead:

"I would be very grateful if you would explain to the men the immense part they have played in the battle. It is difficult for them quite to realise the magnitude of their achievement as the main break-out of our armour was accomplished on another part of our front, thus could not be seen by them. But I am quite certain that this break-out was only made possible by the homeric fighting of your Divisional sector.

The main mass of heavy and medium artillery was concentrated on your Divisional front. It was obvious that the enemy meant to resist any advance along the coastal route and, as we now know, they concentrated the whole of the Panzer Corps against you in the northern area.

Your fighting gave the opportunity for the conception of the final break-through in the centre, but this could never have been carried out if your front had been broken."

The CO announced the policy of resuming training including on the individual level. A large group of reinforcements had arrived, it having been deemed appropriate to hold them in rear while the Bn was committed. The LOB group rejoined.

Under the CO, the senior postings at this time were:

2/ic and OC HQ Coy	:	Maj J R Broadbent
A Coy	:	Lt Tony Nicholson
B Coy	:	Capt Colin Pitman
C Coy	:	Capt John Dinning
D Coy	:	Capt George Reid

Large reinforcements arrived and "X" list, wounded and others returned. For their benefit and for integration, there were conducted visits to the battlefield, and training simulating the forming-up and procedures that had been so recently undertaken for real. Gratifying promotions were announced. Those specially gladening were that Eric Blundell and Ken Gibb had been commissioned in the field. Both were beyond the age for the OCTU but their service, experience and status were widely admired and now fairly acknowledged.

Newton commented about Blundell: "A quiet and unassuming manner hides a very alert brain and a steely courage in peace and war." He said: "Ken Gibb was a grazier in the

Cootamundra district and in 56 Bn prior to 1940. He served on in his 15 Pl until wounded in New Guinea."

Another to return commissioned was Lt J D "Spanky" McFarland who returned from OCTU and was later to become the Adjt. Almost to the distress of some, the Adjt, Arthur Newton, moved out to a staff course. His great service had culminated in his jobs in the battle. Calm, effective and practical in every time of stress he watched against or fixed errors and exhibited humane understanding and humour. He remained forever akin to the spirit of 2/17 Bn. A J Wright became the Adjt.

A reconnaissance and assessment was made of the areas allotted to the Bn for salvage and burying of dead. Pioneers and Ack-Ack Pl do most of the duties.

30 yds ranges were established and practice ensued.

Padre Byrne conducted a service to formalise the burials in the cemetry.

A Bde Church Parade was held at which the Bde Comd complimented the Bde on recent operations and sounded several warnings which, presumably, were noted but are now not remembered.

On 22 Nov all Offrs, who were not with the Bn during the operation, visited the battle area under guidance of Maj Broadbent.

On 24 Nov the effective strength was 28 Offrs and 757 Ors. "Every man to be fully occupied", was the CO's order. Each day he visited all platoons to inspect training.

The Bn received visits from the Divisional Comd and the Corps Comd, speaking formally and informally within the Bn.

Pressure of rumours was satisfied when an advance party was sent off to Palestine and arrangements begun for the move and giving praise.

A message from Montgomery was read throughout the Bn as follows:

EIGHTH ARMY

Personal message from the Army Commander

1. When we began the Battle of Egypt on 23 Oct I said that together we would hit the Germans and Italians for six right out of North Africa. We have made a very good start and today, 12 Nov, there are no German and Italian soldiers on Egyptian Territory except prisoners. In three weeks we have completely smashed the German and Italian Army and pushed the fleeing remnants out of Egypt, having advanced ourselves nearly 300 miles up to and beyond the frontier.

2. The following enemy formations have ceased to exist as effective fighting formations.

Panzer Army	**20th Italian Corps**
15th Panzer Div	Ariete Armd Div
21st Panzer Div	Littorio Armd Div
90th Light Div	Trieste Div
164th Light Div	

10th Italian Corps	**21st Italian Corps**
Brescia Div	Trento Div
Pavia Div	Bologna Div
Folgore Div	

The prisoners captured numbered 30,000 including nine Generals. The amount of tanks, artillery anti-tank guns, transport, aircraft etc. destroyed or captured is so great that the enemy is completely crippled.

3. It is a very fine performance and I want, first, to thank you all for the way you responded to my call and rallied to the task. I feel that our great victory was brought about by the good fighting qualities of the soldiers of the Empire rather than by anything I may have been able to do myself.

4. Secondly, I know you will all realise how greatly we were helped in our task by the RAF. We could not have done it without their splendid help and co-operation. I have thanked the RAF warmly on your behalf.

5. Our task is not finished yet; the Germans are out of Egypt but there are still some left in North Africa. There is some good hunting to be had further to the West, in Libya, and our leading troops are now in Libya ready to begin. And this time, having reached Benghazi and beyond, we shall not come back.

6. On with the task, and good hunting to you all. As in all pursuits some have to remain behind to start with but we shall all be in it before the finish.

    SIGNED: B L MONTGOMERY
                   GENERAL
                   G.O.C. in C., EIGHTH ARMY.

Nov 30: Warm weather continued, everybody occupied packing for move to Palestine. The new RMO, Capt Hughes, reported for the month that: "The most prevalent disease was clinicial dysentry — during the period 104 personnel reported with diarrhoea — 34 were evacuated with the above diagnosis. In general, the health of the Bn is excellent."

The events of December may be covered in the Commander's Summary for December 42:

"On 1 Dec the Bn moved from its position near Sidi Rahman for Palestine. The Bn Comd was OC 'D' Convoy which comprised 2/17 Bn, 10 Coy, AASC, 2/8 Fl Amb. Staging for the four-day journey was Wadi Natrun, Suez Canal and Asluz and Julis Camp. During the four days the convoy worked like clockwork. The whole operation was a credit to the administrative staff, tpt platoon and battalion RPs. The convoy arrived at Julis Camp at 1115 hrs on 4 Dec. Tents had been erected by a working party from 20AITB under direction of Maj Alison, 2 i/c and the troops soon settled in to their new home. On Saturday, 5 and Sunday, 6 December large parties of the officers and men went to the 6 AGH at Gaza to visit their wounded friends. Many happy reunions took place. Transport was provided for those men still receiving treatment but, fit to travel, to visit their friends in the unit. On 7 Dec training began in earnest. Training areas were allotted in an area just east of Julis Village. The RSM began a cadre for recently promoted NCOs. For the whole month weather was perfect and training continued uninterrupted, except for the Christmas festivities. On Dec 14 B, C and D Coys spent the day at Nuseirat range."

Casualties during the battle had for shorter or longer periods imposed greatly increased responsibility on individuals beyond their normal rank and experience. Examples on the coy level included Lt 'Ocker' Hannaford, newly commissioned, having to take over A Coy and on his death, Cpl Bevan Ellison having to act for a while as O C A Coy. In B Coy, Sgt Eric Williams had a short period of command after the death of McCulloch. But down on the Section level, a corporal casualty meant that a senior man, or the natural leader that emerged, had to act. Some very fine contributions were made by men who suddenly found themselves with these duties. There was no reported failure. The end of the battle did not mean they were divested. In many cases they were not readily replaceable. The simple awarding of rank was not sufficient, either as an unasked 'thank you', or an exploitation. Continued faith had to be shown in them from above and kept from below. Urgent cadre training was begun under the control of RSM Dave Dunbar, including minor tactics and section leadership. In almost every case, this was successful. The psychology and the remedy were to be remembered and applied again when a similar situation arose after the New Guinea campaign.

The Bn had been singular in that no one was charged with any failure to do their battle duty. One factor was the alertness of the CO to the relief of strain as seen becoming significant or suggesting risk. An example was his compulsory two days at B Echelon for those in and surviving the outburst of fire and explosions among the 2/48 Bn trucks on the night the Battalion first relieved them.

Despite the CO's direction that every man was to be occupied, there was opportunity and requirement for swimming, sunbaking and general restoration of vigour. Some, too, were got away for leave in Alexandria and Cairo.

The second half of December involved some very emotional happenings. In brief, the new colour patch, the Gaza Parade, Christmas greetings from home and the announcement of bravery awards.

From embarkation on *Queen Mary* through all the Middle East fighting the Bn had worn the miniature black over green diamond colour patch of the original 17 Bn with a broader grey field showing the shape for the Div. The background originally had been the 7 Div diamond shape and, in Tobruk, the corners cut off to give the circle background for 9 Div. Other units had similar insert of the colour patch of their corresponding War I unit. There could be no uniformity or system through such minatures.Gen Morshead decided in expectation of the Div's ultimate return to Australia that 9 Div should have a new and unique shape colour patch with systematic colourings but applying, as far as practicable, traditional ideas. Hence, for infantry the senior (the lowest numbered) Bde colour would be green, next red and finally blue. Bn colours within the Bde to be in seniority sequence — black, purple and white. Hence, 2/17 Bn found itself issued with the colour patch it now regards as famous. The foreshortened "T" shape, with the centre white imposed on the familiar rifle green for 20 Bde and grey background for 2nd AIF. There was much sewing on to puggaree and tunics, some regret, but the General's purpose was accepted as a necessary step and a proper symbol of the Div entity and morale.

Rehearsals for a major parade are never popular and rightly are never omitted. They were endured without the results producing much flush of hope. The formalities of forming the Bn into four large companies, sized from flanks to centre and numbered, meant every man knew his exact place, and such variations as stepping out or stepping short as his position might, on the day, require. The usual few without felt hat, or other disarray, were hidden in the centre rank or excluded.

On 22 Dec, reveille was at 0415 hrs. While insistance at any inspection was anticipated, every man readily made his individual effort for immaculate appearance. For everyone who went on the parade, it was to be the greatest, most emotional and successful ceremonial parade of his life.

The grass parade ground on the Gaza airstrip was well laid out with exact lines and marks to ensure perfect alignments and intervals for the parade companies exactly numbered for equal sized groups of every unit in the Div, all placed from right to left in traditional seniority. The front of the parade faced the road Gaza-Beersheba, then hidden by the dias for VIPs and the grandstand for selected visitors, and spectator areas for the wounded and sick from hospitals and the red caped white veiled nurses.On the face of the alignment stood flag poles, one for each unit to carry its new flag with T colour patch, subsequently to be always flown in its camp lines. It is not inappropriate, but probably just chance, that the Beersheba Road in this region, is now an avenue marked on each side by several rows of well-established, weeping type Australian gum trees.

The Parade proceeded with total steadiness for the arrival of the Div Comd Morshead and the British Comd in the Middle East, Alexander. The traditional general salute, "Present Arms", was marked by the clear three sounds characteristic of that arms movement then a total stillness while the salute sounded. Gen Alexander stood in an open vehicle and drove the length of the front line for his inspection. Nobody glanced to see him come or go but,to the eyes looking straight ahead as he passed, his upright bearing seemed to show his respect for the men he saw.

He returned to the dias with its immediate backing of full-dressed officers of all Services, politicians and other importants.He gave a relatively short but telling address which, in the background silence and thanks to the amplifying system, was clearly heard throughout the Parade. His terms are quoted below. Later the text was printed and a copy given to every man.

> "Officers, warrant officers, non-commissioned officers and men of the Australian Imperial Forces; these great days we are living in are a time for deeds rather than words, but when great deeds have been done there is no harm in speaking of them. And great deeds have been done.
>
> The battle of Alamein has made history, and you are in the proud position of having taken a major part in that great victory. Your reputation as fighters has always been famous, but I do not believe you have ever fought with greater bravery or distinction than you did during that battle, when you broke the German and Italian armies in the Western Desert. Now you have added fresh lustre to your already illustrious name.
>
> Your losses have been heavy indeed and for that we are all greatly distressed. But war is a hard and bloody affair, and great victories cannot be won without sacrifice. It is always a fine and moving spectacle to see, as I do today, worthy men who have done their duty on the battlefield assembled in ranks on parade, and those ranks filled again with young recruits and fresh reinforcements.
>
> To these future warriors I extend a warm welcome and greet them as brothers in arms who have come to join the forces in the Middle East which it is my honour to command.
>
> What of the future? There is no doubt that the fortunes of war have turned in our favour. We now have the initiative and can strike when and where we will. It is we who will choose the future battlegrounds, and we will choose them where we can hit the enemy hardest and hurt him most.
>
> There is a hard and bitter struggle ahead before we come to final victory and much hard fighting to be done. In the flux and change of war individuals will change. Some will come; others will go. Formations will move from one theatre to another, and where you will be when the next battles are fought I do not know. But wherever you may be my thoughts will always go with you and I shall follow your fortunes with interest and your successes with admiration. There is one thought I shall cherish above all others — under my command fought the 9th Australian Division."

Years later, Field Marshal Alexander visited Sydney. Some short time was made available for meeting 9 Div ex-servicemen. It was arranged that Broadbent would meet him at the Airport. It was simple and informal. Broadbent said: "Sir, your Address to us at Gaza is widely remem-

2/17 Bn — Gaza Parade

bered. Probably many men may ask you to sign their copy. This one belongs to my Brigadier, Windeyer, which I will ask you to sign but perhaps you would care to read it. You may need a reminder more than we do." He read it and passed it to Lady Alexander, saying: "Not a bad speech, eh!" The requests for signing happened as forecast.

Thoughts of the past and sentiments from the speech submerged as Gen Morshead called the Parade to attention. Then followed tribute of the 12,000 on parade in the Salute to Fallen Comrades. What happened on the "Present Arms", the lowering of the flag and the sounding of the "Last Post" was uniformly felt as men stood at "Present Arms", Offrs saluting. It was sensed but not seen from those positions until later screenings of the Parade showed many close-ups. Emotions were intense. Tears ran down many faces,but there is nothing in the book to say that can't happen, only that you must stand still. The serious faces stayed wet while "Reveille" sounded and the flag hoisted to the masthead.

Formalities for the March Past began. The bands played *Advance Australia Fair* and moved forward to positions near the saluting base. Gradually units marched to the right to take their turn in the final ceremonial. It was a left wheel and then a left turn and the coys found themselves in line facing down a gradual slope. Thanks to the initiative of the RSM 2/13 Bn, (Jock Borland) who had laid out the parade ground, the march to and past the saluting base was crossed at short intervals by a series of white lines. As you marched they could be seen coming and each front rank was automatically checked in alignment with the crossing of each line. As a result, there was no surging forward or back. No endless glancing to the right. No shouted corrections. Fixed bayonets gleamed at their correct angles. The perfect symmetry was sustained down to, and through, the "Eyes Right" salute as the culminating gesture.

Christmas in Julis Camp was with a good army standard of Christmas food and beer. Long tables set up outside in fine, but cold, weather. Offrs and Sgts acted as mess orderlies.An orderly but relaxed mood was helped by Gen Morshead and Brig Windeyer chatting informally and with the goodwill of the men.

Personal mail and parcels had been received as well as many general greetings with particular appreciation for the message from the groups of mothers, wives and sweethearts who worked to raise the Bn Comforts Fund and the encouraging thoughts from the old 17th.

During this month the following messages appeared in Routine Orders:

"OC Cairo area has stated that during recent leave, 9 Aust Div Troops were the best behaved in Cairo. As a mark of his appreciation he has arranged to welcome the first draft of 100 personally at Cairo main station on 7 Dec and to turn out the band of a Highland Regiment and provide refreshments for the first five drafts."

Prime Minister of Aust has cabled GOC AIF Middle East as follows:

"President Roosevelt has sent me the following personal message which I should like you to promulgate to the officers and men of the 9 Aust Div. 'I wish to extend my heartiest congratulations to you and the officers and men of the 9th Division on the heroic part it has played in the recent victory in the Middle East.'"

Sir Leslie Morshead issued a special order after the parade which read:

"I wish heartily to congratulate all ranks on yesterday's parade. From beginning to end there was the fullest evidence of preparation, keenness and effort by every unit and every single individual, and of efficient and careful staff work. The arms drill and marching were excellent and I have *never* seen troops steadier and with higher bearing on parade. You all did credit to yourselves. Also the bands are to be highly commended on their performance.

Altogether it was a parade which we shall often recall and we shall always remember that salute to our Fallen Comrades."

From 2/17 Bn Comfort Funds, Sydney:

"Members are thinking of you all at Christmas and send best wishes for New Year. More money forwarded for Christmas."

From Gen Sir Thomas Blamey:

"Heartiest seasonal greetings from all comrades in Australia. We are delighted with your successful operations. AIF in the Middle East is continually in our thoughts and those of the Australian community."

From Gen Sir Bernard Montgomery:

"Please convey to all ranks in 9 Aust Div my best wishes for Christmas and my very kind regards. I cannot adequately tell you how much I miss your Division, it was a great blow when you left my army."

From the Hon F M Forde, Deputy PM and Minister for the Army to Lt Gen Sir Leslie Morshead, GOC AIF ME:

"On behalf of the Government and people of Australia I extend to you and to every member of the AIF under your command the heartiest Christmas and New Year greetings and best wishes for your future success and well being. It is also my privilege to send the cheers of comrades who were with you earlier in the year and who have had a special adventure in thrashing the Japanese. We have watched with profound pride and admiration the achievements of the AIF Middle East during recent months which have won the unstinted praise of the Allied Nations. Not only have you played a vital part in the great victory which has lately been won in North Africa, but you have added fresh distinction to the glorious name of the AIF. Our hearts are with you all and the Australian nation which has unshakeable confidence in you and will support you at all times to the limit of its strength. Kindly convey this message to the officers and men under your command."

Perhaps the message which may have been most appreciated at that now far distant Christmas was the briefest which read:

"From Imperial Service Club Sydney — Well done, seasons greetings. Old seventeenth."

Always there is excitement at the announcing of the decorations. On 31 Dec, the Bn welcomed the news that the CO, Lt Col N W Simpson, was awarded the DSO. The MC was awarded to Capt I McMaster and Capt J H Dinning. The DCM was won by Sgt J F Cortis and Cpl E Harris. L/Sgt Vic Rae of the RAP had won the MM. It was known to a few that the Bn's confidential files included many handwritten notes reporting the bravery of many others. It included a list of persons recommended by the CO for Mention in Despatches but, for reasons unknown, none was so acknowledged. The CO sent for Broadbent and told him that his name had been put on the list of officers suitable to command. Broadbent had to ask what was this list and, through the drudgery in New Guinea, Colonel Simpson frequently remarked that something should happen about it. He would have been entitled to, but did not begrudge, the ironic culmination when Broadbent was appointed to take his place.

On 1 Jan 1943 unit strength was noted as 34 Offrs and 872 Ors. That day marked the physical arrival of some 75 reinforcements which were drafted to "E" Coy for the moment, not to be taken on Bn strength. Transport was provided to allow a lot of men to visit the hospital and convalescent depot.

About this time Maj "Blue" Allan had returned to the Bn and, with his seniority, was 2 i/c.

He was to stay with us on the return to Australia, passing on much valuable information gleaned in his long background in New Guinea.

During the month a number of coy tactical exercises were conducted. A quarter guard was mounted daily at the entrance to the Bn lines. General camp routines were observed as the occupant strength built up with reinforcements and a lot of 'X' list returning from other duties and from convalescence. Perhaps someone saw the future. Maj Broadbent with some other officers,with like rank from other Bns of 20 Bde were sent for a few days introduction to the amphibious warfare center on the Bitter Lakes.

14 Jan effective strength 38 Offrs and 943 Ors, 4 Offrs and 120 Ors attached. For those who had had no leave in the Middle East, including reinforcements, there were special arrangements to spend one day in Jerusalem

Picture shows were on in the evenings at the Julis camp cinema.Day parades were held there to allow everyone to see unedited films of the Parade. There were also shows by the AIF Concert Party commanded by Lt Col Jim Davidson, the well known Sydney dance band leader who had a big team of performers and got the characteristic reactions and cheering happiness from the Army audience. 9 Div itself had a small concert party which gave many welcome performances to small groups in the field. Concerts of a certain type seem always in place in Army life. There had been a famous concert in Tobruk. In the Alamein area, where circumstances allowed, small groups would arrive and give welcome entertainment in an improvised situation. B Coy had its own small concert one evening coming into reserve from Tel el Eisa but the Bn peak of famed entertainment was to come with the formation of the Bn Concert Party in the last year of service.

Inter-unit and other football matches were played but departure became imminent when universal kit bags and officers' trunks were handed in to kit store.

On 20 Jan, effective strength 44 Offrs and 968 Ors, with 4 Offrs and 155 Ors attached. At 0830 hrs, all kits were cleared and tents struck and packed. After an early lunch the Bn convoy moved off at 1240 hrs under Comd of Maj Broadbent with the CO in charge of a larger total convey including 2/3 Fd Amb and 10 Coy AASC. The bivouac for the night was at Asluz the petrol point partway into the Sinai desert. Next day the convoy halted at the east bank of the Suez Canal at 1715 hrs.

With long experience, drivers achieved excellent convoy discipline. Orders designated the number of vehicles to a mile and the standard speed. If one was to watch a convoy coming over a rise, each next vehicle would appear with consistent stopwatch accuracy confirming its interval and speed. Check points watched, counted and sometimes made difficulties including for one Italian vehicle seized after the battle. It had been a mobile dental surgery, but given to the RMO, Capt Hughes, it made a worthwhile RAP. He tried to give it to a hospital but, eventually it was abandoned the day we embarked at Suez.

The rest of the journey there was partly by MT and partly in train, with a hot meal ready on arrival at the transit camp.

On Anniversary Day, (now Australia Day), the posted strength was 49 Offrs and 1114 Ors. Swollen coys filled in with route marches, PT, and quaint efforts at coy drill.

27 Jan: Reveille 0345 hrs. It was operation "Liddington" — return home. Troops embarked on *Aquitania* in marching order plus sea kit bags. By about 0945 hrs all were berthed on E, F and G decks. The ship sailed at 1300 hrs. With some 7,000 passengers available area was rationed so that each coy had allotted deck space for one hour, per day. By 31 Jan the ship joined *Queen Mary* at Massawa where sunken shipping could be seen.

Finally, on 3 Feb the convoy left Massawa, having added *Ile de France, Nieuw Amsterdam,* the armed merchant cruiser, *Queen of Bermuda* and HMS *Devonshire* with several destroyers. Passenger total is said to have been 30,985 of whom 390 were AANS and VAD.

In 5 days the convoy reached a then unknown location, Addu Atoll in the Maldive Islands. Refuelling completed, the convoy left on 10 Feb, having in passing an exciting view of this British Eastern Fleet of battleships, cruisers and destroyers.

Shipboard life becomes very regulated. Initial ration problems had been sorted out and meals came on time. Deck space was used for exercises. Indoor space was seized for officers' classes. Boat station drills ran smoothly. Miscellaneous Orderly Offrs, OC troops, Brig Windeyer and the Captain, or his representatives, made inspections. Units take turns to do ship's duties. At night, all on deck search for the first glimpse of the Southern Cross.

17 Feb; A clear day, allowed after 2 years and 4 months the first glimpse of Australia at Fremantle. 7 bags of mail came on board for the Bn. Wharfies having jacked up, troops loaded rations.

The convoy sailed again south of Tasmania and, at about 1300 hrs, 27 Feb entered Sydney Harbour to berth at Woolloomooloo at 1600 hrs. A big crowd gave welcome. The Bn was taken in 2 groups by bus to Narellan where staffs and camp facilities worked through the night on leave arrangements to which the Sydney residents were moved in the morning of Sunday, 28 Feb. The soldiers for various country homes were moved off as soon as practicable. The Bde's few from Victoria had remained the rear party on board ship with Captain Newton and moved off on the Sunday morning.

Sydney welcomes the return of the 2/17 Bn

CHAPTER 13

THE JAPANESE THREAT TO PORT MORESBY

The Mandated Territory of New Guinea was invaded by Japanese forces on 23 Jan 1942 with a landing at Rabaul on the Island of New Britain. The overwhelming strength of the invaders decimated the gallant resistance of the 2/22 Bn of the 8 Aust Div and small groups of Volunteer Rifles. About 400 survived having withdrawn over the steep mountains on the Island and embarked for the Australian mainland on 9 Apr. The enemy landing at Rabaul occurred about the time the remnants of the 8 Div were withdrawing across the Straits of Jahore with British and Indian troops to the Singapore Island which fell to the Japanese on 15 Feb.

General Hyakutake, Comd of the Japanese XVII Army, established a main base at Rabaul for further operations against mainland New Guinea, the Islands of Fiji, Samoa and New Caledonia where the Americans were preparing air and sea bases. In Mar 42 the Japanese 51 Division, commanded by Major General Tomitaro Horii, landed on the mainland of Papua New Guinea at Lae, Finschhafen and Salamaua. Enemy plans to capture Port Moresby by sea were negated by an American and Australian victory in the Battle of the Coral Sea 7 to 8 May, supported by land based air attack. Japanese survivors of the battle were compelled to return to Rabaul.

Following the defeat of the enemy in the Coral Sea battle, General Horii sought another approach to Port Moresby and units from Salamaua moved inland and south along the coast to Gona and Buna with a view to finding a route across the precipitous Owen Stanley Ranges which separated his Division from its objective. Moreover, the plan was to execute a double thrust towards Port Moresby by land across the steep jungle-clad ranges and by sea to seize Milne Bay on the southern tip of Papua pursuant to a seaborne offensive along the southern coast of the peninsula.

General Douglas MacArthur, Comd of the Allied Forces in the South West Pacific Area, occupied Milne Bay with his forces in June and prepared an Allied base. Repeated attempts were made by the Japanese from Jun to Sep 42 to dislodge the Australian Militia, A.I.F. and support units, including the RAAF flying "Kittyhawks", with troops seaborne from Rabaul supported by naval and air forces. In the mud and slush of rain-sodden Milne Bay, Japan suffered its first decisive defeat of ground forces since its invasion of Northern Malaya on 8 Dec 1941. The Australian victory was an important turning point in the war with Japan and the myth of the invincibility of the Japanese Army in jungle warfare was dispelled.

The American Navy partly gained its revenge for Pearl Harbour in the Battle of Midway, 3 to 6 Jun 42, and depleted the effectiveness of the Japanese Navy. Having lost two naval battles and the land battle at Milne Bay, the Japanese concentrated forces aimed to capture Port Moresby overland from Gona on the north coast of Papua where landings had commenced on 21 Jul. The axis of the advance was the mountain track via the Kokoda Village.

The Japanese fought tenaciously against the gallant Australian infantry and reached Iorobaiwa on 16 Sep 42, about 30 miles from Port Moresby. From a vantage point General Horii viewed the southern coast of Papua and the waters of the Coral Sea. He was prevented from achieving his goal by the Australians in a last ditch stand on Imita Ridge.

The Japanese Army Comd in Rabaul was heavily committed to operations against the Americans in the Solomon Islands. Under constant pressure from offensive patrolling and renewed attacks by the Australians, also with problems of supply, sickness from malaria and dysentry and without reinforcements, General Horii commenced the withdrawal of his force on 26 Sep, back over the Kokoda trail, culminating in defeat at Oivi Village on 11 Nov where the General with others died from drowning.

With the enemy cleared from the Kokoda trail, Australian units, reinforced with armour and the Americans, continued the advance along the coast and captured Gona in early December, then Buna and Sanananda in Jan 43. Fighting was exceptionally bitter and exhaustive in battle casualties against a stubborn enemy.

Concurrently with the thrust over the Owen Stanley Ranges, the Japanese had moved inland and occupied Mubo in the hinterland east of Wau on 31 Aug, harried by Australian Independent companies that were part of "Kanga Force" which operated from the Wau area. Successful raids were made by these units on enemy located at Salamaua as early as Jun 42 and later on 11 Jan 43 at Mubo. The Japanese had not abandoned their aim to capture Port Moresby and in a third attempt the 51 Div reached the outskirts of Wau on 29 Jan. Under heavy attack, "Kanga Force" was reinforced with units of the 3 Aust Div airlifted to Wau, and forced the enemy's withdrawal towards Mubo.

A convoy of Japanese reinforcements was sent from Rabaul with a view to an advance from the mouth of the Markham River through the Snake River Valley. The convoy was devastated by Allied fighter and bomber squadrons in the Battle of the Bismark Sea, 2/3 Mar 43 and only about 900 survivors reached Lae.

Meanwhile, General MacArthur had directed General Thomas Blamey, Comd Allied Land Forces, and Lieutenant General Walter Krueger, Comd American 6 Army, to plan operations aimed at the capture of the Lae-Salamaua-Finschhafen-Madang area, establish bases and airfields on Kiriwina and Woodlark Islands and occupy western New Britain. General Blamey's plans to capture Lae included heavy pressure on the enemy in the Salamaua area to waste its strength while preparing the attack on Lae. Almost incessant hard fighting in the Salamaua area engaged by 3 Aust Div and later 5 Aust Div lasted three months. During the battle for Salamaua Woodlark and Kiriwina Islands were occupied by the Americans for airfield construction and airfields were also constructed at Tsili Tsili and Goroka while protected by Australian infantry.

General MacAthur issued an operation instruction on 13 Jun 43 extract as follows:

"Forces of the South West Pacific area supported by South Pacific Forces will seize the Lae-Salamaua-Finschhafen-Markam Valley area and establish major elements of the Allied Forces therein to provide from the Markham Valley area general and direct air support for subsequent operations in Northern New Guinea and Western New Britain."

General Blamey planned an amphibious landing east of Lae by the 9 Aust Div, commanded by Major General George Wootten, a paratroop landing at Nadzab and an overland attack down the Markham Valley by the 7 Aust Div to Madang, commanded by Major General George Vasey. The Australian Corps Comd at the commencement of the operation was Lieutenant General Sir Edmund Herring who had commanded the Armed Forces in New Guinea since mid 1942.

The Assault on Lae began on 4 Sep 43. Thereafter the 51 Japanese Division was fighting on two fronts and the Australians pressed forward relentlessly and captured Salamaua on 13 Sep.

Remnants of the 51 Div were ordered to withdraw on 8 Sep. Fortunately, they were assisted in their escape to Lae by the onset of heavy rain, flooding the rivers and creeks and delaying the Allied pursuit.

The Author trusts that the foregoing brief outline of main events and strategy of the protagonists in the New Guinea campaign, has served as an introduction to the arrival of the 9 Aust Div in New Guinea and the integration of the 2/17 Bn in the Lae operation. Beforehand, the soldiers of the 9 Div were returning from leave after their two and one half years on active service in the Middle East.

EQUIPMENT CARRIED BY BATTALION MEMBERS FOR
OPERATION "POSTERN" - THE LAE LANDING 3 SEP 1943

SOLDIER	ARMS	AMMUNITION	OTHER	WEIGHT
BREN GUNNER No1	BREN	5 MAGAZINES	1 ON GUN+ EXTRA BASIC POUCH	35 lbs
BREN GUNNER No2	RIFLE+SPARE PARTS	6 MAGAZINES 50 ROUNDS 2 GRENADES	2 UTILITY POUCHES	33 lbs
BREN GUNNER No 3	RIFLE	6 MAGAZINES 50 ROUNDS 2 GRENADES	2 UTILITY POUCHES	33 lbs
OWEN GUNNER	OWEN	7 MAGAZINES 2 GRENADES 3 BOXES 9mm AMMO	1 ON GUN+ EXTRA BASIC POUCH	37 lbs
RIFLE BOMBER	RIFLE+CUP DISCHARGER	5 GRENADES –7 Secs 2 SMOKE GRENADES 50 ROUNDS	EXTRA BASIC POUCH SHOVEL OR PICK	32 lbs
RIFLEMAN	RIFLE	150 ROUNDS 2 GRENADES	SHOVEL OR PICK	29 lbs
MORTARMAN No1	2 INCH MORTAR	4 BOMBS PISTOL	EXTRA BASIC POUCH	34 lbs
MORTARMAN No2	RIFLE	16 BOMBS	EXTRA BASIC POUCH	42 lbs
TANK/A RIFLEMAN	TK/A RIFLE	10 x 55 ROUNDS 2 GRENADES		40 lbs
RIFLE BOMBER FOR TANK/A	RIFLE+ CUP DISCHARGER	4 No 68 GRENADES 100 ROUNDS 2 GRENADES – 7Secs	UTILITY POUCHES SHOVEL OR PICK	32 lbs
ASSISTANT FOR TANK/A	RIFLE 10 x 55 ROUNDS	4 No 68 GRENADES SHOVEL OR PICK 100 ROUNDS 2 No 36 GRENADES	UTILITY POUCHES	34 lbs

SUMMARY OF ARMS

SECTION STORES	SECTION	PLATOON HQ	COMPANY HQ
1 PICK	1 BREN GUN	4 RIFLES	2 OWEN GUNS
1 TOMAKHAWK	2 OWEN GUNS	1 x 2 INCH MORTAR	TANK/A RIFLE
2 SHOVELS	5 RIFLES	-	DISCHARGER CUP
2 BUSH KNIVES	1 DISCHARGER CUP	-	6 RIFLES
2 MURRAY SWITCHES			

CHAPTER 14

TRAINING FOR WAR IN THE SOUTH WEST PACIFIC AREA

In March 1943, while Brig Moten's 17 Bde, 3 Aust Div, patrolled against the Japanese 51st Division near Mubo, soldiers of the 2/17 Bn assembled throughout Australia for onward movement back to their Unit.

The 2/17 Bn Comd's summary of activities for Mar 1943, by Lt Col N W Simpson, read:

> "Personnel began to return from leave on 23rd and 24th; the Wallgrove group (HQ Coy and Bn HQ) was transferred to Narellan Camp. Country personnel and those whose leave had been extended for various reasons reported in during the last week of the month. Further special leave was granted in many cases. All companies took their personnel on long daily route marches in preparation for the ceremonial march of 9 Div troops through the city of Sydney on 2 Apr."

Being originally recruited in New South Wales, the Bn, led by Lt Col Noel Simpson, marched in the 9 Div Ceremonial Parade through the City of Sydney on 2 Apr. The Division's March in Melbourne was held on 31 Mar, and the 20 Bde Contingent with about 40 from the 2/17 Bn from Victoria and Tasmania was led by Capt Arthur Newton.

On 7 Mar 1943, tragically Brig J W Crawford, died in an air accident. Arthur Newton recorded this sad event:

> "Our original CO, John Crawford, Comd of 11 Bde in the Townsville area accompanied by one of his CO's, Lt Col P H G Cardale, took off by plane to fly to the Tablelands from either Cairns or Townsville. The plane flew into a mountain side and John Crawford and some of the crew members and passengers lost their lives. Lt Col Cardale and an airman survived but were badly injured. Brigadier Crawford was in his 44th year. The 2/17 Bn owes a lot to this very fine officer and gentleman. Let us not forget him."

On 17 Apr, sub-units of the Bn commenced movement by train to the Atherton tablelands in Northern Queensland. After staging through Redlynch Training Camp near Cairns, the move was completed on 22 Apr to a new camp site at Python Ridge near Kairi. A tented camp from the outset, there were no facilities such as mess and recreation huts. No time was lost in making the Camp habitable before training commenced. Reorganisation was also implemented on the Tropical Scale which varied markedly from the Middle East War establishment to meet the tactical requirements of tropical warfare. Arthur Newton commented on these changes:

> "The Tropical Scale for an infantry Bn was much less in numbers and vehicles to the Establishment we were used to in the Middle East. As at 30 Apr, the strength was 42 offrs and 892 ors. This included 'E' Company, a holding company not on an establishment, where 'B' Class soldiers and those awaiting boards were held with soldiers not yet absorbed into vacancies. Many of our excellent drivers who had carried out their onerous tasks with skill and dedication in the Middle East could no longer serve as drivers and were transferred and

191

retrained for duty with a rifle company or in some cases transferred to other units. One in this latter category was Tom Russell whose worth I respected when I had been QM in Tobruk. He was an older man than most and was transferred to an artillery unit but was killed during the New Guinea campaign.

Before the main body of the Bn arrived at Kairi, an Offr (Lt McKenzie) and 2 Ors of the 2/31 Bn reported to lecture on conditions in New Guinea and help the Offrs and men with hints on tactical and administrative problems of jungle warfare."

With a strength of 44 Offrs and 850 Ors, on 2 Apr, the Bn commenced 10 weeks of intensive training to culminate in Bde exercises. On 28 Apr, Lt Col N W Simpson issued a Training Memorandum:

"1. The following paragraphs record some of the main principles which will govern the conduct of battle operations. These principles are applicable to operations in any theatre of war.

2. Knowing these principles and appreciating that non-observance of any of them may lead to failure in battle and often to disaster, commanders of all ranks should be able to understand more clearly the requirements of battle and organise their training accordingly.

3. The battle must be fought in accordance with these fundamental principles. THE OBJECT OF TRAINING IS SUCCESS IN BATTLE

4. Therefore nothing must be taught during the training period that would not be done in operations. No commander must ever say: 'In actual practice we would be doing this in such and such a way.'

5. One of the outstanding feature of the operations in the Western desert was the fact, fully appreciated by all ranks, that they applied the knowledge and training gained during the training period, in the fighting of the battle, and were never asked to do anything contrary to the principles which were considered essential for success. The 'way of doing things' had been so instilled into all ranks that despite casualties among the Comds, there was never any breakdown in the fighting capacity of the unit or sub-units.

6. DISCIPLINE: No undisciplined unit has ever been successful in battle. Discipline depends mainly on the the officer and N.C.O. Where there are large numbers of troops, as in a unit, who have had battle experience the reputation and traditions of the unit are often an incentive to these troops to maintain a high standard, but where considerable reinforcements without battle experience and lacking knowledge of regimental traditions form part of the Bn the DISCIPLINE MUST BE TAUGHT INTENSIVELY AS ANY OTHER SUBJECT.

    An ill-disciplined unit out of the line will be an armed mob in battle. There will be no sudden magical change. The reaching and maintenance of a high standard of discipline must be the inflexible aim of every commander. Much can be achieved by personal example.

7. FIGHTING SPIRIT: Mere physical fitness, proficiency in the use of weapons and a knowledge of tactics, is not sufficient. All ranks must be imbued with the spirit of determination, and the will to win. They must be taught to be determined, enthusiastic and to overcome all obstacles that would prevent the final and complete destruction of the enemy. Training carried out in a half-hearted manner merely because that particular subject is on the syllabus, is useless. When troops are tired and exhausted, then more than ever, must that 'aggressive eagerness' be insisted upon. Troops must go into battle confident of this ability to overcome the enemy. They won't unless they are trained to do so.

8. INDIVIDUAL AND SUB-UNIT EFFICIENCY: In all types of operations, once the Bn is committed to battle, the issue passes to the junior leader and the sub-unit. Whilst the battle must never get out of hand as far as the Bn and coy commanders are concerned, in close or in jungle country control will be difficult and increasingly so as the sub-units are further committed.

9. Success will largely depend on a high standard of skill, initiative and vigour of the platoons, sections and individuals. Particularly does this apply to the junior leader.

10. During individual and collective training vigorous action must be taken to reach a high standard of sub-unit efficiency.

11. Mistakes made by junior leaders during training must be corrected and where it is clear that further training is necessary then the training syllabus must be adjusted to include recapitulation of subjects which require further emphasis.

12. BATTLE DRILL: One of the main purposes of battle drill is to ensure that in the Bn and each sub-unit — company, platoon and section — of the Bn that there is a common approach to the battle problem.

13. Orders issued are never in sufficient detail for each sub-unit commander to act on them without filling in the details of the application of their military knowledge and common-sense. Much of the essential procedure of preparing troops and sub-units for the battle, be it offensive or defensive, can be taught as a drill, eg; quick deployment, quick concentration of fire power of weapons within the sub-unit and of supporting weapons, quick concentration and employment of battle power, composition of 'R' and 'O' Groups positioning of HQ and chain of command.

14. Battle drill must be sufficiently flexible so that it helps and does not hinder the command.

15. The teaching of battle drill to all ranks will ensure maximum co-operation throughout the unit during the battle, even when casualties necessitate replacement of commanders and the absorption of reinforcements while in actual combat.

16. It is by no means necessary that each company has exactly the same battle drill. There must, however, be no great variation between company and company, nor must it conflict in any way with the Standing Orders for battle of the unit.

17. STAGE MANAGEMENT FOR THE BATTLE OPERATIONS: The prior preparations of committing troops to the battle must be sound. If the unit or the sub-unit dispositions are unbalanced initially the fighting troops are hindered from the moment they start.

18. For example, the positioning of reserves of men and fire power, the location of HQ and the system of evacuations must be based on sound appreciation and deductions.

19. It is always difficult to correct initial errors in stage management once the troops are committed. Stage management and the conduct of the battle must be understood by all officers, at least insofar as their own command is concerned.

20. SOME RULES TO OBSERVE IN BATTLE: Whenever the situation is vague and indefinite and information of the enemy is scant:

a.Recce widely for information

b.Keep your main force concentrated.

c.Secure ground which will assist your further operations and give you an advantage over the enemy.

d. Strive always to gain, and keep, the initiative. Vigorous offensive action will be the only means by which you can achieve this object. Without the initiative you cannot win.

21. OFFENSIVE ACTION: All commanders must learn to deal with situations that are vague and indefinite. In all phases of collective training subordinate commanders must be confronted with problems that will test their mental alertness and ability to do something to overcome the problem and do it quickly. Their solutions may be less sound than if they had a greater time to overcome the problem, but to do nothing is a fatal alternative.

22. It must be impressed on every soldier that to fight offensively is his primary duty. To do that he must have confidence in his leaders, be self confident and self reliant. All training must stress the value of initiative and the offensive spirit.

23. TRAINING GENERAL: Training must be hard. All ranks must get accustomed to march over long distances on the minimum of issue rations, essential for their physical well-being. They must live hard without the comforts of amenities that established camps afford.

24. There is to be no apology given to anyone for the hard living, hard training and hard fighting essential to victory.

25. A great deal has to be done, and the time available is too short for other than vigorous and robust mental application by those whose responsibility is to train and lead, on the one hand, and a spirit of co-operation and willingness to get on with the job, by all concerned.

26. ADMINISTRATION: Nothing can be accomplished without sound administration.

27. It is so vital to success in training and operations that not only should every commander continually observe and apply the principles, but every soldier must be trained in his individual responsibility.

28. The great difference between bad administration and bad tactics is that regarding the latter, incompetency is so often overcome by the dash and courage of the fighting soldier and in spite of an unsound tactical plan, success is achieved and the incompetency is never brought to light.

29. No amount of personal effort on the part of the fighting soldier will produce rations, water, ammunition, medical supplies, etc. at the time and place required if the persons responsible have failed in their part in the administrative plan. They will nevertheless hear about it in double quick time.

30. MORALE: Much has been said about morale. It is the big factor in war. If troops are well led, have sound training and good equipment, are physically and mentally fit and know why they are fighting, their morale will be high and with all that they are more than a match for the enemy, without, they lay themselves open to defeat by uncivilised natives armed with spears and bush knives."

HQ Coy Comd, then Maj John Broadbent, wrote of the training period on the Atherton Tablelands and the Cairns Coastal area:

"The Bn's good fortune in being able to take leave on return to Australia was followed by an excellent opportunity to prepare itself for duty in two very new aspects:

1. General fighting in mountainous, jungle country;

2. Specialised technique in amphibious landings.

This opportunity was realised and exploited to the full with a definiteness of purpose which characterised Colonel Simpson and which by now had impregnated the Unit although it was, in many ways, little more than could be expected from men of common sense and experience who knew the value of preparation and the tasks to be undertaken and in whom there remained elements of sentiment and ideals which had led to their initial enlistment. There was also a certain novelty about the new terrain, conditions and amphibious training with the Americans which encouraged interest. The culmination was that, when the Bn embarked for the Lae operation, it matched the efficiency and morale with which it moved to the FUP at El Alamein.

To some extent the Bn applied its mind to training for the new role before coming to the Tablelands. In the Middle East we had the advantage of some attention to mountainous warfare and perhaps by less of a coincidence myself and a party of Offrs had been sent for a short 4-day period at Kabrit, the amphibious training centre at the Bitter Lakes where, with other Offrs of the Division we were given an introduction to amphibious warfare. This was passed on in several periods of Offr Training on board *Aquatania*. Maj Blue Allan gave talks on New Guinea terrain and tropical warfare which was studied in the same classes. These preliminary studies were found to be of great advantage when the occasion for the actual training of the Bn arrived.

Initially training was directed to familiarising troops with the different types of 'jungle' country including the vicious pockets of vine scrub, learning 'bush' craft as it applied to such terrain including the many personal problems of how to evade or remove leeches, know the stinging tree, sharpen and use a machete, cook the newstyle rations. Scrub typhus first raised its ugly head here and soldiers learned the application of mite repellent and most soldiers were extra serious about it.

The building of the vine bridge was an illustration of jungle pioneering and various types had to be studied. Attention was also given to other ways of crossing water obstacles including the problem of men who could not swim and getting them across on logs, marching along creek beds constantly in water yet managing to keep a few things dry.

During this initial period attention was also given in HQ Coy to developing the specialist knowledge relevant to the platoon in its more technical forms giving the recapitulation of some individual training a more advanced nature, eg. many of the sigs got their first knowledge of elementary electricity and the MMGS studied indirect fire technique. Following the individual training came the collective training by sub-units and finally by the unit as a whole. Exercises were done in open country as well as in jungle country. There had to be realised the almost complete impossibility of any effective recce made by commanders in the jungle terrain, the need for deployment drills to ensure that the Bn came out in almost single file along a track and be got on the move and into action quickly despite the problems of intercommunication. All these matters required substantial practise. A special test exercise was prepared by Maj Blue Allan under the direction of the CO, the Bn to be commanded by myself. Beginning with attack and advance over open country with exploitation down to the Barron River with river crossing then a move into the jungle where the directing staff provided a series of situations involving first elements up to a Company strength and culminating finally in a Bn attack, the whole period being operational requiring tactical positions to be adopted for securing at night, all necessary patrols and so on. This exercise was virtually the culmination of the 'Jungle Warfare' training and thereafter a return to amphibious training. The timings taken by umpires on these occasions showed that the Bn had reached a very high standard of efficiency.

During this period we had the advantage of visits from several very well selected Offrs from 6 and 7 Divs who had had experience in New Guinea. They gave very useful talks and engaged in most co-operative discussions, a relationship in which there was no trace of inter-divisional rivalry.

First official contact with Americans was with an instructional party sent up from the Boat and Shore Regiment (2 ESB) on 1 July 1943, with which we were later to train. Under their supervision at Kairi we practised the drill of embarkation in mock-up boats marked off by rope. They also gave us some instruction to principles as they knew them and made available copies of SOP, their Standing Operational Procedure, which was their Bible in all matters to which they rigidly and unimaginatively adhered. Later at Cairns, Brig Windeyer spent many hours persuading some of their senior officers that flexibility was desirable. Very close and friendly relations developed with the Americans. Neither the Unit we worked with nor the others which worked with the other battalions had any operational experience but they were conscientious and enthusiastic and looked forward to the possibility of doing a job with us. This never actually eventuated but later at Finschhafen we were to receive some visits from some of them and Maj Pike one day went down to Dreger Harbour to see them and received a great welcome. On that occasion he was able to bring back some very practical tokens of the Americans' esteem. He was only there a few hours and when he was leaving, they hurriedly rushed round their lines with sacks calling on everybody to produce anything they could send to the Bn and as a result several bags were filled with general canteen stores, including such unfamiliar things as plugs of chewing tobacco. There were many apologies that the call had come at the wrong time in relation to when their canteen supplies arrived.

The training here was not purely a matter of listening to the Americans. The Bn had its own side to work out, including landing tables, determining the groupings within the Bn into boat loads and wave loads, the study of the problems of re-grouping and re-organising ashore and tactical exploitation, the whole procedure with the clear realisation of the maxim, 'the object of training is success in battle'."

The Commander's summary of the War Diary for May 1943, read:

"In the Bn's first week at Kairi a severe program of long treks over rough mountainous country had done a lot to get the men fit for their new period of training. In the first fortnight of the period particular emphasis was placed on individual training and TOET (Tests of Elementary Training) then gradually working up to section stalks and platoon exercises. This early period of solid elementary training should prove invaluable during our next operational period as in the change over to Jungle War Establishment many specialists such as MT drivers and carrier personnel were transferred to rifle companies. We also have a large percentage of reinforcements who have never seen action. A miniature range was constructed near the camp and except for a very small percentage, all men have twice passed satisfactorily in grouping, application and rapid fire with both rifle and Bren. Tests were also carried out with the Owen sub-machine gun. A jungle assault course was constructed by the Pnr Pl, the object being to give all ranks a chance to practise forward scouting under jungle warfare conditions when in contact with the enemy. One platoon per day was put through the course using ball ammunition and by the end of the month the whole unit with the exception of part of HQ Coy and Bn HQ had completed the course.

The 2 i/c Maj Allan with two Ors from each company constructed a typically NG native vine bridge across Juara Creek to give all ranks an idea of what the bridges are really like.

During the month every NCO in the unit was put through his paces in a five day cadre, particular attention being paid to NCOs who were previously in specialist jobs such as MT and carriers and who have now been absorbed into rifle companies. At the latter end of the month a Potential NCO's course was started and further intakes will be continued in June.

The Sig Offr began a company orderlies course to teach orderlies rudimentary elements of map reading and signal procedure. Some men from each company have been sent to a signal school run by Div Sigs. This should provide the Bn with a good nucleus of reinforcements for the Sig Pl.

During the month the greater majority of 'B' Class personnel left the unit on draft to 9 Div Staging Camp. Visitors during the month included Gen Sir Thomas Blamey, GOC Land Forces SWP, Lt Gen Sir Leslie Morshead, GOC 2 Aust Corps and Maj Gen G F Wootten, GOC 9 Aust Div.

Amenities in the division were generally bad at the beginning of the month but a gradual improvement was made until, at the end of the month the men were quite happy in their new camp. A mobile cinema operated once a week in the Brigade area, 14 men from the unit were able to go to Atherton pictures each night, company canteens began to function as supplies became available, organisation for supplies of tobacco, cigarettes and beer for the division improved considerably and the erection of a YMCA hut in the Bn area with a wireless set was a great boon.

Two race meetings at Kulara on 23 and 30 May provided relaxation and a good day's fun for about 300 of the Bn. Earlier in the period under review a rodeo at the same place was patronised by a party from the unit."

On the Atherton Tablelands there originated within the ranks of 9 Div the group cry "HO! HO! HO!" which may be likened to that heard from a drover encouraging his dogs during the muster or draft of sheep on a rural property. With many soldiers of country background it is not surprising that the cry was familiar with them for use in lighter moments of training while on exercise when an animal was accidentally flushed from its sacred territory in the bush to hasten it on its frantic way. Regrettably, exuberance led to abuse where silence in training to avoid enemy detection of movement is paramount.

Depending on the standard of discipline within the particular unit, in some instances, the cry degenerated to taunt a senior Comd who was recognised sometimes from a distance by the red tabs on his jacket and red hatband. This discourtesy, bordering on insubordination, in general had no regard for whether the Comd may have a proven record of exemplary leadership. The instances of misuse of the cry were kept within bounds in the 2/17 Bn, due to the discipline demanded by Lt Col Simpson and the respect in which he was held by the troops.

The cry, "HO! HO! HO!", perhaps the "War Cry" of the 9 Div, is now traditionally one of acceptance, welcome and acclaim for a respected formation Comd. When Lt Gen Sir Leslie Morshead returned as Corps Comd to visit the 9 Div at Finschhafen, the Division he had commanded with great distinction and dignity during the Siege of Tobruk and the Battle of El Alamein. He was welcomed vocally by the men in the traditional manner. There was on this occasion and always thereafter no misunderstanding the warmth of welcome and respect given by a team of fighting men to a senior Comd of proven ability, expressed by a group of soldiers to one of their own.

In Nov 1987, 45 years after the Bn's first training period on the Atherton Tablelands, sadly the death occurred of a great soldier, Maj Gen the Rt Hon Sir Victor Windeyer, Comd of the 20 Bde at El Alamein and in both the New Guinea and Borneo Campaigns. Sir Victor, a man of great dignity, visited without exception the 2/17 Bn Anzac Day Reunions since the War, to be welcomed in the traditional manner. His response, in addressing the gathering always began vocally in the like manner to his welcome.

Additional entries in the War Diary not in the Summary (Comments by Arthur Newton) were the visits also of:

a.   Lt Gen Sir John Lavarack, GOC First Aust Army who visited the Div Area on 5 May. (I particularly recall this visit as at this time I was Staff Capt Learner on HQ 20 Bde. When Brig Windeyer returned to the HQ in the evening after accompanying Sir John in the Bde area one of the Offrs in the Mess asked him (our Brig) if there had been any 'Ho Ho Ho-ing' during the visits to the units. 'Oh yes,' replied Brig Windeyer in a whimsical manner, 'but after all the soldiers do not have the opportunity to "Ho Ho" an Army Comd every day in the week.')

b.   Maj Gen J J Murray, the original Comd of 20 Bde and who at this time was Comd York Force, visited the Officers' Mess with other Senior Offrs on 23 May when the Bn celebrated its 3rd birthday. Free beer and supper of pork, bread and butter were provided for troops out of Bn funds.

c.   The Governor General, Lord Gowrie visited the Bn area on 25 May. Some representatives of the Bn were included in the Guard of Honour.

d.   On 28 May the Div Comd, Maj Gen Wootten and the Bde Comd, Brig Windeyer visited the Sgts' Mess for the evening meal.

The war in Africa ended on 12 May 1943. This resulted in the exchange of messages between various Comds and the text was published in Routine Orders:

"From Gen Morshead to Gen Alexander: Everyone of us sends you greetings and the most cordial congratulations. We rejoice with you and wish you many more successes."

Gen Morshead's message to Gen Montgomery read: "With all ranks of 9 Aust Div I offer you and all our old comrades of 8 Army our warmest congratulations. We have followed your progress and success with the greatest interest and satisfaction. We knew you would do it."

The reply from Monty read: "Am grateful to you for your kind message from the Officers and Men of 9 Aust Div. We missed you greatly in later phase and wished you could have been with us at the kill. Good luck to you all."

During the month of June training continued on the Tablelands and the Comd's Summary by Lt Col N W Simpson read:

"For the period under review training was in two periods:

a.   Training leading up to Bn exercise June 15-18.

b.   Specialist training and eradication of faults arising from the Bn exercise.

During period a., coys carried out 2 to 3-day bivouacs. All personnel were enabled to use their rifles, LMGs and Owen guns on the miniature range and also to transverse the Bn jungle course. Just prior to the Bn exercise two deployment exercises were carried out to enable reinforcement personnel to become acquainted with battle procedure. From June 15-18 the Bn carried out a 4-day bivouac, the nature and scope of which were:

a.   Battle procedure

b.   Bn in attack in close country

c.   Protection on the move

d.   Protection at rest (perimeter defence)

e. Opposed river crossing

f. Offensive operations in jungle country

Lessons learnt from the exercise were noted and made the subject of further training during period b. These were incorporated in Bn Exercise No. 2 which took place on June 24, the nature and scope of which were:

a. Battle procedure

b. Bn in attack in close country

c. Reorganisation on capture of objective

Both Bn exercises were preceded by a sandtable TEWT (tactical exercise without troops) conducted by the CO and attended by all Offrs and NCOs in comd of pls.

During period b. all specialist training was proceeded with and both A/Tk Pl and MG Pl carried out shoots on their respective ranges. The object of the A/Tk shoot was to zero all guns, while the MG Pl carried out a classified shoot at 500 yards at their range.

Amenities improved considerably during the month. All coys now have enclosed mess huts, a large recreation hut and a canteen have been constructed in Bn lines. Another race meeting was organised by Div at Kulara track, and approx 250 members of the Bn attended. On 22 June, the Bn organised a dance at Kairi and 150 from the Bn were in attendance. Sport is now on a strong footing and both inter-unit and inter-coy games have taken place in union and league codes. Inter-coy hockey, softball, basketball and soccer competitive games were also conducted.

Some matters not mentioned in the Summary but which were in the War Diary were:

a. On 13 June Maj H T Allan left to take up a new appointment as Chief Liaison Officer between American and Aust Forces.

b. 200 Offrs and Men visited Lake Euramo and under supervision of Engr personnel were instructed in the use of Recce boats and Assault Landing Craft on 19 June.

c. On 21 June, Capt C G Pitman left the Bn to take up appointment at the LHQ Tactical School, Beenleigh, Qld.

The Bn struck tents on 4 July 1943, and with the arrival of 60 trucks from 131 General Transport Company, sub-units embussed on 5 July and moved to a tented camp site north of Cairns at Dead Man's Gully on the coastal strip near Trinity Beach. In this location, being awakened over the PA System each morning to the song "Beautiful, Beautiful, Queensland", the Bn began an intensive period of training in amphibious operations.

Typical of a day's activity, the urgency of preparation for the New Guinea Campaign, is revealed in the War Diary for the first three days after arrival in the new camp.

6 July: Location Dead Man's Gully. 0800 hrs: Coy Comds' Conference. 0900 hrs: CO at Bde Conference. 1300 hrs: Coy Comds' Conference. 1530 hrs: Representatives from all coys and Offrs from all attached arms attended a demonstration at Trinity Beach. A lecture was given by Capt Butch, IO 2 ESB.

7 July: 0620 hrs: Bn moves off for Trinity Beach and in position by 0800 hrs. 0830 to 1000 hrs: A demonstration of embarkation and disembarkation of personnel from 2 ESB. 20 Inf Bde and all attached units witnessed the demo. 1030 to 1130 hrs: Lectures were given by the shore and boat companies on the organisation of the shore coy, the boat coy and resupply. 1330 to 1600 hrs: The Bn and all our supporting arms practised embarkation and disembarkation from the LCVPs. Our supporting arms are at present: One Bty 2/4 Lt AA Regt, one section 2/3 Fd Coy, one platoon ex B Coy, 2/2 Mg Bn, B Coy, 2/3 Pnr Bn less two platoons, 2/8 Fd Amb less

three coys, ASC HQ. Draft of 18 ex hospital and schools rejoin unit. Our A/Tk guns arrived in the new area.

8 July: At 0715 hrs, the Bn moved to North Palm Beach for further training in embarkation and disembarkation of stores. This was carried out between 0900 and 1200 hrs. From 1400 to 1600 hrs, all coys trained in re-organisation after disembarkation on the far shore. At 1745 hrs, all moved to forward assembly area for night loading. 1830 hrs: First wave in position in final assembly area. 1900 to 1930 hrs: Troops practise loading stores at night. 2145 hr: All coys arrived back at camp.

The QM's, RMO's, and Education Offrs' Reports for the months of June and July taken from the War Diary were as follows :

(a) The QM's report by Capt P O'Brien stated that all weapons had been received except sniper rifles and only 11 out of 40 cups-discharger had been issued. Wooden butts on SMGs had not proved satisfactory and about 15 weapons were rendered unserviceable during training. Steel butts had replaced damaged wooden ones and these were more satisfactory. Rations had been of a high standard both in quality and quantity. Lectures had been given by Army Catering Corps personnel and were most beneficial. A cooking school was also conducted in unit lines. A full issue of anti-malarial stores was received and every man was equipped.

(b) The Medical report for July by Capt H L Hughes stated that the health of the Bn during the present training period had remained excellent. 35 members were evacuated to hospital during the month. 18 were medical cases (including 9 URTI, 3 malarias and 2 pleurisy), 8 were surgical cases (including an accidental gun shot wound in the neck), 2 ENT (ear, nose and throat), 5 skin cases and 2 eye problems (1 acute conjunctivitis and the other a carbuncle on the lower left eyelid). Bill Hughes further stated the training of stretcher bearers had been supervised and the Bn squad was now complete.

(c) Lt J D McFarland reported on the Army Education Service which had become available to the unit towards the end of June. He had been appointed Unit Education Officer and 52 personnel had applied to study various subjects. Chief among subjects chosen were station bookkeeping, sheep and wool classing, accountancy, carpentry and joining and mechanics. Two members applied for matriculation. Lectures were given in the YMCA tent by 20 Bde Education NCO. Subjects being: 1. The people of China, 2. China at War, 3. Japan and the War. Attendances at each lecture totalled well over 200. Spanky ended his initial report by stating: "The AE Service undoubtedly offers great opportunities for increasing one's standard of education, general knowledge and ability; however under conditions such as those encountered by Inf units, study is particularly difficult and facilities for compiling papers and undergoing examinations are very poor. To successfully complete a course a soldier will have to be very keen and determined, sacrificing all his spare time for study."

Lt Col N W Simpson's Summary for July 1943, brings this chapter to a close with the Bn's embarkation completed on 31 July 1943, destination Milne Bay, New Guinea:

"From the point of view of training this month has been one of the most active in the Bn's history. Since our arrival in North Queensland training has been intensive and discipline rigid. The present standard of the Bn more than justifies all the efforts that have been made by Offrs and men.

A new atmosphere pervades the camp — everyone is keyed to concert pitch. We have finished a period of the most intense training the Bn has ever undergone — it certainly was the most interesting. The men are fighting fit — never been fitter and we look forward to whatever lies ahead with no apprehensions. We have never failed yet and we certainly won't fail this time for we are as well equipped as ordnance can make us. This, joined with a healthy mental outlook and a determination to win, makes the Bn a force to be reckoned with. In the words of an American soldier: 'This two stroke one seven Bn is sure a sweet outfit.'

On 2 July the Bn moved from Kairi in the Atherton Tablelands to a camp some 14 miles north of Cairns to train in combined operations in conjunction with 2 ESB, an American formation. The training was intensive but being something different from our work in the past, captured the imagination of the men who responded and did a really grand job. Our work had not been without faults, but these being detected were gradually eliminated. The training culminated in a Bde exercise on 15/16 July in which the whole Bde plus attached arms participated. The period 17/22 July was mainly occupied in equipping every man and subunit according to W.E. (tropical) scale. In between period of issue every effort was made to retain the physical fitness of the unit. This was done by vigorous route marching with swimming and PT parades.

Much of the good atmosphere which exists throughout the camp is due to the untiring efforts of Mr Wood, the YMCA rep and his staff. He accompanied the Bn on all its exercises and whenever possible had some amenity for every man. By providing a broadcast of news and music during rest periods he did much to overcome the lack of amenities. On 26 July Lt K Gibb and 19 Ors left Cairns as a Bn advance party for our new destination. July 28, C Coy embarked with 2/15 Bn. On the evening 31 July, the remainder of the Bn embarked on SS *William Ellery Channing* for Milne Bay, New Guinea.

This summary would be incomplete without some mention of the good feeling and co-operation between the Bn and A Boat Coy and F Shore Coy 532 EB and SR — the sub-units of 2 ESB which were attached for combined ops training. We feel that the period has done a great deal to create a spirit of co-operation between this unit and any units of the US Army with whom we may, in the future, come in contact."

Governor General's visit to Ravenshoe, – 13 Feb 1945 - HRH the Duke of Gloucester talking to Pte A E Rogers of A Coy, 2/17 Bn. The CO, Lt. Col. J R Broadbent on the left.   (AWM 864538)

ANNEXURE "A" TO CHAPTER 14 — TRAINING FOR WAR IN THE SOUTH WEST PACIFIC AREA

GLOSSARY OF TERMS, UNITS, CRAFT ETC.

A US Engineer Special Brigade: A US Army formation consisting of two Regts each of one Boat Bn and one Shore Bn. Used for maintenance and protection of the beachhead and being equipped with small landing craft can be used to transport personnel and stores in a shore to shore operation or supplement the craft of Amphibious Force in a ship to shore operation.

532 US Boat and Shore Regt (or 532 Group 2 ESB: A force consisting of the Shore Bn 532 Regt with portion of the Boat Bn attached. This was under command of US Task Force 76 until landed when it came under command 9 Aust Div.

Landing Craft of this unit comprised

LCV (P)	–	36
LCM	–	10
LCT	–	4
LCS	–	3
38' patrol boats	–	2

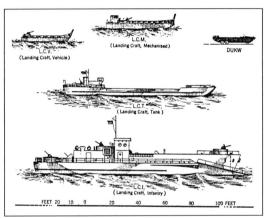

Some of the landing craft used by Allied forces

Equipment included

Bulldozers	–	10
Road grader	–	1
Mobile crane	–	1
Mobile air compressor	–	1

Weapons included

37 mm A/Tk guns	–	6
50 cal AAMG	–	6
30 cal LMG — ground & AA	–	12
60 mm mortar	–	12

LANDING CRAFT:

LCP(R) *Landing craft, Personnel (Ramp)* — Assault craft for personnel — 30 to 36 troops.

LCV(P) *Landing craft, Vehicle — personnel* — Assault craft for personnel and light vehicles 36 to 40 troops or 1 – 1 ton truck.

LCV *Landing craft, Vehicle* — primarily to land vehicles in initial stages of landing. Also used for personnel. Similar capacity to LCV(P).

LCM *Landing craft, Mechanised* — for landing motor vehicle light tank, (Medium tank in Craft Mk III) tractor, gun etc.

LCT *Landing craft, Tank* — for landing medium and heavy tanks.

LCI *Landing craft, Infantry* — to carry approx 200 troops with accommodation, bunks, booking facilities etc. Debarkation along port and starboard ramps projected forward from bow vehicles in initial stages of landing.

CHAPTER 15
FROM CAIRNS TO MILNE BAY

On 28 Jul 1943 the effective strength of the 2/17 Bn was 32 Offrs and 675 Ors. C Coy, commanded by Capt J H Dinning, was detached and boarded the small Dutch M S *Van Heurtz* at 2230 hrs. After several changes of position in the harbour during the intervening days, the *Van Heurtz* cruised off Cairns on 1 Aug to await the rest of the assembled convoy of ships destined for Milne Bay, Papua New Guinea.

The journey to Milne Bay commenced early afternoon on 1 Aug. C Coy had already been on board over three and one half days, almost the time taken for the whole journey. Plans were disrupted by the whims of disconsolate waterside workers, recorded in the following extract from 20 Bde War Diary of 25 Jul 43:

> "1300 hrs orders were received to load the stores for flight 2. A stop work meeting was held this morning by the waterside workers loading the ship on which flight 1 will travel. It was decided at the meeting not to load after 2130 hrs. After 2130 hrs the loading was undertaken by American soldiers. Although the wharf labourers were being paid at holiday rates, it was obvious that they were working at a slow rate. The result of this policy by the waterside workers was that when the troops arrived to embark in the early hours of the morning, the ship was not ready. Embarkation was so delayed that the last troops were not on the ship until first light and it was already daylight before the ship was able to move up-stream. "

David Dexter's Official History stated:

> "Damage caused to the stores and equipment by careless handling and weather had been experienced by both the 9th and 7th Divisions in their movement from Australia to New Guinea. Stop work meetings and go slow tactics by the Cairns wharf labourers had delayed and confused the move of the 20th Bde late in July. "

The 2/17 Bn had left its native land a second time for war on foreign soil, this time not so far away. Passed another landmark in a soldier's life, looking forward to the end of the war, with no end in sight. This time there were not the sirens of Sydney Harbour and the deafening blast of the foghorn on the *Queen Mary* heralding their departure. No small craft with admirers waving flags and displaying placards conveying messages to loved ones setting out on a new exciting adventure to lands far away. A new adventure, yes but not in a luxury liner of yore — instead, in a convoy of many ships, large and small, camouflaged with war paint, sliding silently out of Cairns Harbour towards a passage through the Great Barrier Reef and the Coral Sea.

The war was closer to home this time and the mens' thoughts were intensified towards the ultimate victory over the Japanese. Amongst their lot were those who knew the rigours of the battlefield from their long experiences in the Siege of Tobruk and the hard fighting at El Alamein. These experiences toughened their resolve and the professionalism of their months of intensive training in the art of jungle and amphibious warfare reinforced their high morale in awareness that strenuous times must lie ahead. Others, who were reinforcements, mostly those who joined the Unit in the Middle East after the Battle of El Alamein, were encouraged by "old soldier" mates by their side. Inevitably, as the convoy headed for the open sea, the decline in activity allowed time for reminiscence and reflection on the significance of the events in which they were involved.

Fred Camarsh of the Signal Platoon wrote in his diary:

> "The ship finally draws away from the wharf and heads out of harbour through the Trinity opening of the Barrier Reef followed by several sharks expecting food discharged from the vessel. As the shoreline recedes behind us we have time to reflect back over our four months at Kairi on the Tablelands and at Cairns. Of our treks along the forest trails admiring the beauty of the rain forest and of the deep ravines where we would eat with one hand while hanging on with the other, or removing the countless leaches and watching the platypus families at play in the Barron River. Of our trip to Cairns for our amphibious training when, as the vehicles descended from the plateau, the vast sugar cane fields below us would ripple with the wind like a second sea. Of drives along the shoreline with long sandy beaches on one side and tropical forest on the other. Of mornings when in the pre dawn darkness we would drift in our landing barges some half mile off Trinity or Ellis beaches and then enjoy the beauty of the shoreline as the craft headed shorewards in the dawn; of early cups of tea and breakfast on the beach — and now it all recedes behind us and we look to the future. "

Conditions were relatively comfortable and pleasant for C Coy 2/17 Bn on board M S *Van Heurtz* compared with the experiences of the remainder of the 2/17 Bn on board the American Liberty Ship S S *William Ellery Channing*. Only limited work had been done in converting the "Channing" to troop carrying. It had no portholes, severely restricting the circulation of fresh air below decks, especially at night in "Darken Ship" conditions. Primitive toilets were located on the aft deck. Cooking was done only in daylight on the forward deck in a temporary superstructure. As the lighting of fires in the cook houses was not permitted outside full daylight hours, bread could not be made at night and feeding arrangements became disorganised.

While on board the troops were ordered to carry their water bottles and emergency rations at all times in the event of having to abandon ship. The constant presence of this reserve store of food tempted hungry men and some succumbed to the unpardonable sin of consuming their emergency ration, such action being permitted only on the receipt of a specific order.

A soldier diarist wrote:

> "Tuesday, 3 Aug 43. Still steaming north and enjoying the sight of the numerous small islands with their greenery and sparkling white beaches. We are all suffering the pangs of hunger and cannot understand why the situation exists. We hold a group discussion between decks and vote to commit the deadly sin of eating our emergency ration of tinned chocolate. "

The journey to Milne Bay proceeded without incident so far as the soldiers were aware, the only noticeable activity seawards being nine ships of the convoy which left it for Port Moresby at 1500 hrs on 3 Aug. Space on board both ships did not permit organised training or PT and with the unusual situation of men being left to their own resources, card games were the main preoccupation in the cramped conditions.

The Bn disembarked at Milne Bay on 4 Aug 43 and moved directly to its new camp site on Stringer Bay. Tents had been erected for the Unit by the 22 Militia Bn. The camp site extended along the shoreline to about 400 yards inland from a pebbled beach where the ground rose steeply to thickly wooded hills. The area was covered with barbed wire entanglements and pitted with bomb craters, a grim reminder of the battle for Milne Bay in Aug and Sep the previous year. The close proximity of the camp to the Turnbull airfield and the frequent comings and goings of "Kittyhawk" and "Lightning" fighter aircraft were further reminders that the war was not far away.

A tropical deluge of monsoonal rain welcomed the troops the first night in camp, which flooded the area and this required urgent attention to drainage and to badly sited tents. The monsoonal weather continued for the whole of the time the 2/17 Bn was on the peninsula. Troops became accustomed to being permanently wet during the day, working in deep mud, and expecting the arrival of the monsoon every day as regular as clockwork.

Shortly after landing at Milne Bay a kit inspection was held and a charge laid against everyone who could not produce his emergency ration. The first CO's orderly room was conducted in the atmosphere of the new surroundings, outside a native hut on stilts. The usual procedure for such occasions was followed with an explanation being demanded of each individual by Lt Col Simpson in a way that only he seemed able. A short note was made of each explanation by the soldier and a few terse questions asked of him in a superficial check of his story. Explanations varied between candid acknowledgement of hunger and having eaten the ration, an assertion that it was thought to have been an emergency, and a claim that the ration had been stolen while the soldier was engaged in such important duty as cleaning his rifle. Few men gave an explanation that was accepted but for the most part the CO read a list of so many names, fined so much, grouping them according to the type of story, it being worst of all to have candidly acknowledged the eating.

On 6 and 7 Aug the 2/17 Bn stores arrived. Meanwhile, the hygiene squad had drained the camp area and sprayed bomb craters and slit trenches. Standing Orders contained strict instructions on anti-malarial precautions. Activity for the remainder of August was directed towards preparation for Operation "Postern", the amphibious landing on the Huon Gulf east of the township of Lae. Careful security measures were taken to conceal the location of the landing, known only to those at high level in the planning stage. Photographs of terrain and the intended landing beach, on which names were obliterated, were made available for study by company commanders on 14 Aug. These gave clear detail of the terrain and included close obliques of the beachhead area. The photographs were located in a tent under constant guard and close to the time for embarkation all troops were familiarized with their objectives from the photographs.

Major Broadbent commented on the training period at Milne Bay throughout Aug:

> "Training at Milne Bay became more specific route marching and hill climbing with increase in loads being carried on the man. As usual it began to take the specific turn in relation to the planned activity for the landing although details were not then known. Certain companies began working with the American APDs, the destroyers carrying landing craft, which was a popular assignment and others began to experience the poky conditions on board LCIs. Particular attention was given to the extent of the load which could be carried on the man. A rather too optimistic conclusion was reached but rectified by a decision made at Buna on the way to Lae that the belt rolls containing mosquito nets, certain spare clothing and perhaps miscellaneous personal gear would have to be dumped on the landing. "

Lt Col Simpson in his Summary for the month of Aug mentioned a Brigade amphibious exercise on the 10th and a Divisional exercise at Normandy Island on 20/21 Aug, besides a number of company exercises which completed the Bn's tactical rehearsals and battle drills for "Postern". He further stated:

> "The problems of this coming operation were discussed by all Offrs at several sand table exercises. Administrative work on loading tables and stores to be carried during the

operation was finalized by the 14 Aug. Six Offrs and 55 Ors who comprised our LOB left for Buna on the evening 15 Aug. B Echelon stores were packed and loading began on 18 Aug. On 29 Aug a brigade parade was held at Turnbull Airstrip when Lt Gen Sir Edmund Herring, GOC 1 Aust Corps, inspected the troops and afterwards during an address welcomed the Division and the Brigade to his Command and wished all Offrs and men luck during the coming operation. The amenity side of life for the troops is not quite what we have been used to. The YMCA marquee was functioning until the wireless and electric light plant had to be packed and sent to the LOB base at Buna. Pictures twice per week in an American camp two miles away were well patronised by our troops. Tobacco supplies were adequate and were available at greatly reduced prices. Lt Col A T Allan, Senior LO NGF (our former 2 I/C) paid us two visits during the month. The CO's orders for 'Postern' were given on the afternoon of the 31 Aug. "

The Divisional rehearsal for Operation "Postern" was exercise "Coconut" and involved the embarkation of the Division, less 24 Bde Group, and a practice landing on two beaches on Normandy Island. The craft used were the majority of those actually to be employed in the operation. Several rehearsals were carried out by the assault wave of 20 Bde from APDs and by the follow up waves of LCIs. Loading and unloading of LCTs and LSTs with guns, vehicles and stores was also extensively practised.

2/17 Bn's participation in exercise "Coconut" was recorded in its War Diary:

"20 August: Bn marches to Beach No 1 after breakfast and load on to landing craft for the Divisional exercise on Normandy Island. 1300 hrs: The convoy of 44 craft (LSTs, LCMs, LCIs and APDs) steam out of Milne Bay.

21 August: At dawn the convoy was off the south coast of Normandy Island. First wave of left mission landed on Bunama Bay at 0637 hrs. Second wave landed to right of first wave. Owing to the dense jungle and swamps troops progress was slow but the first phase was completed at 0840 hrs. Bn forward companies, C, A and B continued to make slow progress in the heavy going and the second phase was completed at 0945 hrs. 1130 hrs exercise ends. 1300 hrs; troops begin to reload on to craft. 1730 hrs; disembarkation began at Beach No 1. 1830 hrs; all troops back in camp, tired and wet with the feeling that a day's work had been done. "

Capt P E O'Brien, QM, recorded the following report for Aug:

"All stores arrived from the mainland in good order and condition. Ten A Tk rifles were returned as their retention was not considered necessary owing to the nature of likely operations. Four of these rifles only were then held. Due to faulty ammunition there have been several cases of bulged barrels in Owen SMGs but new barrels were soon received. With the exception of sniper rifles (none held) full W E scale of weapons were held. Rations: practically hard scale continually with a fresh issue at irregular intervals. Bread of excellent quality has been a regular issue. "

Capt H L Hughes, the RMO, stated in the medical report:

"The W. E. Equipment lacks only scissors, SB, 21 pairs. 20 personnel evacuated to hospital during the month including 4 cases of provisionally diagnosed scrub typhus (2 confirmed to date). The main complaint was furunculosis ('boils') some 60 personnel being treated. 25 soldiers had been trained as stretcher bearers. Troops had been lectured on anti-malarial precautions and measures against hookworm, dysentery and infected water. Abscorbic tablets, 1 daily, were commenced on 25 Aug and continued. Salt tablets have been issued to all troops with instructions for use. The standard of individual protection against malaria was in the RMO's opinion, good. The general health of the unit was excellent. "

The nominal roll of 2/17 Bn Offrs with appointments at the end of August, 43 was as follows:

Lt Col N W Simpson	CO	Lt T E Swan	Mor Pl
Major J R Broadbent	2 I/C	Lt J D McFarland	T O
Capt P E O'Brien	QM	Lt K J Gibb	Pl C omd
Capt *P H Pike	OC A Coy	Lt E J Blundell	I O
Capt *L C Maclarn	OC HQCoy	Lt W Forster	Sig O
Capt T C Sheldon	OC B Coy	Lt W M Cooper	MMG O
Capt J H Dinning	OC C Coy	Lt C L Rogers	A Tk O
Capt G T Reid	OC D Coy	Lt B Waterhouse	Pl Comd
Capt A J Wright	Adjutant	Lt P I Pollock	Pl Comd
Lt*R S Rudkin	Coy 2 I/C	Lt K T McLeod	Pl Comd
Lt*J R B Norris	Coy 2 I/C	Lt L A McRae	Pl Comd
Lt*E O Norton	Coy 2 I/C		
Lt*R J Dick	Coy 2 I/C	Chap W L Byrne	Chaplain
Lt H H Main	Pl Comd	Capt H L Hughes	AMC RMO
Lt S G J Waterhouse	Pl Comd		
Lt A E Nicholson	Pl Comd		
Lt N E McDonald	Pl Comd	Supernumerary to EST were:	
Lt S M Williams	Pl Comd	Lt J M Male	
Lt R J Bennie	Pl Comd	Lt N G West	
Lt A P Craik	Pl Comd	Lt W A Graham	

*Note: Capts Pike and Maclarn were promoted to Major effective 4 Sep 43: Notification was not received by the Bn until 19 Oct 43. Lts Rudkin and Norris were promoted to Captain effective from 7 Sep 43: Notification was not received by the Bn until 6 Nov 43. Lt Norton was killed at Scarlet Beach on 25 Sep 43: Notification had not been received by the Bn of his prior promotion to Captain. As late as August Lt L C Simpson was attending the LHQ tactical school. Lt K Sabine was evacuated on 14 Aug with a compound fracture of tibia and fibula which happened on the improvised field firing range when he jumped across a ditch into deep mud: He was promoted to Captain effective 19 Aug 43 and the Bn was notified on 6 Nov 43. Lt Dick became the A Tk Offr for the Lae Landing vice Lt Rogers who was LOB.

On 21 Aug the posted strength of the Bn, offrs excluded, was 1 WO1, 5 WOs 2, (1 def) 5 CQMSs, 34 Sgt, (3 surplus) 65 Cpls, (1 surplus) 604 ptes, (28 deficient) — attached were 2 AAPC, 4 AAMC, 1 AAOC, 4 AEME, 1 AA Post, 24 AACC.

CHAPTER 16

THE HUON GULF - LAE

On 2 Sep, 1943 Operation "Postern" began when Battalions of the 20 Brigade moved at 0700 hrs in boat groups to Stringer Beach for embarkation. The scene on embarkation was described by Alan Dawes, a newspaper correspondent:

"Roads and tracks were swarming with green shirts. They resembled nothing so much as the long lines of chlorophyll-coloured ants that march up and around the trees of the rain forests of New Guinea and North Australia. Packs that bristle with jungle knives, axes and spades; MT bashing the mud under loads of ammo and HE, guns and gear, everything from a bullet to a bulldozer, it was all there, a perfect picture of battle eve."

The embarkation at Stringer Beach proceeded with practised precision as each assemblage of rain-soaked troops put on their equipment and moved forward in its turn to meet the arrival of the allotted craft.

Capt Pike's A Coy 2/17 Battalion, which formed part of the first assault wave on "Red Beach", embarked in Landing Craft Personnel – Ramps (LCP(R)s) which took the men and equipment to the USS *Humphries*, one of four Assault Personnel Destroyers (APD) lying at anchor in the bay. Other troops of the Battalion's fighting echelon embarked up the dual ramps of their respective Landing Craft Infantry vessels (LCI).

The 9 Division convoy of 41 LCIs, 4 APDS, with a number of LSTs and LCTs left Milne Bay at 1300 hrs on 2 September and in inverse order to the speed of its components rounded East Cape and steamed adjacent to the Papuan coast towards Buna and the Morobe coast.

An hour before sunset, the destroyer transports which had departed from Milne Bay later than the other ships, caught up with the rest of the convoy. Never before had the natives of Papua witnessed off their shores such an impressive armada in the Solomon Sea.

The convoy arrived off Buna at 0700 hrs on 3 September and the troops disembarked at 0800 hrs for relaxation in the area occupied by LOB personnel. Some men sat about the beach, others swam or listened to music and took hot refreshments in the YMCA or Salvation Army tents, also taking the opportunity to write letters. Two hot meals were provided before re-embarkation at 1400 hrs.

Capt Pike's A Coy did not go ashore at Buna and stayed on board the USS *Humphries*, where its personnel were hosted by the Americans. They were the envy of the remainder of the Battalion whose accommodation was comparatively less exuberant on board the LCIs.

Having been brought together with a common purpose to defeat the enemy at close quarters, there could not have been a better or more friendly relationship between the soldiers of A Coy and the sailors of the USS *Humphries*. The Australian soldiers never forgot the hospitality of the Americans on that occasion.

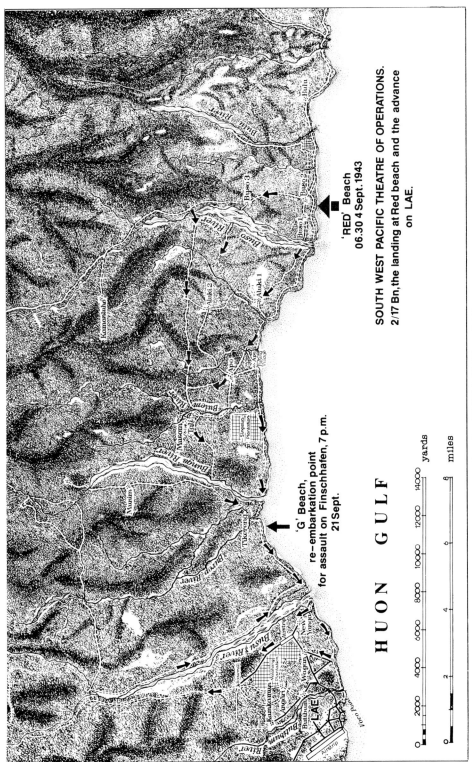

Landing HUON GULF — LAE

Once out to sea the guessing about the location of the beachhead ended. All were informed that "Red" and "Yellow" beaches with which they had become familiar from maps and photographs, were in the Huon Gulf, the nearest about 15 miles east of Lae. The beachheads were chosen amongst other considerations, having regard to the distance they were outside the range of known enemy artillery in the Lae area.

All located enemy defences were in and around Lae itself. They consisted of numerous well dug strongpoints covering all approaches and sited in depth. There were no evidence of defences east of the Busu River though concealment was easy, and there were unconfirmed reports of enemy beach defences along the whole of the southern coast of the Huon Peninsula.

The area in which the Division proposed to approach Lae consisted of a flat coastal plain to an average depth of three miles before rising into the rugged foothills of the inland mountains. West of the Burep River the plain broadened into the valleys of the Busu, Butibum and Markham Rivers, the two former being divided about two and one half miles north of Lae by the Atzera Range, the southern slopes of which dominated the town. The coastal plain was covered with dense jungle interspersed with patches of kunai grass eight to ten feet high and with mangrove swamps in the immediate coastal areas.

Between the main landing beach "Red Beach" and Lae the plain was intersected by five rivers and numerous small streams; apart from the Busu, these were not expected to present any real problem. There were no roads. The landing beaches, "Red Beach", to the east of the mouth of the Buso River and "Yellow Beach", near the village of Hopoi, were approximately 20 yards wide of firm black sand. Behind the beaches swamp allowed few exits. Between the Buso and Busu Rivers other beaches were subsequently found and developed, the most notable was at the mouth of the Burep River, later known as "G" Beach.

The outline plan for the 9 Div Operation was as follows:

The landing was to be carried out in three main groups on 4 Sep 43. H hour was 0630 hrs.

Group 1:   20 Bde (2/13, 2/15, 2/17 Bns) and 26 Bde (2/23, 2/24, 2/48 Bns) with 532 BSR and supporting and maintenance units were to land at "Red" and "Yellow" Beaches preceded by naval bombardment from H-11 to H-5 minutes. The main landing was to be at "Red Beach". 2/13 Bn with dets of Arty, AA and RAE were to land at "Yellow Beach" to protect the eastern flank and to secure an alternative beachhead.

Group 2:   The balance of 20 and 26 Bdes (rear details) and proportion of Divisional troops with vehicles and bulk stores were to land at 2300 hrs on D day. This group was carried in six LSTs.

Group 3:   24 Bde (2/28, 2/32, 2/43 Bns) to land on the night 5/6 Sep.

The intention was:

(a) to capture "Red" and "Yellow" Beaches.

(b) to secure a covering position for and establish a beach maintenance area at "Red Beach".

This was to be carried out with a view to simultaneous maintenance development and protection of the beachhead and the earliest possible commencement of a rapid advance towards Lae.

The Division's Commander, Maj Gen G F Wootten, was warned that if Lae was captured quickly he might be required to provide a Bde Group at short notice to capture Finschhafen.

Concurrently with the operation of 9 Div an airborne operation was to be carried out by 7

WAVE	TIME	COMPOSITION	CRAFT	TPS
		STREAM COCONUTS TRACK SWAMP TRACK ←180″→ ←320″→ ←360″→ BEACH MARKING SIGNS		
1	H	A COY 2/17 Bn 2/15 Bn 12 11	8/LCP (R) 2APD	20 BDE
2	H+10	B COY C COY 24 23 22 21	4LCI	20 BDE
3	H+15	D COY 20 34 33 32 31	4LCI	20 BDE
4	H+30	45 44 43 42 41	3LCT 2LCV	RAA RAE ESB
5	H+35	57 56 55 54 53 52 51	7LCI	2/23 BN 26 BDE DIV HQ
6	H+50	68 67 66 65 64 63 62 61	8LCV	ESB
7	H+53	78 77 76 75 74 73 72 71	8LCV	ESB
8	H+60	88 87 86 85 84 83 82 81	4LCT 4LCM	ESB
9	H+75	98 97 96 95 94 93 92 91	6LCM 2LCV	ESB
10	H+85	108 107 106 105 104 103 102 101	8LCV	ESB
11	H+92	118 117 116 115 114 113 112 111	8LCV	ESB
12	H+105	126 125 124 123 122 20 121	6LST	2/24 2/48 DIV TPS
13	H+110	137 136 135 134 133 132 131	7LCT	BULK STORES

Landing Diagram for Lae Operation

RED BEACH   9 AUST DIVISION

Div with the object of attacking Lae from the north and preventing the movement of enemy reinforcements down the Markham Valley.

The 2/17 Bn Operation Order for "Postern" had been issued on 26 Aug 43. It covered in great detail information on terrain, weather, water supply, beaches, egress from the beach area, all known factors pertaining to the Japanese (their strength, possible intentions, the defences of Lae, supply systems, morale etc). The estimated enemy strength in the Lae area was stated to be: — Field troops 3520, Anti-Aircraft units 860 and line of Communication troops 1090. Weapons were estimated to be not less than 141 LMGs, 42 MMGs, 44 artillery guns, (37 mm to 105 mm) and 42 A/A guns. There was a warning note stating: "Due to ease of concealment, photographic interpretation is approximate only. "

Under 'Enemy morale' there was a significant paragraph which read:

> "The psychology of the Japanese makes an assessment of morale extremely dangerous. They should never be judged on the reaction of German or Italian troops faced with similar circumstances. "

The general plan was for the 20 Bde to land with one Bn on "Yellow Beach" and two Bns on "Red Beach".

(a)"Yellow Beach" — 2/13 Bn.

(b)"Red Beach" — 2/15 Bn and 2/17 Bn.

The additional troops with and in support of 20 Bde were 2/12 Fd Regt, less one battery, (Artillery) 12 Lt AA Bty, (Anti-aircraft Artillery) 2/3 Fd Coy, (Engineers) 2/8 Fd Amb, (Medical) and 2/23 Bn on landing to come under command 20 Bde.

In support of the 2/17 Bn was 23 Bty, 2/12 Fd Regt, one platoon, 2/3 Fd Coy, a Light ADS of 2/8 Fd Amb and some PIB, it was stated, may be attached to contact villagers and for reconnaissance.

The intention of the 2/17 Bn was to land and secure the left flank of a beachhead to permit the landing of the 20 Bde reserve.

The operation was to be carried out in four stages :

STAGE 1 : (i) Landing and immediate capture of the beach and the jungle fringing the beach including the coconut plantation.

(ii) Penetrate inland and capture of the line of the first objective.

STAGE 2 : (i) Capture of the line of the second objective. (ii) This stage was to commence immediately companies had secured the first objectives. Until 2/23 Bn lands at least one company was to be kept in reserve within the area of the first objective, which was not to be committed without the prior approval of Bde HQ.

STAGE 3 : (i) Capture and consolidation of the line of the third objective to secure the beachhead with forward outposts to control the tracks leading into the beachhead area.

(ii) The establishment of a bridgehead near the mouth of the Buso River.

(This stage was to commence when ordered by Bn HQ).

(iii) Movement of 2/23 Bn inland to reserve position. Role : Holding of the position and to be prepared to counter attack the established line of the third objective.

STAGE 4 : (i) Establishment of bridgehead area — Buso River at the track crossing (From Buso to Aluki villages) by 2/17 Bn.

(ii) Preparation of 2/17 Bn for an immediate advance along both coastal and inland routes when the bridgeheads are reported secure.

The Bn Operation Order No 4, (summarized above) appeared to cover all requirements and had a number of appendices. A gridded map enlargement of the beachhead area appended an overlay showing the Company objectives at each stage of the operation. Administrative Order No 6 for the operation issued from the Adjutant, Capt Wright on 28 Aug. This covered the many details regarding rations, ammunition, clothing, transport, water, hygiene, salvage, prisoners, recovery, medical, burials, natives, etc. Lt Col Simpson's plan displayed his usual military efficiency; it was simple, his directions were clear and concise and his attention to detail was comprehensive.

The soldiers of the 2/17 Bn were naturally proud of their Unit's record against their earlier adversaries in the Middle East. In Tobruk the 2/17 Bn was the first infantry unit of the Allies in the 39/45 war to halt and stem the tide of the German Panzers. The Unit's outstanding success against the Germans and Italians continued later in the devastating battle of El Alamein. There, with other units of the 20 Bde given the task, the Bn led the assault to capture and hold vital ground, without relief throughout the entire battle, despite its numbers having been reduced by casualties to about a company strength. The soldiers of the 2/17 Bn therefore welcomed with pride and humility the opportunity, with sister Bns of the Brigade and supporting arms, to execute the first assault landing by Australian soldiers by sea since their forefathers stormed ashore at Gallipoli on 25 April 1915. Moreover, they were conscious of the historical importance of the events about to unfold and approached the landing at "Red Beach" with confidence and dignity to uphold the reputation and traditions of their Bn in both world wars.

At the suggestion of Capt Reid, OC D Coy, Major Broadbent, who was to command the inland group of the 2/17 Bn, called the troops on deck near to last light on the eve of the landing, a time when infantrymen were accustomed to "standing to" and he addressed the troops to the effect; "You have done things in the past of which you are proud — you have learned how to do the landing in the morning — it is a new world and a new medium — there is no basis for not having confidence in each other and in the plan, as you have been committed to a job by commanders you know and a country you are still here to serve: now, go about things quietly tonight and in the morning you will be right. " Sadly, the understanding, gallant Company Commander, Capt George Reid, was killed in the campaign.

The men of Capt Reid's D Coy returned to their bunks below deck in the confined space of the LCI. Soldiers do not usually sleep well on the eve of a battle. It would have been a disturbed sleep for most, if not all men in the strange surroundings. Many were awake when the warning bells sounded before dawn. By 0600 hrs it was light enough to recognise the objective from air photographs and photo-maps which had been widely distributed. The bombers had already completed their softening up work and as troops put on their heavy equipment, rumblings echoed across the water from the bombardment of supporting destroyers. Some soldiers near hatches to the deck moved out to watch the impressive display of naval firepower. The intensity of the barrage and the spectacular sight of tracer shells from the destroyers engendered confidence in those who watched, waiting for their part to play in the attack.

As shown on the diagram for the Division's landing on "Red Beach," the four LCP(R)s on the left of wave 1 contained Maj Pike's A Coy 2/17 Bn group with support weapons. The troops disembarked from USS *Humphries* by scramble nets to the assault craft and landed at 0633 hrs on the left of the brigade beachhead. The remainder of the Bn, with the exception of B Echelon, were transported in LCIs comprised in Wave 2: Capt Sheldon's B Coy & Capt Dinnings C Coy groups, Lt Dick's A Tk Pl and Bn HQ. Wave 3: Capt Reid's D Coy Group and Duplicate Bn HQ. B Echelon were in wave 13 on an LCT.

The extensive and detailed planning of the landing for Operation "Postern" was not tested by enemy action, for the landings on both "Red" and "Yellow" beaches were unopposed. It was not seriously expected that the former would be occupied as no evidence of enemy defences had been located. At "Yellow" beach, however, about 30 enemy had abandoned a strongpost in the face of the invaders.

After landing, subunits of the 2/17 Bn made good progress through the thick rain forest, mangrove swamp and secondary growth to achieve the objectives of the first two stages of the operation. The fifth wave of the landing, which comprised the 2/23 Bn and Main Div HQ was not so fortunate, suffering an air attack from 1500 feet by 6 enemy fighters and 3 bombers. These straffed and bombed the LCIs as they approached the beach and dropped 12 bombs, one of which exploded on the deck of LCI339 just forward of the bridge, and killed the CO of the 2/23 Bn, Lt Col R E Wall, E.D., a Coy Comd, Capt R K Reid, M.C. and five men, and wounded twenty-eight including six officers. LCI 341 had a large hole blown in its side from a near miss and water flooded two of its compartments.

By last light on "D" day all 20 Bde objectives on both beaches had been secured and the 26 Bde with 2/17 Bn under command had begun the advance towards Lae. The 2/17 Bn led the advance in two main groups:

(a) A northern group commanded by Maj Broadbent which comprised Capt Dinning's C Coy and Capt Reid's D Coy.

(b) A southern group commanded by Lt Col Simpson which comprised Maj Pike's A Coy and Capt Sheldon's B Coy. Lt Dick's A Tk Pl, less its two guns and crews commanded by Sgt T George left for protection of the beachhead, advanced independently via the coastline.

No opposition was encountered by the 2/17 Bn on "D" day. The day was a trial of physical endurance in the high humidity and the exertion required in making tracks through the vegetation, especially as all arms, equipment and ammunition, including mortar bombs in 3 bomb containers were carried on the man. To lighten the load, the soldier's belt roll, which contained a blanket and mosquito net wrapped in a groundsheet, was dumped soon after landing. These were never seen again by their owners due to the shortage of boat transport and when other items of supply were given precedence. The absence of this precautionary measure against malaria became detrimental to the general health of the troops after incubation of the disease in the fullness of time.

The northern group moved inland at 0900 hrs according to plan in search of the east- west government track. A large area of timber fallen at an awkward height and difficult for laden troops to cross, interpreted on air photographs as native garden, was encountered early in the advance. This delayed progress and by midday only about 3 miles had been traversed without reaching the intended Buso River crossing. Fortunately two natives were met, one of whom was an ex-policeman who spoke pidgin english and who guided the column northwards to meet the east-west track to Lae. Thereafter, good progress was made until 1730 hrs when the group bivouaced for the night about 1200 yards west of the village of Aluki. A 108 wireless set was lost fording the Buso River and other wireless equipment was ineffective due to the screening of the thick rain forest. Line communication to the rear was cut and the group was therefor completely without communication.

The southern group of the 2/17 Bn had similar physical problems. The troops waded the fast flowing Buso River near its mouth where some equipment became water damaged. Search for a track shown on air photographs was unsuccessful and the alternative of making a track through the rain forest or kunai grassed areas was very slow. The group bivouaced for the night 1000 yards east of a place named the "Nest" about 3 miles north-west of the mouth of the Buso River.

Lt Dick's A Tk Pl less its two guns and crews, after wading the Buso River, followed an indistinct track to the west along the coastline through dense mangrove vegetation and was out of communication with 2/17 Bn HQ after 30 minutes progress. In crossing one of the several narrow deep creeks the wireless operator was recovered after he had sunk out of sight with the wireless strapped on his back. The platoon bivouaced for the night astride a track junction about 2500 yards east of the Apo fishing village. A patrol sent out at dusk along the inland track to investigate small arms fire and contact the southern group was unsuccessful.

If any troops of the 2/17 Bn had difficulty sleeping the night before the landing, none had the same problem the night after the event. Despite a high standard of physical fitness gained in preparation for the operation, few if any men would not have been tired after the demands made on their endurance during the first day.

The evacuation of any stretcher casualties from the northern group for at least the first two days of the advance was a problem considering the distance back to the CCS at the beachhead without transport. There was no answer to the problem except a long carry by stretcher bearers. (Helicopters were not then part of war equipment.) Making the most of the available resources, the RAP personnel were divided into two sections: The RMO, Capt Hughes moved with the northern group assisted by Sgt Bingley, and Sgt Vic Rae moved with the southern group. Sgt Bingley was much older than most soldiers and one of the most liked and conscientious of the men who provided medical care for the Bn.

Maps were unreliable and the northern group, without communication and restricted observation in the thick forest, resumed the advance at 0800 hrs on 5 Sep along the track leading generally in a south-westerly direction. An unsuccessful attempt was made to determine exact location by two men climbing a large tree for observation. Maj Broadbent sent Capt Reid's D Coy to secure the area of Apo Village if the southern group had not already reached the village, while Capt Dinning's C Coy skirted to the north of a large kunai grassed area and at 1400 hrs reached the groups objective in the area of the Buiem River near the village of Tali. Signal wire ran out 800 yards short of the position and phone connection with Bde HQ was established at the end of the line at 1700 hrs.

Meanwhile, the southern group was frustrated by muddy tracks leading north-west through many native gardens and eventually the leading element of Capt Sheldon's B Coy contacted a patrol from D Coy commanded by Cpl Les Garner at 1500 hrs. By nightfall the 2/17 Bn had reached its immediate objective where it held a firm base east of the Buiem River with the Bn in the area of the Singaua plantation except Capt Dinning's C Coy located on the inland route in the Tali Village area. Lt Dick's A Tk Pl was located near the mouth of the river.

The 2/23 Bn had moved to positions ready to pass through the 2/17 Bn and resumed the advance early the following morning. Having regard to the Japanese likely reaction to the landing at "Red Beach" in time and space and the nature of the river obstacles available for their exploitation, it was reasonable to expect that the luxury of any further advance by friendly troops without opposition should have ended. On taking over the advance at 0735 hrs on 6 Sep the 2/23 Bn contacted a party of Japanese about 100 strong moving in an easterly direction half a mile west of the Buiem River. After a sharp engagement the enemy withdrew leaving 30 dead. A series of successful actions by companies ended in an ambush near the Bunga River and forced remnants of the enemy back in the direction of Lae. By last light the 2/23 Bn had crossed the Bunga River.

During the 2/23 Bn's initial encounter with the enemy, subunits of the 2/17 Bn which had moved along a track on the eastern side of the river in the plantation area and Lt Dick's A Tk Pl, located near the river's mouth, came under enemy mortar fire. There the 2/17 Bn suffered its first battle casualties in the New Guinea campaign where one soldier was killed,[1] two soldiers died of wounds,[2] and five soldiers were wounded. The Bn, less Capt Dinning's C Coy, proceeded north on the eastern side of the Buiem River and concentrated with C Coy in the Tali area at 1400 hrs.

Increased numbers of natives came through the northern area throughout 6 Sep, all anxious to help defeat the Japanese and were despatched to Apo village and organised into carrying parties. During the night 6/7 Sep very heavy rain fell, flooding the creeks and making the tracks almost impassable. Despite the impediments, the advance along the coast was progressing rapidly but the distance of the forward troops from the beachhead was accentuated by the absence of tracks and the difficulties of their construction in the marshy country in which they were operating. Also the same night stores and supplies were transported along the coast by landing craft and thereafter this became a normal means of supply.

On 7 Sep the 24 Bd had taken over the advance on the coast and the 26 Bde moved upstream along the Burep River with the aim of crossing the Busu River in the hinterland with a view to an advance on Lae towards the line of the Butibum River, thus outflanking the strong enemy defences known to exist in the area of the Malahang Airfield and cutting all roads and tracks leading to the defended enemy localities between the Busu and Butibum Rivers.

Advancing along the coast on 8 Sep, the 24 Bde's 2/28 Bn reached the mouth of the Busu River and found it a formidable obstacle, worsened by the recent heavy rainfall. (A series of torrential channels, the main channel was then 5 feet deep, 60 yards wide and with a flow of 10 to 12 knots.) Further north, the 26 Bde's 2/24 Bn had also reached the Busu River where its banks narrowed the flow of the water and caused an even more forceful torrent than at the river's mouth. Though bridging upstream would have been possible, the terrain did not permit the transport of equipment to the site. Several attempts were made by engineers attached to the 2/24 Bn at felling trees across the river but the timber was short of the span required. Enemy opposition on the far bank of the river was encountered and hampered both Bns.

Early on 7 Sep Maj Pike's A Coy 2/17 Bn had been sent to Apo Village to faciliate supply from B Echelon which was out of communication with the Bn. Capt Sheldon's B Coy remained in position while the 2/17 Bn, less A and B Coys moved to the west bank of the Bunga River where it bivouaced at 1100 hrs located about 1000 yards east of Munim Village. One day's supply of rations to the Bn was received by the joint effort of carrying parties operating in relay from A and B Coys. Lt Dick's A Tk Pl patrolled south to Kiasia Village, assisted by native guides, where it remained overnight without enemy contact.

8 Sep brought some respite to the 2/17 Bn from the intense physical activity since the

---

[1]
The soldier killed was Pte Alan Robert Davis of B Coy who served In the Middle East after El Alamein and enlisted from Coonabarabran, NSW.

[2]
Pte Eric Herbert Vincent (DOW) was a signaller attached to B Coy and served in Tobruk, El Eisa and El Alamein. He enlisted from Cammeray, NSW. Pte Patrick John Sparkes (DOW) was also from B Coy and served in Tobruk, Tel El Eisa and El Alamein. He enlisted from North Ryde, NSW.

landing, although patrols were sent out to the north, south and west. Men bathed, washed clothes and were glad of the day's rest.

On the night 8/9 Sep two 25 prs Mk II guns were moved by LCM from "Red Beach" to "G Beach" at the mouth of the Burep River. By 1930 hrs 9 Sep the 2/17 Bn, less Capt Sheldon's B Coy which remained in the Munim area with a platoon at Kiasia, was relocated on both sides of the Burep River about 3000 yards from its mouth as protection for the guns of the 24 Bty 2/12 Fd Regt. A divisional forward supply dump had been established at the Tikereng Village. The Burep River bed was jeepable and this relieved the supply problem previously experienced by the 2/17 Bn. Brigadier Windeyer, the 20 Bde Commander, visited the Bn on 9 Sep. Followed a wet and most uncomfortable night.

The discomfort of drenching rain interspersed with the deafening muzzle blast of 25 pdr gunfire in front of the guns at close range experienced by the 2/17 Bn at the Burep River was kindly compared with the problems that beset the 24 Bde's 2/28 Bn on 9 Sep. Several attempts were made by the 2/28 Bn during the morning to get patrols across the mouth of the Busu River. The current was too strong and the enemy hampered the troops with small arms fire from the far bank. In the late afternoon two companies of the Bn forced the crossing upstream and though men were washed away and some drowned and two thirds of the total weapons were lost in the struggle to get across the river, a bridgehead was secured. Determined enemy attempts to dislodge the companies were repulsed. The success story of the 2/28 Bn's opposed river crossing at the Busu, revealed its members' resourcefulness, initiative and determination and its subsequent defence of the bridgehead was an epic with a proud place in the annals of Australian military history.

During the night 10/11 Sep, 4 Bde arrived at "Red Beach" and on the following day relieved 20 Bde of the duties at the beachhead.

On 11 Sep Capt Sheldon's B Coy rejoined the 2/17 Bn at the Burep River and was sent to protect a troop of the 2/12 Fd Regt 1500 yards north of the existing Bn area. Also the Bn's B Echelon relocated from down stream to 400 yards south of Bn HQ. Regrettably, the move of B Echelon resulted in a direct hit on its new location from a high level bombing raid by 14 enemy planes on 12 Sep, obviously intended to silence the guns of the 2/12 Fd Regt. These numberered 14 guns in-all which fired from the east bank of the Burep River. B Echelon personnel suffered six soldiers KIA[1], one DOW[2], and fourteen wounded including the RMO, Capt Hughes.

After the successful crossing of the Busu River by the 2/28 Bn, in the ensueing three days the remainder of the 24 Bde was moved across the mouth of the river partly by LCV ferry and partly by folding boat ferry. Some heavy fighting took place on the west side of the river, particularly the 2/28 Bn was involved when it extended along the coast to an enlarged bridgehead.

On 13 Sep the advance of the 24 Bde continued with the 2/28 Bn following the coastal track and the 2/43 Bn on a parallel track about one mile inland. At 1700 hrs the 2/17 Bn was

---

[1]
  The soldiers killed were : L/Cpl Philip John Acres, an original member who enlisted from Corrimal, NSW. Pte John Stevenson Filbee was an original member of C Coy and served in Tobruk, Tel Eisa and El Alamein campaigns. He enlisted from Newtown, NSW. Pte George W Holland was an original member who was the Bn's butcher and served in the Tobruk, Tel Eisa and El Alamein campaigns. Pte Colin Lincoln Lewis was an orignal member of C Coy and served in the Tobruk, Tel El Eisa and El Alamein campaigns. He enlisted from Berala, NSW. S/Sgt C M (Toby) O'Brien was an original member and WW1 veteran who was CQMS C Coy and served in the Tobruk, Tel El Eisa and El Alamein campaigns. Pte Mark Wallace Wright was an original member who served in the Tobruk, Tel El Eisa and El Alamein campaigns. He enlisted from Cowra, NSW.

[2]
  Pte William Lester Kelly (DOW) was attached to B Coy from the AACC and enlisted from Newcastle, NSW.

ordered to move to the mouth of the Busu River where the unit was ferried across to protect "D Beach" which had been established west of the river to supply the 24 Bde. By 0030 hrs on 14 Sep the last troops of the Bn reached the east bank of the river and companies were disposed in the Old Yanga area. At 0700 hrs Capt Reid's D Coy moved from reserve to a position astride the track at New Yanga. It was forward of this position about 200 yards along the track leading to the Malahang Airfield that a protective patrol from D Coy led by Cpl R S Smith first encountered the enemy at close quarters. This is how Cpl Smith described the action:

> "We started out through 17 Pl's listening post where there was a small track running parallel to the main track. Ross Edmunds was the scout and I followed him with the section at about 20 yards. I was counting the paces and had reached 190 when I heard Ross call back 'Look out!' His Owen gun jammed as he tried to fire at about five Japs ten paces in front of him. While this was happening I looked to my left and not more than five yards away there was another Jap pointing his rifle at me. I disposed of him before he could fire. The section had moved round on my left and began firing at the Japs in front of the scout who managed to rejoin us. After firing nearly all our ammunition at the retreating Japs I ordered my men back to the Coy."

When the patrol returned Capt Reid, who had heard the firing, had already organised another patrol which was standing by for orders and after receiving Cpl Smith's report he decided to attack the enemy immediately. Cpl Smith resumed his story:

> "Capt Reid told me to move my section down to where I had killed the Jap and take up a position there astride the track. We were to fire on to where I thought the enemy were. He explained how he was going to move over well to the left of the main track, work down to about where they were and come in on a flanking attack. At this time we did not know what we had struck as the Japs did not return the fire when we first opened up. We did not know whether it was an enemy post, a patrol or stragglers — I took up the position as ordered and we opened fire. I was afraid Capt Reid's section would put in the attack before our fire cut out. I could only catch glimpses of them as they moved down on my left. When they had reached a position opposite where I thought the post was I ordered firing to stop. No sooner had we ceased firing when on our left the enemy opened up with everything, including a heavy machine gun. We remained in that position for more than half an hour. By this time the enemy firing had ceased and all we could hear was a jabber of voices on our left, evidently Japanese. I went back to investigate movement in rear to find Lt (Barry) Waterhouse with a patrol."

Pte Jack Rowland of Guilford was a member of the fateful patrol led by Capt Reid and recalled what happened:

> "Capt Reid led the patrol consisting of Lofty Beness, Freddy Shaw, Edgar Smith, Jack Urquhart, Gordon Frost and myself. Capt Reid halted us with finger to lip : this brave man who undoubtably was facing a machine gun post some 25 to 30 yards ahead, motioned us to get down. He then brought Lofty Beness closer to him and pointed ahead, said something to Lofty who opened fire with his Owen gun. The response from the enemy was rapid and withering fire power which cut down Capt Reid before he was able to do anything else. He died instantly. Lofty, who was wounded, spiralled back some 15 yards before falling. Freddy Shaw (as later learned) slightly wounded, was able to get back to Coy HQ and report. Edgar Smith and Jack Urquart were also slightly wounded and together with Gordon Frost and myself, we managed with Bren, rifle fire and grenades to hold on until Lt Waterhouse appeared and ordered our withdrawal with covering mortar fire. As we passed Lt Waterhouse

we told him that Capt Reid had been killed instantly. I understand that Jack Harris and Jimmy Cranna with others later recovered Capt Reid's body. "

Pte R S (Lofty) Beness briefly described the final moments in the life of Capt George Reid, one of the 2/17 Bn's finest and most respected soldiers:

"Capt Reid and myself were the forward scouts and we had not moved very far before we sighted an enemy post about 15 yards ahead of us. We had not expected a post to be there. He told me to let them have it with the Owen gun and as soon as I did the Japs opened up with heavy rifle and MG fire. I was kneeling alongside the Captain when a 'Woodpecker' opened fire and I saw the Captain, who stood up to throw a grenade, fall fatally wounded from the machine gun. His last words were 'Carry on'. Just as he spoke I was wounded in the throat which put me out of the picture. "

Lt Hugh Main, who assumed command of D Coy on Capt Reid's death, ordered Lt Waterhouse to establish a defensive position with his platoon near the enemy post. Mortar fire was directed on to the enemy positions and about 40 enemy dead were found in vacated positions the next day.

The respect with which Capt Reid was held by all members of the 2/17 Bn was eulogized by Arthur Newton in a post war newsletter of the 2/17 Bn Association:

"The loss of good friends during and since the war is something we survivors have all experienced. In retrospect, many of them appear to have been 10 feet tall. Mighty men, splendid soldiers. George Thyne Reid was undoubtedly one of these. I believe no single death affected the Bn more than George's passing.

At the outbreak of war George was a grazier at Yass. He was a Lt in the local Light Horse Regiment. He was highly respected and in his quiet unassuming fashion had contributed much to the area by his good deeds. For example, after his death, I recall reading an article in the Sydney *Bulletin* in which it stated that George, prior to the war, had donated the X-Ray equipment to the Yass Hospital. He resigned his commission and joined the 2/17 Bn as a private soldier. George reached the rank of Sergeant while we were in Australia and before we sailed had been recommended for his commission. This had not been granted before we embarked on October 19, but as the CO had anticipated it would have been gazetted before that date, George was allotted accommodation with recently appointed officers including Alan Wright, Vaude Burgess, Alf Tuckwell and myself. A few weeks earlier all of us had been in the sergeants' mess together. George was extremely regimental, he was always out of bed before the rest of us. He insisted on calling us 'Sir' despite our protests and was back in the cabin each night before the 'sirs' had returned. That is except one night when he had obviously celebrated in the sergeants' mess. We had returned and were already in bed when the door opened and George entered with a glorious smile on his face and then began to apologise profusely for his behaviour! When we arrived in Palestine George was commissioned and he and I were platoon commanders in C Coy for the next few months. In Tobruk George remained in C Coy and was involved in as many patrols as anyone who served in that desert fortress. His men were well cared for and I believe many wore socks sent to him by his wife Mary. His quiet strength, ability and cheerfulness endeared him to all. And so the months and years rolled on until that sad day in September 1943 when George Reid, still concerned for the men under his command, was killed by Japanese machine gun bullets — I have never heard in all the long years since 1943, anyone say a harsh word of George Reid. I feel very priviledged to have known and served with him. "

While the 24 Bde Bns pressed on west of the Busu River along the coast, the 26 Bde's 2/24 Bn in the hinterland had difficulty in its efforts to cross the Busu. Not until the morning of 15 Sep was the Bn able to achieve a stable bridgehead. Thereafter the 2/23 Bn passed through and by 1200 hrs 16 Sep had advanced to Kamkamun Village on the east bank of the Butibum River about the same time as the 24 Bde's 2/28 and 2/43 Bns reached the river on their dual axis in the direction of the river's mouth and Lae's Chinatown respectively. Only enemy stragglers were encountered.

On the night of 14/15 Sep a report was received of the capture by 7 Div of an enemy order for the evacuation of Lae showing their probable routes. Thereupon the 2/24 Bn was withdrawn from 26 Bde to 9 Div command with orders to recross the Busu and move immediately to the village areas of Musom and Gawan in the mid reaches of the Busu and its eastern tributary the Sankwep River respectively. The aim was to block all escape routes leading from Lae through this area. The 2/4 Independent Coy was ordered to hold Kunda Bridge, the main track crossing the Busu about 10 miles from its mouth. Subsequent information indicated that large numbers of Japanese moved along these routes prior to the arrival of the Australian forces in the area.

The 15 Sep had been a quiet day for the 2/17 Bn concentrated near the coast and west of the Busu River. Other units of the 20 Bde had crossed the river and the Brigade was divisional reserve as the attack on Lae developed. At 1330 hrs on 16 Sep the Bn had moved to the area of the track and road junction one mile east of Lae's Chinatown.

During the night 15/16 Sep Cpl George William Birch of B Coy 2/17 Bn was unfortunately killed by small arms fire. He was an original member who served in Tobruk and enlisted from Aberdeen NSW.

On 16 Sept, with the simultaneous advance of the 7 Div converging on Lae along the axis of the Markham Valley Road, the township was there to be taken, deserted by the Japanese. Following an airstrike and 9 minutes of artillery concentrations on enemy posts on the west bank, the 24 Bde crossed the Butibum River without opposition and reported at 1420 hrs that it held ground in Lae from the eastern end of Mount Lunaman to the sea. At 1415 hrs a signal was received at HQ 9 Div indicating that 7 Div troops had occupied Lae. There was unspoken rivalry by both divisions to be the first to capture Lae. By chance it was fitting if only in a numerical sense that the 2/31 Bn (7 Div) and the 2/32 Bn (9 Div) junctioned in the town. By last light Lae was fully occupied and the Commander 26 Bde was placed in control of the town which was indescribably filthy and had been very thoroughly wrecked.

The following extract from Colonel E G Keogh's *South West Pacific 1941–45* recorded high level decisions made by the Japanese commanders which profoundly influenced subsequent events in the Allied operations and directly affected the soldiers of the 2/17 Bn and other 9 Div units in the next encounter with the Japanese at Finschhafen, some of whom had escaped from the trap activated by the 7 and 9 Divs at Lae:

> "Lae had been captured without the major battle that had been expected. When the Allies had landed on both sides of Lae, General Adachi quickly arrived at the realistic conclusion that with both of his practicable lines of communication cut, prolonged resistance could result in the loss of the garrison. General Imamura agreed with his recommendation for an immediate withdrawal across the Finisterre Range to the north-east coast, provided Finschhafen and the Ramu Valley were held. Accordingly, Adachi ordered the Lae garrison to withdraw by the selected route. At the same time he ordered 20 Div, less one regiment, to move from Madang to Finschhafen. Carrying food for ten days, the first echelon left Lae on 12 Sep. The march over the mountains was a nightmare. "

David Dexter's Official History summed up the Lae operation with the following:

"The total number of Japanese in the Lae-Salamaua area early in September was about 11,000. Casualties inflicted by the two Australian divisions were at least 2,200. In return the Japanese had inflicted 547 casualties on the 9th Division, including 77 killed, 397 wounded and 73 missing. The 7th had suffered 142 casualties- 38 killed and 104 wounded. About 2000 Japanese were killed in the final drive on Salamaua. The badly led and often beaten fighting units of the 51st Division, (Japanese) together with portions of other fighting units, had carried out a creditable defence of Lae in the face of the onslaughts of two of the finest divisions on the allied side. Had the flooded Busu not delayed the 9th Division for such a period the enemy would in all probability not have escaped. Fortune and nature however, favoured a valiant defender despite the equally valiant striving of the attackers. "

The soldiers of the 2/17 Bn remembered the Lae operation mainly for the loss of their comrades; for their battle against the elements and natural obstacles; for the demands on their physical fitness; for the numerous torrential rivers, thick jungle, swamps and areas of tall stifling hot kunai grass traversed in the high tropical humidity. These unpleasant conditions were bearable with the integration of comradeship and common achievement from the Bn's team effort.

With few exceptions almost all of the Bn's casualties occurred when the soldiers were denied by chance the opportunity to meet the enemy with the dignity of close combat, the traditional expectation of an infantryman. However, casualties from bombs and shells launched from near and far have always been considered fair and reciprocal to the infantry soldier and an inevitable hazard encountered on the battlefield.

The Japanese fought stubbornly west of the Busu River in vital areas on the approaches to Lae in a similar manner to the tactics encountered by the 7 Div in the Markham Valley, long enough to cover the evacuation of the garrison. The enemy in other areas was elusive and scarce on the ground and the soldiers of the 2/17 Bn walked many miles in a short time in search of their adversary. In retrospect, they would have preferred to have confronted more Japanese sooner in the attack on Lae, rather than later in defence of the small village of Jivevaneng on the foothills of the Sattelberg Mountain which overlooked the beautiful tropical harbour of Finschhafen and Langemak Bay.

The pilgrimage to "Red Beach" east of Lae – 50 years after the landing. Veterans visit the Lae War Cemetery.
L-R: *J R Broadbent, A J Wright, P H Pike, A Fletcher (2/13 Bn), W J Macmillan, D Leece (17 RNSWR),*
H E Zouch, R J Moran, A Tarrant.

Following the capture of Lae the 2/17 Bn moved towards a divisional concentration area about four miles upstream on the eastern side of the Busu River. Being unable to cross a footbridge before dark on 17 Sep, the move to its new bivouac area was completed the following morning. The CO, Lt Col Simpson and the Adjutant, Capt Wright attended a conference at HQ 9 Div on 19 Sep in preparation for the next operation at Finschhafen and the Bn moved to the mouth of the Burep River where it remained for two days. 20 Sep was a day of re-organisation and re-supply. Troops washed clothes and experienced the luxury of rest in the sunshine. On 21 Sep, after further preparation, all troops moved to an assembly area and embarked for Finschhafen at 1930 hrs.

When companies of the 2/7 Bn were about to embark, a flight of enemy air force high level bombers appeared. Fortunately for the assembled troops (some moved quickly into a mangrove swamp nearby for concealment) the enemy aircrews were more interested in the ships and overlooked a prime target on and near the beach. The enemy bombs were seen to fall but missed the deployed ships.

When the Battalion landed on "Red Beach" on 4 Sep its effective strength was 31 Offrs and 703 ORs and it suffered the following casualties during the Lae operation: KIA or DOW - I Offr and I I ORs, Wounded - I Offr and 21 ORs. On embarkation for Finschhafen on 21 Sep the effective strength was 29 Offrs and 627 ORs.

Soldiers of the 2/17 Bn who died in the Lae operation were:

NX16098	Pte P J Acres 12/9/43	NX16524	Pte C L Lewis 12/9/43
NX14856	Cpl G W Birch 16/9/43	NX16302	S/Sgt C M O'Brien 12/9/43
NX81859	Pte A R Davis 6/9/43	NX13893	Capt G T Reid 14/9/43
NX17332	Pte J S Filbee 12/9/43	NX24341	Pte P J Sparkes 7/9/43
NX21501	Pte G W Holland 12/9/43	NX34618	Pte E H Vincent 7/9/43
NX89713	Pte W L Kelly 12/9/43	NX15992	Pte M W Wright 12/9/43

LEST WE FORGET

"Scarlet Beach" and "North Hill" seen from Siki Cove – October, 1993

CHAPTER 17
THE HUON PENINSULA — FINSCHHAFEN

To introduce the Finschhafen Operations, extracts from David Dexter's Official History *The New Guinea Offensives* presents a broad picture of earlier plans and events as a preliminary to the amphibious operation in which the 2/17 Bn took part:

"The day after the fall of Lae, McArthur called a conference at Port Moresby to discuss accelerating the assault on Finschhafen. He and Blamey agreed that a brigade group of 9 Div should be sent to the Finschhafen area as soon as possible and that Herring should determine the date. Because of the uncertainty of enemy strength at Finschhafen, Blamey thought that more than one brigade was necessary. (Accordingly, plans were made by Herring for an additional brigade group to move to the Finschhafen area immediately after the assaulting force had made the landing).

Confidence and boldness marked the planning of this operation. It was unusual in three respects: Allied troops rarely undertook large infantry assaults through jungle at night, let alone after landing on a hostile shore; the notice for mounting the operation was so short as to be probably unique for an amphibious undertaking of such size, particularly when it was considered that the troops were a long day's march from their assembly areas; the information about the enemy available to the commander could have hardly been more nebulous. (Estimates of enemy strength in the Finschhafen area by higher formations varied greatly from 4,000 to 350.) Windeyer had received only the Corps estimate when he made his outline plan and thus all he knew was that some people considered that the brigade would encounter only about 350 Japanese and some that it would encounter 1,800, and that no sizeable fighting force would be round Finschhafen. It was known there were several enemy garrisons on the coast towards Madang. Substantial movement of enemy troops had taken place southward as was later discovered. By 22 Sep the enemy strength in Finschhafen was approximately 5,000 all ranks.

20 Bde was selected for the landing as it already had the experience of carrying out the initial landings east of Lae and was also relatively fresh. Wootten felt that the task was too much for one brigade and wished to use the division less one brigade. Herring explained, however, that a brigade group was the maximum that MacArthur would allow, taking into account the opposition expected, the difficulty of maintaining a larger force, and the limitations of the available naval forces.

Brig Windeyer's plan briefly amounted to an assault on the beach-head by two Bns, the 2/17 Bn on the right and the 2/13 Bn on the left. After the beachhead had been secured the 2/15 Bn would advance south along the main road towards Finschhafen — Windeyer stated his intention simply: '20 Bde will land on Scarlet Beach with a view to the capture of the area Finschhafen–Langemak Bay. ' With each of the three Bns would be a battery of the 2/12 Fd Regt, a platoon of the 2/3 Fd Coy and a light ADS from the 2/8 Fd Amb. The 10 LAA Bty and a company of the 2/2 MG Bn would be responsible for the beachhead area, while two

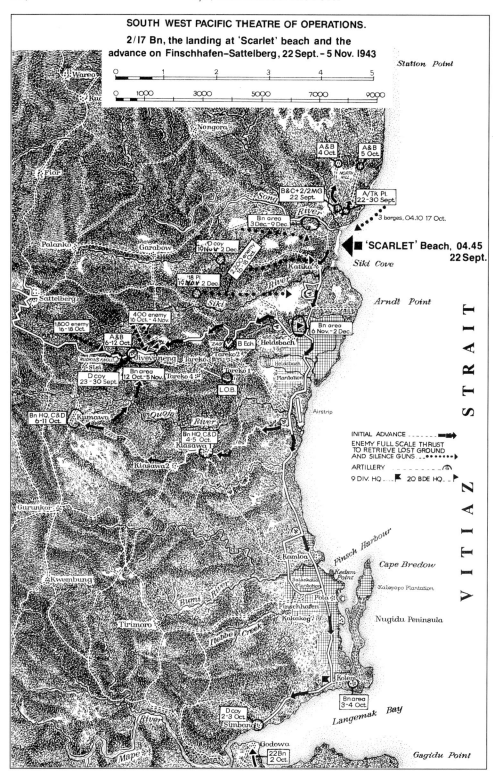

SOUTH WEST PACIFIC THEATRE OF OPERATIONS.

2/17 Bn, the landing at 'Scarlet' beach and the
advance on Finschhafen–Sattelberg, 22 Sept.–5 Nov. 1943

Landing at Scarlet Beach

platoons of the PIB would be used to patrol the coastal track to Bonga, the inland track to Sattelberg, and assist Angua to collect natives.

With the object of unloading the LSTs in two hours and a half from the time of beaching, the 2/23 Bn, the 2/48 Bn, the 2/2 MG Bn and the LOB of the 20 Bde were ordered to provide sufficient men to supply two companies, each of about 100 men, to each of the six LSTs. After unloading at Scarlet Beach the men would travel in the LSTs back to Buna and would then load and accompany the first resupply mission about five days later.

The 21st was a day of great activity for the 20 Bde. Unfortunately there were not enough good aerial photographs of the landing area, and in the morning, while the rain pelted down incessantly, a continuous stream of visitors called at Bde HQ to inspect the few air photographs. The lack of proper photographs was due to the fact that only one aircraft fitted with equipment essential for beach photographs was available. (This aircraft had taken a colour photograph disclosing a shoal in the water off the southern side of Scarlet Beach and thus prevented disaster to the equipment carried by half the LSTs).

The troops had moved to the ship assembly areas on the jungle fringe of 'G' Beach at 1630 hrs. The embarkation, which was arranged by the navy and Wootten's staff, proceeded according to plan except that one LCI failed to arrive because of engine trouble. (This required changes to the 2/13 Bn loading plan). The convoy pulled out from Lae at 1930 hrs and steamed east and then north through the night to meet its destiny. During the night enemy aircraft shadowed the convoy.

The target, Scarlet Beach, lay in a small indentation in the coast making a well defined bay with headlands. It was about 600 yards long and 30 to 40 feet wide with good firm sand which would take LSTs. At the northern end of the sandy beach was the mouth of the Song River and at the southern end a small headland and then a small cove into which Siky Creek flowed. South from Scarlet Beach to Finschhafen lay a narrow coastal strip varying from half a mile to 300 yards in width. To the west the mountainous and difficult country of the

Troops assembled on beach prior to embarkation

Convoy of LSTs approaching the assault beach

Kreutberg Range rose steeply. Creeks and rivers were fordable, but usually ran between deep banks and were not easy to cross, thus constituting good defensive positions for the enemy. Along the coast were coconut plantations overgrown with vegetation to a height between four and eight feet.

Reveille was at 0245 hrs. Broadly Windeyer's plan was that two companies of the 2/17 Bn would land on the right of the beach and two from the 2/13 Bn on the left. Each of these companies had therefor embarked in one of the four APDs which had been instructed to land their barges at definite places. Windeyer intended that the right company of the 2/17 Bn should land as near as possible to the northern end of Scarlet Beach to enable it to capture quickly a dominating feature called North Hill on the northern headland and that the left company of the 2/13 Bn should land in Siki Cove so that it could, as speedily as possible, capture Arndt Point, the southern headland.

This time as the craft carried the invaders northward towards Scarlet Beach, the troops could not see the green jungle fringe of the beach. All that could be seen by the assaulting troops as H–hour approached were the dim outline of funnels and barges about to be lowered from the davits. There was no comforting sight of neighbouring craft, nor was there any impression of the might of the invading force. There was a final burst of speed by the APDs and when according to radar, Scarlet Beach was abreast the APDs trembled to a stop. 'Lower barges', 'Get ready to land', 'Away the landing force. ' This was now a familiar routine for the men of the four assaulting companies — Capt Sheldon's and Maj Pike's of the 2/17 Bn and Capt Deschamp's and Maj Handley's of the 2/13 Bn.

For eleven minutes before the landing five destroyers bombarded the shoreline from 5000 yards, the flashes of the explosions lighting up the blackness of the beach and giving the barges from the APDs some idea of direction in the darkness. The destroyers were using red tracer which looked like giant fireflies — Under cover of it the barges sped to the shore. Windeyer reported later 'Generally the whole wave beached much to the left of appointed places. Most of the assault troops were thus landed in Siki Cove or further left on the southern headland of the bay at Arndt Point. ' Nor did they land in order for the barges of both assaulting Bns became hopelessly mixed in the darkness. Capt Sheldon's Company of the 2/17 Bn on the extreme right, together with the A Tk Pl, appeared less disorganised than the other three because it had landed generally in the Scarlet Beach–Song River area and was soon under control. The next company to the south was Maj Pike's of the 2/17 Bn. Landing in the Siki Cove–Arndt Point area, his troops became so badly mixed with those of the 2/13 Bn he decided that as he had no opposition the best course would be to move inland about 100 yards and wait for daylight. This sensible action enabled the two assaulting companies of the 2/13 Bn on his left to get clear. Although the early waves were landed in such confusion, it did not take long to clear the jungle fringing the beaches."

There was considerable deliberation between the navy and the army in the selection of H–hour for the landing. Initially Admiral Barbey stated his reasons for desiring 0200 hrs for H–hour. He was anxious that the landing should take place soon after moonrise on "D" day. The Official History continued:

"On 22 Sep moonrise would be at 25 minutes past midnight. The Americans were anxious to unload the craft and leave the beach before first light because of the danger of air attack. Windeyer did not favour landing in darkness because he doubted whether the navy could land them on the correct beach, and in this Wootten supported him."

Brig Windeyer's timing for H hour was at first light; 0515 hrs. After discussion between Generals Herring and Wootten and reference to Brig Windeyer, a compromise was reached for 0445 hrs. HQ 20 Bde War Diary for 22 Sep stated:

"0440 hrs — during preliminary bombardment first wave set out for shore on time."

20 Bde troops were making the first opposed landing by Australians since Gallipoli. Only two craft of wave 1 were landed in the right place by the Americans. These were the two LCP(R)s numbered from the right on the approach to the beach, both 2/17 Bn, (No. 1) Lt R J Dick's A Tk Pl with PIB, and (No 2) Lt R J Bennie's 10 Pl with duplicate B Coy HQ. About midway on the approach to the shoreline, No 2 craft personnel were able to observe in the semi darkness the craft on their left suddenly veer left in the general direction of Siki Cove. After first hitting a sand-bar about 100 yards from the shore the No 2 craft beached with the ramp down to reveal immediately in front on the beach a solidly constructed pill box, fortunately unoccupied. Minutes later, when well into the jungle, the noise of the opposed landing on the left of the beachhead was heard as these fortunate platoons proceeded without opposition towards their objectives.

Lt A E Nicholson[1], commander of B Coy's 11 Pl, 2/17 Bn in wave 1 (craft No 3 from the right) related his unfortunate experience:

"On landing we were to cross the beach and move to our right towards the Song River. Almost immediately we came under heavy fire from the jungle on our left as we moved parallel to the beach and casualties occurred very quickly, three being reported killed[2] in

---

[1]
Lt "Tony" Nicholson was a good officer. He was hospitalised for ten months and then transferred to the reserve of officers as it was clear he would never be fit enough to return to the 2/17 Bn.

[2]
Those killed were all from small arms fire, namely: Cpl Jack Hansen from Botany, NSW, Pte James Neylon Graham from Cumnock NSW and a stretcher bearer, Pte William John Williamson, from Orange, NSW Both Cpl Hansen and Pte Graham were veterans of the Middle East campaigns.

WAVE 1. Two Coys each from 2/13 & 2/17 Aust Inf Bns.
2. 40mm Guns on flanks.
Balance 2/13 & 2/17 Aust Inf Bns.
Advance details of Sp. Arms etc.
3. 2/15 Aust Inf Bn.
Bde HQ - HQ Sp. Arms.
4. E.S.B.
5 E.S.B.
6. Eqpt Stores etc Personnel.
7. Eqpt Stores etc Personnel.

WAVE	TIME				CRAFT
1	H / NAVY NO.	□□□□ APD ⑬	□□□□ APD ⑪	□ □□□ APD ⑫ □□□□ APD ⑩	16 BARGES FROM 4 APD
2	H PLUS 20	◊◊ □□□□□□□□ ◊◊			8 LCI 4 LCM
3	H PLUS 35	□□□□□□□			7 LCI
4	H PLUS 40	□□ ◊◊◊◊◊◊ □□			6 LCM 4 LCV
5	H PLUS 60	□□□□□□□□□			11 LCV
6	H PLUS 80	⌂ ⌂ ⌂			3 LST
7	2230 HRS "D" DAY	⌂ ⌂ ⌂			3 LST

Landing diagram Finschhafen operations

the two leading sections and others wounded. We continued on our way and very soon we came to a pill box. I fired a few rounds into it but it was not occupied. I then saw a Japanese silouetted beside a tree and he was eliminated and as I advanced, turning slowly left, I was hit and seriously wounded by a Japanese machine gun about 5 yards away on my left. I saw the muzzle flash clearly. I was thus left behind in the attack which proceeded towards the Song River. I was picked up, perhaps an hour or more later by a doctor and his sergeant from the 2/13 Bn and was given some attention and then put on a LCP(R)s with others being moved further along the beach and became a patient in a CCS operated by the 2/8 Fd Amb."

CSM of A Coy 2/17 Bn, WO2 Pat Conti, was in wave 1 and remembered the landing:

"We got into our LCP(R)s and set off for Scarlet Beach, or so we thought. The noise from our guns was deafening but also reassuring. However, it was not long before tracer bullets started to come from the shore and I realised this was not an unopposed landing, this was Gallipoli all over again. Our craft swung violently to the left and headed for a short time in a southerly direction. We again swung east and crashed into the rocks of the headland (Between Siki Cove and Arndt Point). Luckily the craft was high and dry on the rocks which we stumbled over in almost complete darkness to thick undergrowth which further slowed our progress."

Pte W G Shaw was with C Coy 2/17 Bn in wave 2 on an LCI and related his experience:

"Packed together on the open deck and without a vestige of cover, we had no means of answering the enemy fire which seemed to be getting thicker every moment. Thank God for the darkness. Our LCI was almost touching the boat on our left and we could see bursts of Japanese tracer bullets bounding off the plates not more than a foot below the exposed deck. Already some of the men had been hit, and stretcher bearers groped around in the inky blackness searching for the wounded. Just before we hit the shore the American gunners opened up with their forward oerlikons and much credit is due to them for ably assisting the assault. We grounded on the rocky point between the two beaches and immediately lost our starboard ramp. One by one we ran down the port ramp and jumped into a void, hoping for the best. As it happened some men had already fallen into a deep submerged hole near the ramp and being laden down with heavy battle equipment had to be helped out of the water on to the rocks. As more men poured out of the assault craft our automatic weapons returned the enemy fire and the opposition weakened. After about 20 minutes the enemy fire in the beach area ceased."

In the fierce action at Scarlet Beach, Sgt W B Pearce of C Coy displayed outstanding bravery. When a number of men, heavily laden with equipment, fell into deep water from an LCI and were in danger of drowning, he disregarded the heavy fire from enemy machine guns a short distance away, dragged them out of the water and guided them to the beach. His action in saving more than one life was recognised by the immediate award of the MM for valour.

Pte J A Crawford of the Mor Pl related his experience after landing from an LCI:

"We were Wave 2 this time andwe had expected that the first wave of diggers would have 'done over' the Japanese before we hit the sand. Ahead and above us, on top of the headland about a hundred feet away, a Japanese machine gun opened fire with tracer. The third burst

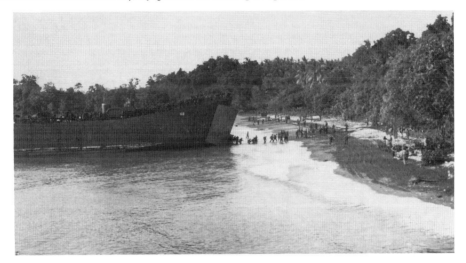

Top : *Troops landing on assault beach from an LST.* **Above:** *An LST landing troops at Scarlet Beach.*

crashed over my head and hit two men behind me. [1] I heard them cry out as I jumped on to the coral and splashed through to the beach. The machine gun poured another burst into the boat, hitting it in the conning tower and killing (so we heard later) its American skipper. We began to climb the thirty foot sloping bank. Two signallers with a heavy coil of signal wire reached the top, slipped, and came crashing down. The rest of us reached the top. The Americans on the LCIs simultaneously opened fire with all their 20mm guns, firing into the treetops and undergrowth to kill the enemy snipers. This intense fire of white tracer passed at first about two feet above our heads. The noise was terrific and for a momemt I thought that a low flying aircraft was coming in from the sea strafing us. When the firing ceased we went on to the top of the bank to stay. About twenty feet from the edge was a freshly dug trench with cartridge cases littered about. The gun-crew had run for it, taking their gun with them."

Sgt Jack Littlewood of the MG Pl in wave 2 remembered the day:

"Bang! We had landed on the rocky point, ramps went down, the port side on to the rocks and the starboard into the water. There was a Jap bunker in front of us firing away. The gunners on the LCI did a good job on the bunker. No 1 Sec went on to the rocks, No 2 into the water. Col Martin was shot, had to be taken from the water, and got a trip to Australia. On landing we went in 200 yards or so to wait for orders to move which came the next day. The Yanks came and put up their camp. They asked us to breakfast the next morning and put us first in the line. What a breakfast of flapjacks and bacon! Bad luck orders came through, we had to move before lunch."

Close in from the timber-line off Scarlet beach the ground rose sharply to a small escarpment about 20 to 30 feet high. This had not been detected from air photographs as the rise in the ground was concealed by the trees adjacent to an area of kunai. Neither were firers of supporting weapons on the landing craft aware that when firing into the trees they were endangering troops moving on to the escarpment. One of the supporting shots pierced the cap of Lt Col Simpson and grazed the top of his semi bald head. This was a lucky escape for him but the sight of the dignified CO, 2/17 Bn with a shell dressing on the crown of his head kept in place by a bandage, neatly tied with a bow under his chin, was light relief in an otherwise serious situation.

Brig Windeyer's simple plan was disorganised from the beginning of its execution as the Americans had landed the infantry on the wrong start line and in the wrong order. In the face of enemy opposition, the speed with which order was restored throughout the day was achieved by the initiative and experience of competent commanders and well trained troops.

It became apparent that the Japanese's plan, with a relatively small force, was firstly to impose the maximum casualties on the attackers with MG fire from prepared positions adjacent to the beach near the timber line, when troops were most vulnerable on their disembarkation — thereafter, withdrawal to more defendable and strongly constructed delaying positions in depth, based on the higher ground of the Katika Spur. The merits of the plan soon became apparent.

The mix-up of the attacking troops could not have been worse. Wave 2, intended to land 20 minutes after wave 1, in most instances, was first ashore in landing craft not suitable for the purpose. Even wave 3, in some instances disembarked under enemy small arms fire. It was

[1]   Pte G W Kearney, an Aboriginal soldier of the Mortar Platoon (2/17 Bn), was wounded at the landing and later died of wounds. Being an original member of the platoon, he was held in high regard by his fellows, having served in Tobruk with the 2/17 Bn's "bush artillery", and at Tel El Eisa and El Alamein.

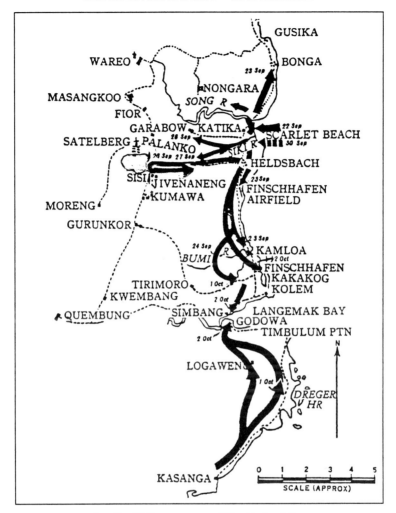

Landing 22 Sep to capture of Finschhafen 2 Oct

daylight before reorganisation of sub-units enabled them to move to planned objectives. With a task of left flank protection of the beachhead, A Coy 2/17 Bn's objective was the Katika feature. The company commander, Maj Pike, related the extraordinary situation of three companies, each from a different Bn of the Brigade which engaged a company of Japanese that resisted stubbornly on the Katika feature:

"After reorganisation, A Coy's leading platoon (7 Pl, commanded by Lt A P Craik) followed a track towards Katika Village and on reaching a clearing was fired upon, suffering casualties. The following platoon (9 Pl, commanded by Lt K T McLeod) did a right hook and struck more opposition. The Japanese reacted by moving around our left flank. Walky-talky communication was not always reliable in close country but on this occasion I welcomed the intrusion on my Company's frequency by Maj Len Snell, a 2/15 Bn company commander, who said he would take care of them. Our third Pl (8Pl) mounted an unsuccessful attack on the enemy positions, suffering casualties. The Platoon Commmander, Lt S G J Waterhouse[1] and Cpl B C Culey[2] were killed. To add to the confusion, a company of the 2/13 Bn arrived on the scene commanded by Capt Cribb and launched an attack with mortar support. This attack was also unsuccessful and the company suffered heavy casualties. The battle for Katika was finally resolved mid afternoon when the defenders did not wait for an assault by two companies of the 2/15 Bn after a mortar bombardment and withdrew leaving eight dead. On subsequent inspection of their defences I was surprised to find the extent of well concealed and strongly constructed pillboxes."

WO2 Pat Conti, CSM A Coy, remembered the heroism of the two brave men of 8 Pl (2/17 Bn) in its attack on the defenders of Katika:

"The platoon was pinned down by a 'Woodpecker'. In response to orders to move forward if possible, Lt Waterhouse attempted a frontal assault when he and Cpl Culey were killed as they clambered over the rise in the ground behind which they had been sheltering."

While other companies of the 2/17 Bn did not meet the strength of opposition encountered by A Coy, they were not without their troubles with the Japanese. Capt Sheldon's B Coy overcame resistance in the jungle near the beach as did Lt Main's D Coy. C Coy's 15 Pl, commanded by Lt K J Gibb captured a defended post, killing seven Japanese. Pte A L Spratt[3] knocked out the post before most of his platoon had left the LCI and before he was mortally wounded on the rocks. Cpl R S Cooper[4] of C Coy was wounded on the landing and later died of wounds. Both men were fine soldiers and held in high regard by their fellows over their long period of service.

The northward progress of Lt Dick's A Tk Pl was delayed by fire from guns on the assault craft plastering the headland north of the Song River. Efforts to stop this unnecessary shooting which endangered troops after they had landed by shouting from the shore over the noise of the guns was hopeless. 20 Bde Operation Order was specific on this point:

"In the event of enemy resistance from the north and south headlands, weapons of the flank LCIs will be prepared to engage during the approach to the beach, but not after H+15 mins."

Total casualties of the 2/17 Bn for "D" day were 4 Offrs and 25 ORs as follows:
KIA — 1 Offr, 5 ORs   DOW — 2 ORs   WIA—3 Offrs, 18 ORs

The Official History continued:

"From prisoners and documents captured on the first day, Windeyer learned that an enemy

---

[1] Lt Stretton Gustavus John Waterhouse of Killara was a quiet, likeable man whose spectacles accentuated in his eyes a ready sense of humour. His mother, Mrs Beatrice Waterhouse of Rose Bay, in response to a letter of condolence, was beautiful in her thoughts of her son, so brave in her grief, as she wrote of the tragedy of war in an everlasting tribute to the men who gave their lives: "Terrible as the war is, it has shown us all the capacity of our men for sublime heroism and devotion to duty. War will pass, life will pass but these great qualities hammered out on the terrible anvil of fighting and suffering will endure forever. Stretton was always so gentle with his father who is very frail, so courteous to all, and when he was young, so sensitive. It amazed me that he took to the army life so happily. He never in any of his letters had a complaint. I feel sure that when he went into action on that day of fate, it was the supreme hour of his life."

[2] Cpl Bruce Culey was a fine upstanding young man who joined the Bn in the Middle East, firstly with C Coy; in Syria he became a carrier driver. Displaying qualities of initiative and leadership he was foremost in sporting activities, particularly on the football field. When the carrier platoon was disbanded he was posted to A Coy as a section commander.

[3] Pte Alfred Lines Spratt was an original member of the 2/17 Bn and a veteran of the Bn's earlier campaigns. He enlisted from Guildford, NSW.

[4] Cpl Roy Selwyn Cooper was also a Middle East veteran and an original member of the 2/17 Bn. Before the war he served in the 17 Bn militia and enlisted from Wollstonecraft, NSW.

force of 300 to 400 had been holding the Scarlet Beach–Katika area at the landing. These Japanese defenders had killed 20 Australians, including 3 Offrs and wounded 65; 9 were missing. The Japanese defenders were companies from the 80th and 238th Regiments. The survivors had withdrawn along the Katika track towards Sattelberg."

The vital ground of the Katika spur west of Scarlet Beach featured again in subsequent operations as important to attackers and defenders alike in the struggle for the possession and security of the beachhead. The first day of the landing found nightfall with all sub-units of the 2/17 Bn located in security of the Beachhead and after some regrouping the plan for the advance on Finschhafen was ready to go early on 23 Sep. The responsibility of the northern approach to the beachhead from North Hill and the coastal strip was taken over by Capt P Nicholls' A Coy of the 2/2 MG BN under command Lt Dick's A Tk Pl of the 2/17 Bn, thus relieving Capt Sheldon's B Coy 2/17 Bn on North Hill to strengthen the NW approach.

The first night on shore was uneventful except for a successful air drop of 9mm boxed ammunition on a kunai patch near Bde HQ in the B Coy 2/17 Bn locality. Having regard to the difficulty of the operation at night, the skill of the RAAF Boomerang crews and Capt R C Garnsey, the Air Liaison officer, (previously IO 2/17 Bn in Tobruk), guided only by a limited supply of torches, was remarkable. The end of the air drop was a relief to the troops nearby who, understandably, did not fancy such heavy missiles raining in quantity from the sky. Of the 115,000 rounds dropped112,000 were recovered.

Quotations from the Official History mentioned the duties of two of the 2/17 Bn Offrs who were seconded for special tasks in the operation:

"On the beach itself Major Broadbent's task was to co-ordinate the defence of the beach, the movement of stores, the development of the beachhead, the requirements of small craft, and the control of the traffic. Broadbent, quick, energetic and full of initiative, proved an excellent choice, and in the succeeding days the force owed much to his drive and flair for improvisation. Broadbent carried out his tasks in conjunction with Pagan of the 2/4 LAA Regt, Brockett of the 532 EBSR, and Capt Nicholas whose company of the 2/2 MG Bn provided 12 vickers guns for beach defence."[1]

"By 1100 hrs on the 22nd Windeyer's adviser on native affairs , Lt Col Allan appreciated the labour difficulties, brought in the Luluai of Tareko and sent out messages through him to tell the 'Kanakas' to come in to work. In Allan the Brigade Commander had the support of an Officer not only widely known and respected throughout New Guinea but one who had served with the Brigade in its Middle East campaigns both as a regimental officer (2/17Bn) and as its Brigade Major."

The Official History continued:

"Windeyer's orders for the next day (23 Sep) were 'The 2/15 Bn would lead the advance to the Bumi River; the 2/13 Bn would assemble in the Heldsbach Plantation–Launch Jetty area, ready to move at 30 minutes' notice'. Thus the Brigade was geared for an advance to the south, but Windeyer could not neglect possible threats from the north or west, and his orders were to be ready for Sattelberg after Finschhafen. General Wootten had told him before he left Lae that he should get at least a company on Sattelberg as soon as possible.

1
  The involvementof the 2/17 Bn Beach Group members in the landing and later in the Scarlet Beachhead is mentioned as a postcript to this chapter.

General view of Scarlet Beach
looking north

At the time neither realised how inaccessible Sattelberg was and both thought of its occupation merely as a method of guarding the open right flank of the advance."

Before the 2/15 Bn began its advance towards Finschhafen on 23 Sep, the 2/13 Bn was located in the Launch Jetty area and extended SW to the village of Tareko. "Zag" was the name given to the feature at the sharp bend in the road to Sattelberg, north of the Tareko villages. Capt Sheldon's B Coy and Lt Main's D Coys (2/17 Bn) moved at 0515 hrs to take up positions at Katika and "Zag" respectively, with a role of preventing enemy approach from the west on to the beachhead. At 0830 hrs regrouping of the 2/17 Bn was complete with A, B and C Coys all in their new positions covering approaches to the beachhead. Lt Dick's A Tk Pl (2/17 Bn) under command 2/2 MG Coy was 500 yds south of Bonga. At 1730 hrs the 2/17 Bn, less A and D Coys, was placed on two hours notice from 0600 hrs 24 Sep to move south as brigade reserve. Lt Main's D Coy was ordered to move west towards Sattelberg, leaving one platoon at "Zag". The Bn's MG Pl commanded by Lt W M Cooper was then at Tareko.

Leading elements of the 2/15 Bn commanded by Lt Col C H Grace reached the Bumi River soon after midday and suffered casualties in the first contact with the Japanese. Heavy fire came from strongly fortified wired positions on the south bank of the river in the Salankaua Plantation. On a pre-arranged plan, Lt Col Grace detached two of his companies with supporting elements led by Maj R A Suthers, to swing off the coastal track and continue the advance along the ridges to the west in an outflanking move. The men had an arduous experience as they hacked through creeper and dense jungle on the flat then uphill on the steep jungled slopes of the Kreutberg Range. Any man who carried a heavy load had it passed up to him. Just after last light Maj Suthers' companies had reached the forward slopes of a spur to a place later known as "McKeddie's OP" (named after Lt J E McKeddie of the 2/12 Fd Regt and featured in the artillery support for later attacks).

The 2/13 Bn, commanded by Lt Col G E Colvin, meanwhile had been warned to follow Maj Suthers who would secure a bridgehead over the Bumi through which the 2/13 Bn would pass and capture Finschhafen. Due to the lateness of the hour the 2/13 Bn's move was deferred until 0415 hrs 24 Sep.

On 24 Sep Maj Pike's A Coy 2/17 Bn took over Capt Sheldon's B Coy's task at Katika and the 2/17 Bn less A and D Coys, then brigade reserve, moved south following the advance towards Finschhafen of the 2/15 and 2/13 Bns to the north of the Bumi River. At 0930 hrs on the same day Lt Main's D Coy of the 2/17 Bn moved up the steep Sattelberg track preceded by a platoon of the PIB commanded by an Australian sergeant and reached the village of Jivevaneng by last light. The Company reported that considerable work was required to make the track jeepable.

At 1230 hrs on 24 Sep the Japanese Air Force enjoyed unusual success when 12 bombers and over 20 escorting fighters attacked the 2/12 Fd Regt gun positions at the north end of the air strip: the guns had been shelling the enemy positions in the Kakakog and Salankaua Plantation areas. Although the 60-odd bombs which were dropped did not damage the guns, 18 casualties[1] were inflicted on the gunners and the 2/3 Fd Coy (Engineers) lost 14 killed and 19 wounded. The air liaison party of the Fifth Air Force lost all its equipment and its commander, Capt Ferrel, was killed.

The resupply of Major Suther's companies of the 2/15 Bn was made difficult by the precipitous nature of the terrain and C Coy 2/17 Bn, commanded by Capt J H Dinning, provided 60 men as a carrying party for this purpose on 24 Sep. Their task was particularly arduous over a distance of about 6,000 yards and they then returned in the darkness; the men held signal wire in their hands to guide them as they stumbled and slid down the hillside.

The FDLs of B and C Coys 2/17 Bn faced the Japanese across the Bumi river. The enemy positions gave an impression of strength, those visible consisted of pillboxes with overhead cover supported by coconut logs and surrounded by barbed wire; these were clearly visible from the FDL's, a distance of about 150 yards.

24 Sep began badly for the 2/15 Bn in reconnoitering a crossing over the Bumi River. Two of its Offrs, Capt E McN Christie of Ingham, Qld and Lt N L Harpham of Dalby, Qld were sniped and killed. When Capt Christie was shot Lt Harpham went to his aid where he also was shot. Both had a reputation of exemplory service in their Bn. With artillery and Machine gun support Capt L Snell's Company of the 2/15 Bn crossed the Bumi river which was waist deep and seized a bridgehead at 1330 hrs with the loss of one man killed.

On 25 Sep a bulldozer was used to clear a jeep track for about one mile towards Maj Suther's companies, which relieved 2/17 Bn personnel from carrying party duties. At 2030 hrs Capt Sheldon's B Coy 2/17 Bn moved north to the gun area in the Heldsbach plantation following reports that a small party of Japanese had landed on the coast between the jetty and the airstrip, potentially to threaten the gun positions. After a difficult move in the intense darkness, troops holding the bayonet scabbard of the man in front to maintain contact, the Company reached the gun area at 2315 hrs and reported NMS. During the day three bombing raids were made by the Japanese on the Scarlet Beach area between 0445 and 0730 hrs when 8 of the Allies were killed and 40 wounded. Of these the 2/17 Bn LOB personnel suffered Capt E. O Norton[3] and Pte A T Jackson[4] killed and ten others wounded. The Allied Air Force, which had been

---

[1]
These included Capt P W Nelson, M C. ,(KIA) who had been a member of the 2/7 Fd Regt with which the 2/17 Bn had close ties in the Middle East, before he joined the 2/12 Fd Regt.

[2]
Lt Harpham was the IO of the 2/15Bn at El Alamein and was with the party from that unit responsible, with the 2/17 Bn's tape laying party, for the 20 Bde start line on 23 Oct 42.

[3]
Capt Eric Oswald Norton joined the 2/17 Bn at Tobruk in June 1941 and was a grazier who enlisted from Walcha. His reputation in the Bn was a fearless and capable officer.

[4]
Pte Alan Thomas Jackson served with the 2/17 Bn in the Lae Campaign. He enlisted from Toongabbie West.

concentrating mainly on nearby Japanese airfields, retaliated at 0935 hrs when about 20 Bostons and Vultees bombed and divebombed positions in the Finschhafen area.

Lt Main related D Coy 2/17 Bn's first contact with the Japanese on 25 Sep:

> "On proceeding past Jivevaneng the sigs were having trouble with communication and the line was cut in rear. Our men on the flank shot enemy presumably trying to get behind us. Sigs Bob Anson and Joe Murray did a lonely and great job repairing the line. The forward scout of the PIB contacted the enemy and no doubt surprised them when he put up his hand and called out 'Japan man he stay!' There was an exchange of fire. Brig Windeyer OK'd our withdrawal back to Jivevaneng where we had a field of fire and observation of surroundings. There we took up a position of all round defence with the PIB in rear."

Cpl Charles E Lemaire, who was with the leading D Coy Platoon (17 Pl, commanded by Lt B Waterhouse) which had advances hundreds of yards west of Jivevaneng, recalled :

> "At the insistence of the PIB scouts who sensed danger, we left the track to climb a hill and when about 30 yards from the crest Les McCarthy's section killed two Japanese, one a sergeant, we believed were leading elements of troops on their way to ambush our men on the main track. On returning to Jivevaneng, weapon pits were dug. With darkness, everyone was on piquet and it was not long before the first attack came. There was no moon, visibility was poor, although it favoured us as from our weapon pits we waited for silouettes to emerge. One bullet from Pte Gordon Kibby's Bren in 18 Pl killed a Japanese carrying an LMG who fell only a few yards away from his position. Pte Lennie Guest of 18 Pl, always a cool customer, proved that a Japanese officer's sword was no match for his Owen gun at close quarters."

On 26 Sep, D Coy 2/17 Bn at Jivevaneng followed up its success of the night before and patrolled towards Sattelberg without enemy contact. Offensive patrolling was the order of the day also for Maj Pike's A Coy, 2/17 Bn in the Katika area. The Japanese were showing a growing interest in the beachhead area. Lt McLeod's 9 Pl, engaged an enemy party and killed an officer and two others when Sgt J. L Tregilgas was wounded — he had been wounded twice before, at Tobruk and El Alamein. A patrol from 7 Pl commanded by L/Sgt T P Brightwell moved west on a track leading from Katika and when rounding a bend, made contact with the enemy. In the immediate fire-fight L/Sgt Brightwell and Pt Healy were wounded. Enemy casualties were not known. "Exhibiting qualities of outstanding courage, capacity to command, and complete disregard for his personal safety that were an inspiration to his fellows," was the citation for Cpl B B Moore, who organised withdrawal of the patrol and received the immediate award of MM for valour.

Persuaded to relate the story of that fateful patrol, late in his life, Cpl Billy Moore, gave his thoughts for posterity to Arthur Rogers, who was the Bren gunner on the patrol. These were the words of the soldier who became the welter weight champion of the 20 Bde on board the *Queen Mary* en route to the Middle East; a man of extraordinary determination and courage:

> "When Percy Brightwell[1] got hit, I said to you and Eric Sweetman, I'll go and get him out; then I said I'll want a bit of cover, as you know there was a bit of shooting going on. When I got out to Percy he said, (these were the words of a brave man) 'Get 'em out! (his section) Get 'em out ! you can leave me here!' I said, no be buggered! I'm going to get you out. Then I said, can you get on my back ? I didn't think I could lift him, as you know he was a big

---

L/Sgt Thomas Percival Brightwell from Artarmon, a fine and gallant soldier, died of wounds while being carried back to the CCS near Scarlet Beach. He was aged 23 years and an original C Coy member of 2/17 Bn, having served at Tobruk, Tel El Eisa El Alamein and Lae.

chap, about 12 stone. He said, 'No —leave me!' I said, no—be buggered! I don't know how I did it but I got one hand under his knee and the other under his arm and lifted him as if he were a baby. This meant that I had turned my back on the Japs. I started to carry him back waiting for the burst that would hit me in the back. Then they let fly; I finished on my back with Percy on top of me. They had hit him on the foot on one side of me and on the hand on the other side of me, missing me altogether. It had shot my hat off or the wind from the burst had. I picked him up again and got him to that rise — you will remember — and got a stretcher bearer to attend to him. When they were taking him back with us someone came to me and said, Perce wanted to see me. I went back to him. Perce said 'Billy Moore you are a gentleman, I want to shake your hand. ' His final words were, 'I'll see you back in the Kings Head. ' This was a pub we all used to talk about for having a party. He also gave me his watch which I did not want and I gave to his great mate Dutchy Holland."

The Japanese officer killed in the encounter with Lt McLeod's 9 Pl, (2/17Bn) mentioned earlier in the day's activity, was in a party of about 30 and he carried on his person an operation order. This disclosed Japanese plans for attack on 26 Sep with a Bn moving from Sisi to the Heldsbach Plantation, aiming to split our forces and destroy our artillery. This was the first reliable information of the enemy strength in the Sattelberg area. Appreciating the vulnerability of our forces in the area of Heldsbach, the plan was masterly in its concept. The deep, penetrating offensive action into the enemy's positions on 26 Sep by the 2/17 Bn's companies supported by artillery bombardment (Maj Pike's A Coy west of Katika and Lt Main's D Coy from Jivevaneng) had pre-empted preliminary moves and upset the enemy's plan.

26 Sep was a day of bitter fighting for the 2/15 and 2/13 Bns in the process of expanding the bridgehead over the Bumi River on to the Kreutberg Range. Maj Suther's two companies advanced to the high ground towards the south-east and the 2/13 Bn, with a company commanded by Maj E. A Handley, advanced south-west on a spur towards the track from Tirimoro. The two companies of the 2/15 Bn, (commanded by Capt L Snell and Capt M R Stuart respectively) attacked and captured a strongly defended kunai-capped hill (later named "Snell's Hill"). The troops pulled themselves hand over hand for about 200 feet and on reaching the summit, with a bayonet charge put to flight the defenders who were naval marines, the Corps d'elite of the Japanese armed forces. Enemy casualties were about 100 compared with 10 of the 2/15 Bn.

Maj Handley's Company of the 2/13 Bn was not as successful in cutting the Tirimoro Track, and was ordered by Lt Col Colvin to disengage for the night after attacking an enemy position and sustaining 9 casualties. To establish a tenable position, the Company withdrew about 150 yards and the next day captured the enemy's dominating position over the Tirimoro Track with a surprise assault. The Company held the position suffering problems of resupply, aptly named "Starvation Hill", where it stayed for the next seven days, protecting the western approach to the Brigade positions in the Finschhafen area via the Tirimoro Track.

Apart from enemy mortar fire landed in the Capt Sheldon's B Coy area, 27 Sep was a quiet day for the main body of the 2/17 Bn. At Jivevaneng shots were exchanged between opposing patrols east of Sattelberg. Also between 1730 and 1815 hrs the Japanese launched three attacks against positions at Jivevaneng all of which were repulsed with at least 10 enemy dead and no casualties to Lt Main's D Coy, 2/17 Bn. The attacks were repetitive from the same direction, mostly on the axis of the track, bunched, shouting, blowing whistles and bugles. In trying to bring fire on to the enemy, the FOO with the company was wounded in the arm[1]. The company became short of ammunition which was shared around as evenly as possible.

Following disclosure on 26 Sep of the Japanese plan in the captured operation order to

---

1
VX30899 Lieut A.G. Rickardson 2/12 Fd Regt.

attack positions in the Heldsbach Plantation, the next day Brig Windeyer made an urgent request to Maj Gen Wootten to send another Bn to Scarlet Beach. Also, with no change in the location of the 2/17 Bn less A and D Coys, on Sep 28 Maj L C Maclarn, (acting 2 i/c) was ordered to establish a HQ at Tareko with under comd Maj Pike's A Coy and Lt Main's D Coy , reinforced by Lt Dick's A Tk Pl which moved from the north side of the Song river to Tareko. Maj Maclarn's command was referred to as "Sattelforce". At first light four Japanese were found stalking D Coy positions at Jivevaneng and were killed.

From reports of enemy movements by the PIB and the noise of water craft the night 28/29 Sep there were indications that the enemy may be withdrawing from Finschhafen. However, there was no evidence of withdrawal by the enemy opposing the 2/13 and 2/15 Bns. (Captured documents later indicated that the Naval Units were ordered to stay and fight.) Brig Windeyer ordered the 2/13 Bn to capture the Kakakog ridge which dominated the Japanese positions in the Salankaua Plantation. (The attack did not eventuate until October 1.) Throughout the day the artillery, and the Mortar Pl 2/17 Bn commanded by Lt T E Swan, were active firing on enemy positions which continued into the night.

On 29 Sep Brig Windeyer issued an operation order with the intention to isolate the enemy at Salankaua Plantation and capture Finschhafen. This entailed regrouping of the Brigade and was contingent upon the arrival by sea on the night 29/30 Sep of the 2/43 Bn commanded by Lt Col R Joshua to relieve "Sattelforce" as early as possible on 30 Sep. The regrouping required relief of the committed companies of 2/17 Bn (A and D) and its A Tk Pl to rejoin the Bn and Capt Sheldon's B Coy 2/17 Bn to move to the north bank at the mouth of the Bumi River to relieve Capt W Angus' C Coy 2/15 Bn at Kamloa, enabling the latter to rejoin its Bn for the offensive. 29 Sep was the first really wet day since the landing. Although unwelcome by troops slipping and sliding on steep hillsides in the forward area, the rain was welcomed by the troops at Jivevaneng. Dry weather had created a problem with water supply, obtainable only at a spring outside their defended locality where enemy ambush was likely. Hard rations of bully beef and biscuits, canned heat and tobacco were also in short supply. Notwithstanding these privations the troops kept in good spirits. Cpl Jack Harris equitably distributed the meagre hard rations with banter, he offered as "Ham and Vo Vo."

With portend for the future, almost a daily occurrence, the Japanese attacked Lt Main's D Coy 2/17 Bn at Jivevaneng in the morning of 30 Sep with about a platoon, then withdrew having left three of their dead. Later in the day the Company was happy to be relieved by Capt Grant's A Coy, 2/43 Bn. With its heavy gear transported by jeep, (luckily the track was then free of enemy penetration) the D Coy Jivevaneng contingent, except for a rear party of six, moved back down the Sattelberg track for a good night's sleep in the Launch Jetty area, removed from the constant threat of Japanese that crawled to infiltrate their positions. The Company had maintained a magnificent defence in its isolated position and when Lt Main handed over the Jivevaneng defences to Capt Grant his Company had had only three men wounded and had killed 30 Japanese. Lt Hugh Main, who began his soldiering pre-war with the 56 Bn in the Riverina, revealed at Jivevaneng he was a worthy successor to predecessors in command of D Coy, 2/17 Bn, all of high regard in earlier campaigns, namely; Maj John Balfe, Capt Ian McMaster and Capt George Reid.

On arrival of the 2/43 Bn, Brig Windeyer gave Lt Col Joshua the immediate tasks; (a) the relief of "Sattelforce", (b) the control of all routes leading into Scarlet beach and Heldsbach areas, and (c) the capture of Sisi and Sattelberg. Due to the buildup of the Japanese forces in the Sattelberg area this was not entirely achievable but the offensive action generated by the tasks would have hindered, if not forestalled the development of the enemy's plans. For the time being therefore, the Bde Comd was able to concentrate his three indigenous Bns (2/13, 2/15 and 2/17) to maintain the aim , "the capture of Finschhafen and Langemak Bay," without constantly looking over his shoulder in concern for the security of the beachhead and the gun areas.

At 1500 hrs on 30 Sep A and D Coys 2/17 Bn and the A Tk Pl were relieved by the 2/43 Bn. By 1800 hrs Maj Pike's A Coy, D Coys 16 Pl from "Zag" commanded by Lt J D McFarland, and Lt Dick's A Tk Pl had arrived in the Bn area North of the Bumi River, adjacent to Kamloa. At 1500 hrs Capt Sheldon's B Coy 2/17 Bn moved to Kamloa to relieve Capt Angus' C Coy 2/15 Bn beforementioned at the north bank of the Bumi River. The main body of Lt Main's D Coy which stayed overnight in the Launch Jetty area reached the Bn area at 0900 hrs the following day.

1 Oct was a decisive day for the 20 Bde. The general plan was for two Companies of the 2/13 Bn to capture Kakakog with one company in reserve. 2/15 Bn was Brigade reserve located in the area of "Snell's Hill" and the 2/17 Bn had two companies ready to exploit into Salankaua Plantation. Fire support was an air bombardment on Salankaua Plantation not before 1100 hrs and not later than 1200 hrs, and artillery on to the objectives from 1115 hrs with companies in position by 1045 hrs. Although the Companies were in position on time, the attack by the 2/13 Bn varied in execution of the planned objectives. The dive bombing by ten "Vultee Vengeances" and eight "Boston" aircraft began before time at 1035 hrs. It was a day of hard fighting and mixed fortunes for the infantry companies of the 2/13 Bn (Forward; Capt B G Cribb's on the right and Capt P Deschamp's on the left; Capt H H Cooper's was in reserve.) Acts of heroism, the initiative of junior commanders and bayonet charges by the troops carried the day and turned the tide in favour of the Bn. Although the 2/13 Bn did not gain its objective on 1 Oct it was close to it and the threat to Kakakog caused the Japanese to abandon some of their positions in Salankaua Plantation.

While the 2/13 Bn attacked the Japanese on 1 Oct the 2/17 Bn, less Capt Sheldon's B Coy, (which fronted the enemy across the Bumi River at Kamloa) and 13 Pl of C Coy, (which secured the Kiasawa track from the NW to the Bn area) moved to cross the river upstream at an old bridge. At 1035 hrs B Coy had a grandstand view of the dive bombing of the enemy positions across the river a few hundred yards away. At 1100 hrs Maj Pike's A Coy, 2/17 Bn relieved D Coy, 2/15 Bn at Snell's Hill and Capt Dinning's C Coy, 2/17 Bn less 13 Pl relieved two platoons of the 2/13 Bn near Ilebbe Creek. A patrol from 14 Pl C Coy, 2/17 Bn moved east on the South side of the river and was fired on from a position covering the road to Finschhafen. At 1200 hrs the enemy positions south of the Bumi River were bombarded with artillery and mortars and raked with MG fire, causing the enemy to reply with mortars. At 1525 hrs Capt Sheldon's B Coy 2/17 Bn on the north bank at the loop of the Bumi River gave a diversionary display of fire power. As if in defiance, the Japanese retaliated at dusk with rifle and automatic weapons along the whole front. This was their "last hurrah" in their defence of Finschhhafen.

With the 20 Bde Group main force now poised to execute the final blow on the Finschhafen defences, the battle for Jivevaneng developed where the 2/43 Bn was undergoing similar pressure from the Japanese to that experienced by D Coy 2/17 Bn in its earlier defence of the Village. The soldiers left on 30 Sep as a rear party on the relief of D Coy's 17 and 18 Platoons were, Cpl M R Lee, L/Cpl E McKee, Ptes R Painter, H B Hanna, G U Kibby and J Campbell. By last light only two platoons of Capt Grant's A Coy relieving force had reached Jivevaneng. It was intended that the third platoon and a second Company of the 2/43 Bn should reinforce Jivevaneng next morning. At 0930 hrs 1 Oct however, the telephone line in rear of the forward position was cut and Capt Grant's third platoon was ambushed with heavy casualties in attempting to rejoin the company which had been attacked repeatedly since dusk the previous day. Attempts by the CO of the 2/43 Bn over several days to relieve the pressure on the inadequate and beleagured platoons, finally with a two company attack, were unsuccessful against stubborn enemy resistance.

Cpl Lee of 2/17 Bn related the experiences of the men of the rear party at Jivevaneng which prevented their return to their unit as planned:

"At approximately 1830 hrs on 30 Sep the Japanese attacked down the Sattelberg track on to the left of our position. The attack failed and the enemy suffered heavy casualties. The 2/43 Bn had one killed and three wounded. At about 2130 hrs he attacked again along the same route as before and cut the track behind and between our position and the main body. Early next morning he attacked the rear of our position without success, when Ptes Kibby, Painter and L/Cpl McKee did a good job claiming many victims. Following unsuccessful attempts to relieve us throughout the day the artillery FOO with 2/43 Bn HQ did a very effective shoot on the Japanese positions just before dark. A few hours later the Japs opened with a Woodpecker and mortar killing a PIB soldier and wounding three of the Company. We were amused by firecrackers and bugle calls that followed soon afterwards, despite the unpleasantness of the situation.

Next morning (1 Oct) our artillery blasted hell out of us causing two of the PIB soldiers to leave; I heard later they got back to Bn HQ and gave information regarding the irregular artillery shoot. By this time ammunition and rations were very light without a chance of replenishment. We spent two days without water and food and the wounded were in a very bad way and could not be evacuated. The Bn made another attempt to relieve us with a two company attack. Owing to some mistake C Coy 2/43 Bn withdrew when they were only a few yards from our posts leaving their D Coy isolated and the unsuccessful attack resulted in heavy casualties to our troops. The same afternoon the enemy attacked us again and failed. Through lack of sleep and no food we were in a pretty bad condition. It was practically unbearable with dead Japanese, pigs and dogs round our positions. That night it rained heavily and was a godsend to us after being without water for so long. The uncomfortable conditions were tolerated without a moan.

At first light (3 Oct) a Japanese sergeant major, with three first class privates, crawled to within a few yards of our position, gave a few yells and came in swinging a sword. The Bren gunner got two of them and his no 2 shot the third who fell across the Bren. The sergeant major then attacked the two Bren gunners, causing terrible wounds on the arms, shoulders and backs of the two men. Lt Beaton eventually shot the assailant and claimed the sword.

Next morning (4 Oct) one of our boomerangs flew over our positions and dropped two messages for Capt Grant, ordering him to get out the best way he could. Later a PIB sergeant major (WO2 T H Scott-Holland) and two privates sent by Bn HQ reached our position after several days in the jungle finding a way out for us and with a message for Capt Grant from the CO. That morning we left Jivevaneng and moved along a creek leaving a section to cover our withdrawal and managed to get out without contact with the enemy. At about 1500 hrs we struck the Sattelberg track in rear of 2/43 Bn HQ at a point where most of the 2/43 members were buried. We had one stretcher case who was wounded the first day. The going was hard and the walking wounded showed wonderful endurance. A meal was ready for us and the best of all was a cup of tea. We then moved back to 'Zag' where we had a few days rest before rejoining our Bn."

The CO 2/43 Bn sent a message to the CO 2/17 Bn praising the soldiering and courage of the six men who were by unforseen circumstances left behind at Jivevaneng to fight alongside the men of his Bn. The defenders had suffered 12 casualties including 2 killed. Capt Grant estimated that 50 of the enemy were killed in the many encounters with his troops.

Brig Windeyer's tactics at the approaches to Finschhafen gained just reward on 2 Oct. Lt Gibb's 15 Pl 2/17 Bn set out at 0600 hrs from about the junction of Ilebbe Creek and the Bumi River and moved east to Kedam Point after sending a section north to contact Capt Sheldon's B Coy, 2/17 Bn by semaphore across the mouth of the Bumi River and a section sent south towards Finschhafen for about 400 yards. The Japanese had gone, showing signs of a hasty departure, leaving equipment, maps and even coins of the realm. Cpl Hal Pearce wrote in his diary, "one of the boys picked up twenty five pounds of N G Shillings." At 0730 hrs Capt Sheldon's B Coy, 2/17 Bn prepared to cross the Bumi River at the ford near its mouth and formed a bridgehead at 0915 hrs with a platoon at Kedam Point and a platoon making for Salankaua Point. Capt Dinnings C Coy, 2/17 Bn less one Pl moved east at 0900hrs and together with Lt Main's D Coy, both companies of the 2/17 Bn were moving south at 0930 hrs along the main coastal track from the River Bumi to Finschhafen. A and B Coys of the Bn followed C and D Coys on their southern drive.

At this time the 2/13 Bn was still in the positions gained the previous day although their patrols had scoured the base of Kakakog Ridge. After trying a few rounds of artillery on to Kakakog to test any enemy reaction, there was no response and the 2/13 Bn advanced to the objectives of the previous day without opposition, mopping up, and counting the enemy dead amongst quantities of discarded equipment, indicating a hurried evacuation. For the loss of 10 killed and 70 wounded the 2/13 Bn had killed between 80 and 100 Japanese during the fight for Kakakog.

While the 2/13 Bn occupied Kakokog and patrolled the Kreutberg Range, the 2/15 advanced to Simbang and the 2/17 Bn advanced along the main Finschhafen Road to Kolem, mopping up as it went.

Lt Dick's A Tk Pl and Lt Cooper's MG Pl of the 2/17 Bn were left at Salankaua Pt and Kedam point to protect the beach in these areas for landing stores. At 1400 hrs all Companies of the 2/17 Bn were grouped in the Kolem area until Lt Main's D Coy was sent to Simbang, where three enemy stragglers were killed. Capt Sheldon's B Coy patrolled Nugidu Peninsular. A Coy, 2/17 Bn captured a PW in the Kolem area; this was the Bn's second for the day as C Coy had captured one at about 1000 hrs near Pola. C Coy's prisoner was a tall, rangy marine and was discovered lying in the jungle with a rifle in the firing position near where Capt Dinning was giving orders, map in hand. Lt W A Graham grabbed and overpowered him with his bare hands after a violent struggle. A Coy's PW was of different ilk; a small, bearded Korean cook sporting a goatee who bowed and scraped and was obviously delighted at being captured.

The sight of Langemak Bay was picturesque, later described by Pte Jack O'Shea:

> "Nature had done her work perfectly, for beaches of yellow sand surrounding the water were just right to merge blue into green to make Langemak Bay a beautiful place. War had only come this far so did not have time to mar the beauty of the bay by crowding it with ships and landing craft."

The arrival of Lt Main's D Coy 2/17 Bn in the Simbang area on 2 Oct coincided with patrols from the 22 Bn in the Godowa area. The 22 Bn, commanded by Lt Col C W O'Connor, had been chasing the Japanese along the coast from Hopoi since 22 Sep and the liaison of friendly troops across Langmak Bay found them each dealing with a small party of the enemy which had little chance of escape. The occasion is related in the history of the 22 Bn by Graeme MacFarlan, extracts as follows:

"After greetings had been exchanged across the water, our patrol managed to indicate the presence 200 yards up river of two Japs who by this time had sought cover— unsuccessfully as far as our patrol was concerned. In the mean time Lt W M Keys (patrol commander) decided to attempt a crossing using a Jap folding boat one of many found lying around the area. Shakily paddling with Jap rifle buts, Keys and two of the patrol set off. In midstream the boat commenced circling, completely out of control. To those on either side of the river it was funny, until the two Japs opened fire on the gyrating victims. The situation was saved when the 2/17 Bn men, with fixed bayonets, set off in hot pursuit of the Japs. The watchers on the south bank from their grandstand seats described it as one of the 'neatest' pieces of bayonet work they had ever seen. By this time the rotating boat had straightened itself and was making good progress to the other bank."

The 20 Bde Group had captured Finschhafen and Langemak Bay in eleven days from the landing at Scarlet Beach after bitter fighting. The Finschhafen campaign, however, was far from over. Intelligence reports indicated that the remnants of the Finschhafen garrison had withdrawn in the direction of the mountainous peak of Sattelberg which dominated the coastal strip. Reliable reports from the PIB and from the local natives also revealed that strong enemy forces were reinforcing the Wareo–Sattelberg area from the north.

2/17 Bn casualties including the landing at Scarlet Beach and up to the capture of Finschhafen, were:

KIA and DOW – 2 Offrs 10 ORs, WIA – 1 Offr 22 ORs

The Bn landed at Scarlet Beach with an effective strength of 29 Offrs and 627 ORs. On the capture of Finschhafen this was reduced to 25 Offrs and 519 ORs.

Soldiers of 2/17 Battalion who died in the capture of Finschhafen:

NX 23056	L/Sgt Brightwell T P 27/9/43	NX 18319	Pte Kearney G W 22/9/43
NX 54554	Cpl Cooper R S 22/9/43	NX 34884	Capt Norton E O 25/9/43
NX 60529	Cpl Culey B C 22/9/43	NX 77698	Pte Smith J 11/10/43
NX 26856	Pte Graham J N 22/9/43	NX 18827	Pte Spratt A L 22/9/43
NX 27031	Cpl Hansen J 22/9/43	NX 60288	Lt Waterhouse S G J 22/9/43
NX 84357	Pte Jackson A T 25/9/43	NX 54552	Pte Williamson W J 22/9/43

LEST WE FORGET

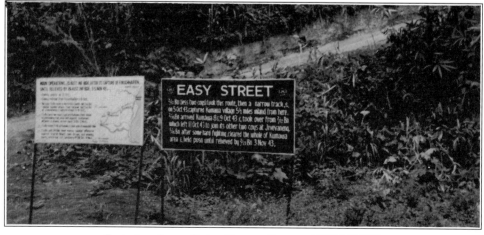

Beginning of steep climb to Kumawa Spur.   (AWM 71387)

Postscript

BEACHHEAD
by John Broadbent

For the performers, the Scarlet Beach operation was a rush. Broadbent, given the title, "Military Landing Officer" was to set up and command the beachhead area. Staff was to come from the LOB personnel of the Bn, a highly anomalous role for such a group — but the team worked. He studied the air photographs and made a layout plan with defensive dispositions including seawards.

The orders basically consisted of the diagram of the layout. Competence was added by his personal knowledge of most of the Offrs to be in charge of the troops concerned. Checking the landing tables, he found that a place had not been allocated for himself and his batman. He had had a previous contact with the APD taking A Coy to Lae. Now it was to land in the centre of the beach and it carried the American representative responsible to raise the Scarlet light marker to guide in subsequent waves. The MLO went there.

Under the tracers of the Naval bombardment, the 16 landing barges had come up line-abreast and headed for the beach. Suddenly, the barge No 3 from the right started to veer to the left. The outline of the land could barely be seen and subsequent enquiries could not confirm the suggested enemy fire. Craft in line-ahead from each APD might have handled the situation but line-abreast caused a disastrous domino effect distorting the direction to the coral shelf previously rejected as unsuitable for landing. The beach centre was remote but the light was vital.

Broadbent with batman and representative with light and sig with wireless ran through the confusion to Siki Cove. In the jungle fringe, Capt Sheldon could be heard shouting, "Throw a grenade, Mr Nicholson". There was enough light to see the LCIs of Wave 2 drifting in, one just in landed the CO and part of HQ 2/17 Bn. By this time Broadbent and the rep were alone. The CO allotted Sgt Mangan to protect them and the rush to the beach centre resumed. No one had landed there. Other Wave 2 craft had diverted left and Wave 3 could be seen faintly approaching.

The purpose was delayed by Mangan and the American shouting to Broadbent to come back. The Yank had the light, so he went back to find them pointing to a small group of Japanese packing up their Woodpecker gun. With pistol proving ineffective and grenade in his basic pouch forgotten, Broadbent seized Mangan's Owen gun, fired a long burst and remembered their job. They rushed along the unoccupied beach in the gloom and put up the light.

The evident uncertainty in Wave 3 seemed to lift and they headed for the beach but without the usual run ashore momentum. None hit a sandbar, it was not located. Dropping the ramps after an indecisive run ashore allowed swaying movement in the hulls of the LCIs. As the craft rolled, the ramps alternatively lifted slightly and slid back, walking the LCI into deeper water. LCIs seemed to forget driving forward with their engines, or were prevented by the ramps then had their bows afloat. Desperate men with their duty of landing slid down the ramps into deeper water. The casualty of a 2/13 Bn mortar man carrying a base plate was inevitable.

By daylight, further beach markers had been erected. The turmoil from the 50mm forward guns on the LCIs firing at an imaginary enemy in the trees stopped. At last these craft cleared from the beach and, in later waves, none knew that anything had happened. In the beachhead team everyone went about their duties and developments soon began. While assault coys were pushing out, Capt Pat Nicholas with 2/2 MG Bn A Coy was setting up defences and reconnaissance for light ack-ack positions was made by 2/4 Lt AA Regt, Bty Comd, Maj Jock Pagan.

Broadbent, examining the beach area, found no sniper positions in trees but saw a pair of Japanese heels in the rear of a shallow covered and camouflaged weapon position undamaged by the bombardment. A terrified Japanese soldier was hauled and ultimately given to a reluctant LST which threatened to discard him at sea.

It is surprising how men, intent on their job, can soon make a beachhead appear functional. The plan disposed of installations mainly back from the timber line along the beachfront and under the trees surrounding a long kunai patch. Although perhaps not visible from the air, it was evident where they had to be.

In the Middle East, it had been realised that outside the line of flight of aircraft the possibility of bombing could be ignored. On the early morning after landing, the drumming noise of Japanese planes could be heard. Looking up through trees, it could be seen their line of flight would be directly overhead. Suddenly, there were the popping sounds which had been explained as indicating "bombs away". Rush warnings were shouted. Ack-ack fire opened and bombs plastered the beachhead. One sad casualty was Capt Eric Norton who, with Keith Sabine, had been the first reinforcement Offrs to arrive in Tobruk and, subsequently, to be distinguished for deep patrolling at Tel el Eisa.

The pattern of bombing was to continue with some devastating effect among the 500 American boat and shore engineers in support. An ammunition dump set on fire added to local hazards.

While beachhead protective patrols made no contact, an earlier patrol by 2/17 Bn had captured enemy documents indicating a prospective attack by land and sea. While the Bns of 20 Bde pursued the aim, for the moment, the exposed beachhead area was not harassed by land. Somehow, after arguments, the need to reinforce the area was at last realised on senior levels. The 2/43 Bn was got in by night and some movable casualties evacuated. It seemed slowly, but the situation developed and more troops were got in. 2/3 Pnr Bn built up its Coy allotted to the defence of the landing.

The sign erected at Katika Village to record the Unit activities   *(AWM 71411)*

CHAPTER 18

JIVEVANENG — KUMAWA

THE JAPANESE BUILD-UP IN THE SATTELBERG—WAREO AREA

During the 20 Bde advance on Finschhafen the Japanese withdrew forces from the area south of the Mape River via an inland track to Sattelberg. By 2 Oct 43 this move had been completed and with the remnants of the naval garrison which had withdrawn from Finschhafen, the total enemy strength in the Sattelberg area was estimated at 4,500. Also substantial reinforcements totalling 6,200 were moved down the coast and overland to the Sattelberg—Wareo area. As later revealed, the enemy intention was a build-up of strength in preparation for a counter offensive for the recapture of Finschhafen. All attempts by the Australians to advance on Sattelberg were strongly resisted by the enemy.

AN OUTLINE OF 9 DIV TACTICAL CONSIDERATIONS

On 1 Oct 9 Div was given the following tasks:

(1) Defend Finschhafen

(2) Develop Finschhafen as a Base Sub Area.

(3) Gain control of the east coast of the Huon Peninsula up to and including Sio.

To carry out these tasks a period of reinforcement and preparation for the offensive was required.

For the defence of Finschhafen it was appreciated that the vital ground in the area was the Sattelberg Mountain feature and the long narrow ridge running west from Gusika on the coast to Wareo. Along a track which followed the crest of this ridge, the enemy conveyed inland the supplies which had been brought down the coast in barges. Possession of the ridge would cut this supply route to the Wareo-Sattelberg area and deny the enemy extensive observation of the coast line as far south as Dreger Harbour.

Wareo, at the western edge of the ridge, was on a 2600 ft plateau which dominated the entire Song River valley and the country inland from Scarlet Beach to Sattelberg. It was also the junction point of many important tracks, all of which were routes of supply to the enemy forces in the area and accessible to the enemy for attacks on Allied forces in the Scarlet Beach and Finschhafen areas.

The capture of the Gusika—Wareo line would both secure the Finschhafen area and provide the ground from which an offensive could be launched to drive the Japanese from the east coast of the peninsula.

COMD 20 BDE AIMED TO CAPTURE SATTELBERG

With the inadequate forces immediately available to him, Brig Windeyer, Commander 20 Bde, relied heavily on offensive action to gain time for the ultimate defeat of the enemy. He had planned before the capture of Finschhafen the relief on the Sattelberg Track of the 2/43 Bn, less two companies, with the 2/17 Bn. The whole of the 2/43 Bn would then have been available

Evacuating the wounded from the forward areas

for the close protection of Scarlet Beach while the 2/17 Bn would have moved along the track from Jivevaneng to the objective, Sattelberg. The execution of this plan was forestalled by the enemy action which had begun on 1 Oct when Capt Grant's Company of the 2/43 Bn became isolated at Jivevaneng, from where it withdrew by a devious route and rejoined the main body of its Bn located east of Jivevaneng.

As it was apparent that the enemy was in strength on the Sattelberg Track, Brig Windeyer attempted an outflanking move to the south with the 2/17 Bn, less two companies. It was a quick turnaround for the Bn from where it was located in the Kolem area on 2 Oct, the day Finschhafen fell to the Australians.

At 0800 hrs the next day the first elements of the Bn were lifted northwards by motor transport to the airstrip near the mouth of the Quoja River where by 1400 hrs all subunits of the Bn were assembled. Maj Pike's A Coy and Capt Sheldon's B Coy became the Brigade's mobile reserve commanded by Maj Maclarn, the OC HQ Coy, and later in the day moved to the Heldsbach Plantation.

2/17 BN DIVIDED — ATTACKS NORTH OF THE SONG RIVER

Early warning was received on 2 Oct of a strong enemy force approaching Scarlet Beach via the coastal track from Bonga and this force eventually established a position astride the track opposite the defensive position of 11 Pl, 2/3 Pnr Bn, north of the Song River. Maj Maclarn's 2/17 Bn two company group moved northward by motor transport from the Heldsbach Planta-tion at 0830 hrs on 4 Oct to deal with this development. Both companies were in an assembly area on the slopes of North Hill at 1700 hrs with Maj Pike's A Coy forward and Capt Sheldon's B Coy in reserve.

At 1815 hrs, after an artillery bombardment, A Coy's 7 Pl commanded by Capt R S Rudkin crossed the start line, the edge of the kunai grass and timber. Very soon its forward sections came under effective automatic fire from the reverse slope in the jungle and three men were wounded, one of whom later DOW[1]. The forward sections had hardly moved from the light of the open kunai grass to the comparative darkness of the jungle when the enemy fire struck them. Owing to the lateness of the hour and the difficulty of locating the enemy positions in the failing light, the two company group bivouaced for the night on North Hill in anticipation of a resumption of the offensive in the morning.

On 5 Oct at 0645 hrs, the enemy positions north of the Song River, estimated one company strength, were engaged with artillery by one battery of the 2/12 Fd Regt and the 2/17 Bn mortars. The enemy reaction revealed the right flank of its defensive positions. The attack was resumed at 1500hrs further to the flank than the previous day after a concentration of 10 minutes artillery fire, and 5 minutes MG fire by a platoon of Capt Nicholas' Coy, 2/2 MG Bn. Maj Pike's A Coy advanced to the east without opposition after passing through B Coy holding a firm base on North Hill at the timber line and at 1710 hrs came upon vacated enemy positions astride the coastal track. Contact was made with 11 Pl 2/3 Pnr Bn to the south and a patrol sent 600 yds north towards Bonga revealed many diggings, all showed signs of recent occupation and hurried evacuation. Two dead enemy were found recently buried and there was ample evidence that casualties had been inflicted. The night passed without incident.

2/17 BN DIVIDED— THE KUMAWA OFFENSIVE

The Japanese withdrawal route from Finschhafen was believed to be the track running north from Simbang through Kumawa and Sisi Villages which joined the main Sattelberg Track west of Jivevaneng. If soon enough, an advance to Sattelberg via Kumawa could therefore also aim for the destruction of any enemy that used this route. Without opposition on 4 Oct, Capt Dinnings' C Coy and Lt Main's D Coy, with Bn support weapons, comprised in the group commanded by Lt Col Simpson, advanced in that order from the area of the airstrip to Kiasawa 1 Village, as a preliminary move in an offensive operation to occupy the Kumawa Village area.

The track was steep, rough and slippery, then impassable for jeeps and was ironically dubbed "Easy Street". The troops struggled up in some places the one in three gradient, two steps forward and slid one step backward, ankle deep in mud, at times being frustrated also by clinging liana vines while carrying 48 hours extra rations. The walk was especially arduous for soldiers carrying MGs, filled water cans, mortars, mortar bombs and signal equipment and under these conditions the long journey seemed to the men an eternity. Leading the advance, Lt W A Graham's 14 Pl C Coy prepared an ambush in the vicinity of the track junction forward of Kasiawa 2 Village which controlled the tracks from Kumawa and another leading north from the Bumi River.

C AND D COYS, 2/17 BN OCCUPY KUMAWA

Lt K J Gibb's 15 Pl, C Coy patrolled forward to Kumawa on 5 Oct with PIB scouts and reported at 1100 hrs that the village was occupied by 16 Japanese who had vacated their flooded defensive positions and were sheltering from the rain underneath the huts. Cpl Hal Pearce of 15 Pl recorded in his diary :

> "Fired on 100 yds from Kumawa Village by MG and small arms. We formed a very wide front and opened fire. The Japs fled thinking we were a much larger force, leaving one dead and one badly wounded in the Village. Another lying 'doggo' 10 yards in front of my post got away in the jungle. Lt Graham's 14 Pl killed three at the ambush position in rear."

1

L/Cpl Joseph Godfrey Dwyer joined the 2/17 Bn in the Middle East and served in the Lae Campaign. He was hospitalised due to his severe wounds from which he did not recover and died in Australia on 6 May 44.

On the night 5/6 Oct Capt Dinnings' C Coy 2/17 Bn was in occupation of the Kumawa area which controlled the track junction, Kumawa to Sisi, near where Lt Col Simpson located his HQ. Lt Main's D Coy was moved to the track junction 400 yds south-east of Kumawa. The 2/12 Fd Regt shelled Sisi Village at dusk and several times later during a wet night. At 2030 hrs six grenades probably from an enemy cup discharger exploded wide of C Coy's area in reply.

C AND D COYS, 2/17 BN PATROLS LOCATED THE ENEMY DEFENCES

At 0830 hrs 6 Oct, Lt L A Mc Rae's 13 Pl, C Coy patrolled out along the track towards Sisi Village with a section of PIB and after proceeding 500 yards discovered enemy of about two platoons in ambush along the track and positions that extended westward on the rising ground. Capt Dinning's C Coy was moved forward and occupied positions astride the Sisi track which fronted the enemy. Lt Main's D Coy, less Lt P I Pollock's 18 Pl, left in an ambush position at a track junction in rear, moved forward to Kumawa.

A section patrol commanded by Cpl Ross S Smith of D Coy was sent from Kumawa to reconnoitre the ultimate direction of a track from the north-west corner of the Village. Cpl Smith related its activity:

> "Charlie Lemaire was the forward scout followed by myself, 'Brig' Murray, 'Ocker' Ryan, Jack Blair, and Pat Smith who was dragman. We had not gone 30 yards from the village clearing when Charlie swung around half right and let go a burst at several helmeted Japanese watching the progress of the patrol. On my signal the remainder of the patrol moved on my left and began firing. I fired a long burst from my Owen at a Jap 10 yards away after which a general hubbub broke out and about 15 Japs that seemed to come from nowhere ran out to the right further into the jungle, firing shots haphazardly as they went. None of us was injured and after a pause of ten minutes I returned with the patrol from whence it came."

Lt Col Simpson instructed Cpl Smith to return to the area of contact and attack the enemy. Cpl Smith resumed his story:

> "This time we intended to work down towards the enemy's right flank and then move through in extended line, firing as we went to keep their heads down until we overran them. The enemy had heard our approach through the thick bamboo and chattering all over the place was loud enough to wake the dead. I saw movement everywhere, estimated at least a company strength and dismissed the idea of a successful section attack. I moved the section to within 15 yards of the enemy positions where we fired all our weapons and threw about 20 grenades. The enemy's response was only a few rifle shots fired at random. After using up nearly all our ammunition we returned to our positions at Kumawa."

After he received the patrol report from Cpl Smith, Lt Col Simpson was convinced that he was confronted with a strong enemy force. With enemy pressure and infiltration from the south and west the ground held by Capt Dinning's C Coy was contracted on 7 Oct and the defence coordinated with the movement forward of Capt Main's D Coy, less 16 Pl left in an ambush position with a section each from 17 Pl, the MG Pl and the Pnr Pl at a track junction in rear. Fire was exchanged many times throughout the day. Ammunition and one day's rations were brought forward, part of the way by native carriers. Very heavy rain fell during the day and continued during the night 7/8 Oct. All defensive positions became filled with water and the area became a quagmire occupied by drenched troops.

D AND C COYS, 2/17 BN DEFEATED ENEMY ATTACKS FROM THE REAR

Lt J D McFarland's 16 Pl, D Coy with sections of the 2/17 Bn's MG and Pnr Pls at the track junction ambush position in rear, were soon in contact with the enemy en route from Finschhafen to the Sattelberg area, as told by Cpl Les Garner:

"On the first afternoon, even before we had properly settled in, our listening post observed four Japs, evidently forward scouts, coming up the steep track leading from Simbang. Some of our gear was still lying on the track and although we were absolutely quiet, the equipment was noticed by the enemy scouts who were cautious and decided to withdraw. Cpl L Keogh then took out a small patrol and on return reported no movement seen.

We set a booby trap about 20 yds out and awaited developments. Sentries were doubled that night although with the additional firepower provided by the MG Section and the Pioneers we were confident.

Next morning at about 0530 hrs an enemy scout tripped the booby trap and Reg Miller immediately fired the Bren. Any surprise the enemy had expected was lost with the abrupt end to the silence of the night which awoke everyone. Jabbering voices were heard from the main body of the enemy about 60 yards down the track. The attack soon came, estimated one company strength, straight up the track. Although our Vickers, Bren and Owen guns laid down a wall of fire, the Japs managed to get an MG into action only 12 yards from the Bren. Cool and accurate rifle fire drove the crew back.

The enemy used a rifle bomber who sent over three grenades to the far end of our positions, one of which landed a yard from the MG and killed Cpl Carr-Boyd[1] who died with his Owen gun in his hand facing the enemy. Two of the MG section were wounded. Pte Carpenter[2] manned the Vickers gun and although he and Pte Darel Luck were crammed in a small hole with the body of Cpl Carr-Boyd, they continued with effective fire on to the enemy.

The condenser can and tub were riddled with bullets.

After failure with the frontal attack, the enemy moved to a flank making for high ground which dominated our positions; this threatening to split the Kumawa defences. Lt Mc-Farland called for support from Kumawa and Lt Gibb's 15 Pl, C Coy was sent to strengthen the position. Meanwhile, the enemy was engaged in several costly tactical errors. They began by forming up too close to our right flank and were devastated by our automatic fire. Also the party which tried to reach the high ground was surprised by 15 Pl and suffered heavy casualties. In withdrawing, the remnants of this party moved too close to our post with more disasterous results. After this the Japanese gave it best and although they harrassed with fire throughout the remainder of the day, there were no further attacks."

Lt Mc Farland's ambush platoon ran short of ammunition and in response to an S.O.S., a patrol from Lt Dick's A Tk Pl at Kasiawa commanded by Sgt K Denny carried forward a case each of 303 ammunition and grenades and arrived in time while the fight continued. The patrol returned to Kasiawa with walking wounded.

C AND D COYS, 2/17 BN DEFEATED MORE ENEMY ATTACKS

While the heavy fighting was in progress down the track in rear on 7 Oct, the main force at Kumawa clashed with strong enemy detachments. Attempts were made at infiltration and

---

1
  Cpl Beresford Reginald "Barry" Carr-Boyd served the 2/17 Bn in the Middle East campaigns and in the Lae operation. He enlisted from Balgowlah, NSW.

2
  Pte W L Carpenter kept his vickers gun in action throughout the entire day until it was disabled by a mortar bomb. He received the immediate awarded of the MM for his tenacity, bravery and coolness which contributed largely to the failure of the enemy to pierce the defences.

small parties tried to isolate the ambush force resulting in a steady increase in their casualties. One enemy party crossed the Kumawa track between Lt Col Simpson's HQ and Lt Gibb's 15 Pl C Coy.

Ptes D Benham and R Huntingford from Coy HQ, who manned a listening post, killed three of the enemy with rifle fire. One of the enemy ran forward with an LMG to within 10 yards of the command post and was killed with a rifle shot by Pte R Bevan of Bn HQ.

Considering the extent of the fighting during the period 5 to 7 Oct and the heavy casualties inflicted on the enemy, Lt Col Simpson's force in the Kumawa area had remarkably few casualties; only 1 Or killed and 1 Offr[1] was wounded with a bullet through his mouth, and 4 Ors wounded. This says much for the training and fighting skill of the team effort. All casualties had been evacuated safely to the ADS near Kiasawa Village. By comparison, the body count of enemy found dead after actions from 5 to 10 Oct was 37.

It was still raining when dawn came on 8 Oct. Enemy fire on to Lt Pollock's 18 Pl west of the village started the troops vigorous bailing and they soon had their trenches emptied of water. The heavy rain made the track through Kasiawa unfit for jeep traffic and caused a long and difficult carry for supplies. Since 5 Oct only nine scanty meals were consumed and no further rations were held on the night of 8 Oct. On this day Lt Gibb's 15 Pl engaged with Bren guns and obvious success a large party of Japanese fully laden which moved north along a ridge about 200 yds west of the track. 14 enemy dead from this action were found by a later patrol and were included in the 37 bodies previously mentioned.

During the morning of 9 Oct several attacks were made on Lt Main's D Coy at Kumawa. All were repulsed without loss to the defenders and four enemy dead were counted. Line communications from Bn HQ to C Coy and Bde HQ had been severed by the enemy and this was restored. A few enemy continued in occupation of positions west of the Sisi track and Kumawa Village.

Lt Col Simpson's war diary for 9 Oct stated:

> "The enemy caused us no trouble during the morning but our stomachs did. Breakfast rations did not arrive till 1200 hrs.
>
> A patrol left accompanied by PIB to investigate the track north of Sisi and if possible to locate the left flank of the enemy and reported the enemy still held a line NE and SW across the Kumawa—Sisi and Kumawa—Mararuo tracks."

2/17 BN DIVIDED — THE JIVEVANENG OFFENSIVE

While Lt Col Simpson's group was successfully inflicting casualties on the enemy in the Kumawa area, Maj Maclarn's group was also on the offensive. It may be remembered this narrative left the two company group on 5 Oct after it had forced the withdrawal of an enemy party estimated at a company strength which had threatened the Scarlet beachhead in the area of the coastal track north of the Song River.

As 20 Bde reserve it was not intended that Maj Maclarn's group would stay north of the Song River. For the time being however, strengthening of the defences in the area was required due to the enemy's apparent interest in the beachhead and on 6 Oct Maj Pike's A Coy came under command 2/43 Bn, registered artillery defensive fire tasks and patrolled north-east to the coast and west to the high ground without contact. Capt Sheldon's B Coy remained under command Maj Maclarn in position near the Song River.

---

[1]
  Lt W M "Tom" Cooper, the MG Offr, a Middle East veteran who enlisted from Wagga Wagga, NSW.

With the immediate threat to the beachhead removed, Brig Windeyer had not changed his original plan for the relief of the 2/43 Bn on the Sattelberg track by two companies of the 2/17 Bn and to regroup the former for the defence of the beachhead. Having received an operation order in the late afternoon the previous day, Maj Maclarn's HQ and Capt Sheldon's B Coy moved part of the way by MT thence by foot from the Song River area at 0800 hrs on 7 Oct and relieved D Coy, 2/43 Bn in positions east of Jivevaneng Village at 1400 hrs.

Soon after arrival Lt R J Bennie commanded a strong 10 Pl, B Coy patrol with PIB scouts and investigated ground and tracks preparatory to an offensive towards Sisi Village and located the northern flank of enemy positions on a small feature which dominated the Sattelberg track about 500 yards south-west of Jivevaneng. This was the same feature on which Lt Barry Waterhouse's 17 Pl, D Coy had encountered the enemy on 24 Sep, two days after the landing at Scarlet Beach: It was named the "Knoll". The enemy's southern flank was also located by a strong patrol from 11Pl, B Coy commanded by Lt N E McDonald. To have obtained this information so soon after arrival in the area was a considerable achievement and in the nature of Maj Maclarn, whose reputation in the Bn was an audacious soldier who was always keen to take the fight to the enemy.

Violent storms were experienced the night 7/8 Oct. Troops of the Kumawa contingent of the 2/17 Bn were not the only ones thoroughly drenched. It was Lt S M William's turn in the morning and he commanded a patrol from 12 Pl, B Coy in search of suitable ground for an attack on the enemy positions located by Lt Bennie's patrol the previous day. Owing to the nature of the ground, the patrol was unable to cover the intended distance and the patrol returned without incident.

After a heavy concentration of fire by the 2/12 Fd Regt at 1500 hrs 8 Oct, Lt McDonald's 11 Pl, B Coy proceeded west along the axis of the main Sattelberg Track and demonstrated with fire against the enemy positions, aimed to draw fire. The enemy's response revealed the location of two MG posts covering approaches along the main track. On the patrol's return the enemy's positions were again bombarded with artillery and the MGs located with B Coy, 2/17 Bn targeted the Knoll with an effective shoot.

THE KNOLL

Captured by B Coy ½ Aust Inf Bn 9 Oct 43 after road surprise assault from north of road. Enemy made 5 counter attacks but all repulsed with heavy casualties. ½ Bn patrols operated against enemy posns west & north of this point until Bn relieved 5 Nov 43.

B COY, 2/17 BN GAINED SURPRISE AND CAPTURED THE KNOLL

Enemy information was enough for Maj Maclarn who decided that capture of the Knoll on 9 Oct was necessary to improve his tactical situation. Maj Pike's A Coy, 2/17 Bn was relieved by subunits of the 2/43 Bn north of the Song River, and after the steep climb up the Sattelberg Track, rejoined its two company group in the Jivevaneng area and formed a firm base at the Village where Maj Maclarn established his HQ.

Soon after A Coy arrived in the area, at 0930 hrs, Capt Sheldon's B Coy (10 and 12 Pls) moved from positions east of Jivevaneng Village to north of the main Sattelberg Track, along the route previously reconnoitred by Lt Bennie's patrol on 7 Oct. Leading troops cut their way along an old disused track with machettes down into a deep reentrant which extended for about 500 yds to a small clearing, the recognizable forward assembly area for the attack. This was about 200 yds north-west of the objective.

At 1030 hrs, Capt Sheldon reported by phone his forward elements 50 yds from the enemy positions and Lt McDonald's 11 Pl, less one section left at Jivevaneng, moved forward to concentrate the Company. The artillery fired on the objective from 1030 to 1045 hrs. The plan of attack was an assault with 10 Pl forward, 11 Pl in support and 12 Pl in reserve. The quiet approach to the objective, in the order, 10,12,11, guided by PIB scouts up a 45 degrees spur was along a slippery track, closed in on both sides by tall trees and dense undergrowth. There could be no deployment to the right of the track as the ground fell away sharply into a deep ravine which extended from the start point.

The main enemy positions were dug in deeply on the objective, south of the Sattelberg Track. (Some fox holes were ten feet deep.) The approach of the attackers was dominated by an enemy "Woodpecker" (HMG) sighted also to cover the main track. For 10 Pl troops to reach the enemy's main positions on the objective the "woodpecker" and its supporting posts needed to be silenced and thereafter a steep bank at least 8 ft high climbed.

Lt Bennie's skilful close reconnaissance established the location of the "Woodpecker" and contributed greatly to the success of the attack which commenced at 1110 hrs with 10 Pl's assault, supported by fire from 11 Pl. 10 Pl had sneaked unnoticed by the enemy to within 10 yards of the first enemy post. The leading section led by Cpl E S Grant had to crawl the last 20 yds on the slippery, steep track before reaching the open ground. Pte R L Stanton, an original member of B Coy and a veteran of earlier campaigns who enlisted from Dee Why, NSW, was a member of Cpl Grant's section and told the story:

"Owing to the nature of the ground, only one platoon could move into the attack. It was raining heavily but it helped to conceal us and deaden any noise we made. As soon as the shelling stopped we fanned out for the assault. We left the jungle and were almost on the enemy when all hell broke loose. As if a miracle had happened, the rain suddenly stopped and we charged up a very steep slope on our hands and knees midst a shower of grenades from the Japs. We threw some of our own but these rolled back down the hill and exploded amongst us. We eventually reached and crossed the track in front of a 'Woodpecker' which opened up on us from a flank. With the exception of Larry Grant[1] who fell mortally wounded,

---

[1]
Cpl Eldrick Stuart "Larry" Grant previously served with the 2/4 Bn 6 Div in Libya, Greece and Crete before he joined the 2/17 Bn and served at Tel el Eisa, where he was wounded, and the Lae campaign. He originally came from Toowoomba, Queeensland and moved to Canowindra, NSW, before enlistment at Sydney.

all of us crossed safely with lead whistling around us and reached the objective and occupied the Jap foxholes. Another section silenced the 'Woodpecker' and the whole platoon overran the hill."

The second forward section of 10 Pl, with the first section on its right, assaulted along the track. Cpl R C "Clarry" Brooks[1] displayed great coolness and courage as he moved steadily up the slope firing his Bren gun from the hip. He wiped out the 'Woodpecker', killed all the enemy in three posts and demoralized them on that part of the objective. Sadly, Pte K A Miller[2] was killed in the assault.

Behind Cpl Grant's section, then led by Pte E H "Shorty" Meredith, the second and third sections of 10 Pl overran the objective as they chased the enemy that fled before them. Lt Bennie related the difficulty of hitting a moving target while climbing a slippery hill. He resolutely led his platoon to the objective while he threw grenades and shot at least two of the enemy. When Capt Sheldon was wounded in the knee by shrapnel on the same afternoon in an enemy counter-attack and was evacuated, Lt Bennie[3] assumed command of B Coy, organised consolidation on the objective and the defeat of numerous counter-attacks.

B Coy, 2/17 Bn had surprised the enemy, an often sought after advantage in the attack seldom achieved in the tactical battle. Complemented by the skill, determination and courage of Lt Bennie's 10 Pl, ably supported by Lt McDonald's 11 Pl which also contributed in the consolidation on the right flank, the attack was an outstanding success. The supporting fire from 11 Pl achieved its purpose as the enemy gun crew that manned the "Woodpecker" directed fire down the main track towards Jivevaneng instead of at the soldiers assaulting their position and may have been partly responsible for their own demise.

B Coy casualties, two killed and four wounded, (including one remained on duty) were light compared with those inflicted on the enemy in a strong defensive position. (8 enemy dead were counted on the objective, four in one foxhole, plus a sword which was duly souvenired.)

Capt Sheldon's B Coy HQ was established on the feature at 1210 hrs. In readiness for counter-attack, 10 and 11 Pls covered the south and west approaches respectively and 12 Pl manned the old "Woodpecker" position and the approaches from the north, including the main Sattelberg Track. The Company was strengthened with Lt K T McLeod's 9 Pl, A Coy which arrived via the Sattelberg Track from Jivevaneng in time for the first counter-attack and occupied a close reserve position North of the track.

---

[1]
Cpl Rupert Clarence "Clarry" Brooks enlisted from Sydney and was a veteran of the Tobruk, Tel el Eisa, El Alamein and Lae campaigns. For valour on this occasion in the assault and his alertness and resolution in the face of subsequent counter-attacks in a vital position where the enemy made determined efforts to break through the defences, and his encouragement to others, he received the immediate award of the MM.

[2]
Pte Ken Allen Miller served with B Coy in the Tel el Eisa, El Alamein, and Lae campaigns and enlisted from Mortdale, NSW.

[3]
Lt Robert J Bennie who enlisted from Nowra, NSW, was a veteran of the 2/17 Bn's earlier campaigns at Tel el Eisa, El Alamein where he was wounded, and Lae. For his valour on this occasion he received an immediate award of the MC.

B COY, 2/17 BN CONSOLIDATED AND DEFEATED NUMEROUS COUNTER-ATTACKS

After the loss of the Knoll, the enemy had fled into the jungle to the south of the feature but were soon reorganised and mounted the first counter-attack against 10 Pl, preceded by bugle calls, whistles and yells. Before the first attack was defeated the enemy had come within 20 yds of 10 and 11 Pls with a shower of grenades and snipers' bullets from the dense undergrowth. During this attack Pte Peters[1] was killed by a sniper from close quarters, where he effectively manned a Bren gun in a weapon pit at least 15 feet ahead of the other members of his Section. After dusk, an attempt was made by Ptes Meredith and Brown to recover Pte Peter's body without success when Pte Brown[2] also was killed by a sniper's bullet fired from close range.

A second counter attack at 1845 hrs was also repulsed and came from the same direction as the first. Like the first it developed into a grenade throwing contest with a decided advantage for the defenders with strong arms on the higher ground.

On the night 9/10 Oct, Lt Bennie's troops were quietly active and consolidated positions in preparation for the inevitable counter attacks that followed. During the night the enemy paid more attention to the HQ positions at Jivevaneng Village with 6 artillery rounds at 1900 hrs that appeared to have been fired from about 2000 yds forward of B Coy FDLs. Enemy parties also attempted infiltration of the Jivevaneng defences during the night without success. The enemy artillery fire ceased on being engaged by a troop of the 2/12 Fd Regt.

All soldiers were alert from "stand to" in the morning of 10 Oct and they were surprised by the blasts of a mountain gun which fired 31 shells mainly on B Coy's 11 Pl over direct sights from about 100 yds west along the Sattelberg Track. Already damaged by friendly artillery, shells from the enemy's gun almost denuded the feature of its remaining vegetation. Ptes H Daniels[3] and J F Neil[4] of 11 Pl were killed by direct hits and casualties grew in numbers. Despite the intensity of the bombardment and the loss of their mates, the troops were steadfast and volunteers came freely to fill in the gaps. One such volunteer, Pte S H Fitzhenry[5] of 12 Pl was mortally wounded by direct shellfire while he attempted to reach a forward fox hole and died before he could receive attention.

After the enemy shells and mortar fire stopped, only a broken note was heard from the bugler, which suggested he became a casualty. The next frontal attack came once more against 10 Pl in the familiar pattern with hand grenades and snipers' fire. The heavy fire from automatic weapons and grenades of 10 Pl commanded by Sgt J Woods, who had succeeded Lt Bennie, repulsed the attack.

Counter-attacks were repulsed during the remainder of the day and came so frequently that some soldiers lost count. Lt Bennie however, knew there were five. With each attack the shells

---

[1]
Pte Frederick William Peters was a veteran of the Tel el Eisa, El Alamein and Lae campaigns. He enlisted from Kurri Kurri, NSW.

[2]
Pte Thomas Brown was a veteran of the Tobruk, Tel el Eisa, El Alamein and Lae campaigns. He enlisted from Glebe, NSW.

[3]
Pte Harry Daniels served with the 2/17 Bn in the Lae campaign. He enlisted from Cammeray, NSW.

[4]
Pte James Frederick Neil served with the 2/17 Bn in the Lae campaign. He enlisted from Surry Hills, NSW.

[5]
Pte Stephen Henry Fitzhenry was an original member of the 2/17 Bn who served at Tobruk, Tel el Eisa, El Alamein and Lae. He enlisted from Kogarah, NSW.

and mortar bombs reached a greater intensity, seemingly in attempts to blast the defenders from the face of the earth.

At the height of the attacks, Sgt J Woods[1] exposed himself to enemy fire frequently in organising his platoon, manned a Bren gun when its No 1 had been wounded and brought effective fire on to the attackers. Reorganisation became necessary as casualties caused gaps in the defences. Pte E R Ryan and R A "Snowy" Hall of 12 pl were two among others who were ready volunteers and filled positions.

Lt N E McDonald's 11 Pl, with weapon pits facing north-west towards Sattelberg, also suffered gaps in its defences. After a hammering with the mountain gun and with men temporarily away, only Dave Dunning, Gordon Broome, Gordon Simes and himself were holding the platoon front. CSM Harry Wells and company orderly Charles Alderdice with others filled the gap on this occasion until the men returned.

Fatal casualties on this day were, in addition to those already metioned, Cpl C J "Clarry" Anderson,[2] DOW, and Pte D B Harding,[3] KIA.

The repulse of so many counter-attacks was a considerable drain on B Coy's first line ammunition, particularly in the expenditure of grenades. On 10 Oct, resupply was sent forward by Sgt John Baker, the Bn's Pay Sgt, who filled the position of acting RSM for Maj Maclarn's group, the RSM, WOI Dave Dunbar, being with Bn HQ at Kumawa. Ammunition carried forward by A Coy personnel were 12,000 rds of 9 mm, 9,000 rds of .303 in cartons, 3,000 rds of .303 in bandoliers, 12 boxes of 36 grenades, and 3 boxes of 2 inch mortar HE. Two day's emergency and one day reserve rations and water was also carried forward to B Coy during the day.

The total casualties sustained by B Coy since the operation began in the Jivevaneng area were 9 Ors KIA or DOW, 1 Offr and 9 Ors wounded, and 9 Ors wounded remained on duty.

The Japanese obvious annoyance at the loss of their FDL was revealed by their indulgence in numerous repetitive, unsuccessful counter-attacks and emphasised the tactical importance of the feature. The direct artillery fire in support of the counter-attacks was a traumatic experience for B Coy soldiers; nevertheless they were undaunted and not an inch of ground was recovered by the attackers while costly casualties were inflicted upon them.

An estimate by the defender of the enemy casualties was difficult. Time after time the pathetic cries of the enemy's wounded indicated their casualties were numerous. It was generally believed that the Japanese carried their dead some distance away before burial and a body count after a prolonged action in close contact was not therefore an accurate indication of their losses.

20 BDE REGROUPED FOR THE ADVANCE ON SATTELBERG

After the capture of Finschhafen, Brig Windeyer's aim was the capture of Sattelberg. With the immediate threat to the Scarlet Beachhead removed, he concentrated two of his indigenous Bns on dual approaches to the mountain. On the direct approach he used the 2/17 Bn on the axis of the main Sattelberg Track and the 2/15 Bn on the left flank via the Kumawa Spur. The 2/13

1
   Sgt John Woods served with the 6 Div in Libya before joining the 2/17 Bn for the El Alamein and Lae campaigns. He enlisted from Bowral, NSW. For his valour on this occasion he received the immediate award of the MM.

2
   Cpl Clarence John Anderson was an original member of the 2/17 Bn and served at Tobruk, Tel el Eisa, El Alamein where he was wounded, and Lae. He enlisted from Canley Vale, NSW.

3
   Pte David Bruce Harding was a university student who, according to his early enlistment number, had previous service in the 2nd AIF, details of which regrettably are not known to the writer. He enlisted from Wollstonecraft, NSW.

Bn, depleted in strength after the Kakakog battle, remained in the Finschhafen area in the early stage of the operation. The 2/43 Bn had continued responsibility for the protection of the beachhead. While the regrouping of the Bde was taking place, reinforcements in the area were imminent with the expected arrival of the balance of 9 Div less the 26 Bde group. The advance HQ of 9 Div arrived on the north shore of Langemak Bay on 10 Oct and relieved 20 Bde of the responsibility for the maintenance of Finschhafen.

2/17 BN REUNITED AT JIVEVANENG

The 2/15 Bn began the march north from Finschhafen to Kumawa on 8 Oct and was in the Kumawa area on 10 Oct, ready to take over from Lt Col Simpson's group of the 2/17 Bn. The same day a patrol commanded by Lt Graham from C Coy 2/17 Bn with the specific task, found a suitable route from Kumawa to Jivevaneng for the movement of the Kumawa force. Capt Rudkin commanded a 7 Pl, A Coy patrol routed south of the Sattelberg track from Jivevaneng to Sisi Village and found it unoccupied. Close enemy small arms fire from the rising ground west of the village apparently directed at a friendly "Boomerang" low flying reconnaissance plane revealed enemy using the area.

Lt Col Simpson's group was relieved at Kumawa on 11 Oct by the 2/15 Bn and set out at 0930 hrs along the route found by Lt Graham across the deep reentrant of the Quoja River and arrived in the Jivevaneng area at 1630 hrs. The 2/17 Bn, less the A Tk Pl on its way from Kiasawa, was united as a fighting unit after eight days' separation.

The Japanese gave up their plan to recapture the Knoll after their last counter-attack on 10 Oct and paid more attention to the Jivevaneng defences. The 2/17 Bn's reinforcement of the area with two more rifle companies and its complement of support platoons enabled relocation of subunits, strengthening of the defences and subunit relief, especially for Lt Bennie's

immunity from the enemy's infantry in the situation of all round defence. The enemy, if not sufficiently deterred by offensive patrols or other means such as defensive fire from artillery, was free to approach under concealment of the terrain or by night to a chosen part of the defended area.

On 11 Oct, Maj Pike's A Coy moved to support Lt Bennie's B Coy in the area of the Knoll while Capt Dinning's C Coy and Lt Main's D Coy improved defences in the Jivevaneng Village area. Lt Col Simpson visited the Knoll for a reconnaissance. Those with him were concerned for he wore his peaked officer's cap with the obvious risk that he may have become a casualty from enemy sniper fire. He had not left the area when a soldier was wounded by a sniper's bullet near where the CO had earlier viewed the front.

On this day, sadly, Pte J Smith[1] of the 2/17 Bn's Intelligence Section died of wounds he suffered near the Bumi River on the advance to Finschhafen while attached to B Coy. He was buried in Bomana War Cemetery, Port Moresby.

Lt Col Simpson ordered Maj Pike to extend the FDLs forward to a small jungled feature occupied by the enemy on the north of the track and used as a snipers' haven. This feature became known as "Rudkin's Knoll" and was the beginning of a long narrow spur that extended west towards Sattelberg held in depth by the enemy. The obvious enemy dominance of this straight stretch of track cut into the spur with a continuous steep embankment, ruled out the

---

[1]
    Pte Jack Smith had served with the 2/17 Bn in the Lae Campaign and enlisted from Young, NSW.

approach from the south with only a platoon strength and without flank protection. The north approach was via a 20 feet cliff, impossible to climb unaided by equipment. There remained only a frontal assault which was undertaken by Capt Rudkin's 7 Pl on 12 Oct. After a fierce firefight in which Pte B C Blanch[1] was killed and three were wounded, including Section Commander Ron Percival, Lt Col Simpson ordered the Platoon to withdraw. Sgt P Cunningham's A Coy Pl had moved to a position below and south of the track but did not take part in the attack and was also withdrawn to the FDLs.

The next three days were relatively quiet for the 2/17 Bn which patrolled and attacked the enemy during daylight with Artillery, 3 inch and 2 inch mortar harrassing fire. On 13 Oct, Cpl L C Burrell[2] of 8 Pl A Coy was killed. C and D Coys relieved A and B Coys in the forward positions on 15 Oct. Also on 15 Oct Lt MacFarlane's 10 Pl, PIB again became attached to the Bn to assist with patrols, and Brig Windeyer visited the Bn area.

9 DIV PREPARES FOR JAPANESE COUNTER OFFENSIVE

During the period 6 to 15 Oct the 9 Div forces in the Finschhafen area were reinforced to include the 24 Bde, 2/2 MG Bn and the 2/3 Pnr Bn. Maj Gen G F Wootten's immediate aim was to advance to Wareo. Preliminary moves were the capture of Sattelberg, and the opening of the Wareo feature to attack from the east by a move along the spur from the direction of Gusika Village. This would also cut the enemy supply line from the coast.

With this plan in view and with concern to secure Finschhafen from attack, tasks were allotted on 11 Oct as follows:

(a) The 24 Bde to protect the Scarlet Beach area in depth against any attack from the west or north-west, and with not less than two companies gain control of the track junction near Bonga.

(b) The 20 Bde to continue pressure towards Sattelberg with a view to its capture.

(c) The 22 Bn to protect the area south of Mape River.

While preparations for the plan were being made, strong evidence indicated that an enemy attack was imminent. As it was not possible for 9 Div to anticipate the enemy in resuming the offensive, orders were issued on 15 Oct which laid down the policy for the defence of the Finschhafen area against attack from land and sea. Included in the ground considered by Maj Gen Wootten as vital to the defence and to be held at all costs, was the high ground and the Sattelberg track near Jivevaneng, held by the 2/17 Bn. Other vital ground involved in subsequent tactical developments was: The track junctions near Bonga; North Hill; the high ground about two miles west of Scarlet Beach between the Song River and the Sattelberg track near Jivevaneng; and Kumawa.

On 16 Oct, the main enemy concentrations were astride the track Palanko–Katika, astride the Sattelberg track west of Jivevaneng, on the Sisi Track north of Kumawa and in the Sattelberg area.

An operation order captured on 15 Oct and other orders with maps captured later showed that the Japanese had planned three coordinated attacks:

A. A diversion in the north by two companies to advance south from Bonga.

---

[1] Pte Bruce Charles Blanch was a veteran of the 2/17 Bn's Middle East and Lae campaigns. He enlisted from Lismore, NSW.

[2] Cpl Leslie Cuthbertson Burrell served with 2/17 Bn in the Tel el Eisa, El Alamein and Lae campaigns. He enlisted from Strathfield, NSW.

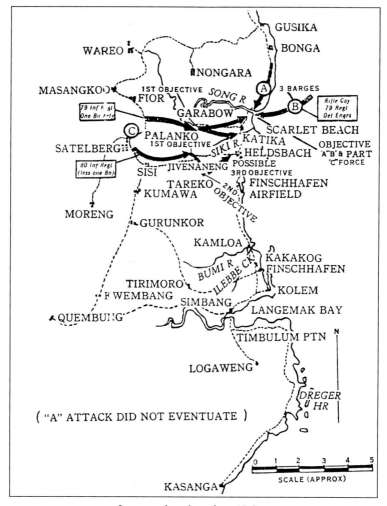

Japanese plan of attack on 17 Oct

B. A seaborne attack by an infantry company and a detachment of engineers equipped with explosives and demolition charges, to land at Scarlet Beach during the night to destroy dumps, artillery positions, tanks, barges etc.

C. The main landward attack of one regiment to attack eastward astride the Sattelberg Track to capture Heldsbach, and one regiment further north to move eastward to capture Scarlet Beach and Katika areas.

The determination of the enemy's "X" Day for the offensive was to be indicated by a bonfire on Sattelberg Mountain.

2/17BN DEFENDED JIVEVANENG AGAINST ENEMY ATTACKS IN STRENGTH

The effective strength of the 2/17 Bn when it was attacked by elements of the Japanese 80 Infantry Regiment at 0445 hrs on 16 Oct, as part of its plan for the capture of Heldsbach Plantation, was 22 Offrs and 447 Ors.

The enemy's first attempted infiltration at the PIB positions at Jivevaneng was perhaps by chance but more likely by design, as it would be unlikely that a prior reconnaissance would not have been made in daylight for such an important and large scale planned operation by the Japanese 80 Regiment. The PIB Pl presented by the nature of its troops a weak spot in the outer defences. This developed into a fierce attack on the 2/17 Bn HQ position which lasted until approximately 0930 hrs. Lt E J Blundell, who was the IO, related how the attack began:

"Lt Bill Forster, the Signal Offr, and I were asleep under a two man tent on the cleared ground near the track when I was awakened by the sound of a rifle shot coming from the area occupied by the PIB Pl. About two hours later the Lt in charge of the Papuans, Lt Macfarlane, reported to Lt Col Simpson there was movement down the reentrant in front of his position.

Soon after there was an exchange of shots and a Papuan was shot dead[1]. The PIB, attached for patrol activity, were not trained in, nor were they expected to take part in defensive operations, and the Lt withdrew his platoon immediately after he advised Lt Col Simpson of his intention; this left a gap in the defences.

The brunt of the first attack was taken by the left forward section of Lt Dick's A Tk Pl north of an old hut, once a missionary school house. Commendation was due to Pte R A Gillespie, who fought with an enemy MG crew at a range of about 50 yds, destroyed them and broke up the attack.

The RAP came under direct fire and Ptes E Bade and W McCarthy were wounded. The RMO, Capt H L "Bill" Hughes thereupon moved the RAP about 100 yds inwards for protection."

For two hours from 0730 hrs the main track and positions occupied by Sgt R Reay's MG Pl and Lt T Swan's Mor Pl were subjected to severe shell fire from a 70 mm mountain gun and a 75 mm gun.

Lt Blundell continued his story:

"We were shelled and mortared in daylight and then the Japs brought up a small mountain gun and fired point blank into the trees above our heads, causing air bursts. The sound of the gun fire and the explosion of the shot was instantaneous and we could not locate the gun. We knew it was close but nobody realised then it was only 60 yds away.

Pte R Bevan of Bn HQ and some of the signallers climbed the big trees at risk of being sniped and tried to locate the gun but undergrowth obscured their vision."

Throughout the day four more attacks were made on the defences and at 1515 hrs Bn HQ was heavily bombarded with 81mm mortar fire when Sgt Harry Tasker[2] of the MG Pl was killed by shrapnel. Both 2 inch mortar and cup discharger were used by the enemy throughout the day. All attacks were successfully repulsed.

Lt Blundell recorded events of the second attack:

"It came at about 1600 hrs from the north-east after a heavy bombardment of mortars. Fortunately, Lt Col Simpson had just moved A Coy into the area and with the help of the

---

1
PN682 Pte Ketapipia, PIB.

2
Sgt Eric Donald "Harry" Tasker was an original member of C Coy and a veteran of the 2/17 Bn's Middle East and Lae campaigns. He enlisted from Wagga Wagga, NSW.

right forward section of the A Tk Pl commanded by Cpl M Ready, was able to kill the attack before it gained momentum.

Sgt Tom Johnson[1] of the Pnr Pl was fatally shot when a Jap party crossed the track and got into the bamboo between Bn HQ and the main Village. The enemy party cut communication with our troops holding the Knoll. Lt Forster was wounded in the shoulder when he was about to set out with a line party to attend to the break. Later in the day the line was relaid to the Knoll and the track between the localities was patrolled hourly thereafter for several days."

Cpl M Ready related his concern for a likely enemy approach and the inadequate strength he had in his locality:

"Lt Dick placed Cpl Tasker's Section under my command which gave us two Brens and four Owens but we still had a blind spot on our right flank. The sections were under orders not to fire until they saw a definite target. The result was that during the attack in the afternoon Cpl P Bascombe, RAP, shot and killed a Jap at 6 yards and Pte A Fogarty killed two Jap mortarmen with one burst of the Bren at four yards. The rest of us plastered the bamboo with grenades which were supplied to us by Pte Bevan of Bn HQ. Within a few minutes of our opening fire, Pte N Moylan, with two others from A Coy dashed across the track, dived into a hole and got their Bren gun into action on our right flank. With the three Brens on a twenty yard front it put 'finis' to any plans the Japs may have had in that quarter."

Lt K J Gibb's 15 Pl, C Coy was withdrawn from the Knoll to strengthen the defences in the Bn HQ locality and although the position was exposed and troops had to remain in their holes all day, reasonable security of the HQ was restored without the constant threat of being overrun by the enemy, located as near as 50 yds away.

Mystery surrounds the disappearance of L/Cpl L "Mick" O'Brien who commanded a small patrol on 16 Oct from Lt Pollock's 18 Pl, D Coy which aimed to destroy an MG post that harrassed Bn HQ. Pte S V Turnbull, who was forward scout of the patrol told the story:

"The patrol consisted of L/Cpl 'Mick' O'Brien,[2] Gordon Kibby, 'Ocker' Ryan,[3] Col Nash,[4] 'Jimmy' O'Neill, Jack Blair and myself.

Mick hadn't gone 10 yds before he kicked a booby trap. Although none of us was hurt, it was the beginning of our bad luck. I was leading scout and rifle bomber about 15 yds in front of Mick when I came to a suitable position to fire the grenades. I halted the section and called Mick up to discuss where he would have me fire them.

We were about 20 yds in front of the section, spread in a slight curve in the track. Mick was lying on his left side supporting his head on his elbow and I was kneeling about a foot away from him. As we talked briefly we were fired on from about 10 yds slightly left of our front and I took cover in a clump of cane about 5 yds behind us. Only about a dozen shots had been fired when I unintentionally blocked the fire of the rest of the section. Mick said 'help

---

1
Sgt Thomas Johnson, DOW, was a veteran of the 2/17 Bn's Middle East and Lae Campaigns. He enlisted from Brooklyn, Hawkesbury River, NSW.
2
No trace was found of L/Cpl L "Mick" O'Brien, despite an extensive search of the area. He was posted missing, presumed dead. He joined the 2/17 Bn in the Middle East and served in the Lae campaign.
3
John Luke "Ocker" Ryan, KIA, served with the 2/17 Bn in the Middle East and Lae campaigns. He enlisted from Bondi Junction, NSW.
4
Colin Francis Nash, KIA, served with 2/17 Bn in the Middle East and Lae campaigns. He enlisted from Tamworth, NSW.

me Sid, I've been hit in the stomach'. I saw four Japs running back to where I thought was the post we set out to destroy and I fired several shots and probably hit one, who gave a lurch.

After the Japs had disappeared I went to Mick but seeing out of the corner of my eye that someone was hit behind us, I asked Mick if he could walk. He said he thought so and I got him out of his equipment and to his feet. He seemed all right so I went back to see how the rest were.

I found that Col Nash and 'Ocker' Ryan had been killed. We decided to get them back but the Japs had other ideas. They came at us from a another direction, so we decided the best thing to do was to get to cover and try to pick up Mick, who we thought was going back on a track which led to our positions. The Jap continued to fire at us and a number of other shots were heard, probably fired at Mick. We decided to get back and make a larger patrol to get the boy's bodies out but due to the failing light this did not eventuate. So ended a patrol when I lost three of the best mates I ever had."

Failing in their attempts to dislodge the defenders, the Japanese dug in on the reverse slope in an area of cane north of the village. They were as near as 50 yds from the Bn HQ, close enough to inhibit the use of 3 inch mortars and artillery on their forward positions and for them to employ the sneak sniper tactic at which they were adept.

From pay books found in the area, the attacking force was identified as part of 2 Coy, 8 Bn, 80 Regt; estimated strength, 50 to 70. Judging from the cries of the wounded many casualties were inflicted on the enemy during the day. Only 6 dead bodies were counted but there was evidence that many others had been dragged away for burial.

Casualties suffered by the 2/17 Bn on 16 Oct were 3 KIA, 1DOW, 1 Missing, presumed dead, and 1 Offr and 13 Ors wounded.

The 17 Oct was comparatively quiet by the standard of the previous day. However, there was one casualty, Pte R S Holder[1] of D Coy, from sniper fire. Early afternoon heavy bombing and straffing from "Mitchell" and "Marauder" aircraft was seen and heard in the Sisi—Sattelberg area and pamphlets were dropped in and around Sattelberg. Enemy 81 mm mortar fire on A Coy at 1700hs was soon silenced by the Bn's 3 inch mortars.

The morning of 18 Oct revealed that the enemy had cut the main Sattelberg Track east of Capt Rudkin's B Coy locality, up till then a relatively quiet place. Loss of line communication to Bde HQ was from experience an indication that the enemy was on the L of C. A patrol located the enemy position at 0900hrs, estimated strength one platoon, well dug in amongst bamboo astride the track east of a bend known as "Cemetery Corner", so named where soldiers of the 2/43 Bn were buried in an earlier action. The enemy positions were registered by artillery but the engaged results were not known. Unfortunately, a smoke shell during the registration struck some 36 grenades and caused four casualties in the 2/17 Bn. Lt Ken Gibb of 15 Pl, C Coy was accidently wounded on reconnaissance and his place was filled by the IO, Lt Eric Blundell. Enemy snipers and grenades from cup dischargers throughout the day confined most soldiers to their holes in the Bn HQ locality and an A Tk soldier for the second successive day was sniped; on this accasion the soldier survived his wound.

At 1200 hrs 19 Oct, the enemy position east of B Coy, 2/17 Bn was effectively shelled by 12 guns of the 2/12 Fd Regt; 25 rounds per gun. The effect of the artillery concentrations caused

---

1

Pte R S Holder KIA, joined the 2/17 Bn in the Middle East and served in the Lae Campaign.

the enemy to move close to Capt Rudkin's B Coy, perhaps to avoid further artillery concentra-tions and to find a more suitable location. Whatever their intention, they were dealt a severe blow by the Company with small arms fire and grenades at close quarters and 7 enemy, including an officer of a platoon force, were killed; the remainder withdrew to the prepared positions astride the track from whence they had come.

Soon after the enemy attack on B Coy, Maj Broadbent arrived via a track from New Tareko to resume his posting as 2 I/C of the Bn, accompanied by Lt N West and 6 LOB personnel and a PIB Sgt with 3 Ors. The patrol returned via the same route to the CCS with wounded comprising 3 stretcher cases and 5 walking wounded.

As MLO, Major Broadbent had handed over the responsibility of the Scarlet Beachhead to the Comd 24 Bde, Brig Evans. He, and a small group from 2/17 Bn got themselves to 20 Bde HQ in Heldsbach plantation. He got permission to take his party and some additional "X" list persons to get to Jivevaneng with much needed medical supplies. A Sgt with four PIB soldiers were joined for scouting and any local liaison. The party set off on suggested track lines shown on a revised edition of a Sattelberg map. There were numerous Tareko villages but no occupants were found. A climbing and exacting track was followed. It seemed the right direction but there was no outlook to decide exact locations. After a guarded resting halt, the Sgt reported that his scouts would not go further — "There were Japs". Questioned, it appeared they were not seen, but could be smelt. Broadbent moved forward and with signs of slight confidence the scouts resumed a cautious advance. He directed them to skirt a slight clearing in the undergrowth that led up a slight rise. The leading scout turned back with a great smile and beckoned forward. He had reached the Sattelberg track at the bend below Jivenaneng and lying in the centre of the road was a dead Jap. Looking from the scrub at the side of the road leading up a straight stretch, Broadbent could see Rudkin. A simple, cautious detour was all that was necessary to ensure the party's arrival.

Elements of the 2/3 Pnr Bn were in contact with the enemy further east down the Sattelberg Track. Due to the terrain and lack of visibility there was a problem that persisted throughout operations against the enemy positions, wedged between friendly forces, to determine on the ground their exact location and thereby take measures to prevent casualties to own troops. Commanders were confronted with the reality of the problem when, in support of an attack by a platoon of the 2/3 Pnr Bn on 20 Oct, its Bn's 3 inch mortars bombarded Capt Rudkin's B Coy, 2/17 Bn. 7 salvos of 7 bombs were fired at minute intervals before a message to stop firing via the diverse lateral line communication achieved the desired result. Although no thought would have been given to such matters by those on the receiving end at the time, who counted the "pops" from a distance and prayed as the bombs whistled their perpendicular decent, the pattern of the beaten zone surrounding Coy HQ was a lesson in the effective use of the Bn support weapon. It was extraordinarily lucky that only one soldier was injured and a Bren gun left on the parapet was damaged.

Having been unsuccessful in repeated attempts to dislodge the 2/17 Bn from the Jivevaneng feature, the Japanese had embarked on a policy of containment and the Bn was effectively surrounded on three sides from the east, north and west. With the jeep track from its B Echelon at Zag to Jivevaneng cut by the enemy, a new supply route was necessary. This situation was not new to the Bn with the experience of the 9 Div in Tobruk where for nine months the alternative supply route was by sea. On a smaller scale, the difference at Jivevaneng was a sea of jungle and a route across the hazardous, steep reentrant to the jeephead at Kumawa, able to be traversed only by foot and wide open to enemy ambush from all directions.

The track taken by Maj Broadbent's party on its return to 2/17 Bn on 19 Oct via the Tareko

Villages had established a more direct and comparatively more secure alternative route for re-supply and casualty evacuation. This route was subsequently used in preference to the more arduous and difficult one especially for stretcher casualties across the deep Quoja River re-entrant between Jivevaneng and Kumawa.

The 2/17 Bn soldiers knew the defence of Jivevaneng was temporary and the time would come for an attack to end their stay. They also knew full well the meaning of the term "offensive defence"; to gain and retain the initiative, "turn the tables" and give the enemy no respite. The Bn's background and long experience of its offensive desert patrols in the Siege of Tobruk and at Tel el Eisa came to the fore in the tropical surroundings of Jivevaneng. During the period that followed, when they destroyed or defeated all the enemy around them, when remnants of the last pocket of resistance withdrew on the night 4/5 Nov, the fight was taken to the enemy in every way possible with the resources available. The policy of offensive action against their active enemy was limited only by the Bn's fighting strength; the firepower of manned weapons on the ground; commensurate with holding at all costs the area of vital ground entrusted to it. Lt Col Simpson's words, "What we have we hold", underwent a most stringent trial, for more than ever, each and every soldier had an important contribution to make to the defence.

Each day's offensive activity almost became routine over a protracted period as enemy dispositions were located and harassed with patrols and firepower. Two day's war diary are extracted below as an example of the 2/17 Bn's activity in its state of semi-siege. There were days of greater activity but the first was selected for an obvious reason.

"23 Oct: (The anniversary of the Battle of El Alamein.)

During the day patrols contacted enemy positions at 58956620 (estimated 12 men), and 591663 where enemy listening post was engaged and sounds of movement were heard. The 81 mm mortar position reported on 17 Oct was found by a patrol situated in a small grass clearing. The mortar was not in position and several 3 inch mortar craters in the area indicated a successful 3 inch mortar shoot on the 17th. 1140 hrs: Usual native carrying party arrived with rations. 1250 hrs: Capt G Holtsbaum, Brigade LO and Lt Westley Smith, IO from 1 Aust Corps visited and gave us a review of the situation generally in this area and the operations of the 7 Div in the Markham Valley, including the drive to Madang. Maj Pike and 7 Ors returned to the LOB detachment at New Tereko. Maj Maclarn succeeded Maj Pike as OC A Coy. 1530 hrs: 2 Inch mortar shoot on enemy positions at 58956620 — results unknown but all bombs appeared to be well in the target area."

"24 Oct: 0645 hrs: 15 parachutes with large cylindrical containers attached were dropped by the enemy on the north-west slopes of the Sattelberg feature. 1330 enemy LMG fired on 9 Pl A Coy area. This was replied to with cup dischargers with unobserved results. 1423 hrs 3 inch mortar shoot by 2/13 Bn on enemy positions at 594661 1503 hrs: Air strike by Bostons on Sattelberg area and Coconut Grove at 593681. Tac R had identified this latter position as a probable enemy strongpoint. 1400 hrs: LOB party proceeded from New Tareko to the Bn position encountered small enemy force astride the track at 594658 and were forced to withdraw having suffered one casualty[1] During the morning a B Coy patrol tried to locate the enemy's southern flank astride the Sattelberg Track at 594661 (Cemetery Corner). The flank was estimated to be 60/100 yards east of the above map reference. No estimate of enemy strength could be ascertained."

1

Cpl William Keith "Bluey" Bartlett was wounded with the LOB party and died of wounds on 28 Oct. He was an original member of the 2/17 Bn and served in the Middle East and Lae campaigns. He enlisted from Mudgee, NSW.

The administrative problems encountered by the 2/17 Bn in its isolated position were related in its CO's summary signed by Maj Broadbent for the month of October, 1943:

> "The rationing of the Bn proved at first a problem but this was overcome by using the track from Kumawa North to Jivevaneng. Each day a ration party consisting of up to 120 carriers, supervised by personnel of the 2/15 Bn made the journey and at no time did the ration question become acute as an ample reserve was built up. Evacuation of sick and wounded presented a real problem as they had to be moved over two very difficult routes — the ration party route south to Kumawa and thence by jeep to the ADS and secondly by route to New Tareko at the present location of our LOB personnel."

The medical report for Oct by the RMO, Capt Hughes, gives more detail of the medical problems and the state of health of the troops who had been in action with varying degrees of enemy contact since the Lae landing at Red Beach on 4 Sep:

> "During the greater part of the month the Bn was in close contact with the enemy. The unit covered a great deal of country and began to show signs of weariness in the first week. For the next three weeks the Unit was stationary, surrounded by the enemy. This period was a difficult one medically as well as tactically as the casualties were evacuated by native porter and in many cases had to be held 24/36 hours, in some cases for 48 hours.

> Owing to the large area all men were essential and for the last two weeks of the month all cases of clinical malaria were treated in the lines with good results. Mosquitoes were not troublesome, as the site was 2,000 feet high and 1,000 feet from the nearest water. Nets were not available and could not have been used if they were (tactically), but repellant was available in limited quantities and atebrin was taken. Two companies were without atebrin for 2/3 days but no great increase in cases of fever were noticed from them. The general health of the Bn throughout all this period remained good but the long hours of piquet and the tension made the troops noticeably weary. No cases were evacuated N.Y.D.N.(Not Yet Diagnosed Neurosis) but two personnel were given sedatives and retained in the RAP for 24 hours before being returned to the lines.

> An attempt was made to clean the area, bury all enemy dead, construct latrines etc but it was impossible. Finally section latrines were dug and functioned satisfactorily. Flies were extremely numerous however and diarrhhoea and the majority of the cases of clinical dysentery responded to sulphaguanadine and only two cases were evacuated with this complaint. During the month the RAP staff suffered casualties — Cpl chiropodist wounded and an orderly killed."

Capt Hughes did not mention that during the enemy's attack on Jivevaneng, when there was an evacuation problem, he performed an emergency operation to save the life of a soldier by amputating his leg with an old wood saw which was found in a native hut. The soldier survived the ordeal.

THE JAPANESE PLAN TO RETAKE FINSCHHAFEN FAILED AT KATIKA

After the bonfire was lit on Sattelberg mountain at 8.30pm on the night of 16 Oct, and following the translation of documents captured on 15 Oct, Maj Gen Wootten was privy to most of the important information concerning the Japanese plan of attack on the Scarlet Beach — Heldsbach area. The odds were therefore weighted in his favour. Maj Gen Wootten and his opponent, General Katagiri, Commander of the Japanese 20 Div, had both arrived in the Finschhafen area about the same time; both were reinforcing as quickly as each's circumstances permitted and both were intent on the offensive.

Plan A, the enemy's diversion in the north at Bonga in the coastal sector, to the defenders

---

1
WX8350 Pte W J Field AAMC was KIA on 3 Nov 43 (see page 271)

was nothing more serious than a patrol clash on 16 Oct with elements of D Coy, 2/43 Bn near Gusika and was not assessed as the diversion for the main attack.

At 0300 hrs on 17 Oct, a heavy air bombardment raid on the Finschhafen area which lasted for one hour without damage heralded plan B, the seaborne attack. At 0415 hrs three barges glided towards Scarlet Beach with muffled motors close to the northern cape. Originally there were believed to have been at least 7 barges, four having been reported sunk by PT boats south of Sio on 15 Oct. Their approach from Bonga was monitored by coast watchers en route. However, in the immediate area of Scarlet Beach, due to the rain, darkness and noise of the surf, they were not detected until near the mouth of the Song River.

The enemy barges were engaged by Bofors of 2/4 Lt AA Regt, LMG's and rifles of 2/28 Bn and a 37 mm gun and 50 calibre MGs of the American 532 ESB Regt. Two of the barges were disabled on the sand spit at the river's mouth and the third was hit but managed to retract and withdraw north with casualties. Mortally wounded, a 50 mm gun crewman of the 532 ESB Regt, Pte Nathan Van Noy Junior was awarded America's highest award for valour, the Congressional Medal of Honour. Of those who landed, 39 enemy were killed on the beach and 36 escaped across the mouth of the river where they were mopped up during day patrols of the 2/43 Bn. Many weapons including flame throwers, mines, demolition charges and bangalore torpedoes were recovered on the beach.

Plan C, the main enemy landward attack began on 17 Oct against the 2/3 Pnr Bn on the vital ground west of Katika. Unbeknown to the defenders, the previous day the enemy had passed its 79 Regt group between the widely dispersed forward companies of the 2/3 Pnr Bn into a concentration area about one mile west of Katika. Patrols of the 2/3 Bn had clashes with the enemy on 16 Oct, most likely flank guards of the enemy's advance, but they were unable to assess the strength involved.

The enemy had early success on 17 and 18 Oct and forward elements reached the sea at Siki Cove and the field gun positions south of the Siki River. This drove a wedge between the 20 Bde and the 24 Bde and severed land communication between 24 Bde HQ and 9 Div HQ. The 2/13 Bn, less two companies was moved from the Finschhafen area to the vicinity of Heldsbach and with under command a company of the 2/23 Bn, fulfilled the tasks of preventing the enemy's movement south of Siki River to; (a) attack the gun areas at Heldsbach Plantation and (b) cut off the 20 Bde units on the Sattelberg Track from their supply base at Launch Jetty.

The Commander 24 Bde, Brig B Evans, withdrew subunits of the 2/43 Bn from the Bonga track junction area to create a reserve of two companies south of the Song River. Three companies of the 2/3 Pnr Bn on the high ground west of Katika that had become isolated from their Bn HQ were also withdrawn to a contracted perimeter in the area of Scarlet Beach.

Two areas of vital ground to be held at all costs under the 9 Div plan of defence had been left to the enemy. Loss of the vital ground at Jivevaneng held by the 2/17 Bn would have impacted seriously to the detriment of the 9 Div's battle in progress. This, of course, was never envisaged by the 20 Bde, nor by the members of the 2/17 Bn and contributed to the defeat of the enemy's original plan of an advance to Heldsbach with the 80th Regiment.

Reinforced with the arrival in the Fischhafen area of its 26 Bde, and after fierce encounters with the enemy, the 9 Div's battle for Katika lasted until the night 25/26 Oct when the Japanese commenced withdrawal along the route from whence they had come. Thereafter, the 24 and 26 Bdes pushed their FDLs forward and during the period 26-29 Oct strong fighting patrols with artillery support harried the retreating enemy and inflicted many casualties. General Katagiri, with originally only 7 mountain guns had no answer to the effective firepower of the 2/12 Fd

Regt and the 2/6 Fd Regt which made great contributions in support of the infantry units to the defeat of the enemy counter-attack at Katika.

The Japanese losses in the counter-offensive were extremely heavy. Enemy dead counted were 679, many others had been buried and many were probably never discovered. A conservative estimate of enemy battle casualties was 1500. Own battle casualties for the period 16-28 Oct were 228 including 3 Offrs and 46 Ors killed.

The defeat of the enemy counter-offensive allowed the 9 Div's resumption of the offensive and the immediate aim was the capture of the high ground Sattelberg Palanko by the 26 Bde, with a view to a subsequent advance to the Gusika-Wareo line. The plan involved the relief of the 20 Bde by the 26 Bde and as a preliminary, the elimination of the enemy pocket astride the Sattelberg Track east of Jivevaneng.

These lines would be incomplete without mention of the sterling work performed by the pilots of the "Boomerang" reconnaissance aircraft that flew fearlessly at low altitude over enemy territory in search of information. Often they would drop packages to the 2/17 Bn at Jivevaneng which contained tobacco and cigarettes, always welcome commodities.

JIVEVANENG

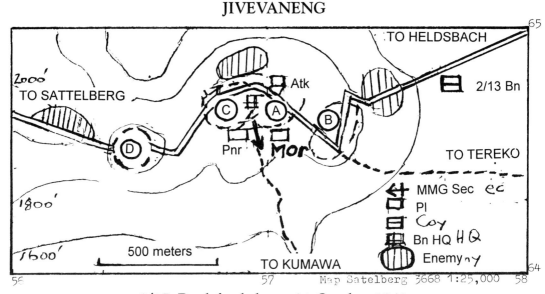

2/17 Bn defended area 31 October 1943

A COY & 12 PL, B COY 2/17 BN WITH 2/13 BN REOPEN THE L OF C

On 25-26 Oct, when the enemy commenced withdrawal from Katika, 2/17 Bn patrols were active and the enemy was harassed with artillery, mortars, LMGs and Cup Dischargers. Elements of the 2/13 Bn were in position east of the enemy's positions across the Sattelberg Track at a place named "Coconut Grove". A new direct signal line was laid to Bde HQ via Tareko and lateral communication with the 2/13 Bn was maintained to co-ordinate future operations.

The enemy targeted listening posts on Jivevaneng FDLs by infiltration and sneak sniper attacks. These tactics achieved some success and casualties were sustained mainly when the posts were being relieved. On 27 and 28 Oct 8 Pl A Coy had a soldier killed[1] each day in these circumstances.

During the 29 Oct, the usual movement was observed among the enemy positions forward of 2/17 Bn HQ. This was always engaged by cup discharger grenades and mortars. Late in the afternoon 3 inch mortars and MGs engaged the enemy position. On this day Brig Windeyer visited 2/17 Bn and reviewed the situation. On a reconnaisance at Cemetery Corner, the position of B Coy 2/17 Bn's daylight standing patrol, which overlooked the area of bamboo where the enemy positions astride the Sattelberg Track were ensconced, he used the phrase, "squeeze them out". B Coy's 12 Pl, commanded by Lt Stuart Williams, was moved quietly to a concealed platoon locality with one section's Bren facing directly down the track at an enemy bunker occupied by four men with a "Woodpecker" at about 20 paces. The enemy bunker had previously been located by a patrol commanded by L/Sgt Eric Sullivan of 12 Pl when the southern flank of the enemy's positions was determined. To have occupied the position under the nose of the enemy in daylight and undetected was a remarkable achievement. The platoon settled in for the first night and improved the position, as each shovel full of earth was handled gently and quietly; so gently that almost all night was required to complete a slit trench.

The story of the following day when the Platoon indicated their presence to the enemy was told by Lt Williams:

> "In the early morning an enemy patrol walked right up to our positions and received a grim welcome. The survivors withdrew having lost 4 killed and several wounded. From then on we had searching small arms fire from the enemy but offered no targets. The Bren gun position was in a reasonably obvious area but they could not pinpoint it — nor could we locate their snipers. We used the rifle and grenade cup discharger from an area just in rear of our positions."

During the afternoon of 29 Oct a small B Coy, 2/17 Bn reconnaisance patrol, commanded by Sgt F P Plunkett, endeavoured to contact the 2/13 Bn troops at Coconut Grove and was ambushed near a track about 150 yards west of the grove when Sgt Plunkett[2] and Pte E J Walmsley[3] were killed. The story was told by Pte R E Lucchinelli of the Bn's Intelligence Section who was with the fateful patrol:

> "Our plan was to move down a minor ridge and when sufficiently far down cut across, recce the area and ultimately to link up with the 2/13 Bn. Slim Walmsley, the scout, had moved from the valley to the top of the ridge leaving us spread out at the bottom. He reached the top, looked about and turned to beckon to us when all hell let loose. He went down immediately and the Japs turned their fire down the valley and moved up the track firing down at us. It was so thick where we were that our vision was almost negligible. Frank Plunkett had started to rise and was about to move us forward when the firing started. He got a burst and by the time we tried to apply a dressing he was gone. Rifle fire could not achieve much in the circumstances and grenades were thrown but it was impossible and the

---

1
   Pte William John Buckett served with the 2/17 Bn in the Tel el Eisa, El Alamein and Lae Campaigns. He enlisted from Lismore, NSW. Cpl Harold William Vernon Priest served with the 2/17 Bn in the Middle East and Lae campaigns. He enlisted from Hobart, TAS.
2
   Sgt Francis Peter Plunkett was an original member of the 2/17 Bn and served in the Tobruk, Tel el Eisa where he was wounded, El Alamein and Lae Campaigns. He enlisted at Glebe, NSW.
3
   Pte Edward James "Slim" Walmsley served with 2/17 Bn in the Middle East and at Lae. He enlisted from Yass, NSW.

only alternative seemed to be to return as quickly as possible by the way we had come. Apparently we had been under observation almost from the time we had moved from the top of the small ridge and they were waiting for us in ambush.

We returned to a debriefing by Lt Col Simpson and Brig Windeyer. Frank Plunkett's patrol was not altogether fruitless as evidenced by the Brigade operation order issued that night and by the events of the next few days. The bodies of both men were recovered on 31 Oct near where they were killed; Sgt Plunkett had been moved on to the track."

Brig Windeyer issued an operation order at 2330 hrs on 29 Oct aimed to open the main Sattelberg Track between the 2/13 Bn and the 2/17 Bn positions. The method required close cooperation between the two Bns on timings, a movement forward by the 2/13 Bn under cover of diversionary fire from the 2/17 Bn to gain ground for an attack, and continued pressure on the enemy by the 2/17 Bn at Cemetery Corner. The plan included the ambush of various enemy supply and escape routes.

At last light 30 Oct, the 2/13 Bn had made some progress towards the enemy positions and with the track cut for 13 days on 31 Oct, there had been the discomfort of incessant rain for 48 hrs. The morning of 1 Nov was spent on reconnaissance for an attack on the enemy positions east of Cemetery Corner by 9 Pl, A Coy, 2/17 Bn, commanded by Lt K McLeod, and this eventuated at 1130 hrs. The attack made only 20 yards progress in the thick bamboo and the platoon withdrew having suffered 2 casualties.

On 1 Nov Lt Col Simpson, with only a brief warning, left the 2/17 Bn to administer command of the 24 Bde and Maj Broadbent, 2 I/C, administered command of the 2/17 Bn in his absence.

The attack on the enemy's positions at Cemetery Corner was resumed at 1000 hrs 2 Nov by Maj Maclarn's A Coy, 2/17 Bn after a diverson by the 2/13 Bn. Lt McLeod's 9 Pl led and reached its objective on the northern side of the track but an effort to move Lt West's 7 Pl through on the right flank failed after the Platoon suffered 6 casualties from withering enemy MG fire. A stalemate developed until 1500 hrs when the 2/13 Bn attempted to move west and made some progress before positions were stabilized for the night. During a reconnaissance, Maj Maclarn was wounded in the leg and Lt Stuart Williams, Commander of 12 Pl, B Coy in support, thereafter took command of the operation.

Only about 150 yards separated the forward troops of both Bns but the enemy was firmly wedged in between them amongst the bamboo. By arrangement, "Tally Ho – the Red Fox", Lt Col Simpson's nickname, was called out by men of the 2/13 Bn to indicate their position to their counterparts of the 2/17 Bn opposite. This no doubt would have intrigued any English speaking Japanese soldier that may have listened.

The 2/17 Bn's MG Pl made an important contribution to the attack with two Vickers guns. Apart from the effect of the supporting fire, its destructive volume of bullets had cut down the cane, and laid the enemy's positions bare and untenable to the Japanese psyche.

The story was told by Cpl Roy Roach:

"On 2 Nov my section was given the task of a rapid fire shoot of 2000 rounds to cut down the bamboo which gave the Japs complete cover for their machine gun nest that caused so many casualties. Sgt Toby Harris, DCM, was badly wounded the day before trying to reconnoitre around the corner. A Coy's efforts had failed to silence the MG and because the ground fell away so sharply from the track at Cemetery Corner, our bullets had passed over the enemy's positions.

On orders from Sgt Reay, I chose a new position for maximum results and with 'Mickey'

Rooney as No 2 we did a 5 minute shoot of 8 belts of ammunition, while 9 Pl A Coy was in position on our right, waiting for H hr at 1000 hrs. The shoot went to plan until a smoke bomb from 2/13 Bn nearly suffocated both of us.

The first 9 Pl section to hit the corner ran into concentrated MG fire and 'Blue' Smith, Joe Williams, Paddy Nolan and others were wounded. Then Cpl Bruce Brown's gun went into action with Dave Hall, Derek Cunningham, Bert Kelps and Jim Wilson. Jim Wilson and Dave Hall became casualties. Stretcher Bearer Rapp's work was commendable. We did sporadic shooting with both guns during the day as harrassing tactics."

The 2/17 Bn casualties for the day were 1 Or[1] killed and 1 Offr and 8 Ors wounded.

On the night 2/3 Nov, L/ Sgt Eric Sullivan's forward section of 12 Pl, 2/17 Bn at Cemetery Corner heard nothing unusual, only slight movement below the road. There were however three rifle shots fired in quick succession during the night, heard at 2/17 Bn's B Coy HQ. This was unusual and may have been an enemy signal in a planned withdrawal, for in the morning the positions astride the track were empty except for 5 dead Japanese and much abandoned equipment. An inspection revealed the extent of strongly entrenched positions with overhead cover supported by coconut logs.

The Sattelberg Track was once more open to Bde HQ and the L of C was intact for resupply and casualty evacuation by jeep transport. The semi-isolation of the 2/17 Bn had ended after an uncomfortable period of 17 days.

On 20 Oct, 18 tanks comprised in Maj Hordern's C Sqn, 1 Tk Bn were unloaded at Langemak Bay. Tanks would have greatly assisted in opening the Sattelberg track and saved casualties in the difficult operation. Soldiers of the 2/17 Bn were aware of this. They were also aware that Maj Gen Wootten required the tanks as a surprise weapon in the attack on Sattelberg, where the main approach was a defile which made easy the construction of obstacles to tanks and the effective use of mines. Elaborate precautions were therefore made to conceal the presence of tanks in the area, especially as the Sattelberg Track was under observation from the Sattelberg—Wareo feature. Part of the plan required the tanks movement by night and their noise covered with artillery fire. 9 tanks reached east of Jivevaneng where they were hidden in the cane on 9 Nov, four days after the 2/17 Bn had left the area.

2/17 BN'S C COY GROUP REMOVE LAST ENEMY POCKET AT JIVEVANENG

With the Sattelberg Track open to Jivevaneng, the relief of the 20 Bde began. Maj Gen Wootten was prepared to complete the relief before the enemy pocket north of Jivevaneng was removed but Brig Windeyer informed him the 2/17 Bn would perform this last remaining task. At 1030 hrs on 3 Nov a reconnaissance party of the 2/24 Bn arrived in Jivevaneng in preparation for relief of the 2/17 Bn and at 1130 hrs Brig Windeyer and parties visited the Bn area.

During the morning Capt Dinnings' C Coy planned an attack on the enemy's positions north of Bn HQ. The plan was a frontal assault from the Company's FDLs with Lt W A Graham's 14 Pl right; Lt L A McRae's 13 Pl left; and Lt E J Blundell's 15 Pl in reserve. The attack

---

[1] Pte Ernest Robert Foster KIA joined the 2/17 Bn in the Middle East and served in the Lae Campaign. He enlisted from Drummoyne, NSW.

commenced at 1330 hrs and 14 Pl was able to move forward to the edge of a ridge about 40 yards forward of Bn HQ to thick bamboo. The platoon met fierce opposition and 13 Pl was unable to move the required distance. Fierce fighting at close quarters of about 20 yards ensued the whole afternoon.

Soon after the attack began L/Sgt B G Dawes[1] had one of his Section of 14 Pl killed and three others wounded; Lt Graham was mortally wounded and although only a short distance from the enemy fire, L/Sgt Dawes dragged all casualties to safety and arranged their evacuation while he maintained his Section in action.

Further progress by the forward platoons was not possible but the enemy was held off. At about 1500 hrs, L/Sgt Dawes' Section was counter-attacked by about 25 of the enemy that brought with them a "Woodpecker". The whole enemy force was annihilated by Owen gunners and the accurate fire of the Brens, the barrels of which ran hot and had to be replaced. L/Sgt Dawes had waited until the enemy were within 10 yards before he gave the order to fire. He then established himself in a forward position later found to be only 7 yards from the enemy and despite flood rain and sniper fire, harrassed the enemy for 36 hours. He threw about 60 grenades during this time and his aggressive example helped force the enemy's withdrawal.

At 1600 hrs Cpl J Littlewood's MG Section with Ptes P Larkin and A Mills was positioned on the left flank and supported the attack with effective fire. By last light the forward platoons had partly dug in and consolidated their positions overnight on the ground won. Their slit trenches were just over the edge of the slope and looked down into bamboo and jungle with limited observation. Some enemy positions were tunnels with small peep holes only big enough for a head and shoulders. Pte D McCaffery killed three enemy and had mistakenly cursed his bad markmanship as a helmeted head appeared repeatedly in the same spot. He was relieved to find later three of the enemy dead at the spot, one on top of the other.

The forward platoons were supplied ceaselessly with ammunition and support especially from 15 Pl. Cpl Ian Moore on his own initiative walked into a hail of enemy fire several times to carry Bren gun barrels forward and help wounded back, including Lt Graham whom he carried on his shoulder. Sgt W Pearce also did gallant work with the supply of ammunition. Later 15 Pl moved forward and filled gaps between 13 and 14 Pls caused partly by casualties and the men dug in under heavy rain. Pte R Bevan, the Bn HQ Clerk, was another who risked his life time and again beyond the call of his duty. He died from a sniper's bullet and Capt A J Wright, the Adjutant, remembered his last moments:

> "Bobby was an excellent soldier in his administrative role; cheerful, helpful and efficient but he was beginning to feel the urge to take a more active part in the Bn's warlike efforts. He expressed a wish to take part in the attack some way. He climbed into the lower branches of a rubber tree and was calling out any signs of movement ahead of the troops. A Jap sniper shot him through the chest and the look of surprise and mystification on his face was so terribly apparent as he was helped to the ground. Everyone was fond of Bobby who was younger than most and it was a sad morning for us all. His loss to the efficiency of the Bn HQ staff was very great."

The attack by Capt Dinnings C Coy was described by Cpl Mayne Ready of the A Tk Pl:

> "The most vivid memory I have of Jivevaneng was the final C Coy attack. The memory of

---

[1] L/Sgt B G "Snowy" Dawes was an original member of the 2/17 Bn and served in all its Middle East Campaigns and at Lae. For his valour and contribution to the success of the attack on this occasion, he was awarded the immediate award of DCM. He enlisted from Queanbeyan NSW.

men moving silently forward to face, suddenly, a terrific barrage of fire from the enemy at close range; of men going down and not all getting up; of a bare headed man smoking a cigarette exposing himself to all the elements, giving a word of encouragement here, an order there (Capt John Dinning, MC). The memory of Bob Bevan of Bn HQ, like Clancy of the Overflow, coming out to lend a hand, carrying Bren mags, full ones forward and empty ones back. I remember men diving forward a yard at a time, the continuous chatter of machine guns and ceaseless bursting of grenades and darkness suddenly falling, and rain."

At 1900 hrs the eastern positions at the village were hit with 40 mortar bombs, 81mm, and these caused casualties, 2 killed and 3 wounded. The total casualties for the day's fighting on 3 Nov were 1 Offr DOW[1], 8 Ors KIA[2], and 10 wounded, with 1 remained on duty.

Torrential rain fell during the night 3/4 Nov and filled most of the diggings to a depth of two or three feet with water. Both the command post and the intelligence room were full of water and much valuable equipment and records were damaged. The 2/17 Bn area became a quagmire, in some places covered with about six inches of slimy mud. Forward companies, especially Capt Dinnings' C Coy spent a most unenviable night but everyone remained in good spirits.

Capt Wright remembered the night:

"The rain continued well into the night and being soaked to the skin, everyone was very cold indeed. After the command post filled with water, I remember sitting on a box, back to back with J R B (Maj Broadbent) under our groundsheets trying to get warm. I can also remember seeing a shadowy figure gliding past as we sat. Whether the figure was one of us or a 'Nip' we didn't find out, nor made any effort to, because of the cold. There was concern for the morning with everyone forced above ground."

At first light 4 Nov, L/Cpl F G Mahalm[3], of 14 Pl C Coy, when he endeavoured to take food to his Section, was sniped and died of wounds. Throughout the day fire was exchanged and hand grenades were constantly thrown by both sides.

During the morning of 4 Nov Capt Rudkin's B Coy and Lt Main's D Coy, 2/17 Bn were relieved by companies of the 2/24 Bn. The relief also included Sgt Reay's MG and Lt Swan's

---

1
  Lt William Arthur Graham, DOW, served with the 2/17 Bn in the Lae Campaign. He enlisted from Cooma, NSW.
2
  Pte Robert Mulholland Bevan KIA, served with the 2/17 Bn in the Tel el Eisa, El Alamein and Lae Campaigns. He enlisted from Marrickville, NSW.
  Pte George Calder, KIA, served with the 2/17 Bn in the El Alamein and Lae campaigns. He enlisted from Ryde, NSW.
  Pte Laurence Vincent Cronin, KIA, joined 2/17 Bn in Tobruk and served in the Middle East and Lae campaigns. He enlisted from Balmain, NSW.
  Pte Ronald William Doidge, KIA, served with the 2/17 Bn in the Tobruk, Tel el Eisa, El Alamein and Lae campaigns. He enlisted from Bankstown, NSW.
  Pte William James Field, KIA, was a stretcher bearer attached to the 2/17 Bn from the AAMC. He enlisted from Harvey, WA.
  Pte Norman Thomas Kenyon, KIA, served with the 2/17 Bn in the Tel el Eisa, El Alamein and Lae campaigns. He enlisted at Paddington, NSW.
  Pte Norman John McNeilly, KIA, joined the 2/17 Bn in the Middle East and served in the Lae Campaign. He enlisted from Hurstville, NSW.
  Pte John William Ratcliffe, KIA, served with the 2/17 Bn at Tobruk, Tel el Eisa, El Alamein and Lae. He enlisted from Redfern, NSW.
3
  L/Cpl Frederick George Malhalm DOW served with the 2/17 Bn in it Middle East and lae Campaigns. He enlisted from Waverley, NSW.

Mor Pls. In the late afternoon there was more enemy mortar and artillery fire targeted in the defended area but no casualties were sustained by the 2/17 Bn.

The informative and succinct War Diary of the 2/17 Bn for its last day at Jivevaneng Village is recorded hereunder in tribute to the diarist:

"5 Nov: First light revealed that the enemy positions forward of C Coy had been vacated during the night. It was a scene of desolation with bodies and equipment everywhere. The distance between enemy positions and those of C Coy varied from 3 yards to near 14 Pl to 20 yards forward of 13 Pl. This gives some idea of the task undertaken by C Coy and how well they stuck to their job. 10 bodies only were counted in the area but there was ample evidence that many more casualties had been inflicted. We were now in the pleasant position of being able to hand over the area to the 2/24 Bn, clear of the enemy. The work of the Bn had been of great tactical importance as the area could be used as a base for further offensive operations against the Sattelberg area. From paybooks etc. the enemy force was identified as elements of I Bn 79 Regt, a new unit in the area. Evidently a relief had been effected during the last few days with 2 Coy, 8 Bn, 80 Regt, the previous unit identified in the area. Several types of enemy equipment were recovered (listed) and were returned to salvage. A Coy relief was completed by 1400 hrs, C Coy by 1415 hrs and Bn HQ by 1430 hrs. Sub-units marched to the new Div reserve area near Heldsbach. YMCA provided tea and biscuits as companies moved through Bde HQ to Heldsbach Village."

On 6 Nov the effective strength of the 2/17 Bn was 20 Off-rs and 437 Ors. Everyone took full advantage of the first day of rest; without exception they washed their clothes which they had not taken off for many weeks. Clothing issues were made and there was a general canteen issue. Plenty of material was available to make shelters comfortable and a new atmosphere pervaded the place. Maj Broadbent administered command of the Bn and he congratulated Capt Dinning's C Company for its fine effort in destroying the last Japanese pocket of resistance at Jivevaneng.

The Queen's Colours of the 17 Bn, laid up at peace in St Thomas Church at North Sydney, bear the Battle Honour, "Jivevaneng - Kumawa". This Chapter has related some stories of the battles, told by men who were there. It was impossible to record in the pages all that happened and every brave deed; inevitably much has remained "unseen or unsung". The deeds of some men who suffered wounds and others have been partly lost in time, as these pages have been written long after events, when many survivors of the battles have passed on, including some who have contributed to these lines. Time has not however, removed records of the main events concerning the history of the 2/17 Bn and these have been mentioned in the narrative.

When the soldiers of the 2/17 Bn first came upon the tiny village of Jivevaneng, it was on a hot day and after they had climbed a steep dirt track, laden with their weapons, ammunition and equipment. There was a cleared and level place for a short rest under the shade of a large rubber tree; a few paw paws to eat; some coconuts to open and quench the thirst, like "nectar from the gods" compared with the chlorine tainted contents of a water bottle. Nearby there were a few deserted native huts; one had been a schoolhouse. The enemy was expected somewhere further along the track. It was a beautiful place.

Later the soldiers came again and fought relentlessly to hold Jivevaneng, as these pages have revealed. Its possession was vital to defeat an enemy counter-attack and stage a later battle further up the Sattleberg Mountain.

Many men of three countries suffered and many died in the Village. Of the dead and

---

1

Cpl Carr-Boyd was killed in action at Kumawa.

wounded, many more were Japanese than were Australians and Papuans. The stately tree, overlooked by the mountain, became an aiming mark for enemy artillery and mortars and all became ugly in the destruction and carnage of warfare.

Because there was a risk of more death, the bodies of some soldiers lay and decomposed where they had fallen until it was perhaps safe to recover them for burial. The soldiers' privation with shot and shell was worsened by the heat and persistence of flies by day, the cold at night, and rain in deluge which filled their trenches, and their existence thereafter became even more uncomfortable in a quagmire of mud and slime.

In defence of the vital ground on which the Village stood, the high spirits of the Australians never wavered and when the time came for attack their courage was indomitable against a brave and determined enemy. In the thoughts of the men who survived, the words "Jivevaneng" and "Kumawa" became not only a Battle Honour but a small part of Australia's hallowed ground abroad, with the last resting places of their Comrades who died there, in the War Cemetery at Lae.

The years since 1943 have returned the Mountainside to its natural beauty. If the Jivevaneng Village survives, may it continue to have a schoolhouse and may its children study something of their Village history, when brave men from foreign lands fought, suffered and died for its possession. Perhaps the children of the school, far removed in time from the arrows and spears of their Village ancestry, in an enlightened age, may ask themselves, "Why was it so?"

POSTSCRIPT

Post World War 2, the 2/17 Battalion AIF Association undertook two return visits to the battlefield in the Finschhafen area. The first occasion was in October 1993 to commemorate, fifty years thereafter, the Battalion's operational success during the War.

The second occasion was to dedicate a Memorial at Jivevaneng to commemorate the fortitude of the Battalion, with support, in the defence of the area during the months of September to November, 1943, and in memory of fallen comrades. On each occasion the Touring Party paid homage to fallen comrades by a visit to their graves in the Lae War Cemetery.

The Tour Leader on both occasions was Maj General John Broadbent who administered command of 2/17 Bn during the last stage of the enemy's defeat in the battle for Jivevaneng and for part of the time in the pursuit to Sio.

In 1993 the visitors were fortunate for the assistance of Lt Col Colin Baker of the Matheson Library, UNITECH, Lae, who, with the help of his wife Sandra, fostered the party, arranged for transport, accommodation, rations and medical requirements at Dregerhafen and throughout the tour.

The experience of the earlier tour helped planning of the 1997 tour and great assistance and co-operation was forthcoming from Maj Brad Hampton and Capt James Dickson of the Australian Defence Staff located at the Papuan New Guinea Defence Academy in Lae. Capt Dickson supervised the building of the Obelisk, and Maj Hampton did the over-all local administrative planning which he executed in a competent and efficient manner, in keeping with the high standard expected of the Australian Army. The support throughout of Lt Col Bill Kavanamur, Commander of the Lae Area of the Papua New Guinea Defence Force, and the work of the cadets of the Papua New Guinea Defence Academy who built the Memorial, is acknowledged with thanks. The Tour Party was especially appreciative of the hospitality extended by Maj Hampton with wife Victoria, and Capt Paul Hobbs with wife Christine, who were joint hosts in their quarters at Igam Barracks, when twice the Bn members staged at Lae overnight.

The Memorial, constructed of river stones and cement, is near the location of the Bn's HQ in 1943. It features two plaques, one in English and the other in Pidgin and was dedicated on 13 November, 199'7 in the presence of the Village Committee and local population. Maj Gen Broadbent addressed the throng in English, and his words were duly interpreted into Pidgin English. Lt Col Kavanamur then spoke in Pidgin. Following the speeches, each man simultaneously unveiled the plaques draped in the Australian and Papua New Guinea flags respectively. Maj S (Tex) Morton, an Ex - 9 Div Chaplain, completed the dedication ceremony, followed by traditional drum music from the Village Band.

Soldiers of the 2/17 Bn who died north of the Song River, at Jivevaneng or Kumawa were:

NX 16022 Cpl C J T Anderson 10/10/43	NX 2450 Pte D B Harding 10/10/43
NX 16125 Cpl W K Bartlett 28/10/43	NX 77843 Pte R S Holder 17/10/43
NX 8390 Pte R M Bevan 3/11/43	NX 23798 Sgt T Johnson 16/10/43
NX 47960 Pte B C Blanch 12/10/43	NX 37187 Pte N T Kenyon 3/11/43
NX 25410 Pte T Brown 9/10/43	NX 51608 L/Cpl F G Mahalm 4/11/43
NX 46796 Pte W J Buckett 27/10/43	NX 94575 Pte N J McNeilly 3/11/43
NX 55590 Cpl L C Burrell 13/10/43	NX 41766 Pte K A Miller 9/10/43
NX 57044 Pte G Calder 3/11/43	NX 46963 Pte C F Nash 16/10/43
NX 22438 Cpl B R Carr-Boyd 7/10/43	NX 91491 Pte J F Neil 10/10/43
NX 29076 Pte L V Cronin 3/11/43	NX 85704 L/Cpl L O'Brien (MPD) 16/10/43
NX 57297 Pte H Daniels 10/10/43	NX 46385 Pte F W Peters 9/10/43
NX 21264 Pte R W Doidge 3/11/43	NX 17455 Sgt F P Plunkett 29/10/43
NX 82953 L/Cpl J G Dwyer 6/5/44	NX 58646 Cpl H W V Priest 28/10/43
WX 8350 Pte W J Field 3/11/43	NX 52334 Pte J W Ratcliffe 3/11/43
NX 21759 Pte S H Fitzhenry 10/10/43	NX 58783 Pte J L Ryan 16/10/43
NX 83417 Pte E R Foster 2/11/43	NX 50991 Lt W A Graham 3/11/43
NX 23665 Sgt E D Tasker 16/10/43	NX 14254 Cpl E S Grant 9/10/43
NX 60374 Pte E J Walmsley 29/10/43	

LEST WE FORGET

Location of enemy road block east of Jivevaneng, 1943.   (AWM 71184)

CHAPTER 19
PURSUIT TO SIO

The Bn had gone into action at Scarlet Beach with a strength of 31 Offrs and 703 Ors. It came out of Jivevaneng with 20 Offrs and 432 Ors, including many reinforcements. Those figures tell their own story of the worst operational conditions in the history of the Bn. The ordeal at Jivevaneng was much more severe physically than at Tobruk. The rations were never sufficient and, during the frequent rain the men lived for days on end in clothes which could not be changed or dried. They will never forget those weeks in the mountains below Sattelberg.

After relief by 2/24 Bn, the Bn moved on 6 Nov some 6,000 yds down the Sattelberg track to the Heldsbach Plantation where companies were dispersed and developed an all-round defensive position. As part of the Coast Defense Policy, the unit became brigade reserve with responsibility for the defence and co-ordination of all units in the Launch Jetty Beach area. One company was detailed for immediate notice to move to Launch Jetty area on advice from Bde HQ, and the remainder of the Bn was on 2 hours' notice to move within the brigade sector.

Evacuations caused by malaria and dengue fever increased every day and, in November, the total reached 208. Those men were replaced by 116 reinforcements and 103 troops who returned to the Bn.

These evacuations caused many problems and it is interesting to note that, in the period between 13 Nov/3 Jan, there were 6 changes in command of the Bn. This of course had repercussions at company, platoon and section levels and, together with a high number of reinforcements, created a number of problems. It was fortunate that our operational activity was relatively low-key during this period.

Maj John Broadbent was administering command of the Bn as Lt Col Noel Simpson was temporally in command of 24 Bde.

The first few days were spent in building comfortable shelters from the old corrugated iron and other material lying about the plantation. Mosquito nets and new clothing were issued, and large quantities of mail and parcels were delivered, which had been impossible to send up to Jivevaneng. Plenty of fresh water flowed by the company areas and the men lived in comparative luxury.

C Company moved to a position astride the Sattelberg Road near Heldsbach on 8 Nov, and 10 Pl of B Coy was sent to a coast-watching station known as The Jetty but the rest of the Bn remained at the plantation, where a program of training and defence works started.

It was discovered that the average age of the reinforcements arriving each day was only 19 and that they had had little training and no battle experience. The veterans were reshuffled among the companies to train the newcomers A potential NCOs cadre was started under the guidance of the RSM, WO Dave Dunbar, to overcome the shortage of junior leaders. Instruction in section leading and administration, map reading, patrolling and preparation of patrol reports was crowded into four days.

While other units prepared for the attack on Sattelberg heavy shellfire blasted the Japanese

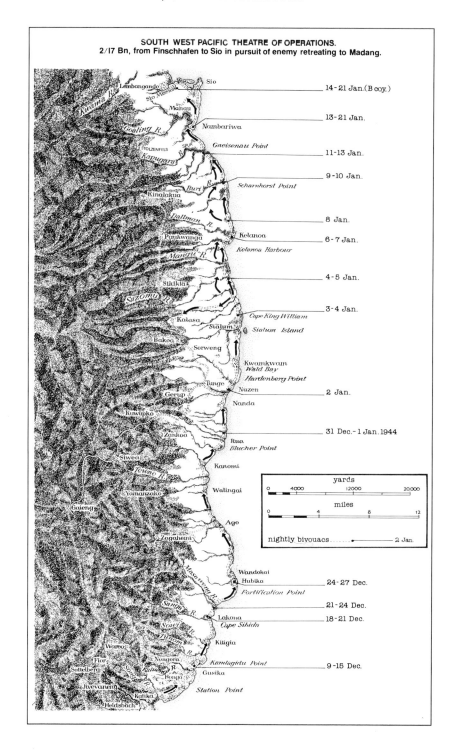

SOUTH WEST PACIFIC THEATRE OF OPERATIONS.
2/17 Bn, from Finschhafen to Sio in pursuit of enemy retreating to Madang.

positions, and at night Matilda tanks moved forward to help the infantry. Bulldozers, graders and supply vehicles turned the main road through Heldsbach Plantation into a sloppy mess.

On the 15 Nov the outline plan for 26 Bde advance towards Sattelberg became known. It was to be a three Bn attack with 2/23 Bn from Kumawa, 2/48 Bn supported by tanks from Jivevaneng and 2/24 Bn from Siki. D Day was 18 Nov and, as the Bn had been so involved at Kumawa and Jivevaneng, these activities were followed with interest by members of the Bn.

On 18 Nov D Coy Comd by Lt Hugh Main and the A/Tk Pl moved beyond Katika to positions overlooking the Song River valley not far from Scarlet Beach. Coy HQ and two platoons formed one group astride the main track and 18 Pl and the A/Tk Pl were about 1,000 yds further west. These two positions gave an excellent view of Sattelberg and Wareo, and 2/6 Fd Regt soon took advantage of them as observation posts.

On 26 Nov orders were issued at 20 Bde HQ for forthcoming operations. The intention was to capture Nongara Village with subsequent exploitation to Wareo feature. The 2/17 Bn role was to assemble on the south bank of the Song River on D minus 1 day. On D day the Bn would advance on the left with 2/15 Bn on the right and 2/13 Bn as Bde reserve.

On 27 Nov Bn orders were issued and all Pl Comds, Pl Sgts and Section Leaders viewed air photos of the area north of Song River and west of Wareo.

A great deal of recce and preparation had been made for this operation and all was ready to commence on 27 Nov. However, following the successes of 26 Bde in the Sattelberg area and a visit by Generals Berriman and Wootten, it was decided to re-assess the whole plan. This resulted in a change to a two-pronged attack by 26 and 24 Bdes on Wareo and the Gusika-Wareo ridge respectively. 20 Bde was reallotted to the coastal thrust towards Sio.

About this time a Pl patrol, led by Lt Barry Waterhouse with some Papuan Infantry, to the Nongara Village found the area had been abandoned by the Japanese. However, on 1 Dec, 2/15 Bn, with Maj Rod Suthers administering Comd, was ordered to advance to this area and beyond and encountered some stiff opposition from scattered Japanese groups.

On 2 Dec, 4 Militia Bde, Comd by Brig Edgar, was concentrated in the Bonga area. Gen Wootten had given a Warning Order to Brig Edgar that: "on a date to be notified, the 4 Inf Bde will advance by the coast route to the mouth of the Masaweng River". It was also decided that the "resting" Bns of the three AIF brigades would provide "experienced AIF personnel" to act as "advisers" to each Bn of 4 Bde. Each team consisted of 3 Offrs, 9 NCOs and 9 Ptes capable of leading sections. Our unit provided a team for attachment to 29/46 Bn to advise and instruct.

The 4 Bde advance commenced on 5 Dec and continued against stiff opposition until this objective at Masaweng River was reached on 20 Dec. During this period, they suffered heavy battle casualties of 65 Killed and 136 Wounded.

The Bn moved forward on 9 Dec to provide flank and rear protection for the Militia Bde, a task entailing much patrolling over rough country. 2/13 Bn took over the coastal advance from 4 Bde after they had crossed the Masaweng River, and on 20 Dec captured Fortification Point.

Members of the Bn were fascinated by a display of 25-pdr sniping just before Fortification Point was occupied. It sounds impossible, but gunners supporting the advance achieved it. Part of the Bn was stationed on a high feature overlooking the Masaweng River, on the far side of which stretched Fortification Point, and nearby was an artillery observation post. Now and again one or two Japs could be seen emerging from cover and setting off across the long track leading around Fortification Point. Every time this happened the delighted gunner on duty would order "Shot one!" The artillery had the range so accurately that the shells landed close to the Japs every time. The point was too distant for MG fire and the infantrymen had to stand and watch the artillery "sniping".

With the capture of Fortification Point, the remnants of the Japanese division, which had threatened Scarlet Beach 10 weeks earlier, became a fleeing rabble chased by 20 Bde.

The Bn, which was in Brigade reserve, did not move until 24 Dec, when it passed beyond Fortification Point through open and hot kunai grass patches to the tiny village of Hubika. Decomposed Jap bodies littered the area and the stench was almost unbearable in some places.

In this hot, dry, evil-smelling place the Bn spent its fourth Christmas. The Christmas feasts of previous years were only a memory. Turkey and ham were served but the helpings were so small that some of the wits called for microscopes. The contents of Australian Comforts Fund parcels helped improve the meal. There was not even one bottle of beer in the Bn. To get a drink of water it was necessary to walk about 2 miles up a creek bed to where a tiny spring of clear water had been found. A Church Service was held in the morning and an impromptu concert at night.

The Bn followed 2/15 Bn to Wandokai, from which was planned an amphibious attack on Sialum further up the coast. This proposal was cancelled and the unit marched on to Walingai.

On 4 Jan 1944, the Bn became the advanced guard for 20 Bde and, with D Coy leading, moved up to the southern side of Kelanoa Harbour. Two Jap stragglers were killed and a sick one captured. One was killed by a patrol led by Sgt Bill Taylor of 18 Pl D Coy.

17 Pl went forward as a patrol along the shores of the Harbour and killed three more Japs who had been unable to keep ahead of the swiftly-moving Australians. It came under long-range MG fire from Chissi Point on the far side of the Harbour but had no casualties, although a bullet went through one man's haversack. Pte L Guest, the Pl's forward scout, was approaching the Mangu River when he was suddenly confronted by two Japs whom he killed.

The hardest task on these long, weary marches up the coast of the Huon Peninsula was that of the inland column, which had to move along about 1,000 yds from the sea. The route usually lay over a series of rough coral ridges slashed by deep gullies and interspersed with islands of hot kunai grass.

When B Coy reached Chissi point it found that the Japanese had moved on. Patrols to the Dallman River reported that the only signs of the enemy were the bodies of some of them and items of abandoned equipment.

The other companies moved forward on 6 Jan through Kelanoe Village to the Dallman

C Coy moving through Kunai grass

River. The Japanese opened up with machine guns at extreme range from the other side of the river but most of the fire fell well short of the unit positions. Patrols killed a few Jap stragglers.

The next day, a strong patrol from C Coy was sent north along the western bank of the Uenaga River, where scattered equipment revealed that the Japs had had an engineers' dump.

About this time, Capt Alan Wright, OC Coy, reports another example of artillery "sniping". His forward platoon had reported that they had reached a very deep, sheer ravine which was dominated by a MG post on the other side covering the approaches from every direction. There was no sign of Jap activity but the Arty FOO was taken forward and asked if his guns would deal with it. The FOO studied his map with some misgiving but was keen to give it a go anyway. The gun lines were back on the Song River, so he was close to maximum range. However, he radioed his fire order and shot one was on its way. The gun was heard by all and almost immediately followed by the arrival of the shell which slammed bang into the MG post blowing it to pieces. Everyone stood there goggle-eyed with amazement — especially the FOO. After congrats all round and no further Jap activity, the advance continued.

The tracks leading down to the river had been mined and the ridge was honeycombed with pillboxes. This was the first attempt that the Japs had made to form a defence line against the Australian advance up the coast but they had failed to occupy the positions and the way lay open for the next stage of the move towards Sio.

After crossing the Dallman River, A Coy, Comd by Capt Jim Dick, took over the advance towards Scharnhorst Point. The flank guard, 9 Pl under Comd of Lt Harry Lindsay, moved out early some 1,000 yds to pick up the inland track and move abreast of the main body moving along the coast. However, with the nature of the country, they were soon out of radio contact and were not heard of again until the afternoon of the following day.

The vanguard moved forward along the coastal track and soon after crossing the Dallman River the forward scout[1] was killed and the second scout was slightly wounded in the leg in going to his assistance. 7 Pl, under Comd of Lt Rutledge, was ordered to do a "left hook" to find the enemy flanks, while 8 Pl gave harassing fire to keep the enemy's head down.

7 Pl made the jungle over open ground without incident but then ran into Jap-defended positions. Lt Rutledge was wounded in the hip soon after entering the jungle, but continued to direct operations and report results over the Walkie-Talkie set to Coy HQ. The Platoon, which was only about 11 strong, were outnumbered and were ordered to withdraw. Two men went to assist Lt Rutledge out and, as they were picking him up, a Jap stood up in his fox hole and threw a grenade. The grenade wounded both men and it was thought that Lt Rutledge had been hit again and killed. The two men crawled out and were picked up by the rest of the platoon who then withdrew as ordered.

The Company was ordered to pull back and a troop of 25-pdrs was moved up to fire over open sights at the Jap positions indicated by A Coy Comd. Also a section of MMG was brought forward to fire at the same targets.

After this barrage, a patrol from A Coy was sent forward to recce the area and it was found to be unoccupied. Lt Rutledge was found still alive by this patrol, but badly wounded, having been hit again in the shoulder by our own 25-pdrs.

Lt Rutledge had joined the Bn as a Reinforcement Offr on 24 Dec and had little opportunity to meet many members outside his Comd during his short stay. Fortunately, he recovered from this harrowing experience, but did not return to the Bn.

---

1   VX91739 Pte Gordon Edward Harris, A Coy — KIA 8-1-44, aged 26 years. He enlisted from Mansfield, VIC.

By the middle of the afternoon C Coy, by-passing the enemy position, had crossed the Uenaga River and captured its objective, a dominating hill. The Japs who were not killed escaped into the thick jungle.

A Coy set off next morning with a troop of Matilda tanks which, however, soon became bogged on the soft inland track. The presence of several dead Japs showed how accurate the fire of the 25-pdrs and machine guns had been.

B Coy, Comd by Capt Ray Rudkin, passed through A Coy and the advance Pl, Comd by Lt Chicka Rogers, contacted about 30 Japs armed with one MMG, two LMGs, one light mortar and rifles holding a line of the creek. In the subsequent attack our losses were 1 KIA,[1] 1 DOW,[2] and 4 wounded, but with Arty, Mortars and Tank support, B Coy captured the enemy positions across the Buri River and remained overnight. At "stand to" the next morning, two Japanese hiding in the bunkers committed "Hari Kari" on being challenged by our troops.

At this time it is appropriate to mention the work of the A/Tk Pl or Tank Attack Pl as it was then called, in its new role of flank protection. Since leaving Sialum area on 4 Jan, half the platoon, with an attachment of PIB scouts were used to move along the inland routes, checking back tracks, abandoned dumps and camps. The PIB men also checked native reports of Jap movements in the area. On 11 Jan, one of the Pl patrol crossed the Kapugara River to reach a sheer cliff face 20ft in height with wooden ladder destroyed. It is alleged that Ptes "Kanga" Gillespie and Les Barber scaled the cliff, captured a Jap prisoner, found some rope which enabled the advance to continue. The patrol moved on and occupied the 550 feature, the highest part of the Stolzenfels Spur where it was later joined by an artillery observation party.

Meanwhile, Capt Wright reported that C Coy was called down from the heights to go into Bn reserve and given permission to have a clean-up with a beach parade. At about 1800 hrs, with most of the Coy either in the water or drying themselves on the beach, two American "Lightning" aircraft turned in and strafed the beach – they came in for a second run very low with sand and water flying everywhere. They turned again but this time, evidently realising their error, they waggled their wings as they flew away. It was amazing and decidedly fortunate that, with 100-odd men exposed, not a single member was hit or injured. The CO was not amused and neither were the members of C Coy.

The Japanese obviously attached great importance to the Kapugara Gorge in the Stolzenfels Spur area which had been used as a staging camp, but the whole area was abandoned in a disgustingly filthy state. At the mouth of the river, there was ample evidence of the destruction caused by the American PT boats where two wrecked barges, an armed patrol boat and a submersible barge were found. Fortunately for us they decided not to defend the area.

Following the route made by the A/Tk Pl, A Coy resumed the advance up the coast on 13 Jan and reached the Goaling River opposite Nambariwa. The crossing of this wide, sluggish river was made in boats that the demoralised Japanese had left on the near bank. Another prisoner was taken and Nambariwa occupied.

C Coy arrived at the river but was too late to cross before dark. It killed 4 Japs and settled down for the night, and A Coy killed an officer and a private at dusk. Equipment captured included 2 mortars of a new type and a 75mm field gun.

Forward patrols reached the Bde objective, Sio Mission, next day and the rest of the Bn

[1] NX43432 Pte John Terance Reilly, B Coy — KIA 9-1-44, aged 21 years. He enlisted from Billinudgel, NSW.
[2] NX200978 Pte Arthur George Croft, B Coy — DOW 9-1-44, aged 27 years. He enlisted from Moree, NSW.

Rope ladder erected at Gneisenau Point

moved up from the Kapugara Gorge. It was obvious that Sio had been used as a staging area for more than 1,000 men who, according to the natives, had left a fortnight before.

2 Japs were killed and 2 were taken prisoner next day. The bodies of 15 others were counted, evidence of how malaria, typhus and dysentery had reduced the strength of the virile enemy who had fought so doggedly around Finschhafen and Sattelberg.

With the other coys settled in between Sio Mission and Nambariwa, B Coy and the A/Tk Pl established a firm base at the mission, from which vigorous patrolling resulted in the death or capture of many more Japs who had been too sick or demoralised to keep ahead of the Australian advance.

During the clean-up operation, the death occurred of a gallant ANGAU Offr, Capt Lou Pursehouse, who was shot by a lone sniper south of Sio lagoon. He had been attached to the Unit during the advance and his local topographical knowledge was of great assistance. He interrogated about 350 natives collected by the Bn during this time. Capt Pursehouse had been part of a Coast Watching team in the coastal area since March when he witnessed the battle of the Bismarck Sea. This team had provided valuable information of every movement prior to and during the battle for Finschhafen. As an old boy of North Sydney Boys High School, he was well known to a number of members of the Bn.

All members of the Bn became excited when 6 Offrs and 30 Men were detailed for "special duty". Everybody hoped that this was the advance party for the return to Australia.

Patrols spent the following days clearing the Sio area of the enemy, helped by the Papuan Inf, which combed the foothills and outlying country. Scores of Japanese dead lay among the scattered dumps of guns, rifles and equipment.

The advance party of 4 Militia Bn arrived on 18 Jan to take over the Sio Mission area. This was the end of the 9 Div campaign in New Guinea, a campaign which had resulted in the capture of Lae, Finschhafen, Sattelberg and all the Huon Peninsula. His operational bases safely held, Gen MacArthur had already begun his big island operations in the north. The danger of a Japanese invasion of Australia had gone and the great net of Allied land, air and sea power had begun to close in on Japan.

The 20 Bde advance from the Masaweng River to the Sio Mission was tame compared with earlier operations but it had meant a lot of walking over rough country in hot humid conditions which made the long marches tiring and irritating. The last 26 miles of the 52-mile advance were covered by 2/17 Bn in 11 days. Incidentally, that does not sound an impressive achievement until it is realised that the flanks had to be continually patrolled and the column was held up for more than a day in places while deep patrols probed the foothills.

During the advance, the Bn had killed 65 japs, counted 72 bodies and taken 7 prisoners. Our losses were: - 2 KIA, 1 DOW, 9 WIA, 1 MPD (Angau).

The Salvation Army officer attached to the Bde, earned the gratitude of the troops in the march up the coast by supplying them with amenities. Many times, even when they were moving forward, he prepared hot, sweet coffee for every man.

The 4 Bn took over the Sio Mission and the Bn returned by landing craft to the Saparo River, where a training program was introduced. Many of the men were comparatively new reinforcements and needed intense instruction in infantry operations.

All coys moved back to Kelanoa Harbour on 28 Jan, and 2 days later to the Masaweng River behind Fortification Point. By this time, there had been substantial evacuations as a result of malaria, dengue fever and hookworm and the unit strength at the beginning of February was only 16 Offrs and 372 Men.

The Bn spent its most pleasant month in New Guinea here on the Masaweng River. Training was restricted to a few hours a day, and picture shows and impromptu concerts were held.

It was not long before the wide river was denuded of fish for about a mile. Grenades were plentiful and the dull boom of explosions was frequently heard at the camp. The stunned fish were collected as they floated downstream. They made a delicious addition to the monotonous rations.

The divisional commander, Maj-Gen Wootten, enjoyed the Bn's sports meeting on 12 Feb so much that he stayed until the last event was over. Coy rivalry was keen and the points-score competition resulted in a dead-heat between B and C Coys with 26 points. D Coy was close third with 25; HQ with 17 and A with 4. Individual results were:

100yds: J Faulkner (HQ), 220yds: C Brede (D), broad jump: J Faulkner (HQ), shot putt: T Cottee (C), hop, step and jump: T Gardiner (B), high jump: H Gillham (B), long kick: P H Bascombe (HQ), 440 and 880yds relays: D Coy, tug-o'-war: C Coy.

The Bn was well beaten in the Brigade sports a few days later. 2/15 Bn gained 54 points, 2/17 Bn gained 36 and 2/13 Bn gained 19.

After a series of small coy trials, the Bn held its swimming championships at Coconut Beach. The starting board kept falling apart and sinking but the competitors and spectators were undeterred. Pte D Cunningham (HQ) had narrow wins in the 50 and 100 yds freestyle, and Ptes R Sullivan and A McHugh, both of HQ, were not extended in the 200 yds freestyle and 100 yds backstroke respectively.

The Bn had an easy victory at the Bde carnival 2 days later. 2/15 Bn was second and Bde HQ third, but 2/13 Bn was stationed so far away it was unable to compete. Ptes Cunningham and McHugh won their events again and Sullivan was just beaten in the 200yds freestyle.

The 20 Bde team finished second of the 4 teams in the Divisional Carnival. McHugh won the backstroke race and Cunningham and W Shaw of C Coy were narrowly beaten in the 50yds freestyle. Cunningham came 3rd in the 100yds. The water polo team, including Sullivan and McHugh, won its heat but was beaten by 2 goals to 1 in the final. Lt MacPherson of D Coy outclassed the other competitors in the springboard and high diving.

The five Bn representatives were members of the 9 Div team which beat the rest of the Corps at the next carnival. Interference robbed McHugh of a win in the backstroke and he and Sullivan were members of the water polo team which won by 8 goals to nil.

Cunningham, Sullivan, McHugh and Shaw finished a close third in the relay and Lt MacPherson won both the diving events easily.

The month of rest, sport and comparatively good food improved the general health and the troops were fit when they moved by trucks to the Song River on 26 Feb, the final step leading to embarkation for Australia.

Before the Bn left its bivouac area on 2 Mar to board the steamer "Klip Fontein", 7 Offrs and 138 Ors, Comd by Capt R S Rudkin, represented the Unit at the dedication of the War Cemetery near the Bumi River at Finschhafen. The long rows of white crosses were in two sections, Australians on one side of the road and Americans on the other. Just inside the entrance to each section stood a concrete monument like the one at Tobruk.

So ended the Bn's part in the New Guinea campaign, in which it had lost 63 all ranks either KIA, DOW or MPD, 160 WIA and hundreds evacuated sick.

The Bn had triumphed over its new enemy. It had found him tough and willing to die and, although it had had some anxious moments at Scarlet Beach, Kumawa and Jivevaneng, its Members had considered themselves superior to him at all times. Not once had the unit yielded ground in the face of an attack.

Physically, the campaign was the most severe that the Bn had ever endured. The long marches through the humid jungle, the nerve-racking fighting at close quarters, the days on end of incessant rain when no clothes could be kept dry and the inadequate food were reflected in the thin faces and lean frames of the troops when they landed at Brisbane on 9 Mar 1944. They had suffered in heart-breaking privations but they were proud that the achievements of their Bn had not been surpassed in the bitter fighting that wrested the Huon Peninsula from the Japanese.

The remains of Soldiers of the 2/17 Bn who died in New Guinea, were exhumed and reinterred at the Lae War Cemetery - except for Captain Pursehouse, whose body may have been washed out to sea and L/Cpl O'Brien, who was missing at Jivevaneng. Both soldiers have no known grave. Those who died on the pursuit to Sio were:

NX200978	Pte Croft A G 9/1/44
VX91739	Pte Harris G E 8/1/44
PX178	Capt Pursehouse L 17/1/44 (ANGAU attached) (MPD)
NX43432	Pte Reilly J T 9/1/44

LEST WE FORGET

The soldiers' remains have been exhumed and moved to the War Cemetery at Lae, except for Captain Pursehouse, whose body may have been washed out to sea, and L/Cpl O Brien, who was missing at Jivevaneng. Both soldiers have no known grave.

CHAPTER 20
RETRAINING

Having returned to Australia and gone on well deserved leave during April 1944, virtually all of the Battalion were suffering not only from the physical strain of the campaign but more especially from the medical consequences of the tropical jungles of New Guinea.

At a parade on arrival back in Brisbane, Lt Col Simpson announced that he had relinquished comd of the battalion and had been appointed to comd 2/43 Bn.

Lt Col J R Broadbent was appointed to command 2/17 Battalion on 28 February 1944.

NX12225 John Raymond Broadbent, CBE, DSO, ED, was born at Manly on 24 June 1914, and was a solicitor in civil life. Before the War he served in the Sydney University Regiment, being commissioned on 9 February 1937. He was an original member of 2/17 Bn, joining in May 1940, and served with the Battalion throughout the War, being promoted Captain 1940, Major 1942 and Lt Col 1944. He was

J R Broadbent

a dedicated officer, strict in maintaining discipline and unrelenting in ensuring that all under his command were thoroughly trained and physically fit. He led by example.

In post war years, in addition to pursuing his legal profession, he made time to continue soldiering, being promoted Brigadier 2 July 1955 to command 5 Infantry Brigade and Major General on 1 December 1963, as General Officer Commanding 2 Division, Citizen's Military Force. He was awarded the DSO on 21 April 1944 and the CBE in 1967.

During May personnel gradually returned from leave and moved to a new camp site at Ravenshoe in the Atherton Tablelands. On return their chief occupation was devoted to improvement of their new camp and, towards the end of the month, commenced organised sports. Reassembling the Bn was a slow process due to the high incidence of malaria amongst all ranks, with daily evacuations at times exceeding the numbers returning from leave.

June and early July saw more returning from leave and hospital, plus general reinforcements joining the Bn. Training was intensified including the start of a jungle course and field firing. It became clear that there was need for considerable training by all ranks in patrolling, particularly among new arrivals who had no previous experience. A large draft of ORs from the disbanded 5 Inf Bde joined the Bn bringing strength nearer to the war establishment. On 8 July the Bn set out on a march to Mt. Garnet, arriving there on 11 July. On 14 July a divisional review was held on the racecourse with the troops being inspected by General Sir Thomas Blamey who was accompanied by Lt Gen Sir Leslie Morshead. The following day a race meeting was held which was much enjoyed.

Major F A Mackell, who had rejoined the Bn on 11 Jun as Bn 2 i/c, was seconded on 17 July to take up duties on the Combined Ops Staff at the War Office London.

At the political level there was a great deal of uncertainty about the future role of Australian troops. MacArthur's planning at one stage envisaged a couple of Australian divisions being used, as part of the American forces, for operations in the Phillipines, but this would have involved re-equipping Australian troops with American weapons and equipment and placing Australian divisions under American Command. Blamey and the Australian Government would not agree to such a move.

Despite this higher level uncertainty, training continued to be comprehensive at individual, company and battalion level. In the middle of August Bn exercises were held with a battery of 2/12 Artillery Field Regt and mortars and heavy machine guns in support. In September the Bn moved to a camp in the vicinity of Trinity Beach for training in amphibious operations over a few days.

The Bn was to begin a very long training period but that could not then be known. Throughout the period sometimes large batches of reinforcements arrived consequent on the disbanding of units not in the main AIF Divs. Reinforcement officers also arrived who ultimately took the unit beyond establishment.

They arrived as strangers, the assimilation required understanding and effort. Surplus officers were of considerable advantage. Assistants could be posted to various appointments including Adjt and IO. Routine duties were more widely spread and special duties easily filled. Availability for umpiring in field exercises was real, assistance in enforcing the tactical lessons.

In the period, Padres and RMOs were to change. Capt T A R Dinning had been a well accepted replacement of 'Snow' Hughes but had had to leave on medical downgrading. The MO to arrive and be with the Bn to the end was Capt Frank Ritchie. His efficiency, virile approach and keen participation in Bn activities made him popular and valuable.

Broadbent was intent that new and old would be integrated into one efficient team capable of matching the Bn performances of the past with intensified individual abilities. The latter included developing the acute discernment and alertness of forward scouts to almost unbeliev-able standards of calm efficiency.

Another critical factor for the safety of the individual and collective success involved ability in firing from the hip. Jungle firing courses were established and used repeatedly to practice and test the individual in quick and accurate response. In battle practices the training was repeated in more open country.

At this stage there was a remarkable decline in the incidence of malaria due to the introduction of daily dosage of atebrin.

A range allowing Bn weapons was located in a harsh, arid mining area to the west. A visiting team of some six Canadian officers had been sent to view the Bn attack exercise with live firing of Bn weapons. They found it hard to believe that nothing was pre-known of the ground or attack except to the CO and IO, and that deployment and commitment were so rapid, with fire plan on time. Drama and adventure developed as the dry grass countryside caught fire from mortar bombs and smoke. Sig cables chasing the forward coys were on fire as the reserves moved through to complete Phase 2.

During October and November training continued with another 3-day amphibious exercise at the end of November on an LS1 at Cairns. By this time, reinforcements that joined the Bn

Pte Creber winning 440yd race

had reached a reasonably high standard of training. December and January saw less intensive training and many sports activities. Christmas week came and was much enjoyed by all ranks, with many types of sporting activities. On Christmas Day the officers and sergeants did the honours in the men's messes for dinner. Although considerable disappointment was felt by most of the original members of the Battalion in having to spend their fifth Christmas away from home, all messes were happy scenes. They had all been decorated with greenery and sketches "having a shot" at a number of the officers. The troops looked fit and well. Most of them had developed a healthy tan from being able to give their undivided attention to sport.

February and March were very wet with a lot of heavy rain and long periods of misty rain making conditions miserable. Small numbers were proceeding on leave but no major drafts departed. On 11 March all members were warned of pending embarkation for overseas service. Although most members were disappointed that they would not receive leave prior to sailing, the prospect was well received and all ranks were ready for action after the long and intensive training period.

On the night of 15 March a concert was staged in the YMCA hut by members of the battalion under the direction of Pte R Brierley. The Bde Comd, CO and personnel of HQ Coy attended, and the concert was acclaimed a great success, consisting of numerous and varied acts. The CO paid tributes to the individual efforts of organisers and players.

The following night A and B Coys attended the Bn Concert Party's performance and again it was voted first class, with the cast being more relaxed and less self-conscious.

The third night of performance was well attended by C and D Coys and the concert party had proved such a success that its season was extended to allow 2/13 and 2/15 Bns to view the performance. (See *Appendices* for History of Concert Party.)

On 19 March A, B, C and D Coys marched out to carry out night attack exercise in continuing wet and squally weather. Meanwhile a Ceremonial Brigade Guard under Capt H Main rehearsed for the visit of the Governor of NSW, Lord Wakehurst, which occured on 21 March.

During the afternoon of 23 March the battalion moved out for participation in an attack exercise on 24 March. The exercise was intended as practice in "battle innoculation" and battle practice with a final brigade objective, 2/15 Bn right, 2/17 Bn left and the battalions changing over during the afternoon and repeating the attack. 2/8 and 2/12 Fd Regts provided artillery support while Bn MMG'S and mortars concentrated on flank protection. The attack commenced with forward companies "leaning" on the barrage, but some arty fire fell too close to the

A Platoon drill competition under the command of Lt R H Fletcher – Ravenshoe Qld –18 Jan 1945

14 Pl during training

start line and there were three casualties. Maj Colin Pitman received a nasty shell spinter in the leg, having to be evacuated and had a long sojourn in hospital. Capt Wright and one OR received minor injuries. The attack was pressed home and the objectives were taken without further incident.

At 1330 hours the attack again commenced with the two reserve companies of the morning taking the forward positions. A perfect barrage this time with safety precautions improved on the morning's display — no casualties — and the attack was pressed home with vigour. The exercise ended at 1630 hours and, after a hot meal in the bivouac area, the troops were transported back to camp. The exercise had given reinforcements a further example of how artillery can be used to the maximum advantage.

On 31 Mar, 26 general reinforcements marched in as band personnel to HQ Coy. So, after an absence of almost three years (during which time the band instruments had few players to use them), the formation of a battalion band was welcomed. It was not long before they were performing to good effect on parades, route marches and for the general entertainment of the troops. Within a month they had developed into a good combination.

The Concert party and Band provided entertainment of a high standard and planned holding concerts during the foreshadowed voyage.

On 6 April the CO, Adjt and 10 were warned for movement at 12 hours' notice and on 9 April they departed as the planning party. Maj Maclarn assumed adm. comd of the Bn. As the Bn's move overseas would probably be at very short notice packing of equipment in readiness for the trip was speeded up. As a result the latter part of the month could not see general training continue and activity was confined to route marches and general administration.

On 1 May all companies moved out at 0830 hrs on individual all day route marches. A movement order was received and at 1100 hrs the coys were recalled. At 1315 hrs a first draft of 340 moved out in AASC transport: this draft consisted of elements of HQ Coy and B Coy and was under comd of Capt Rudkin. A conference advised that the remainder of the Bn would leave for Townsville at 0800 hrs next morning and, after staging in transitcamp, would board USAT *David C. Shanks*. There was much activity for the remainder of the day striking tents and completing packing of stores.

At 0330 hours 2 May the stores and loading party left. Reveille was at 0500 hours and the rest of the Bn moved off at 0800 hours in AASC trucks for an uneventful trip to Innisfail where they entrained and after lunch moved out at 1500 hours. On arrival at Townsville at 2245 hours they detrained and moved into Oonoonba staging camp. The next three days were spent in the staging camp. Limited leave was granted to personel with relatives or close friends in Townsville — from the large number of applications for leave, one would be entitled to think the Bn was formed in Queensland, not NSW!

On 6 May embarkation on *David C. Shanks* was completed by 1430 hours and at 1800 hours the voyage to Moratai commenced. News was received of VE Day shortly after departing from Townsville. This was a very trim Liberty ship and provided exceptionally good conditions for wartime. There was a general feeling that this was going to be the last big show and morale was high that the War would be finished for good. During the voyage training continued and there were lectures on Borneo. While passing the Finschhafen-Sio coast, the ship moved close inshore and all personnel who had participated in the operations in the area refought the battles of the previous year.

On 11 May the "Shanks" steamed into Biak which was a hive of activity as the Americans had quickly made this island into an important L of C base. Next day and most of the following day were spent at Biak until about 1800 hours when three transports, with two escorting corvettes, steamed out into the setting sun. Disembarkation at Moratai was effected on 16 May and the Bn moved to the staging camp. Next day A Coy moved to the 9 Div area several miles outside the American perimeter to begin clearing the Bn area. By 20 May the whole Bn was concentrated at this Sabit area, the clearing of which had entailed arduous work by the troops and served as a good hardening exercise after the sea voyage.

The planning party rejoined the rest of the Bn on 19 May after an absence of more than 5 weeks. Planning for this operation — OBOE–6 had been both comprehensive and thorough, although subject to several changes and uncertainty in many areas. Fortunately, it had been possible to withold any uncertainty over planning from subordinate commands and eventually present a single stable plan. All troops had, by 27 May, been put in the picture, regarding terrain and the main features of the immediate amphibious operations, from sand table models and air photographs. However, place names had not been disclosed except to those personnel necessary for the planning stage.

Training had consisted of route marches and practice on scrambling nets, and instructions in dealing with Japanese mines and booby traps. On 26 May the Bn moved to the staging area and various supporting arms arrived. Marrying up into boat loads and waves was now complete, ready to move to LS1 HMAS *Kanimbla* the following morning. This move began at 0815 hours

29 May with troops marching one and a half miles in full marching order under a hot sun and humid conditions. They embarked on LSM's and soon reached *Kanimbla* and then boarded via scrambling nets. Aboard, the quarters were stuffy but there was ample space for sleeping on deck. Meals were most satisfactory but the water position was bad. Next day the troops assembled on troop decks in preparation for the disembarkation exercise the following day. The troops moved by waves to the scrambling nets, descended to the landing craft and then returned to the troop decks. Next morning, 31 May, the full exercise was carried out, with the landing craft approaching the beach but the troops not landing. Next two or three days were spent aboard and then, at 1300 hours 4 Jun, *Kanimbla* moved to her convoy position.

OPERATION ORDER — OBOE 6

The Bn operation order was issued on 24 May 1945 and the following are the salient points of the order:

Own Troops 9 Aust Div (less 26 Bde Gp) is to capture the Brunei Bay area to permit the establishment of an advanced fleet base, and to protect oil and rubber resources in the area.

24 Bde Gp is to capture Labuan Island.

20 Bde Gp is to capture area Brunei Bluff — Brooketon and Muara island with two Bns forward.

    (a) Right: 2/17 Bn will land on Green Beach and capture
        Brunei Bluff — Brooketon.
    (b) Left: 2/15 Bn will land on White Beach and capture Muara Island
    (c) Bde reserve 2/13 Bn.

Shipping LS1 HMAS *Kanimbla* is to carry 2/17 Bn Gp.

Intention 2/17 Bn Gp will capture:

    (a) Green Beach
    (b) Cowie Ridge
    (c) Brooketon

Method Summary of Op

The op will be in 3 phases:

    Phase I Amphibious assault on Green Beach.
    Phase II Attack on Cowie Ridge
    Phase III Attack on Brooketon.

PHASE I — Green Beach

Landing

    (a) The Bn Gp will be launched from HMAS *Kanimbla* and will land on Green Beach.
    (b) "H" hour (notified later) expected to be approx 1.5 hours before full tide.

Tps and Objective

    (a) Right D Coy with 4 Pl (less guns)
    (b) Left C Coy will capture Green Beach and 200 yds inland.

Action on Capture — Right

    (a) Mop up.
    (b) Proceed to Phase II immediately

Action on Capture — Left

       (a) Mop up and secure left flank and front of beach head.

       (b) Patrol 1000 yds East to clear beach line.

       (c) Strong fighting patrol to Sand Line to determine:

           (i) Strength and dispositions of enemy in area.

           (ii) Suitability for tanks.

       Ground gained will be held.

PHASE II

Tps and Objectives

       (a) Extreme Right: 4 Pl Task: Clear beach line and capture Brunei Bluff.

       (b) Right: D Coy Objective: Bt Cowie.

       (c) Left: B Coy Objective: Barracks area 615554.

       (d) Reserve: A Coy.

Reserve — Probable Roles

       (a) Assist capture of Derby (Cowie Ridge 610555).

       (b) Execute Phase III.

Action on Capture — Extreme Right — 4 Pl

       (a) Secure Bluff.

       (b) Contact patrol to D Coy.

           Right — D Coy

       (a) Exploit to Derby and Route 6.

       (b) Support B Coy in capture of Geelong Knob (611552).

       (c) Secure line of Cowie Ridge and block Route 6 to West.

       (d) Be prepared to establish standing patrol at junc 601551.

           Left — B Coy

       (a) Support D Coy in capture of Derby.

       (b) Block Route 6 to East.

       (c) Capture Geelong Knob (611552)

       (d) mop up Geelong and secure approaches from South.

       (e) Be prepared to sp Phase III.

PHASE III — Brooketon

Summary of Op   Two Coy attack on Brooketon in SE direction. Plan will operate if A Coy NOT committed in Phase II. Code word "Brooke".

Tps and Objectives

       (a) Right: A Coy Objective Yellow Beach West.

       (b) Left: C Coy (less one pl left flank protection).

       Objective: Yellow Beach East.

Other Services and Supporting Arms

       Naval Bombardment and Support Craft

       Support Fire Control Post will be with Bn HQ.

       Air Support

       Direct air sp is to be given as follows:

           (a) Anti-personnel bombing of area Green Beach, Cowie Ridge

and Brooketon from H minus 35 to H minus 15.

(b) Aircraft will be on air alert to answer calls.

(c) An Air Liaison Post will move with Bn HQ.

Tanks

(a) On landing tks will move along beach line to assembly area and form part of Bn reserve. Tp comd report to Bn HQ.

(b) Phase II probable role of attack on Derby.

(c) Phase III probable roles:

   (i) Tk and inf assault ech with A Coy.

   (ii) Sp C Coy and destroy pillboxes on Sand Line.

15 Bty

(a) Landing: One tp with assault waves on White Beach and one tp on Red Beach.

(b) Phase II: Fire sp as directed by FOO to travel with D Coy.

(c) Phase III: Program will be varied by observation of FOO.

(d) It is noted that sp for Phase III is directly with line of advance of fwd tps.

58 Bty

(a) Landing: One tp (4x75mm) will land Green Beach will NOT be available until assembly completed (probably not before H plus 45).

(b) Phase II (if available) as directed by Bn HQ FOO waits Bn HQ.

(c) Phase III (if available) by observation of FOO, who will move with C Coy.

(d) Bty HQ with Bn HQ.

Mortar 3"

(a) 3 Pl will land all mortars and sp Phase II and III.

(b) Mortar Fire Controllers: one with each B and D Coys and, if directed, one with each A and C Coys.

(c) Number of mortars and amn allotted will be controlled by Pl Comd subject to directions from Bn HQ.

MMG 2 Pl

(a) Phase II: One sec under comd each B and D Coy, Pl HQ with B Coy.

(b) Phase III: If available from Phase II.

   (i) Pl will sp on targets from vicinity Geelong Knob and Derby.

   (ii) After fire plan one sec will cover approaches to Brooketon from South and engage opportunity targets.

MMG B2 Pl 2/2 MG Bn

(a) On landing will come under comd C Coy and assist in protection of left flank.

(b) Phase III: If fire posns available will sp from vicinity left flank.

MMG B3 Pl 2/2 MG Bn

(a) On landing pl will come into res with Pl HQ with Bn HQ.

(b) Guns will be mounted to cover beach line to East and manned by minimum crew.

(c) Remaining personnel will assist unloading under comd QM 2/17 Bn, Capt L.C. Simpson.

RAE

(a) Recce dets (each 3 OR) with C and D Coys on landing Duties normal.

(b) One det (7 OR 1 bulldozer) in sp tank tp.

Pioneers 5 Pl

(a) Two secs local protection Bn HQ. One prepared to move with Tac HQ.

(b) Two secs under comd Capt L.C. Simpson for unloading unit stores, thereafter part of Bn res.

Tpt

(a) One jeep and trlr will land at Green Beach from LCM and report to Bn HQ.

(b) Remainder of Bn tpt will land Yellow Beach and on landing:

(i) Complete initial de-waterproofing.

(ii) Proceed to B Ech area.

(c) Grease and plugs removed in de-waterproofing will be retained for future ops.

It was an imposing convoy made up of approximately 100 vessels in total, comprising the craft to take part in three simultaneous landings at Brooketon, Muara island and Labuan Island. It was a clear indication of the decline in Japanese control of that part of the islands as the convoy passed close to the Halmaheras which were still occupied by the Japanese. Continuing preparations for the operation were carried out during the voyage with a briefing area set up on B deck, with a relief model, maps and air photos of the Brooketon area, and all platoons had full briefings. There were also frequent exercises of movement from the troop deck to scrambling net stations. Likewise there were lectures by BBCAU (British Borneo Civil Administration Unit) officers on Borneo and these were willingly attended and the troops generally very interested. The voyage was quite without incident, with no scares from either aircraft or naval units. 9 Jun saw the convoy steaming down the west coast of Borneo and during the night arrived off Brunei Bay.

Green Beach and Brunei Bay - June 1945

Convoy viewed from Kanimbla

Lt Kennedy briefing his Pl

Concert aboard the Kanimbla

As the Battalion approached their assault landing area the posting of officers was:

CO	Lt Col J R Broadbent		**B Coy**
2 i/c	Maj P H Pike	OC	Capt R S Rudkin
Adjt	Capt J D McFarland	2i/c	Capt K T McLeod
Ass/Adjt	Lt H R J Lindsay	10 Pl	Lt D A Williams
IO	Lt B Waterhouse	11 Pl	Lt M P Trudgeon
RMO	Capt F L Ritchie	12 Pl	Lt R E Kennedy
Ass/IO	Lt B Cunningham		
			C Coy
	HQ Coy	OC	Capt A J Wright
OC	Maj L C Maclarn	2i/c	Capt E J Blundell
1 Pl Sigs	Lt G Brooks	13 Pl	Lt B I Delves
2 Pl MMG	Lt D H Vickers	14 Pl	Lt J W Mussett
3 Pl Mort	Lt P I Pollock, Lt H J	15 Pl	Lt G Simpson
Philp			
4 Pl A/Tank	Lt R J Moran		
5 Pl Pioneers	Lt D M Wood		**D Coy**
6 Pl Adm	Capt L C Simpson	OC	Maj N B Trebeck
TO	Lt A J C Hewitt	2i/c	Lt B Forster
		16 Pl	Lt J B Clarkson
	A Coy	17 Pl	Lt G R Chrisp
OC	Capt G F J Holtsbaum	18 Pl	Lt P B Powell
2i/c	Capt P K Murphy		
7 Pl	Lt F J Fink		**Unallocated**
8 Pl	Lt L F Graham	Later to 15 Pl	Lt J D Andrews
9 Pl	Lt G L Horsfall	Later to 4 Pl	Lt N N Fletcher
		Later to 6 Pl	Lt W J Wasley
		Later to 7 Pl	Lt C W Vock
		Later to 11 Pl	Lt D R McLeod

Brunei township – June 1945

CHAPTER 21
OPERATION OBOE 6

At 0800 hours 10 Jun, troops began moving to net stations, and all were supremely confident. Half an hour later the naval and air bombardment began, with a most effective bombardment of the landing beach and the high ground to the right, Brunei Bluff and Cowie Ridge, which overlooked the beach. The first wave began descending the scrambling nets into the landing barges which, as soon as loaded, circled nearby until all were ready and then, in extended line, headed for the beach. As they approached, four LC1 rocket support craft discharged their rockets into the fringe of the landing area. At 0915 hours the first wave landed unopposed but the beach had been incorrectly marked and the landing was 1000 yards east of the intended area and the ground inland was tangled growth and wet swamps. This meant that D Coy had an additional 1000 yards to their objective, Cowie Ridge, and the going was slow and wet.

Being unopposed the advance proceeded smoothly, although D Coy and 4 Pl moving towards Cowie Ridge and Brunei Bluff, found the going slow and difficult and, for a while, were out of touch with Bn HQ through having insufficient signal cable. B Coy contacted the only enemy party in the area, killing two and taking another wounded as a prisoner. By 1230 hrs the whole of the Brooketon area was cleared, a troop of Matilda tanks and a troop of 75 mm guns had landed and, finally, 2/13 Bn had landed on Green Beach and was preparing to take over responsibility of the area to enable 2/17 Bn to advance towards Brunei.

Following a rapid reorganisation of the Bn, A Coy set off as advance guard along the Brunei Road — known as Route Six — at 1400 hours. News of the other landings were coming in and it was learned that 2/15 Bn had captured Muara Island and 24 Bde were firmly established on Labuan Island. By 1700 hrs, the Bn were in allotted dispositions for the night 4000 yards along Route 6.

Towards 2100 hours there were sounds of a vehicle approaching and shortly a two and a half ton truck with headlights alight appeared from the direction of Brunei. Two machine guns and crews were in position covering the road and they opened up with a hail of fire. Five Japanese were killed and one, badly wounded, was taken prisoner, but two others managed to escape into the darkness.

On 11 Jun, C Coy took over the role of advance guard and moved off at 0800 hours. Although signs of recent enemy occupations were found at frequent intervals, no contact was made, and very rapid progress was made towards Brunei.

At about 1030 hours the Commander-in-Chief, Gen MacArthur, visited tactical HQ which was moving with the advance company. He was accompanied by Lt Gen Sir Leslie Morshead, Maj Gen Wootten, Brig Windeyer and Vice Admiral Royal. Gen MacArthur congratulated the unit for the progress being made and wished it luck. It was encouraging for the troops to see the supreme commander taking a personal interest in the operations of the Bn.

In sweltering heat and humidity, made worse by about six-foot high grass on either side of the tracks and road being followed, and without the slightest vestige of breeze, it was like marching

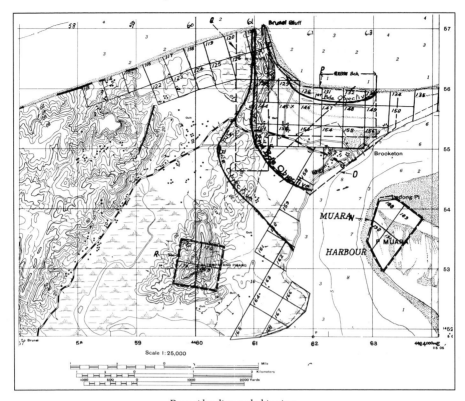

Brunei landing and objectives

through hell, and many suffered heat exhaustion. Nevertheless, a good distance was covered and about 1600 hours a halt was called. The CO, with a couple of scouts, moved forward to recce an area for the Bn positions that night. After moving forward about 2000 yards they found a good place, then noticed movement on the road which proved to be a Japanese. They fired a few shots each and one scored a hit but the Japanese managed to reach thick cover. The Bn moved forward and took up defensive positions for the night after an advance of some 13,000 yards.

Next morning D Coy took over the advance guard role and soon reached the junction of the Berakas—Brunei roads. Here there was clear evidence of the devastating effects of the naval bombardment and at the road junction D Coy captured two trucks driven by Indian drivers who had been taken prisoner at Singapore. These were the first POWs to be released by 2/17 Bn. B Coy then moved forward and occupied the Brunei airstrip. Leading south from the airstrip the road led through a defile dominated by a sharp razorback ridge, on the left.

Following the capture of the airstrip without opposition 12 Pl B Coy commanded by Lt Reg Kennedy, led the advance and made contact with minor opposition after some 300 yards. The leading scouts observed movement approx 250 yards forward, but experienced difficulty in identifying whether it was native or Jap until, eventually, firing determined the question. Observation was difficult because of thick scrub on either side of the road but the platoon moved forward as rapidly as possible with the left forward section unsuccessfully firing on a Jap moving across the road. The road was mined at intervals and this Jap exploded a mine with a time fuse.

Contact was again made by the right forward section and, following firing, the enemy

Above left: *Down scramble nets.*
Above right: *First wave boarding
landing barges.*
Left: *Landing barges touch down of
Green Beach.*
Below: *Out of barges and sprint for
tree line.*

Lt Waterhouse, Lt Col Broadbent, Capt Wright

withdrew. Considerable talking could be heard from the small feature on the right of the road. Movement on the road was under observation from a series of features on the left of the road, so one section took up a position covering the right of the road, and another section covering the road and features on the left. The remaining section moved on the left flank to clear any enemy from the features and occupy the ground in order to assist movement to the right of the road. By good use of fieldcraft and aggressive action this section captured an enemy post, killing three and the remainder fled. Pte F. McGrath displayed first class ability and coolness which earned him the Military Medal.

11 Pl, commanded by Lt Milton Trudgeon, was committed to the long narrow feature to the right of the road which was the only remaining ground preventing further advance along the axis of the road. The attack, with 2 sections forward, was across 150 yards of swamp covered with tall grass. These sections were supported by fire from the other section, 2 inch mortar and 12 Pl across the road. The tall swamp grass gave cover from view, allowing the troops to reach the base of the feature without coming under fire. They sighted five Japs apparently prepared to catch anyone emerging from the swamp. The two sections of 11 Pl assaulted firing from the hip and the Japs, evidently wounded, were driven off the feature into the swamp beyond, where five bodies were counted next day.

The enemy engaged our troops with small arms fire and grenades, wounding three including Cpl Broome and Cpl Allgood, but Cpl Allgood and Pte Neindorf remained on duty. By this time, a section of MMGs were in position where they could cover the whole of the feature, and also the mortars were in action.

This ridge feature presented a problem as it was covered by enemy fire whilst swamp on both sides impeded movement. The Pl Comd asked for fire support while the enemy's positions were probed on either flank. Movement on the right came under heavy fire both from the ridge and also from the swamp. Probing on the left met with success and, following the fire support program, 11 Pl advanced killing five Japs including 1 Offr. Pete Taylor[1] was killed in the operations. Mopping up of the objective continued being a slow process among the tall grass, but a further two Japs were killed in their holes. B Coy held the ground through the night with Jap activity on all platoon localities, including 4 Pl which had come under comd B Coy to defend the right flank[2].

1
  Pte Reuben John Taylor, aged 26 years, enlisted from Barellan, NSW.
2
  4 Pl suffered 2 KIA, 2 DOW and 2 WIA on 12/13 June (see Postscript on page 308)

Above: En route to Brunei
Below : Having a rest

Above: En route to Brunei
Below: Members of C Coy in Brunei

By late afternoon the Bn was established in positions to the South end of the airstrip for the night. About 1930 hrs enemy parties attempted to infiltrate, and opened fire on the position held by 4 Pl, which resulted in 1 killed and 3 wounded. A little later a number of heavy mortar bombs fell in the vicinity of D Coy HQ, and MG Bn personnel suffered 2 casualties. An airstrike was requested for the morning of 13 Jun and, in the very early hours of the morning, more mortar bombs fell in D Coy area. The supporting artillery engaged the enemy mortar firing positions. There were also sounds of enemy transport movement.

As dawn was arriving a party was seen approaching C Coy from the direction of Brooketon. At first there was some doubt whether they were natives but, as soon as 15 Pl halted them, it became clear that they were enemy. They split into two groups and fled. One party of seven raced across the airstrip and were completely annihilated by 14 and 15 Pls. The other group of five or six moved towards C Coy HQ and on the way ran into Lt George Simpson who was found bayoneted to death some 25 yds from his Pl HQ and it was not known why he was alone there. The Japanese then moved back towards the airstrip and were all killed by fire from C Coy HQ.

At 0925 hrs the airstrike, that had been requested to bomb enemy positions 1000 yds forward of B Coy, fell 600 yds short of the objective and dangerously close to B Coy positions. A second bomb strike at 1100 hrs fell on the objective originally allotted and proved to be most effective as, together with artillery fire, it was responsible for the withdrawal of nearly a battalion of the enemy troops. The enemy positions were found to be very well prepared and, had the enemy continued to hold them, they would have been very difficult to dislodge.

Following the second airstrike D Coy moved out on the left flank high ground to eventually come in at the back of Brunei town, with A Coy leading the way along the main road. 9 Pl of A Coy had moved along the river and secured Gadong Ferry. After moving some distance A Coy were fired on from the spur on the left, and a patrol from C Coy went off to clear this ridge, killing two enemy. Then a patrol from D Coy further out on the left moved to contact C Coy and encountered three Japanese, killing two and wounding the other one.

The Gadong Ferry area was consolidated and a patrol from A Coy crossed at the ferry and found a native prison compound in Gadong estate. They found three English speaking natives and about forty others all of whom were fettered with handcuffs or leg irons. In one hut there were five dead natives chained to posts and a number of others in pitiful condition. The Japanese guards had left a day or two previously but an anti-British Javanese police sergeant-major was in charge. He was taken into custody to answer for his cruelty.

D Coy patrols captured a prisoner at Kumbang Pasang village and in a sharp encounter with five enemy moving out from Brunei, two of the enemy were killed and one badly wounded. The Coy then moved on to Tasek reservoir, killing another Japanese on the way, and found it to be undamaged and unprotected.

C Coy, which had taken over the advance guard, had been pushing on and by 1445 hrs were securing Brunei town, being involved in almost street fighting at times. At 1445 hrs they reached the water front. While mopping up the town area, a section of 14 Pl encountered a party of eight Japanese led by an officer who staged a Banzai charge. The section displayed great coolness in killing all the enemy and suffered no casualties themselves.

By 1600 hrs the battalion had completed its initial task of capturing Brooketon and Brunei. The 17 mile advance had been completed in less than four days which was a very satisfactory achievement. The enemy opposition had been weak and nothing more than rather unco-ordinated delaying actions. Conditions had been very exhausting especially as heavy loads were carried. Apart from unconfirmed casualties the Japanese had lost 52 killed and 2 prisoners.

11 Pl B Coy had taken over the Clifford Bridge approaches and reported movement seen

on the west bank of the river. The Bridge, an arched concrete construction of considerable span, appeared to have been prepared for demolition with boxes of picric acid explosive and aerial bombs stacked across the bridge at the crown of the arch. On the far side of the river was a small hill that could have been used by Japanese to cover the bridge and have a firing party to detonate wired up explosives.

Lt Underwood of 2/3 Fd Coy Engrs, crept up to the pile of explosives under cover of evening light and found that several wiring circuits had been set up ready for demolition and it had to be assumed that these were connected to an exploder probably set up on the small hill on the far side of the river. Next morning 11 Pl sent a Section across the bridge under cover of mortars and smoke shells fired by 2/8 Fd Regt and the Engrs removed the detonators and dumped the explosives into the river.

2/17 Bn became Bde reserve. 2/15 Bn, which had moved up the Limbang River from Brunei Bay, continued the advance in the direction of Limbang. 2/13 Bn was warned of a possible landing down the coast.

14 Jun was spent with all companies remaining in the Brunei area carrying out offensive patrolling. A thorough search of the town area was instituted for documents and valuables. The town was divided into four sectors and small parties under an officer moved through all buildings. A patrol from C Coy encountered enemy east of the town and the Japanese attacked. The patrol killed five without loss to themselves, but then had to withdraw due to lack of ammunition. The artillery and mortars then took up the fight and, when C Coy moved forward later, they found the enemy had evacuated.

D Coy patrols to Tasek reservoir found the reservoir undamaged and not prepared for demolition. They killed a couple of enemy as they moved further and eventually saw 20/25 Japanese running along a ridge some 400 yards from them. A patrol from A Coy towards Kumbang Pasang village were warned by three natives of an enemy force just ahead, and they went with the patrol to point out where the Japanese were. In the patrol attack they killed seven enemy without casualty to the patrol.

The Dyaks, the small stature head-hunting men of Borneo, were waging an unrelenting war against the Japanese with spears, poison darts and keen-edged pahrangs. On the morning of 15 Jun they brought in two Japanese whom they had hog-tied and carried on poles, suspended by their hands and feet, for eight miles. One of these prisoners, a 2nd Lt, was very pleased to be delivered to the Australians and was keen to talk. Not all Japanese were so fortunate and many of the inland tribes of Dyaks added smoked Japanese heads to their trophies in their long-houses.

B Coy as a mobile gp, with under comd one sec MMGs, two dets mortars, a det of engineers, and in support one battery Arty, tank recce party and Naval Bombardment party, commenced the advance towards Tutong shortly after 1000 hrs on 15 Jun. The coy improvised with sandbagged jeeps used by 12 Pl as the advance guard and a captured truck. They advanced 10 miles without contact, the only sign of the enemy being two abandoned trucks and evidence of an attempt to blow up the road. However, the road was in good condition and quite usable by tanks. The distance advanced the first day waslimited by the range of the Arty and the Bn's tropical scale of transport as the vehicles were required to return to Brunei to ferry C Coy forward the following day.

On 16 Jun the Tutong force became a two company detachment under command of Maj Pike, who left Brunei at 1000 hrs with a small HQ party. C Coy embussed in motor trucks and had reached B Coy area by 1220 hrs, with B Coy continuing the advance and, although numerous road blocks were met, no contact was made and Tutong was secured at 1850 hrs

Lt Col Broadbent surveys ruins at Brunei

Clifford Bridge

without opposition. This advance to Tutong was acclaimed by high comd at the time as being the fastest up to that date by Allied land forces in the South West Pacific area.

Back in Brunei, A and D Coys continued their patrol activities with occasional contacts. At 1315 hrs on 17 Jun the Sultan of Brunei arrived at Bde HQ and expressed his gratitude for the liberation of Brunei by Australian forces. The dignity of the occasion was somewhat marred when the Sultana was being helped from the canoe by his highness and almost fell into the river. The regal party, which included three canoe loads of entourage, then proceeded to the palace and 2/17 Bn provided a detachment under Sgt Holland, to guard the Sultan.

Meanwhile, a B Coy patrol reached the Danau Ferry at Kuala Tutong and there found three large pontoons on the near bank of the river. Acting on native reports a patrol moved upstream eight miles and found a launch suitable for towing the pontoons.

On the morning of 18 Jun, crossing by the Danau Ferry commenced and C Coy moved as the advance guard towards Seria. At 1000 hrs Bn HQ moved by truck to Tutong, leaving Maj Maclarn in command of A and D Coys still in Brunei. Danau was occupied without contact and C Coy advance continued along the beach. The speed of advance was limited by the bottleneck at the ferry. The beach was broad and hard, fringed by tall casuarina trees with thick swampy jungle beyond the trees. B Coy began crossing the ferry on 19 Jun and, by late afternoon, Bn HQ had crossed and was established at Danau. At last more motor vehicles were being ferried across and Bn HQ and pioneer platoon began moving along the beach by motor transport at 0930 hrs on 20 Jun to join C and B Coys. The sounds could be heard of naval and air bombardment supporting 2/13 Bn group landing at Lutong down the coast.

The beach provided satisfactory movement for transport and there were sturdy bridges

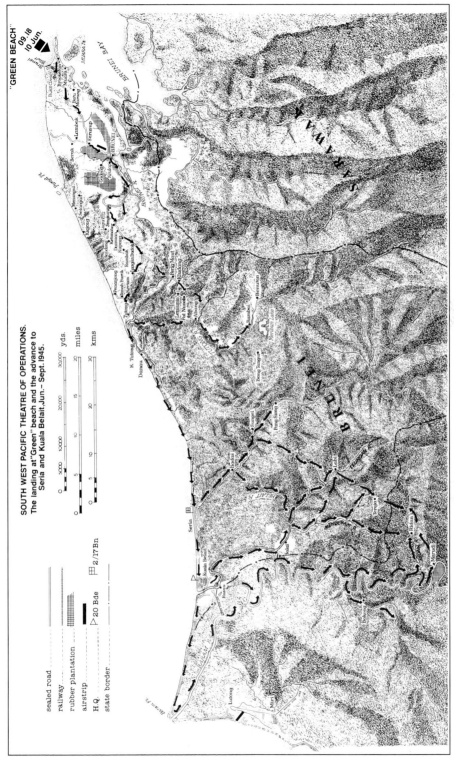

Landing to Seria and Kuala Belait

across all the streams that cut through the beach. By 1515 hrs C Coy had reached the outskirts of Seria and found the oil fields in that area intact, although further on wells were burning furiously. At 1630 hrs first contact was made and 13 Pl, who were moving along the road some hundred yards in from the beach, engaged a small party of Japanese and suffered one wounded. Another platoon moved inland and immediately met another party of enemy and a sharp fight ensued. Our artillery engaged the enemy positions. By 2000 hrs both bridges over the Bira River had been captured and C Coy had a platoon securing each bridge, with a bridgehead on the far bank. In this engagement there were 12 Japanese killed for the loss of two wounded.

At first light next morning, patrols were pushed forward and reported no sign of enemy. At 0930 hrs a Pl from C Coy was sent to cut the light railway to Badas, while the remainder of the company were disposed to secure the Bira River bridges. At 1130 hrs B Coy passed through C Coy and moved into Seria and the area to Seria River had been secured by 1500 hrs and Bn HQ moved forward to the B Coy area. Information was received from natives that the Japanese had withdrawn from the whole of the Seria-Belait area and that they had massacred a large number of Indian POWs who had been held in a compound at Kuala Belait.

There were 45 oil wells blazing fiercely in the Seria field with huge columns of dense black smoke billowing up for thousands of feet. The heat was so intense that nearby roads were impassable and detours had to be made around the fires.

Colonel Aikyo, the Japanese officer in command of Seria-Miri oilfields area, had given orders on 10 Jun that the oil wells were to be fired and this work continued for approximately three days. Of the 45 wells burning, two were almost pure gas, the remainder consisting of low and high pressure oil wells.

On 22 Jun, 3 Pl 2/3 Aust Fld Coy, with the assistance of A/Tk Pl and Pioneer Pl, started extinguishing as many fires as possible, and some civilian oilfield personnel were recruited to assist. The low pressure wells were less of a problem than the high pressure wells and these were the first to be got under control. Three of these wells were extinguished in one day. At the end of July 17 oil wells were still burning in Seria and were the more difficult ones to control. They eventually required an American expert on oil fires to be called in.

(A fuller report on the oil fires appears in the appendices.)

Since the original landing the battalion had captured Brooketon, Brunei and Tutong, and advanced 75 miles to reclaim the valuable Seria oilfields in a matter of twelve days. In that period the Bn had accounted for 85 killed plus 22 unconfirmed killed, 8 wounded and 12 prisoners — a total of 127 against their own casualties of 6 killed and 10 wounded.

Next day four escaped Indian POWs were recovered, while extensive patrolling was carried out without contact.

On 23 Jun, A Coy and one section 2 Pl arrived by truck from Brunei. B Coy and Bn HQ moved forward to the western outskirts of Seria, and Bn HQ was established in four bungalows along the sea front. From their position half way to Kuala Belait, A Coy pushed forward next day and entered Kuala Belait, and found it completely free of enemy. They found the prison compound where the massacre of the Indian POWs had taken place. It was impossible to make an accurate estimate of the number of victims as the buildings had been burnt, but the charred bones and corpses made it clear that there had been a great many.

A patrol from C Coy to Badas reported that the narrow guage railway from Seria was intact and they found an undamaged locomotive and trucks. Two other engines were salvaged and next day the patrol returned to Seria with the three engines and the engineers soon had the two larger engines working. The patrol had also found the pump station in reasonably good order and, by

Capt Murphy detailing patrol route

Patrol setting out

11 July, the pumps were re-started. This was invaluable in providing the necessary water and mud for the fire fighting and extinguishing of the oil well fires.

On 25 Jun D Coy arrived from Brunei by truck and settled in at Penaga golf course between Seria and Kuala Belait. The Bn was once more together except for the A/Tk Pl which was guarding the Tutong Abang road junction. Meanwhile, 2/13 Bn had made a successful landing at Lutong, near Miri, and late on 26 Jun, an A Coy patrol made visual contact from one bank of the Baram River with a patrol from 2/13 Bn on the other bank. So now 20 Bde controlled over a hundred miles of the coast from Brunei Bluff to Miri.

From this stage onwards, the Japanese showed no serious intention of fighting for Brunei, and their aim was clearly to withdraw inland and try to concentrate in British North Borneo. This action was full of danger for them, firstly because many of the routes to the north had been cut by Australian Forces in various places. The second danger lay in the fierce Dyak tribes who, fighting in their native land, comprised an unrelenting, unseen enemy who constantly preyed on the demoralised Japanese remnants as these weary troops struggled through the dense Borneo jungles.

Along the coastal area the BBCAU took over administration of the local population and it was not long before the area became a hive of industry. Many workers were required on the oilfields: the gardens, so long neglected, were quickly put back into production: long grass, growing profusely on once well tended playing fields and along the roadsides, was cut down, drains were cleared and refuse carted away and burnt.

A Coy despatched a patrol, under command of Capt Murphy, by canoes paddled by Dyaks or Malays to establish a base at Balai and patrol from there. This base was increased and Capt Murphy had 7 and 8 Pls under his command at Balai and Bde advised that a DUKW would be at the Bn disposal for supply of the Balai force.

An interesting sight was witnessed at Kuala Belait when this DUKW (an amphibious vehicle) returned one day carrying an important Dyak as a passenger. He was perfectly at ease while travelling in this "boat", but as the DUKW headed towards the sandy beach he started showing signs of apprehension. As the crash of the boat became more imminent to him, he climbed on to the side of the boat, and the look of disbelief and amazement on his face was something to see as this boat turned out to be a vehicle and drove safely up the beach!

C Coy, which had a Pl established at Badas, moved to that area for operations in the Bukit Puan area where reports indicated a fairly large enemy force.

By the close of Jun only 17 oil well fires were still burning. A total of 41 Indian POWs had been recovered plus 3 Javanese who had come in. A demonstration of force to impress the locals of the Australians' ability to hold the area was made at Kuala Belait, using mortars and artillery. The demonstration was so successful that many natives made for the jungle and were slow to return.

Postscript

NOTES ON OBOE 6

The Brunei operation was planned and prepared in great detail; even to the distance from the shore that tin hats would be piled by those in the Coy who preferred their felt hats. Progress was quick at the landing stage and assiduously reported to Bde. In reply came multiple demands for reports. Ultimately, a Staff Offr had to admit that he should have been sending the questions to another Bn.

Sleep before a landing is often broken by thoughts. The sustained din of fire into the enemy truck on the first night had added to fatigue. Progress on the following morning was again interrupted by multiple messages from Bde. The Bn was to halt and an important thing was to happen. Nothing seemed important enough to stop the advance and it continued. Eventually, the important thing happened with the arrival of McArthur the C-in-C SWPA————in the pleasant company of Morshead, Wootten and Windeyer. MacArthur was gracious and accepted that the War should not stop. The passing troops could see his chat with the CO.

The CO was known to have discussed with the Brigadier the unnecessary responsibilities created by senior officers being too far forward. When the CO himself with batman and a couple of scouts had disappeared ahead of the point section, shots rang out. The Brig then arrived, asking for the C.O. Loyalty delayed obedience to the answer. Eventually, the little party on reconnaissance returned. The C.O., Seeing the Brig from afar, prepared his plan to change the obvious subject to be raised. He was pleased that he had used his rifle to fire the first aimed shot of the escapade.

The tank support plan had failed. Moving along the road, tanks had crushed some culverts. They were ordered to desist. The Bn was never to understand why the order caused them to drop out instead of continuing to support, using the time available with the infantry rate of advance, to by-pass culverts.

The non-event at the Clifford Bridge after Brunei had its dramatic moments before success. Water and mangroves seemed to block any crossing except on the bridge. The pile of explosives in its centre were formidable and the ground opposite gave much scope for a hidden Japanese to detonate. All available fire-power and smoke were turned on in the plan prepared by Rudkin. Trudgeon had to designate his forward section, and with it ran through the risk of crossing the pile of explosives.

Capt Glynn Stark of the Naval Bombardment Group had been in support for the advance. Contact appropriate for a shoot was not made but there were threatening features away from the road. It was accepted that these gave sufficient justification for a demonstration of fire-power. The advancing troops were given this advantage.

The Flying Fortress circling over Brunei as a co-ordinator of planes coming in for airstrike, was a new scene. It was unwelcome that the strip markers of our forward troops were torn by bomb fragments, but the noise helped frighten the Japs.

In the short stay in Brunei town, stray Japanese were sighted at night. None appeared ready to return the walkie-talkie radio thrown by Shortie Bowker an orderly with C Coy when suddenly confronted by a Jap on the first entry into the town.

Bde had issued the order to advance towards Tutong. Broadbent, assessing the enemy resistance and his friendship with the arty, had decided to try a motorised advance, using sandbagged jeeps for a forward scouting element and borrowed artillery trucks to carry the close support. For their own movement the gunners had squeezed up their personnel and towed their guns in tandem. At first the progress was only at the rate of a scout on foot, as the roadside was given detailed surveillance. A few harsh words of encouragement soon produced the knack of motorised advance.

The river at Tutong seemed to offer significant delay. It was too wide and deep to ford and the surf and sandbar too remote and indefinite. News was gained that the civilian launch which towed the ferry was somewhere upstream. Two famous friends and soldiers from A Coy, Ding Dong Bell and Billie Moore, volunteered to go searching by canoe with a couple of locals. Broadbent gave them clear authority to shoot if there was treachery. Instead, there was quick success soon doubled with the arrival of engineer resources. A detailed crossing sequence was prepared and controlled effectively and, with urgent efforts, a satisfactory force was crossed to rest overnight and begin an early advance along the beach.

The small local contacts occurring throughout the campaign were all handled quickly and effectively.

The campaign had involved a number of small happenings. Many are mentioned. Risks calling for initiative and courage were taken and mostly rewarded without casualty. Sometimes with a fulsome sense of purpose, there was flirting with obedience. A plan for a heavy shoot-up of suspected enemy staging area with all three guns that were available, appeared to be frustrating for the opening salvos when there came a direction to fire a warning shot in case there were civilians. The gunner officer pointed out that it was not indicated where the warning shot should be fired. It was fired out to sea!

Down the little railway line to Badas, C Coy had discovered a chest of Canadian Ross sniper rifles packed in their original grease. They were sent to Bn HQ where somehow it was thought a good idea that they be cleaned and instructions in firing given to some promising Dyak supporters.

Broadbent made two trips to a burnt out area littered with galvanised iron sheets in searching for the Indian prisoners. Locals pointed and disappeared. Eventually, skin and bone bodies with bayonet stab marks were discovered half burned on the periphery. Burnt bones were everywhere under the tin. Skulls seemed an appropriate item to count the casualties but none could be found. Eventually, a pile was found on turning over a sheet of tin near on what had been a corner. Within days, two Indian soldiers insisting their duty called for a report to the CO, stood in weakness and a state of collapse to tell him. A warship seen off the coast had threatened invasion. The Japanese, under their cruel Sgt-Maj, had withdrawn inland. Prisoners left to fend for themselves had found and consumed some rice. The enemy had returned and decided to punish by killing the lot. The victims, herded and jabbed into one room, had been bound, then dragged to another and beheaded. Chance had left unbound the two escapees who had struggled to fall through a window and crawled far enough away to avoid roasting when the place was set on fire. Broadbent was later to see the Sgt-Maj in the Labuan prison camp. His abuse to him was thorough as the Jap stood shuddering through a malarial rigor. It did not seem to matter that he understood no English. The accompanying Japanese officer did.It is believed a later war crimes court did justice.

A lighter tone marked the later activities at Seria. An inter-platoon football competition was conducted. Broadbent played League with the Bn HQ team and everybody had their chance. It was lucky that the Brig went to Div as otherwise the beer prize would have only been twelve bottles. Football was in very short halves and could be stopped at the discretion of the RMO who learned the rules to umpire or a coy cook who already knew them. It was a short walk to dive in the warm brown surf.

The Concert Party's great turns were amplified by the RMO writing up his memory of the drama, "Ten Minute Alibi".The training of a team for a spectacular performance.

Broadbent and Rudkin chose to see a responsibility to stay and long and sincere friendships were distrupted by the departure ofthe 5-Year discharge team.

Training did not stop with the surrender. Books providing elementary instruction in letter-writing and mathematics were issued. Each platoon commander had to become a school teacher. On a visit a Div Col Chief of Staff found it difficult to believe that even 2/17 Bn would still have supported these orders.Finally, on Labuan the Bn had to move around the shoreline and parade on an airstrip. Lord Mountbatten was to visit the Div with congratulations. There were orders that he wanted everybody to close in around the dias so that he could speak intimately. It happened. He was seen at close quarters. He spoke well. The shudders on how the crowd would be undone proved unnecessary.

At last the time came for the final Bn nucleus to be designated. The small group left Labuan together by Liberty ship, eventually to end up at Ingleburn within yards of the start.After dealing with demands for return of typewriters issued in May 1940 Broadbent found himself from the first 20 to the last 2 in 2/17 Bn.

POSTSCRIPT

In consolidating the right flank of the Objective captured by 11 Pl on 12 June, 4 Pl had Pte G A O'Sullivan KIA and Cpl A E V Jones DOW (14 June) from sniper fire. Effective fire from an LMG soon after first light caused Pte J R Menzies to be KIA and Pte N P Donovan to DOW on 14 June. Ptes J Carroll and L P F Murphy were wounded. NX 95343 Pte Norman Patrick Donovan age 19 of Killara, NSW. NX 59919 Cpl Albert Edward Victor Jones age 28 of Marrickville, NSW. VX 91690 Pte John Robert Menzies age 24 of Albert Park, Vic. NX 83039 Pte Gerald Andrew O,Sullivan age 26 of The Rock, NSW.

CHAPTER 22
THE NIPPON SUN SETS

The beginning of July marked the end of a phase, and the start of a new phase. 2/17 Bn were established with HQ at Seria while 20 Bde HQ was at Kuala Belait. The rather arbitrary drawing of straight lines on a map to denote the limits of the divisional area led to restriction of activities in which the Bn could engage. As a result, this new phase meant that companies acted in independent roles, controlled by Bn HQ, and the only realistic way to continue the story is to follow each company's separate operation.

C Coy was firmly established at Badas with two 25 Pdr guns in support. Native reports indicated Japanese occupation of Bukit Puan a few miles up the Belait River, and native estimates could have indicated anything up to 300 being in that area. The artillery was used to pound the Bukit Puan area, and 15 Pl and 14 Pl advanced on the area intending to capture the enemy stronghold, and prepare ambush positions on the escape track. The village of Bukit Puan was secured in the late afternoon without contact, and the natives reported that the Japanese had withdrawn earlier in the day, moving south towards Labi. A patrol along the Labi track before dark found an abandoned Browning MG but were unable to make contact with the enemy.

While one platoon remained at Bukit Puan, and a section of guns of 16 Bty moved from Badas to Bukit Puan, patrols by the remainder of the company continued to move towards Labi, but were not able to catch up with the escaping enemy. There was hard work by supply parties taking rations and signal wire to the forward patrols, some eleven miles distant in the Labi area.

About this time Bde HQ advised the CO that the Bde comd did not want too large a force committed to the Labi area as he regarded 2/17 Bn as his Bde reserve. So instructions were issued for a Pl to move south along the track to Labi and make contact with a Pl from A Coy at the track junction east of Teriam. On 5 July, 14 Pl, C Coy, and 7 Pl, A Coy, effected this meeting and any threat to the Seria area was removed. From that time C Coy continued several fruitless patrols along muddy, slippery tracks but sighted no more enemy. On 12 July, 13 Pl left Bukit Puan by canoe on a two-day paddle to Kuala Belait while, on 13 July the rest of C Coy moved back to Seria, a platoon of the 2/2 MG Bn having taken over at Badas.

The A Coy river force of Capt Murphy at Balai was joined by the rest of A Coy, with D Coy taking over the original A Coy positions at Kuala Belait. Patrols pushed forward and reached Simburu, Teriam, Simpang and Mendaram without sighting a single Japanese. After having made contact with 14 Pl, C Coy, A Coy moved on in a southerly direction, and Coy HQ with 7 Pl set up at Simpang. On 8 July a patrol continued beyond Mendaram and reached Bukit Teraja where a bivouac area was found with indications that the Japanese had occupied it the previous night, but no enemy were seen.

Two sections of the Pioneer Pl moved up to Mendaram to establish a base, while a section of artillery got their guns into position at Simburu. From their base at Mendaram, 8 Pl patrolled along the track to Ridan on 9 July returning on 11 July. During this patrol natives gave

Tea break at Seria. L-R (rear):
———, C R O'Neill, C G Meyer.
(front): Pte A A Porter,
Capt E J Blundell, Lt N N Fletcher.

Left: Tea break at Seria
Below: Seria surf carnival

information that the Japanese still had Indian POWs with them and were making for Linei south of Marudi. On 16 July a patrol from 8 Pl at Ridan was informed by some Dyaks that Japanese were moving towards them and the patrol, moving fast, rejoined the rest of their platoon. This party of Japanese was about 40 strong and were moving from Marudi — more is told of them in D Coy operations. 8 Pl had a fight with them from an ambush position they set up killing four and, after a short fire fight the 8 Pl patrol broke off contact because of the superior enemy fire power and returned to their base.

The troops stationed at Seria had plenty of opportunity for surfing. A Surf Carnival was organised for 11 July but, due to pouring rain that day, it was postponed until the following day. 12 July was bright and clear and the carnival was a great success, due in no small measure to the basic organiser, Lt Peter Cunningham. There were a good number of nominations for all the water events and beach events with entrants from 16 Bty 2/8 Fd Regt, B3 Pl 2/2 MG Bn, Sup Dep Pl AASC, Air Force and Navy as well as the Battalion. The best individual performer for the day was A.J. Mathieson of C Coy. The variation of events was good and the enthusiasm of the organisers received the reward it deserved.

A side effect of the Surf Carnival was the development of keen aquaplaning, supported by the CO. Jeeps, with 60 to 80 feet of rope, towed a board which the rider manoeuvred in the

Top left: On board LCM at Kuala Belait. *Top right:* Moving up Barem River. **Above :** Landing at Kuala Ridan

Top left: *Patrol moving out from Mardui.* **Top right:** *D Coy men talking with recovered Indian POWs.* **Above left:** *Pte Fells paying Dyaks.* **Above right:** *Maj Trebeck and Pte Fells paying Dyaks.*

HMAS Tigersnake at Marudi

Inspecting Clunere Temple

hallow water with varying degrees of skill. It was all great fun until a report from the LAD regarding the effect salt water was having on the jeeps resulted in an instruction from Bde that this pastime was to cease!

On the night of the Surf Carnival the Bn Concert Party gave its first show in Borneo.

Before operation Oboe 6 started SRD (Special Reconnaissance Department) units were operating in various parts of Borneo. In April one of these units dropped into the Baram River basin and was commanded by Maj Toby Carter. Toby Carter was a New Zealand born oil surveyor who had been working in Borneo and his SRD unit soon had many Dyaks and other natives organised into resistance fighters. The SRD were a collection of a few somewhat remarkable fellows: Carter's 2 i/c was Capt Fred Blondell, an English offr who had done about a dozen operational parachute drops into occupied Europe before coming out and being dropped with the SRD into Sarawak. On 10 July Carter's party entered Marudi but, following a stiff fight in which they killed 11 Japanese, they were forced to withdraw from the town. The enemy party was well led and were evidently combat troops who had moved from the Miri area via Bakoeng to Marudi. Following his party's forced withdrawal from Marudi, Carter flew by Catalina to 20 Bde HQ where he asked for assistance from Brigade troops. It was decided that 2/17 Bn should support Carter and, accordingly, arrangements were put in hand.

On 14 July, a river force under comd of Maj Trebeck, consisting of D Coy plus a detachment

17 Pl and det of Mortars at Bakoeng

of mortars, signals, engineers and the RMO, departed from Kuala Belait in three LCMs escorted by one LCM gunboat and the SRD motor schooner HMAS *Tigersnake*. The small convoy moved along the coast and entered the mighty Baram River and moved up river to the village of Tudan, where the force staged for the night in a rather uncomfortable swampy area. The Baram River is in Sarawak and is indeed a great and wide river, navigable for well over 100 miles by ships of several hundred tons. Next morning Trebeck and Carter transferred to the gunboat and the force proceeded up river, receiving reports from natives in canoes that a party of 40 or more Japanese were at the junction of the Ridan River and the Baram. At about 1200 hours, having arrived at Kuala Bakoeng junction with the Baram, a section of 16 Pl went ashore and reported the area clear of enemy, so the force continued up river. They had to wait about ten minutes just around the last river bend until the arrival of the flight of 6 Spitfires that had been on call. Then, with the gunboat leading and firing into the area where the enemy had been reported, the Spitfires bombed and machine-gunned the area. Under cover of rockets from the gunboat, 16 Pl and 17 Pl landed to find that the Japanese had withdrawn. These two platoons proceeded to move across country along the track to Marudi, while the remainder of the force proceeded by river around the peninsular to Marudi and landed there without opposition. Defensive positions were quickly organised and by nightfall the force was firmly established, with the Union Jack flag having been hoisted.

Next morning, 16 July, Lt Clarkson and 16 Pl set out on a patrol, to follow the enemy party that reports indicated had evacuated Kuala Ridan when D Coy landed, was under way and they were headed towards Ridan. The patrol was also to contact Lt Graham's Pl at Ridan. The remainder of D Coy set about local patrols in the Marudi area, while Trebeck posted the proclamation of Martial law in Marudi bazaar. He and Toby Carter inspected the town and the British Residency on top of the high ground and moved their joint HQ into it.

The 16 Pl patrol staged that night in the village of Sunga Pasil and next morning moved on along a track that traversed many swamp areas. About midday they sighted a party of 12 Japanese, but these enemy withdrew towards Ridan before they could be engaged. About two hours later 16 Pl encountered the Japanese party of about 40 with 4 LMGs and engaged them,

Watching air strike on Japanese positions

D Coy HQ at Bakoeng

endeavouring to circle the enemy positions. However, the enemy positions were well sited on slightly rising ground, while 16 Pl were in swamp. After a hot fire fight, in which 10 enemy were thought to have been killed, Lt Clarkson was forced to break off the engagement and ordered the patrol to withdraw. Cpl Ted Howard, an original of the unit, was killed and two were wounded — one Dyak was also killed. The patrol made a difficult return to Marudi in darkness carrying the wounded men with the untiring help of the Dyaks. This Japanese party was again in contact with an A Coy patrol on 18 July, after which the remnants disappeared into the swamps, heading south and westwards.

On 17 July a patrol under comd of Lt Forster, mainly 17 Pl, departed by LCM accompanied by the gunboat, to Bakoeng and found the village to be unoccupied, so the patrol moved on further up river. Natives reported that 18 Japanese were coming down by canoe, so a water ambush was set up. However, no enemy appeared, probably having heard the LCM engines, so the patrol moved on and, rounding the river bend near the junction of the Arang and Bakoeng Rivers, was met with MG fire. Bullets penetrated the ramp of the gunboat and Pte Griffiths was killed. Fire from the gunboat silenced the enemy positions but the nature of the river banks made a landing impossible, so the craft were turned about and the patrol returned to Bakoeng

Next day the patrol concentrated on trying to find tracks forward to the enemy position encountered the previous day. An organised air strike and mortar concentration all fell in the target area. Late on 21 July this patrol returned to Marudi.

On 20 July, Lt Powell and 18 Pl left Marudi for Ridan which they reached late on 21 July, having found the track clear of enemy. They remained at Ridan until 25 July, when they return again to Marudi, having made contact with Lt Graham's 8 Pl A Coy and established that the track was now clear.

D Coy worked in close co-operation with Carter's SRD unit, operating in the general area. Marudi proved to be a much more important centre than had at first been thought. The rubber resources of the area were extensive and a sizeable quantity of raw rubber was stored in Marudi warehouses. A large complex of rivers — and therefore communication — was controlled by Marudi, and it was also of considerable political significance in pre-war days. So the re-occupation of the town did much to restore British prestige. Maj Trebeck, as unofficial Acting Rajah of Sarawak for that area, was visited by several Dyak chiefs, one of whom wanted to present him with five smoked Japanese heads!

17 Pl, less 1 section, was established at Bakoeng and recce patrols up river to the Arang area found that the enemy had withdrawn from those positions. On 27 July, acting on native reports that there were 6 Japanese at Arang, Lt Chrisp set out on a patrol with 4 and 6 sections, but found the enemy had gone. Lt Chrisp with 6 section returned to Bakoeng along the river track, while 4 section, under Cpl Lemaire, moved via the inland track. This section had gone some distance and, when in the area in which they had previously located some enemy tunnels, they were ambushed by a party of 8 Japanese. In the engagement that ensued, Pte Williams was wounded and one Dyak killed. A Japanese officer and two others then charged, and Lemaire killed the officer. One of the others was killed by Bren fire, while the third was speared by one of the Dyaks. L/Cpl Giffen assisted the wounded Williams and then disappeared, and while looking for Giffen, Lemaire encountered another Japanese whom he killed. The patrol made repeated efforts to find L/Cpl Giffen but to no avail. Cpl Lemaire then led his section in a difficult withdrawal through swamp, and met Lt Chrisp with a party who had gone out from Bakoeng looking for 4 section. Cpl Charlie Lemaire had shown considerable resourcefulness and coolness throughout the engagement and was awarded the Military Medal. (Some days later, the body of L/Cpl Giffen was found in long grass.)

Natives reported that two strong enemy parties were approaching Bakoeng and it was decided to withdraw the patrol to Marudi, and this was effected at 1130 hrs on 27 July. On 28 July, 17 Pl plus detachment of mortars and section MGs moved back to Kuala Bakoeng. Next day, Lt Forster took a small patrol overland to Bakoeng and found it unoccupied, so 17 Pl with the detachment of mortars and section MGs moved from Kuala Bakoeng and established at Bakoeng.

On 29 July, Lt Col Broadbent went up to Marudi by a re-supply craft from Kuala Belait and spent the night at Marudi. 70 pounds of gelignite were included in supplies for demolishing the Japanese tunnels at Arang. Next day, 30 July he, accompanied by the RMO Capt Ritchie, returned by Catalina from Marudi to Seria.

The situation in Marudi was stable and already local inhabitants were flocking back from up river and the population was now about 1000. Marudi was beyond the boundary line of the Divisional area, and this imposed considerable restrictions. On 31 July, D Coy HQ and 16 Pl transferred to Bakoeng, leaving 18 Pl and the SRD in occupation of Marudi. On 2 Aug 17 Pl patrol went to the tunnel area at Arang with engineers and blew in the tunnels with the gelignite received. No enemy were encountered

In a small clearing on the jungle-lined bank of the Bakoeng river, some 2000 yards upstream from its junction with the Baram, a small Dyak hut served as HQ for D Coy. Each evening a few would gather around the wireless set, which was their only link with the outside world, and listen to the news from Radio America. And so it was on the night of 6 August that they heard the news consisting of the announcement that an Atomic Bomb had been dropped on Hiroshima, followed by graphic detail of what had happened, and the expectation that peace would come within days.

Meanwhile, for Bn HQ, most of HQ Coy, and B Coy stationed at Seria, life was pleasant, with plenty of surfing by day and, by night, the mobile cinema and the Bn concert party. About the only real activity was a 10 Pl, B Coy, patrol on 25 July when natives reported five Japanese at Taunggling, and the patrol took into custody 3 Formosans and 2 who were believed to be Japanese, but also claimed to be Formosans.

August 1945 will be remembered by all as the month in which, after nearly six years of conflict, the world finally saw the end of World War II.

The early part of August was somewhat unreal with increasing rumours that the War was nearly over. On 10 August, a most important message from Bde HQ advised that if Japan surrendered, military precautions and discipline must in no way be relaxed. Next day, 11 August, the C in C, Gen Sir Thomas Blamey, visited the Bn and intimated that the end of the War was imminent. On 13 August, Bde issued instructions to cease offensive operations. Then on 15 August, VJ Day arrived with the confirmation that Emperor Hirohito had accepted the Allied terms of surrender. Difficulties were expected, and were experienced, in ensuring that the Japanese in Borneo received the surrender instructions and complied with them.

On 17 Aug a Bn commemoration parade was held at Seria attended by the whole unit with the exception of A Coy and D Coy which were represented only by troops attending a potential NCO cadre. The CO, Lt Col Broadbent, delivered the following address:—

"We are on parade that as many of us as possible may be together to remember the efforts and sacrifices made by the men of this battalion in the winning of this war. The fighting effort is now over. We all know this unit was not the only one which helped in the winning, but every one of you can be proud of the way in which the 2/17 Bn has always demonstrated its sense of duty. In the past we have remembered. Those who were there will never forget how, after Alamein, the Division held a great memorial parade on the plains of Gaza. It was for many the most emotional moment of their lives. Then there were times less formal, as when we came together in the grass at Heldsbach Plantation. In the future there will be many times when we shall gather to renew the ties of comradeship that have bound us during our service. Then we shall recall, to the doubtless boredom of any listeners, our own escapades. We shall think of those disabled by wounds who miss the full advantages of we luckier ones. But mainly, we shall remember those many men from Cpl Edmondson to L/Cpl Giffen, who lie protected from the drifting sands in Tobruk, or in the arid hardness of that ridge behind Alamein, or those in that sacred piece of ground reclaimed from the jungle of Finschhafen, and lastly those who will ultimately rest at Labuan."

It was 5 September before the first Japanese moves were made for surrender, and 10 September when Japanese General Baba signed the surrender at Labuan. Following this signing, final moves were put into operation for the withdrawal of the A Coy and D Coy troops from upcountry and, by the end of September, the only remaining troops upcountry were 17 Pl D Coy, then at Marudi.

More and more personnel departed under the 5 Year Scheme for demobilisation, and the depleting of battalion numbers was increased when 150 personnel proceeded to Singapore to help released Australian POWs return to Australia.

The last military operation carried out by 2/17 Bn was on 6 Oct when 17 Pl from Marudi moved back to Bakoeng, and then up river to Beluru, where 174 Japanese POWs were picked up, together with 19 Indian POWs still being held by the Japanese. Then, at Nakat they picked up another 47 and, next day, a further 62 POWs, delivering all these to 2/13 Bn at Kuala Baram. 17 Pl then finally rejoined D Coy at Seria on 7 October.

On 12 Oct, the historic event occurred and 2/17 Bn was declared a redundant unit. After five years and seven months, it entered a period of waiting for the ultimate fate of the unit to become known. During October drafts of long service personnel marched out for discharge.

On 20 Oct an advance party of 2 Off-rs and 22 Ors left for Kuala Betait to embark for Labuan. With the moving out of the advance party there was much speculation by all personnel that it seemed to be the first stage of the long awaited move back to Australia.

On 29 Oct 2 Off-rs and 120 Ors left Kuala Belait for Labuan while, on 31 Oct as LST pulled into the beach at Seria, the remainder of the Bn finally embarked and late that night headed for Labuan.

Over the years, many memories had been accumulated, with ups and downs, good times and bad, easy and tough, as fate dictated. The men of 2/17 Bn had fought against the fighting soldiers of Germany, Italy and Japan, and they had never been defeated. No battalion can hope for a better record.

During the month of November efforts were made to acquaint personnel in demobilisation procedures and matters regarding their return to civilian life. A program of education, amenities and sport, designed to enhance physical and mental well being was carried out.

The final break-up of the Bn came suddenly in the second week of December, 1945. The bulk of personnel, other than those for discharge, marched out to the 2/2 MMG Bn for detachment to the BBCAU supply depot and to guard PWs. By 10 December, effective strength was 4 Offrs and 21 Ors comprising the Bn's Administrative Cadre, formed to complete all records and wind up the Bn.

On 10 December the Adm Cadre embarked on the Pachaug Victory, and the 9 day voyage took them via Torres Straits to Brisbane. On 23 December the Cadre arrived at Ingleburn Camp where the Bn had been formed. The 2/17 Australian Infantry Battalion was disbanded on 8 February 1946 after over five years and nine months of service.

Battle casualties sustained by the 2/17 Battalion in the Borneo Campaign were KIA and DOW, 9 and WIA, 15. Those who died were:

NX 95343	Pte Donovan N P 13/6/45
SX 19112	L/Cpl Giffen J C 27/7/45
QX 55465	Pte Griffiths R L 17/7/45
NX 17655	Cpl Howard E J 17/7/45
NX 59919	Cpl Jones A E V 14/6/45
VX 91690	Pte Menzies J R 13/6/45
NX 83039	Pte O'Sullivan GA 12/6/45
NX 4302	Lt Simpson G 13/6/45
NX 125839	Pte Taylor R J 12/6/45

LEST WE FORGET

CHAPTER 23
POSTSCRIPT

17TH/18TH INFANTRY BATTALION
(THE NORTH SHORE REGIMENT)
1948–1960

The major contribution of 2/17 BN AIF towards building up the effectiveness of the post-war Citizen Military Forces in the period particularly covered by the years 1948-1960 deserves recognition. It is hoped that this postscript to the Battalion's distinguished war-time history will show the extent of this contribution.

It is fortunate that when the CMF was re-activated in 1948, 17th Battalion was one of the units selected for raising on the reduced Order of Battle, even though this was to be in linked form with its sister battalion, the 18th.

The 2/17 Bn AIF Association had thus an interest in the CMF through its successor battalion in the post-war Army. This encouraged the enlistment of a number of former members of the 2/17 Bn into the newly formed CMF Battalion. This led to a close association from the outset between the two parties which was a source of mutual satisfaction and benefit.

In April 1948 the former CO of 2/17 Bn AIF, Lt Col J R Broadbent, DSO, was appointed to raise and command an infantry battalion on Sydney's North Shore. This new unit was designated 17/18 Infantry Battalion and was to be raised in the former recruiting areas of the pre-war 17th Battalion (North Sydney Regiment) and 18th Battalion (Ku-ring-gai Regiment).

Having accepted this appointment, Col Broadbent commenced to interview potential officers for his new battalion in April 1948, and within a few weeks had screened in excess of 100 applicants from whom most of his final selection was made.

His aim was to gain the best experience offering from the many war-time units represented by the potential officers offering their services, and his final selection reflected this intention. The effect upon 17/18 Bn was that its founding officers represented a spectrum of war-time experience rarely found in other units, which was of great benefit to it.

This policy was also extended to the selection and appointment of warrant and senior non-commissioned officers, and this served to firmly base the new battalion upon a war experienced cadre of considerable calibre.

Well known identities of 2/17 Bn who elected to resume their military careers in 17/18 Bn, were the following:

Ray Rudkin	Alan Tarrant
Dave Williams	Bob Settree
Tom Holland	Bob Reay
Alan Kennedy	Harry Wells

On 1 May 1948, 17/18 Inf Bn came into existence, and the cadre of newly appointed officers and senior NCOs commenced training in preparation for the first intake of recruits in June at the various depots allocated to the Battalion. HQ and some sub-units were located at Kooringa

Road, Chatswood and other sub-units at Pittwater Road, Manly and at Ernest Street, North Sydney.

By 1948, the precarious war-time alliance between Russia and the Western Powers had collapsed, and there was a widespread belief that war in Europe was imminent. It was against this background that the Battalion took shape, and Lt Col Broadbent formulated his policies for the preparation of his Battalion for war in the foreseeable future. There was a concentration on training of a practical nature, carried out at every opportunity in the field. Particular emphasis was placed on weapon skills and minor tactics. Special attention was paid to Offr/NCO training both within the unit and at external schools. Also the attendance of other arms and services at unit training was encouraged. Great value was placed upon patrolling by day and by night and patrol skills were highly regarded throughout the Battalion.

Officers and NCOs alike were required to be qualified for rank held, and preferably for the next rank above. However, the custom of temporary promotions and provisional appointments which was unfortunately prevalent in some units of the CMF was frowned upon in 17/18 Bn. This was a primary reason for the high standard of performance of the Battalion throughout its existence.

The first camp of continuous training was held early in 1949 at Greta in the Hunter Valley, and coincided with a record wet spell.

Notwithstanding the severe weather, this first camp was highly successful, enabling the lessons learned at home training parades to be put into full effect in the field under the most testing conditions.

With the training routine of the Battalion now established and working effectively, Col Broadbent turned to those aspects necessary to foster that esprit de corps, which was becoming evident in the unit.

An early target was the revered Unit Associations related to both 17th and 18th Battalions in their various forms since the Great War. These Associations were encouraged to participate in the activities of the new battalion, and within a short while they became an effective support group. With a linked battalion, care had to be taken to see that as far as possible neither battalion was favoured above the other, and generally an even-handed approach was possible, although this sometimes required the wisdom of Solomon.

Both groups of Associations presented trophies on behalf of their former units for competition in soldierly skill within 17/18 Bn. In this category, special mention must be made of the 2/17 Bn AIF Association's gift of a trophy for section patrol competition. This was in the form of a bronze statue of a typical infantryman, dressed and equipped for jungle warfare. It was competed for usually during annual camps. In the early years the competition was judged by a panel from the Association. Presented in 1949, it was fiercely contested by each company, and played an important part in developing patrol skills in the Battalion to a high standard.In order that neither of the linked battalions should be favoured above the other, Col Broadbent decided that the unit would not have a regimental badge, but would use instead the badge of the Royal Australian Infantry Corps. In the same vein, it was decided that the unit's territorial title would be "The North Shore Regiment".

The formation of a band was an early objective, and throughout its existence the Battalion was noted for the excellence of its brass band. Naturally, this led to the selection of a regimental march, and the CO decided that the Battalion would adopt "Boys of the Old Brigade". Although this had been the regimental march of 17th Battalion in both wars, and between wars, it was appropriate to this linked battalion, the components of which had served as sister battalions in the same brigade (5th) during the Great War. However, the Regimental March of 18th

Battalion, "Men of Harlech", was always played on ceremonial and other occasions so that, to all intents and purposes 17/18 Bn had two marches.

During the World War II, the King's and Regimental Colours of 17th and 18th Battalions had been laid up in the custody of their respective garrison churches at North Sydney and at Gordon for safe keeping. At an early stage, both sets of Colours were taken up by 17/18 Bn from St Thomas' and St John's Churches respectively, and thereafter placed in service with the Battalion.

In similar traditional vein, the historic mess silver and trophies of the old battalions was retrieved from Ordnance, where it had been stored for safety during the War, and once again graced the various messes.

Former alliances with famous regiments of the British Army had lapsed with the disbandment of 17th and 18th Battalions during the War. These alliances, with the East Surrey Regiment (17th) and the South Wales Borderers (18th), were confirmed and approved in 1951 for 17/18 Bn. These were no empty alliances — there was visiting between unit representatives as occasion arose, and an active exchange of correspondence and information between units.

The study of regimental history and customs, not only of the ancestral battalions but also of the Allied Regiments was required of all ranks, and taught to all recruits. Members of the earlier battalions were at times invited to speak of particular operations in which they had taken part, so that students had the benefit of eye witness accounts of the history which they were studying.

As an illustration of the standard of tactical training achieved in the second year of the new battalion's existence, 17/18 Bn carried out training up to battalion level in a weekend camp prior to annual camp in 1950. Observers from all units of 2nd Division attended this demonstration. The annual camp of continuous training for 1950 was held at Glenfield, west of Sydney and, whilst consolidating the work of the previous year, prepared the way for an ambitious battalion group exercise in which Col Broadbent was anxious to test his battalion.

This major exercise — Operation AUDAX — was held over the weekend 24/26 November 1950. It involved the Battalion, with major elements of 7th Fd Regt, 2 Div Column RAASC, 2 Div Provost Coy and 1st Lt AA Regt, either under command or in support, in an advance to contact and encounter battle exercise in the Mulgoa area.

AUDAX was the most ambitious exercise attempted by any CMF unit up to that time and demonstrated the high level of tactical competence of which well-trained and led CMF soldiers were capable.

The 1951 Annual Camp was held at Singleton, a venue with which the Battalion was to become familiar over the next few years. This was a most active camp which included night operations at battalion level, an exercise not to be lightly taken at any time, but which was most successful.

In July 1951, Col Broadbent relinquished command of the Battalion to his former 2 i/c, Lt Col P H Pike, himself a former officer of 2/17 Bn. During his three years of command, Col Broadbent brought the Battalion, which he had formed, to a state of readiness for war, the necessity for which was demonstrated by the outbreak of the Korean War just a month earlier.

Although each of the succeeding COs were equally as successful as Col Broadbent, all would agree that it was the policies and principles he laid down which formed the firm foundation upon which the enviable reputation of the Battalion was built and maintained. It is for this reason that more attention has been paid to this founding period of the Battalion than the succeeding years.

At this stage, the volunteer element was at a sufficiently high level to allow realistic unit training. However, the worsening international situation which resulted from the outbreak of war in Korea, and Australia's commitment to United Nations Forces in that theatre, caused the Government to introduce a system of National Service, utilising the existing CMF framework to absorb trainees after they had completed their initial continuous training.

The first intake of National Service trainees marched in to 17/18 Bn late in 1951, and was rapidly and effectively integrated with the volunteer element.

Although not without its problems, the worst of which was the fairly rapid fall-off in volunteer enlistments, National Service contributed much to the Battalion, which maintained itself at near full establishment through to the end of National Service in 1960.

The appointment of an Honorary Col, which had been initiated by Col Broadbent, was now made, and this was a former CO of 18th Battalion between the Wars, Brig C E Cameron, MC and Bar, ED. The new Honorary Col inspected his Battalion at a parade for this purpose held at Chatswood Oval on 5 February 1952. Brig Cameron was a great asset to the Battalion and a most active Honorary Col. He retained this appointment until 1960.

Annual Camps 1952 and 1953 were both spent in the Singleton area, most of the time in the field. All phases of open warfare were practised in exercises up to battalion level, and the inevitable drop in efficiency in tactics, which had resulted from the change to National Service, was rectified.

Camp 1953 was particularly notable in that, whilst the Battalion was developing a defended area during an exercise, a surprise drop of paratroops onto the vital ground took place, supported by RAAF fighters in a ground support role. The plan was devised in secrecy at HQ 8th Bde and sprung on the Battalion to test its reaction. The senior observers who had just "happened to call in" at that time were impressed by the speed and professional manner in which the Battalion's counter attack force carried out its task of regaining this ground. Brigadier Dougherty, who as CO of 2/4 Inf Bn, had himself experienced paratroop drops at Heroklion in Crete in 1941, was particularly complimentary of the manner in which the Battalion had reacted to this surprise situation.

At this time, 4 Sergeants of the Battalion were selected to proceed with the Australian Coronation Contingent to London to take part in the Coronation of HM Queen Elizabeth, and at the same time Lt Col Pike was awarded the Coronation Medal, being one of the few CMF commanders to be so honoured.

Following the loss of the Ernest Street Depot to 1st Light AA Regt, RAA, B Coy was relocated at Gosford in January 1954 where it subsequently became a tower of strength to the Battalion and closely integrated with its local community.

On 4 Feb 1954, the Battalion took part in the lining of George Street, Sydney on the occasion of the first visit of HM Queen Elizabeth to Australia. This was an experience which those present will never forget, recalling the intensity of feeling and emotion aroused by that first visit of the Sovereign to Australia.

Annual Camp 1954 was largely spent on the Singleton field firing range, each company in turn having to carry out a tactical exercise involving the live firing of all company weapons, with battalion heavy weapons in support. Preparations were then put under way for a major all arms exercise later in the year.

On the weekend 19/21 Nov, 17/18 Bn carried out a battalion group advance and encounter battle exercise in the Campbelltown-Appin-Cordeaux Dam area, code-named AUDAX II. This was the most ambitious CMF exercise carried out up to that time. It involved RAAF reconnaissance and ground support sorties, together with major elements of armour, artillery, provost, transport, engineers and air support signals, either under command or in support.

At this time, few units were prepared to attempt major exercises of this nature with National Service soldiers, but this problem did not affect 17/18 Bn in carrying out this most successful exercise.

In late February 1955, the advance party of the Battalion had moved into Singleton to prepare the annual camp, when disastrous floods devastated the Hunter Valley. Singleton was particularly badly flooded. The Battalion's advance party, under Maj E S Marshall, played a leading role in rehabilitating the town. For his leadership in this crisis Maj Marshall was made an Officer of the Order of the British Empire. Warrant Officer Class II E. Jackson was awarded the Medal of the Order of the British Empire.

Emphasis in training had now swung away from open warfare. The 1955 Annual Camp was spent in Pokolbin State Forest studying and practising jungle warfare techniques. Although Australia had led the world in jungle warfare only 10 years before, no pamphlets were available to set out official doctrine. The Battalion overcame this difficulty before camp by producing and printing its own doctrine on minor tactics in jungle conditions. This was adopted by all units of 2nd Div until official pamphlets became available later on.

In July 1955, command of 17/18 Bn passed from Lt Col Pike to his former 2 i/c, Lt Col E S Marshall, OBE. Like Col Pike, the new CO had been commissioned in 17th Battalion and had subsequently served with 2/33 Bn AIF during World War II.

For the first time, the Mount Royal State Forest area was made available for military purposes and provided a superb setting for jungle warfare training.

After a detailed reconnaissance of the new area, planning commenced for the next annual camp in 1956, to be held there. However, Mount Royal had one major drawback — it had only one means of vehicular access, which was subject to extensive flooding. As might have been expected after a long spell of dry weather, prolonged rain set in as the unit moved into camp, and the advance party was marooned at Mount Royal.

At short notice, the Battalion changed its bivouac and exercise area to Monkey Place Creek in the foothills of the Brokenback Range between Cessnock and Broke. In what turned out to be a highly successful camp, the Battalion demonstrated its expertise in patrolling before the Governor General, Field Marshall Sir William Slim, who showed great interest in the 2/17 Bn Association Patrol Competition.

Training exercises in 1956 were directed to raising the efficiency of sub-units, and in the production and development of officers and NCOs. As a result of this concentration on basics, the Battalion became the first CMF unit to achieve complete posted strength in all ranks.

In March 1959 the Battalion moved into Mount Royal for its annual camp. As had been forecast, the area had great potential for training in jungle warfare up to brigade level, so this potential was exploited to the full.

During the latter part of 1957, C Coy was constituted as the Bn's Cadre Company with the charter of giving recruits their initial training, and conducting special promotion courses for NCOs and first appointment training for potential officers. A team of first class instructors was developed. As graduates were returned to their sub-units, the efficiency of the intensive training which they had undergone advanced the professionalism of the Battalion as a whole. Its weakness, perhaps, was that the Cadre Coy tended to operate somewhat at the expense of sub-units in its early stages by siphoning off their best instructors. Nonetheless, the concept of a Cadre Coy was a bold and imaginative step which produced positive results in the enhanced standard of efficiency which it promoted. This scheme attracted much inter-unit interest, and visitors and observers were frequently present at its activities.

In October 1957 a new depot was occupied by D Coy at Hornsby.

Annual Camp 1958 was held in the Mount Royal area, with concentration on deliberate defence and the full development of defenced localities in jungle terrain. The 1959 Camp was held at Singleton to allow training for the forthcoming presentation of New Colours. However, a major battalion exercise in advance to contact and deployment for battle was still carried out in mountainous country in the Pokolbin State Forest.

On 7 June 1959, 17/18 Bn was presented with new Queen's and Regimental Colours for both of the old battalions on the Sydney Church of England Grammar School Memorial Playing Field at Northbridge. This was the first occasion on which two sets of Colours were presented to the one unit at the same time. The Colours were presented by the Governor, Sir Eric Woodward, KCMG, CB, CBE, DSO.

On 1 July 1959, the, by now, traditional handover ceremony was held at Chatswood Depot, when the retiring CO, Lt Col E S Marshall, OBE handed command to his former 2 i/c, Lt Col D H Wade-Ferrell, MC, who had also been commissioned in the former 17th Battalion.

The new Commanding Officer, who had been decorated with the Military Cross for gallant conduct in Bougainville in 1945, brought a wealth of experience and enthusiasm to his new command.

Unfortunately, as the Battalion moved towards the centenary year of 17th Battalion in 1960, plans were already in train to cut out National Service and to use this as a reason to introduce wide-ranging restructuring of the CMF, particularly in its infantry components. The effect of this was to substantially reduce the command potential of the CMF to compete for senior appointments in the event of war.

This disastrous reorganisation, which was known as the Pentropic Concept, was planned to take effect from 1 July 1960. It fell particularly heavily upon the existing infantry battalions, all of which were to be disbanded and re-formed as companies in battalions of new State Regiments.

This plan was finally unveiled in December 1960 and provoked a storm of protest not only

Consecration of new Queen's and Regimental colours

Last parade of 17/18 Bn

from CMF officers throughout Australia, but also from the RSL, local citizens' organisations and councils. Although both Government and Army were shocked at the depth of feelings against this proposal, it went ahead, and 1 July 1960 was set for the end of National Service and for the re-organisation to take place.

The effect of this decision upon units now largely composed of National Service personnel, and preparing for annual camps in the near future, was little short of disastrous. The Government gave the clear signal that, although it expected National Service soldiers to fulfil their obligations up to 30 June, nothing would happen to them if they did not. Units were thus in the position of having to prepare for camps, without any confidence in the numbers likely to be attending. Notwithstanding, this last year of the Battalion's existence was as busy and as effective as ever. An early activity was the laying up of the old King's and Regimental Colours of the 18th Battalion in St John's Church at Gordon.

The dedicated work of the Battalion's highly regarded Chaplain, the Reverend Noel Goodsell, was recognised in the New Year's Honours List by the award of Member of the Order of the British Empire. This was well received by all ranks who considered this recognition to be well deserved.

The Battalion's last annual camp was held at Singleton in Feb/Mar 1960 with about 90% of National Service soldiers attending. This in itself was a tribute to the effectiveness of the unit and the impression that it had made on its National Servicemen due to the personal exertions of Officers and NCOs.

It is to the credit of the CMF that, even though this was to be its final camp in its present form, high level exercises continued. The Battalion was tested by HQ 8th Bde in a major field exercise in the Muswellbrook area involving covering force operations by day and night. The professional manner in which 17/18 Bn carried out its operations was favourably commented upon by senior observers.

The spirit of all ranks in this last camp was exemplified in this quote from the Sydney *Bulletin* of 23 March 1960:

"Eyewitness notes an unusual tribute paid by the North Shore Regiment (17/18 Infantry Battalion) to their CO, Lt Col D H Wade-Ferrell, MC, during their final camp at Singleton (NSW). The last night of camp, the troops formed up and marched in perfect order behind the band through the Battalion's lines, giving the CO 'eyes right' as they passed him. Not one officer was on parade, which was arranged purely by the troops — and there was not a man absent!"

Even though 17/18 Bn was now in the last months of its existence, Col Wade-Ferrell was determined that his Battalion would not just wither away as could easily have happened. His leadership at this time was an example to all, and home training continued at the usual high level of activity. This included two major tactical exercises, without troops, for Officers and senior NCOs, one of which was an RAAF/Infantry co-operation exercise, involving an actual airlift and airlanding exercise. A battalion range practice was held, also various unit courses, all of which were carried out with a high level of attendance and enthusiasm.

In keeping with this policy of "business as usual" the Bn 2i/c, Maj H P Boland, qualified by examination for the rank of Lt Col; one of four only CMF Infantry Offrs to so qualify in 1960.

On 29 May, a Centenary Review of the Battalion by its Honorary Col was held in St Leonard's Park, the original parade ground of 17th Battalion's ancestral corps, the St Leonard's Rifle Corps. The old King's and Regimental Colours of 17th Battalion were paraded through the streets of North Sydney and then ceremonially laid up in its Garrison Church of St Thomas.

An achievement of which the Battalion was proud was the provision of three middle rank officers in succession to the United Nations Military Observers' Group for extended tours of duty on the disputed border between India and Pakistan[1]. The diplomacy and soldierly conduct of these officers was favourably reported by their United Nations superior officer upon their return to duty with 17/18 Bn.

As from midnight on the night of 30 June/1 July 1960, 17/18 Bn (North Shore Regiment) ceased to exist as an operational battalion, and became an administrative cadre, responsible for winding up the affairs of the former battalion, and arranging the transfer of personnel and equipment to 2nd Battalion, The Royal New South Wales Regiment, into which the old battalion had been absorbed. National Servicemen who did not elect to serve on as volunteers were discharged. Those members for whom there were no jobs in the now severely reduced establishment of the CMF were either placed on the Reserve of Officers, or discharged.

It was to be many years, however, before the Army made good the loss of experienced officers and non-commissioned officers which it suffered throughout the CMF, by its wasteful and ill-considered actions at this time.

On disbandment, 17/18 Bn provided two coys to the new 2nd Battalion, The Royal New South Wales Regiment. B Coy, (The North Shore Company) was located at Kooringa Road, Chatswood, whilst Support Company (The Ku-ring-gai Company) was located in a new depot at Pymble.

Senior Officers of the former 17/18 Bn were given important appointments in other areas of the Eastern Command structure, and on the HQ of the new 2 Bn, RNSWR Battle Gp, which was located at Millers Point. These Offrs played decisive roles in maintaining CMF infantry standards through the several years of the sterile Pentropic exercise, when so many of the best Offrs and NCOs produced by the CMF over years of devoted, professional training, were lost to the Army through its indifference.

2/17 Bn AIF was fortunate that its traditions, and those of its predecessor in World War I, passed into the hands of Commanding Officers of the calibre of those who commanded 17/18 Bn during its 12 years of existence. This spirit was to survive the Pentropic fiasco through those Officers and Soldiers who continued to serve Australia well and faithfully until such time as common sense dictated recognition of the vital role played by CMF, and particularly CMF Infantry, in the defence of Australia.

In December 1961, Australian Army Order No 135 directed that the Battle Honours listed

1
  Maj R S Rudkin MC. ED., Maj D A Williams MBE. ED., Capt D I Aspinall ED

therein for 2/17 Bn, AIF be borne by 17th Battalion, even though the Battalion at that time was classified as "inactive". Together with those awarded to 17th Battalion, AMF for the Great War, a selection of ten of the Honours won during World War II, were authorised to be borne on the Queen's Colour (which had been presented in 1959). This was done, and these Colours were subsequently laid up in St Thomas' Church, North Sydney in 1963, where they rest today.

17/18 Bn was virtually an extension of 2/17 Bn, and to its disbandment in 1960, maintained many of the characteristics and attitudes of an AIF Battalion, particularly as regards readiness for war, unit pride, loyalty and comradeship, and high standards of weapon training, tactics and battle procedures. These are achievements of which those former members of 2/17 Bn who served with 17/18 Bn may rightly be proud. Through their efforts, and those who came from other sources, the spirit and efficiency of the AIF, of which 2/17 Bn provided such an example, were maintained at a high level until 1960, and that was no mean achievement.

FROM THE PENTROPIC REORGANISATION
UNTIL THE PRESENT TIME

The term "Pentropic" was the name given by the Australian Army to a tactical organisation based upon "fives" rather than the traditional "threes". It was first suggested by the eminent British military writer, B H Liddell Hart, in his book "Defence of the West" published in 1950. Liddell Hart explored several alternatives for achieving greater flexibility of command on an atomic battlefield in North West European conditions. His suggestions were not taken up by the British Army.

About 1957, the United States Army experimented with this theory, naming it "Pentomic". One Regular and several National Guard divisions were involved, but the concept was dropped.

At about the time that the "Pentomic" concept was being phased out in the United States Army, it caught the attention of Australian Army planners, and the decision was made to reorganise the CMF in accordance with this concept, suitably adopted for use in tropical warfare. Whilst it was nominally adopted by regular infantry battalions, those on service outside Australia remained on the well-tried standard tropic establishment.

As conceived by the Australian planners, the Pentropic Battalion involved a dramatic increase in both manpower and weaponry, with a fifth rifle company being added. Intermediate HQs (brigades) were abolished and battalions were controlled directly by Divisional HQ. However, for detached operations involving two or more battalions, a Task Force HQ was formed which directly controlled the operations of its battalions. As these Task Force HQs could not be formed on an ad hoc basis, they in fact simply became brigade HQs under another name.

Experience in tropical warfare during World War II had shown how difficult it was to reinforce and maintain standard battalions at an acceptable level for operational tasks. Most informed thinking, based on personal experience, indicated that the answer lay in overcoming these manpower and supply problems rather than experimenting with the grossly enlarged and unwieldy infantry battalion establishment now proposed.

Perhaps the kindest thing which might be said of the planners was that they appeared to confuse conditions in North West Europe with those in New Guinea. Therefore, in the nature of all bureaucrats, having made a blunder, they fought a rearguard action to save face to the bitter end.

The HQ of a Pentropic infantry battalion was in fact an enhanced brigade HQ in its own right. It was commanded by a full Col who was usually, but not always, CMF, and who had as a deputy commander a CMF Lt Col. The COs principal Staff Officers were an Executive Officer

(Lt Col) and a GSO 2 and DAA & QMG (Majors) who were Regular Officers. Two CMF Majors were "shadow" GSO 2 and DAA & QMG. All other appointments usual in an infantry battalion HQ were present.

Each of the Pentropic battalions formed a battalion of the newly created state regiments: in New South Wales this was the Royal New South Wales Regiment (RNSWR) which, at this time, existed rather as a concept than as a reality.

In New South Wales, three battalions were formed:

1st Battalion RNSWR was based upon the former 1st Commando Company, and took the form of a three-company, special task battalion based in Sydney. The various university regiments maintained their former roles, without significant alteration to their structure. The two Pentropic battalions shared the rest of the State between them, with the exception of the Far North Coast, which went to the Royal Queensland Regiment for some years.

2nd Battalion RNSWR (of which the former 17/18 Bn formed part) was responsible generally for that part of New South Wales above an east-west line north of Sydney Harbour.

3rd Battalion RNSWR was responsible for that area of the State lying south of that line.

Initially, 2 RNSWR had its HQ at Millers Point, but this was subsequently moved briefly to Carlow Street, Crows Nest. At this stage it had depots at Crows Nest, Chatswood, Pymble, Gosford, Newcastle, Cessnock, Maitland, Taree, Grafton, Macksville, Coffs Harbour, Kempsey, Orange, Dubbo, Parkes, Lithgow and Bathurst. Those former battalions incorporated in 2 RNSWR were:

> 2nd Battalion (City of Newcastle Regiment) as C Company (The Newcastle Company) and Band.

> 6th New South Wales Mounted Rifles as E Company (The Mounted Rifles Company).

> 13th Battalion (The Macquarie Regiment) as D Company (The Macquarie Company).

> 17th/18th Battalion (The North Shore Regiment) as B Company (The North Shore Company) and Support Company (The Ku-ring-gai Company) and Regimental Band.

> 30th Battalion (The New South Wales Scottish Regiment) as A Company (The New South Wales Scottish Company) and Pipes and Drums.

On 1st July 1960, Brig the Honourable S.L M Eskell, ED, MLC, the former Commander of 14 Bde, assumed command of 2nd Battalion RNSWR Battle Group with his HQ at Millers Point.

It had been decided by Army that for their formative year the Pentropic Battalion Battle Groups would be commandedby former Brigade Commanders. In view of the complex structure of the new HQs and the introduction of senior Regular Officers with CMF "learners" of equal rank, coupled with the need to have Commanding Officers of sufficiently high rank and experience to push their requirements forcefully at higher levels of command, this was probably a wise move. Nonetheless, it had the bad effect of retarding CMF promotions for at least another year at levels where they would be most needed in the years to come. This block in promotions was also exacerbated by retaining Officers who had already completed terms of command with former battalions as Deputy Commanders, thus denying qualified Officers a further opportunity of promotion and gaining experience for war. The protocol of allowing graduates only to command university regiments also denied many first class Officers the opportunity of advancement. This made a one-sided convention that it was acceptable for University Regt Offrs to command Field Force units, but not vice versa.

2 Bn RNSWR was faced with forming a cohesive battalion across virtually the northern

half of the State with minimal transport resources and restrictions upon air travel when this was obviously the sensible and most economic answer to this problem.

The space and travel problems of the new 2 Bn RNSWR were immense. Coys occupied areas which had formerly been Bn areas. The problems of administering, supervising and controlling these enormous areas with minimal transport or alternative travel arrangements were enormous. As though these problems were not enough, they were compounded by shortages of Regular Cadre Staff, and the dispersion of CMF Offrs and NCOs. Inevitably, the amount of time required of CMF Offrs and NCOs was so great, particularly in far flung country areas, that it clashed to an unsupportable degree with family and employment obligations. This led to the loss of many of the best members of the unit who, in less stressful circumstances, had been major contributors to their old units. Of course, as most of this attrition was caused by unacceptable dispersion, these losses were usually where they could not be accepted. A simple look at a map of New South Wales should have revealed these potential problems to Army planners at the outset, and they need not have occurred had any reasonable forward planning gone into the Pentropic Concept.

Of necessity, training had to revert generally to section and platoon level. Those opportunities to control large bodies of troops in the field, which had been such a feature of life in most of the pre-Pentropic CMF battalions, no longer existed. This in turn led to a diminuition of opportunities and skills in administrative areas, which could only be partly redressed at TEWTS.

The opportunity for CMF Offrs and NCOs to attend Army schools or courses of instruction had never been great, but they seemed to be even less available at this time.

Other problems were to be faced if the new battalion was to become effective. Sub-units were still fiercely loyal to their former battalions. They were resentful at seeing comrades, with whom they had served happily for years, thrown on the Army scrap heap through redundancy only and no fault of their own.

A major error by planners was to allow territorial titles related to former battalions to be used by companies of the new Pentropic battalions. This indulgence, which was only a sop, had the effect of keeping alive loyalties which should have been directed to the new battalions. At TEWTS and exercises, and in annual camps, this parochial tendency was particularly evident in the first couple of years. Eventually, the passing of time and some plain, hard talking to the Offrs and Senior NCOs began to break down these very real barriers to integration.

As might have been expected, the 1961 Annual Camp was not a happy one. It took all of the very considerable diplomatic skills and toughness of character, with which Brigadier Eskell was amply endowed, to bring this camp to a successful conclusion.

Both 2 RNSWR and 3 RNSWR were brigaded under 1st Task Force for this camp and exercised in the Mount Royal area. The unsuitability of the Pentropic establishment for tropical warfare in mountainous terrain was amply demonstrated, and did little to build up the confidence of senior and middle rank Officers in its effectiveness. Old skills at section, platoon and company level were of a high standard, and this compensated to a great degree for an otherwise depressing camp.

It should not be thought, however, that 2 Bn RNSWR Battle Gp was alone with its problems. This was not the case, as the Pentropic reorganisation had the same disastrous results Australia-wide throughout the CMF. In fact, Brig Eskell's leadership at this stressful time was critical to the emergence of his unit as an effective force during his period of command.

On 21 July 1961, Comd of 2 Bn RNSWR Battle Group passed to a former CO of 17/18 Inf Bn, Col P H Pike, OBE, ED, who, since his last Comd, had spent the time in various Staff and

P H Pike

Training postings at Eastern Command. With the introduction of the Pentropic establishment, Col Pike had spent the last year as DAQMG (CMF) at HQ 1st Task Force. He was thus familiar with the Pentropic Concept and his new Comd.

By now, HQ of 2 Bn RNSWR Battle Group had been re-located at Carlow Street Depot, Crows Nest, and an early decision of the new CO was to move his HQ to Pymble Depot, where HQ 2/17 Bn RNSWR is still located.

Army HQ Training Directives seemed to be based on the belief that CMF units were incapable of training at higher levels than Pl and Coy, much to the disgust of Senior CMF Offrs whose experience went far beyond that. It was often difficult to obtain facilities for Specialist Pl training, and there was always a shortage of sufficient ammunition and other stores to bring Specialist Pls up to the level considered desirable by the new CO.

The Bn had by now sorted out its identity problems to a large degree, and this was reflected in better co-operation between sub-units.

However, to reduce the possibility of this problem arising in the future, Col Pike took particular pains to gain the support of influential ex-members of former units, including past COs, particularly in country areas. This provided effective local support groups from whom isolated Pl and Coy Comds could obtain advice and assistance if need arose, before approaching Bn HQ.

A somewhat sad task for the new CO over a period of some months was to carry out the Laying Up of the Colours of the former Bns from which 2 Bn RNSWR was raised. Impressive ceremonies were held at the respective Garrison Churches at Newcastle (2 Bn), Orange (6 NSW Mounted Rifles), Taree (13 Bn), Crows Nest (17 Bn), Gordon (18 Bn) and Sydney (30 Bn, NSW Scottish). This marked the passing of an era in which serving CMF units had close associations with their war-time equivalents. It also heralded a period of decline in recruiting in country areas which in past years had proudly supported their own local unit or sub-unit, directly connected with the locality.

Despite the problems created by distance between HQ at Pymble and sub-units scattered throughout the northern half of the State, unit schools and courses were conducted, and remarkable uniformity in examination marking was achieved by the preparation of detailed guide lines for examining Offrs and NCOs, to follow in assessing candidates. It would have been fatally easy to have adopted the soul-destroying 'bull ring' method of instruction throughout the Bn and, indeed, this view was urged on the Bn from time to time by Formation HQ, but this pressure was stoutly resisted by Col Pike.

Although Bn level exercises were frowned on, HQ Staff took every opportunity to use the movement of sub-units in the field to set up command post exercises which, without interfering with the sub-units' movements or exercises, enabled Bn HQ to be exercised at the same time. On one occasion at Mount Royal, the Div Comd paid a surprise visit in the field but was even more surprised to find a complex withdrawal exercise on two axes in progress and, further, that it was being professionally conducted by a CMF-manned HQ.

The three years of Col Pike's Comd were not easy years. There was a mental block amongst the older members of the territorially named coys against whole-hearted integration in the new Bn; and a view that the coys were cadres of the former Bns, simply awaiting re-activation in the future.

This parochial view was not so evident in the new generation of recruits now coming forward as they had not served with the old Bns. Consequently, their loyalties generally lay with 2 Bn RNSWR, in which their experience lay.

Throughout the period of his Comd, Col Pike worked strenuously to overcome these difficulties and to rebuild confidence in the future of CMF Inf throughout his Comd. It is to his credit that, in these difficult circumstances, he was able to do this.

On 1 July 1964, Comd of 2 Bn RNSWR Battle Group passed to Col E S Marshall who had succeeded (then) Lt Col Pike as CO, 17/18 Inf Bn. Like Col Pike, the new CO came from Staff and Training appointments to his new Comd and this experience was to be of great value to him in dealing with the complex Comd and Training problems inherent in the geographical 'spread' of Pentropic Bns.

Regular Bns had been far less affected by the Pentropic re-organisation than their CMF counterparts, because their sub-units were concentrated; and, as Australia's commitments in South East Asia began to escalate, one after the other the Regular Bns reverted to tropical establishment.

It took the re-introduction of National Service in 1965 to finally kill off the Pentropic establishment in CMF Inf units and on 30 June 1965, 2 Bn RNSWR Battle Group was disbanded, and 2 Bn RNSWR and 17 Bn RNSWR were re-activated with effect from 1 July. Col Marshall took over Comd of 17 Bn RNSWR and set to work enthusiastically to rebuild the new Bn on the well-tested tropic establishment.

The area from which the Bn was to draw its recruits was still far too large and travel distance between HQ at Pymble and sub-units was still excessive and wasteful of time. However, it was a great improvement on what had formerly been expected under the Pentropic Concept.

Sub-units of 17 Bn RNSWR were located at Pymble, Crows Nest, Erina, Lithgow, Bathurst, Cowra, Orange, Dubbo, Parkes, Forbes, Chatswood, Katoomba and Blacktown.

The first Annual Camp of 17 Bn RNSWR was held in the Mount Royal State Forest area, with training generally confirmed to Pl and Coy level.

By now the effects of National Service were beginning to show, and persons eligible for National Service could elect, as an alternative to two years full-time service in the Regular Army (with possible service in Vietnam) to serve for six years part-time in CMF.

As these recruits began to arrive in the Bn, they brought with them the old problems inherent in compulsory service. Chief amongst these were the time-consuming procedures involved in dealing with those soldiers who, whilst subject to the National Service Act, still tried to evade CMF service. As had happened before in the 1950s, key personnel spent an inordinate amount of time on this sterile and unproductive area of administration, to the detriment of the unit as a whole. Within a few years however, former National Servicemen, who had completed a tour of operations in South Vietnam, began to join the CMF, introducing experience of war into their units for the first time since Korea .

Having guided 2 Bn RNSWR Battle Group and its successor, 17 Bn RNSWR, successfully through this transitional period, Col Marshall handed over Comd later in 1965 to Lt Col F.S Hallissy who had formerly commanded 5 Bn (Victorian Scottish).

With Col Marshall's departure from the Bn, that strong link with the pre-War 17 Bn (North Sydney Regt) which hadbeen shared by all COs, with the sole exception of Brig Eskell was severed. One only of the succeeding COs, Lt Col Douglass Aspinall had served with 17/18 Bn, during which time he had served for two years in Kashmir on the United Nations Military Observer Group.

Col Aspinall was also responsible for having Pymble Depot designated as Suakin Depot in honour of 17 Bns Senior Battle Honour. He also arranged for the access road to be named Suakin Street; and for a memorial to be erected in the depot grounds to honour 2/30 Infantry Battalion, AIF.

Thereafter, whilst the traditions of 17th and 2/17 Inf Bn AIF still provided a source of inspiration to serving soldiers they were now history, and not living memories within the Bn.

The story of 17 Bn RNSWR must hereafter be briefly told, as space does not permit the achievements of the COs who followed Col Marshall to be dealt with in detail. This is not to say that what they did, and are still doing, is not just as important as the past, but rather that by the passage of time it is now of somewhat less relevance to those to whom this history is primarily directed, the former members of 2/17 Bn AIF.

The abolition of National Service in 1972 saw the Bn faced again with the problem of building up to acceptable strength with volunteers from a community which, particularly in the country, was disenchanted with the Vietnam experience, and viewed military service of any kind with distrust. It was a long time before this resistance was overcome and volunteers began to come forward in sufficient numbers to enable sub-units to reach effective strength.

In the period which followed the Vietnam War, numbers of ex-National Service veterans of that conflict joined the CMF or, as it later became known, the Army Reserve (ARES). They had shared experiences, often in the same unit with regular soldiers with whom they were now serving, and it brought Regular Cadre and ARES NCOs and Offrs much closer together than in the past.

The need for ARES Inf to be trained to the highest possible level, consistent with the constraints imposed by part-time soldiering, began to be recognised by AHQ planners, and ARES sub-units became more frequently involved in major regular Field Force exercises. Sub-units attended the School of Land Warfare at Canungra for intensive training in lieu of attendance at Annual Camps, and a more flexible and supportive attitude towards problems of ARES units began to show.

During this period, a number of important events in the life of 17 Bn RNSWR took place which are briefly recorded:

(a) Queen's and Regimental Colours of new pattern were presented to the Bn by the Hon Col RNSWR, His Excellency, Sir Roden Cutler, VC, KCMG, CBE at Victoria Barracks on 21 July 1968.

(b) To mark its Golden Jubilee Year, on 17 Sept 1978, Ku-ring-gai Municipal Council granted the Bn: Freedom of Entry to the Municipality.

(c) On the occasion of the anniversary of 75 years of local government in the Municipality of Ku-ring-gai, and the 21st Birthday of the Royal New South Wales Regt, a ceremonial parade was held on Regimental Park at Killara, on 28 June 1981. This was followed by the Exercise of the Grant of Freedom of Entry to the Municipality by the Bn.

(d) On 17 Aug 1985, the first Suakin Dinner was held by the Bn's Officers to honour the New South Wales Soudan Contingent Centenary. This Dinner is now an annual function.

In 1987, it became apparent that, with declining strengths in some areas, some Bns of the Royal New South Wales Regt could not remain effective and must be either disbanded or linked with other Bns. It was decided to link two Bns in each Bde and, on 5 Dec 1987 at a ceremony held at Newcastle, 2 Bn was formally linked with 17 Bn to form 2/17 Bn, The Royal New South Wales Regt.

On 16 April 1988, in conjunction with Ku-ring-gai Municipal Council, 2/17 Bn RNSWR celebrated the 200th Anniversary of the Founding of New South Wales with a Drumhead Service held in Memorial Park, St Ives. This was followed by the Exercise of the Right to Freedom of Entry to the Municipality.

Well established patterns of training including overseas and major exercise participation have continued, whilst a significant contingent from the Pipes and Drums took part in the British Army Scottish Division's Beating Retreat in London, 1990.

In 1990 the Battalion was involved in the Newcastle earthquake cleanup, and in April 1990 provided assistance in the Nyngan floods. Since then the Battalion has adjusted to changed home area boundaries, now generally at Central Sydney and the Central Coast.

To enable the long planned conversion of Suakin Depot, 2nd/17th RNSWR was temporarily relocated to Silverwater, near Parramatta, while work was carried out to convert the old depot to a multiple usage depot, to be shared with 7 Field Regiment RAA.

On 13 April 1996, after exercising its Right of Freedom of Entry to the Municipality of Ku-ring-gai, 2nd/17th RNSWR formally re-occupied Suakin Depot.

2nd/17th RNSWR played a major role in the multinational Exercise Kangaroo '95 in which the unit performed very well. New interoperability concepts were tested with RAAF in the harsh conditions of northern Australia and different command and control arrangements within the Battalion group were tested. The unit consistently produced the best ready-reaction times achieved during this major exercise.

In May 1997 a company group formed from E Company, Arncliffe, and including a platoon from C Company, Newcastle, went to Battle Wing, Canungra for individual and collective training in a realistic and challenging environment. Also in May the Battalion formed part of Exercise 'Rhino Charge' near Broken Hill, conducted by 9 Brigade at Kenswick Barracks, South Australia and practised individual and collective skills in the unfamiliar area.

Whatever changes in organisation and equipment have taken place since 1945, the role of infantry remains unchanged. As it has been throughout history, it is still to seek and close with the enemy, to kill or capture him, to seize and hold ground and to repel attack by day or night, regardless of season, weather or terrain.

Today this is the primary role of 2nd/17th Bn RNSWR. In addition, because all of its soldiers are volunteers for service anywhere if called out, it constitutes part of the 'follow up' force which will be next for battle after the regular component of Field Force is committed. Additionally, like other ARES Inf Bns, it has a special task which varies from unit to unit. In the case of 2nd/17th Bn RNSWR at the time of initial deployment of Field Force, this is to provide 'round out' elements for 1 Div if called upon. This means that sub-units may be called forward from the Bn to serve as sub-units of a regular Bn which needs its war establishment 'rounded out' before operations commence. Our successor Bn in ARES is worthy indeed to carry on the traditions of 17th and 2/17 Bn AIF and does so proudly.

2/17 Aust Inf Bn is fortunate indeed that it did not vanish into history as so many notable Bns did at the end of the War. It has been represented worthily in one form or another since 1948 on the Order of Battle of the Australian Army, by CMF and ARES Bns, and members of the Bn should be proud of the worthwhile achievements of their successors over the last 40 years.

The Regimental Motto of 17th Battalion (The North Sydney Regiment) says it all FACTA PROBANT - Deeds Prove.

COMMANDING OFFICERS
SINCE THE SECOND WORLD WAR

17/18 Infantry Battalion (the North Shore Regiment)
1948-1951	Lieutenant Colonel (later Major General) J R Broadbent, DSO, ED
1951-1955	Lieutenant Colonel (later Colonel) P H Pike
1955-1959	Lieutenant Colonel (later Major General) E S Marshall, OBE
1959-1960	Lieutenant Colonel (later Colonel) D H Wade-Ferrell, MC

2nd Battalion, Royal New South Wales Regiment (Battle Group)
1960-1961	Brigadier The Honorable S L M Eskelf, ED, MLC
1961-1964	Colonel P H Pike, OBE, ED
1964-1965	Colonel (later Major General) E S Marshall, OBE, ED

17th Battalion, Royal New South Wales Regiment
1965	Colonel (later Major General) E S Marshall, OBE, ED
1965-1968	Lieutenant Colonel (later Brigadier) F S Hallissy
1968-1971	Lieutenant Colonel D I Aspinall, ED
1971-1974	Lieutenant Colonel J C Southwell, ED
1974-1975	Lieutenant Colonel A T Pembroke, MC
1975-1978	Lieutenant Colonel K J Kirby, ED
1978-1981	Lieutenant Colonel (now Brigadier) D R Leece, RFD, ED
1981-1984	Lieutenant Colonel (now Brigadier) B A Trimble, RFD
1984-1986	Lieutenant Colonel (now Major General) B A McGrath, RFD
1986-1987	Lieutenant Colonel L A Wood, AM, RFD

2nd/17th Battalion, Royal New South Wales Regiment
1987-1989	Lieutenant Colonel L A Wood, AM, RFD
1989-1991	Lieutenant Colonel (now Colonel) A S Morrison, RFD
1991-1993	Lieutenant Colonel D D Shearman, RFD
1994-1996	Lieutenant Colonel G N Oakley, RFD
1997-	Lieutenant Colonel A Henderson, RFD

B Coy 2/17 RNSWR on a MOUT Exercise (Military Operations Urban Terrain)
at Singleton Camp, February 1997

NOMINAL ROLL

NX69167	Abberton T W	
NX84643	Aboud M	
NX19192	Acorn W S	
NX16098	Acres P J *KIA* (NG)	
NX41540	Adams A V	
NX21267	Adams R J	
NX17062	Adamson L A V	
NX172712	Affleck J W	
NX14503	Ahearn J A *DOW* (A)	
NX4657	Ahearn R L	
NX21674	Ainsworth G S	
NX16428	Akins J	
NX55508	Alderdice C W *WIA* (A)	
QX45644	Aldridge A P	
NX20037	Alexander C B	
NX50757	Alexander F L	
QX22538	Alexander L E *KIA* (A)	
NX130786	Alford J	
NX70327	Alison A M Major	
NX18810	Allan H H	
NX12229	Allan H T Lt Col	
NX16241	Allen F J	
VX26493	Allen G B	
VX129254	Allen J H	
VX141393	Allen J W	
NX14861	Allen L J	
NX89831	Allgood J E *WIA* (B)	
NX58004	Allison E *WIA* (T)	
NX83661	Allshorn A D	
NX21783	Allsop L P *KIA* (T)	
NX21782	Allsop R J	
VX150507	Anderson A	
NX14994	Anderson C A	
NX16022	Anderson C J T *WIA* (A)	
	DOW (NG)	
NX156281	Anderson J A	
VX146991	Anderson J D	
NX190941	Anderson K W	
NX50171	Anderson L	
NX17188	Anderson N E *WIA* (A)	
	WIA (NG)	
NX119478	Anderson R E	
NX90688	Andrew H D	
VX146393	Andrew J D Lieut	
NX69605	Andrews E J *WIA* (BA)	
NX14370	Andrews R	
NX46126	Andrews S W	
VX55929	Angel R S *WIA* (NG)	
NX13537	Angus J R *WIA* (A)	

ACC	Accidental deaths
DOI	Died of Illness
DOW	Died of Wounds
KIA	Killed in Action
MPD	Missing Presumed dead
MUR	Murdered
POW	Prisoner of War
(A)	Alamein
(AU)	Australia
(B)	Borneo
(BA)	Before Alamein
(BH)	Benghasi Handicap
(NG)	New Guinea
(P)	Palestine
(S)	Syria
(T)	Tobruk

NX21261	Angwin W
NX92479	Anslow A C
NX71608	Anson G *WIA* (A)
NX17871	Anson R J *WIA* (BA)
	WIA (A)
NX142844	Applebee R T
NX16379	Appleton L
NX17856	Archibald R
NX17782	Armstrong C E *WIA* (T)
NX16467	Armstrong C T
NX19644	Armstrong R F
NX90614	Arndell G C
NX28704	Arnold J E *WIA* (A)
NX89685	Arrighi J L
NX13943	Ash C
NX23168	Ashby A J
WX40246	Ashby H W
WX26702	Ashman H G
NX56027	Ashton E F
NX17255	Askew R R
NX16996	Askildsen R D
NX16064	Asquith J S
NX14779	Atkins S G *WIA* (T)
	WIA (NG)
NX21478	Atkinson A W
NX43347	Atkinson K G *WIA* (A)
NX24314	Auckett R V
NX35723	Auswild J
NX23135	Avery R *KIA* (A)
NX166050	Badcock E G
NX58834	Bade T E
NX17584	Baillee H E J

VX146064	Bailey A W
NX21680	Bailey C G
NX21673	Bailey J H
NX18670	Baker C
NX21836	Baker F C
NX123838	Baker J C
NX21838	Baker J O
NX16738	Baker S V
NX125846	Baker W R
NX12329	Balfe J W Major
VX57044	Banfield A W
NX156058	Banks H A
NX14409	Barber L *WIA* (T)
NX34089	Barber W J
NX58824	Bard J B
NX2571	Barker A *WIA* (A)
NX21644	Barker C R
NX20987	Barker F W
NX2577	Barker R
NX22902	Barnard D J
NX22283	Barnes A
NX126653	Barnes R V
NX58834	Barnes W *WIA* (NG)
NX79425	Barney S W W
NX66440	Barnett E A
NX21074	Barnett P C
NX14951	Barrell C P
NX39892	Barrell L R B
NX37023	Barrett F W
DX563	Barron F C
NX45097	Barrow J
NX55688	Barry D J
NX17745	Barry G H S
NX39057	Barry L T
NX56297	Barry W J
NX172702	Bartlett A
NX16125	Bartlett W K *DOW* (NG)
QX27021	Barton C G L
SX11298	Bascombe P H
NX126593	Basham F W
NX21199	Bassett J S *WIA* (A)
NX46750	Battese J *WIA* (NG)
NX17219	Bateson H
WX12263	Batty C E
NX14463	Baverstock H L
NX165398	Baxter E T
NX46916	Beale D H
NX96424	Bean H
NX16551	Beard E J

NX50503	Beard K E Lieut	
NX60500	Beasley A C	
NX125784	Beath B V	
NX17185	Beaumont R	
NX90168	Beaumont R F	
QX53348	Beaumont W G	
NX68954	Beavan E F *WIA* (NG)	
NX55112	Beaver K E	
NX15937	Becker E A	
NX171368	Beckhaus A H	
NX17784	Beezley A J *DOW* (T)	
NX60169	Bell A	
NX79700	Bell B V	
NX17458	Bell C S *DOW* (T)	
NX21849	Bell E E *WIA* (T)	
	WIA (A) *WIA* (NG)	
NX20736	Bembrick K R	
NX66348	Beness R S *WIA* (NG)	
NX18666	Benham D G	
NX21957	Benn M A *WIA* (T)	
NX68979	Bennett C C	
NX15455	Bennett C W L *WIA* (A)	
NX67784	Bennett R	
NX29288	Bennett R C	
NX21259	Bennett R J	
NX92061	Benny V E F	
NX34299	Bennie R J Lieut *WIA* (A)	
NX59329	Bennie R J *WIA* (A)	
NX14372	Benson F A	
NX93098	Bersene C E	
NX22217	Berg A W L	
QX26797	Berger C H	
NX14835	Berry S	
QX19715	Berryman J H	
NX58830	Berwick H T	
NX21384	Berwick K E	
NX8390	Bevan R M *KIA* (NG)	
NX54959	Bevan T T	
NX41622	Beveridge C	
NX24486	Bingley P J	
NX14856	Birch G W *WIA* (T)	
	KIA (NG)	
NX13939	Bird C R Capt	
NX109013	Bird J M	
NX21205	Bird K R *DOW* (T)	
NX22620	Birks N B	
NX12211	Bjelke-Petersen D G Lieut	
NX78224	Black A J *WIA* (NG)	
NX16359	Black R J	
NX90052	Blackall R G	
NX16286	Blackburne W K	
NX17344	Blacklock J S	
NX66490	Blacklock W G *WIA* (T)	
	WIA (A)	
NX16877	Blackwell T E	
NX21420	Blair A	

NX17259	Blair D	
NX17260	Blair J	
NX17582	Blair J	
NX21419	Blair W *POW* (T)	
NX17767	Blaker B J	
NX47960	Blanch B C *KIA* (NG)	
NX17990	Blanch H R	
NX126651	Blight C H	
NX174187	Blockley J R	
VX16593	Blore J	
NX17528	Blundell E J Capt	
NX190940	Blundell H W E	
NX12370	Blundell J B Cap *DOI* (AU)	
VX130039	Blythe H	
NX20790	Bodkin W A	
NX18370	Bodley P W	
NX6944	Bohannon A	
NX17385	Booth A F *WIA* (A)	
NX90283	Booth A G	
NX4948	Booth H J *WIA* (A)	
NX83144	Borthwick J J	
VX90519	Bott W C A	
NX74116	Bourke J F	
NX77957	Bourke J R	
NX156513	Bourke L J	
NX10990	Bourke V H	
NX44181	Bourke W E	
WX26667	Bovell T A	
NX17006	Bowden B	
NX16776	Bowden G H	
NX57215	Bowden R W	
NX60592	Bowditch F C *WIA* (T)	
NX168549	Bowers H H J	
NX83086	Bowker G W	
NX14609	Bown H C	
NX22255	Boyce D	
NX15956	Boyce J W *WIA* (T)	
NX91476	Boyd J R	
NX15670	Boyland J *WIA* (T)	
NX22125	Boyland P E J	
NX16977	Boyle F H	
NX17510	Brabin C A *WIA* (T)	
NX41908	Brackenreg A W *WIA* (A)	
NX14388	Brady H M *KIA* (T)	
NX43305	Brady N J *WIA* (A)	
NX15652	Bray J W Lieut	
WX39083	Brede C C	
NX18104	Brennan W H	
QX57117	Brent P T H	
NX170816	Bridger R F	
NX12298	Brien L C Major *WIA* (A)	
NX84089	Brierley R J	
NX164306	Briggs J H	
NX21475	Briggs O	
NX23056	Brightwell T P *DOW* (NG)	
NX21773	Brinckley W H *KIA* (T)	

WX28254	Britten L A	
NX17213	Britton J I *WIA* (NG)	
NX12225	Broadbent J R Lt Col	
NX154835	Broadbridge A J	
NX60656	Broadhead D *WIA* (A)	
NX14837	Brock B E *KIA* (T)	
NX94307	Brodie K	
NX4022	Broinowski S M	
NX24386	Bromwich A R T	
	WIA (NG)	
NX148597	Bronson R P	
NX9660	Brook G R Lieut	
WX5557	Brooks J W Lieut	
NX27607	Brooks R C	
NX20784	Broome G G *WIA* (B)	
NX60164	Brotherton W L	
NX21262	Broughton R	
NX77998	Brown A B M	
NX92995	Brown A F *DOI* (AU)	
NX164112	Brown A H	
NX91620	Brown B M	
NX92620	Brown C C M *WIA* (NG)	
NX14415	Brown D McD	
NX89985	Brown H G	
NX125783	Brown H J	
NX18906	Brown H M	
NX21390	Brown H S	
NX176056	Brown J A	
NX191862	Brown J J	
NX16212	Brown J S	
NX22284	Brown L	
NX24698	Brown L J *WIA* (T)	
NX21389	Brown S G *WIA* (A)	
NX25410	Brown T *KIA* (NG)	
NX157831	Brown T G	
NX22215	Brown W S	
NX16000	Brownlow N G	
NX24645	Brown-Parker R A	
DX580	Bruun P D *WIA* (A)	
NX24218	Bryant A F *WIA* (T)	
NX17918	Bryant F	
NX22201	Bryant G R	
NX21457	Bryant H W	
NX164659	Bryant J E	
NX22216	Bryant T N	
NX91511	Bryce J A	
QX44056	Bryde E A	
NX16230	Brydon W	
QX55835	Bryen R S	
NX55245	Bryson W S	
NX66250	Buckett D H	
NX46796	Buckett W J *DOW* (NG)	
NX32697	Buckingham W G	
NX23678	Buckley R G	
NX171573	Budd F C	
NX19224	Budden T	

VX79203	Bugge R J	
VX2477	Buist B C	
NX56862	Bulley S L	
NX66330	Bulliman D	
NX80621	Bulliman L J	
WX27368	Bunce G	
NX17593	Bundy R A	
NX16742	Bundy S V	
VX119048	Bunting R A	
WX26615	Burch O	
WX26668	Burch W J	
NX27164	Burford P L J	
QX26797	Burger C A	
NX58854	Burgess H J	
NX22429	Burgess R	
NX17372	Burgess R F WIA (A)	
NX15891	Burgess R V Lieut	
	WIA (BA)	
NX77957	Burke J R	
NX60453	Burke J T	
NX21463	Burns F WIA (T)	
	WIA (T) KIA (A)	
NX174663	Burns L S	
NX17776	Burns R A WIA (NG)	
NX55590	Burrell L C KIA (NG)	
NX90424	Burrell R H	
NX60574	Burrows E	
WX8575	Burton H Lieut	
NX143172	Burton H V	
TX6790	Burton M C	
NX2550	Burton S T	
NX22834	Butcher S R	
NX93357	Butler J	
NX22802	Butler W	
NX16094	Butt R C	
WX21743	Buttel P M	
NX172184	Byers W	
NX49251	Byrne A F	
NX91192	Byrne C	
NX58410	Byrne M E	
NX171361	Byrne P R	
VX47864	Byrne W L Chaplain	
NX22434	Byrnes B J WIA (BA)	
	WIA (A)	
NX21203	Byrnes T WIA (A)	
NX53097	Byron H J	
NX162161	Caffyn A	
NX21391	Cain W	
NX57044	Calder G KIA (NG)	
NX19077	Caldwell J S	
NX17583	Callaghan J J WIA (T)	
NX53586	Calvert N A	
NX21480	Camarsh F T	
NX23059	Cameron E A KIA (A)	

NX60361	Cameron G S WIA (A)	
NX16232	Cameron I W WIA (A)	
NX24418	Cameron W	
NX174306	Camilleri V	
NX25284	Campbell A WIA (T)	
NX21612	Campbell C T	
NX91473	Campbell J H	
NX23799	Campbell L M	
NX95025	Campbell N J	
VX92428	Campbell R J	
NX90160	Campbell S N	
VX128626	Campesato G	
NX14460	Cannon J D	
NX89264	Capewell P N WIA (NG)	
NX14806	Carey D M	
NX47116	Carey W L WIA (BA)	
NX200247	Carlin B T	
SX99	Carnegie A D	
NX21392	Carney G	
NX112845	Carney M T	
NX125751	Carpenter E G	
NX59910	Carpenter W L	
NX50677	Carr J W	
NX22438	Carr-Boyd B R	
	KIA (NG)	
NX23163	Carrett R C	
NX21432	Carrick J J WIA (NG)	
NX161924	Carroll J WIA (B)	
NX34024	Carroll K S	
NX14883	Carroll P D	
NX46358	Carter B L	
NX21681	Carter C	
QX37157	Carter C D	
NX24575	Carter J W G	
NX200335	Carter R J	
NX122496	Carthew A	
NX17092	Carthew G H	
NX21370	Cartledge B H WIA (T)	
NX21913	Cartledge D J T/Major	
	WIA (A)	
NX18654	Cartwright C A WIA (T)	
NX93510	Cassels M McK	
NX173349	Cassidy R J	
NX79939	Castle-Roche W F M	
NX21513	Catlin J H WIA (NG)	
NX139271	Chaffey G	
QX40247	Chalmers K L	
NX21221	Chambers A	
NX35375	Chambers T S	
NX33461	Chamberlain D G	
NX19282	Champion J WIA (NG)	
NX21464	Champley S W D WIA (T)	
VX124805	Chandler R F	
NX32825	Chaney E C WIA (NG)	
NX18308	Channon R W WIA (NG)	
QX30475	Chapman A	

NX12420	Chapman E T Capt	
	KIA (T)	
NX34881	Chapman G H T/Capt	
NX17752	Chapman H C	
NX16210	Chapman N J	
NX17753	Chapman S J WIA (NG)	
NX21271	Chard R F	
SX30740	Chardon R F	
NX119351	Chennock L J	
NX78106	Chigwidden W A	
NX22900	Chilcott J A WIA (A)	
NX17703	Chilvers P S WIA (A)	
NX25429	Chrisp G R Lieut	
NX19515	Christian E O	
NX79247	Christie D H	
NX162187	Christopher J A	
NX24429	Church A R	
NX15662	Churchard A WIA (T)	
	WIA (NG)	
NX23079	Churchard J T	
NX17717	Clark B H WIA (A)	
VX94745	Clark D L DOI (B)	
NX17124	Clark F G KIA (T)	
NX30305	Clark R A	
NX86466	Clark S J	
NX60569	Clark W H WIA (T)	
NX42871	Clarke A E WIA (NG)	
TX9217	Clarke B N	
NGX76	Clarke G A Lieut	
NX86741	Clarke R S	
NX147635	Clarke R V	
NX167771	Clarke T J E	
NX144854	Clarkson J B Lieut	
NX93793	Clavan H T	
NX22433	Cleary D	
NX95485	Cleary J W	
NX46939	Clegg W J	
NX16438	Cliff G S	
NX18672	Clint J A	
NX110280	Close L W J	
NX23661	Clout W R	
NX44344	Clutterbuck P	
WX19644	Coates A H	
NX20753	Coates E H	
NX170894	Coates W H	
NX89695	Cobley K H	
NX17201	Coburn F E	
NX171452	Coffey A N	
NX140857	Coffey J E	
NX23159	Coffey S W	
NX46968	Coffey S W	
SX31751	Coffey T J	
NX125821	Cole F J G	
NX23131	Cole H M	
NX78945	Cole R E	
NX125819	Cole R V	

NX13265 Cole R W	NX10579 Cottee F	VX60264 Crowther J
NX190383 Collett E F	NX10858 Cottee T J	NX18638 Crowther J H
NX171472 Colley D N	NX41603 Cotten E N	NX18288 Crowther S H *WIA* (A)
NX10461 Collier R H	NX168484 Couch C D	NX21379 Cruickshank H
NX23081 Collingwood G A	NX119473 Couch H G	NX34136 Crute N *KIA* (T)
NX90079 Collins A G	NX52998 Coughlan T E	NX58506 Cruwys C E
NX57000 Collins F A *DOI* (P)	NX55794 Coulter A J	NX21339 Culbert A W
QX50631 Collins N R	NX11466 Coulton S R Lieut	NX87897 Culbert J A
NX17053 Collins R M *WIA* (T)	*WIA* (A)	NX52407 Culbert T A *WIA* (A)
NX93399 Collyer B F K *WIA* (NG)	NX20753 Coutes E H	NX60529 Culey B C *WIA* (T)
NX200085 Comber R J	NX21839 Coventry A R	*KIA* (NG)
NX52185 Commins F *KIA* (BA)	SX22684 Cowan G A	NX10521 Cullen J *WIA* (NG)
NX15039 Condon E *WIA* (A)	NX21287 Cowling L S M	NX125399 Cullen J B
NX24480 Condrin J T *WIA* (T)	NX169924 Cox D S	NX83045 Cummings H
NX57226 Conlon P H	NX15268 Cox G N C	NX169864 Cummings H L
NX21237 Conlon R T *KIA* (T)	NX21375 Cox H	NX98879 Cunnane R F
NX16289 Connell J C S	SX31702 Cox L B	NX986 Cunningham D R
NX138385 Connellan J S	NX46938 Cox R J	*WIA* (NG)
NX171874 Connelly A W	NX27098 Cox R P	NX20674 Cunningham P B Lieut
NX16235 Connolly C B	NX171374 Coyte K J	NX22923 Cunningham W J
WX37451 Connolly J E	NX70966 Craik A P Lieut	NX150777 Curnow N H
NX24582 Connolly J L	NX21785 Crain H A *WIA* (A)	NX36354 Curran J
NX18165 Connor F *KIA* (A)	NX134982 Crampton J T	NX92506 Curran J W *WIA* (NG)
NX58732 Considine A J	NX52160 Crane A L	NX32737 Currie A H
NX16223 Conti H P	NX20615 Crane N C *DOW* (A)	NX31091 Currie E
NX19782 Conway A J	NX32824 Cranefield F D	NX143925 Curry M
NX23101 Cook A *WIA* (A)	NX53210 Cranna R J	NX20891 Curry N F
SX32501 Cook A H	NX44163 Crawford J A	VX124764 Curtin J C
QX53309 Cook J R	NX378 Crawford J W Lt Col	NX50083 Curtin R W
NX93458 Cook L G	NX69794 Crawley J W *WIA* (NG)	NX116696 Curtis F T
NX31051 Coombes C W *WIA* (A)	NX82763 Craven E C	NX85215 Curtis V J
WX28729 Cooney L J	NX168469 Creamer G G	NX17060 Cusick J
NX21299 Cooper C A	NX37002 Creber G B	NX14800 Cutler C B Lieut *WIA* (A)
NX89471 Cooper C F *WIA* (NG)	NX39100 Creber J H *WIA* (A)	NX20757 Cuttriss W J
NX21338 Cooper F C *WIA* (A)	NX14968 Cremin H	
NX54554 Cooper R S *DOW* (NG)	NX82453 Crews C T	NX11629 Dad B L
NX202135 Cooper W A	NX22644 Crisdale A D *WIA* (T)	NX71411 Dale A O
NX14851 Cooper W M Lieut	NX139272 Crisp R D	NX39506 Dale J R
WIA (NG)	NX18668 Critchley C	NX114422 Daley K D
SX29374 Cooper W P	NX80063 Crockart J *WIA* (NG)	NX47280 Daley P R
NX15680 Coote G D *WIA* (A)	NX200978 Croft A G *DOW* (NG)	NX91064 Daley R
QX37151 Copnell W N	NX17831 Crofts G P M	NX93829 Dalton E R
NX16242 Coppin D C	NX24050 Crofts G T	NX21324 Dalzell W
NX33594 Copus W J	NX82939 Crofts R B	VX48267 Dalziel A L
NX24483 Corby O C	NX89700 Croke K P	NX23129 Dangarfield J
VX134230 Cordwell J L T	NX21841 Crompton C W	NX57297 Daniels H *KIA* (NG)
NX1195 Cordwell W D *WIA* (A)	NX29076 Cronin L V *KIA* (NG)	VX102092 Darcy E J
NX101724 Core M T	NX190387 Crook A M	NX39625 Dare J A
NX200541 Cork H J	NX58238 Cross A P T	NX26928 Dargan A L
NX85164 Corney R J	NX17568 Crossland G W	NX200805 Darley J P
NX169567 Corr H	VX89700 Crosthaite S A	QX40205 Davidson G W
NX16031 Corrie A E T	NX18549 Crothers N	SX30662 Davey F R
NX14480 Corstorphan C L	NX32820 Crothers W J	NX23126 Davies H
NX13746 Cortis J F *WIA* (A)	NX21298 Crotty W	NX21642 Davies N *WIA* (T)
NX22032 Cosgrove W J	NX26423 Crowe L E	NX72774 Davies O E
NX191861 Cottam J W	NX10645 Crowley J W	NX33444 Davies O T

'X156515	Davis A J	NX14995	Dixon J E	WX28352	Dunston F A
'X81859	Davis A R *KIA* (NG)	NX18406	Dobie H *WIA* (NG)	NX21668	Dutton I A *WIA* (NG)
'X60537	Davis C	NX21265	Docksey W A	NX82953	Dwyer J G *DOW* (NG)
'X15466	Davis C J	NX41013	Dodd C A	VX130998	Dyball J E
'X559	Davis F A	NX166384	Dodd F S		
'X60289	Davis L	NX21756	Dodd G W *WIA* (T)	NX17220	East P S *KIA* (A)
'X60611	Davis R		*KIA* (A)	NX14393	Easterbrook E N
'X25203	Davis S *WIA* (A)	NX46383	Dodds E M A *WIA* (NG)	NX94928	Eastment A C *DOI* (NG)
'X45206	Davis T C	NX108494	Doherty W J	NX60664	Eccleston H J R *DOW* (A)
'X18420	Davison E M	NX21264	Doidge R W *KIA* (NG)	NX38225	Eccleston W L *DOW* (A)
'X21309	Davison L E	WX32716	Doig M J	NX15705	Edmondson J H *KIA* (T)
'X22835	Davy G	NX17342	Dominey N W	NX91403	Edmonds R L
'X137200	Dawe F F F	N 442711	Donald B M	NX48290	Edwards C A
'X15984	Dawes B G *WIA* (A)	NX17684	Donaldson D D	NX175858	Edwards C J
'X9107	Dawes J	QX45833	Doneman H J	NX92342	Edwards C M
'X80012	Dawson J H J	NX32474	Donnelly R *DOI* (A)	NX19502	Edwards E W *WIA* (A)
'X18440	Dawson L T *KIA* (A)	NX47176	Donohoe M *DOW* (T)	NX14970	Edwards H
'X202244	Dawson R E	NX95343	Donovan N P *DOW* (B)	NX67293	Edwards H S A *WIA* (A)
'X60578	Day H G E	NX53636	Donovan P A *WIA* (BA)	NX18371	Edwards J A J
'X21544	Dearden V G	NX23181	Doran D McL	NX15686	Edwards L S
'X164747	Deaves J B	VX92847	Dorman V H	NX178838	Edwards L T
'X25035	Debus B C	NX21813	Dorse H J	NX19222	Edwards R G
'X139097	Dee J	NX190539	Douglass N W	NX66552	Edwards W A *WIA* (BA)
'X42044	Deem G W	NX156279	Doust L M	NX168425	Egan J
'X18113	Deering J	NX60237	Dowd F R *WIA* (A)	NX15775	Eisdell M A M *WIA* (T)
'X102896	Delaney A H	NX16120	Dowd J T	NX23655	Eley W H
'X14867	Delaney J	QX57078	Dowe F W	NX26687	Elford R H *WIA* (NG)
'X17656	Delaney N E	NX125775	Downes L E	NX83320	Ell E W
'X53030	Delaney T G	NX15076	Downing J N Lieut	NX55654	Ellicombe J A A
'X126627	D'Elboux J M		*KIA* (T)	NX168462	Elliott A A C
'X203064	Delmas N L	NX26216	Doyle J T *WIA* (NG)	NX27980	Ellis H J B
'X69775	Delves B I Lieut	NX125857	Doyle R S	NX200567	Ellis O K
'X79586	Dempsey H F	NX21814	Dransfield G	NX22619	Ellis T J
'X109123	Dempsey N C	NX21371	Dredge C D	NX20775	Ellison B *WIA* (T) *WIA* (A)
'X116744	Denmeade F J	NX22256	Dredge R F	NX49377	Elrington J
'X33542	Denne A K	NX51675	Dreghorn A D *DOW* (A)	NX168912	Elrington R F
'X20609	Dennis A G	NX166696	Drew L S	NX23103	Elsbury G
'X29372	Denton G E	NX83662	Driver C J	NX170609	Esley J F
'X21268	Derrick J J	NX22172	Druce P H	WX26491	Elton N P
'X167281	Dettman W R	NX21842	Dryley F W B	NX72358	Englert J B
'X14947	Devine J A	DX881	Drysdale A S	QX45831	Enoch D C
'X14591	Devlin J A *WIA* (NG)	NX175891	Dubois F P	TX15182	Enright A J
'X111576	Devlin R J	NX67211	Ducrou S	NX166661	Entwistle J A
'X542	Devlin T	NX57514	Duffy W T R *WIA* (NG)	NX169509	Epple N J
'X20857	Devulder R	NX16229	Duggan L G	NX17741	Ernest A R
'X21297	Dew E	VX125108	Duggan M H	NX58740	Ernest H G *WIA* (A)
'X17100	Dick R J Capt	SX19270	Duggan S F	NX119913	Eschbach R E
'X23543	Dickinson W S	NX16216	Dunbar A E	NX70003	Etheridge C G H
'X90104	Dickson R H	NX15757	Dunbar D C	NX21446	Evans A E
'X14878	Diethelm G	NX19531	Dunlevey R F	NX14931	Evans A G
'X17417	Dillon L H *KIA* (T)	NX96263	Dunlop I M	NX83379	Evans D B
'X17247	Dinnen T M	QX1628	Dunn R C *KIA* (T)	NX19518	Evans G W
'X14374	Dinning J H Major	NX24578	Dunn V A	NX58742	Evans H J
'X26733	Dinning T A R Capt	NX67408	Dunne A M	NX27308	Evans J
'X59991	Dixon A L	NX23127	Dunning D C	NX126613	Evans K
'X60481	Dixon C A *WIA* (A)	NX22218	Dunning H B	NX37716	Evans L *WIA* (A)

NX176415 Evans L R	NX23122 Field F W *WIA* (A)	NX18005 Foster D W
VX125484 Evans L W	NX15783 Field J W	NX83417 Foster E R *KIA* (NG)
NX21388 Evans N	NX17552 Field P	NX19447 Foster H F *WIA* (A)
NX22815 Evans R E	WX8350 Field W J *WIA* (A)	QX5623 Foster W D *WIA* (BA)
NX20976 Evans S	*KIA* (NG)	NX20669 Fowler S F
NX177402 Evans W G	NX17332 Filbee J S *WIA* (T)	NX17771 Fox C R
WX26617 Evans W T	*KIA* (NG)	NX21678 Fox G A *WIA* (A)
NX18248 Everett H C	NX203290 Fincham H	QX57980 Frankcom R W
VX81437 Everett K	NX17699 Findlay J K *WIA* (A)	NX30367 Frankland G P
NX59262 Everson A E *WIA* (BA)	QX8529 Fink F J Lieut	NX114475 Franklin A
WIA (NG)	NX19223 Finlay D E *WIA* (T)	NX21521 Franklin E F
NX15561 Ewin D H	NX56084 Finlay L A G *WIA* (NG)	NX60295 Franklin E S *DOW* (A)
NX36997 Eyre P W E *KIA* (A)	NX52925 Firth C F *WIA* (T)	NX9618 Franklin L
	NX16021 Firth W A *WIA* (T)	NX20787 Fraser A F
NX91964 Fahey A R	SX33556 Fischer G H	NX16239 Fraser D C
QX56662 Fahey J H	NX89800 Fisher C L	VX124896 Fraser L W
NX157106 Faint H L	NX102026 Fisher R J	NX23800 Freeberg *NER POW WIA* (BH)
NX126282 Fair N L	NX17031 Fitzgerald C G	TX14763 Freeman H J
NX90748 Fairall A W	NX13994 Fitzgerald H R	NX14952 Frew C
WX28353 Fairclough C R	NX155080 Fitzgerald K H	NX94568 Frew K L
WX28111 Fairclough R M	NX21759 Fitzhenry S H *KIA* (NG)	NX36915 Friend L G *KIA* (A)
NX14799 Fairfax J M	QX2353 Fitzpatrick T E	NX78671 Froggatt T
NX17126 Fairhall C H	NX20786 Fitzpatrick V J	NX72589 Frost F G
NX157107 Falconer D G	NX174684 Fitzsimmons K R	NX60615 Frost G
VX140545 Falls N G	NX91506 Flanagan J G	WX28337 Fruin D
NX29436 Farrand A A *WIA* (NG)	NX119479 Flannery R T	VX88292 Fry D J
NX23060 Farrand E W *WIA* (A)	NX21840 Fleming R McD	QX55920 Fry J
NX66274 Farrant R A	NX60291 Flemming D C *KIA* (T)	NX16439 Fuller A L
NX16441 Farrar-Pugh G A *DOI* (AU)	NX17186 Fletcher G C	NX155072 Fuller S J P
NX32985 Fardy L V A *WIA* (NG)	NX31289 Fletcher J W	NX171362 Funnell D J
NX18194 Farrell B T	NX25132 Fletcher N N Lieut	NX41466 Furner C N *WIA* (A)
NX17619 Farrell D *WIA* (A)	*WIA* (A)	NX17057 Furner R G
NX155763 Farrell W E	VX3012 Fletcher R H Lieut	QX43930 Fursey W T
NX60325 Farrelly W H *KIA* (A)	NX14464 Fletcher W L B	NX23055 Fyffe R M *KIA* (T)
NX48794 Fathers S F K *WIA* (NG)	NX41989 Flint V	
NX18063 Faulkner J *WIA* (NG)	NX79970 Flynn T A *WIA* (NG)	NX18853 Gagan R S
NX19277 Fawell E	NX26530 Fogarty A M	NX44221 Gain R E
VX18204 Fawell R W	NX173172 Fokes G H *WIA* (B)	NX32648 Gallagher G R
NX56899 Fawkner F H P	NX9682 Foley J *WIA* (A)	NX17030 Gallagher J R
NX66375 Feggans J	NX86767 Foley L D *WIA* (NG)	QX57861 Gallagher K W
NX16224 Fell J *ACC* (BA)	NX19526 Folley E G	NX125785 Gallagher S T T
NX175458 Feneck A	NX124493 Foran W J	VX118137 Galley H J
NX22593 Fenn S	QX52154 Forbes H G	NX155848 Galvin E R
NX484 Fenton A G T/Lt Col	NX36986 Ford E J	NX14850 Gambling J S
NX60300 Ferguson A N	NX16237 Ford G H	NX22036 Gane C W
NX94590 Ferguson D C	NX156527 Ford K A	NX22813 Gardiner T J
NX42844 Ferguson O T	NX22436 Ford R A F *POW* (T)	NX168931 Gardner A
NX82937 Ferguson W K	NX17373 Ford R C	NX167770 Gardner N R
NX92545 Ferguson J R	NX105371 Forlonge L R	SX29334 Garland R
VX23 Fergusson M A Lt Col	NX51166 Forrest G R	NX155161 Garner H
NX50183 Ferrer W J	WX28354 Forrest L M	NX23084 Garner L W
NX17970 Ferris J	NX20769 Forster B Capt *WIA* (NG)	NX51115 Garnsey R C Capt
NX17581 Ferris R G *WIA* (T)	NX89174 Forster L J N	NX60662 Garry J G *WIA* (A)
WIA (NG)	NX56375 Forsyth D	*WIA* (NG)
NX18134 Ferry T W	WX26704 Forwood R L	NX21317 Garton J
NX21620 Field A G	NX14832 Foster A	NX18179 Garvan O P

X100862	Garven E W	
X21399	Gash E A *KIA* (A)	
X17797	Gatenby C A	
X58757	Gates R E *WIA* (A)	
X30796	Gauci L	
X176318	Gaudry L J	
X21396	Gautby G R *WIA* (T)	
X30096	Gavin J N *WIA* (NG)	
X10388	Geale A *WIA* (A)	
NX190939	Geale A J	
NX17343	Geaney J F *WIA* (BA) *WIA* (A)	
NX21406	Geary E C *KIA* (T)	
NX17025	Geddes G *WIA* and *POW* (BH)	
NX93457	Geddes J W	
NX12372	Geike W B A Lieut *WIA* (T)	
WX31155	Genoni A C	
NX11946	George A R *WIA* (A)	
NX24546	George T O'D	
NX18004	George V W *WIA* (T)	
NX19087	Geoghegan W *DOI* (AU)	
VX91517	Gerecke L J	
SX32801	Gerrard A	
NX33215	Gersback J *KIA* (A)	
NX146728	Gibb C G	
NX33058	Gibb H	
NX14839	Gibb K J Lieut *WIA* (T) *WIA* (NG)	
NX77768	Gibbons L T	
QX27187	Gibbs C A	
NX17921	Gibson F A	
NX87747	Gibson G J	
NX24756	Gibson R	
NX173930	Gibson S C	
NX22439	Giersch S J *WIA* (NG)	
SX19112	Giffen J C *KIA* (B)	
NX17051	Gifford A B *KIA* (T)	
VX118684	Gilbert R J	
VX140887	Giles F J	
SX29925	Giles L	
NX17063	Giles L M	
NX17226	Gilfeather B F A	
NX170552	Gilholm J F	
NX24467	Gill B W *WIA* (A)	
WX40513	Gillatt C	
QX14308	Gillespie R A *WIA* (NG)	
VX147723	Gillett L	
NX193919	Gillham H	
VX91833	Gillick A V	
NX23156	Gilligan T P	
WX29403	Gilmore F C	
NX22099	Gilmour J L ACC (BH)	
WX37744	Gimbel A	
WX28396	Gimbel C	

NX2637	Gjedsted R E Lieut	
NX29774	Gladwin R	
QX33337	Glasser C W	
NX24087	Glassop J L	
QX49145	Gleadhill G G	
NX201703	Gleeson C	
NX14367	Gleeson L K	
NX24438	Gleeson L M *WIA* (NG)	
NX16060	Gleeson W P *WIA* (T) *WIA* (A)	
NX55208	Glennie B S Lieut	
NX22037	Glossop H J G	
NX5836	Glynn S J	
NX21285	Godber V A N *WIA* (T)	
QX45979	Goelder D M	
NX72672	Goffett C	
NX168466	Gold L R	
SX19257	Goldner P L	
NX52962	Goodall J	
NX155163	Goodfellow R H	
NX15194	Goodman E G	
NX18090	Goodwin F G	
NX78256	Goodwin P L	
NX124427	Gooley E A	
NX164664	Gordon B S	
NX39421	Gordon D J *WIA* (NG)	
NX16456	Gordon G A	
NX16209	Gordon J P	
NX169157	Gordon L	
NX166698	Gordon N C	
NX21283	Gordon W C *WIA* (T)	
NX125409	Gorham K V	
NX156517	Gorham V V	
NX26322	Gould L *WIA* (A)	
NX48897	Gow J	
NX124411	Gowans A L	
QX5840	Grace P E	
NX203082	Graham F N	
NX170172	Graham F W	
NX26856	Graham J N *KIA* (NG)	
NX59113	Graham L F Lieut	
NX154554	Graham O J	
NX162932	Graham V M	
NX50991	Graham W A Lieut *DOW* (NG)	
NX84777	Grainger D S	
NX4500	Grant A H W Lieut	
NX66643	Grant C W H	
NX14254	Grant E S *WIA* (BA) *KIA* (NG)	
NX12327	Grant J D Capt	
NX52291	Grant N A	
NX60273	Grant R S *WIA* (T)	
VX15889	Grant T R	
TX15113	Grave D H	
NX170891	Graves E J	

QX33472	Gray A J	
SX18206	Gray A J	
NX92514	Gray D F	
NX126649	Gray E R	
NX84893	Gray M A *WIA* (NG)	
NX162172	Grayston D	
NX202183	Green A G	
NX156083	Green B L	
NX20678	Green D A	
NX17052	Green G	
NX60419	Green J C *WIA* (T)	
NX190388	Green J L	
NX14617	Green R N R *KIA* (A)	
NX13281	Green W E B	
NX84729	Greenaway E W	
SX19219	Greenfield C E	
NX24422	Greenup A E	
NX200879	Greenway P L	
NX16036	Greenwood C F	
QX53701	Greer R V	
NX19327	Greer S M	
QX33197	Grey J F	
NX20785	Grey R B *WIA* (A)	
VX121127	Gregory A R	
NX60554	Greig A V	
NX60670	Gribble W C	
VX141052	Grierson H C	
NX170712	Griffen H E T	
NX129421	Griffiths A E	
NX36991	Griffiths E L *WIA* (A)	
NX22797	Griffiths F J	
NX168927	Griffiths K	
QX55465	Griffiths R L *KIA* (B)	
NX16202	Griffiths R L A	
NX19622	Grigg J W	
NX156064	Grimson S C	
NX91618	Grooms H N *WIA* (NG)	
NX60474	Grunsell F H *WIA* (T)	
NX16290	Gubbins W L	
QX3403	Gudge C	
NX57219	Guest L H *WIA* (A)	
NX28752	Gunning J A	
NX21038	Guy E L *WIA* (A) *WIA* (NG)	
NX57197	Guy J *WIA* (T) *WIA* (NG)	
NX57198	Guy M	
NX164036	Guy W R	
NX40518	Habgood W	
NX90682	Hadlow C T *WIA* (NG)	
SX19505	Haggett F L	
NX171618	Haig A J	
NX27109	Hair J G S	
NX82826	Haiser S G	
NX169493	Halcrow B	

NX17050	Hale D B	
NX22739	Hale V H	
NX22621	Hales W A *WIA* (A)	
NX56631	Haley J J	
NX21482	Hall A W	
NX90170	Hall C D *WIA* (NG)	
NX172417	Hall C J	
NX90418	Hall L J	
NX22724	Hall R A	
NX60471	Hall S A	
NX104173	Hallam R F	
NX13766	Halloway R A Lieut	
NX168428	Halls R C	
NX24224	Halpin H J	
WX28248	Hamersley V T	
NX17285	Hamilton F J	
NX19487	Hamilton F P	
NX93424	Hamilton J A	
NX52651	Hamilton J G	
NX18384	Hamilton O M	
NX143267	Hammond S C G	
NX105093	Hancock H C	
WX29193	Handyside L F	
NX144491	Hanigan J W	
NX60579	Hanna N B	
NX20774	Hannaford R A Lieut *KIA* (A)	
NX27031	Hansen J *WIA* (A) *KIA* (NG)	
VX91677	Harnden J	
Q144881	Hardgrave J W	
NX23827	Hardie G *WIA* (NG)	
NX29961	Hardie R A	
NX17065	Hardiman B A	
NX14068	Hardiman D J	
NX2450	Harding D B *KIA* (NG)	
NX16461	Hardy A C	
NX18193	Hardy G *WIA* (T)	
NX29961	Hardy R A	
NX174634	Harland B K	
NX169833	Harland B S	
NX154389	Harlovich C S	
NX17103	Harney J	
NX15040	Harper C J	
NX155506	Harper F J	
NX70023	Harper F S	
NX51654	Harper R G	
TX15191	Harper R J	
NX21243	Harris C	
NX21416	Harris E *WIA* (A) *WIA* (NG)	
NX167549	Harris G A	
VX91739	Harris G E *KIA* (NG)	
NX26839	Harris J	
NX30756	Harris J	
NX46652	Harris M L *WIA* (BA)	

SX30760	Harris N G	
NX17773	Harrison A H *WIA* (BA) *WIA* (A)	
NX28404	Harrison C G *DOW* (T)	
NX42589	Harrison J R	
VX141083	Hart C W	
QX47634	Hartvigsen C E	
NX14449	Harvey A J *WIA* (A)	
NX171373	Harvey E C	
NX90389	Harvey L W C	
NX164591	Harwood C W	
NX22613	Hassen E *WIA* (T) *WIA* (NG)	
NX66700	Haverstein M C	
NX14780	Hawkins A G	
NX24589	Hawkins A J *KIA* (A)	
NX66147	Hawkins B *WIA* (T)	
VX29887	Hay G S *WIA* (A)	
NX21337	Hayward A *WIA* (NG)	
VX2455	Hayward J E	
NX21444	Hazel A T	
NX17251	Hazel S N J	
NX21316	Hazell S P S	
NX91954	Healy G A *WIA* (NG)	
NX17058	Heap A J	
NX171371	Hearne C J	
NX37928	Hearne J H	
NX202452	Heatley J	
NX15996	Hedges J W H *WIA* (BA)	
NX82108	Heffernan T P	
NX14481	Hellman A L *WIA* (T)	
NX91939	Helps H C	
NX17130	Hemme S R *WIA* (A)	
NX79013	Hemphill J D	
NX147112	Henderson G McK	
NX11557	Henderson W G *DOW* (A)	
QX59306	Hendry N A	
NX17182	Hennessey R J *WIA* (T)	
NX36967	Hennessy R F	
NX14456	Hennessy R I C *WIA* (A)	
NX82349	Henson H S	
NX21538	Henwood W J *WIA* (T)	
WX28298	Herbert R W	
NX21791	Hermon J C *DOW* (A)	
NX17885	Herps N K	
NX27602	Hesketh J B	
NX14834	Hewitt A J C Lieut	
NX33646	Hickey H J	
NX19132	Hickey W	
NX168417	Hickman R	
NX52186	Hickson J F	
NX125886	Higgins C P	
WX26597	Higgins *KIA* C	
NX23802	Higgins M D *POW* (T)	
NX14996	Higgins M L H	
NX39611	Higgins R F C *WIA* (A)	

NX168926	Higgs E J	
NX89101	Hill C R *WIA* (NG)	
NX174739	Hill C W *WIA* (B)	
NX14860	Hill D McK	
NX147754	Hill E F	
NX157998	Hill F L	
NX18066	Hill F T P	
NX22618	Hill G T	
NX56226	Hill J W *WIA* (T)	
NX195405	Hill N A	
NX24016	Hill N G	
NX16435	Hill R M	
NX89711	Hill S R	
NX22739	Hill V H *KIA* (T)	
NX71460	Hillier G	
QX46554	Hillier J	
NX53379	Hillier J	
NX57529	Hills F E	
NX60027	Hills J J *POW* (T)	
NX174117	Hilton E J	
NX16453	Hilton J H	
NX49216	Hindmarch J J	
NX28867	Hinds F A *KIA* (A)	
NX58750	Hindson H R B *WIA* (NG)	
NX26248	Hinksman L J	
VX14848	Hipkins E H C Capt	
NX21273	Hird K E	
NX17652	Hobbins M P	
NX19443	Hobbs L K	
NX23894	Hobday N J W	
NX90689	Hocking J A	
NX22213	Hockley S L	
NX51081	Hodder E	
NX123852	Hodder F J	
NX18414	Hodge J W	
NX86067	Hodges J A	
NX24734	Hodges W H	
VX142000	Hodgkins J W	
NX32928	Hodgson W B *WIA* (BA)	
NX66352	Hodson A	
NX21300	Hogan A E	
NX200347	Hogan F J	
NX91489	Hogarth T	
NX155000	Hogg M D *WIA* (B)	
NX77843	Holder R S *DOW* (NG)	
NX82316	Holder W C	
WX28159	Holgate P S	
QX45810	Holland E R	
NX21501	Holland G W *KIA* (NG)	
NX21378	Holland J V	
NX22222	Holland T W *WIA* (NG)	
NX92555	Holliday D C	
NX13904	Hollier E J	
NX17783	Hollingsworth F J *DOW* (A)	
NX22267	Hollis R J	
NX5964	Hollonds R P *WIA* (NG)	

'X28227	Holloway N R	
'X16453	Holman H J *WIA* (T)	
'X19078	Holmes A J	
'X135447	Holmes F D S	
'X52196	Holmes J W	
JX22861	Holmes K M	
JX24477	Holmes W *KIA* (A)	
QX11381	Holmes W J H	
VX28205	Holt J	
JX29407	Holtsbaum G F J Capt	
JX125360	Homan F B J	
VX28226	Horner A J	
'X131361	Horsfall G L Lieut	
JX157084	Hosler J	
JX119479	Hoswell C H	
JX60675	Hourigan T	
JX17655	Howard E J *KIA* (B)	
JX130678	Howard H E	
JX15742	Howard J *WIA* (A)	
JX79577	Howard J R *WIA* (NG)	
VX120750	Howden W T S	
VX90394	Howe S L	
NX21403	Howell E W	
SX32531	Howell E W	
NX23182	Howes A L A *WIA* (NG) *DOI* (AU)	
NX32354	Howie L *WIA* (T)	
NX20985	Howieson D W	
NX17340	Hoyer J E	
SX19314	Huddleston M C	
NX19442	Hudson F J *WIA* (T)	
NX53581	Hughes H J	
NX70236	Hughes H L Capt *WIA* (NG)	
NX16171	Hughes W J *WIA* (T) *WIA* (NG)	
NX170021	Hugo V	
NX60657	Hume A H *WIA* (A)	
NX9799	Humphries E H	
NX132879	Humphries H R	
NX18178	Hunt A T	
NX20760	Hunt H J *WIA* (A)	
NX29269	Hunter F	
NX90657	Hunter W D J	
NX18307	Huntingford R F	
NX14175	Huntley P W	
NX39526	Hurel L M H	
NX18116	Hurley T S	
NX14401	Hurling S W *WIA* (BA)	
NX170676	Hurst J E	
NX172437	Hussey R C	
NX168488	Hutchings H D	
NX17545	Hutchinson R J	
SX30769	Hutton S E W	
TX9064	Huxley E A	
NX18101	Huxley N J	
NX17079	Hyatt F R	

NX156961	Hyde A E	
NX125822	Hyde J V	
NX167262	Hyland G W	
NX17778	Hynes P O	
NX17064	Hynes W A *DOI* (AU)	
NX22425	Ife N R *KIA* (A)	
SX19235	Iheup M A	
NX13734	Ikin C A *WIA* (A)	
NX16521	Illingworth J	
NX21883	Inglis S C *WIA* (A) *WIA* (NG)	
NX124464	Ings L H *WIA* (B)	
NX18136	Innes J A	
NX18917	Innes N R	
NX17258	Inskip V	
NX21209	Insole R G *WIA* (A)	
NX59023	Ireland H J C *WIA* (A)	
NX14368	Ireland K W	
NX90102	Irvine S M	
NX66141	Irwin N T *WIA* (A)	
NX34046	Ison W K	
NX21320	Jacob P J	
NX171370	Jacobs J P	
NX92510	Jackson A S	
NX84357	Jackson A T *KIA* (NG)	
NX27023	Jackson C J	
QX59638	Jackson C J	
NX171866	Jackson H F W	
QX31998	Jackson H W F	
NX126647	Jackson L L	
NX125864	Jackson L T *WIA* (B)	
NX125773	Jackson N M	
NX74139	Jackson W G	
NX13729	Jaggers M G *KIA* (T)	
NX27156	Jamieson C M	
NX157108	Jamieson D A M	
NX68744	Jamieson J R *KIA* (A)	
NX92185	James J	
NX125358	James L S	
NX85719	James R M	
NX25271	Jansen C	
NX21843	Jarman A B *DOI* (AU)	
NX32584	Jeffery A H	
NX155770	Jeffery C W	
NX60530	Jeffery J R	
NX80788	Jeffery L T	
NX17404	Jeffress S E P	
NX19902	Jeffriess P T	
NX157959	Jeffs L G	
NX15017	Jenkins E	
NX16096	Jenkins J	
NX202384	Jenkins K E D	
NX33102	Jenkins R	
NX22973	Jenkins W J M *WIA* (NG)	

NX19505	Jepson T L W	
NX20990	Jesperson W J	
NX92160	Jessop L E A	
NX17143	Joass L H	
NX112896	Job C	
NX28862	John H K	
QX55648	Johns H J *WIA* (B)	
NX168492	Johns L J Lieut	
NX22527	Johns N McL *WIA* (T)	
NX60015	Johnson A E	
NX78588	Johnson B	
SX12966	Johnson B	
VX123721	Johnson C R	
NX16217	Johnson D *DOI* (AU)	
NX21757	Johnson H *WIA* (T) *WIA* (T)	
NX31031	Johnson H J *WIA* (T) *WIA* (A)	
NX172276	Johnson L E	
NX43968	Johnson L W	
NX18103	Johnson R *DOI* (AU)	
NX23798	Johnson T *WIA* (T) *DOW* (NG)	
NX50419	Johnson W *DOW* (A)	
NX21761	Johnson W L *POW* (T)	
NX27816	Johnston C E	
NX123873	Johnston J D	
NX22214	Johnston J R	
NX21017	Johnston L	
NX21310	Johnston M J A	
NX82365	Johnston R G	
NX21729	Jones A C	
NX59919	Jones A E V *DOW* (B)	
NX14869	Jones L H	
NX21763	Jones P C	
VX36421	Jones R W	
NX21714	Jones T	
NX108210	Jones T A	
NX20739	Jones V	
NX16221	Jordon W A *DOW* (A)	
NX51922	Jordan W L	
NX22340	Joy J	
NX28657	Jury D A *WIA* (BA) *WIA* (A)	
NX20793	Kalachoff I G *WIA* (NG)	
NX10560	Kane A S	
NX53678	Kane H *WIA* (T) *WIA* (A)	
NX86698	Kane M R	
NX153053	Kawelmacher R C	
NX28721	Kay R	
NX51446	Kean J A *WIA* (A)	
NX164501	Keaney D	
NX18319	Kearney G W *WIA* (A) *DOW* (NG)	
VX136929	Kearney J T	

NX45231 Kearney M	TX15448 Lacey K L	NX194586 Leslie S A
NX14519 Kearney V J *WIA* (A)	NX19638 Lackey A F	NX179363 Lester G A
SX22174 Keegan T J	NX21427 Lackey A F	NX14236 Levy D A
NX21405 Kelaher J D *WIA* (T) *WIA* (NG)	VX91287 Ladd R L	NX16524 Lewis C L *KIA* (NG)
	NX60646 Lambert E R *WIA* (A)*	NX38366 Lewis H
NX13901 Kellie N D F	NX17078 Lambourn W R J *POW* (T)	NX94021 Lewis W M
NX172641 Kelly A	NX23136 Lane C *WIA* (T)	NX12172 Lewis-Mathias A Lieut
NX60437 Kelly A C C	*WIA* (BA) *DOW* (A)	NX16238 Liddiard J N
NX91505 Kelly C R	NX51388 Lane F M	QX47850 Liddle J W
NX17131 Kelly D J	NX17253 Lane J C	NX15682 Limn G G Lieut *WIA* (T)
NX200237 Kelly E	NX22221 Laney N J	QX3359 Lindburgh V C
NX171207 Kelly J L	NX16458 Langford H H	NX82856 Lindsay C C
NX26986 Kelly J	NX125361 Langford L V	NX49268 Lindsay E P
NX21762 Kelly K P	NX92075 Langford G W	NX14354 Lindsay H R Lieut
NX89713 Kelly W L *DOW* (NG)	NX14114 Langman W C H	NX91530 Lindsay J
NX203080 Kempshall T G C	NX47957 Larkin A	NX22171 Lindsay L D
NX26767 Kendall M J	NX47743 Larkin E *DOW* (T)	NX92517 Lindwall H A
NX22223 Kennedy A *WIA* (NG)	NX26911 Larkin P J	NX17547 Linn D
NX17215 Kennedy C L	NX126648 Larkings S	NX17266 Littlewood J H S
NX97419 Kennedy G K	NX17740 Larnach J M	NX20181 Livingston S J
NX59787 Kennedy H C *WIA* (A)	NX60280 Larsen R G	NX168932 Lloyd F W T
NX22365 Kennedy J	NX17654 Latter D B F *WIA* (BA)	NX16720 Lloyd J A *WIA* (T)
NX166458 Kennedy K B	*WIA* (A)	NX59927 Lloyd J T *KIA* (A)
NX4384 Kennedy L K	NX135609 Launt P D	NX22427 Lloyd N E
NX18061 Kennedy P E	NX23801 Lavallee P *POW* (BH)	NX94830 Locke W A
Nx104115 Kennedy R E Lieut	NX23659 Lavis J *WIA* (T)	NX57095 Lockwood H C
NX190006 Kennelley F J	WX38799 Law F G	NX154698 Lodge F W
NX13750 Kenniwell A J *WIA* (BA)	NX16416 Law J W G *KIA* (T)	NX168939 Lofts R A
NX37187 Kenyon N T *KIA* (NG)	NX17345 Lawler J J	NX18355 Long C V
NX57715 Keogh L *WIA* (A)	NX200469 Lawler W H	NX59224 Long T H
NX177826 Keogh W D	NX99809 Lawlor C	NX202855 Longhurst J L
WX39056 Keown S K	NX24215 Lawlor V P *WIA* (T)	NX17245 Loomes H W
NX51680 Kerim E A	NX25562 Lawrence E W *POW* (T)	NX192881 Lopes P E
NX14753 Kerr K R Lieut	QX22994 Lawrence H Chaplain	WX26673 Lord C J
NX82721 Keys P	NX16597 Laws J E *POW* (T)	NX50030 Lord L D *WIA* (NG)
NX21873 Khan R G	NX72975 Laycock E C *DOW*	NX72850 Lord S T
NX18006 Kibby G U *WIA* (T)	VX140848 Lazzaro B J	NX77910 Lorrane O
NX34561 Kidd A G	NX14414 Leaman W M	NX37075 Love W R
NX21348 Kidd D *KIA* (A)	NX14381 LeCouteur G S Lieut	TX3244 Lovegrove L A
NX24342 Killain J G *WIA* (T)	NX22643 Legge F G *KIA* (T)	VX91611 Lovell A F *WIA* (NG)
NX17239 Killalea J V	VX125370 Lee H E W	QX47958 Lovelock G
NX26803 King F R	NX22435 Lee J	NX15610 Lovelock R W C
NX43203 King J P	NX32738 Lee J	NX135610 Lovett R B
WX12524 King K B	NX60184 Lee M R	NX91197 Lowe A E *WIA* (NG)
VX91633 King W H *WIA* (NG)	NX14594 Lee N *DOW* (A)	VX10627 Lowrie A L
NX36611 King W R	NX84077 Lee R B	NX66697 Lowry S
NX142568 Kingdom G L	NX92906 Lee R	NX600 Lucas J C
NX19095 Kinsella A J	QX52107 Lee S C	VX115881 Lucas J P
NX23137 Kirkham J M	NX14927 Leech W J *WIA* (T)	NX78292 Luchinelli R E
VX141072 Kirley F J	NX169810 Leek C A	NX171879 Luck C B
NX87905 Kirton W	NX201697 Lehman R G	NX23155 Luck D N *WIA* (A)
SX38170 Kite M V	NX172275 Leighton K J	*WIA* (NG)
VX64190 Knevitt H *DOI* (NG)	NX65985 Lemaire C E *WIA* (A)	NX14534 Luck H W
QX55816 Knickle C E	NX142412 Lennon A E O	NX95550 Luck R G
NX83101 Krause J H	NX14804 Lenon G J	NX21288 Luck R W
NX157085 Kristensen E H	NX8955 Leseberg W J *WIA* (A)	

* Lambert later DOI in Australia.

X17077	Lund J C	
X44060	Lunney R G	
X21650	Lupton C J J	
X168545	Lutherborrow E	
X133204	Luxford L J	
X60614	Lynch C J WIA (A)	
X21685	Lyneham D V	
X66135	Lynn J	
X15174	Lyons F M	
X70099	Lyons W A	
X22225	Mabbott V G	
X128983	MacDonald J N	
X59402	MacDougall N	
X20986	Macey L E	
X5398	Mackay H	
X12231	Mackell F A Major	
X23349	MacKenzie B D	
QX58072	MacKenzie J R	
X12228	Maclarn L C Major	
	WIA (A) WIA (NG)	
X6960	Maclean D	
X15591	MacLeod A	
X21325	MacLeod A C	
NX93739	MacLeod H B	
X18495	Macmillan W J C	
VX136810	MacNamara S F	
NX14105	Madden P T	
NX34934	Maddern N P Lieut	
NX14833	Maders W D	
NX12306	Magno C K M Major	
NX51608	Mahalm F G KIA (NG)	
NX20890	Maher A T	
QX57375	Maher C L	
NX21376	Maher D F	
NX17847	Maher H T KIA (T)	
NX200088	Maher J L WIA (B)	
NX17679	Maher R	
NX125363	Maher S P	
NX47428	Maher T J WIA (A)	
NX17849	Mahoney G N	
NX51499	Mahoney H W	
NX14840	Main H H Capt WIA (T)	
NX20888	Mainstone C E	
NX79635	Maizey A F	
NX171379	Malcolm R M	
NX60607	Male J M Lieut	
NX90418	Mall L S	
NX14638	Maloney L N	
NX50804	Maloney P L WIA (A)	
NX22220	Malthouse H L Lieut	
	WIA (T)	
NX19105	Mancer A F	
NX21630	Mangan J F L	
NX21631	Mangan L G WIA (A)	
NX24387	Mannion C J	

NX154552	Mannion P G
NX25464	Manns J J WIA (A)
NX169838	Manuel S E
NX44366	Marchment F
NX22101	Marcus L J KIA (A)
NX126612	Markham J C
SX39291	Markwick J M
NX34649	Marriott L A M
NX175490	Marsh R S
NX54819	Marshall E R
VX91635	Marshall V R
QX30683	Marshall W G McA
NX20835	Marstella O E POW (T)
NX13944	Martin A W WIA (T)
NX14586	Martin C E WIA (NG)
NX41099	Martin F G
NX24316	Martin H R
NX37004	Martin J T DOI (P)
NX21294	Martin T P
NX32736	Martin W E
NX16457	Mason G R DOW (T)
WX38638	Mason T
NX165730	Massey T P
NX21282	Masters G J
NX91999	Mathes C J
NX109629	Matheson D R
NX23111	Mathews A E KIA (T)
NX84028	Mathews H W
NX23064	Mathieson O J
NX44482	Matthews A E
NX176036	Matthews J
QX3100	Matthews R E
NX168350	Matthews R F
NX42351	Matthews T
NX33335	Maude J
NX21991	Maude W J S
NX16004	Maxwell A P
NX90190	May D
NX17317	May H J
QX36271	Mayers N J
NX90259	Mays A A
NX58614	Mazzetti M
NX16696	Mealing M
NX58993	Meaney L O
NX60330	Mears C W
NX8230	Mears R P
NX29574	Meincke E P
NX21328	Meldrum H W P
NX89496	Mellon R J
NX22034	Melville R
NX18135	Mendham H S WIA (A)
NX12526	Mendham P M Lieut
NX14823	Menser L A
NX155500	Menzies B
VX91690	Menzies J R KIA (B)
NX81490	Mercer C R H

WX3417	Mercer D L Capt
NX28868	Meredith E H
WX26565	Merifield F A
NX17056	Merrick J R
NX18806	Meyer C G
QX28327	Mickan S S
NX70309	Millar C K
NX4718	Miller A A
NX23662	Miller C L
NX6172	Miller D F
VX139087	Miller D O
NX19000	Miller E H
NX18332	Miller H N
SX19472	Miller H G
NX157149	Miller H K
NX132415	Miller J C
NX91242	Miller J H
NX41766	Miller K A KIA (NG)
NX147221	Miller K R
NX125787	Miller L
NX52130	Miller R J
NX91241	Miller V WIA (NG)
NX20765	Milligan K F WIA (A)
	WIA (NG)
NX18663	Mills A D
NX22642	Mills C L WIA (T)
QX28605	Mills R H
NX57916	Millward F T
NX79911	Milne A W
VX136385	Milne J W J
NX17195	Minehan A W KIA (A)
NX79434	Minnikin G A
VX133792	Mitchell C R
NX20989	Mitchell G W WIA (A)
NX1990	Mitchell H T
NX24141	Mitchell J W W
NX66659	Mitchell L J WIA (BA)
	WIA (A)
NX16231	Mitchell P J
NX14283	Mitchell S A
NX15886	Mitchell S E WIA (A)
	WIA (NG)
NX125405	Mitchell T C
NX60247	Mock L M
NX12328	Moffatt J G S Lt Col
NX21296	Molloy A F WIA (A)
NX20758	Molyneux E
NX96698	Molyneux E J
NX21689	Monaghan S C H
	DOW (A)
NX65951	Monahan V J F WIA (A)
	WIA (NG)
NX19225	Moncrieff J A WIA (T)
	DOW (BA)
VX135009	Montgomery N D
NX175554	Moody R W

NX16044	Moon H C R	
NX17597	Mooney J T	
NX17128	Moore A J	
NX19113	Moore B B *WIA* (T)	
NX91836	Moore D V	
NX19287	Moore I S	
NX15008	Moore J	
NX18007	Moore J F	
NX18832	Moore L G	
NX15990	Moore N	
NX19525	Moore P O *WIA* (A)	
NX16599	Moore R F	
NX89302	Moore R W	
NX179664	Moore T W	
NX37936	Moore W	
NX105125	Moore W J	
NX170102	Moran F G	
NX37719	Moran H A	
NX4510	Moran R J Lieut	
NX90411	Moran T A	
NX22259	Morgan G E	
NX23053	Morgan G R *WIA* (NG)	
NX24262	Morgan J A	
NX23663	Morgan J L	
NX27474	Morgan L J	
NX23133	Morgan N E	
QX33014	Morgan S W *WIA* (NG)	
TX13134	Morgan V A	
NX49642	Morris E J	
NX18377	Morris J *WIA* (A) *WIA* (NG)	
NX171378	Morris W A	
NX60630	Morris W J	
NX53866	Morrison A E	
NX91553	Morrison A F	
NX18178	Morrison J L	
NX89171	Morrow J E	
NX93431	Morton K W Lieut	
NX79377	Moses K A *WIA* (NG)	
NX32353	Mott E A J *WIA* (NG)	
NX124461	Mouldt E D	
NX60336	Mould L H *WIA* (A)*	
NX60239	Mould R G *WIA* (A)	
NX91102	Moylan J J	
NX78079	Moylan N	
NX91025	Muddell J H *WIA* (NG)	
NX20839	Mudie E *WIA* (T)	
NX172451	Muir W M S	
NX1192	Mulcahy M H *WIA* (NG)	
NX142968	Mulholland P A	
NX93507	Mullins V J	
NX126650	Mullins W T	
NX58638	Mulvihill J M *WIA* (A) *WIA* (NG)	
NX14949	Muncaster F G	
NX17061	Munday J A *WIA* (T)	
NX20759	Munday R E	
NX21318	Munns C W	
NX60263	Murdock K J	
NX51685	Murdock N W J *DOI* (AU)	
NX42828	Murphy G J A *WIA* (BA)	
NX125853	Murphy J H	
NX23085	Murphy J T	
QX8839	Murphy L P F *WIA* (B)	
NX70701	Murphy P K Capt	
NX17174	Murphy W D N	
NX17286	Murphy W H	
NX21758	Murray A *KIA* (A)	
NX34525	Murray D G	
NX13926	Murray J	
NX8397	Murray J J	
NX55335	Murray J P *WIA* (NG)	
NX60689	Murray J R *WIA* (A)	
NX17101	Murray T M	
NX13480	Murray W J	
NX19115	Murrell P W	
NX123482	Mussett J W Lieut	
NX23057	Musgrave J D'A *KIA* (T)	
NX27338	Myers W *WIA* (A)	
NX125896	McAdam J I	
NX14631	McAndrew J R *KIA* (A)	
NX21479	McAulay A H	
NX2033	McAuley G M *WIA* (A)	
NX67383	McCaffrey D *WIA* (NG)	
NX99586	McCall A E	
WX19096	McCallum D B	
WX19091	McCallum K	
NX24332	McCann P E *WIA* (A) *WIA* (NG)	
NX15784	McCarthy A E	
NX14827	McCarthy A W	
NX19360	McCarthy D Capt	
NX16451	McCarthy H *WIA* (A)	
NX44689	McCarthy J F	
NX 17811	McCarthy L J *WIA* (A) *WIA* (NG)	
NX6629	McCarthy N	
NX72268	McCarthy W C *WIA* (A)	
NX17748	McCarthy W E *WIA* (T) *WIA* (A)	
NX96241	McCauley T	
NX17132	McCool A N	
NX18114	McCoole M G	
NX45275	McCormack G	
NX16427	McCormick W J	
NX17744	McCosker A W	
NX27975	McCosker C L *POW* (A)	
NX56997	McCoughtry W G Lieut	
NX21804	McCoy J H	
NX93339	McCullagh G A	
NX12408	McCulloch E M Capt *KIA* (A)	
NX202986	McCullock J E	
NX37780	McCully J R *KIA* (A)	
NX21385	McCrimmon F	
NX21207	McDermott A E	
NX89125	McDonagh A J	
NX133031	McDonald A G	
NX91545	McDonald B	
NX67392	McDonald D	
NX16318	McDonald E C	
NX22666	McDonald F M	
NX16694	McDonald H *WIA* (A)	
NX39870	McDonald H E *KIA* (A)	
NX19441	McDonald H N *WIA* (T)	
NX60404	McDonald J E *WIA* (T)	
NX126631	McDonald M A	
NX21812	McDonald M R	
NX59131	McDonald N E Lieut	
NX24695	McDonald S J	
NX126630	McDonald S R	
NX23052	McElroy R McL Lieut *WIA* (A) *KIA* (A)	
NX84764	McEntyre C	
NX24708	McFarland J D Capt	
NX19179	McFayden J O	
NX172300	McGeecham W R Lieut	
NX15970	McGillivray W J	
WX26812	McGlenchy A J	
NX156243	McGlynn A A	
NX126279	McGlynn A H	
NX124096	McGlynn B K	
NX60252	McGrath C M *WIA* (A)	
NX57283	McGrath D D *WIA* (A)	
NX18326	McGrath F J	
NX22616	McGrath M F	
NX55020	McGreal B T	
VX93706	McGuigan W G	
NX14680	McGuire N E	
NX16093	McHenry H J *WIA* (A)	
NX20202	McHenry L V	
NX14494	McHenry M *DOW* (T)	
NX16455	McHugh A R	
NX92559	McIntosh R W V	
NX22212	McKay D W J *POW* (T)	
NX14831	McKean A J	
NX83627	McKechnie J V	
NX17846	McKee E *WIA* (T)	
NX161832	McKee J	
NX17314	McKenna A W	
NX21200	McKeon P	
NX146817	McKenzie E I	
NX93145	McKenzie K J	
NX22795	McKenzie L *WIA* (T) *WIA* (A)	
NX18359	McKenzie W D H	
NX70735	McKinley J F Lieut	
NX17920	McKinley V E	

* Mould later DOI in Australia.

'X17265	McKinnon J D	QX45835	Nelson B J	NX23058	O'Donnell G P
'X20771	McLachlan H D	NX175823	Nelson H A L	NX126655	O'Donnell G P WIA (B)
'X23657	McLaren J	NX23630	Nelson J M	NX49229	O'Donnell L H WIA (NG)
'X60617	McLean C R	SX32857	Nelson S L J	NX82697	O'Dwyer J
'X52727	McLean R R	NX66426	Nesbitt D Y	NX66802	O'Flanagan W
'X123848	McLennan A D	NX17866	Nesbitt R A WIA (T)	NX12305	Ogle R W G Major
'X53569	McLennan A L WIA (T)	NX60187	Neuss D M DOW (A)	NX90339	O'Grady F T J
	WIA (A) WIA (NG)	NX60170	Neuss K E	NX96346	O'Grady R F
'X37099	McLeod D R Lieut	NX19157	Newberry C H	NX125359	O'Keefe E M
'X17142	McLeod F J	NX60213	Newell S C WIA (T)	NX60589	Oldfield E W
'X65452	McLeod K T Capt	NX21490	Newlands J L	WX33228	O'Leary D C
'X21361	McLeod W R C	NX130778	Newman A E	NX119943	O'Leary P M
'X14385	McLucas H D	NX119758	Newman A G	NX14844	Oliver A J
'X44754	McLure J	NX15587	Newman G H	NX21492	Ollis C B
QX50632	McMahon A	NX93460	Newman T L	NX34603	Olsen J
'X17019	McMahon M E	NX19226	Newton A G	NX82764	O'Mailey R R
'X125770	McMahon S A	NX15834	Newton A J C Capt	NX168916	O'Malveney B W
'X16143	McManus A W F DOI (P)	NX68824	Niass A C	NX37021	O'Neill C R
'X12510	McMaster I F Capt	NX14668	Nicholls M A WIA (BA)	NX21164	O'Neill J
	DOW (A)	NX14826	Nicholls R J	NX170514	O'Neill J J
'NX155165	McMillan A T	NX49587	Nichols L J	NX23161	O'Neill J M A
'NX26127	McMillan N A WIA (A)	NX15147	Nicholson A E Capt	NX166792	O'Neill J T
'NX16313	McMullen A W KIA (A)		WIA (NG)	NX53596	Ord R
'NX14922	McMullen W R	NX22885	Nicholson G A	NX17334	O'Reilly P J
'NX12215	McNab D Capt	NX60354	Noakes A D	NX56380	Osborn D J
'NX31506	McNamara J B WIA (T)	NX95196	Nolan A	NX22031	Oselton H R
VX56934	McNamara K L	NX20634	Nolan P WIA (NG)	NX92484	O'Shea J C
VX136810	McNamara S F	NX9788	Nolan W J	NX23162	O'Shea T P
NX 98569	McNamee W J	VX93422	Norquay D E	NX83039	O'Sullivan G A KIA (B)
NX94575	McNeilly N J KIA (NG)	NX156522	Norris F D	NX50034	Oughtred D S
NX46618	McPherson N K Lieut	NX15055	Norris J R B Capt WIA (T)	NX22028	Owen E E
NX46957	McPhillips L J		WIA (A)	NX12362	Owen J M Lieut WIA (T)
NX17754	McQuilty E WIA (NG)	NX53626	Norris W T KIA (A)	NX15047	Owen P W
NX165286	McRae A J	NX34884	Norton E O Capt	NX57115	Owen W H
NX 17338	McRae G DOW (T)		KIA (NG)	NX22501	Owens N R
NX32139	McRae G R	NX28008	Norvill B WIA (A)	NX20277	Oxman G G
NX46633	McRae L A Lieut				
NX104646	McRae R W	NX20776	Oatley C A G WIA (T)	NX22424	Paddle C R
NX21270	McShane M H	NX15707	Oatley W R	NX171865	Padmore W
NX65230	McVey J W	NX16302	O'Brien C M KIA (NG)	NX69730	Page A G
NX17588	McVicar A	NX95822	O'Brien D B W WIA (NG)	NX47058	Page C O J
NX17293	McWhinney L H	NX157483	O'Brien E T	NX60450	Painter R J
V207064	McWilliams W A	NX66993	O'Brien F J	NX90552	Palmer C J
		NX86322	O'Brien J O	VX92204	Palmer K A
NX17775	Nagle P F	NX60302	O'Brien J P WIA (A)	NX16437	Palmer W T
NX21260	Nance H A	NX85704	O'Brien L MPD (NG)	NX84782	Park A G
NX46963	Nash C F KIA (NG)	NX12445	O'Brien P E Capt	SX19686	Parish K
NX23158	Naughton F B	VX26586	Ochiltree J G Major	NX95332	Parker A J
NX68931	Naylor J R	NX21857	O'Connell E	NX16967	Parker J E
NX20673	Naylor W R	NX65709	O'Connor H M	NX50083	Parker P
NX43365	Neasmith T H	NX54997	O'Connor J M P DOW (A)	NX14829	Parker J P
NX16263	Neave K O	NX91949	O'Connor R A	NX44336	Parkes W H
NX18665	Neely L J	NX95204	O'Connor T W	NX94194	Parks D H D
NX21474	Neil E D A	NX17242	O'Connor W J MUR (AU)	NX18907	Parkinson J S
NX91491	Neil J F KIA (NG)	NX14998	O'Dea L H WIA (T)	NX15098	Parnell L P
NX139847	Neindorf E G WIA (B)	NX19326	O'Donnell C T WIA (BA)	VX92195	Parry L G

NX175456 Parsons R	VX91210 Phelan C J	NX60571 Pullen T M
NX17059 Parsons R W S *WIA* (NG)	NX50929 Phillips A J C	VX148612 Purcell R
WX22589 Paterson J S	NX84027 Phillips J T	NX78672 Purdue V K
NX14836 Patman H F	QX38756 Philp H J *Lieut*	PX 178 Pursehouse L *Capt MPD* (NG)
NX33476 Patman W H	NX88206 Phinn L W	WX28308 Purser E J
QX2854 Patterson A T	NX16896 Phyland A R *WIA* (A)	NX17879 Quick A J
NX24500 Patterson H W	NX170676 Pickering S P	NX54916 Quillan S V E *WIA* (NG)
NX17978 Patterson W J	NX21833 Pickford R J	NX29031 Quinn A D *WIA* (A)
NX18115 Patterson W J	NX123329 Pickup F E	NX18545 Quinn J W *WIA* (T)
NX89791 Pattison D T	NX12220 Pike P H *Major*	NX1839 Quinn R P *WIA* (NG)
NX24174 Paul E F	NX16965 Pike W F	NX58931 Quinn S G *WIA* (BA)
NX126609 Payne A G	NX20770 Pincham C A N	NX29032 Quinn V M
NX43071 Payne V D	NX69593 Pinchin K R	NX141291 Quinnell F W
SX19683 Payne V R	NX90742 Pink R	
NX32673 Peachey A G	NX19076 Piper K H *WIA* (A)	NX93433 Rabjones L C *WIA* (NG)
SX19504 Peacock W H	NX70231 Pitman C G *Major*	NX130787 Radnedge L P
NX17208 Pead G R	NX119429 Pitt F I	NX172099 Rae R
NX66222 Pearce A E	NX17214 Pitt-Owen R J G	NX42385 Rae R A
NX140848 Pearce E J	NX79459 Plaister A B	NX50437 Rae V *WIA* (A)
NX43957 Pearce G A	VX62927 Pleydell K M	NX200843 Rainey C C
NX14853 Pearce H W *WIA* (T)	NX17455 Plunkett F P *WIA* (BA)	NX101698 Rainsford P H
NX14877 Pearce W B	*KIA* (NG)	NX2012 Ramage G A
NX89946 Pearce W J	NX19861 Pocock F L	NX24709 Rand E J *DOW* (A)
NX17514 Pearse A G	NX89527 Pollard M P	NX60502 Ranson G
NX18591 Pearson J H	NX90401 Pollard O J *WIA* (NG)	NX82396 Rapley C
NX24221 Peck R W	NX15683 Pollock P I *Lieut*	NX5142 Rapp W *WIA* (A)
NX21469 Peckham H	NX20773 Polson C B *KIA* (A)	VX38332 Rasleigh H H
NX60381 Peddell E C	NX15754 Porter A A	NX17127 Ratcliffe C T
NX80064 Peel E R	NX49763 Porter F K	NX52334 Ratcliffe J W *KIA* (NG)
NX18351 Peelgrave F W	NX116689 Portors D E	NX56693 Read A G
NX1603 Peirce D C *Lieut*	NX14493 Portsmouth H D	NX56692 Read E L *WIA* (T)
NX16459 Pellow R A	NX59913 Potter W F	NX89159 Read W H
NX19023 Pemberton L W	NX39525 Potts D C	NX19372 Reading G
WIA (NG)	WX28747 Povah W A	NX24694 Reading R *KIA* (A)
WX22508 Pengully G M	QX38618 Powell A E	NX55380 Readman G
NX66451 Penington W J	VX136385 Powell C H	NX40591 Ready M A E
NX22363 Pennington H	NX113719 Powell F B G *Lieut*	TX14675 Reardon R J
NX91507 Penrose W C *WIA* (NG)	NX5388 Powell M J *WIA* (BA)	NX14380 Reay R J
NX17066 Perceval R A *WIA* (A)	NX124948 Power J	NX44420 Rebett J R T
WIA (NG)	NX60457 Power J T *WIA* (A)	NX90485 Reece L E
NX34855 Percival S M *Lieut*	NX60212 Power L G	NX14369 Reeves R H D
NX20988 Perkins D H *WIA* (NG)	NX33797 Power R J *WIA* (A)	NX58544 Reid C G
WIA (NG)	NX164851 Powyer G H	NX55952 Reid D W
SX3202 Perkins R A *Major*	NX21806 Pratt G H	NX156514 Reid F A
NX21417 Perry A R *WIA* (A)	NX60527 Pratt K S	NX13893 Reid G T *Capt KIA* (NG)
NX32279 Perry E	NX72001 Pressick S T	NX20772 Reid I B *WIA* (T)
NX32902 Perry G G *McC*	QX45828 Price S E	NX60410 Reid L T *WIA* (A)
NX66173 Perry R E	NX58646 Priest H W V *WIA* (NG)	NX85047 Reid P
NX46385 Peters F W *KIA* (NG)	*KIA* (NG)	NX29404 Reid W
NX14219 Peterson A C *WIA* (A)	NX23132 Priest R *WIA* (A)	NX22199 Reilly C J
NX174575 Petrie W W	*WIA* (NG)	NX43432 Reilly J T *KIA* (NG)
NX21743 Pettit C V	NX125852 Pringle W R	NX36934 Reynolds A E *WIA* (A)
NX131606 Pettit N D	NX168921 Prosser J T	NX16026 Rhoades P *WIA* (A)
NX82760 Peyer A	NX20788 Proud R S	NX37087 Rice F J *WIA* (A)
NX156426 Pfeiffer R H	NX29883 Proudlock W L *WIA* (A)	NX23130 Rice R A
NX154224 Pfitzner A H	NX154699 Pullen A R	DX532 Richards A J

NX94813	Richards C
NX90643	Richardson E J
NX17181	Richardson H L
NX23328	Richardson H L
WX37533	Richardson J H
NX52021	Richardson O C
NX16092	Richardson T K *WIA (A)* *WIA (NG)*
NX22211	Rickard H J
NX22030	Rickerby S A
VX87323	Ricketson K H C
SX29895	Ridge A M
NX17991	Ridgway J D W
NX18062	Riley C J
NX41074	Riley R T *WIA (BA)* *WIA (NG)*
NX168364	Ring K F
NX203245	Ritchie F L Capt
NX138485	Ritchie H W
VX91200	Ritchie J M K
NX26210	Ritchie R
NX169903	Roach K T
NX23205	Roach R
NX72510	Roach W *WIA (NG)*
NX15697	Roberts A H
NX60246	Roberts F O *DOW (T)*
NX126656	Roberts R A
NX119460	Roberts R R
SX19397	Roberts R T
NX125085	Roberts W R
NX168940	Robertson A A
NX17553	Robertson A D
NX65228	Robertson J D Lieut
NX14417	Robertson K S
NX70152	Robertson N R Capt
NX7465	Robertson R W *WIA (A)*
NX15052	Robertson R W T
NX39762	Robertson W T
NX83647	Robertson W W
NX26683	Robinson C R
NX173303	Robinson C R
NX78760	Robinson L C
NX136645	Robinson W T C
NX18350	Robson E J
NX14645	Robson H J
NX46509	Rogers A E *WIA (NG)* *WIA (NG)*
NX16360	Rogers C L Lieut
NX67393	Rogers F W
NX15132	Rogers W G
NX57005	Rollings F T R
NX19281	Rollings S T *WIA (T)*
NX54512	Ronan W T
NX24726	Roper R E J
NX17724	Rooney P W
NX23102	Rooney W H *WIA (T)*

NX80458	Rose H C *DOI* (NG)
NX27958	Rose J
NX15968	Rosen A *WIA* (T)
NX38505	Ross A J
NX21817	Ross C H K *WIA* (T)
NX24576	Ross D A
NX142347	Ross M A
NX60461	Ross T B Lieut
NX60249	Rouen C M
NX21393	Roughsedge R W
NX29077	Rout D J *WIA* (NG)
NX69244	Routley C F
NX30513	Rowe L J
NX91053	Rowland J L
NX58529	Rowell C J J *DOW* (T)
NX14585	Rowell E A
NX47587	Rowles F
NX124462	Rowling E C T
NX14875	Rudkin R S Capt
VX148366	Runnalls R
NX89732	Russell A P
NX90354	Russell B T
NX125863	Russell F G
NX17008	Russell T J
NX83444	Russell W
NX14295	Rutledge D Lieut *WIA* (NG)
NX169520	Ryan C
NX54514	Ryan E J *WIA* (A)
NX68828	Ryan E R
NX175538	Ryan E R
NX58783	Ryan J L *KIA* (NG)
NX20802	Ryan J S *WIA* (T)
VX124827	Ryan K C
NX21769	Ryan L J
NX25016	Rymer B *WIA* (NG)
NX34889	Sabine K B Capt
VX121379	Sammutt A W H
NX190045	Sampson G E
NX68827	Sanders F C *WIA* (BA)
NX22833	Sandstrom J
NX119474	Sargent L F
DX610	Sargent M G *WIA* (NG)
NX81875	Saul N L
VX66240	Saunders C E F
NX16472	Saunders H D Le'T
NX24159	Saunders L
NX60492	Savage R R *WIA* (A)
NX92476	Sayers R J
VX145719	Scanlon J T
NX17330	Schellack F C
NX77754	Schenk P W *WIA* (NG)
VX134226	Schodde W K
NX134312	Schofield A D
NX201251	Schofield C B

NX77885	Scholfield J W
NX9315	Scholz L J *WIA* (A)
NX21346	Schrader G D
SX19300	Schubert L L
SX29783	Schultz H V
WX25167	Scott A R C
NX23387	Scott D McD
NX14846	Scott H
NX31315	Scott S
NX99168	Scott S F
NX14702	Scott T E
NX192629	Searle A B
NX14945	Searle R J
NX90674	Searson P B *WIA* (NG)
NX18146	Seaton E
NX93443	Seddon R J
NX92548	Segaert J K
NX21901	Seibright N
NX22273	Selfe L T *WIA* (A)
NX2016	Sellars G *WIA* (NG)
NX174820	Settree J R
NX125425	Sexton L J
NX15777	Shanahan J J
NX58606	Shanahan M W
NX22389	Shannon F
NX157110	Sharp A H
NX22614	Sharp C N *WIA* (BA) *KIA* (A)
NX21280	Sharp I *WIA* (T)
NX194607	Sharpe H W *WIA* (B)
NX34118	Shatten R J *WIA* (T) *WIA* (A)
NX15188	Shaw A *WIA* (A)
NX47687	Shaw F A *WIA* (NG)
WX26566	Shaw N R
NX16452	Shaw W G
NX17273	Sheargold L W J
NX43528	Sheargold M
NX125357	Sheather G A
NX156055	Sheedy A T
NX15986	Sheedy C R
VX92074	Sheedy T J
NX16141	Sheehan F C *KIA* (T)
NX20843	Sheehan J
NX28415	Sheldon T C Capt *WIA* (A) *WIA* (NG)
NX16517	Sheldrake S S
NX24833	Shepherd C A
QX41519	Shepherd J A
QX41496	Sheppard H C Lieut
NX60204	Sherd G P *WIA* (BA)
NX91834	Sherriff M A
NX16279	Shields S J *DOW* (A)
NX67772	Shilper J G
NX14474	Shipton A E
NX174270	Shipway A C

NX169980	Shoolman D	NX16454	Smith H E	NX72576	Stallworthy J E
NX131049	Shuttleworth K	NX77698	Smith J DOW (NG)	NX51649	Standen W R WIA (BA)
NX12297	Silverstone J Major	NX21751	Smith J	NX6106	Stannard A J
SX19490	Sim D W	NX39663	Smith J F	SX30789	Stansborough A H
NX90330	Simes G J	NX17762	Smith J H	NX78114	Stanton D R
NX154541	Simington F	VX93681	Smith J I	NX22437	Stanton R L
NX21989	Simmonds B S	NX155722	Smith J J	NX20892	Starr A
VX91818	Simmonds J V	NX20030	Smith J R WIA (T)	NX85049	Starr R H
NX79665	Simmons C	NX79529	Smith J R	VX93788	Startup I W
VX29018	Simmons D S	NX154311	Smith J W	NX21951	Steain F
NX16662	Simonds A A	WX39255	Smith K	NX23054	Steel A B
NX24169	Simons B R	SX32502	Smith M S	NX14398	Steel W
NX18809	Simpson A E	NX60448	Smith N A	NX15674	Steel K J J
NX4302	Simpson G Lieut KIA (B)	NX14999	Smith N J	NX16732	Stephens J C
QX41496	Simpson H C Lieut	NX82624	Smith P A	NX68046	Stephens K G
NX52928	Simpson L C Capt	VX69967	Smith R	NX93508	Stephens L A
NX12221	Simpson N W Lt Col	NX60497	Smith R A WIA (NG)	NX17779	Stephens S T WIA (A)
NX78845	Simpson R M	NX6630	Smith R E	QX17670	Stephenson P G
NX92468	Simpson R F	NX32653	Smith R G	NX139199	Stephenson R P
NX16226	Sims C	NX14825	Smith R J	NX41984	Steward C D
NX21418	Sims C J WIA (T)	SX21945	Smith R S	NX38342	Stewart A G WIA (A)
NX23261	Sims W G	NX31103	Smith R S WIA (NG)	NX73422	Stewart D
NX33807	Sinclair A E J	VX92405	Smith S	NX21647	Stewart J B
NX72539	Sinclair S R	NX18489	Smith S E WIA (A)	NX81265	Stewart J J
NX20792	Sindel G S		WIA (NG) WIA (NG)	NX60540	Stewart J L WIA (T)
NX60661	Sivell D	NX21382	Smith T L	NX60250	Stewart K A
NX89415	Skinner F J	NX23160	Smith T M C	NX171880	Stewart L C
SX31601	Skinner L E G	NX16155	Smith V	NX125835	Stewart R
NX41395	Slack G S WIA (A)	NX23134	Smith V DOW (T)	NX22035	Stewart R M
NX16006	Slattery C J	NX125774	Smith V A	NX16032	Stewart W A G
NX82695	Slattery J E	NX14402	Smith W A T	NX60548	Stirling R S KIA (A)
NX130278	Sligar V C	NX17768	Smith W H	QX33203	Stirling W J
NX22004	Small A J	NX19279	Smythe T	NX17263	Stoddard O A D
NX17012	Smith A	NX17013	Snell W R	QX8982	Stone W M WIA (NG)
VX66997	Smith A A	NX15023	Snelson F	NX57582	Stoppelbein J C W
NX18102	Smith A E L	NX17359	Soden F T WIA (NG)	NX90297	Stormon L J
NX66814	Smith A G	NX16300	Solomon J G A	NX60505	Stoyles F J
NX27646	Smith A H	NX39036	Soorley J F KIA (A)	NX19221	Stoyles G W
NX10387	Smith A J	NX23167	Southee F R J	NX141264	Stratton J M
NX157383	Smith A T	NX119453	Spackman F W	NX17275	Stratton N C
NX20791	Smith B H	NX125834	Spackman R C	NX17121	Stuart L M WIA (T)
NX1742	Smith C	NX50386	Spare S L		WIA (T)
NX20789	Smith C A	NX124337	Spargo H F	NX17993	Stubbs L A WIA (NG)
NX119470	Smith C C	NX24341	Sparkes P J DOW (NG)	NX21401	Styles W J WIA (A)
NX27954	Smith C G Lieut	NX200816	Sparks A G		WIA (A)
NX171922	Smith C P	NX60665	Spencer R W	NX93409	Suaerbier W
NX11014	Smith C R S	NX85574	Spinks A A	NX193450	Sugden J E
NX26977	Smith E G	NX26453	Spinks R H KIA (A)	NX124412	Suitor W E
NX60498	Smith F A WIA (A)	NX66228	Spittle R L	NX22253	Sullivan A E
	WIA (NG)	NX126635	Spleit H N	NX21369	Sullivan E E
NX44778	Smith G C	NX139837	Spleit P R	NX12279	Sullivan J F Capt WIA (A)
NX6572	Smith G E	NX21677	Sprague E J	NX14838	Sullivan R WIA (T)
NX89660	Smith G H	NX18827	Spratt A L WIA (A)	NX60251	Sullivan W A
NX4024	Smith G P Lieut		KIA (NG)	NX172420	Summers J T
NX56812	Smith H C WIA (A)	NX16193	Stafford R O'C WIA (A)	NX53079	Sutherland F J
	WIA (NG)	NX59457	Stage W J	NX60290	Sutherland J

NX90108	Sutton K J	
NX67427	Svanberg S O	
NX66676	Swan T E Capt	
SX8162	Sweeney J	
NX46499	Sweetnam E J *WIA* (A)	
NX21347	Swift R A	
NX54688	Symington C G	
NX26578	Symon P *WIA* (BA)	
NX123845	Symonds L	
QX46639	Tacey M A	
NX17246	Tait R A *WIA* (T)	
	WIA (A)	
VX92730	Talbot A A	
NX20740	Tallon A V J	
NX24163	Tallon S G	
NX18065	Tanner A S *WIA* (T)	
NX26159	Tansey T J *WIA* (NG)	
	WIA (NG)	
NX101008	Tapp G T	
NX15724	Tarrant R A B	
NX23665	Tasker E D *KIA* (NG)	
NX39711	Tasker G F *WIA* (A)	
	WIA (NG)	
NX47800	Taylor A *WIA* (A)	
NX91065	Taylor A J	
NX21402	Taylor E J *WIA* (T)	
NX58782	Taylor E L D	
QX57864	Taylor F	
NX16362	Taylor G	
NX46502	Taylor H J *POW* (A)	
NX21404	Taylor J G *WIA* (T)	
NX168393	Taylor J G	
NX176317	Taylor N C	
NX56487	Taylor R C *KIA* (A)	
NX125839	Taylor R J *KIA* (B)	
NX17331	Taylor V	
NX17772	Taylor V E *WIA* (A)	
NX19384	Taylor W E	
NX18064	Temple A D	
NX91386	Tesch H E *WIA* (NG)	
NX90739	Thibou R D *WIA* (NG)	
NX71906	Thirkell E T	
VX70163	Thomas A J	
NX17826	Thomas G	
SX19309	Thomas M	
NX56903	Thomas W R P	
NX17196	Thompson A A	
	WIA (NG)	
NX89807	Thompson C A	
NX21549	Thompson F C	
NX47294	Thompson F W *WIA* (NG)	
WX26559	Thompson G E	
NX14948	Thompson H E	
NX82700	Thompson J	
NX60423	Thompson J J	

NX56431	Thompson J K Capt
	WIA (BA)
NX34389	Thompson L
WX36397	Thompson S W
NX21645	Thompson W H
NX17244	Thompson W J
NX17197	Thompson W K
NX21272	Thorley J B *WIA* (T)
	WIA (NG)
QX37662	Thorn A D Lieut
NX48773	Thorn R T *WIA* (A)
NX28333	Thornley S
NX176663	Thornton E G
QX37399	Thorogood S J
NX60680	Thorp J O
NX60279	Throsby G
NX125867	Ticehurst A W
NX83746	Tidd A H
NX52005	Tilbrook W N
NX47647	Till A H Lieut
SX19365	Tilly C J
WX37138	Timms J B
NX44504	Tink I M *KIA* (BA)
NX20984	Tinker H A
NX16189	Tipping A G
NX174150	Tobin J W
NX60455	Todkill A J *WIA* (T)
NX174438	Tognolini A J
NX87129	Toner T
VX140806	Tonkin R J
WX29399	Tooke H A
QX52119	Towner J C
NX23063	Towns R W
NX23204	Townsend J H
NX21671	Towsey D B
NX42633	Trask J
NX157111	Traves A F
NX12371	Trebeck N B Major
NX21302	Tregilgas J L *WIA* (T)
	WIA (A) *WIA* (NG)
NX20264	Tremble L L
NX147037	Tremble R J
NX91492	Treseder H C *WIA* (NG)
NX16015	Trevena J A *WIA* (T)
	DOW (A)
NX21308	Trotman O H C
NX21266	Trousdale R
SX19373	Trowse C H
NX65621	Trudgeon M P Lieut
NX47930	Trute W J *WIA* (A)
NX 14997	Tuckwell A E Lieut
	KIA (T)
NX14521	Tuffnell T H
NX54863	Tunks W P
NX162091	Turl L T
NX190541	Turnbull A P

NX17854	Turnbull J A
NX54498	Turnbull J B
NX79631	Turnbull S V
NX15853	Turner C J
NX15041	Turner G F
NX174321	Turner H C
NX16050	Turner H E *WIA* (T)
NX171449	Turner H W
NX89260	Turner J L
NX60522	Turner J V
NX21211	Turner N A *WIA* (A)
NX20743	Turner R E
NX13999	Turner R L
NX44143	Turner S *WIA* (NG)
N267366	Turnlove A P
NX19444	Tutton A D
WX19257	Tutton S J
VX120639	Tyzack R C
NX17287	Unicomb G L *WIA* (T)
VX128436	Upton L H
NX22422	Urquhart A H Lieut
	WIA (A)
NX55094	Urquhart J W *WIA* (NG)
NX26348	Usback A A *WIA* (T)
	WIA (A)
NX60377	Utting A C
NX34435	Vallotto G J *WIA* (NG)
NX60524	Venables W H *DOW* (A)
NX14477	Verrinder A W
NX38063	Vick H T *WIA* (BA)
WX4368	Vickers D H Lieut
NX142566	Vickery A
NX22796	Vickery F
NX12984	Vidler I P K
NX16684	Vincent A J
NX34618	Vincent E H *WIA* (A)
	DOW (NG)
NX17876	Vincent G D Lieut
	WIA (T)
NX15744	Viney A E A
QX40103	Vock C W Lieut
NX17347	Wade J
NX51427	Wade L W J
VX141154	Wade N R
NX22266	Wade R W
NX58834	Wade T E
WX41257	Wager R
NX60639	Walcott H V
NX43127	Waldron A J *WIA* (A)
NX29949	Waldron J W *WIA* (A)
QX11006	Waldron R R E
NX15025	Walker A J
NX23508	Walker C F

NX68739	Walker C J	
NX89327	Walker H F J *WIA* (NG)	
SX37167	Walker J A	
NX17262	Walker J F	
NX154182	Walker J F	
WX36726	Walker J R	
NX116695	Walker M	
NX59294	Walker R R *WIA* (A)	
NX16715	Walker S	
NX200835	Wallace N F	
NX90361	Wallace P	
NX53402	Waller C J *WIA* (A)	
NX166289	Wallis B B	
NX19042	Wallis J	
NX60374	Walmsley E J *KIA* (NG)	
NX54336	Walsh D F	
NX26560	Walsh G J	
NX23237	Walsh J	
NX17687	Walsh J M	
NX17747	Walsh K B	
NX83494	Walsh R C	
NX17848	Walsh W E	
NX52355	Walshe V J	
NX200894	Ward A W J	
NX43298	Ward H S	
NX47883	Ward W J	
NX174492	Warden J L	
NX174889	Ware J M	
NX66343	Warner L E	
NX97734	Warren K C	
VX75353	Wasley H J Lieut	
NX17867	Wass G O	
NX14133	Waterhouse B Lieut	
NX60288	Waterhouse S G J Lieut *KIA* (NG)	
NX93389	Waters N	
NX17561	Waters W	
VX113850	Watkins R G	
NX144498	Watling E R	
NX190385	Watmore D G	
NX34074	Watson B H Chaplain	
NX136831	Watson E A	
NX26901	Watson R	
TX14457	Watson R F	
NX55079	Watts G A	
NX78353	Watts G R *WIA* (NG)	
NX78251	Watts K	
NX81189	Watts T	
NX58797	Waugh R A J	
NX47936	Weary B *KIA* (A)	
NX60514	Webb C E *WIA* (A)	
NX58778	Webb J W *WIA* (BA)	
NX135135	Webb P	
NX78255	Webb W	
NX16215	Webdale G T	
QX16281	Weedon R F K	
NX22346	Weekes H E
NX21676	Weeks H E
NX7379	Weeks W W
NX85272	Weeks-Chalmers E
NX16701	Weingott J
NX83761	Weir M J *WIA* (NG)
NX19495	Weissel J B
NX21882	Welsh D A *WIA* (T)
NX24615	Weldon A C *WIA* (A) *WIA* (NG)
NX125404	Weller C J
NX27792	Wells H D B *WIA* (T) *WIA* (NG)
NX23658	Wells K F *WIA* (T)
NX125844	Wells L A
VX15120	Wells N Lt Col
NX51074	Wells R J *WIA* (A)
NX16992	Welsh V
NX18546	Wentworth-Perry B A
NX21279	West A C
NX17054	West F A
NX25269	West H A
NX15013	West N G Lieut
NX126607	West W W
NX66583	Weston H L *KIA* (A)
NX90271	Weston J
NX17374	Wharton J A S
NX125860	Wheatley A E
NX119471	Wheatley M A S
NX16196	Wheaton J W *DOI* (BH)
NX119463	Whitaker A E
NX14852	Whitaker H J A
NX123811	Whitaker T J A
NX50168	Whitbread E N *DOI* (NG)
VX90703	White A W
NX53726	White J
NX21284	White K F
NX21424	White L
NX15748	White N
NX167752	White N I F
NX57919	White R C
NX17007	White V N
NX49194	White W J
NX15991	Whitechurch R C *WIA* (T)
NX18149	Whitelaw P G W
WX37886	Whitely B F
NX32498	Whitmore J G
NX90565	Whitton W G *WIA* (NG)
NX34527	Whitty P C L
WX28262	Whyte J McP
NX7049	Wicks P H
NX22226	Widdowson K *WIA* (NG)
NX21760	Widerberg J C *ACC* (BH)
NX20977	Wiggins W H

NX15066	Wight B McD
WX22394	Wightman F D
NX24448	Wilcox W A
NX20858	Wilkes F A
NX13902	Wilkinson A *KIA* (T)
NX167404	Wilkinson J G
NX16095	Williams A
NX123846	Williams A J
NX46531	Williams C J
NX47414	Williams C L
NX45318	Williams D
NX91482	Williams D *WIA* (NG)
NX104283	Williams D A Lieut
NX47829	Williams E F *POW* (A)
NX21502	Williams E J
NX16214	Williams E M *WIA* (A)
NX92879	Williams E S
NX22252	Williams F D *WIA* (A) *WIA* (NG)
NX170714	Williams G
NX17397	Williams G E
NX125879	Williams G W *WIA* (B)
NX17979	Williams J C *WIA* (A) *WIA* (NG) *WIA* (NG)
NX24484	Williams J E K
NX21484	Williams J H *WIA* (NG)
NX12296	Williams J M Major
NX125868	Williams J T
NX16575	Williams K W
TX15117	Williams L
NX37085	Williams M A
NX125828	Williams M G
NX17527	Williams O N *WIA* (T) *WIA* (NG)
NX17383	Williams R B
NX16297	Williams R C
NX91467	Williams S A *WIA* (NG)
NX52495	Williams S M Lieut
NX125836	Williamson R
NX54552	Williamson W J *KIA* (NG)
NX3922	Wills R N
NX17470	Willson O A
VX80206	Wilmott F S
NX60434	Wilsdon K F J *WIA* (A)
NX6636	Wilson A
VX87965	Wilson A C Lieut
NX56593	Wilson A E *WIA* (A)
NX84152	Wilson A O
NX12212	Wilson C H Capt *WIA* (A)
NX140768	Wilson D M
NX21322	Wilson F
NX169712	Wilson G L
QX23350	Wilson H D
NX18306	Wilson J
NX18981	Wilson J H
NX90731	Wilson J R *WIA* (NG)

NX170517	Wilson K E	WX26860	Wood H		
NX26929	Wilson N A	NX4541	Wood J N	NX17360	Yarwood L
NX60446	Wilson N J *WIA* (A)	NX125881	Wood R	NX14787	Yates N
NX9574	Wilson R	NX14606	Wood R W *WIA* (NG)	NX14928	Yates T A *WIA* (T)
NX14590	Wilson T G	WX19616	Wood W P	NX31300	Yeend S H Lieut
SX19549	Wilson W H D	NX21869	Woolridge R W *POW* (T)	NX21327	Yeomans R F
NX12224	Windeyer H F Capt	NX55005	Worlock J	NX40521	Yeomans W
	DOW (T)	NX46532	Wormald A E *WIA* (NG)	NX21407	Young A K
NX16222	Windeyer O A	NX58816	Worthington N S G	NX18166	Young G T *KIA* (T)
NX10914	Windley R G		*POW* (A)	NX15751	Young J W
NX10050	Windybank E C C *DOI* (S)	NX18129	Wray F	NX15728	Young M J
NX26354	Winstanley H	NX58449	Wray G R Lieut	NX56049	Young S J
NX125845	Wirth D W	NX14738	Wright A J Capt	NX60305	Young V H
NX60472	Withers T J	NX93718	Wright J J	NX21377	Yule B
WX36699	Witt F	NX15992	Wright M W *KIA* (NG)		
NX88525	Wolfe E F	NX85340	Wright V *WIA* (NG)	NX60160	Zickby C J
NX82689	Wolstenholme C F	NX17365	Wright W E	NX60436	Zouch H E
NX16646	Wood D M Lieut	NX17198	Wroe W C		
NX173628	Wood F	NX23157	Wynne A W		

NON-BATTLE CASUALTIES
DIED OF ILLNESS

The following soldiers died of illness while serving with the 2/17 Australian Infantry Battalion:

NX12370	Maj Blundell J B (AU) 24/12/46*		
NX92995	Pte Brown A F (AU) 7/12/43		
VX94745	Pte Clark D L (B) 31/10/45	NX18103	Pte Johnson R (AU) 8/5/44
NX57000	Pte Collins F A (P) 19/12/41	NX60406	Sgt Lambert E R (AU)14/10/43
NX32474	Pte Donnelly R (A) 9/11/42	VX64190	Pte Knevitt H (NG) 29/11/43
NX94928	Pte Eastment A C (NG) 2/11/43	NX37004	Pte Martin J T (P) 31/l/42
NX16441	Sgt Farrar-Pugh G H (AU)16/8/45	NX16143	Cpl McManus A W F (P) 1/11/41
NX23182	Pte Howes A L A (AU) 31/12/44	NX60336	Pte Mould L H (AU) 5/l/46
NX17064	Pte Hynes W A (AU) 3/3/47*	NX51685	Pte Murdoch N W J (AU) 21/3/44
NX19087	Pte Geoghegan W (AU) 30/10/42	NX80458	Pte Rose H C (NG) 10/10/43
NX21843	Pte Jarman A B (AU) 24/2/45	NX50168	Pte Whitbread E N (NG)12/11/43
NX16217	Pte Johnson D (AU) 15/9/40	NX16196	Pte Wheaton J W (BH) 7/3/41
		NX10050	Pte Windybank E C C (S) 7/4/42

MURDERED

NX17242	Pte O'Connor W J (AU) -5/4/44		* Died Post War

LEST WE FORGET

2/17 AUSTRALIAN INFANTRY BATTALION - CASUALTIES

	KIA & DOW		MPD		ACC		POW		WIA	
	O	OR	O	OR	O	OR	O	OR	O	OR
BATTLE CASUALTIES MIDDLE EAST (a) Libya 27/2/41 to 23/10/41 (including Tobruk)	3	36	1	0	0	2	0	14	8	119
(b) Egypt Tel El Eisa 25/7/42 - 22/10/42	0	3			0	1			2	35
El Alamein 23/10/42 – 6/11/42	3	59					0	4	13	190
NEW GUINEA 21/9/43 – 20/1/44	4	57	1	1					8	152
BORNEO 10/6/45 – 14/8/45	1	8							0	15
TOTAL	11	163	2	1	0	3	0	18	31	511

SUMMARY	Officers	Other Ranks
BATTLE CASUALTIES	44	696
OTHER (a) Died Of Illness		
Middle East		6
New Guinea		4
Borneo		1
Australia	1	11
TOTAL		22
(b) Murdered		1
TOTAL CASUALTIES	45	719

Figures compiled from initial information supplied by the Central Army Records Office, Melbourne, in conjunction with the Australian War Memorial, World War II records. AWM Roll of Honour cut off dates were 3 September 1939 and 30 June 1947 which caused some adjustments made between the categories advised by CARO.

Tobruk War Cemetery – Cyrenaica

APPENDIX 2
HONOURS AND AWARDS

Awarded to members of the 2/17 Australian Infantry Battalion

VICTORIA CROSS — (VC)
NX15705	Cpl Edmondson, J H

DISTINGUISHED SERVICE ORDER — (DSO)
NX378	Lt Col Crawford, J W
NX12221	Lt Col Simpson, N W
NX12225	Maj Broadbent, J R

BAR TO DISTINGUISHED SERVICE ORDER — (DS0)
NX12221	Lt Col Simpson, N W

ORDER OF THE BRITISH EMPIRE

Officer — OBE
NX12229	Maj Allan, H T MC
NX12296	Maj Williams, J M
NX12328	Lt Col Moffatt, J G S

Member — MBE
NX15834	Capt Newton, A J C

Medal — BEM
NX23135	Sgt Avery, R

MILITARY CROSS — (MC)
NX12329	Capt Balfe, J W
NX12231	Lt Mackell, F A
NX12228	Capt Maclarn, L C
NX12510	Capt McMaster, I F
NX14374	Capt Dinning, J H
NX34299	Lieut Bennie, R J
NX51115	Maj Garnsey, R C
NX17528	Lieut Blundell, E J
NX14840	Lieut Main, H H
NX14875	Capt Rudkin, R S
NX12279	Capt Sullivan J F

DISTINGUISHED CONDUCT MEDAL — (DCM)
NX13446	Sgt Cortis, J F
NX21416	Cpl Harris, E
NX15984	L/Sgt Dawes, B G

MILITARY MEDAL — (MM)
NX23052	Sgt McElroy, R McL
NX16216	L/Cpl Dunbar, A E
NX16060	Cpl Gleeson, W P
NX50437	A/Sgt Rae, V
NX14877	Sgt Pearce, W B
NX65985	Cpl Lemaire, C E
NX18326	Pte McGrath, F
NX4541	A/Sgt Wood, J N
NX27067	Pte Brooks, R C
NX59910	Pte Carpenter, W L
NX19113	Pte Moore, B B

MENTIONED IN DESPATCHES — (MID)
NX12229	Maj Allan, H T, MC
NX12212	Capt Wilson, C H
NX12510	Capt McMaster, I F
NX12228	Lieut Maclarn, L C
NX70231	Lieut Pitman, C G
NX15013	L/Sgt West, N G
NX27792	Pte Wells, H D
NX378	Lt Col Crawford, J W, DSO, ED
NX17100	Lieut Dick, R J
NX12372	Lieut Geikie, W B A
NX14850	Sgt Gambling, J S
NX16060	Cpl Gleeson, W P
NX12408	Maj McCullock, E M
NX13893	Lieut Reid, G T

NX16441	Sgt Farrar-Pugh, G A
NX12298	Maj Brien, L C
NX18194	Pte Farrell, B T
NX12510	Capt McMaster, I F
NX56431	Capt Thompson, J K
NX16093	Sgt McHenry, H J
NX17879	Sgt Quick, A J
NX14999	Sgt Smith, N J
NX16222	Sgt Windeyer, O A
NX21689	Cpl Monaghan, S C H
NX19384	Cpl Taylor, W E
NX60689	L/Cpl Murray, J R
NX12228	Capt Maclarn, L C
NX12445	Capt O'Brien, P E
NX24708	Lieut McFarland, J D
NX15757	WOI Dunbar, D C
NX24575	Pte Carter, J W G
NX22900	Pte Chilcott, J A
NX22222	Pte Holland, T W
NX47930	Pte Trute, W J
NX8390	Pte Bevan, R M
NX16597	Pte Laws, J E
NX21849	L/Cpl Bell E E
NX12221	Lt Col Simpson, N W, DSO
VX26586	Maj Ochiltree, J G
NX13939	Maj Bird, C R
NX18475	Sgt Macmillan, W J C
NX14133	Lt Waterhouse, B
NX14844	WOI Oliver, A J
NX14738	Capt Wright, A J
NX16036	Sgt Greenwood C F
NX60361	Sgt Cameron G S

Awards For Post War Service

COMPANION OF THE ORDER OF THE BATH — (CB)

Maj Gen N W Simpson, CBE, DSO & Bar, ED

ORDER OF THE BRITISH EMPIRE

Knight Commander (KCB)

Lt Col Sir Charles Cutler, ED

Commander (CBE)

Maj Gen N W Simpson, DSO & Bar, ED
Maj Gen J R Broadbent, DSO, ED
Lt A H Urquhart

Officer (OBE)

Lt Col F A Mackell MC ED
Col P H Pike, ED
Lt R E Kennedy

Member (MBE)

Maj D McCarthy
Maj J D McFarland
Maj D A Williams
WO1 A J Oliver
Mr P N Capewell

Medal (BEM)

Mr L O Meaney, ISM
Mr A S Tanner

AUSTRALIAN ORDERS

Dr H L Hughes, A.O.
Lt A H Urquhart A.O. C. B.E.
Maj R J Moran O.A.M.
Mr K F Ring O.A.M.

ORDER OF ST MICHAEL & ST GEORGE

Commander (CMG)

Dr T A R Dinning

APPENDIX 3
ABBREVIATIONS

A	Acting	CCS	Casualty Clearing Station
AA	Anti-Aircraft	Cdo	Commando
AAG	Assistant Adjutant-General	CGS	Chief of the General Staff
AAMC	Australian Army Medical Corps	C-in-C	Commander in Chief
		Col	Colonel
AAMW's	Australian Army Medical Women's Corps	Comd	Command, Commander, Commanded
AASC	Australian Army Service Corps	CO	Commanding Officer
		Coy	Company
Admin	Administration, administrative	Cpl	Corporal
Adj	Adjutant	CQMS	Company Quarter Master Sergeant
ADMS	Assistant Director Medical Services	CRA	Commander Royal Artillery
ADS	Advanced Dressing Station	CRE	Commander Royal Engineers
Adv	Advanced	CSM	Company Sergeant Major
AEME	Australian Electrical and Mechanical Engineers	CSO	Chief Signals Officer
		Det	Detachment
AFV	Armoured Fighting Vehicle	Div	Division
AGH	Australian General Hospital	DLI	Durham Light Infantry
AHQ	Army Head Quarters	DOI	Died of Illness
AIF	Australian Imperial Force	DOW	Died of Wounds
Amb	Ambulance	DP	Dual Purpose
Angau	Australian New Guinea Administrative Unit	DR	Despatch Rider
		EBSR	Engineer Boat and Shore Regiment
AP	Armoured Piercing		
APD	Assault Personnel Destroyer	Engrs	Engineers
Approx	Approximately	Eqpt	Equipment
Ares	Army Reserve	Fd	Field
Armd	Armoured	FDL	Forward Defended Locality
Arty	Artillery	FOO	Forward Observation Officer
Asst	Assistant	FUP	Forming Up Place
ATK, A/Tk	Anti-Tank	Gd	Guard
AWAS	Australian Women's Army Service	Gen	General
		GHQ	General Headquarters
BBCAU	British Borneo Civil Affairs Unit	Gnr	Gunner
		GOC	General Officer Commanding
Bde	Brigade	Gp	Group
BM	Brigade Major	GSO	General Staff Officer
Bn	Battalion	HQ	Head Quarters
Bty	Battery	HF	Harassing Fire
BW	Bullet Wound	HMG	Heavy Machine Gun
Capt	Captain	hrs	Hours
Cav	Cavalry	Hy	Heavy

I/C, i/c	In Command		Pte	Private
Indep	Independent		PW, POW	Prisoner of War
Inf	Infantry		PWCP	Prisoner of War Collection Point
Int	Intelligence			
ITB	Infantry Training Battalion		RAA	Royal Australian Artillery
KIA	Killed in Action		RAAF	Royal Australian Air Force
LAA	Light Anti-Aircraft		RAC	Royal Armoured Corps
LAD	Light Aid Detachment		RAE	Royal Australian Engineers
L/Cpl	Lance Corporal		RAF	Royal Air Force
LHQ	Allied Land Forces Headquarters		RAAF	Royal Australian Air Force
			RAP	Regimental Aid Post
L of C	Lines of Communication		RAN	Royal Australian Navy
Lt	Lieutenant or Light		Recce	Reconnaissance
LCI	Landing Craft Infantry		Regt	Regiment
LCM	Landing Craft Mechanised		RMO	Regimental Medical Officer
LCP(R)	Landing Craft Personnel (Ramp)		RSM	Regimental Sergeant Major
			R of O	Reserve of Officers
LCT	Landing Craft Tank		R/T	Radio Telegraph
LCV	Landing Craft Vehicle		RTR	Royal Tank Regiment
LCV(P)	Landing Craft Vehicle - personnel		SA	Small Arms
			SAA	Small Arms Ammunition
LCS	Landing Craft Support		Sec	Section
LMG	Light Machine Gun		Sgt	Sergeant
LOB	Left Out of Battle		Sig	Signalman
L/T	Line Telegraph		Sigs	Signals
Maj	Major		SMG	Sub-machine Gun
MG	Machine Gun		Spr	Sapper
Mil	Military		Sqn	Squadron
MLO	Military Landing Officer		S/Sgt	Staff Sergeant
MMG	Medium Machine Gun		SW	Shell Wound
MT	Motor Transport		SWPA	South West Pacific Area
NCO	Non-commissioned Officer		Tac R	Tactical Reconnaissance
NEI	Netherland East Indies		TCP	Transport Control Point
NMS	No Movement Seen		Tk	Tank
NG	New Guinea		Tpr	Trooper
NS	National Service		Tps	Troops
OG	Orders Group		TSMG	Thompson Sub-machine Gun
OC	Officer Commanding		URTI	Upper Respiratory Tract Infection
OCTU	Officer Cadet Training Unit			
Ops	Operations		USAAF	United States Army Air Force
Ors	Other Ranks		USN	United States Navy
OSMG	Owen sub-machine gun		VAD	Voluntary Aid Detachment
PIB	Papuan Infantry Battalion		WE	War Equipment
Pl	Platoon		WIA	Wounded in Action
Pnr	Pioneer		WOI	Warrant Officer Class One
POL	Petrol Oil Lubricant		WO2,WOII	Warrant Officer Class Two
PT	Patrol Torpedo (boat)			

APPENDIX 4

THE 2/17 BATTALION AIF ASSOCIATION

By Bill Shaw

THE INAUGURATION

The idea of forming a group of all ex-2/17ers arose, naturally, in a pub. About mid-1945, quite a few of the boys who had been lucky (or unlucky) enough to have been discharged early, used to gather at Alma's Bar in the Angel in Pitt Street, and this developed into the main ex-2/17 watering hole. The notion of keeping a list of those who called in at the Angel occurred to Harold McLachlan, and in June 1945 this list was used to arrange an initial meeting of 2/17ers at Cliff Polson's home in Wollstonecraft. It was decided to hold regular meetings, the first of which, in effect an inaugural meeting, was held at Sargents Restaurant on 7 July and elected Claude Brien as President, John Baker as Secretary and Harold McLachlan as Treasurer. The Committee included Bev Ellison, Swede Weldon, Col O'Donnell, Goff Schrader, Bill Leaman and Vic Walshe.

During July 1945 a proposed Constitution was prepared by Harold McLachlan and John Baker, assisted by Lt Col McKenzie of the original 17th Battalion (Bruce McKenzie's father), who was a great stalwart of our Association during its formation.

From July onwards, monthly meetings were held at the offices of Shipping Newspapers in Bond Street, Sydney. Membership forms were printed and issued, often by hand in the pub, and a letter was sent to the CO, 2/17 Inf Bn, then in Borneo, inviting each member of the unit to become a member of the Association.

The first General Meeting was held on 17 Jan 1946 in the Surf Lifesaving rooms in Hamilton Street, Sydney. The Constitution was adopted and Officers elected, and so the Association came into a formal existence. The 1946 Committee was

PRESIDENT:	Claude Brien
VICE PRESIDENTS:	Phil Chilvers, Pat Conti
SECRETARY:	John Baker
ASSISTANT SECRETARY:	Bill Leaman
TREASURER:	Harold McLachlan

COMMITTEE:		
	Vic Walshe	John Broadbent
	Swede Weldon	Jim Dick
	Bev Ellison	Bob Reay
	Rex Auckett	Peter Bryant
	Cam Oatley	Claude Pettit

THE "FORTIES"

The "Forties" was a period of development in the Association. Regular meetings were held at various locations — Winns, Marrickville Anzac Hall, Philip Street, Millers Point and the 17 Bn Drill Hall in North Sydney. In April 1946 our membership was 429, and the annual sub was two bob (2/-). The first "Smoko" was at Sargents Restaurant in December 1945 (entry 1/-), for which invitations were largely by word of mouth in the pub. This was followed in June by an invitation from the 17 Bn Association to their annual get-together at Winns Cafe in Oxford Street. "Smokos" became regular events and were held at the above locations, also at the Australian Hall and the Union Jack Hall in Hamilton Street. In 1947, a dance was arranged at Grace Bros Auditorium, and 2 years later, 1949, the first Battalion Ball took place at the State Ballroom.

320 members of 2/17 Bn marched through the City of Sydney on Anzac Day for the first time in 1946, a number which has since been rarely exceeded. In these first years there were no organised Anzac Day reunions for our Association. Members tended to frequent the city hotels after the March. On one or two occasions, Smokos were held on the day before, at 17/18 Bn Drill Hall, North Sydney

The organisation of all these activities was largely in the hands of John Baker, Secretary during those formative years. The Committee gave active and wholehearted support, yet special tribute must be paid to John Baker for the enormous amount of work which he devoted to the detailed arrangements, not only for the monthly meetings but also for the social functions and even preparation of the News Sheet.

A sub-committee, consisting of Harold McLachlan, "Swede" Weldon and Fred Wray, was formed to produce a News Sheet, the first of which was mailed to members in November 1946. John Baker, Spanky McFarland and Goff Schrader also became involved, and News Sheets were issued, somewhat irregularly, when there was "something to say".

A Golf Day was organised in 1946 and became a popular yearly event. In April 1948, a Cricket Match was arranged with the Spit Swimming Club.

In April 1946, 17 Bn Association invited 2/17 Bn to their annual pilgrimage to the Pozieres Cross at St Thomas' Church, North Sydney. 10 of our members attended and this became a regular yearly function. At another Service in 1949, the Colours of 17 Bn were lifted and presented to 17/18 Bn AMF.

1947 saw the formation of the 9 Div Council. John Broadbent and Goff Schrader were our members on the Council, with Brig Windeyer as Chairman.

THE '50S AND '60S

During these years the Association broadened its activities, with emphasis on social events and the Newsletter. Membership had increased to over 730, and subs raised to 10/- per year. In 1950 Country Vice-Presidentrs were elected to help keep in touchwith 2/17 members in their district and to report items of local interest. These were:

Chicca Rogers (South Coast)	Rowley Savage (ACT)
Stepper Stephens (North Coast)	Mayne Ready (North West)
Charlie Cutler (West)	John Moore (Newcastle)
Max Dunlevey (Riverina)	Spanky McFarland (South)

THE NEWSLETTER

The Newsletter, much as we know it today, was introduced in 1952 edited firstly by John Baker, then by Peter Bryant, followed by a sub-committee comprising Peter, Charles Alderdice, Alex

Crisdale and Athol Roberts. Initially, 5 issues per year were increased from 1956 onwards to 6 issues per year.

From 1958 to 1963, the Newsletter was edited by Duncan McNab, to whom we have always been indebted for his dedication, especially in those days when contributors were relatively few and material for each issue was difficult to obtain. In November 1963, Noel Grant was appointed Editor and has assumed this important role ever since.

SOCIAL AND ANZAC DAY

Social occasions flourished, especially in the '50s, with annual Smokos, also Annual Balls from 1950 to 1965 at RSL HQ, the Hotel Australia and the Monash Hut in Rose Bay. In 1965 a 25th Anniversary Dinner was arranged at the Hotel Metropole, with Gen Sir Victor Windeyer as Guest of Honour.

As popularity of the Annual Balls waned, 1968 saw the first Dinner Dance (Ladies Night) at the Combined Services Club. These continued to attract a good number of members and ladies for many years.

Golf Days were organised regularly, and the first Bowls Day took place in 1965, against 2/13 Bn at Cronulla.

Around this time, 9 Div Reunions came into fashion, and these included both city and country locations.

Anzac Days continued to be well attended by our members, despite the long march. In those days the Anzac March finished in the Domain. In 1955 a Reunion after the march was arranged at the Chatswood Drill Hall which continued up to 1969. From the early '60s, 17 Bn Association combined with 2/17 Bn to hold one Anzac Day Reunion and it was decided that, from then on, the 17th members would be our guests for the day. In 1957 a guessing competition (raffle) was started and proved to be a successful fund raiser for some years.

WELFARE

In the earlier years, welfare was mainly in the hands of individual Committee members. It must be remembered that everyone was much younger and, consequently, there were fewer hospital patients to look after. However, a Hospital Committee was formed in 1957 consisting of Ted Mudie, Vic Dunn and Ted Jenkins, who devoted much time to this work. In 1968 Leo Meaney was appointed as Welfare Officer and performed a dedicated service visiting members in hospital and attending funerals.

CHURCH ACTIVITIES IN THE '50S AND '60S

Attendances of our members increased, both at the Remembrance Day and Anzac Day Services at St. Thomas' Church, North Sydney. As agreed by the Committee, the wreaths used in these services (also at the funerals of members) were in the Battalion Colours, white and green, in a "T" shape.

In 1953, it was decided to have a memorial plaque placed in St Thomas' Church, with the inscription:

"IN MEMORY OF THOSE MEMBERS OF 2/17 INFANTRY BATTALION WHO GAVE THEIR LIVES 1939-1945"

A sub-committee was appointed to implement this decision, including John Broadbent, Geoff Coote, Gordon Broome, John Baker, Charles Alderdice, Harold McLachlan and Phil Pike, assisted by 17th Bn Association. Lengthy unforeseen difficulties arose in designing the plaque, arranging production and organising the Service in the Church. It was finally unveiled in March 1956. Brig N.W. Simpson performed the ceremony, with over 100 of our members amongst a congregation of 800 in the Church. This was rightly hailed as an historic event in the Association's history.

Early in the '50s it was proposed to bring a wooden cross of a 2/17 Bn member, who died in New Guinea, and place it in St Thomas' next to the Pozieres Cross. This cross (of Bobby Bevan) did finally arrive, but this project also met insurmountable difficulties with Church authorities, and the original proposal was unsuccessful. The cross was eventually presented to the Combined Services Sub-branch in 1962.

In October 1963 a ceremony took place for Laying Up of the Colours of 17 Inf Bn at St Thomas' Church. This was preceded by a "Review" at North Sydney Oval. The Colours were escorted by a troop from the 2 RNSWR from Chatswood Drill Hall to St Thomas'. Maj Gen Simpson was the Reviewing Officer.

OTHER ITEMS IN THE '50S AND '60S
2/17 BATTALION TROPHY

The association readily adopted the suggestion of Lt Col J R Broadbent as CO of 17/18 Bn CMF that a trophy be given for annual competition on section level.

The plan was for a model figure of an infantryman. Charles Alderdice introduced Jack Pender a Work associate who had ability and enthusiasm. He spent time checking dress, equipment, rifle etc then built a plastic model depicting much detail. One hot day he found the model sagging and softening. Urgently he coated it with plaster. Some detail was lost but it was possible to break up the plaster, remove the contents, and end up ready for casting. The result has been a realistic figure with personality as of a man in action. Some $80 was donated for the metal to make the solid figure. Beyond that members assisted with casting and the solid polished wooden base. Messers Taylor and Kelly were thanked for this work.

The competition was for rifle sections on the subject of preparing for battle, going from assembly area to field firing. It was first held in Liverpool area and about 60 members of the Association attended. Marking was done by persons who had been Section Comds in 2/17 Bn.

Similar marking and support was given in later years. Once by rush of green and white ties arrived to be worn for the time. Later conditions led to the competition being judged on a patroling on which War II had seen much performance and ability in the Bn.

Throughout the '50s, Phil Pike, who succeeded John Broadbent as CO, developed close, and continuing, relations with the CMF of 17/18 Bn. This liaison was to stand the Association in good stead in years to come.

1953:   Bn tie introduced and was very popular with members.

1956:   John Edmondson VC Memorial unveiled at Liverpool by Sir John Northcott. 18 members attended.

1959:   Name badges introduced.

1964:   John Broadbent appointed as Major General — a great honour.

1967:   Lapel badges instigated by Ray Turner.

THE '70S AND '80S

The '70s and '80s saw some of the Association's greatest achievements. This was due in no small measure to the wonderfully gifted leadership of Colin Pitman, whose term as President continued until he passed away in 1989. During his Presidency, Colin initiated many projects and guided them, with meticulous planning, to a successful conclusion. Tribute is also paid to Phil Pike who diligently organised various social occasions during this period, and especially for his detailed work on the Battalion History.

MORE ON THE NEWSLETTER

The Newsletter continued as the most important function of our Association, being the one direct link with all members. The '70s and '80s saw a large increase in members' contributions to the Newsletter including many special articles of interest. Of major benefit were the War History Notes by Arthur Newton, which are covered later in this supplement.

The format of the Newsletter was improved in 1987, both to contain costs and also to re-design the cover sheet to show Battle Honours. Noel Grant has been Editor for the last 26 years, during which time he introduced a number of new features, and is applauded for his long and dedicated service.

MEMBERSHIP

Membership declined over the years (510 in 1989), although a concerted drive to introduce younger members of the Bn met with some success. Inevitably, there was an increase in the number of widows on our mailing list and these ladies provided enthusiastic support, including many contributions to the Newsletter. District Representatives were appointed in 1979, and in 1986 a Victorian Branch was established by Ralph Watkins, who organised various functions in Victoria.

MORE ON WELFARE

Welfare work continued through the '70s and '80s, during which time Leo Meaney was a constant visitor to our sick and disabled members in hospital. Recognition of his outstanding service was made by his award of the British Empire Medal. In 1988, Leo's health began to suffer and Bruce Wentworth-Perry took over as Welfare Officer.

FINANCE

The Association's financial objectives were maintained, in that funds be adequate, but not excessive, to meet the objectives set out in the Constitution. John Blockley has done an excellent performance as Treasurer since 1974, and Harold McLachlan as Auditor since 1954.

REUNIONS

Anzac Day remained as the highlight of each year, when city, country and interstate members assembled in remembrance, and gathered for reunion and friendship. In 1970 the Anzac Day Reunion was switched from Chatswood to the Drill Hall at Carlow Street, North Sydney, and continued there ever since. Also from 1970 onwards, catering for the day was organised by "Blondie" Wilcox, and this proved to be a most popular arrangement.

Bn reunions were held outside Sydney, in 1985 at Murwillumbah, organised by Charlie Lemaire, and then in 1988 at Cowra, organised by Bert Oliver. These were magnificent occasions, enjoyed by ladies and families as well as members, in a magical atmosphere of good fellowship and relaxation. During 1989, plans were formulated for a 50th Birthday Reunion to be held at Gosford the following year.

In addition to their normal reunions in October each year, 9 Div Council arranged a mixed reunion in March 1987, organised by Phil Pike. This was held at Victoria Barracks where over 60 of our members and ladies had a most enjoyable day, including an inspection of the historic Barracks.

MORE ON SOCIAL

"Guest Evenings" were initiated in 1970 in order to entertain those people who had helped the Association during the year. These evenings became an annual event and were held at the homes of Ivan and Ruth Dutton, and Jack and Val Doyle.

The "Ladies Nights" at the Combined Services Club continued to be popular for some time until interest waned in 1982.

During the '70s and '80s, Platoon Reunions and Sergeants' Dinners were held from time to time and demonstrated the continuing bond within the Association.

In 1989, the Committee arranged a luncheon for widows at the Anzac Memorial Club, Cammeray. This was a "Getting to Know You" occasion, and the result was an overwhelming success.

Regular Golf Days continued, despite reduced numbers due to advancing years. Bowls Days were revived in 1985 and flourished under the capable hands of Harold McLachlan.

ST THOMAS' CHURCH

Early in the '70s a new form of service was introduced for our Anzac Day and Remembrance Day Services, which was printed and presented to the Church. Attendances of our members increased considerably and, in 1979, 17 RNSWR participated for the first time. Each year since then, they provided a Colour Party which greatly enhanced the Remembrance Day Service.

On what was one of the most moving occasions in the life of the Association, the new 17 Bn Memorial area in St Thomas' was dedicated in 1984. This was the culmination of five years of work devoted to the realisation of an idea by our president, Colin Pitman. The project involved extensive reconstruction and paving of the Memorial area, with a floor plaque which reads:

"THIS DEDICATED AREA
HALLOWS THE MEMORY OF ALL
WHO IN WAR AND PEACE
SERVED THE INFANTRY TRADITION
OF 17 BATTALION"

Replacement of the 80 year-old flags, and detailed restoration of the Pozieres Cross was completed. In addition to the many years of working with Church authorities to convert the idea to a reality, Colin was also instrumental in raising the funds for this project. Construction was finally completed and, with St Thomas' filled to capacity, the dedication took place on Remembrance Day 1984.

Previously, in 1983 embroidered kneeler cushions were dedicated, 18 of which bear the names of 2/17 members. These were the result of many years of painstaking work by the St Thomas' Embroiderers Guild, some of whom were wives or widows of 2/17 men. Inclusion of our members on these memorial cushions was again due to the initiative of Colin Pitman who spent much effort on the background work involved in this project.

17TH BATTALION AIF ASSOCIATION

By 1973, the numbers of the "Old & Bold" had come down to about 70, and it was becoming evident that, due to infirmity, their Association needed help with administration. Their members were incorporated in the 2/17 mailing list, and their activities reported in the Newsletter. In 1979, our Association was entrusted to administer the affairs of 17th Bn Association, and Charles Alderdice then presided over their quarterly meetings. These developed into regular quarterly Luncheons at the Combined Services Club at which the "Old & Bold" were entertained by some of the 2/17 members.

SUNDRY ITEMS IN THE '70S AND '80S

1976:   2/17 Plaque introduced.

1981:   Replica of the Owen Gun handed over to 17 RNSWR at Pymble in a joint presentation by Phil Pike and Paddy Owen.

1984:   Harry Wells' book produced, "B Company 2/17 Infantry".

1986:   Constitution updated and distributed to all members.

THE 2/17 BATTALION HISTORY

The preparation of a Battalion History has been a problem for successive Committees since the formation of the Association. From the late 1940s, sub-committees made initial efforts to produce a history by extracting data from the Official War Diaries. A professional writer, Lawson Glassop, was engaged in 1951 but, after 4 years, progress had floundered and by reciprocal agreement Mr. Glassop was paid off.

At this stage, Dudley McCarthy, who had participated in writing the Official Australian War History, started to re-write the initial sections of our own History. Dudley's work was masterly but, due to ill health, he was unable to continue at that time.

In 1957 another writer, John Laffin, was engaged to edit the History, but he left for overseas and this arrangement lapsed. The same year saw another setback in that the manuscript representing the vast work done by previous sub-committees disappeared.

By 1959, Dudley McCarthy had re-commenced writing but, having heavy business commitments, progress over the next 3 years was slow. From 1962, due to his commitments in the Department of External Affairs and the Diplomatic Corps, the writing of our History virtually ceased. John Broadbent visited Dudley in New York in 1964, and 3 years later Colin Pitman saw him in Mexico but, despite his optimistic expectations, there was no real progress. By 1968, Dudley had completed 5 chapters, up to the end of Tobruk, but his continuing pressure of work precluded any further writing. In 1974, upon request, Dudley returned all material, including the 5 chapters already written. This was, in effect, the nett result of nearly 30 years during which time very little was achieved, perhaps because no one could really devote the full time work necessary to produce the history.

Finally, in the 1980s, there arose three conditions favourable to success:—

(1) It was actually in 1978 when Arthur Newton started his notes from the War Diaries in Canberra; these started in the Newsletter in February 1980. Not only were these notes of absorbing interest to our members but, over the subsequent 9 years, they formed a record of events upon which our Bn History could be based. Also of great value at this time were the 8 maps supporting the War History notes, as first proposed by Don Stewart. AfterPhil Pike pursued the basic data, Alex Crisdale undertook the painstaking work of drawing the original maps which were then printed by Paddy Fenton.

(2) In 1987 Colin Pitman recognised Arthur's notes as the means by which a History could at last be published, and he determined to proceed where all had failed in the past. Colin's plan was to divide Arthur's notes into 4 sections for initial action:

	Action By:
Formation of the Bn up to the end of Tobruk	Bruce Trebeck
Palestine, Syria, Alamein and the return to Australia	Phil Pike
	John Broadbent
Jungle & Amphibious Training Milne Bay, Lae, Finschhafen	Ray Rudkin
Tablelands, Morotai, Borneo	Bruce Trebeck

As well as planning the operation, Colin established a substantial fund, by his own personal representations, to meet the initial costs of producing the history.

(3) In 1988, a History Committee was formed, consisting of Colin Pitman, John Broadbent, Phil Pike, Ray Rudkin, Bruce Trebeck, Alastair Urquhart with Arthur Newton as the Canberra Researcher at the Memorial. Phil Pike assumed the role of Director, to collect and update material. Alastair Urquhart arranged for the Advance Bank to provide typing services and later, after the Committee decided to purchase a word processor, printer etc., he arranged for accommodation at St Leonards Branch of the Bank, which enabled them to set up their own production centre. The bulk of the work of producing a manuscript fell to Bruce Trebeck, Ray Rudkin, Phil Pike and John Broadbent, but great assistance was given by many volunteers who collected stories, anecdotes, photos and other material to complete the work for presentation to the Printer.

The application and resolution of Arthur Newton, Colin Pitman and Phil Pike were indispensable to the final publishing of 2/17 Bn History in 1990, surely the greatest achievement of the Association. This History was only produced as a result of their dedication, and will surely be treasured by our members for all time.

THE 90s:

As more members retired from work their leisure time increased for Association activities. Anzac Day remained the yearly highlight. The luncheon venue was changed in 1997 to the Masonic Centre CBD, where commercial caterers have eased the burden on Jack Doyle and Bill Wilcox and the small group of willing members who had worked for many years attending to members' needs.

Country reunions, initiated by Charles Lemaire at Murwillumbah, followed by Bert Oliver at Cowra, continued under the gifted leadership of Phil Pike and local Committees:

1990	Gosford	- 50th Anniversary of Battalion's formation.
1993	Canberra/Queanbeyan	- 50th Anniversary New Guinea Campaign.
1995	Wollongong/Fairy Meadow	- 50th Anniversary, end of World War II.
1996	Liverpool District	- To commemorate Bn's first move in 1940
1997	Katoomba	- To commemorate Bn's visit to Katoomba -in 1940.

Members' contributions to the Newsletter have increased. In addition to Arthur Newton's historical notes and supplementary notes from Fred Camarsh, there were numerous articles on wartime experiences, personal reminiscences, humourous anecdotes and commemorative tours of battlefields. Organised tours of Borneo and New Guinea by Phil Pike, John Broadbent's 9th Division tour of the Middle East and lastly, Ray Rudkin's in New Guinea, were as follows:

1992	Brunei/Durussalam	- Goodwill tour.
1992	El Alamein/Tobruk	- 50th Anniversary, Battle of El Alamein.
1993	Lae/Finschhafen	- 50th Anniversary of Landings.
1995	Brunei/Durussalam	- 50th Anniversary Borneo Campaign.
1997	Lae/Finschhafen	- Dedication of 2/17Bn's Memorial at Jivevaneng.

The 2/17 Battalion's Memorial at Jivevaneng, built with the assistance of the Papua New Guinea Defence Academy, displays two bronze plaques, one inscribed in Pidgin and the other in English: each feature the Australian Commonwealth Military Forces Rising Sun Emblem and the Battalion's Colour Patch. The inscription reads:

**THIS MEMORIAL WAS PLACED BY THE 2/17 BATTALION ASSOCIATION
TO COMMEMORATE THE FORTITUDE OF THE BATTALION
WITH SUPPORT, AT JIVEVANENG
AND IN MEMORY OF FALLEN COMRADES
DURING THE DEFENCE OF SCARLET BEACH
FROM SEPTEMBER TO NOVEMBER 1943.
DEDICATED ON 13th NOVEMBER 1997.**

Planning has commenced for the erection of a memorial to fallen Comrades in the State of Brunei and to commemorate the Battalion's part in the recovery of the State's Oilfields and the restoration of the Sultinate in 1945.

MEMBERSHIP,

Overall membership inevitably declined in 1997 to: Battalion members, 409; Widows or relatives, 155; 17 Bn AIF, 3.

PERSONALITIES

Noel Grant retired in 1997 after 34 years of dedicated service as Editor of the Newsletter. Bob Pink replaced him. Sadly, long serving Treasurer, John Blockley, died in 1993 after 19 years in that capacity. John Carter replaced him. Revered First AIF veteran, Bill Pincott, died in 1995 at the age of 100. On separate occasions, John Broadbent and Phil Pike were honoured by members of the Association of the 17th Battalions in celebration of their 80th birthday at the Anzac Memorial Club, Cammeray. Ray Rudkin was elected President in 1996 on Phil Pike's retirement.

Norma Holland and Joyce Dunn organized mixed luncheons in the CBD, and light luncheons after the Church Services at St Thomas' Church, with the assistance of members' ladies.

Committee members with long service are:

	Years		Years		Years
John Broadbent	47	John Chilcott	24	Owen Windeyer	13
Harold McLachlan	44	Colin Pitman	23	Julian Clint	12
Gordon Kibby	36	Ivan Dutton	22	Peter Bryant	12
Charles Alderdice	34	John Blockley	21	Col O'Donnell	12
Noel Grant	34	Leo Meaney	20	Gordon Broome	11
Joe Wallis	33	Bill Shaw	16	Goff Schrader	11
Jack Doyle	30	Alex Kenniwell	14	Fred Camarsh	11
Phil Pike	27	Jack Smith	14	Eric Blundell	10
Ces Greenwood	26	Athol Roberts	13	Ray Rudkin	10

Deserving of special mention was the untiring and selfless service of Bruce Wentworth - Perry to his fellow members in welfare matters, such as the acquisition of service and disability pensions, hospital visitations and attendance at funerals. In these activities he has been assisted by his caring wife, Iris. Sadly, Bruce died in 1997. Tom Frogatt replaced Bruce as Welfare Officer.

INTERSTATE REPRESENTATION.

Ralph Watkins established a Victorian Branch, followed by Gordon Fischer in West Australia (1992) and Jim Dinning in South Australia (1993). These have flourished with the enthusiastic support of their members.

ASSOCIATION PRESIDENTS

PERIOD	NAME	YEARS OF SERVICE
Jul 1945 - Aug 1946	Claude Brien	1
Sep 1946 - Aug 1947	Goff Schrader	2
Sep 1947 - Sep 1949	Eric Blundell	2
Oct 1949 - Sep 1950	Arthur Newton	1
Oct 1950 - Sep 1952	Blue Allan	2
Oct 1952 - May 1954	Harold McLachlan	1.5
Jun 1954 - Apr 1955	John Baker	1
May 1955 - May 1956	Alex Crisdale	1
Jun 1956 - Nov 1963	Duncan McNab	7
Dec 1963 - Apr 1964	John Broadbent	4 months
May 1964 - Apr 1966	Bob Halloway	2
May 1966 - May 1989	Colin Pitman	23
May 1989 - May 1996	Phil Pike	7
May 1996 -	Ray Rudkin	

LOOKING TO THE FUTURE.

With most members in their late seventies and some past eighty years of age, the Association continues to be strong. Inevitably, as happened with the First 17 Battalion AIF Association, that handed over its Administration to the 2/17 Battalion AIF Association, at some future time, the latter will look with confidence to its successor, The Association of 17th Battalions, to proudly carry on the Tradition.

Editor's footnote:Bill Shaw, who compiled these notes, has been dedicated and outstanding in his appointment as Secretary since 1981. Bill retired due to illness in December 1997 and was succeeded by Ian Startup.

*The men behind the successful Anzac Day reunions – **L-R:** Co-caterers "Blondie" Wilcox and "Jack" Doyle, with permanent helpers, WAG Stewart, WA Wilcox, LJ Rowe, J Wallis, JT Doyle.*

APPENDIX 5

2/17th WOMEN ON THE HOME FRONT

By Joyce Balfe

The AIF Women's Club was formed in 1940 by Lady Mackay and meetings were held every Friday afternoon at YWCA in Liverpool Street to enjoy companionship, a chat, news from the various war zones and afternoon tea. There were hostesses (some of them 2/17) and the very large hall was arranged in sections each with a notice reading 6, 7 and 8 Division. It was important for families and friends to make contact and it became especially so for 8 Div.

Some of the 2/17 womenfolk knew each other, some just by being introduced when visiting the camp at Ingleburn or Bathurst and when the men sailed away, they gradually made contact seeking news, and as time went on NEWS became more and more urgent.

The idea grew that we should form a 2/17 Comforts Fund and towards the latter part of 1941 we were given the use of a meeting room in Culwalla Chambers. Mrs. Gladys Crawford was our first President; Mrs Mary Brien, Treasurer and I was the Secretary.

We arranged a luncheon party at David Jones where a photograph was taken and Mrs Crawford sent a copy overseas to the Colonel who proudly showed it around the Battalion.

2/17 Battalion Womens Comfort Fund. **Standing**: *Gwen Brown, Mrs Maclaren,—, Gladys Crawford, Mrs Crawford Snr, Jinny Fowler, Joyce Balfe, Mary Brien, Nancy Wray, —, Mollie Pike, —, Mrs Tuckwell, —.* **Seated:** *Lillian Broadbent, Mrs Windeyer, Mrs C Sheldon, Lady Moreshead, Phyl Magno, Barbara Lloyd, —, Mary Windeyer.* **Not accounted:** *M Collins, M McLachlan, M Dick.*

We originally held our meetings on Friday morning and began to arrange theatre parties and card parties which were well attended and raised money to buy comforts for the men serving in the Battalion. After our meeting, we would have lunch in the City and then would all go to the AIF Women's Club at the YWCA.

I remember well a wounded soldier in uniform limping into the crowded hall and everyone began to clap as Michael Eisdell, smiling and waving his walking stick made his way down the full length of the hall to the stage and microphone. He was given a stirring welcome and we all clung to every word he said. He was a good speaker and first hand news was so very precious — then he was inundated with questions.

Eventually we were given the use of a shop in Rowe Street, across the street from the Hotel Australia. It was an instant success. By now, word of our venue had got over to the men in the Middle East and they wrote home and told their families about the Comforts Fund Shop. We had absolutely no shortage of helpers and the shop was opened five days per week, and wives, mothers, fiancees, sweethearts, sisters, aunts and friends were all available for roster. Many fathers and uncles working around the City, or visiting Sydney would pop in to make themselves known, give us some news, or bring in something to sell.

Incredible friendships were formed and the first thing that was asked by those working each day would be, "Did you get a letter?"

When a mate's name was mentioned in a letter, it was always important to get in touch with his family and pass on the news, and so the shop became a popping-in place, especially at times when the mails were held up. On 8 Dec 1941 our boys got the news that we were at war with Japan and air-mail was at a stand-still and we all felt our separation more than ever.

About the middle of February 1942, Lt Col Crawford was transferred from 2/17 Bn and returned to Australia. Lt Col Noel Simpson replaced him and his mother, Mrs. Simpson, became the president of the Comforts Fund.

An agreed proportion of AIF were returned from the ME to Australia and there was some disappointment for those left in the ME and then when the news came that Singapore had fallen, our men were really unsettled, everyone felt so far apart and all we could do was to write letters and help cheer and support each other.

Lady Moreshead now became President of the AIF Women's Club and each week encouraged us with her charming manner of speaking. She often had a message for us from Sir Leslie.

Brig John Crawford came up to the YWCA and spoke from the stage to everyone in the hall and then came around to each one us in the 9 Div group. He gave us first hand news of the men who were dear to his heart.

It was not long before country people, who had letters from 2/17 soldiers abroad, began calling in to the C.F. Shop and, of course, they didn't come empty-handed. Our food and clothing was rationed by this time, but people were bringing in home-made jams constantly, even though they had to sacrifice their food coupons for the sugar. If I stayed with friends overnight, they would always run up a couple of batches of cakes to sell in the shop and lots of cakes were made by all those on the roster and friends outside the Bn.

All these goodies became much sought after by the guests at the Hotel Australia. We would sell out practically every day. During that time I made the shop almost a full time job organising rosters, etc. and all of us helpers would wonder, "What can I take in today?" My sister-in-law had given me a red necklace and I decided I would donate it to the shop. I arranged it in the window amongst other things, and who was one of the first customers? Yes, John's sister! We seemed to always have theatre party tickets for sale and people could come to the shop, choose from the theatre plan and purchase their tickets — we always sold out Another time I had stayed the night with some friends and in the morning walked from their house to the railway station - it was to me an unfamiliar area and I passed a huge camelia bush loaded with magnificent blooms. Without hesitation I went and rang the doorbell and asked absolute strangers if I could have the flowers to sell in the Comforts Fund Shop. Women on the home front did strange things! Many others could tell similar tales, but the shop was kept stocked. We had some very valuable ornaments given to us from time to time and these we would take and have valued by an antique dealer — often we would get a better price from him than we would if we sold it in our shop.

It was a fun day when someone would bring in a parcel of lovely hats, the laughter and comments as they were tried on! Because of the rationing they sold very well.

We purchased traced linen to be embroidered and the helpers would take it home (some had never tried to embroider) and bring it back completed to be sold in the shop. We purchased as much khaki wool as we could — in order to do this we had to get clothing coupons from people and the ladies would knit socks, balaclavas, gloves, etc. and then a parcel would be sent to the Bn.

As Minister for Education, The Hon Clive Evatt unveilled a memorial to Cpl Edmondson at Hurlstone Agricultural College and afterwards asked me to just let him know if there was anything at all he could do for us. I think he was shocked when immediately I asked if he could arrange for us to buy wool without coupons for the Comforts Fund. "No, very sorry." Always the Comforts Fund shop was a hive of activity, but essentially it became a refuge, where we all understood each other and there was always someone to listen and to advise.

Of course, the people at home suffered from the everyday ailments as usual, but many were alone, and the effects on families of casualties was sometimes shattering. Some elderly mothers were left absolutely alone when sons were captured or killed and they were devastated and bewildered. The mother of Bill Johnson who was taken POW also had a son POW with 8 Div and found working in 2/17 Comforts Fund shop and attending the AIF Club was her salvation. We saw some tragic circumstances.

As the men came home wounded or had been returned to Australia to help train the men here, such as Bruce Trebeck, Bayne Geikie, Joe Blundell, it was very natural for them to call in to the shop and not uncommon to see 2/13 there as well. These bearers of news from the ME created an excitement in those times and were made very welcome.

The position of the shop was absolutely super — the Hotel Australia being so close, we used their phones and if we wanted to sit and talk with someone, we just automatically went into the large foyer and were indeed most comfortable. Our card parties continued very successfully. It was decided that we would hold a large scale function and involve the relatives and friends of the whole Battalion. I contacted the Army and asked if we could get the names and addresses of next-of-kin of the whole Battalion and to my amazement they agreed. There was a black-out at night and Mary Brien and I went out to the Sydney Showground, night after night and copied by hand from Army Records the names and addresses of every man's next-of-kin. Looking back, it is hard to believe, but that is exactly how we got them.

Then we made an advance booking at Sargents Restaurant in Market Street (which was very large) for an Afternoon Tea on Saturday, 6 Nov 1942. We wrote an an invitation/letter and sent it out to everyone and invited as special guests Lady Moreshead, Mrs V. Windeyer and Mrs John Crawford. We carried on organising, there was a job for everyone, the hall was to be set out in Companies, hostesses, flowers, afternoon tea menu, entertainment, everything arranged to the final detail, and now we had to wait for the day. Acceptances and money rolled in from far and near and we knew were going to have a capacity crowd.

As the day approached we began to get news of casualties from the Battle of El Alamein. People were coming into the shop seeking news of their loved ones, the cable lines were jammed and almost no details were available. I was going to the Red Cross two or three times a day with queries for more information about the casualties. We had been advised that the Red Cross could get a "bulk" cable through and individuals were asked not to send cables because of the overloading. It was indeed a grim and heart rending time for the people at home waiting and hoping and praying that they would not get the next cable.

We had news that Ian McMaster, Keith Magno, Claude Brien and many others had been wounded and then Saturday morning, 6 Nov 1942 came. I had arranged to leave home early because I had the keys of the shop and we were all meeting there, some bringing flowers to decorate the hall, some special dishes etc. Just as I was leaving, my telegram arrived to say that John was wounded - I phoned his family but I just had to go on. When I arrived at the shop members were waiting and the first thing I heard was that Keith Magno had died of his wounds. Somehow it all seemed strange that this long awaited function with our well laid plans was about to happen amid such turmoil and anxiety, but we all just had to carry on.

Right on time people began to arrive from far and near — it was a most successful gathering. People were so generous, many had brought things for the Comforts Fund to raffle or sell in the shop. The guests were each taken to the areas set aside for the various Companies and then out came the letters and photographs. It was wonderful to see them meeting people that they had heard about in letters, the mother, wife or girl friend of their son's or husband's best mate — just to be all together and have the companionship of each other at this devastating time. I have never stopped marvelling how this function turned out to be almost a miracle. Although it wasn't planned that way, many people were all brought together at such a critical time when they really needed each other, many lasting friendships were made and I really saw "the 2/17 family" That day.

I received a letter from Brig John Crawford dated 3 Dec 1942:

"I am very grateful to you for writing to me the sad details of the recent casualties. As I read your letter I kept wondering how the old battalion will fare with so many of the best dead or wounded, and my stout old John Balfe commanding the 32nd, the latter fact I am very proud of. The 17th has found a fine parcel of CO's for other units.

I shall be glad to know the extent of John's wounds and that they are not serious. He has been exceptionally lucky and I assume they are not serious. By rights he should have been killed five or six times, at least, but beyond a scratch on the nose he remained unscathed. I am glad to hear of Lt Col Ogle's DSO but am distressed at the extent of his wounds.

Thank you for your kind congratulations and for all you are doing for the Comforts Fund."

This just had to be one of the last letters that Brig Crawford wrote before he was killed.

The Hospital Ship arrived in Sydney on Saturday, 9 Jan 1943 and the troopship a few days later. Our men were all back in Australia again. At the first meeting of the Comforts Fund after they arrived home, Lt Col Noel Simpson attended and presented Mary Brien and myself a cut glass vase from the Comforts Fund. Mrs. Victoria Maclarn was elected the new Secretary and the Treasurer.

The Bn moved up to Atherton and then New Guinea and business carried on as usual at the Comforts Fund Shop and we all still "popped in". When Lt Col John Broadbent took over as CO his mother, Mrs Lillian Broadbent, became President.

Without a doubt the concern and help for each other practised in the Comforts fund, continued over post war years and played its small part in strengthening the bonds of our 2/17 Battalion AIF Association.

Dedication of the 2/17 Battalion memorial at Finschhafen – 13 November 1997. **L-R:** *P K Murphy, D Luck, S Morton (Salvation Army), J R Broadbent, W J M McMillan, K J Hall (2/13 Bn), and R Pink.*

The Dedication of the John Edmondson VC Memorial Plaque at Rowes Lagoon, Federal Highway. NSW. 1995
L-R standing: *A H Roberts, J A Clint, J Harris, R S Grant, R S Rudkin, J S Gambling, J W G Carter, L G Power, J R Broadbent, R E Kennedy. Front: S Morton (Salvation Army), M C Haverstein, R Mackell (with son Austin), S Rudkin.*

Left:
*The Australian
El Alamein Memorial.*

Below:
*The 2/17 Bn Association at the
Australian War Memorial on
Labuan Island, 1995.*

APPENDIX 6
SERIA OIL FIRES

NOTES BY LT E B UNDERWOOD (MBE) RAE NX40095

When 20 Bde of 9 Div landed on 10 Jun 45 on the shores of Brunei Bay, the 2/3 Fd Coy RAE was assigned in support to the Bde Comd. Maj R F Eastick was in comd of 2/3 Fd Coy.

The three platoons of the RAE Fd Coy were each assigned to a Battalion of the Brigade and to 2/17 Bn was assigned 3 Pl, Lt E B Underwood in comd. To him were detached bulldozer units from the 2/1 Mech Equipt Coy RAE.

Having occupied the town of Brunei, the 2/17 Bn group proceeded through Kuala Tutong at a fast pace and then along the beach to Seria, essentially an oil field area. They found that the Japanese had left a spectacular and heavily damaged "scorched earth" area comprising the whole of the oilfield and its installations. The oilfield extended about an average of a half mile inland from the beach and about 2 miles long coastwise, the field having been developed from swamp jungle.

The whole area was sandy, the roads having been built up by digging deep ditches on either side and three small rivers or creeks with timber bridges. The roads were narrow and mostly tar sealed.

The creeks and roadside ditches had clearly been filled with oil and set on fire. The main damage, of course, was that the timber bridges, to a major extent, had been burned out as had oil and gas collecting stations dotted about the field. The main oil storage tanks had all been fired and were collapsed. The stores and machine shops had all been fired and damaged considerably. Clearly the intention of leaving the oilfield in a highly damaged condition and difficult to recover in production had been rather thoroughly carried out.

37 oil wells were still burning, some relatively small, others very large indeed. Smoke from these billowed well into the air and in parts the noise was intense. At night, parts of the oilfield were lit up as though it was daylight. On some of the fired wells, steel production derricks had collapsed over the burning well heads and on others even drilling derricks had collapsed likewise. The major complication was that these were complete with drilling engines, winches, pumps etc, all lying over and around close into the well heads. The majority of the wells had by this time built up large mounds of coke around the well heads and about the collapsed steelwork.

The Sappers of 3 Pl were quite thinly stretched out along the line of advance of 2/17 Bn and were hard put to it to fulfil their normal support duties to the Bn. They had men stretched from the base at the town of Brunei, bridge repair work between Brunei and Kuala Tutong, operating a ferry-deficient river crossing at Kuala Tutong and elements up with the leading units of 2/17 Bn whose Comd had set a considerably fast pace.

Thus, with the bridge repair work necessary in Seria, the Sappers were very much under-manned and under-equipped for quite a time and the Pnr Pl of 2/17 Bn provided very valuable assistance in getting bridges in some sort of shape to carry support and supply vehicles and artillery as required for the forward movement of the infantry and gunners. On one of the bridge

sites, the largest repair job required, just beyond the bridge a number of oil well heads were found to be booby trapped. These consisted of bombs set against the oil well heads with trip wires laid in the long sword grass. Fortunately these were discovered early and dealt with, otherwise not only would casualties and damage normally expected of a booby trap of this nature been experienced, each such well head would have been put on fire. These traps had been cunningly chosen as such fires would have made the construction of a crossing over this particular river quite difficult indeed. In the event the repair work had to be carried out in three stages before the bridge could be used without careful supervision. The contribution by the Pioneers was much welcomed by the Sappers.

Beyond this bridge, there were large well fires quite close to the main road and the heat from these was such that the tar surface of the road had been burned off and a small stretch of the road so hot and the hot sand so dangerous that by-pass tracks had to be constructed. Here again the Pioneers contributed material help in its construction under quite difficult conditions.

A search of the main installations of the oilfield had revealed a number of the bombs set about as booby traps in quite vital positions, eg against lathes in the machine shop. These were dealt with satisfactorily and the collection of these bombs was later found to be useful to the Sappers in their oil well fire fighting efforts. They, of course, needed water and their only initial source was to use these bombs to blow craters in the beach. These proved to be of limited value only as the craters soon filled up with sand by wave action. Still, it was a start.

From a member of the oilfield operating staff, the first to return after the arrival of 2/17 Bn, it was learned that the normal source of water for the oilfield, its installations, residences etc, was at Kuala Badas, some 4 miles into the jungle. This place had been chosen as a source because there was a good river supply and also a clay deposit for the manufacture of mud for oilwell

drilling operations. It was approached along a clearing cut through the jungle and along which pipelines and a narrow gauge Decauville railway had been laid.

The Sappers asked 2/17 Bn to accompany them with an infantry patrol to clear the area as necessary so that an estimate could be made of the possibilities of getting at least the water supply system working again. The patrol, then organised, advanced to Badas and found the plant undamaged by any explosive or fire action but much in need of maintenance attention, as with any installation operated by the Japanese during the war period. In a separate Appendix this operation of reaching Badas by a 2/17 Bn detachment is described in detail.

The area was completely deserted but eventually the operators resident on the site came in from the jungle and arrangements were made to leave a small detachment of Infantry and Sappers on site to get the plant running. This guard was necessary as it was not clear whether the Japanese might or might not return. However, after a few days the detachment returned to Seria and a water supply plus indeed, a mud supply, was established. Damaged storage tanks at the Seria end were found to be of limited but adequate capacity.

Once the road communications had been set in some sort of order and the Bn had settled in, mainly in the Seria-Kuala Belait area, more members of the Sapper Pl and assigned bulldozers came on foward to Seria and some work could be started on the job of fighting the oil well fires.

None of the engineers — nor any of the troops — had ever seen an oilfield, not even an oil well, and certainly not an oil well on fire! A few days after their arrival in Seria, an Officer of the Dutch East Indies Civil Administration Unit, Capt Beukema, arrived. Before the War he had worked on oilfields in the Dutch East Indies and was able to advise Underwood of the design, method of drilling and final assembly of oil wells and of their above-surface fittings called the "christmas tree" through the valves and pipes of which the oil and gas were produced. He also advised on the procedures and equipment used to separate oil and gas at the production stations dotted about the field. He was impressed with the light nature of the Seria oil, the high proportion of gas produced and the obviously copious flow and high pressures at the wells. Unfortunately, his stay was short as he was called to another area. However, at least the Sappers now had some knowledge of what they were trying to deal with, although Beukema had never had experience of oil well fire fighting.

Fire fighting equipment was non-existent but bits and pieces of small mobile water pumps of Japanese origin were found here and there. The magnetos had all been removed, but these were fortuitously found dumped in one of the rivers, by Sappers and Pioneers carrying out repair work. The LAD attached to 2/17 Bn did a fine job in getting a few of these operating. In association with the Sappers, the LAD were also very helpful in making up portable shields from galvanised iron sheets of which there was ample supply from damaged buildings together with frames welded from the plentiful supply of steel bars. Similar steel mats were made up to enable the Sappers to get closer in to burning wells as the surrounding sand for up to 30 feet out from the well head was extremely hot and so powdery that it would carry no weight at all.

Four of the burning wells were clear of any collapsed steel and coke and it was judged that the main control valve of the "christmas tree" appeared to be undamaged and the Sappers envisaged that, if they could get long-handled (about 20 feet) "spanners" with pronged fingers on the end, they may be able to insert such a tool into the wheel spokes of the valve and turn it off. The LAD made up these "spanners" and, using these together with the portable shields and steel mats, the Sappers were able to shut the valve, thus extinguishing the fire and closing in the well at the same time.

For their next step the Sappers selected the smallest of the well fires with the intention of endeavouring to smother the fire with sand, bulldozed gradually up into a mound to cover the "christmas tree" and the hot coke around it. This well was near the beach and the rather unsatisfactory bomb-crater source of water mentioned above was used together with the small pumps put into operation by the LAD. This was before it was known about the water supply from Badas. The water was intended mainly to keep the bulldozer and its driver cool. Covering the "christmas tree" with sand proved fruitless as the sand always heated up and even with this relatively low pressure well the effluent always kept on fire. Fortuitously, the fire was put out when a little water was directed at the right spot onto the hot sand. Underwood realised immediately that steam was the answer. This well was cooled off, the sand heap removed and the "christmas tree" valve closed. The well was thus under control, apart from very minor leaks due to fittings damaged by heat.

When 2/17 Bn arrived at Seria all the normal field operating personnel had taken refuge in the jungle. Gradually they came back to the field and various workshops were made operative. To meet the Sappers' requirements of gas for firing boilers to raise steam, some of the wells were brought into production.

Together with these operators who knew the field well, the Sappers aided by 2/17 Bn Pioneers arranged for portable boilers to be moved to each well fire site. Tanks were positioned nearby for water and mud storage and some large portable drilling mud pumps were put in order and used to pump mud into each well once the fire had been extinguished. More water became available and more fire fighting water pumps, more tractors and bulldozers were brought in. All of this equipment was set up around a well fire site and pipework laid out to suit each particular case to provide steam jets to be directed from various positions right into the base of each fire. With most wells, work had to be done using explosives, bulldozers and steel wirelines to clear the well heads of obstruction of coke and collapsed steel derricks, etc.

Of outstanding assistance in all of this work was a field foreman, Mr Joseph Brodie, who knew the field well and all the workmen and who spoke Malay, Chinese and English. Also of particular help was Mr Ng Sum, foreman of the oilfield machine shops complex. These men worked very hard in supervisory and also practical capacities, often with ingenious improvisation. As to the names of Sappers who did particularly outstanding work in this whole effort it is unfair to try to rely on memory for names; suffice to say that many worked beyond the normal calls of duty for Sappers associated with a front line infantry battalion — particularly after the declaration of peace.

Once everything was ready, the first step was to cool down the area around each fire as far as possible with water jets. This was done while waiting for an onshore breeze which, on clear days, could be expected at about 1030 hrs. The boilers were sited to windward so that, when the fire was extinguished by the steam, the gas and oil still flowing strongly from the well head was carried in the opposite direction.

On one occasion, the breeze was late in arriving, the sky being lightly clouded. The fire had been extinguished by steam later than usual, but the crews working on the well head were unable to complete the work necessary to prepare the well for control of the oil and gas flow before daylight failed. The situation then was a massive outflow of gas and oil to the atmosphere with all attendant dangers, and the Sappers had to take the only safe decision possible which was to set the well on fire again and try again next day which they did successfully.

With this experience a source of induced wind was sought. A monoplane, with an engine maintenance man as operator, was acquired from the RAAF in Labuan. The wings were stripped off and, when used at each well, the tail of the fuselage was manoeuvred as close as possible to the fire site on the windward side. Then it was strapped down to steel pickets driven into the ground, to stop it turning turtle, and the engine started. The draught from the propellor was very effective. It was necessary on each occasion to continually hose the fuselage and fuel tank to prevent the heat effects. Because it was not flying, and in danger of over-heating, the engine had to be watched carefully also. This machine proved a boon and was used always, even when the steam extinction procedure was dropped and another technique adopted, as detailed below.

When using the steam extinction procedure, once the fire had been extinguished, the surroundings to each well had to be cooled off before crews could move in and work on the well head. Small dams were built up around the well in a circle of about 30 feet diameter and filled with water. The heat of the sand below these kept this water actually boiling for about a half hour. Numerically small crews then went in to the well head in rotation. It was impossible at the well head site to hear any discussion of what to do about what, depending on each situation as it presented itself on close inspection. Working in the oil and gas flow was a very dangerous operation as one spark from say, a steel tool striking another piece of steel, would have restarted the fire with dire results for those working at the well head. Of course, fire hoses were used to minimise this possibility. Crews were changed as each man could stand only short periods working in the oil and gas. The RAP of 2/17 Bn were on hand. One major effect on the crew members was nausea for which plenty of sweetened tea was taken as a palliative — usually after vomiting. But the worst effect was temporary blindness. Various eye washes were tried, but none could give quick relief which was essential to get a picked man back onto the job. Finally, after many treatments, the RAP came up with castor oil drops which worked wonderfully. The heavy hand tools required to be used on the well head for this work had been gathered together after much searching and were carefully husbanded. But that little bottle of blue glass with the castor oil and its dropper and waddings was treasured in a small box as an essential on site before any work started.

When a few of the pre-war managers arrived from abroad, the work of ensuring gas, water and mud supply was taken over from the Sappers who were then able to concentrate on the burning wells, ably assisted by some of the field operating staff who had come back in from the jungle and from inland river settlements. The War was clearly easing to an end at this stage and the Sapper support for the Bn operations was reduced to some water transport duties plus a detachment off with a group of the Bn out in the jungle searching for a number of the Kempei Tai who had committed shocking atrocities in Kuala Belait before the advance troops of the Bn could reach there.

Eventually, two oil well fire fighting experts arrived from the USA, a father and son team Mr H & Mr Chips Patton. They were very impressed with the evidence of the high pressure nature of the Seria field wells and with the high gas content of the light oil which characterised this field. They concluded that their usual method of "snuffing out" oil well fires with explosive charges was of very doubtful value and were unimpressed by the lack of facilities and services available to them as compared to what would have been readily accessible in a fire emergency on their home ground.

Underwood was very conscious of the dangerous nature of the work so far carried out and still to be done, and also of the fact that all his Sappers had the very natural ambition to finish the War as returned soldiers. Some still with this platoon of RAE had enlisted in September 1939, had been sent to the UK, back to Syria, then through Tobruk and both battles of El Alamein, the Lae and Finschhaffen operations in New Guinea and finally through Morotai and on to Borneo. He had been wrestling with the problem of finding a way of handling the oil well fires with reduced danger. Together with a couple of the normal field operating staff, he had developed an idea of how to go about this. On one particular well, he had managed a method of directing the oil and gas stream away from the well-head so that the crews could work at the well-head in comparative safety and comfort. But this was a particular case, suited fortuitously to this one well. However, the idea was persisted with but without any practical result. The difficulty really reduced to ignorance and lack of experience with oilfield equipment and operations. The basic idea was to work out a method of "stabbing in" a wedge-shaped pipe into the main pipe of the "christmas tree" to be able to divert the flow of gas and oil and somehow then bring the well under control.

This objective was discussed with the men from Texas and they could see that the idea may be developed, provided certain items of equipment could be found and provided the workshop's capacity (which had been badly reduced as part of the Japanese "scorched earch" activities) was up to the job of putting everything together as necessary. After much sketching of possibilities and discussion, searching for component parts and some excellent effort on the part of the workshops, a "stabbing in" assembly was put together which, if successful, would not only divert the flow of oil and gas, but would also be capable of manipulation to enable mud to be pumped into the well to bring it under control. In order to carry and handle this equipment, the Sappers acquired a large track-mounted crane from the stores' unloading unit in Labuan complete with operator who was essentially given practice training when the whole assembly was put together. It was cumbersome and the skill necessary to work it to fairly fine limits of movement had to be achieved — and was.

The American experts preferred to go ahead with this method of attacking the job as they too could well appreciate the dangers associated with the steam process of putting out the fires and then working on a gushing well head.

While all this assembling and manufacturing of components took some time, the Sappers continued on with the necessary preliminary work of clearing away from the burning well heads the masses of coke, twisted steel and other machinery which had collapsed around the "christmas trees". They endeavoured to remove parts of the "christmas trees" so that there was an open pipe into which the equipment being fabricated could be stabbed. Also, they prepared the surrounding area for a reasonably level approach for the tracked crane, water supply, water pumps, mud supply, mud pumps and other ancillary equipment required at each well.

In removing the mass of rubbish around each well head, the Sappers used explosives — quite large charges — in cases wrapped in asbestos cloth and mounted on steel sledges. These were pushed into position by bulldozers along sand ramps previously built up to suit each situation. The sledges, made up of welded steel pipe, were designed for each occasion to suit the individual needs at each well. The sledge with its load of explosives was edged into position and was hosed to prevent early detonation by heat. When in the desired position the charges were blown from an exploder set behind the rear of the bulldozer.

One well, cleared and prepared ready, proved stubborn in clearing up the "christmas tree" in that the top valve of the "christmas tree" remained in position sitting on top of about a 5 foot high vertical pipe — the main pipe of the "christmas tree". The situation thus was that there was no open pipe into which to stab the equipment. The problem was to cut this pipe and, while the Sappers knew how this could be done with the right kind of explosives correctly positioned, this was impossible in such hot conditions. The Americans thought that suitable steel sawing equipment could perhaps be found in the USA but that it would have to be carefully selected to do the job and would take a long time to obtain in any case. The Sappers thought of armour piercing projectiles and considered the range from the a/tk rifle to 25-pdr shells. The selection had to be carefully made and eventually the decision was taken to discuss possibilities with the a/tk 6-pdr gunners attached to 2/17 Bn. The main point was that the cut had to be clean and, if necessary, done in stages as the wrong kind of projectile could quite possibly make matters worse at the well-head. The gunners felt confident and a gun was set at about 30 yards range from the well, firing out to seaward. With careful aim the gunners put the first shell through the exact centre of the thick-walled steel pipe as neatly as could be. With two more shots, one left of the centred hole already cut, and one to the right of it, the pipe was cleanly cut. This, undoubtedly, was the first time in history — and probably the last — that an oil well "christmas tree" had been so treated. The gunners were delighted, as were all others concerned, and eventually the open pipe so produced was stabbed, the fire extinguished and the well brought under control.

In using the "stabbing-in" equipment mounted on the crane, some experimentation was found necessary at first and some adjustments to its design had to be made. But in the main, it proved to be the answer and good teamwork with the American experts, the Sappers, the field operating personnel and everyone involved, made it work. It required a study of the conditions at each well and proper preparation work so that, at the right time, all effort came together. Undoubtedly, it was a much less dangerous way of going about the job, particularly in view of the high pressures and the high gas content of the Seria field wells.

It was thought that the Japanese had started the work of their scorched earth programme on the Seria field on the day of the landing at Brunei Bay, 10 Jun, and it would have taken a few days to take it to the thoroughly designed stage that they achieved. The 2/17 Bn reached the field on 19 Jun. The War ended on 14 Aug. The last oil well fire was extinguished on 24 Sep. Perhaps it is worth recording that the last well did not call for controlling by filling the well with mud as the "christmas tree" valve was found to be operable. When a pressure gauge was fitted to the well, the well head pressure was found to be 2340 pounds per square inch. Near the well head, about 15 feet out, were the 4 concrete derrick foundations and one of these concrete foundations had melted — a rare sight indeed!

2/17 Bn and its attached and support troops had thus contributed to the recovery of a valuable oilfield, sadly, stupidly, yet easily destroyed to a large extent by the Japanese. The well fires were almost certainly the worst ever encountered anywhere in view of the total number on fire and of the high pressure nature of the Seria field. The field was operated by British interests and its early return to production and expansion was important to that nation which had suffered so immeasurably, as well as to the people of Brunei who also had felt their full share of oppressive occupation.

Above: Men of 14 Pl – C Coy en-route from Seria to Badas (Brunei). **L-R:** L/Cpl Clarke, Ptes Wilson, J W Hodgkins, B Menzies, K Shuuleworth, H Fincham, Williams. **Below:** Men of D Coy load water drums on landing craft at Kuala Belait (Brunei) before leaving for Marudi. **L-R:** L/Cpl R A Roberts, Pte S Grimson, Cpl A Jackson.

APPENDIX 7

2/17TH CONCERT PARTY

SOME OBSERVATIONS AND INCIDENTS OF INTEREST
By Ron Brierley (written in 1945)

I write these memoirs, hoping that they will interest the members of the Concert Party, for every recollection brings a laugh or a sigh. I'm sure we'll all remember the days we've spent — and nights — rehearsing, planning and making costumes, the hectic moments before the curtain rose, the successes of some nights and the failures of others.

These memories will probably last a lifetime — they've been rich enough to do so. So, here I go, trying to bring to life all those little incidents. The great "I" will occur more than often. But, then, that is surely my privilege.

Ever since a child of eight years, my "predominating passion" has been the arrangement of a concert. The kids from the whole block used to ransack their mothers' wardrobes for costumes and turn out for the show in the most stunning creations. Usually Mother's new hat — or latest gown — was worse for wear. Many paid for their artistic tendencies with sore backsides — but "the Show must go on" — and on it went. At every opportunity, throughout the last ten years, I've organised a concert party for some purpose or other. So you can see that I was only following the old tradition and impulse when I got to work on forming a concert party to do a "smoko concert" at B Coy Mess last March at Ravenshoe.

The piano (always the greatest of all worries) was promised to me by the Salvation Army Representative, 2/43 Bn in return favour for my services which had been given quite frequently. I then combed the Bn for talent, eventually taking a handful of fellows down to 2/43 Bn for a rehearsal, to see what they were made of.

I received a surprise — they were OK. There was Ron Keogh (comedian), Alf Greig (tenor), Frank O'Brien (western singer), Bernie Carlin (tenor), Allan Verinder (harmonicist), Clarrie Greenfield (recitist) and Blue Bartlett (a healthy acquisition to the chorus numbers). So it was that our Concert Party started off. Dick Blackwell joined us the day before the show.

The Smoko Concert was voted a great success. The mess was crowded, approx 250 were present. S/Sgt Williams (our QM) helped to enlarge the mess for the show. Mr Khron, YMCA representative, lent a microphone and the 2/23 Bn Dance Band assisted with the program. The CO, Col Broadbent and other officers were present. Well, that first night was the start of many footlight parades and everyone was enthusiastic about doing further shows.

Dick Blackwell introduced me to "Irish" O'Malley who also had ideas about a Bn concert party. We arranged a meeting to discuss the matter and this was held at D Coy mess. There were forty present, including the Amenities Officer, Mr Williams and the YMCA rep, Mr Khron.

It was beer night and I had some trouble getting them there — everyone was merry and bright and the meeting went along at a quick pace. Here is the company as formed:

Ron Brierley	Producer and Musical Director
Irish O'Malley	Dialogue Director
Dick Blackwell	Stage Manager

Trevor Bevin	Doug Colley	Bernie Carlin
Len Sexton	Jack Hillier	Harry Grierson
Darkie Miller	John Moore	Harry Andrews
Bill Whitton	Frank O'Brien	Bert Coffey
Danny Keaney	Jim Lee	Denz Schofield
Hugh Cummings	Curly Broadbridge	Mr Grant
John Carter		

The first rehearsal was held at 2/43 Bn (the home of the piano) and three other rehearsals were held in various spots which were most unsuitable. We had not found a home and felt rather lost. Mr Khron then came to our assistance and gave us the use of the YMCA. So we settled down to some steady work.

In the meantime, our friends from 2/23 Bn Dance Band requested a return favour from us. We jumped at the suggestion. We performed the same program as we did at B Coy Smoko. It was rather dull — everything felt dull. The audience (about 200 in number) was very quiet and unresponsive. Of course, some of Irish's jokes were "hot". The audience was polite and so were we, but we didn't like each other much. However, they gave us a steak and egg supper and that was OK.

The rehearsals for "Revue Number One" were going fine by this time. Particularly humourous was the first rehearsal of the "ballet". The ballet (supposedly a group of very lovely lissome creatures of the female sex) consisted of the following:

Len Sexton	Jack Hillier	Danny Keany
Bill Whitton	Blue Bartlett	Doug Colley

a more hefty ballet you could not have imagined. On this first rehearsal night they had fortified themselves with the old amber and it took a lot of effort to get them there. In this state, flitting around like so many butterflies was just child's play to Hillier and Coy and they did enjoy it! They broke two tables in the Sergeants' Mess, also churned up the floor! But then —"the Show must go on".

Both Irish and myself were directing the ballet. When one tired of showing Bill Whitton how it was done, the other would have ago. Poor Bill was hopelessly tangled, and gracefully retired after a while, and was received very warmly in the ranks of the chorus. The dates were decided upon, stage erected in the YMCA and costumes ready per Yours Truly. And, now to the Show!

15 Mar was a very busy day, and I was right in the thick of it. The stage had to be dressed, costumes ironed and hundreds of other little things to do. As usual, when tea time came, I'd "had it".

1930 hrs — that pulsating hour — found the dressing room in a state of turmoil. Everyone was nervous but, I must say, patient. There was no panic — not then! With the "girls" dressed and the chorus set up with sashes and white shirts that fitted, I called the company on stage and gave some last minute instructions. The "girls" by the way, caused quite a stir among the company. The fitting of "busts" was a very interesting procedure. I couldn't help but feel a deep satisfaction when I noticed the quiet and confident way the whole company trusted in me.

Nearly all of them were new to amateur theatricals, but carried on as though they were old hands.

The YMCA was crowded out. Footlights lit up our new curtains and the whole atmosphere reminded me of the moments before the overture at the "Royal" during my last leave. I entered through the back of the hall, made my way through the dark to the piano and a thin ripple of applause greeted me. Over the phone Dick said all was ready to go, so away we went.

The band consisted of the following:—

DRUMS	Hugh Cummings
PIANO	myself
CORNET	Curly Broadbridge

I was compering the show from the band alcove, with microphone:

". . . and now we take you to the Cafe Balalaika, where life is gay with wine, women and song!" The curtains parted and the old ever popular "Al-a-zuga zay", with Bernie Carlin, and the dance by Irish and Harry Andrews, hit the boards.

The crowd was undecided whether to take it, or laugh. The female impersonators were the main trouble. They kept laughing, enjoying the joke themselves. Danny Keany was the main offender in this. But who was to stop laughter on a stage like this — it is usually a hard job making amateurs smile at all. So on we went. Irish and Coy put over the first of the famous sketches that were to become so notorious in later days. Doug Colley made his Ravenshoe debut in "Cuban Pete" a song and dance rumba with the chorus. Irish excelled as Senor Royallio Omarlio, the impressario of the famous "Rushing Ballet".

This number brought the house down and had to be repeated. Blue Bartlett lost his brassiere and was quite embarrassed too. All kicked a shapely leg in the most angelic style.

Trevor Bevin, our "operatic tenor", Dick Blackwell, baritone and popular vocalist Bernie Carlin all gave excellent performances. Len Sexton, the big, beautiful doll in the "Gay Nineties" Selection, was impressive in picture hat complete with parasol. The boys made a Victorian dash in their white boaters, assuring everyone that they "just loved to be beside the seaside". By the way, Lennie Sexton's "doll" frock caused quite a stir behind the stage, I believe. Half a dozen fellows pulling and Len screaming and squirming — all because we had no eyes and hooks, so the waistline had to be sewn up to fit as near as possible. Len told off a couple of them, including Dick Blackwell who had practically dragged him on stage for the Gay Nineties, half dressed. I thought I noticed something rather drawn about the smile Len gave him during the number!

Well, so came the finale. The CO made some very complimentary remarks and I answered accordingly. "Wish me luck as you wave me goodbye" was our finale number. After that, supper on the stage and lots of cross talk — criticism, constructive and otherwise, but mostly constructive. The show on the whole had been good, but there were a few changes to be made. The show was too short for a start (a bet I won with Dick Blackwell) we got to work on additions for the next day.

That night, the show went over with a real bang! Everyone was intoxicated with the success of it and this time we celebrated with a supper of steak and eggs at the canteen by courtesy of the CO.

The third night was another success — and another supper at the canteen. So ended our first "season" at Ravenshoe.

The following week we invited the members of the 2/15 Bn to a performance but, owing to some last minute change in their syllabus of training, only thirty attended. That was very disheartening, so we decided that from then on we would restrict our efforts to our own Bn.

Bernie Carlin had to be carried to this performance owing to a sprained ankle (football as usual). After this, there followed a few return favour visits. Dick Blackwell, Barnie Carlin and I assisted at concerts (two in number) at the 2/43 Bn and 2/23 Bn, also one at 2/15 Bn. Trevor Bevin and I sang and played at a recital at Brigade. Everywhere we were enthusiastically received but why not — our solosits were better than any other unit could offer.

Revue Two then began to take shape. Irish and I, keen followers of musical comedy, had "Merry Widow" and "Desert Song" in mind. This time we decided to add dialogue to the selections, thus giving them a story. This was probably our most productive period. Irish "went to town" with sketches, and the musical arrangements were very elaborate. We had some new members — Allan Cripps, Julian Clint, Doc Williams, Jim Lee, John Champion, Gidley Wilkinson (who, I forgot to mention, assisted Digger Miller in a mimic number in Revue One). All were very enthusiastic. Julian Clint painted some impressive backdrops for "Desert Song" and "Merry Widow". The new band had arrived and Skeets Palmer was a very welcome newcomer to our C.P.

And so we come to Revue Two. A crowded house, the lights low and the band starts away. The compere, Ron Fawell (another addition), does his preliminary canter before the curtain and it opened on the Can Can (Bring 'em on, bring 'em on!) which was to become a byword throughout the Bn. The choruses were very flat however and everyone seemed "off". The sketches saved the night — they were snappy and got the laughs. As the show went on it improved, but was not up to standard. As Gidley remarked during one of the numbers, "Look at the the producer, he's off his nut!" I *was* tearing my hair in no uncertain fashion. The highlight of this performance (if it could be classed as such) was the "tumbling" act of Hillier and Miller. A classic example of two very merry men, just a little too full to do anything at all. The act resulted in a series of runs from one side of the stage to the other, various trippings and much ado about nothing. Naturally, I was not *very* enthusiastic about it and decided to leave it out of the next performance. The chorus got a piece of my mind after the show. A scratch rehearsal on the following day toned things up a lot.

The second night, 9 April, was a wonderful effort of good singing, acting and continuity. The chorus were on their toes. Bernie Carlin's "Vilia" was perfect. I gave him an encore — it was worth every bit of it. The show was as perfect as I could have desired it to be. Highlights of the program were:

"MERRY WIDOW"

Prince Danilo	Bernie Carlin
Princess Sonia of Moravia	Harry Grierson
Count Vermicelli	Trevor Bevin
Count Otto	Irish O'Malley

"DESERT SONG"

Red Shadow	Dick Blackwell
Captain Damaresque	Bernie Carlin
Wanda	Harrie Grierson

The "Down South" number was very popular too. All agreed that "Desert Song" was the most entertaining number we had done so far.

Mr Grant read the church notices for the week and his choir persisted in swinging the hymns. The schoolroom scene (with Greenbottle, Ron Keogh and Co) was a havoc of humour, and the sketches up to the usual high O'Malley standard. Owing to the indisposition of Trevor Bevin, Bernie Carlin took over all the tenor parts — quite a job entailing some thirteen songs, and none too easy. We celebrated, or at least most of the fellows did with their issue of beer. Bernie saw fit to tell me what he thought of me about the encoring of "Vilia", which had such a reverse effect on me that I "gave the show away" for the night, all soloists included, and swore I would never give another encore to any soloist as long as I lived. Next morning, we patched it up — no more encores! And so ended Revue Two with another performance the following night.

About this time the companies were holding formal dinners. The Concert party was requested to entertain at two of these — firstly C Coy and then at HQ Coy. We were very pleased to do so and had an enjoyable night on both occasions.

Bernie Carlin, Dick Blackwell, Harry Grierson, Skeets Palmer, Curly Broadbridge and I made up the party at C Coy mess. I think the most notable event of that evening was my rendition of Twelfth Street Rag, in as much as I've heard about it ever since! There was beer, of course, that probably accounts for it.

HQ Coy mess was a *big* night — about fifteen of the C.P. were present. The C.P. band gave numbers followed by choruses, solos and sketches by the members. All went very well. The beer flowed and the C.P. certainly had its share. I was pounding the piano for quite some time and the party went on well into the night. Notable drunkards were: Dick Blackwell, Irish O'Malley, Bernie Carlin and, of course, yours truly had his share.

Irish persisted in doing jive with the Coffey and Bernie Carlin danced an old time waltz with much gusto. I think I even had a hand in a version of the Lambeth Walk myself. Julian Clint became very amorous I believe. The night was certainly tops and everyone had a great time. And that ended our activities at Ravenshoe.

The next phase of C.P. work was not so successful as our previous efforts. The "David Shanks" was a crowded ship and had very little room for concerts. Furthermore, the authorities in command were not sympathetic towards us. We managed to do community concerts on deck after dark and these were quite successful, but not spectacular by any means.

Our music consisted of a small church organ and cornets and we did mostly repetition work, keeping our new material for the time when we could give a daylight performance. This did not occur until we boarded the "Kanimbla" but, even then, the authorities were not interested. The actual organisation of a concert was done by the ship's orchestra through Dick Blackwell. Even then we were only allowed an hour.

Irish and Ron Keogh and Co did the right thing by the sketches, and the chorus and soloists did some new work, notably "ShowBoat" and a selection of Strauss Waltzes. It went over very well. Photos were taken — I noticed the chorus became strangely stimulated when the camera came into view! Apart from that, our voyage was uneventful, and we had expected a busy time.

Then came the landing and all thought of footlights faded away until we were firmly established at Seria, North West Borneo. The Adjutant, Capt McFarland, suggested a community concert, so we went to work again. Wednesday, 11 July was the date. The band assisted with a concert party consisting of Irish O'Malley, Dick Blackwell, Frank O'Brien, Bert Coffey and Allan Cripps, plus Ron Keogh and myself. It was a dullish night — mainly because of lack of Concert party members and facilities. Irish was out of sketches — couldn't think of a thing — the first time such a calamity had befallen us. We were also considerably browned off as a result of the lack of interest shown by the authorities on the voyage over. All these things tended to slow down the show. Capt McFarland then decided to give us a "shot in the arm". A meeting was called for Sunday, 15 July at the Command Post, Seria.

At this meeting important matters were dealt with, eg piano, sewing machine (for costume making) locality for performances, time off for rehearsals etc. So, Revue Number Three started off. Capt Simpson, Capt McFarland and Lt Wasely were new members of the show. Other new members were:

Arthur Russell	Lt Cutler
Lt Cunningham	Sammy Ducrow

Old members able to assist were:

Dick Blackwell	Irish O'Malley
Allan Cripps	Frank O'Brien
Gidley Wilkinson	Jack Hillier
Harry Grierson	Doc Williams
Ron Fawell	Julian Clint

and, of course, the boys from the band — Curley, Skeets and the two drummers. Bernie Carlin was unable to help, but promised a "Guest Artist" number.

This turned out to be the most piecemeal show we have done. Both Irish and I were devoid of ideas — racked our brains night after night. Our main difficulty was the lack of soloists and chorus members. We had to build all our numbers with accentuation on the chorus work and leave solos out. We succeeded however, and compensated by obtaining the services of Capt Max Wurthly of Brigade in a Bracket of Guest Artist numbers.

Rehearsals went well — we held them in a house on the outskirts of the suburb, very close to the fires and very noisy. I managed to compose an opening chorus in "On with the show" style and incidentally the first of the few opening numbers. "We've got a cute little show", it ran, "plenty of music and songs that you know". You will notice it called the "little" show. I didn't dare to be over optimistic about it. As far as we were concerned it was a very flimsy affair.

The company was very enthusiastic and that means everything to a show. So, after a solid week of work on costumes, props and rehearsals, Revue Three hit the boards of our new stage (built for the occasion) on Thursday, 2 Aug. To our surprise it was voted the best show so far!

Now to some notes about the show. The band was assisting us this time but, after the show, we doubted the authenticity of that statement. The opening number went off OK. Mr Wasely's "Charlie Cutler Is His Name" (and yours truly is Hugh Wasley) became the vehicle of a number of attempts at character acting by other members. Spanky was a good compere. Irish as "Mo" went over well and Gidley as the "comedienne sophisticate" really excelled. Allan Cripps and Ron Fawell did their "Sailors' Hornpipe" _with vim and vigor and yours truly struggled at the piano (down, off-stage) trying to make myself heard, resulting in a tinkle like a spinet. Capt Wurthly gave three fine renditions, and Bernie Carlin sang in his usual entertaining style. The band went haywire during the Spanish Town Chorus and the dancers lost the routine completely. Otherwise the show went over well.

We had kept our beer issue and made good use of it on stage after the show. So ended Revue Three. First night — last night — same night! This was due to the fact that our auditorium could seat the whole Bn. There was no necessity for a repeat.

After this, a change came over the C.P. It was very noticeable — probably the result of the enthusiastic reception given to Revue Three. All were keen on doing Revue Four. New members were:

Noel Moylan	Norm Elton
Mick Cain	Ron Burns
Lt Lindsay	Capt Ritchie

Capt (Doc) Ritchie brought new vim to our company. We selected him as our new compere (Capt McFarland was too busy with impending cessation work to take an active part in the show). Capt Ritchie's repertoir of "Sultry University Sketches" was very handy to Irish — and were they *sultry*! They blew into a gale before we were through. Our old silvery voiced tenor, Bernie Carlin, became "un"-indisposed and joined us again together with John Moore and Doug Colley. The company now numbered thirty members in comparison with the sixteen of Revue Three.

The Doc, Irish and I now became highly productive — "fertile" as we called it. The opening number I composed eclipsed that of R3. For further fare we built an Eastern Scene around the "Buck Shee-Allah" and gave it dialogue. The setting was the Sultan's Court at Brunei. Our flair for musical comedy was vindicated in a selection from "New Moon", also with dialogue. The Gidley sensuously displaced her charm with real reckless abandon in a sultlry little number of Latin vintage — "A Bit of the Mexican Magic" with the assistance of the chorus.

Bernie Carlin featured a number I had written for him coming over on the "Shanks", named marleta Mia, and Irish and Allan Cripps (now a vivacious blonde) tangoed. Dick Blackwell featured a prayer I had written for the cessation of hostilities (this was our "Victory Show") and Bernie's "Holy Night" made a great impression. The "Liberation Army" (not to be associated with the Salvation Army) was a riot. The lines of Sister Moylan became a by-word for the future. "Sister Moylan will carry the banner next week", reply, "I carried the B—— last week". "Well you'll carry the —— thing again this week!" Doug Colley made a glorious slip with the reply — it's strictly off the record — just in case you want to send this home!

Friday, 17 Aug was the first night. It had rained all day and looked most unfavourable for an open air show. Some of the Five Year boys were leaving us that night, so we decided, hail or shine, the show would go on. There was a huge crowd at the area long before dusk, and the weather had broken.

Off went the opening number. All went well until Gidley entered with his lampshade hat. The Rains Came — with a vengeance! Poor Gid, with only a brassiere on the upper reaches, was half swimming half sliding through the routine. During the next sketch we hauled the piano on stage. It must have looked very comical.

By this time the rains were pouring the usual Cs and Ds. Doc asked the boys if they would rather us postpone the show until Saturday night, but they wanted it to go on. So on we went. After the finale (which I had concocted from the last war melodies with suitable words) the CO bid Good Luck and God Speed to the fellows leaving, and all sang "They are jolly good fellows". I made my faux pas re Dick Blackwell being my "moral and physical support" and got a laugh. Then the CO gave a party which was very welcome.

The following Monday night we gave a performance for other units. And so ended Revue Four — and the War.

And now to the final stages of this narrative: Revue Five was coming up. Before going on to it, however, we did a trip up river to A Coy at Balai. This was a change, and everyone felt enthusiastic about it until we arrived there. Irish and Allan Cripps had gone ahead two days before the main body and had the stage dressed or, at least, composed. The auditorium was a large shed right on the banks of the river. Carlin and Co promptly overturned a canoe but, other than that, all was serene in the C.P. ranks. The enthusiasm of our welcome did not amount to much and we felt rather disheartened. However, after our performance of R3, everyone became more hospitable.

The audience was comprised of some fifty A Coy fellows and probably one hundred natives, all very voluble, particulalrly during the sketches — most of them did not understand English. The singing, they applauded mildly. The following night, Sunday, 26 August, R4 was given a great reception although, from our point of view, it was a bit slow due to lighting effects that caused us some bother.

Following our musical comedy trends, the Doc, Irish and I decided to do a condensed version of "Maid of the Mountains". Irish, assisted by myself and later the doctor, completed a story and dialogue suitable to the material we had and went to work on rehearsals on 31 Aug. After spending a week on it, the company decided at a meeting called to discuss the matter that the cast were unable to carry it through successfully. It was cancelled and the show postponed for four days.

Revue Five — 20 Sep 1945 — RED THURSDAY.

The night before, I had done all the pressing and final stitches which kept me working until 0225 hrs, but considered it was worthwhile. My plan was to have a clear day before the show and not the last minute rush as usual on Thursday. I impressed on the company the necessity of good organisation and entreated them to make this the most orderly show possible.

That night at 1800 hrs, the principals attended a pre-show party at the RAP as per the invitation of Doc Ritchie. Needless to say being Doc Ritchie's party, it was a *party*. The Great Ritchie combines effervescent enthusiasm with potent action. The potency wasn't missing! The result — a jeepful of very merry principals making their way to the stage about 1940 hrs, lustily singing the numbers from "Antonio".

After the boys had dressed at the command post, we carefully picked our way to the stage just on 2000 hrs and, without further ado, away went the opening chorus, another of my concoctions. To say the show was a riot is a sinful under-estimation. The singing was executed as never before.

And now to some details: All went well through the first act, everyone kept his "eyes on the ball". The Intermission however, found the coy in great spirits. Chorus members lay here and there — Gidley parading dans le nude and skipping, dolphin-like about the officers' mess. Len Sexton assured me that we were still mates, and Spanky begged me to "'ave another drink". Dick Blackwell, the mother in our melodrama, was crying that his breasts were not big enough. Bernie Carlin was frantically entangled in his surcoat for "Maid of the Mountains". I retrieved the lanterns from a game of football being played in the dressing room. The CO was hovering around paternally trying to help, and one or two sober members were fixing the stage for the next number. Len Sexton fell down the steps from the dressing room into a jeep, emitting a loud roar, and general pandemonium reigned.

As for myself, I didn't care a damn! It was great fun. Ordinarily, I would have been tearing my hair. Irish said that it was just as well I wasn't sober, someone would have clocked me in the long run. I shall never forget Gidley swaying in the frame for "Sunnyside Up" for all the world like a monkey and completely oblivious to the audience. Rather an embarrassing incident had occurred earlier in the evening. Gidley lost his pants! The result — RIOT.

Well, after the show, the CO entertained us all with another party. That part of the evening is just a haze to most of us, but we all vote the CO, Doc Ritchie and Spanky the best of sports for it was the best evening we've had, and a fitting finale to our activities.

And so ends our day! Five Revues, three Mess Concerts, one shipboard, one community, and other tidbits thrown in. A total of 16 performances.

APPENDIX 8

PERSONAL ANECDOTES

BATTALION HQ & INTELLIGENCE SECTION

SOME OF THE PERSONALITITES
By Noel Grant

MICHAEL EISDELL (I Sec) had been a radio announcer with the BBC in England, and migrated to Australia in the Depression years (1930s) and immediately joined the staff of the ABC. He had just the right voice for such a post. After the War he organised "The Goon Show".

A keen sportsman, he played Rugby in England for the fashionable Roslyn Park Club (he always referred to it as The Park). There would be beer and scones after a game.

His mother had driven an ambulance in England during the German Blitz. He was shot in the knee in Tobruk — we recall his voice that night pleading, "My God, I have been shot".

He sent me a Christmas card in 1980 — from High Street, Kensington, London. It featured Lord's during the Centenary Test, 1980. It read:

> "One thinks of one's old friends when one is absent. Even so I'm too mean to pay the airmail postage — a friend is taking all my Xmas cards back to Australia and posting them locally. Best wishes, hope to see you after my sixth and final return to England — the end of the over as it were."

Sadly, some years ago, he was killed by a motor vehicle (whilst he was a pedestrian).

THE "OWENS" There were three "Owens" in the unit. Lt J M (Paddy) in B Coy. Peter in the I Section. A third brother, Evelyn was withdrawn from the unit at Bathurst so that he might proceed with his invention, the famous Owen gun (which later became such a valuable weapon in the new Guinea campaign).

ALEX CRISDALE (I Sec) was responsible for drawing up the fine maps of the Battalion's campaign. These were distributed over a period with the Newsletter.

R N R "DARBY" GREEN. Our Bn HQ Sgt was a great character who was highly respected by all ranks of the Battalion. He was a Law graduate from Sydney University and in civilian life was a Legal Officer in the NSW Police Dept.

After the Tobruk campaign at his own special request he was given permission to transfer to the Mortar Pl. After attending a school in Palestine where he gained a pass of distinction, he served as Sgt in this Pl during the battle of Alamein and was killed in action. His ability to put his philosophy into verse was known to many and one of his many poems is reproduced here:

Nightpiece in Libya

Fragments of old songs sung in the heart,
Tags of old verses echoing in the mind,
A moon who silvers with fantastic art,
A shell-shocked town and other battlekind,
A breeze whose soft caress revives the smart
Of that last evening, now so oft repined
In this false heaven, you stand a thing apart,
A symbol of desire and faith combined.

Then suddenly the guns crash out their hate,
The flares distort the shapeless battlefield,
And for a while, all hell decides out fate,
Our faith along the one remaining shield,
Silence once more — sham Peace which serves to fill
The mind with thoughts of you, more poignant still.

Tobruk, June 1941

H H "HAPPY" ALLAN. There is the story of the cake. To commence at Ingleburn it was the practice of the CO, Lt Col J W Crawford to have cake available in the Officers' Mess each Sunday, and he became affectionately known as "The Cake Eater".

Later, the following incident occurred in Tobruk. Darby Green had received a parcel of a cake (from his sisters in Sydney) — this would be a very isolated instance. He shared portion of the cake around Bn HQ. To distribute the remainder he called "Happy" Allan (the runner) indicating the Sig Sec and said, "Take this to the cake eaters". "Yes, Sgt Green", said Happy. Happy was no University graduate, but he was a faithful servant. The word "cake eaters" would have been impressed in his mind, for a little later the phone rang and this occurred — "Commander here, thank you, Green, for the cake".

COLIN LEWIS drove the ration truck in Tobruk. He had come up in hard times with the Depression years and not had the privilege of much education. He was not able to write and, on several occasions, he prevailed on me to write a note for him to his wife. He was an obedient, faithful, very competent driver and a happy character.

On one occasion in Tobruk, I accompanied him to an area to collect the daily rations. There was much shelling over the flat that afternoon and after a while, he pondered on what to do. I suggested we could follow "Murphy's dictum", that is to get in quick and get out quicker. I don't think he knew much about "Murphy", still we got in and got the rations and returned (not without much shelling) and we were covered with dust and sand on our return. Sadly, Colin Lewis was later killed in New Guinea.

THE SALIENT AREA, TOBRUK

The practice was to take the sanitary tins from Bn HQ down the wadi each afternoon to a disposal point (there being no Water and Sewerage Board available!). We took it in turns — 3 tins, 2 men. Ray (Spongy) Turner was the Hygiene Sgt, and a very efficient one, too. This afternoon it was my turn, with two others. Half way down the wadi a lot of shelling occurred (much noise with the shrapnel striking the stony area). We went to ground (I was fortunate as

I had pride of place, between two tins. I thought it gave me some security. I recall one of the others saying, "If they hit a tin we will all be 'up the well-known creek'".

D MCD "MAC" BROWN, RSM. I recall being with him at Bn HQ (the salient position). Mac had retrieved an old Lewis gun which he overhauled and put into service — it was his pride and joy. Daily, about midday, a German plane would fly over our position and do a bit of machine gunning. Mac set up his gun this day — about midday — the plane approached from out of the sun, and there was the usual machine gun fire and we got covered with sand and dust. The plane crashed, and when the pilot's body was recovered, there fell onto the desert a photograph of a beautiful German girl, with German writing on the back of the card. It was handed to me and I subsequently placed it with Bn records. The sadness of war!

ARTHUR HELLMAN, The I SGT. He had been in the 1st AIF — at Gallipoli and in France. Pre-war he was a rubber plantation manager in Malaya. Perhaps the best tribute is that written by George Vincent following Arthur's death some years ago:

> "If ever a man was identified with our Battalion that man was Arthur Hellman. There must have been hundreds of us who knew him from 1940 to 1976, trained and fought and played alongside him and who will miss him from now on.

> A vital man in all he did. It was only when we ourselves reached the age of 40 that we realised how hard it must have been to keep up with men 20 years younger and just in the first blush of strength and vigour. And we took him for granted. We regarded him as one of us, expected him to do everything we did. Arthur would not have had it otherwise. It was great to have known you, Arthur."

THE RUM RATION

It was after our stint in the salient, Tobruk. The CO had approved a rum issue. Darby Green (Bn HQ) called on Alan Dixon to organise the ration, with strictly an equal amount for all. Alan noted the names, but he had a query and asked Darby, "What about the Padre?" Darby knew it was a silly question and suggested he contact the Padre, Father Watson. But as Alan turned to go he found Father Watson there with his mug "at the ready".

A LITTLE WHISKY

About June 1941, with the khamsen blowing in from the Sahara, we were at Bn HQ. Darby Green — always on the alert — indicated that through the haze he noted someone approaching. It turned out to be the Adjutant, Colin Pitman — there had been a gathering of Officers at the Command Post, and Colin had ensured that a little surplus whisky would be given us (Darby Green, Arthur Hellman, Mac Brown, myself and maybe some others were there). We appreciated the thought and it sure made our day.

GEORGE VINCENT. A fine athlete from Western Australia. A 1st Grade Sydney Rugby player. He won the race around the deck of the *Queen Mary* (which was some distance).

George had attended an OCTU in Cairo, and has given this report of his leaving Palestine for Tobruk (where he was severely wounded):—

> "We left Kilo 89, which was functioning to bring in reinforcements for various 9 Div units. This is the story as far as 2/17 Bn was concerned. In the party were Ted Chapman, Paul Mendham, Keith Sabine, myself and 20 others, including Sgt 'Taffy' Evans. The whole party had route marched to the railway siding at Gaza and entrained for Kantara for onward movement. At Kantara there was some access to arak (drink) and this fired many brains. Crossing the Canal, and then another train, there occurred some indiscriminate firing of

rifles. Following a stoppage I well remember the difficulty we had in getting some of the men back on to the train.

We went on to Amiriya and to Mersa Matruh — there we had several days adjacent to a camp of Polish officers who had escaped by rowing into Egypt. Then stops at Sidi Barrani, Bardia, Salum. Rumours were flying around about the situation — there was a steady flow of Air Force personnel in full retreat.

Following a hot meal we moved on to the top of Halfaya Pass to await further instructions. The officers of the party were issued with a pistol and the troops with rifles. There were many rumours and we had no idea of the state of affairs. Further west we learned that the Army was in full retreat to Tobruk.

Finally, we got orders to advance and came into Tobruk in time for a German air raid and a few hours before Rommel's forces encircled the town. We went through the town of Tobruk and stopped at Wadi Auda overnight, subsequently joining the unit on the perimeter."

"IZZY" SHARP. According to Arthur Newton's note, Izzy had enlisted in the 1st AIF, but too late to leave Australia. But he was very active during the 1918 influenza epidemic with distinguished service as a hospital orderly. He was early into 2/17 Bn. At Ingleburn in the early days he would be heard each morning singing loudly. He often rendered the song of the day — I remember it well:

> "I've got sixpence,
>
> Twopence to spend, and twopence to lend,
>
> and twopence to give to my wife."

He could have been heard down at Campbelltown. A nice fellow and a lovable character. He was severely wounded, with Harry Malthouse and others, at Tobruk.

I recall another story told by Arthur Newton. Whilst at Ingleburn there was leave for those of the Jewish faith to attend the Day of Atonement. Izzy had made special application for the day's leave and this was approved by the CO. On his return Arthur asked Izzy how he spent the Day of Atonement. Izzy replied, "I went to Randwick Races".

THE "I" SECTION

There was Eric Blundell, Owen Windeyer, Bob Ford, Julian Clint, Geoff Reading, John McVey, Alec Crisdale, Stan Hill, Arthur Russell, Reg Luchinelli, Dal Cartledge, Doug Broadhead, Noel Moylan and many others.

Geoff Reading, born in Dover, England, spent many years in Palestine and Egypt prior to the War. His family had a real Middle East background. Brother Bob was, sadly, a casualty at Alamein. Bob was born in Ibrahimiah, a suburb of Alexandria in 1918. Shortly after World War I (his father served in the Royal Engineers) the family moved, through El Kantara by a Model T Ford, through the Sinai Desert and to Haifa, where his father had been appointed as an Administrator on the Palestine Mandate of the occupied enemy territory authority. Subsequent appointments were: Asst Dist Commissioner and Land Settlement Officer, Governor of Tulkarem, a sub-district in Palestine, and was seconded to Amman in Trans Jordan as Chief British Representative.

SYRIA 1941
By Alan Wright

Our Bde was spread over a wide area of northern Syria. Where the rest of the Div was I can't recall. Our own Bn was widely dispersed, with HQ at Afrine. At this time, 6 and 7 Divs had departed from the Middle East and we who were left in Syria could not believe it when the news of Tobruk's fall came through. We were rather dismayed to hear of Rommel racing across North Africa towards Egypt and the Nips racing south in the Pacific. We were all expecting to be moved somewhere — hopefully home — and towards the end of June furphies were rife as to where we were going. I know that fairly early on the morning of 26 Jun a message came over the phone at C Coy to send someone out to contact the Brig, who was watching D Coy doing an attack exercise, and request his "return to Bde immediately. Stop. Immediately." That was enough to fan the furphy flames more than ever and, next day, the Padre turned up, visiting the Coys and assured everyone 2/15 Bn had already gone. "Gone where?", everyone wondered and, to complicate things the Salvo Rep called in with supplies of writing paper and a further rumour that we were returning to Australia.

"Stepper" Stephens, who had been up in Aleppo, returned to the unit and said the rumours there were that our Bde was to remain in its present position and the other Bdes were moving elsewhere. All very confusing and an OC Conference at Bn HQ confirmed Coy training programs for the next couple of weeks.

Suddenly, on Sunday, 28 June Bn HQ issued Orders to prepare to move. The actual move began on 1 July.

Everyone was instructed to remove and hide Rising Sun badges from hats and Australia badges from tunics, so that no one could be sure who we were. That Div order must have been one of the best of the World War II jokes. An Australian soldier is an Australian soldier, obvious to see, especially in large numbers.

The collection of the Bn was a piecemeal one. Maj Magno was to be OC Train and I had been given the job of entraining everyone. Together we "collected" the train at Meidan Ekbes, where some of A Coy went on board. We then moved on to Hera Dera where B Coy was entrained, and then the remainder of A Coy at Radjou further on. At Kout Kerlek the Chef du Gare told me that he was putting our train into a siding to allow the Toros express to pass through and, because it was late, we would be there for some time. I told the Major that the bastard was refusing to allow us to move on. That was the sort of situation for which Keith Magno had a natural skill in confronting and solving. A screaming tirade in Arabic, French and English ensued. There were important, paying, business men on the express and it was necessary they go past. Keith listened to this in his gentlemanly way whilst fingering the butt of the pistol on his hip and pointed out that our train was full of very important soldiers and it was to move immediately. I don't think Keith actually produced the revolver but it was pretty close. With a shrug of shoulders and palming of hand the Chef du Gare with a look of hatred, gave in and soon after we departed. The unfortunate paying passengers did the waiting.

The remainder of the Bn we picked up at Katma. We were all night on the train and passed Baalbek early afternoon next day, the temple ruins could be seen from the train, and arrived at Rayak at 1600 hrs where everyone detrained.

Rayak was the beginning of the narrow gauge rack railway to Damascus and, because of this and its limitations, the Bn was split up into three train loads. We set off as soon as the changeover had taken place and, in the afternoon after dark, the views of the mountains and the valleys from the train were magnificent. We all arrived in Damascus in our three groups, where we detrained and were given a hot meal.

Once again the Bn was re-grouped — this time into two trains. The first one contained B and C Coys and some of HQ Coy. The last one had the Carriers which were loaded onto flat cars and A Coy in store wagons. I cannot remember where D Coy was but have an idea it preceded the Bn. The last train moved off at about 0300 hrs and in the early morning arrived at Dera where it was possible to wash and shave. Soon after the train began the steep grade down the Yeroo Valley.

It was whilst the train was moving at considerable speed down this winding valley that Pte Blanch was thrown out. The makeup of the train was such that the flats with the carriers were behind the engine and then about eight to ten store wagons. I had charge of the train and was in the first wagon with some of HQ Coy and it was not until we heard the continuous yelling from the rear wagons that we realised something was wrong and only by careful hanging out of the trucks by all concerned were we made aware that the train had to be stopped. Somehow, with further yelling and hanging out from the side from our truck we caught the eye of the engine driver and indicated he had to stop the train. The degree of grade and the speed we were moving was such that it was about 2 miles before the train could be brought to a stop. It was then found what had happened. Blanch had been kneeling and lighting a primus on the floor of his wagon and as he was getting to his feet a sudden lurch toppled him over the top of the closed lower section of the double door.

It looked pretty grim for Blanch — he would have been thrown against a sheer rock face and bounced back under the train and none of us believed he could be other than severely injured.

I then demanded the engine driver reverse the train back up the line to pick him up and was met immediately with the full blast of Arab protest, complete with waiving arms. No way could it be done. No way could the engine push so much weight up the gradient in reverse. Protesting volubly, together with a fireman even more so, he refused to try. Finally after a lot of threats he agreed to drive the train further on to the next siding, five miles ahead, detach the engine and one truck and reverse back with the lighter load. Meanwhile, whilst he was carrying out this manoeuvre some of us set off up hill with a stretcher to pick up what we believed would be a very damaged body. After trudging uphill for about a mile with a great sense of relief we could see Blanch walking down the track towards us. He was very scratched and torn but otherwise all right — no bones broken, but somewhat shocked. We sat down there and then and waited for the engine to come up and collect us.

In due course it arrived with the truck, and the driver gave us the impression that he expected to be publicly thrashed and hanged by the Syrian Railway Chiefs for allowing us to force him to do all this mucking around with his train. We got on board and down we went. Eventually, the train was put together again and we moved on, arriving at Gallilee at midday, and Haifa at 1900 hrs.

A Coy unloaded immediately and joined a train which was in the station, already loaded with the rest of the Bn and which set off within the hour for the Canal.

The rest of us transhipped the Carriers and stores into a Palestine train in Haifa yards, where we had some sort of a clean up and a meal. We all got in the trucks, lay down and went to sleep.

Sometime about 0700 hrs next morning we awoke and found we were at Lydda and there we stayed until midday. This was unfortunate for some Arab water melon growers who had loaded a truck full of beautiful ripe melons on a train standing alongside us. The load was considerably reduced by the time it moved away! We were forced to leave a flat car with two of our Carriers behind at Lydda on account of an overheating axle box.

The journey continued on across the Sinai to Kantara. Once again in the middle of the night I had to stop the train by flashing a torch and putting the Carrier lights on when continuous yelling could be heard from the rear. It was a false alarm and once again the engine driver didn't think much of Australian soldiers. At 1600 hrs we arrived at Kantara and whilst our trucks were being floated across the Canal we had any amount of time to swim and clean up. The two Carriers left behind arrived at midday and everything was across the Canal by 1430 hrs. However, shunting went on and off until 2000 hrs when the guard came and demanded that the Carriers be moved to the centre of the flats. We refused to move them and he just shrugged his shoulders and walked away. By late evening, everyone was sound asleep in the trucks and remained so until 0300 hrs when an air raid awoke us and some incendiaries were dropped, with no damage to the train. By 0700 hrs we were at Ishmalia. By this time it had become our sixth day on the train, everyone had just about had enough, but we pushed on past Tel el Kebia and Zag Azig. By 1700 hrs that afternoon we were about 30 miles out of Alexandria and knew for sure that this was not the way back to Australia.

At Sidi Bishr the RTO told me that we would move on late that night. Early next morning we pulled into the station at Amiriya. There we were met by lorries waiting to take us and our stores to rejoin the Bn somewhere out along the Mersa Matruh Road. So ended our 7-day train journey.

Pte Blanch, about whom this story was initially told, survived the fall from the train, survived the battle of Alamein some months later, but lost his life tragically in New Guinea in 1943.

LAE 1943
By John "Spanky" McFarland

During the very early days of the landing at Lae the Battalion acquired the services of a native named "Penwa" who acted as a guide and supplied certain information of varying degrees of reliability and usefulness. Penwa attached himself to me at the time — I was then Assistant Adjutant and shortly afterwards posted as OC 16 Pl D Coy.

Penwa became an immediate favourite with the troops and the scrounge was on to equip him with a uniform and the necessary weapon to protect himself. Everything went well until boots were required — size was actually 12, but at last a pair of 10s was obtained and great amusement was caused when Penwa put them on the wrong feet complaining bitterly that, "Boota along feet no —— good". I might add his vocabulary was already showing the effects of tuition by 16 Pl.

Duly equipped with trousers JG, shirt JG, boots and a rifle, Penwa was settling in and becoming a most useful member of the Pl and I am quite sure his services as "bunk" builder and general useful were greatly appreciated by my batman. Penwa was most respectful and loyal and I was often amused to overhear, quite accidentally of course, conversations between him and some of the boys, baiting Penwa being a great pastime: "Mr 'Spanky' no good boss", would eminate from one of the boys, and Penwa would be quick to reply, "Mr Spanky . . . good boss you fellas along 16 Platoon no —— good".

The Lae show petering out and we received orders to embark for Finschhafen. Penwa presented a real problem. It did look like leaving him behind until someone got the bright idea that he should be brought along. Of course, I knew nothing of this intention officially and imagine my surprise when one of the troops on board the LCI who I had thought was showing a great deal of suntan turned out to be Penwa — fully equipped — gaiters, webbing, haversack (well-stocked with ki ki), rifle and about 20 rounds. "Me fight along 16 Pl help em buggerup Japan man", was the explanation of his presence.

Penwa scrambled ashore with the Pl, neck deep in water and with the LCI and its cargo receiving a good deal of attention from the beach defenders. When the Pl was finally mustered we pushed inland, having lost touch with most elements of the Bn, and when about 2,000 yards from shore we established a defensive position, it was here Penwa had his first shot at a Jap who was streaking through the kunai. He claimed a hit with a string of language more suitable for a bullock-driver than an uneducated native. Shortly after the Pl rejoined the Bn and pushed off with the rest of the Coy towards Sattelberg. 16 Pl were dropped off about halfway to form a base and hold the track open for supply etc. From this position several patrols were sent out and, resulting from one such venture, Penwa presented me with a couple of chickens which he had demanded from some poor native family. Chicken stew was indeed a luxury for the Pl.

Penwa was called to Angau HQ shortly after and was away from us for about a week. His return was rather amusing to us but not to Penwa. The Pl had been holding the Kumawa track junction and, after a rather difficult few days, was relieved by 2/15 Bn and moved to rejoin the Bn. On arrival at Bn HQ at the village of Kumawa the CO indicated to me that he would like the Pl to occupy a position on the forward edge of the village and (as we soon found out) rather close to the enemy who had a couple of LMGs apparently under nearby houses. We were busily digging in under rather uncomfortable conditions, after making a cautious approach to the position by ways of dead ground and avoiding the beaten track when, to our surprise down the track fully laden and with a toothy smile plods Penwa. Having been directed to the area where 16 Pl would be found, he approached with a loud, "Me come back along 16 Pl Boss". His statement was cut rather short by a shower of fire from the Japs and I will never forget the expression on Penwa's face which by that time was a shade of white nearing that of any of us. However, he was not daunted and brought his rifle into play, although somewhat erratically.

There followed many days of patrols particularly after we had moved to Jivevaneng and Penwa was always a willing member of anything that was on. He was a tower of strength during the "evacuation" patrols when wounded members were carried many miles over most difficult tracks. Many times I heard Penwa with a string of abuse informing the native bearers in no uncertain terms that, "This fella soldier belonga bloody best mob". No doubt penalties for careless handling were aptly described in native lingo.

The boys during this time treated Penwa really well — he got his full share of rations even down to the limited distribution of tobacco, and he likewise was always prepared to share what he had with others. I can recall rolling a few smokes out of his carefully conserved supply when without any myself. 16 Pl were to shortly bid goodbye to Penwa as he went with me when I was posted to 8 Pl, A Coy. There was, I am quite sure, genuine sorrow amongst the boys when Penwa left. "No. 8 Pl no —— good", quoted some of the boys, "You stop No. 16". Penwa's reply was, "Me go alonga Mr Mack — he boss along me". However, during the resting period prior to the push to Sio, Penwa visited 16 Pl on numerous occasions. He would often come back from a visit and say, "Why 8 Pl only got bully beef, b—— 16 Pl get nice big piece meat" — or — "16 Pl get plenty new clothes new boots, 8 Pl get only little". The truth of his observations were never really established. However, on a split up of rations, if Penwa could land the odd tin of jam for 8 Pl, he would certainly do so.

Shortly after the start of the push along the coast to Sio we were to lose Penwa. A representative of ANGAU ordered his return to that organisation. Despite long and fluent protests by Penwa and, I must admit a protest from me on the basis that he was a useful guide and interpreter, he marched out of the Bn having been with us for many weeks. During this time he had become a popular figure and at all times a willing and useful member, though quite unofficial, of 2/17 Bn.

I recall another incident. During the Lae Op when the Bn was Div reserve I was delegated to report to Div HQ as a temporary LO. The purpose was to carry any orders to the Bn should communications break down as they were frequently doing. Penwa tagged along and soon had me installed in a nicely palmed sleeping dingus in the HQ area. The following morning two strange visitors appeared at Div — a tiny native baby and a rather attractive lubra. The story was that the baby was the remaining member of a family killed by bombing and the young girl, a stray from somewhere or other, had been asked to care for the baby. Great efforts were made to have Penwa take an interest in the pair but the prospects didn't seem to appeal to him very much, or I fancy it was the prospect of having a readymade family. Penwa had a long conversation with the young girl, the details of which are known only to them. The result was that Penwa came to me and said, "Mr. Mack, you talk along big fella boss gettum Penwa holiday and take Mary along village". I asked him if he was going to stop with the Mary but he was quick to reply, "No boss, me before sun go tomorrow back along you". Things were duly arranged and off went Penwa with the Mary and the baby. He was back again looking rather tired and, to my enquiry regarding how he felt, he replied, "Me plenty tired Mr Mack. Walkem all day workem all night — plenty tired".

THE SIGNAL PLATOON — 1 PL HQ COY
By Phil Pike

In May 1940, all Specialist Platoons had similar problems in forming a team able to support or service an Infantry Battalion. We were a group of civilians thrown together under a voluntary system by choice or selection. Few of us had special expertise for our posting and it took some time for any civilian talents to be developed to meet the needs of the service. Firstly, there was a requirement for all members to reach a certain standard in basic military training common to all Infantiers.

The Sig Pl had a good mix of old and young from all walks of life with a great range of talents. The early NCOs, "Jock" Fairfax, Cyril Pincham, Norm Ife, Jack Williams, Alastair Urquhart, Billy Macmillan, all played a significant part in developing the Pl into a highly efficient operational unit which serviced the Bn with courage and distinction.

The Pl quickly developed a great spirit and mateship. Our first casualty was Johny Baker who dropped a 5-gall keg on his foot at a "Smoko" at Ingleburn. This caused him to be downgraded medically, but it did not prevent him from fighting his way back to the Bn as Pay Sgt and in the post-war years, he became foundation Secretary of the Unit Association.

The Pl did not reach full strength until we arrived in the Middle East and, by this time, Ted Scott, Angus Smith, Bob Buckley and others had been joined by the brothers, Mauri and Joe Neuss, Alf and Ernie Read, Frank Milward, Rowley Savage, "Tock" Reid, Bob Anson, Fred Camarsh, Joe Murray, "Junior" Warlock, "Bluey" Morrison, Steve Champion, "Soak" Coventry and others. Later Jimmy Lee, "Uki" Cameron, "Boy" Farrand built up a great team.

Our tour of Garrison duty at Port Said provided a great opportunity to get a taste of operational experience manning a Sig Office and communication network. It saw the formation of the Despatch Riders so well narrated by Bob Anson in "The Bloke on the Motor Bike".

There was an incident at Sherif Quay in Port Said where HQ Coy and the Sig Pl were camped in tents on the sand flats which caused the Authorities great consternation. This was the disappearance of some 280 cases of Australian beer (48 bottles per case) from a nearby wharf. Maj "Blue" Allan, who conducted a Court of Inquiry into this heinous crime, had great difficulty in naming the culprits and thus made an open finding that it was caused by "a person or persons unknown". It was interesting to note that the refrigeration qualities of cool sand under many of the Sig Pl tents was a good place to hide the loot. Of course, no inference is drawn.

Well, my close association with the Pl finished early in the Tobruk campaign, but I always look back with pride at my first command in the AIF which maintained a great record of service over 6 years of war.

Many changes took place after I left and some of the stories are told in the following anecdotes:

"THE BLOKE ON THE MOTOR BIKE"
The Best Job in the Battalion
By Bob Anson

At Port Said Egypt, 16 Dec 1940, Lt P H Pike requested 4 volunteers from his Sig Pl. The duties: To ride 4 Norton motor cycles, taken over from the Highland Light Infantry, for duty at Area HQ, Sherif Quay. Bill Bodkin, Alan Morrison, Phil Moore and Bob Anson took one pace to the front.

From 17 Dec 1940 until 9 Jan 1941, this team carried Despatches to units along the Suez Canal. This was their initiation to the best job in the Army — the Infantry Despatch Rider — or just "Don R".

Returning to Kilo 89 Palestine on 10 Jan 1941, these soldiers would not see another motor cycle until they reached the tiny coastal port of Marsa Brega, Libya on 9 Mar 1941. The motor cycles would be captured Italian Army machines the "Gilera" and "Benelli". The roads and desert tracks they would ride on would be the sealed Via Balbia, and the sandy wastes of El Agheila, Marsa Brega, Agedabia hinterland, with its marshy swamps and defiles heavily mined, subjected to the howling sand storms of the Sahara. On 21 Feb 1941, at 20 Bde Signal School, Brig John Murray gave this talk: "In this war we shall use Despatch Riders to provide speedy conveyance of messages between front line units and HQs where wireless or field telephone communication fail. We shall use you to keep mobile and armoured columns in touch. The work before you calls for resourcefulness, integrity, pride in duty and courage, because mostly you shall be on your own."

IN THE FIELD

On 10 Mar at Marsa Brega, Bill Bodkin makes the first Don R run to El Agheila some 45 km west. On 11 Mar, Bob Anson went to Agedabia and Beda Fomm. Returning along the Via Balbia on the 12th, he was greeted by a low-flying Heinkel, north of Agedabia, and survived his first experience of being machine gunned from the air. It was Bob Anson's first initiation to war and it left him a little shattered.

For the next 7 days, the Don Rs were subjected to daylight air straffing along the El Agheila-Agedabia defile, now known by transport drivers and despatch riders as "Bomb Alley Defile". The country offered very little protection, so we developed the ditching tactics of evasion, to be used later in Tobruk. This technique was not without its problems, and Don Rs became wellknown to the RMO, Capt Sullivan. However, the job had merit, it was never boring, had its little spice of excitement, and the thrill of being a 1941 "Bikie".

On 23 Mar, Lt V. Burgess, the Sig Offr, detailed his 4 Don Rs to the motorised column — Bodkin and Morrison to the advance column, Moore and Anson to the rear. The Germans were coming. They were close to the Marble Arch and were expected at El Agheila. As Don Rs, they already had contacts with Kings Dragoon Guards, Royal Horse Artillery. So began the "Benghazi Handicap", the gallop on iron horses from Marsa Brega to Tobruk.

As Don Rs they heard all sorts of rumours, and strangers were treated as hostiles. During the long desert haul of Inf soldiers in troop trucks, riding through the day and night through dust so thick, that the Don Rs had their share of troubles as they weaved to and fro with messages for their CO and other despatches to the various units during the confusion of withdrawal in front of a mobile enemy — always at their heels.

The first casualty was Bob Anson who crashed at Er Regima and broke his left foot. After treatment by the RMO at El Abiar, he mounted the "Gilera" and became the one-booted Don R to Lt Col John Crawford, CO of 2/17 Bn.

At El Abiar, Bill Bodkin was hit by an armd car and badly hurt. He was sent back to 4 AGH at Tobruk, went out on the hospital ship, was bombed, saved from drowning by the Royal Navy and rejoined the unit at the Salient sector, Tobruk, June 1941. The reserve Don R, Alan Cross was so badly injured on the Barce Pass on 5 Apr, that he was never to rejoin the unit again.

Keith "Herb" Hobbs, the lad from Wagga Wagga, volunteered to run the only spare motor cycle left into Tobruk. He set off from Barce and rode all night of 6 Apr across the desert to Guiovanni Berta, thence to Tmimi and reached Fort Pilastrino. That ride was no mean feat! Herb should have become a Don R.

The Duty Don Rs, Morrison, Moore and Anson, had a testing time — they were often on their own trying to locate units. Despatch work became a hit or miss occupation. It was not a case of "take this despatch to this unit", but "find the unit and deliver it". On 6 Apr the 2 Don Rs, Morrison and Anson, decided to keep together. They had heard numerous rumours and both became worried that they might be captured. At night real confusion existed at a desert cross road. It was becoming clear to the 2 Don Rs on the Italian "Gilera" motor cycles that they were getting mixed up with other people — "hostiles".

They headed south across the desert, arrived at 2/13 Bn lines at Martuba Oasis and rode on during the day of 7 Apr to locate 2/17 Bn at Gazala.

At Gazala on 8 Apr, both Anson and Moore reported sightings of German columns as they carried out Don R duties. On 9 Apr near Acroma, Bob Anson lost his mount. He was within 16km of Tobruk, delivering the last despatch to 20 Bde Sigs. Running into a low flying duel between a Hurricane and Messerschmitt, he wrecked the motor cycle, escaped with several abrasions, and was brought into Fort Pilastrino at dawn 10 Apr by 2/48 Bn. Moore and Morrison arrived safe and sound, and they commenced duties in Tobruk with two "Gilera" and one "Benelli" motor cycles, a gift from Maj H.T. (Blue) Allan, the BM. The "Benelli" was Phil Moore's pride and joy throughout the Seige. We never questioned how Maj "Blue" Allan "cliftied" the motor cycle. During the Easter Battle, the Don Rs hardly stopped — messages to the Bn Rifle Coys, to the support groups of 3 Royal Horse Arty, B Bty of 1 Royal Horse Arty and the tanks of 1 Royal Tank Regt. Throughout the Seige, Moore, Anson and Morrison found friends within these British Regiments, that was to carry over to Tel el Eisa in 1942. On Easter Monday, Don R, Alan Morrison, was in the hot seat as he worked to the guns and tanks. As Bob Anson was to say later, "How 'Blue' Morrison survived this day is a miracle — he reminded me of the Charge of the Light Brigade". Anson stayed on as front line Don R till 26 June. He joined Bill Bodkin at B Coy HQ's Salient sector. On 26 July, Alan Morrison joined B Coy HQ at R42 El Adem. They both stayed with the Coy until its relief by 1 Bn Essex Regt on 21 Oct. Throughout the Seige, Phil Moore remained as Bn HQ Don R, and in the latter months of the Seige was relieved by Sam Ducroe.

SYRIA JAN-JUNE 1942

At Bn HQ Latakia, Syria 31 Mar 1942, the CO, Lt Col N W Simpson, signed, sealed and issued Moore, Morrison and Anson with their Army motor cycle licence — they had become Specialists.

In Syria, the Don Rs had the best job in the Bn, no guard duties — they were on duty at all times. Their duties saw them ride long, lonely distances over beautiful country, up and down, across the steppes and mountains that bordered Syria from Turkey. Their diary entries showed the names of places, such as Meidan Ekbes, Azaz, Radju, El Hamman Killis, Katma, Sanju, Kanfra through the Jebel Siman and the Kurd Dagh. They delivered and received Despatches. No hosties were encountered and the job was a "Cooks Tour" on Army Pay, in a pleasant, lovely country that was a tough battle ground for 7 Div the previous year as they fought the Vichi French.

On 18 Apr the good life ended. The motor cycle blokes, on the orders of their Sig Offr, Lt Burgess (maybe from higher up), took to "Shank's pony" and marched the 100 miles from Latakia to Tripoli.

En Route they passed the Castle of the Krak des Chevaliers, a great fortress built by the Crusaders in the 12th Century. Four days later, at Mt Tourbal, Morrison and Anson collected the "Nortons" and started the Don R duties again, visiting such places as Tripoli, Beit Haoutte, Zaboud, Homs, Alma, El Mina, Becharre. The tracks on the Tourbal were terrible, only fit for goats and Cypriot mules and many falls were experienced. Finally Anson crashed near Madjilaya on 1 June and his injuries kept him away from the unit until 23 June. At Azaz resumption of Don R duties was undertaken on 25 June, with a final Despatch to Meidan Ekbes on the border. On 1 July, Morrison and Anson left Afrine on their Nortons for Baalbek, Metulla, Tiberius, Beersheba and crossed the Sinai. On 4 July they ran into the Cairo-Alexandria traffic jam, and finally reached Tel el Shammana some 5 miles east of El Alamein at 2200 hrs on 5 July. The Afrika Korp was almost in the Alexandria doorway. From 9 July, Phil Moore, Alan Morrison, Ewen (Ukie) Cameron and Bob Anson were issued new BSA motor cycles. That evening Anson commenced the Don R runs with a special despatch to 2/3 Fld Coy Engrs, 11 Bty 4 Lt A/A Regt, 1 Pl B Coy 2/2 MG Bn, 57 Bty 2/7 Fd Arty Regt and 2/3 A/Tk Regt. Work at El Alamein had started. On 10 July, Don R contacts and dispositions were logged with 2/15 Bn, 20 Bde HQ, Mobile Section 2/8 Fld Amb, 58 LAD 10 Coy AASC.

So was the life of the Don R throughout July. Moore was sent for a spell to Sig Reserve, and Morrison went to special Sig duty at the Sig Office. Throughout the Bn's long tour of front-line service at Tel el Eisa, "Ukie" Cameron and Anson carried out the daily Don R tasks, to the forward Coys and support groups. On 18 Aug at Tel el Eisa, Anson was wounded and did not rejoin the unit until just prior to the El Alamein Battle. He was sent to B Coy as a Signaller.

Moore was wounded at El Alamein, and Ewen Cameron was killed. Don R duties with 2/17 Bn ceased at Alamein in October 1942.

Throughout the 2 years of Active Service in Libya, Syria, Egypt, "the blokes on the motor bikes", as one C Coy rifleman called them, exhibited all those qualities stressed by their Brigadier at Kilo 89 Palestine, February 1941.

BENGHAZI 21 MAR 41

Bill Bodkin, one of our Don Rs, tells his story;

He badly injured his right arm and leg on the Regima Escarpment and was moved by Fd Amb back to Tobruk Hospital to await evacuation to Alexandria.

Just before Easter we had a big air raid. The Germans used screaming bombs and the noise of our AA was terrific. At 1700 hrs the next night, 6 dive bombers hit the hospital — Wards 9, 10 and 11, causing many casualties. The poor devils never had a chance! The explosions were terrific.

The bombing went on night and day but on Easter Monday the bombing ceased. 2/17 Bn had gone into action for the first time and had given a wonderful account of themselves. The hospital ship arrived at 1500 hrs and the loading of sick and wounded started — a precarious process — and the lighter was bombed on her way out. She finished loading at 1700 hrs and then we started on what turned out to be our worst experience. We cleared Tobruk Harbour and were about 2 hrs' sailing time from Tobruk, when Hell let loose from the skies. At tea time the first bomb struck. There were 8 dive bombers. The first bomb hit the stern with a terrific scream, followed by more. I was thrown to the floor. Then the Hurricanes were amongst the Jerries. Then 2 destroyers were alongside, and one took us in tow. I pay special credit to the nursing sisters who showed wonderful skill and courage.

At 2200 hrs the ship started to list badly on the starboard side and we were ordered to abandon ship. It was some job as the sea was choppy. Then 464 wounded men and crew were transferred. We were cramped, very stuffy, making many sick.

The next day we reached Alexandria. Ambulances met us at the wharf and I was moved to the Naval Hospital, away from the Hell on Earth at Tobruk. I didn't know it then, but I was to be back in Tobruk within a month.

I had lost my paybook on the gallop back, but was able to draw 50 piastres. Next by train to Cairo, to 15 Scottish General Hospital on the banks of the Nile. Then a bit of leave in Cairo. Left by train for Gaza and arrived at 20 ITB (Mughazi/Nuiseratt).

Back to Egypt, passing through El Amiriya and an air raid over Alexandria. Route marches and a little training. Another mate and I had 30 piastres between us and we gave it a go at the two-up school and came out with 7 pounds.

Then by destroyer back to Tobruk — a peaceful trip this time. To the staging camp (in the wadi at Tobruk) and then back to the unit. Then my paybook turned up!

SOME JOTTINGS FROM BOB ANSON'S DIARY

22 OCT 1941 — LAST DAY IN TOBRUK — Allan Morrison, Bruce Latter and I accompany Fred Camarsh, Bob Buckley, Herb Hobbs and Jack Allsop to the War Cemetery. We marched down the road to the foot of the escarpment, and wended our way through the rows of graves, some are not yet completed, some are mounds of stones. Many of the 2/17 Bn's graves are covered with white tiles. We pause a while at Jack Edmondson's grave, a simple white cross with "VC" inscribed. We pause also at the grave of Frank Clark, DCM, MM and also Lance Allsop's grave and many others we know. The words inscribed on the plain memorial at the entrance were in keeping with what we felt, as we pay homage to our fallen mates:

This is hallowed ground;
for here lie those who died
for their country.

On the way back, we can hear the rumble of the gun fire up the front.

WE CROSS A PORTION OF THE DEVIL'S GARDENS

On 6 Nov 1942, as Capt Colin Pitman led the remnants of B Coy over the small ridge of Pt 29, a hell of a place, we still had to cross a bit of random mixtures of booby traps, and anti-personnel mines. They were zones created to kill man at any mistake he made.

Terrified of mines, I trudged along, as though I was treading on hot bricks. It was a cloudy day, and the beastly boxes of death were everywhere. Some numbers of dead lay in the Gardens of the Devil as we called them.

Wherever Colin placed his feet so did I, and Geoff Parry placed his steps in mine. We intended to survive. Eventually we crossed the field, moved over the Mersa Matruh Railway Line and headed for our rest bivouac on the coast. Capt Pitman had taken us through a fiery period of some 12 days. As I settle down to a good long sleep, aircraft drone overhead. Heavy rain falls — the first rain I have seen in the Western Desert and, with the feeling of relief that I made it, I opt for sleep.

On 9 Nov, Capt Colin Pitman, Fred Camarsh, Colin Ikin, Colin O'Donnell and Geoff Perry visit Thompson's Post. I fiddle about with the wireless — 8 Army at Barrani and Sollum, 7 British Armour Div near Sollum, New Zealand Div at Barrani, 51 Highland Div at Fuka. We watch the first supply train transport moving west toward Mersa Matruh.

At this time, I reflected on the past 14 days, as related to Sig duties at B Coy HQ. Eric Vincent, our trained wireless operator, was badly wounded in the first hour of the Battle, and George Henderson an ex 2/4 Bn veteran, had recently joined the Sig Pl. He, like I, had missed the lead up Battle exercises. Therefore, after Eric left a gap in our ranks, the two of us could never cope with the load of maintaining communications at all times. Ross Jamieson, our runner, was killed at Pt 29 on 28 Oct.

When George Henderson was wounded on 29 Oct and died at the MDS, Signaller replacements were nil. We lost 7 KIA and 19 wounded and three of these were to receive their second wounding. 10 Signallers survived the action. Statistically, we had 72% casualties.

Were it not for the help given me by the Coy Comd from the night of the 29 Oct to 3 Nov in looking after phone communications, and allowing me to get some rest, then possibly I too may have been on that statistical list. It was great to be with B Coy throughout the action. Thanks to Colin Pitman and Hugh Main.

THE MACHINE GUN PLATOON — 2 Pl HQ Coy
ALAMEIN — 1942
By John Cortis DCM

An instruction was issued in August 1942 that all Infantry Battalions would raise a MG Pl consisting of 2 Sections each with 2 Vickers guns.

2/2 MG Bn conducted a weapon training school which I attended together with Harry Tasker and other NCOs from the Division. The personnel were recruited from rifle coys and Stan Yeend was appointed in October as Pl Comd.

The training of the Pl prior to 23 Oct was very intense but all members knew their jobs prior to the battle.

On the night of the attack the Pl moved forward on foot with the guns and ammo loaded on trucks and we had no casualties. The second night was the same procedure until the attack was held up by heavy MG fire and the whole scene was brightly illuminated by an a/tk gun which was on fire. Our guns were quickly unloaded and put into action and were most effective silencing most of the enemy guns, enabling the position to be consolidated. Our Sec moved forward through D Coy and dug in and the other Sec remained with B Coy.

We were kept pretty busy from then on and one Sec fired about 20,000 rounds per gun. Our worthy driver brought ammunition supplies and new barrels up the following night which was a mighty job. We stayed in this area until after Black Sunday and the guns were on continuous action.

I was grounded a couple of days later and took no further part in the action. Later, I was sent to OCTU, commissioned and posted to 36 Bn to serve out the rest of the War in New Guinea and New Britain

NEW GUINEA — BORNEO — 1943
By Darrell Luck

The Platoon embarked at Townsville on a liberty ship and were taken to Milne Bay which had recently been the scene of some heavy fighting by 18 Bde. For us it was to be just a starting point for some landings further up the north coast of New Guinea.

We did a bit of real jungle training here and, as I remember, it seemed to rain just about the whole time we were there. Tommy Richardson would keep us amused as he became self-appointed quiz master much in the style of Tony Barber. Many an hour was whiled away in this fashion, the only restriction being, of course, Tommy had to know the answer to his questions.

We moved from Milne Bay to Buna then by LCI for the landing at Lae at 0630 hrs on 4 Sept 1943.

We were in the first wave and got ashore safely without opposition. The second wave followed us in and had no sooner hit the beach and in came the Jap bombers. It felt quite strange seeing the red disc under the wings instead of the black crosses. They scored a direct hit on one LCI and killed quite a few but they were not from our Bn. We gathered into our formations and set off towards Lae until we got to the Buso River. This presented quite an obstacle as it was deep and flowing very swiftly. We had already heard furfies that some chaps had been washed out to sea and drowned, and with all our equipment it was going to be difficult to cross. Bruce Brown volunteered to swim it with a rope tied around his waist which he did by entering the stream some 200yds up from where we wanted to cross. He was a strong swimmer and made it about the spot we wanted and tied the rope to a tree on the opposite side to us and the rest of us pulled ourselves across by hanging on to the rope.

Our next port of call was to be Finschhafen and that was to prove to be a very different kettle of fish. We once again embarked on LCI near the mouth of the Burep River on the evening of 21 Sept for a dawn landing at Scarlet Beach.

The landing at Scarlet Beach took place at 0430 hrs proceeded by a naval bombardment by American warships. As we approached, it became evident by onshore flashes that this was going to be an opposed landing.

Our LCI veered away from the beach to the east and ran ashore against some coral outcrops. As we approached we could see the water we had to wade through to get ashore was being churned up by enemy MG fire.

Bob Reay led us off on the right hand side gangway followed by myself and Col Martin, my No 2, and the rest of the Sec behind. Bob and I made it to the coral and clambered up but Col Martin had been hit by a burst of MG fire with 3 bullets passing through his hips from left to right. He was dragged ashore and made as comfortable as possible. It was pitch dark while all this was going on. We assembled on shore and Bob Reay told Bruce Brown and myself to move forward in front of the Pl and keep a lookout. I don't know about Brownie, but I was a little nervous about this as I couldn't see my hand in front of me but believe me I was listening very carefully.

We now moved eastward along the coast to the region of Heldsbach and one day, while occupying a position and not very well dug in, we came under very heavy fire from 3" mortars. As you will no doubt all agree a mortar barrage is not very pleasant as you can hear the plop as it starts its journey and you can hear it descending and the closer it gets the louder its whistle becomes and you swear it is coming straight for you. The slit trench I was in was about 1ft deep and 6ft long, half covered by logs and dirt at one end. While I was deciding which half of me to put under the covered end I heard someone yelling and knew one of us had been hit. I poked my head out with no great enthusiasm and saw Dagwood Osborn by Tommy Richardson's slit trench and Roy Roach was running to the rear to get a stretcher. Tommy had been badly hit in the legs. Roy came back with a stretcher and a bearer and Tommy was taken out but they were not able to save his leg.

After this it was decided that we would move inland and we proceeded into the mountains up Easy Street. This track seemed to go on forever and, of course, the loads we were carrying didn't help. Besides the normal gear a soldier carries, in our case the Vickers Tripod, weighed 60lb, the gun 40lb, a 2-gall can of water and each box of ammo weighed 28lb. However, we finally reached a fork in the track just below Kumawa and it was decided we should form a perimeter there for the night.

At this time half the MG Pl was attached to D Coy who sent out a patrol to scout the area and they reported back that there were signs of Japanese down the eastern fork of the tracks. Booby traps were set up and a Vickers gun mounted facing down the track. Just before dawn a booby trap went off which alerted us all and soon after the Japs attacked with MG and rifle fire. In the first onslaught Barry Carr-Boyd our NCO was killed. Bluey Fathers, No 2 on the Vickers, was shot through the hand and arm and Norm Capewell received a head wound. Lt Tom Cooper was shot through the jaw, the bullet going in one side and out the other. This left Bill Carpenter alone in the gun pit without assistance but he managed to keep the gun firing. I could hear Dagwood Osborn yelling out to Ken Pratt to come to Bill's assistance but every time "Prattie" attempted to move he would be pinned down by enemy fire. Things looked a bit grim at that end of the perimeter and as there was nothing doing my end I ran down the track and hopped in beside Bill; of course Barry Carr-Boyd was beyond help. We now seemed to have the Japs pinned down as their fire was becoming more sporadic but during the morning they made several attempts to lob grenades into the gun pit in order to silence the Vickers which was the main obstacle in their path but they were not successful, although some landed very close. About 1500 hrs things had been quiet for some time and I said to Bill, "Let's open a tin of bully beef". (We hadn't eaten all day). I picked up a tin from the bottom of the pit and while attempting to open it, a Jap sniper put a bullet through my hair. We forgot the bully and Bill fired a burst in the general direction. Soon after this, Pancho Rose from D Coy circled around through the jungle behind the Japs and shot one or two with his Owen gun, hopefully the sniper. All was quiet again and we all spent a restless night. It was raining by now and we took turns at trying to get a bit of sleep, just lying down in the mud and water. Next morning a patrol went out and discovered the Japs had pulled out, but a few bodies were left behind. Bill Carpenter was recommended for, and received, a MM for his part in the battle. He was the one who kept on firing while alone and under difficult conditions and was probably the main reason the attack was halted.

We now made our way across country to Jivenaneng to join up with the rest of the Bn. A couple of days later we were given the task of firing all 4 Vickers guns on suspected Jap positions. These positions were at extreme range so observation of any strike was a bit haphazard. On completion of the shoot I made the remark, "I don't know if we hit anything or not but I bet the Japs now have our position pretty well pin-pointed". The next day it happened sure enough a Jap mountain gun and 2" mortars zeroed in on our position with great accuracy. The mountain gun shells were hitting the trees above us and exploding, sending showers of shrapnel among us and, of course, into the pits as usual. In the pit next to mine I saw Derek Cunningham jump out of his pit and more or less straight into the blast of an exploding shell. Derek jumped back into his pit rather gingerly, I thought, and I then saw him toss something out. It seems that a 2" mortar bomb had hit him a glancing blow on the shoulder and landed on its side at his feet without exploding. Hence the sudden evacuation and the sudden realisation that the exploding shells were more dangerous than the unexploded mortar bomb; hence his re-entry to the pit and the tossing out of the unexploded bomb. Soon after this I felt a thump in my back and started bleeding, so I knew I had been hit but it didn't seem too bad. When things quietened down I went down to the RMO, Snow Hughes, and he told me to go down to CCS with a few other walking wounded including Col Brown. And, believe it or not, 15 minutes after we went down the track it was cut by the Japs and the Bn was surrounded. From here on I can only give a second-hand account of what happened as I was no longer with the unit. Later that day, Harry Tasker, our Sgt, was killed. In the following days, the Vickers gun was used in an attempt to break the deadlock and it was used in a rather unorthodox fashion. Under covering fire from a rifle coy they had to run and carry their equipment to a pre-selected spot, mount the gun and try to knock out a Woodpecker that was causing us some embarrassment. The main actors I believe were Don Osborn, Bruce Brown, Roy Roach and Dave Hall and it was all done under fire from the Woodpecker. I believe they did the job successfully to the extent that soon after the Japs moved out of their positions to a safe climate, if there was such a thing.

THE ATHERTON TABLELANDS — RAVENSHOE

After leave the Bn was sent to Ravenshoe for further jungle training. A lot of the members of MG Pl were no longer with us due to many things — killed, wounded, sickness (mainly Malaria). Some were classified B class and some were demobbed. Consequently, we had a big influx of reinforcements, some very young. We were to stay at Ravenshoe for over 12 months, the longest time in one place throughout the War. Training became very repetitive. A lot of sport was played which helped break the monotony. Mainly football, some cricket. It kept us fit and produced some fine sportsmen. Inter-Pl, Coy and Bn football was played — all with great enthusiasm. At night there was two-up run by Jack Shepherd and Darby Green, and Bob Melon would always take an SP bet. And if you got sick of that you could bank on someone suggesting a party which was actually a booze-up. Pat Larkin and Col Brown were great party starters. Not always to everyone's delight and, because it would always take place in someone's tent, you either had to join in or put up with a lot of drunks all night. Pat Larkin could get a bit pugnacious when drunk. One night he produced a tomahawk and started cutting the legs off the bunks of anyone he found trying to sleep. Another night, Jack Littlewood was needling a 6 Div Sgt and Pat hopped in to help and promptly got flattened. Another night, Doug Vickers, our Lieut, poked his head in a tent and Joe Flannagan clocked him, not realising who it was. Doug was a good sport and treated it as an occupational hazard.

Of course, there were also some good things like the cans of local chilled milk nearly every day for 3d a mug. Also Cairns beer from kegs in tin mugs which didn't do much for the taste, but beer was beer and went down well. Corn grown by local farmers was dished up to us daily until everyone was crowing and cackling like chooks every time mess parade came around.

Everyone was looking forward to leave at Christmas 1944. The furfies said we were going to get it but it didn't eventuate. This caused a lot of discontent among the troops. Without being melodramatic, we had all joined up to fight and all we were doing was sitting on our backsides. One consolation in the summer was a beautiful swimming hole nearby. Crystal clear water surrounded by cliffs on one side and trees on the other. Many pleasant hours were spent there. All things end and in May 1945 we were transported to Townsville and embarked on ships ending up at Morotai.

BORNEO
(Written with the help of Aub McMillan)

We embarked on *Kanimbla* at Morotai bound for Borneo. A nice ship, good food and an uneventful voyage for most. Not for me. My bunk was a top bunk as it turned out directly underneath her rear 6" gun. Lying on my bunk reading a book one day they fired the gun. The noise was indescribable, reverberating through the steel deck. I thought we had been torpedoed and with my life jacket in my hand I was off and reached the open deck in what must have been record time, only to find the deck littered with bods playing cards, dozing and lounging unconcernedly. As no one was taking any notice of me I tried to look calm and watched them fire the next practice shot.

On 10 June 1945 *Kanimbla* arrived off Brunei. Plenty of naval and air support and at 0918 hrs the Battalion landed on Green Beach against little or no opposition.

The first action for the MG Pl was when Pat Larkin shot up the Jap truck. The truck came along the road towards our position with headlights on. Jack Littlewood in charge of the gun told Pat to fire a burst over it. Pat had other ideas and fired a burst into the cabin, killing the driver and most of the occupants. The truck was bringing up a gun and the Jap officer either didn't know the enemy was there or tried to bluff his way through with lights on. Pat souvenired the Jap officer's sword.

We arrived at Seria and the oil wells which the Japs had set alight. It was an awesome sight — flames going hundreds of feet into the air and they turned night into day. It took many weeks to put them out, in fact, some were still burning months later. Opposition to our advance had been practically non-existent. There was the occasional sniper who had to be dealt with and also they buried metallic objects at intervals on the road which slowed down the advance while the engineers cleared these objects and sometimes there would be a real mine amongst them.

On one occasion, difficulty was experienced in dislodging some Japs dug in on a ridge. We were with D Coy at this stage. Markers were put out for the Air Force to distinguish our positions. However, the planes came in at the wrong angle and, although they dropped the bombs on the Japs, some of them bounced into our position exploding amongst our men causing a few nose bleeds but no major casualties. The Air Strike was called off.

From Seria we moved to Kuala Belait. Not much resistance, a sniper now and then. Around here the fields were full of sweet potatoes which made a welcome change to our diet. From here some of MG Pl accompanied a rifle coy on a deep patrol up the Baram River by boat to Marudi. At night we would land and form a defensive perimeter, and a probing patrol would scout the area for signs of any Japs.One of these patrols brought in a native who had a huge gash in the back of his neck. The Jap who had tried to behead him must have been in a hurry not to have finished the job.

On 15 Aug 1945 the War ended. We were still at Marudi and we were hoping the Japs also knew it was over. When the War ended the Bn assembled at Kuala Belait to await transport home. The time was spent mainly by participating in sporting events, mainly football. This was played almost daily even though we were sitting on the Equator. From here some of the lads joined the BCOF. The only one I know from MG Pl who joined and really went was Ray Mathews.

MORTAR PLATOON — 3 Pl HQ COY
By Lance O'Dea

The Platoon was formed in May 1940 initially from ex-Militia volunteers from country and city:

Lt Ted Chapman, 45 Bn; Sgts Stan Giersch, 17 Bn; Lance O'Dea, 4 Bn; Cpls Don Perkins, 4 Bn; "Paddles" Whitelaw with a big bunch of "South of the Border" lads from the Tweed River Bn — Joe and Herbie Chapman, Charlie Crompton, Ted McQuilty and Fred Dryley; and Terry George, Bill Forster, "Honest" Jim Harney, Ticci Rodgers and Johnny Garner from civvy street.

The march to Bathurst completed, the unifying process began with their competitive efforts to equal, or better, the other HQ Coy platoons, especially the "Mug Gunners" in the Carriers.

Obviously, a small platoon, being but 2 detachments, they eventually finished as 8 detachments, despite the dire warnings of the old World War I soldiers. The growth followed their usefulness in the mobile nature of warfare in the desert as distinct from, the static nature of the Great War. Tobruk, our first engagement, was in defence but a far from useless application of this infantry weapon under direct control of the Coy Comd. Its mobility and high trajectory made it even more so in the islands of the Pacific. It remains in my memory as a "lucky" platoon as we made it back into Tobruk despite running out of fuel in the wilderness behind Derna, then, just before our destination, a burnt-out clutch. Also a very high percentage of those listed above made it back to civvy street.

EMBARKING FROM LAE
By Ray Havenstein

Having finished the Lae Campaign, the Battalion withdrew to a beach area north of Lae, to refit and rest for the coming Finschhafen Campaign.

On the day of embarking, we moved onto the beach where our transport, the LCIs and the LSTs, were anchored in the bay. Just prior to embarking, approximately 10 Jap bombers came over the bay bombing the transport as they went. All the troops on the beach headed for the cover of the jungle. Frank Soden found an unoccupied slit trench and dived in only to find that it was a latrine partly filled in. The result was that Frank ended up half submerged in its contents. Having only the clothes he wore, he made for the river for a good scrub up. Fortunately, Kevin Stewart produced a tin of baby powder to save the day.

LANDING AT FINSCHHAFEN

We were in the second wave coming in to make the landing at Finschhafen. The American skipper of our LCI could not see the beach because it was still dark and we heard him call out, "Where is the beach?", and the next thing we knew we were upon the rocks at the eastern end of the beach. Disembarking as best we could, we were met by Jap MG fire coming from a bunker above the beach some 200yds away. Being in the second wave, we were not impressed. Two of our boys were hit — Darky Kearney and Ted McQuilty. Colonel Simpson was standing amid a stream of tracers telling us to keep moving as we weren't in George Street. As we got to the beach the first wave was landing. The American gunners on the front of the LCIs decided to help by firing their 20mm guns into the Japs' bunkers in the coconut grove above the beach. I was with Tom Clarke and Snow Lawler at the bottom of the embankment, having to wait for the American gunners to finish but before they did they chopped off the top of a coconut palm which fell across Snow Lawler pinning him down. Tom and I pulled the palm from him, not before the green ants from the palm began attacking him in their hundreds.

The last we saw of Snow he was getting out of his clothes as he headed for the water!

MORTAR PATROL AT JIVENANENG VILLAGE

Lt Tom Swan received orders from Colonel Simpson that Sgt Havenstein was to take a patrol of 5 men and clear the Japs from their position in front of Bn HQ. The patrol was to consist of Cpl McHugh, Ptes Rex Burns, Charles Crompton, John Stallworthy and Scrappy Carroll. We set out along the track with Scrappy as our drag man and came onto the Jap position which was unoccupied, much to our relief. So we moved on down the track to a junction of the main track coming from Sattelberg to the beach. We set up a defensive position and sent Cpl McHugh back to Bn to report that the position was clear. The Colonel then ordered the patrol back to its platoon.

On the way back we found fresh Jap foot prints causing much concern. Reaching our position with Scrappy coming in last, we discovered he was wearing a pair of Jap sneakers. He was anything but popular and received much abuse from the rest of the patrol.

ANTI-TANK PLATOON — 4 Pl HQ Coy
By Stuart Williams

In June 1942 it was rumoured that the AIF Infantry Battalions were to be armed with 2-pdr a/tk guns. Lt S.M. Williams and Sgt T. George were sent from Syria to an A/Tk Gunnery School in Egypt. The British officers had fought against German armour and they made sure that the lessons learnt by them were understood. Ptes R.J. Wells and L. Barber also went to a school to learn the skills of Artificer and Technical Storeman respectively.

Meantime, 9 Div were in action in the general area of Tel el Eisa and 2/17 Bn was in reserve. Orders were given detailing the organisation of the Pl and its training. There was a certain sense of urgency.

On 21 July, 9 personnel from 2/3 A/Tk Regt joined the Bn. Personnel from the Coys to form the Pl were obviously hand-picked by Maj Balfe. Two 2-pdr guns and two porter vehicles were received. The condition of the guns necessitated the first of many visits to a very helpful workshop unit.

The third gun must have been received in late July, the fourth and fifth guns were received in August and the sixth arrived on 6 Sept. The seventh and eighth guns were received later in September.

The three months leading up to the Battle of Alamein were hectic. Gun drill — and more gun drill — crew training, a/tk tactics, range firing and more gun drill. We were indebted to Maj George Copeland for his interest in our problems. Sgt Jim Fletcher and the other men from 2/3 A/Tk Regt reinforced the theory of correct siting, camouflaging and tactical use of the guns by explaining what to expect if the jobs were not done correctly.

On 10 Sept, Capt E.M. McCulloch became OC of the A/Tk Pl. The same day, Lt R.J. Dick joined the Pl and he and Lt S.M. Williams were each in charge of a Sec of four guns.

The Pl strength was a follows:

Pl HQ: OC, Captain, WO II, Artificer, Technical Storeman, MT Mechanic, 2 Despatch Riders, Batman, Cook.

EACH SECTION: Led by a Lieutenant with a Batman/Orderly, 4 Gun Crews, each led by a Sergeant.

Capt C.H. Wilson took over command of the Pl from Capt McCulloch towards the end of September. The standard of training was excellent but new crews had to be formed and the incoming personnel trained — gun drill, camouflage and tactics had to be mastered by all ranks as second nature.

The portee was a 4-wheel drive truck designed to transport the guns, crews, ammunition and other equipment. The drivers were proud of their reliable vehicles — just as their gun crews were proud of their "chauffeurs", though such respect was not always obvious.

On taking up new positions, the crews, ammunition, stores all had to be dug in, as well as the gun and it was always a race to get all finished and camouflaged before first light. On no account, during daylight hours, was a gun to be stripped of its camouflage or manned by its crew until the enemy tanks reached our FDLs.

Up to the Battle of Alamein we had no casualties from enemy action. The only unusual activity was that one gun moved with C Coy in their role as Link Coy with 2/15 Bn during the Bulimba raid.

The threat of air attack was always present. Shelling was a problem but the Rifle Coys got more than their fair share.

Our only personal transport at Pl HQ was the BSA motor cycle of the despatch rider. Sgts Jack Asquith and Jim Fletcher both said that the BSA was difficult to extract from bomb craters.

An a/tk firing range was located in 9 Div HQ area. Our visit to the range was on the same day that Mr. Churchill was there. Sgt Jim Fletcher said our crews did very well in both gun drill and shooting.

The build-up of the 8th Army, the planning and preparation for the Battle of Alamein are history. Our fellows under the guidance of Sgts Jim Fletcher and Terry George were well prepared for the job to hand.

Lt Jim Dick was disappointed to be LOB and WOII Jim Fletcher took over Comd of his Sec of 4 guns.

Space would not permit details of the actions of the various gun crews during the battle, even if they could be recalled. The general Pl story is as follows:

On the night 23/24 Oct, the Pl moved with the other A Echelon vehicles along the centre line of the advance with the din of the mighty barrage — each vehicle in the wheel tracks of, and at the ordered distance behind, the vehicle ahead.

During the advance the motor cycle of Pte Carl Lane exploded an a/tk mine, and he and our mechanic, MT Pte Bill Jordon, died from their wounds and Ptes Jack Wells and Stan Edwards were wounded. Capt Wilson decided to send the other motor cycle back to B Echelon.

Our portees were well loaded during the battle. As well as their usual crew and equipment, they carried reserve 2-pdr rounds and a reserve of SAA and grenades. In addition, the Pl Comd, Pl HQ personnel and the two Sec leaders were allocated to various portees.

The guns were deployed to the various Rifle Coys in accordance with our orders, guns were sited, dug in and camouflaged. A very busy night followed by a very watchful day.

On the night 24/25 Oct, while moving forward with A Echelon vehicles, the portee of Sgt Dick Gautby's gun caught fire. Lt Keith Sabine uncoupled the gun which was being towed. The fire attracted a lot of shellfire from the enemy. After some delay the guns were again sited and dug in.

That afternoon, the enemy mounted a counter-attack with tanks and infantry on our Bde front. The attack was beaten off with heavy loss — 18 tanks were knocked out, mainly by the 6-pdr guns of 2/3 A/Tk Regt. Our 2-pdr guns did not fire a shot as the enemy tanks did not reach our FDLs. During the action, Pte L E Alexander was killed, and Capt Wilson, WOII Jim Fletcher and Sgt "Stepper" Stephens were wounded.

On the night 25/26 Oct, we were to take over positions from 2/48 Bn. As our vehicles moved forward, four trucks carrying ammunition for 2/48 Bn blew up. The "fireworks display" was bombed, and arty, mortar and small arms fire was very heavy. None of our vehicles was hit and we finally got around the problem area and were led to B Coy area. There were no 6-pdr guns of 2/3 Regt in the area. They had lost one gun in the bombing and their casualties in the previous day's action were heavy. By this time, it was obvious that the crews would have little time to get dug in before daylight, so the guns were dug in where they were. They must have worked like demons to get settled in by first light.

We put in a most unpleasant day, with German tanks harassing us from a distance, and shelling and MG fire were very heavy. One of our 2-pdr guns was knocked out by a shell from a Mark 4 tank. Pte R Reading was killed and Pte A H Hume was wounded.

On the night 26/27 Oct, the 6-pdr guns from 2/3 A/Tk Regt came forward and our guns were re-positioned to link with them. The following day was just as unpleasant. Orders came through that on the night 27/28 Oct we were to take over the position of 2/48 Bn at Trig 29 area. A reconnaissance group went to 2/48 Bn HQ in the afternoon, arriving just as 2/48 Bn and our C and D Coys came under attack by tanks and infantry. The enemy were beaten off and the situation eased by 1800 hrs.

Our positions were taken over by the Seaforth Highlanders. Further enemy attacks on 2/48 Bn at night held us up — the changeover was at 0200 hrs. No great problems as the gun crews did not have to dig new posts. As on the previous day (and on subsequent days also) tank and infantry attacks were mounted in this area by the enemy but our arty concentrations, MMGs and mortars did not let them get to our FDLs. The enemy MG, mortar fire and shelling by arty and tanks were constant reminders that we were considered to be trespassing. We were lucky that we had air superiority and that the Air Force and Navy had kept the enemy short of shells for their medium and heavy arty.

On the night 28/29 Oct, 2/15 Bn attacked to the north from our area and one of our 2-pdrs was moved to C Coy who were to be a link Coy with 2/15 Bn.

From 30 Oct to 5 Nov, we did not move our guns. As from 2 Nov, after the Durham Light Infantry and the Maori Bn put in their attack, the constant Spandau fire ceased to be the bane of our days and nights. Arty and tank shelling still continued.

By 5 Nov, the enemy had pulled back from the battle area. The lines of 8th Army motor vehicles in close convoy just went on and on — with dimmed lights at night!

On 6 Nov, 2/17 Bn moved to rest area "B" near the coast. One wag (it might have been one of the Hillier brothers) said that Rommel had only pulled out to get away from the soaking rain!

Lt R.J. Dick returned from LOB, and Capt C H Wilson resumed Comd of the Pl on 14 Nov. 2/17 Bn, after rest and training, moved by road convoy to a camp at Julis in Palestine.

Reorganisation, training, leave and the parade of 9 Div before Gen Alexander were the substance of our stay at Julis before the move to Port Tewfik for the voyage back to Australia.

Members of the Pl will remember our mascot, Stuka, who guarded our area from raids by the Arabs on our rifles and other gear. All pets had to be left in the Middle East, but somehow or other she managed to get to Port Tewfik where a good home was found for her with a British unit. We were sorry to lose her.

The gun crews were not happy to be leaving their 2-pdr guns with which they had worked so constantly. However, we were headed for home!

NEW GUINEA 1943
Some Extracts from Les Barber's Notes

The Pl was re-formed in the Tablelands in July 1943 with many new faces as only 11 of the old crew were still with us. The new Pl Comd was Jim Dick, but Sgts Terry George and Bob Askildsen were still with us. After plenty of Jungle Training, range practice and manoeuvres we joined up with the rest of the Bn at Milne Bay and landed at Red Beach west of Lae on 4 Sept.

We left our guns at the beach head and followed along the coast towards Lae, when near Bn HQ we copped a mortar attack and one of our blokes, R. Oxman, was wounded. 7 Div beat us to the punch to occupy Lae, so we moved back along the coast to get ready for our next job. We did not have long to wait as we were soon re-embarked and on the way to Scarlet Beach at Finschhafen where we landed on 22 Sept.

Once again we left 2 guns and crews at the beach head while many of the Pl carried on in a patrolling role. We soon became known as the Tea, Biscuit and Ammo unit, as we protected carrying parties for the forward Coys, using Fuzzy Wuzzy carriers and PIB scouts in our resupply missions. It was in this constant patrolling that we put into practice the bush lore that "Kanga" Gillespie had coached us in during our training periods.

After Finschhafen fell, the Bn took its turn to take the lead on the coastal move to Sio. After Lt Jim Dick was wounded, Lt Bob Moran took over and led the Pl until the end of the Borneo Campaign. The Pl was split into 2 parties, one going along the coastal track and the other moving inland as a flank guard. This group was glad to have the PIB scouts with them as they struck a number of Jap stragglers which were dealt with very quickly.

Finally, we ended up at Sio at the end of a taxing campaign, having many medical casualties and 5 blokes wounded.

BORNEO 1945

Once again with 2 guns and many new faces in the Pl, we set off on *David C Shanks* which took us to Moratai where we stayed for a few days. After a few barge and beach training exercises, we boarded *Kanimbla* which landed us at Brunei Bluff on 10 June.

The Bn led the advance on the move to Brunei Town, and we were attached to B Coy. On the night and early morning of 13 June, disaster struck the Pl and we counted our losses, at first light, to find 4 dead and 2 wounded.

This, of course, was devastating to the Pl, but we pressed on with the rest of the Bn towards Seria. Our next job was to move out on some inland patrolling with Dyak guides. We made our base camp at Labi Village and, although we found no Japs, we learnt a lot about the Dyak customs and their hatred of our enemy. The church missionaries will have a hard job persuading them to cease their "head shrinking" activities which they seem to enjoy. We were all glad that they were on our side as they were good scouts and friends.

When the War finished, we made our way back to the coast at Seria where we moved into Shell Company houses and relative luxury compared with our previous abodes.

So, it was farewell to all the mates whom I had the pleasure of meeting, and sad memories of those lost in battle.

Proud to be infantrymen and to do our bit in whatever task the Bn was given, 4 Pl was clearly the best A/Tk Pl in 2/17 Bn.

With the gunnery role in the Middle East and the patrolling and special duties in New Guinea and Borneo, the fellows did what was asked of them.

The AIF tradition of service was borne out in the team spirit of the gun crews — through all the hard grind they had the example of Terry George to live up to.

CARRIER PLATOON — HQ Coy
By Don "Dagwood" Osborn

For those of us of an age to be aware of the rise of the late Adolf Hitler, prior to the commencement of World War II, the declaration thereof, on the third day of September 1939, was anticipated and sobering.

At that time I saw myself as a potential "fighter pilot" and was pretty keen to get into air crews in that capacity. I had gone through the motor bike stage, and regarded myself something of a rifle shot. I could hit targets thrown into the air, and I would shoot pennies held between a thumb and forefinger some 25yds away. The friend who held the pennies, to this day, holds his hand aloft with fingers spread to indicate all present and correct. He retired only recently from the position of 2 i/c of our oldest Bank which indicates he really was not an idiot. I also enjoyed driving my Lancia and this friend's big 30/98 Vauxhall which in those far-off days could and did do the "ton".

On 4 Sept 1939, I offered myself to the RAAF and rather assiduously pursued this into the first few months of 1940, at which time the Melbourne recruiting centre for air crews decided they could well do without me and my talents. Undaunted by this rejection, I hightailed the Melbourne scene for that of Sydney — to try up there. When Dunkirk highlighted the seriousness of our position, I offered myself to the Army at the Sydney Town Hall, and due to these causes, eventually arrived at 2/17 Inf Bn.

On arrival in Palestine with troops labelled as 2nd and 3rd 2/17 Inf reinforcements, we marched into John Broadbent's Coy at 20 Bde ITB.

J.R.B. decided to interview each of us individually, no doubt in an attempt to determine if it was worthwhile persevering with us. I told him of my unfulfilled ambitions as a pilot, and added if there was a second choice, I would like it to be in armour.

Next I found myself at the Middle East Armoured Training School. I gained the impression this was really intended to give Offrs, WOs and NCOs an awareness of how Bren Carriers should be employed, as apart from myself, there was only one other Or there.

At the conclusion of the course I was pleasantly surprised at finding I had gained the distinguished pass for the school and, as a result, I was duly paraded to Bde HQ and congratulated and informed that I would be held until 2/17 Bn Carrier Pl called for reinforcements.

Because of this I had to watch my mates march out for Tobruk, and spend a few more weeks at the depot. Meanwhile those worthies who had marched out were enjoying themselves at the fleshpots or whatever at Alexandria and/or Cairo. I finally got a straight-through movement to Tobruk and found they had only just arrived there a day or two before.

Someone or more of this group had regaled the Carrier Pl with the alleged "prowess" of this intended "driver", and I soon learned that I was not only a just arrived reinforcement, but also somewhat unwelcome.

I discovered another poor soul somewhat similarly on the "outer" and, pending an ultimate acceptance, aligned myself with him.

On moving into the line at the El Adem road block, my first introduction to the real thing, I passed quite some of the time engaging at target practice with my rifle, and in this I was soon joined with young Bill Wilcox, then and still known as "Blondie". I was dubbed "Deadwood" but, in pretty quick time, with Blondie in tow, and the Women's Weekly cartoon of Dagwood and Blondie featured, the "Deadwood" switched to "Dagwood". As such I was known throughout the rest of my stay with 2/17 Bn.

Throughout my period with Carrier Pl of 2/17 Bn, I drove Tom Fitzpatrick's carrier, and the friendship then developed, continuing until his death in 1987.

Whilst in Tobruk, when the Bn was in the line, some of the Carrier Pl manned one of the front line posts, and on a number of occasions this was the post at the El Adem road block.

On one such occasion, Gen Moreshead had gone out to a conference in Egypt, and Brig Murray was acting Fortress Comd. He exercised this command by instructing that the rum which had been coming in with the supplies as standard British Army issue, and until then not being issued, would now be issued each night. Our first awareness of this was on the arrival of the ration truck one evening, when the driver called the news from his cabin.

This rum was the real "McCoy", heavily overproof, and something to be taken slowly. From this initial issue, Tom Fitzpatrick, who had acquired a liking for a tot of rum in his days as a Shearers' Boss in the back country of Queensland and northern NSW, very carefully decanted half of the slender ration into a souvenired German water bottle, and steadfastly maintained this practice until the end of the Bn's participation in the defence of Tobruk.

He maintained he was building up a something with which he would celebrate this event and, as it grew in quantity, so did our special care for the old chap and his precious bottle.

Ultimately we were brought out of Tobruk by the British destroyer HMS Griffin which had difficulty in berthing because of the offshore wind, and the fact that she was listing fairly heavily due to some damage formerly suffered. She had not even berthed when the rest of the flotilla was heading out to sea. Her skipper disregarded a signal to abandon his attempts, assent by the flagship, and patently did not take offence at the shouted instructions directed at him from his intended passengers, most of such instructions being pretty lurid, and slanted at his navigational skills, or possible lack of same.

Once on board, those of us comprising Tom Fitzpatrick's body guard, manoeuvred him and his precious bottle up a ladder and into one of the forward gun turrets, where surprised gunners were vainly trying to get the message through to the bunch of dumb Australians that "you can't come in here lads".

We were in such a happy state at being on board and on the way out that we did not hold this against the gunners, and very quickly made friends with them — this, no doubt, being partly assisted by the German bottle. They insisted that we eat the delightful hot meals as sent up to them, and were equally insistent on eating our hard tack rations, which we had brought for our own sustenance on the way out.

As a matter of passing interest, it will be recalled that, when the General returned to the fortress and resumed his command, the rum issue continued with the exception of Sundays and, for some forgotten reason, one other night. On this latter occasion, Tom was moved to personally give out a replacement tot to each of us.

Fleas and flies were two of the problems associated with service in Tobruk, and one of the established counter-measures against the former was to spread one's blankets to the rays of the setting sun in such a manner as to highlight the whereabouts of the fleas by the reflection of the sunlight.

On one occasion whilst engaged in this at the El Adem road block post, it occurred to me that the opposition must be similarly troubled and would possibly likewise take advantage of the setting sun's rays to de-flea their blankets. I grabbed a set of binoculars and climbed the observation tower some few yards to the rear of our post and, sure enough, all personnel in the enemy post had their blankets spread and were busily chasing their brand of flea.

The following afternoon, whilst the mirage was still running, I took some lengths of signal wire, a Spandau machine gun, ammunition and the binoculars down to this observation tower and, with the aid of the wire, hauled everything up to the platform at the head of the tower and settled down there to await the evening flea hunt.

At the appropriate time the stage was fully set, our boys were busy de-fleaing their blankets, and Hans and his mates were doing likewise. I balanced the Spandau on the forward guard rail, elevated it to what I judged to be the correct angle for the range involved, and let fly with a full belt, and then closely observed the result with the binoculars.

My elevation had been perfect, and the strike was right among the de-fleaers. Within seconds the opposition were spraying the desert with their own Spandaus, in an each-which-way pattern. Bullet strikes were showing up in all sorts of random directions.

As on the previous evening when the initial observation was made, I again remained still and sat there until after darkness set in. Whilst doing this, I observed a couple of ambulances arrive and load up, and then drive off again, and I was well satisfied with the exercise.

At about mid-morning next day, I was rudely awakened from a deep sleep in my little Italian-made concrete dug-out, by the scream and explosion of a bomb, delivered by a Stuka, and aimed at my own sleeping quarters. It exploded a few feet from the dug-out entrance. The dug-out itself was invaded by a cloud of dense black smoke.

I charged through this to my weapon pit, where I already had a Bren gun mounted for ack-ack defence, and followed the Stuka, as it climbed, with a full magazine from the Bren. During this I was bare-footed and, shortly afterwards, one foot became very painful. On inspecting it, I found a very sore blister of the same size and shape of a spent .303 shell. I had unknowingly stood on it whilst firing at the Stuka.

At this post there was a small stone shed which was used for preparing our meals. It was customary for someone to prepare the breakfast after the morning standto. When the meal was ready, this person, or his assistant, would select one or two Italian hand grenades from a stock held and, after pulling the pin, pitch the thing outside to explode, this being in lieu of the "Come and get it" call.

On one morning towards breakfast time, the opposition sent over a bevy of 50mm mortars which landed within the confines of the post. Next thing, Billy Stewart emerged from his dug-out, mess gear in hand, and a big grin in anticipation of breakfast, and headed toward the mess hut, until someone alerted him to the causes of the "false alarm".

During the Tobruk scene, a strong relationship developed between the Australian soldier and his British counterpart. In fact, in those far off days, we really considered we were also British.

Whilst in the El Adem road block post, we became very friendly with an English Lt Col and his batman. They would make periodical visits to our Col Crawford or someone generally in the direction of Bn HQ. We would observe them travelling by foot, the batman always several steps behind the Colonel, and invariably at a time when the mirage made such movements safer. It became our practice to offer them a cup of tea as they drew near. We learned that they were from the Northumberland Fusiliers, a very effective unit, operating the Vickers MG.

On one occasion as they approached, it was decided we should upset the established caste system. On their arrival, we extended every cordiality to the batman, everyone crowding around him and making everything of him, almost ignoring the Colonel who quickly became concerned that he may have somehow unknowingly offended us.

After we got this message through, we assured him our concern was merely because of their manner of movement which we accepted as proper on the parade ground but, to our minds, was outside the pale in the existing circumstances. As was expected, and already known to us, he was a gentleman as well as a top Brit, to everyone's amusement and satisfaction as from then, the two would be seen to close ranks when still some distance from us on the approach, and to revert to their standards when a similar distance after departing.

On our last day in Tobruk, we were staged in the "birdcage", a wire mesh enclosure, built by the Italians to house prisoners of war. During the day, my friend Frank Commins of the Sig Pl, and later KIA at Tel el Eisa, and myself hitch-hiked back to the Harbour for a swim and a last look at the town.

On heading back toward the birdcage later in the afternoon, we tried to hitch a ride on a 4x4 Morris driven by an Englishman, with his officer as his passenger. As they approached, we gave them the traditional signs asking for a ride but the motor did not change sounds at all and they sped past us without even an acknowledgment of our presence.

Frank had a very big voice when he chose to use it and, at this point, he did choose. "You Pommy B—'". The driver took his foot off the accelerator and looked to the Captain for confirmation and was given the nod of approval. He then hammered the brakes to bring the vehicle to a screeching halt. Frank and I then immediately ran flat-out to them and jumped up into the back with a hearty, "Thanks mate, we didn't think you were going to stop for us".

The driver again looked to the Captain for confirmation, was given the nod of approval once more, engaged the gears and drove forward. He duly delivered us to our destination and then turned the vehicle around to get back to their own destination which was some distance back towards the Harbour.

SPECIALIST PLATOONS — engaged in OBOE SIX

Editor's Note: —

The following narrations were written by unknown authors in September 1945. They are reproduced, except for spelling, basically unedited and relate many humourous incidents and the lighter side of soldiering. The use of nicknames and slang are commonplace and I am sure they are not meant to offend. They do illustrate the irreverent humour of the Australian soldier.

SIG PLATOON NARRATIVE

Contrary to expectations the Borneo campaign for the Sigs, so far as the bullocky work was concerned, was comparatively easy and those with not-so-fond memories of New Guinea were agreeably surprised.

Owing to the swiftness of the advance, we were continually screaming to Bde for more and more cable, giving Capt "Whizzer" Watson a perpetual headache. The cable was usually forthcoming but "Whizzer" managed to give us plenty of headaches later on. That length of pessimism "Blue" Maroney and his team of linesmen performed yeomen work laying and maintaining the Bde line in the early stages. Incidentally, they should be grateful to Tojo for so generously leaving the greater part of the old civil line in working condition. Jack Crowley, once again, our W/T operator from Bde, had a strange lapse of memory this time in that he failed to "dice" his set at the first river. Joe Murray, in his wisdom (?), attached himself unofficially to the Bde line team and was noticed concentrating heavily on the paying out of the line every time the jeep dusted past the hoofing Pl. Despite his length of calf, Joe is definitely allergic to marching.

Jimmie Lee and "Digger" Rollings the first night out happened to be out on a line during the time the "blue" occurred with the Jap truck and spent a cold uncomfortable night, unable to move as every time they did so A Coy, as always alert, would kindly open up on them.

"Furphy" Ferguson is most careful when teeing-in these days to make sure he is on the correct line after once obligingly poling 2 miles of line for the arty on a hot day, due to both 2/8 Arty Sigs and ourselves having a Sig nicknamed "Junior".

"Bluey" Morrison, the Pl's happy man, demonstrated his unique driving ability by nicely ditching a Jeep borrowed from Yanks of the CIC when installing a phone for them at Brunei.

At the Tutong relay post Ernie Read, "Soak" Coventry and Co aided the bored MO of the ADS in breaking the monotony by helping him to drink his uplifting concoctions, the main ingredient of which was pure alcohol. They were heard from occasionally on the line.

Bill Forster and "Junior" Worlock were mighty pleased over the to-the-point wrap up that the CO gave them on the smoothness and efficiency of the last move to Seria.

At our Seria Mansion we received reinforcements when "No-landings" Neuss, Toc Read, "Strings" Champion, "Matt Gabbott" Smith and Chas (Greater than Barrymore) Dickson arrived. "Paddles" Froggatt has fond memories of "Foochow" where he received 16 direct hits in a short but sharp encounter with a wasps' nest.

Tempers became frayed among the line-laying party during the latter stages of the journey from Simpang to Ridan, the Pioneers vowing that they would never be trapped again. "Tank" Maher of the Pnrs and "Lofty" Tacey, the big men of the team could always be relied upon to side-slip gracefully into every swamp.

The Sigs were, for a very short time, the proud possessors of a dashing Ford V8 sedan. Those who had put in a considerable amount of work on it were definitely "agin" the Government when officialdom stepped in and commandeered it.

Alf Read once again upheld the reputation of the Sigs with A Coy even though, on occasions, "Gunner" George Holtsbaum and he did not quite see eye to eye over communication problems.

Peter Goodwin had reached such a rich shade of chocolate that the "Red Shag" has been asking pertinent questions about natives being seen on the premises.

A couple of keen, if unscientific, contests have been fought at Seria, viz. "Garrulous Gabbott" Smith v. Bill Read and "Knock-em-down" Samsu v. "Give-it-a-go" Rollings. In the former bout the contestants dourly fought each other to a verbal standstill, having retired to virtual dumbness to recuperate. In the latter contest, old Samsu possessing greater staying powers won on a KO, the "Hunk" looking like one of Jack Carroll's victims after the event.

"Silent" Fred Camarsh, despite our fears, somehow saw the campaign out and, when the news of his impending discharge was imparted to him, his speed and agility in breaking all records from Ridan to Seria even dazzled the Dyaks.

"Dooker" Cranefield, our quiet and modest driver, became adept at mending lines — reef knots you know — but, sad to relate, it was necessary for a surgical operation to be performed each time he was needed in order to separate his stretcher canvas from his horizontal back.

Our handsome young pounder of the key, Jerry Hosler, keeps his hand in for the Post Office and is never satisfied with anything under 200 groups. "Shorty" Webb, the only Sig Clerk with the infallible system has not yet been caught out, despite several fierce tussles with his opposite number at Bde. "Doc" Doyle our instrument mechanic, disappears each day into his store, whereupon weird sounds emanate periodically but it has yet to be proved whether he ever actually repairs any instruments.

"Spike" Baker is noted for his one-man patrols but to date he has not produced even a pig. It is not yet known whether "Killer" Mouldt has ever actually drawn blood with his trusty knife and now that all Nips are protected animals, his chances look dim. Incidentally, the Sigs' only decoration was presented recently when "Trudgie" collected his DCM.

The "Little Fuehrer" Brooks cared for the Pl for a short time but, by the time he came to us, he had definitely been de-Fuehrerised. His exact and detailed Sig diagrams still hang on the walls of our Sig Office, which is the best the Pl has ever had.

Although he was not with us when he was hit, young Ray Griffiths (afterwards 17 Pl) had been a member of the Pl for so long that we considered him as one of the flag-waggers. He quickly became proficient at Sig work and, without being asked, would always hop in and do his share at any job. The Pl was deeply affected by his death and we all lost a really good pal.

Now that the "show" is over we can laugh at our troubles which, in retrospect do not appear so bad. Everyone worked hard and, when the "power was on" no one was found wanting.

With the War over and the prospect of resuming civilian life around the corner no one regrets the campaign, which in later years will provide food for many good tales.

ACTIVITIES OF 2 PLATOON — MACHINE GUNS

After a pleasant 6-day journey aboard HMAS *Kanimbla*, we arrived off the north-west coast of Borneo.

Reveille on D day was blown at 0500 hrs. Most of the chaps awoke with the usual moans but this soon turned to excitement on realising that this was the great day. At 0600 hrs, breakfast was served — and what a breakfast! The cooks certainly went to great pains to see that everyone was satisfied. We all ate as much as possible because lunch was a long way off. Also, the prospects of eating bully beef again didn't appeal to us.

After breakfast, we all returned to our troop deck to check equipment prior to going ashore. It was extremely hot below decks and, as we were in the second wave, we had to spend quite a while below waiting for the first wave to leave the ship. The time was spent in playing a few games of cards or smoking a couple of nervous cigarettes.

At last our turn arrived and we moved to our boat stations, very thankful to breathe in the fresh morning air. As usual Barrie Rymer was last to appear on deck with his tin hat tangled around his neck.

By this time, the bombardment on Green Beach had commenced, and amid the terrific noise we climbed down the scrambling nets into our landing craft. For the operation, Pl HQ and 2 Sec were attached to B Coy and 1 Sec with D Coy. Landing Craft No K27 contained Pl HQ and 2 Sec and Craft No K28 contained 1 Sec. Plonk Luck and Orderly Mathews had a worried look on their faces as they had to move ashore in the first wave as a recce party.

After pulling away from the ship, the craft started a monotonous circling for 1 hour and, at the same time, the barrage was intensified. We were supposed to keep our heads down, but the interesting sights happening around us were too great and we had to have a look-see. Eventually our coxswain manoeuvred our craft into position and we moved toward the shore. Bombers and fighters patrolled the sky, giving us added confidence. We could see the first wave already on the beach now and, after a few minutes, our craft grounded and the ramp was lowered.

As expected, water was one of our difficulties but was overcome and most of us were only wet up to the knees. Tiger Timms was a little too eager and finished up in the water up to his neck. Opening the waterproof cases delayed us a little, but no time was wasted, and we were soon on our way to rejoin our respective Coys. "Basher Lug Sug", John Sugden, had the honour of firing the first shot (accidentally) and nearly earmarked "Bateye" Shepherd.

Proceeding inland, we reached a swamp and here our morale nearly dropped to zero. "Lusty" Layton got himself lost and was wandering around up to his neck in slush. However, after much toil and sweat, both Sections reached their objectives and took up their positions.

After a well earned rest, everyone started to take a little more interest in the surroundings. Barrie Rymer was studying some huts about 100yds to our front. Suddenly 2 Nips ran out and one fired a shot at us. Their surprise must have been terrific when Jack Shepherd sprayed them with a belt of ammo from the machine gun.

Later in the afternoon we commenced to move to Brunei, camping the night on the right side of the Brooketon-Brunei Road. Everyone was very tired and lost no time in settling down to a well earned sleep. Later on we were deprived of this sleep by the intrusion of Nippon. Apparently not knowing our positions, a party of Japs in a 3-ton truck came driving down the road. The headlights were blazing and offered a good target to our guns. P.J. Larkin and Jack Shepherd, showing brilliant marksmanship, stopped the truck with a couple of bursts and then disposed of the passengers. The sight that greeted everyone in the morning was not very pleasant. However, we were all very pleased with the number of kills, without having any casualties ourselves.

From Brunei we moved by truck along the coast through Tutong and thence onto Seria, where we spent one night. Here we could not obtain much sleep owing to the continual roar of the oil fires. Next morning we were very pleased to move into Kuala Belait and take up positions. 2 Sec was camped in the Customs House near the wharf and Pl HQ and 1 Sec were in the natives' quarters near a bombed church.

Our stay in Kuala Belait was very enjoyable. Everyone readily made friends with all the native children who caused great amusement with their antics and sayings. The children gave Bernie Lazzaro the nickname of "Hung Up" which, in Malayan, means to stutter. However, the name didn't cure him. Barry Rymer felt a bit allergic to rowing and made a very unsuccessful attempt to convert a canoe into a sailing boat. Jack Littlewood, Pat Larkin and Jack Shepherd were introduced to the native wine, saki, which caused some very bad headaches. Ken Pratt, who loved children, spent his time standing on the side of the road issuing sweets and biscuits to the passing children. He was known affectionately as Father Pratt. Dumpy Gilmore's weight led him into strife. The railings of a bridge, unused to terrific weight, collapsed, depositing Dumpy in a very muddy ditch.

From Kuala Belait, Pl HQ and 2 Sec moved up the river to Simpang. On arrival we heard a lot of yelling up the track. Into view came an old Dyak carrying a Jap head which had been lopped off at the shoulders. Naturally we were all amazed, but nevertheless curious, and spent quite a while examining the trophy. After the head was smoked he took it off to hold a celebration where much saki was drunk.

During our stay at Simpang, work consisted of carrying parties to Mendarham. Keith Ricketson worked hard carrying other chaps' loads in exchange for their weekly ration of beer. Murray Ross, alias "Brushmush", received word confirming his engagement. He sang and whistled all through his piquet that night and hasn't been the same man since. R.C. Ford "V8" had a nightmare and let out a horrible moan and we all thought that the Nip had got him. Lt Happy Vickers rushed out in bare feet, flashing a pistol. However, by this time Ron was awake and explained the position.

Ring-a-Dang-Doo Ring was the cook (or thought he was). He had the cheek to yell out, "Come and get it or I'll throw it away". Pat Green carried out a bit of bookmaking on a commentary given by R C Ford. Jack Littlewood and Stan Livingstone were worried about the 5-Year Plan.

During a heavy downpour of rain the river broke its banks and flooded our area. Bert Luck, Scrummy Nelson, Tony Delaney and Bill Hyland all had a great time rescuing gear which had floated down stream. As usual, Norm Taylor was worried about his native banjo which he treated like a long lost brother.

Meanwhile, after leaving Kuala Belait, 1 Sec were attached to D Coy. They proceeded up the Baram River by LCM with a gunboat in support. Bivouac area for the first night was the middle of a swamp. Moving up river next day helped in the assault on Marudi.

After reaching this peaceful spot, a defensive position was taken up on the north-west track. Doovers were erected, then Cpl Plonk Luck took the Sec on a scrounging patrol, arriving back with an old gramophone. That evening "Lubra" gave everyone a great lug bash about leaving the area. George Thompson attempted to catch a rooster by chasing it with a sword. Finished up with George breaking the Scabbard and no rooster. Ned Kelly and Russ Luck volunteered to go on a patrol, but never again, as the chief of the first village wanted them to stay the night in his house, sleeping between two maidens. On seeing the number of heads in the house they decided against it. "Bull Frog" Taylor became mixed up with some saki and croaked his way to bed falling over Strawb McMillan's doover.

Bubbles Andrews and Ray Lee drove everyone mad playing the same records over and over again on the gramophone. Everyone was relieved when it broke down. However, "Gundi Guy" and "Shell Head" Matthews became unpopular by repairing it again. Lusty Leighton became the chief pig shooter. After shooting up everything but the pig it was decided to use him for firing the Victory Salute.

The final stay of the journey was at Bakoeng, then to Seria where the whole platoon relaxed, playing football, surfing and waiting for a discharge.

THE ACCOUNT OF 3 PLATOON — MORTARS

The platoon disembarked from HMAS *Kanimbla* on the morning of 10 June 1945 with the farewell of "Good luck to you, too". During the landing our first casualties were experienced. "Lightning" Pickup, making a fast move from the beach, cut his little finger on a machete, and Cpl Laycock tasted the China Sea by being trampled into the water during the mad scramble by the Arty. The landing went according to plan with the platoon eventually establishing itself 150yds from the beach. Furious digging took place until, to the relief of all concerned, it was discovered that the only opposition was the swampy ground.

After numerous cups of tea, prepared with water from a well sunk on the spot by "Watering" Mellon, the platoon moved forward in an endeavour to get into the picture with "Pete" Pollock leading the column, chewing his pipe (minus tobacco), and muttering, "For Christ's sake! Be in it". After about an hour's march, with mortars at the high port, we eventually caught up with the tail end of the picture related to us by Pete amidst, "actually this" and "actually that", and "including this" and "including that". After much drinking of C Juice and the discarding of surplus gear, such as tin hats and life jackets, we started off on the famous "Route Six Derby".

The first realisation of taking part in a war occurred on the first night when a party of mobile angry men nonchalantly drove into our lines. After a quick disposal of these we spent a very uncomfortable night dodging surplus bullets fired by the multitude into our area. Our "Rhode Island Red" (C O J Page) spent the night creeping and cackling like one of his kind, and was extremely fortunate to be crowing at daylight the next morning.

After much scrambling for positions at the barrier, 3 Sec, piloted by "Daylight Dan" Chapman, and carrying top weight, forged to the front of the column. The day proved uneventful, except for a visit from the Supreme Commander, Gen MacArthur, Gen Morshead and Gen Wootten, accompanied by a horde of sightseers.

Next morning, there was a slight change in positions with "Scissors" Quinn and his "Merrymakers" dashing off in hot pursuit of supposed loot. Their efforts were in vain as the Sons of Nippon halted and so did "Scissors". The Sec Comd having gone forward, "Busty" Hay, imitating Lord Nelson with the Walkie-Talkie to his deaf ear, took control. "Busty", not quite in the picture, decided to take matters into his own hands and "plonk" one down. Nobody knew where the bomb was going — least of all the gun crew led by "Lothar" Faint. That night everything but the kitchen sink was thrown into the fray. In the meantime, "Herr von Havenstein's" No 1 Sec received a social call from a member of the opposition who, after making a minute inspection of the doovers, was allowed to depart unchallenged by "Tracker" James and his Cootamundra China "Casanova" Ticehurst. 4 Sec entertained 3 Sec on the air strip with a delightful rendition of "Danny Boy" by the slumbering Aubrey Lyle Gowans. Brunei was occupied the following day by B and C Coys, the occasion being well remembered by the sterling rearguard action fought by "Timor Red" Baxter in defence of the cemetery.

Following 2 days of fighting nothing more serious than spooks, "Scissors" Quinn and his "Merrymakers" moved off by motorised column to Tutong, leaving 1, 3 and 4 Secs in undisputed control of looting operations. It was later found that most of the consolidation in this field was neutralised by the subversive activities of the Field Security. Dress swords that were early visualised by the ardent looters as adornments of the home mantlepiece, were among the illgotten souvenirs so promptly confiscated. Bicycles, however, were allowed to remain in the possession of the finders and facilitated social calls. All went well with "Scissors'" mob until that night when "Shorty" Fry, forced into a defensive attitude by the swift approach of a supposedly angry man, peppered a buffalo, prefixed by a frenzied shout of, "I'm going to let him have it". The rest of the trip to Tutong was uneventful, except for the welcome of the local inhabitants who waved flags and shouted, "God Save America". One over-enthusiastic native brought up the rear of the column doing the jitterbug.

3 Sec moved the following day under a change of commander, "Zombie" Mathieson. Consequently, many thousand words were spoken during the trip. The remaining two sections proudly undertook the defence of Brunei, with 4 Sec, under Lloyd Chennock, doing most of the fighting. 1 Sec used up all their energy with their social activities. 4 Sec, attached to C Coy, hold the honour of taking over the FDLs of that coy when one of their patrols was chased down a spur by an angry Woodpecker. Feeling insecure in this position, "Dora" Curtis made use of local shotguns set on fixed lines covering trip wires and booby traps constructed by "Camel" Robertson. "Tiny" Bailey, who up to this time had been feeling the pinch, showed no interest in the situation by eating three tins of bully beef, a day's ration of biscuits, and quenching his thirst with the juice of a dozen coconuts.

After pottering around Tutong for a couple of days, our health was such that we were able to continue on with the next phase of the "Derby". We boarded "Queen Mary" at the Tutong Ferry and made a record crossing of the river at the rate of 2 hours to the knot. With no opposition being found on the other side, lunch was taken. It was at this point that "Lightning" Pickup displayed his second turn of speed in the operation. He almost scalped himself getting under a Jeep after someone in a nearby section had accidently fired a shot. Having the principles of war firmly fixed in our minds, we pushed on, setting up camp during a heavy downpour. A comfortable night was NOT spent by all. However, morale was maintained by the arrival of our first batch of mail in which "Monster" Mannion defeated "Snoozer" Doust by one telegram.

The next day proved to be the "day of days". The barrier rose with Bn HQ, ably led by the CO, without equipment, in the front, closely followed by the Pnr Pl with the rear being brought up by "Scissors" Quinn and Co who were seriously hampered at the start by a surplus of information. The pace was terrific! On reaching the bound, all concerned were halted by a party of angry men who did not prevent the Section from sinking numerous wells on the beach. At this stage, 3 Sec went into action again and registered their first confirmed kill. During the heat of battle a shot was returned. "Tug" Baker, the Beckam prop, had the misfortune to make a three point landing on an ant nest. "Snoozer" Doust, who was on his feet for a change, when ordered to ground, looked around with a vacant stare and enquired, "What's going on?" "Zombie", endeavouring to carry out a shoot, became over anxious and, by moving with the forward scout, Sig "Jeep" Drew, much to his dismay, found himself too close to the enemy to use his Walkie-Talkie. Suffering under the strain of battle, "Jeep" decided to rest his war-weary body by positioning his 6 stone beside a supposedly dead Nippon. Instead of becoming relaxed, his nerves became over-heated when he learned that the said Nippon was only wounded and lying doggo.

While the Bn was moving in to occupy Seria, 3 Sec was shocked to learn that it was left behind to provide rear protection for that force. "Lightning" Pickup and "Watering" Mellon moved out on a two-man patrol to investigate movement down the road. Never before in the annals of Jungle Warfare has camouflage been used to such an extent. At this stage, "Zombi" Mathieson decided to obtain some valuable information from a local Chinese. Speaking very unintelligible Pidgin English, he enquired as to the distance to Seria and received the reply, "From here to Seria proper is approximately 5 miles". Undaunted, "Zombie" came again with another flow of jargon to which the Chinese replied, "I beg your pardon, Sergeant".

The occupation of Seria was carried out uneventfully. Little did we know at the time that it was going to prove a place of historical value as far as the platoon was concerned. In the meantime, base wallahs 1 and 4 Secs went from Brunei and pushed forward to lonely outposts.

1 Sec moved into Kuala Belait with A Coy and assisted in the occupation of the town. All troops were billeted in well appointed houses, even to a daily visit from the nightman — in a professional capacity, of course! During our stay there it was decided to hold a mortar shoot for the twofold purpose of practising the gun numbers and impressing the natives. While ranging, one smoke bomb dropped short into a Chinese garden, causing a general exodus from the immediate vicinity. Fortunately, it failed to explode. Sometime later a Chinese caused a second panic for the day by appearing at the door of a rifle platoon's billet, cradling the "dud" bomb in his arms and asking, "What will I do with this?" He ignored the ready reply and deposited it in an unoccupied native hut, where it later exploded, burning the hut to the ground.

For one detachment of 1 Sec the de luxe life at Kuala Belait was of very short duration as, after a couple of days, they headed off up the Belait River in search of fresh adventures. At Kuala Belait they met up with a band of Dyaks and shared a house with them for a few days. One evening when the Dyaks returned from a patrol with a monkey, which a member of A Coy had shot for them, the mortars were invited to assist in masticating the animal and found it quite palatable.

As the river from Sembaru to Teriam is navigable only by sampan, the embryo canoists, notably Donnie Enoch and Charlie Rouen, were given ample opportunity to improve their technique as paddlers. The going was hard and the river traffic heavy so that, apart from the "get out and push" procedure necessary to cross the numerous sand bars, many head-on collisions occurred with sampans laden with refugees fleeing from the Labi area.

Arriving at Simpang, the mortarmen settled in to enjoy a month of what proved to be the most entertaining time we have spent on the island. More fruit, vegetables, eggs and poultry were available than we could possibly cope with. "Bungarra" Buttel later became famous for his monster fruit salads — nothing less than half a kerosine bucket full per meal. On one occasion, when the mortars were ordered to put on a shoot from a position about a mile in advance of our area, it was decided to recruit 6 bomb carriers from a band of Dyaks which had considerably increased since our arrival in that area. When we eventually set out on our mission, we presented a very colourful spectacle. Our 6 carriers had grown to a force of well over 50 Malayans and Dyaks dressed in full battle array with head dresses varying from "pork pies" to peacock feathers, and armed to the teeth with blowpipes, spears and parangs. Just as we arrived at the intended mortar position a Chinese runner arrived with a message cancelling the shoot as the target was out of range. "P for Petrol" O'Dwyer was reluctantly compelled to order an about-turn to the chagrin of the warlike natives who were somewhat appeased by the distribution of tailor made cigarettes.

The arrival of the remainder of the Section at Simpang was the signal for an outbreak of many good natured arguments which continued all day and far into the night for the duration of our stay there. The subjects for discussion ranged from the correct way to write a "t" to the most efficient mode of dress for farm work. The most memorable of all these took place when the Census Form arrived with instructions that an officer had to supervise the filling in of details. Uproar reigned until it was decided to elect "Host Holbrook" Anderson as an adjudicator and from then on the discussion was carried out in the best debating society tradition. Just as midnight was approaching it was decided to place a motion on the books that it was "an insult to a man's intelligence for the Army to decree that an officer had to supervise the filling in of the form". Next day, owing to a shortage of officers and time, we filled in our own forms but, when they were later checked by Lt "Happy" Vickers, it was found that almost without exception they contained many errors — the "insult" appeared to be justified.

It was at Simbang that we first saw concrete evidence of the head-hunting tendencies of the Dyaks (that is, if a Nipponese top-knot could be described as concrete). The head was brought to our position after the smoking part of the ceremony was completed. The headman appeared amongst us as we were in the act of eating our evening meal, nonchalantly swinging the head in his right hand whilst he engaged us in a somewhat one-sided conversation. But with the iron constitution of the mortarmen not even a hair, far less a stomach, turned by the unprepossessing sight — a high compliment to the food cooked by "Uncle Gus" Harlovich who had been ably assisted by "Slim" Sargent.

Most of our time in that region was spent in carrying forward stores and ammo to the other outposts. On several occasions we were invited into the Dyak's homes at Mendarum by the headman who greeted us all at the door with a handshake and motioned us to sit down on the floor of the hut. The barman then came around with a jug of saki and duly did the honours whilst several Jap heads leered down at us from their vantage points along the wall. Even these pleasant visits did not compensate for the rigours of the arduous ammo carry, and many tempers were a little frayed on returning to base. After one particularly solid trip, "Stonewall" Jackson became very annoyed when his billycan capsized into the fire for the third time in as many minutes.

Scorning the customary drop kick, he deftly picked up the offending vessel and neatly punted it far into the green vastness of the jungle hell.

It was with deep regret that we left the green glades of Labi to return to the coast, but we all felt a little curious to see how the other half (the rear portion) of the Army lived.

While 1 Sec were operating in their jungle hell, part of 3 Sec, under the baton of "Jungle Jim" Byrne, moved to the local railway station to board the "Spirits of Salts" — a typical Queensland train — for Badas. After an extremely nerve-racking trip, during which chin straps had to be worn under the chin to obviate the loss of hats (fur felt), we arrived at our destination. Heated argument arose as to whether the section should live in a house or "rough it" in true infantier style. "Zombie" decided on the latter, so doovers were erected. In typical Army style the "Boy Wonder" decided that we must move to the house. "Smacker" Smith became delirious, continually wandering around the area in a pronounced state of coma and blowing the "Derriere" out of canoes. "Professional Killer" Andrews at this stage decided to lay an ambush in which "Jeep" Drew was to play an outstanding role. He was detailed out on the far side of a creek to operate as a listening post. A lonely, unarmed angry man with exquisitely chiselled features entered the ambush. "Stand-to" was ordered and "Jeep", realising his responsibilities of protecting the right flank, made a smart move towards his hole. Unfortunately, his path was marred by numerous obstacles and he finished water-logged in the creek, securely suspended at the point of balance by a stick. A reel and line was organised and Jeep's rescue carried out.

Our next move was to Bukit Puan, and this was uneventful. "Kuala" Blight, "Blue" Fursey, Mick Merifield and "Horse" Langman joined the section at this stage. Mick Merifield proved a passenger by inserting a tomahawk through the middle of his right foot, while the "Horse", terribly conscious of Bilharzia, refused to bathe his loping body in the local water. Needless to say, after a while even his best friends wouldn't tell him. "Herbie" Grooms and "Boley" McDonald, operating as mules, did good work carrying food to forward Sections. At the end of a fortnight we said farewell to the beautiful, tropical paradise of Bukit Puan and returned to Seria where, several days previously, "The Taralga Bull" Cameron had returned from his sojourne with the LOBs. His silk worm squeek was maintained during his absence and was prevalent in the early hours of the morning much to the disgust of "Watering" Mellon and "Snoozer" Doust.

The Bn's objective was to secure the Pl, minus 1 Sec, concentrated at Siestaville, Borneo Soldiers' Club, in the mainstreet of Seria. Our home proved to be extremely comfortable having all mod cons. However, the monotonous cry of "keep the men occupied" changed a life of peace to one of complete hell. Selection of domestic duties took place with "Troop Starver" Keown being duly elected as OC Cook House. He proved a bigger failure than "Troop Starver" Moon of long known fame, much to the sorrow of "Munga" Tyzack. His offsider, "Monster" Mannion, wielding a mighty tin opener, proved to be the only man to "bugger up" pilchards. With the rehabilitation scheme in full swing, the Pl was armed with prehistoric tools and machetes and put through their TOETs as grass cutters. "Sharpy" Cooper immediately became a patron of the YMCA, ably supported in all his moves by "Loafer" Laycock. Naturally, after a time, the Pl became trade grouped as haymakers, and "Palooka" Page engaged "Chopper" Chapman in a hectic 3-minute bout during which Palooka removed his teeth as safety precaution against the powerful left of Chopper. It was a great fight, no direct hits being scored, and the winner was awarded an antique cane chair.

Owing to too many "number two's" on grass cutting tools, the "keep occupied" slogan lost significance and a "keep fit" campaign was introduced. Delightful scenic route marches took place daily from Seria to the Golf Links. No interest was taken in these marches and the lethargic appearance and mechanical action gave the faithful readers of Mandrake in C Coy the scope to nick-name our platoon "The Kordies". Because "Panicky Pete", had rushed away sometime earlier, it fell to "Baron" Philp to dish out daily issue of Kordie Water. It came naturally to Donald Yuill Nesbitt to play the part of a Kordie and he had contemporaries in Wally Birch and "Spencer Tracy" Higgins. "Lothar" Faint proved faithful to Mandrake (Maj Maclarn) by carrying out all duties given to him without a murmur. With the return home of 5-Year stalwarts "Blue" Chapman Snr, "Busty" Hay and Charlie Rouen an NCOs' election was inaugurated in which "Honest Jeep" Drew, "Wog" Smith and "Champ" Chardon were candidates. The "Drew-Smith" policy was: "Less work, more pay, nought piquets and more beer". Consequently, "Champ" Chardon, being extremely conscientious and taking great interest in all pams, won selection and then held the distinguished rank of L/Cpl.

Hostilities having ceased, the disposal of surplus bombs was the order. A shoot was organised and conducted from the football field. The scream of "drop short" brought about some of the fastest moves seen on the field during its operation. The shoot was highly successful in that it proved the Kordies capable of removing the rear portions of "Chicka" Anderson's trousers with a high explosive bomb at 150yds.

Having Siestaville completely clear of grass and debris and subject to Mandrake's approval, it happened again and the Kordies moved to a primitive area on the edge of the jungle. After a completely reorganised "keep occupied" campaign we are now living comfortably in Mandrake's Rest Home, waiting for IT to happen again. Primary schools have started in which "Kid Basher" Watling has taken control of "Dead End Kid" Baccy Ryan,the star pupil. The Kordies were contenders in the Bn Football Compeitition but, owing to the absence of sufficient supplies of Kordie Water, they only ran second. Requisitions have been sent to the QM for adequate supplies for the present competition.

4 Sec, who are at present detached to D Coy and out of communication with the remainder of us, have become known as the "Marudi Mudlarkers". In anticipation of their return in the near future, adequate supplies of cotton wool, steel helmets and shovels have been stored in the area to cope with the horrid tales and bloody battles which will be expounded to us by such celebrities as: "Otway" Fawkner, "Mastoid Basher" Bourke, "Admiral" Bird, "Doc" D'Elboux, "Hollywood Heavy" Tutton, "Shandy" Davis, "Grandpappy" Anderson and the youngster of the mob, Sig Donnie Funnell.

We conclude by hoping that the demobilisation plan becomes supercharged and sufficient shipping made available to return us to our one and only home that WE can return the good wishes of "Good luck to you too" to all concerned.

EXPERIENCES AND ADVENTURES OF 4 PLATOON — Anti/Tank

On the morning of 10 June (D day), the Pl disembarked from HMAS *Kanimbla* into LCV L8 in the first wave, Personnel in the boat comprised Pl plus 3 Naval Beach Gp and Jack Carroll, attached from the Band. Whilst our boat was waiting to move into position, the boys were all very cheerful and our "funny man" and "morale booster", Jack Menzies kept the boys in good spirits by cracking jokes and singing (mostly parodies).

As the first salvo was fired, Arthur McCall put his hand to his head and called out in a loud voice, "Good God, I've had a brainstorm". Although the boys were outwardly very happy, their thoughts and gazes kept turning to Brunei Bluff which was our first objective. It was a very formidable and tough looking feature. As the creeping barrage was laid down on the bluff, there were numerous witty remarks passed by members of the Pl, such as: "Little bit of iron rations for your breakfast, you bastards, don't be afraid to help yourselves, there's plenty to go around". When we formed into line-abreast and headed for the beach at a very fast rate, the water was forced through the ramp and those forward received a good drenching, ie, Lt Moran, Alf Fogarty, "Peanut" Jones, "Red" Murphy and Harold Miller. After passing the rocket firing LCIs we happened to be right in their line of fire. This being our first enterprise with rockets, everybody in the boat received a hell of a fright when the first salvo was fired over our heads — some thought it was return fire from the beach. We were all told to keep our heads down at this stage, but we were too cramped in this position and, apart from that, everybody wanted to see what was going on. Needless to say, up went the heads. The Yankee Commander of the barge drew up alongside and, in a very panicky voice, said, "Keep your bloody heads down, you guys, we think there is a machine gun firing from the beach". This did not help the boys at all, but they still kept on singing and cracking jokes. The Pl theme song, "She'll be comin' round the mountain" was sung very heartily by all at the final burst of speed before hitting the beach. The boat grounded about 50yds out and the first man out, Bob Moran, received a good ducking by falling into the water, being nearly waist deep. He lost his Owen gun in the fall and amused all by groping around trying to retain it. He did so after a few seconds. The Pl was well strung out from the boat to the beach.

On arriving at the fringe of the jungle, Mick Kane declared the battle "on" while attempting to cock his Owen. His hand slipped off the cocking handle which carried a round forward and fired it, narrowly missing Reg Lehman's chest. I don't know who got the biggest shock, Mick or Reg. Alf Fogarty also fired at a movement in a bush and was very surprised when, what should fly out but a poor harmless bird. "Alfie, we're surprised at you!" Moving towards the Bluff, our loads became hardly bearable, tin hats were "diced" on a road approx a quarter mile from the beachhead, and felt hats were then worn to everyone's relief.

On crossing a stream or lagoon a few hundred yards further on, all the Cholera and Bilharzia regulations were completely disregarded by some of the boys as they splashed and lay down in the water — it sure was hot!

This campaign being the first of quite a number, confirmed all reports that they had overheard or were told regarding tropical warfare, heat loads etc. After crossing the lagoon, the Pl had to advance towards the Bluff which, at this stage, was towering above us, along the practically open beach. Nobody was particularly happy about it, although a happy-go-lucky front was held by all. The feature seemed to look down upon us like some sinister monster, ready to pounce upon some unwary victim. All eyes were scanning the precipitous sides of the hill, thinking what an ideal position it was for a surprise attack, and wondering whether we would ever be able to reach the top as it was so steep. Luckily for us, the Air and Naval bombardment had done an excellent job of this sector. Very little of the ground had not been covered with fire of some description.

To counteract everyone's fears, the Navy was standing offshore ready to come to our assistance at a moment's notice. The Navy certainly instils a lot of confidence. It was a relief for all when we had to wade through the surf up to our waists, keeping the temperature down somewhat. Arriving at the point of the Bluff we had to recce right around it, looking for an easy access to the top. It finished up we had to scale a very steep gradient, helped by the use of our ropes. Even then we just made it and were all absolutely done in when we reached the top. I guess not one of us would have reached the top had there been one man with a rifle there. Only one man at a time could go up, and he was absolutely useless as far as a fighting unit is concerned as both hands and feet were utilised to assist his ascent. Tojo had "blown through" for which we were all very grateful, although deep down there was not a man who thought he would be waiting for us, as he received too heavy a pounding beforehand.

It gives one an added sense of security to see all the surroundings flattened before going in. A cup of "cha" was the uppermost thought in everyone's heads, it being lunch time, terrific heat, and everyone utterly fatigued. Whilst a few scouted around clearing the area, the tea was boiled. Needless to say, water bottles were quickly emptied and we dug for water, going down about 18". It was slightly discoloured, but otherwise excellent to drink. "Cha" and more "cha" was put on until every man in the Pl drank somewhere in the vicinity of 3 pints. It was here that Reg Hallam nearly received the "D" for which he was looking so hard. He was told to climb a lookout tower and watch the surroundings, while a Sec was clearing the area. Unknown to Dick Mills and "Knobby" O'Brien, Reg was admiring the view and cooling off, when Dick was heard to say, "There's somebody in that tower, give him a burst, Knobby". Rather a nice thought that, isn't it Reg? However, it didn't eventuate.

After a spell of a couple of hours we were relieved by a Pl from 2/13 Bn and marched up the ridge to join Don Coy at the Rajah's house, or was, as it had been burnt to the ground. In fact, it was still smouldering when we arrived. An hour's spell here, and more "cha". We moved forward and attached to Don Coy with the Bn advancing along the main Brooketon-Brunei Road. The first night spent in Borneo was very lively. A Jap truck was done over by our MG Pl and a couple of Japs escaped, causing a lot of unecessary firing throughout the night. Our Pl was placed in a rather good position on the side of a hill and we were receiving all the backwash from the other Coys. One spent round fell in a bush a couple of feet from Mick Kane's head and another near Reg Hallam. We did not have much sleep that night. Reg Hallam missed two chances of his "D", being nearly shot during the hours of darkness in mistake for a Jap.

The second day of landing was a very unfortunate day for us. Late in the afternoon "Peanut" Jones and "Gerry" O'Sullivan were hit by a Jap Sniper at very close range. Next morning just after daylight we copped it again by LMG fire, this time causing heavy casualties. Jack Menzies, "Buzz Bomb" Donovan, Jack Carroll and Red Murphy were all hit. "Mauler" Menzies died within 2 minutes, "Buzz Bomb" died of wounds, Jack Carroll and Red Murphy were badly wounded. The night of 11/12 June was a nightmare for all, "standing to" all night, with Tojo having a go at us spasmodically with an LMG — no sleep for anyone. It was a very sorry Pl that moved out next morning. Those boys that had been killed ranked high in everyone's estimation. They were all young and were the best of pals. They were sadly missed.

The Pl lost a lot of its pep when we lost "Mauler" Menzies — he was the life of the Pl, never a dull moment when he was about. His wisecracks etc. will live forever among the boys.

There was a particularly funny incident on the second day. It was a very gruelling march along the open road. We had been marching for longer than usual and were halted in an open spot with no shade whatsoever. The sun was belting down very fiercely and everybody was bone dry. On the side of the road was a large drain and for a few seconds we sat on the edge of it, longing and wishing it was safe to drink. To have water so close when we were so dry, and it was hotter than we had ever been in our lives before, was too much for any man. Mauler looked longingly at it for a few seconds then plunged into it, saying, "—— the Bilharzia, —— the Cholera. He stood in it and poured water out of his hat all over him. It wasn't many seconds before the rest of the Pl were doing likewise. "No risk, no fun."

When we took up a perimeter defence at Tutong Ferry, the area was too large for the Pl. Each Section was covering a platoon area. Sections were under strength, there being only 5 men to each, 2 men had to remain on piquet all night. There were only 2 watches in the Pl, meaning that one Section had to take their timing from the nearest watch. The Section that had no watch (No 2) got slightly balled in their piquet and was standing to at about 0300 hrs.

At the Clifford Bridge area one Section had taken up a defensive position at the Western end. One night, "Happy" Parker, who was on piquet at the time, looked up and saw a figure standing in front of him. He tried unsuccessfully to put a round up the spout. In the meantime the figure had moved onto the bridge. We heard next day that a Jap had been picked up at Bn HQ. Luckily unarmed. We have a suspicion that he may have been the same one.

We moved by transport to Tutong Ferry and, on the way, our truck broke down. We finished the last few miles with a tractor pushing us. I have heard of one man being forced into action with a pistol but, I think this Pl has the honour of being the first pushed into action with a tractor!

At the 18 Mile Cross Roads we lived very well, the natives keeping us supplied with eggs, cucumbers, bananas, beans etc. Everybody started to replace their lost weight here, due mainly to the excellent job of cooking done by "Brig" Dempsey. We had a good bludge at Tutong Ferry for a few weeks, then word came through that the Pl had to march to Seria to rejoin the Bn. The idea of rejoining the Bn was OK but the thought of marching 26 miles along the open beach was not so hot. It was about the worst march we have ever done. We did most of it at night, arriving at Seria in 2 days.

TRANSPORT PLATOON

On the trip from Morotai the Pl was split up over two holds. Their job was to relieve the assault Tps of as many fatigues as possible and in this respect were "caught up with" much to the delight of the boys in the Rifle Coys. When not actually working in the mess they were invariably having a cup of brew, for Billy Wright and Blue Cole have no peers at finding one of these no matter how quiet the brewers may try to keep it.

Z-1 arrived with an order that the CO was to inspect all vehicles on the ship and the thought of him losing a few gallons of sweat brought many a chuckle for they had been doing it each day when they went down to start their vehicles. When the inspection was over he looked as though he had been over the side instead of down in the bowels of the ship.

Dave Hall was the "hero" of the landing, being the only member of the Tpt to land at Green Beach. The others became "base wallahs" by landing at Yellow Beach after it had been taken. Speed May and Hec Booth were in a lot of strife towing the 2-pdr guns for as soon as they left the barge they were bogged to the eyebrows. They painted a pitiful picture wielding their shovels while everyone else was busily getting on with the War.

In the period immediately after landing, our job was to centralise all the Bn stores and this brought with it many thrilling rides over boggy patches. Blue Cole holds the record for being bogged the most but he was not the only one to be stuck. Sid Andrews, the "boy" cook grasped the chance of hitch-hiking with Hec Booth to B Ech and on the way put on a very fine trapeze act for, whilst racing through a sand patch, the jeep hit a large bump and Sid went hurtling through the air to land flat on his back.

"Muscles" Chapman and "Black Alf" Crompton commanded a lot more respect after they had taken Gen MacArthur on a tour of inspection. The only trouble is that Muscles hasn't stopped talking about it yet or, if that is not the subject, he can soon find another one.

Much interest was displayed in some of the captured Jap trucks and much work was put in on them in an effort to get them back on the road once again. "Bibs" Cowling and "Bluey" Wormald put on a magnificent performance whilst working on one of these. The truck was parked on the side of the road surrounded by thick scrub and no other Tps were within a mile of them. Suddenly the terrifying crackle of straffing filled the air and Bibs and Bluey, thinking they were the target promptly shot through. Bibs in his flight ran into a pool and was saturated.

A half hour later they staggered into B Ech firmly convinced that they had been the sole target of 6 Mitchells.

Maudy Foster became OC Water Cart having converted a Jap truck for this purpose and he did some death defying dashes in this along a stretch of road near the air strip where some Jap snipers had been reported. Rumour has it that Maudy was going so fast that no Jap bullet could have caught him.

At Brunei some more trucks were found and work on them began at once. Doddy Mock became so engrossed in his work that, on several occasions others walked into him thinking he was part of the truck, the latter being black of course. Doddy had scrounged so many spare parts that he had sufficient to make another two trucks besides keeping the one he had in running order.

From Brunei to Seria, Ian Dunlop and Tommy Budden were the dauntless double who piloted the advance. It was never thought that jeeps would be used as armoured cars but that was their fate after the addition of a few sand bags and a Bren or two. Speed May, Billy Bodkin, Ron Stanton, Hec Booth and Billy Wright completed the complement of drivers on the mobile column. Much panic was caused during the first night of the advance. Tommy Budden, Ian Dunlop and Billy Bodkin were camped close to each other and in the wee small hours of the morning they were rudely awakened by a thunderous crashing in the undergrowth. Rifles and Owens came from nowhere all trained on a poor inoffensive water buffalo.

After crossing the Tutong Ferry, Ron Stanton had an argument with a GMC truck and came out second best. That didn't worry Ron for it meant a trip back to Brunei and a good chance of bashing the spine. Doddy Mock confounded the critics when driving off the ferry for his front wheels were on the wharf when the barge moved out and he made the old truck make a supreme effort and jump the gap.

Coming along the beach from Tutong to Seria, Speed May endeavoured to do the disappearing act when his jeep stalled in the middle of a patch of quick sand, but we still have him with us — a mighty man is our Speed!

Alby McDonagh more often gave the impression of being a junk peddler than the QM's driver. One trailer was not sufficient for him, he tagged a jungle cart on behind for good measure. It was a case of everywhere that Alby went the cart was sure to follow.

Dooker Cranefield wasn't very keen on the War. He preferred to take other people out on scrounging expeditions but strange as it may seem, he didn't get any souvenirs. Perhaps he talked himself out of them.

Now that the War is over everyone is keen to get home. However they seem very keen on going home looking like black men for, if they get much darker, that is what they will be. The RMO will shortly be called upon to perform two major operations to remove the beds from the backs of Ron Stanton and Black Alf Crompton. Bibs Cowling is hoping that he will be able to take his Jap truck with him, for he says that winding it up each morning is good for the liver. Blue Cole, who went on the second batch of 5-Yearers, must have scratched his old bald head when he was put ashore at Leyte instead of Sydney.

Generally, the transport have had a very easy campaign, although at times they were called upon to do some solid work and then they showed that they could be relied upon when called for.

FROM A COY

Few rifle companies in the Second AIF had a better mentor as their first Commander than our A Coy. Capt H T Allan had served in the 17 Bn World War I, his last posting being A Coy Comd, and had been awarded the Military Cross in 1918. I think it is unique that 22 years later, aged 45, he enlists and is posted as A Coy Comd 2/17 Bn. "Blue" Allan, as he was affectionately known to all ranks, did not stay in this posting long as he moved to various jobs at Brigade, Division and finally to New Guinea Command. Here his expertize, gained as a between-wars gold miner at Bulolo, was put to good use, in recruiting of native carriers, his knowledge of the country and his advice on how to survive. Throughout the War "Blue" never missed an opportunity to look up his "old mob", particularly A Coy for which he had a great affinity, and he left his mark.

Claude Brien took over from "Blue", and with "Curly" Wilson as 2 i/c, Peter O'Brien, Joe Blundell and Dick Bird as Pl Comds, Ned Kellie as CSM and Bill Leaman as CQMS, A Coy was under way.

Memories are fading and I apologise for omissions but, when I think of A Coy, these names come to mind. Goff Schrader, Cliff Polson, Toby Harris, Occer Hannaford, Bev Ellison, Billy Moore, "Ding Dong" Bell, Peter Pollock, Harold McLachlan, Billy Wright, Pat Conti, J H McHenry, Phil Chilvers, Bert Portsmouth, Arthur Rogers, Jack Geaney, and many more. Sufficient to say, the Coy had its share of "characters" from all ranks who served the Bn well, and the anecdotes that follow give accounts of some lighter sides of soldiering not mentioned in the manuscript.

By Pat Conti

BENGHAZI ESCARPMENT

The Bn seems completely unaware that their gallant 8 Pl defended unaided this entire escarpment which lay some miles along the Coast Road to the east of Benghasi. How we finally got there only the Almighty would know, certainly not our leader, Sgt Harold McLachlan, as he cheerfully admits to this day. Our defensive position overlooked both the road and the Mediterranean Sea and was located near a local tribe who all appeared to live under this huge tent plus their chooks, farm and domestic animals. We became friends with them and they were most hospitable to us. Mainly through sign language, we found out they hated the Ities because of their conquering of Libya. They would take one of the tribesmen in a plane and drop him over their settlement. The CO must have become anxious about our safety because, after a few days, Dudley McCarthy our IO turned up and ordered us to leave at once. Apparently Jerry was almost on top of us, so we left our position hurriedly and in some disorder and headed back to our trucks and safety.

TOBRUK

A few things stick out in my memory: Nearly being shot by Bruce Blanch following a rifle inspection. Bruce forgot to put his finger on the bullet when he cleaned his rifle and pressed the trigger and it flew past my left ear. A similar mishap from a Bren gun cleaned by Billy Wright at El Agheila had me wondering if my Section really liked me. Then we had a spell at Bianca in a large dingus built above the ground with rocks as the ground was too hard to break the surface. Why the previous occupants had built it thus was beyond us, as it was a great aiming mark for Jerry's daily hate which occurred just before sundown. During the day, it was also used by the Royal Horse Artillery as an OP by an officer and his offsider, a young gunner named Brooks. When the mortar fire began accompanied by bursts from a Spandau, this officer would telephone a fire order to his guns. The orders never seemed to be completed because the bombs would start raining down all around the post and would cut his wire. "Brooks", the officer would say, "the wire's cut". Brooks would jump to it, over the parapet and track down where the cut occurred. Having mended it, he would return for further orders. All this was carried out during intense mortar fire and we were quite incensed by his officer's apparent callousness. A few days later, the officer returned accompanied by a 2/12 Field Regt gunner, Brooks apparently was on advance party as 2/12th were relieving the RHA. When the mortars began that afternoon and the usual break in wire occurred, the officer said to the Aussie, "The wire's cut". No movement from our Aussie gunner, a hard look from RHA who then clambered over the parapet and mended the wire. We were ashamed of our Aussie's lack of guts and our previous assessment of the RHA officer who could take it as well as give it out.

The next day I was ordered to take out a small recce patrol that night. However, before setting out, I was called to Pl HQ and informed that instead of taking out the patrol I was on an advance party, the whole Bn was being relieved. I asked Alf Tuckwell our Pl Comd, who was taking my place. He said, "I am." Something appeared to be disturbing him so I asked if anything was wrong. He said, "Do you know what day it is?" I said, "It's Friday". He said, "Friday the 13th!" His death on that Patrol will always live in my memory. There was no doubt he was superstitious and particularly so that day. He could easily have given that Patrol to someone else or not even put me on the Advance Party. But he also knew I had had a torrid time for a whole week, including sustaining a direct hit on our dingus which incapacitated my Bren gunner and his mates, Tommy Budden and Billy Proudlock, and putting the Bren gun out of action. So he took my place and died. Alf was a very gallant and caring officer whom I will never forget.

Then there was the patrol returning to base who stopped in their tracks hearing an incredible sound in No Man's Land — a rooster crowed! This resulted in messages flowing between Tobruk and Cairo when it was even suggested that the enemy were using birdcalls to make contact with each other's patrols. What had appeared to be a mystery was my old friend, Cpl Bevin Ellison (or was he a Private?). Bevin's movement in rank was akin to a yo-yo but he also fancied himself in the crowing business. Before joining up he was known to come home late at night, a little you-know-what, put his pyjamas on, open his bedroom windows, look out on the calm, still night there would emerge from him a life-like crow. This would immediately be taken up by nearby roosters and then to others like ripples on a still pond. Satisfied with the turmoil created and no doubt giving his well known chuckle, he would close the window, climb into bed and fall asleep. Well, he too was on patrol that night when the urge to crow came over him. You know about the rest of the story.

An amusing incident occurred when we were in the Blue Line, not long after Dal Cartledge had joined the Bn from Cairo OCTU. He was a happy, bright, intelligent and caring officer from the start. However, he had not yet come to full terms with his rank and his charges were all seasoned soldiers. Unfortunately for him, the Pl piquet broke down on the only occasion the CO decided to visit his men to see how they were observing "stand-to". My section was a little closer than Pl HQ to the road and our sentry had roused us all up when the CO's voice was unmistakable from some hundred yards away, "I think A Coy should be about here". The two bods accompanying him agreed almost as if they were talking to God. I looked around very hurriedly, all were in position and alert. Bill Brinkley, our guard, was just a few yards away. I whispered to him, "Bill, don't forget to challenge correctly". "OK, Sarge", he said. I watched the three figures slowly but purposefully advance towards us out of the gloom. "Halt, who goes there?", barked Bill. "Friends", said the CO. "Advance over and be recognised", said Bill. You beaut, I thought to myself. Full Sergeant tomorrow at least. The CO stepped forward. Horrified

I looked at Bill. His rifle and bayonet were lying on his dingus and Bill calmly rolling a cigarette using both hands. All hell broke out. Bill finally got out (he was a stammerer), "We all knew it was you, Sir". I told him we had been fixed on him since his vehicle stopped, but to no avail. "Where's Pl HQ?" Pl HQ was pointed out. Poor Dal, there had been no piquet to awaken them and they were all blissfully asleep. Later Peter Pollock described the scene and the tongue lashing Dal got and how the latter was so upset that Peter thought suicide was on the cards. I then told Peter the piquet had broken down and named the culprit who was afterwards suitably punished. So everything returned to normal.

Finally, just before we sailed from Tobruk, there occurred much activity on the Bn's front which culminated in an attack by C Coy on "Plonk" out through the Post that 9 Pl was defending. As a L/Sgt, I was Acting Pl Comd, not an uncommon happening in the 2/17th. It was to this Post that Frank Windeyer was carried on a stretcher, mortally wounded, but still conscious. His concern was not for himself but for his men as I heard him repeatedly ask for information regarding individuals who accompanied him on this tragic and, to me, unnecessary encounter.

THE LANDING AT FINSCHHAFEN — AN EYEWITNESS REPORT
By Noel Moylan

Due to circumstances, certainly not by choice, I found myself in the bow of a landing craft, being one of four craft of the first wave of those making the initial assault at Finschhafen. The time was pre-dawn on 22 Sept 1943 and the immediate objective was Scarlet Beach.

We had trained for this operation (i.e. the seagoing part of it) on the APD the USS *Humphries* and, if one can recall reasonably happy memories from wartime activities such as these, then the *Humphries* enabled us to do just that.

We were 8 Pl, I was the Pl Runner, and the ship carried, I think, the whole of A Coy.

It was an old ship and I am sure not designed to carry the whole coy of an infantry battalion. I doubt also whether any of us had been on a destroyer before but the novelty of it, coupled with the friendly co-operation of the crew and the quality of the food they provided (no limit to back-ups) had, during the past couple of weeks training on it, provided a most welcome relief to the standard infantry training routine.

Breakfast on the ship at approx 0400 hours on 22 Sept was jocularly and irreverently referred to as the Last Supper which subsequently sadly proved to be true for some of our comrades. After breakfast we assembled on deck and thence down the nets to the landing craft — an operation that we had practised many times during the preceding weeks.

The night, or morning, was very dark and we set off for Scarlet Beach under the control of an American boatswain — we in 8 Pl occupying 1 craft on the left flank of the 4 in line abreast.

It must have been a navigational nightmare for the US Navy men responsible for getting us to the designated area of the beach in the darkness and the supporting gunfire would have done nothing to help their concentration.

Scarlet Beach was bounded at one end by an outcrop of rocks and, as a result of a slight error in our directional path (was it any wonder?), our craft ground to a halt on to these rocks. I believe that this made us first ashore on that fateful morning.

This then became our landing point so the bow gate was lowered and the landing commenced. Our Pl Comd, Stret Waterhouse, was first off and promptly disappeared as the rock on which our craft faltered was not part of the general land area. However, we managed to pull him clear and then proceeded to follow a very wet Pl leader on a stumbling stepping-stone journey to the shore proper. After finally reaching terra firma (a strange description for an area of thick jungle undergrowth with swamps and creeks predominating) and re-grouping (i.e. holding on to the bloke in front) we simply inched forward until some interruption or daylight should appear.

This forward movement involved maintaining contact with the fellow in front in the sure knowledge that none of us knew where we were, where we were going or what was in store for us. It also involved at times wading through waist deep water, holding aloft rifle, (or SMG), ammunition and a precious little plastic (or was it rubber in those days?) bag containing tobacco and pay book.

Our task, of course, was to clear the enemy of the surrounding area of the beach to allow the following waves of our forces to disembark. When daylight appeared we pressed forward up the hill surrounding Scarlet Beach until we met strong resistance from a well fortified defensive enemy post.

Our attack on the post resulted in the death of Stret Waterhouse and a Sec leader, Cpl Bruce Culey, both of whom were killed by small arms fire almost simultaneously. With assistance from a mortar barrage, the Japs abandoned the post with whatever equipment they had with the exception of a number of bags of unprocessed rice with which we supplemented our rations for some time thereafter.

At the end of a long and exhausting day, we prepared a defensive position on the top of a hill. Just prior to sunset, planes arrived overhead and numerous parachutes dotted the sky. We were relieved to learn, after our initial alarm, that it was not the beginning of a counter offensive by the enemy but supplies being dropped for us from the RAAF.

So ended Day 1 of the Finschhafen operation. It was the beginning of a period of some weeks of skirmishing, culminating with the action at Jivevaneng from which we were finally relieved and from all of which we had lost half of the Pl as casualties.

RAVENSHOE
By Alf Toglianini, 9 Platoon

In Ravenshoe, whilst I was a member of 9 Pl and our Bn was away on bivouac, three men had been left behind, having been detailed for guard duty. I was included and the other two were Jimmy Crawley, known as "Brutus", and another younger man, "Tassie" Enright.

Our duties were to guard two detainees who were under detention in the Guard Room. This was an American Bell tent which was enclosed by a barbed wire fence.

The word had got around that a movie of "The Rats of Tobruk" was to be shown in the adjoining 2/13 Bn area. We were all keen to see this film and had made the decision to do so. Having no option we took the two prisoners with us.

Little did we know that our interlude would be discovered, nor the consequence of our action. We made sure that the lights were left on in the Bell tent and environs in order that no suspicion would be aroused regarding our escapade. Little did we know also that the Adjutant, "Spanky" McFarland, had decided to inspect the area in which the Guard Tent was situated.

To Spanky's astonishment, no challenge was given by the guards and the compound was deserted. Truly, this was a very bewildering mystery and Spanky was at a complete loss as to what had happened to the guards and the prisoners.

After a time lapse of some duration, men's voices were heard and four men approached the Guard Tent to be accosted by Spanky who angrily demanded, "Where have you been?" The answer was, "We have been to the pictures to see the "Rats of Tobruk". "You have, have you?" Calling the Regimental Police, Sgt Conway, Spanky placed the guards under arrest also.

There was still one man missing, for one of the original prisoners having asked permission to attend to a call of nature, had not as yet appeared. A search was immediately carried out, with no result. This character had decided to "shoot through", "never to be seen again". A few days later, the furphy had it, the absconder had caught a plane at Mareeba, some chap had been given "the good oil".

The day after this episode, a Court of Inquiry was held, and the accused were marched in and paraded before Spanky. The Investigation went on but, gradually, the seriousness of this crime and King's Rules & Regulations were forgotten, as discussion became that of another topic — the movie "Rats of Tobruk". Spanky and the arrestees discussed this with great enthusiasm and Spanky, carried away with nostalgic memory, let mercy prevail.

The end result was that "Brutus" received a severe tongue lashing in which he was told that, as he was a seasoned and older soldier, it was hoped that he would set these younger men a good example. Brutus, no doubt, thought it was well worth the reprimand. We certainly enjoyed the show.

THE RIVER DYAKS

Having always been interested in unusual people and places, the River Dyaks of Borneo who, very much on our side during our confrontation with the Japanese, I found to be very fascinating

It would seem that these people were not sportsmen (in the true sense) as would be instanced by their peculiar attitude when challenged to contest their skill with the Blowpipe.

These forest dwellers were of picturesque appearance, both male and female sporting waist length hair with a minimum of clothing, the females being topless. In the lobes of these people's ears coins were worn, Straits Settlement dollars being the most common, and many had their teeth imprinted with gold and brightly coloured jewels or stones. On their throats and arms were tattoos of an eagle or some such bird.

Being a communal people, they lived in kampongs in which were Long Houses. These large huts housed approx fifty mixed men, women and children. The moral standard was high, bearing no resemblance to the permissiveness commonly observed in our own present day society.

The women folk would tend the young "Dyak fry" and look after the chores in and around the kampongs. The men would hunt for food and, no doubt, carry out their hobby of "head hunting".

The Long Houses were built on stilts, under which pigs were kept, and were, no doubt, a safety precaution against floods and marauders. The Dyaks were well armed with their 5 or 6 foot long blowpipes complete with a supply of poisoned darts.

On occasions, tests of skill were arranged. Having placed a cigarette box on a convenient tree, the contestants would do their thing with blowpipe and dart. When it was the Diggers' turn to have a shot at the target, if a no-score hit was observed by the Dyaks, they would roar with laughter and make derisive gestures, accompanied by obviously rude remarks. If, however, the target was hit, that was another matter, the Dyaks would become furious and, collecting their blowpipes, would move away in disgust.

One young Dyak by the name of Kunya, was in severe trouble, he was given a "short back and sides" haircut by a mischievous Digger. He was excommunicated by his companions, forever exiled, for he had broken a taboo. Meanwhile, this pathetic pariah had attached himself to 2/17 Bn. He happily joined in with his new found friends, sharing both chores and rations. He proved himself of some use but, as to his ultimate fate, I wonder. Maybe his shrunken head adorns one of the long houses with the knick-knacks which the Dyaks collect. No doubt he would be hanging near an arrangement of Japanese and Chinese heads (the Dyak's favourite trophies). He may even have been swapped for a couple of pounds of potatoes!

As ever, Life has its sad ironies.

SOME TALES FROM BORNEO
(Authors unknown)
8 Platoon, July 1945 — Ridan

On the 16th, while we were out on patrol, a Dyak came running up with the news that the Japs were moving on towards our small holding force at Ridan. A forced march brought us back to the holding force much to their relief. As the Japs did not turn up that day we spent an uneasy night and next morning decided to go out and joust with them. Every sign pointed to the fact that the Japs did not know that there were troops in the area and we looked like giving them a swift sure "kick in the pants".

The first light of the 17th found us ready to move, led by 4 Dyaks and under the leadership of "Trigger" Tregilgas. We had marched for an hour when the Dyaks called a halt, as Japs had been sighted out in front. Bert Lovall sent the Dyaks back and 6 Sec withdrew to a good position about 20 yds to the rear. Harry Byron and Cpl Ings went to the right of the track and the other 6 men went to the left. One of the Dyaks caused Harry quite a little discomfort by firing over the top of his head while sitting in the middle of his back.

4 Japs came around the bend and were all killed by shots from 6 Sec. Jake Ings had a narrow escape when he saw a little angry man taking a bead on him. He fired from the hip and "the little son of heaven" winged his way home. In these half a dozen hectic seconds the Japs had a machine gun in action. 4 Sec, in reserve, had taken up a position on the left flank and 5 Sec was moving across the track which ran parallel to the track on the right. 6 Sec poured fire into the Japs, and Bill Payne, assisted by Lennie Langford, the Pl Mortarmen, had their stovepipe hurling bombs in the Jap direction in less than a minute. A very commendable effort. The Jap was not long in replying with his mortar, but none of the bombs fell in our direction.

Meanwhile, Jake Ings spotted a wounded Jap forcing his way through the thick undergrowth. Jake decided to wait for a better shot when a bullet cut the flesh on the last two fingers of his left hand. A Jap, who had come to the assistance of one of the wounded, was coolly shot by Screw Williams before he could do any damage. It was at this moment that Jake, despite his wounded hand, despatched the Jap before he could reach the cover.

Meanwhile, 5 Sec had been pinned down by automatic fire before they could reach their objective. Sgt Tregilgas directed Wal Petrie, 5 Sec gunner, to have a go at the unseen Jap gunner. Wal let a mag go, but couldn't find the gunner. The Japs, however, got onto the 5 Sec position and poured in a burst, sending our portly Lt "Porky" Graham, to ground smartly. It was then decided that we had obtained our objective by surprising and inflicting casualties on the Japs so we were to retire. As a parting gesture, the 3 grenade dischargers were brought into action and the barrage laid down made an impressive noise.

When the barrage had cleared the Dyaks raced in and obtained some gruesome trophies in the form of heads. 8 Pl had only retired in time because the Japs laid down a barrage of MMG and Mortar right on their vacated positions. We all returned to our area feeling very happy in the fact that we had done a good job.

9 PLATOON
BALAI — MORNING OF 29 JUNE 1945

Having arrived at Belai, Pl HQ and one Section were quartered in a two-storey house, quite close to the river. The other two Sections had an old timber mill in which to sleep. We were amazed to find that our fellow occupants of the house were Dyaks who occupied the lower storey.

Our first impressions of the Dyaks were indeed good. For the most part, they are splendidly proportioned little men and very handsome in their own way. They are liberally tatooed and their teeth are gold covered and studded with brilliant stones of all colours. They are quite friendly little coves after you penetrate their shyness and we had many a good yarn. It was funny to see the boys trying to carry on a conversation with their limited vocabulary. About the only word that was universally understood was "Bagoose" (good). With our fellows, it was very much overstressed.

FINK'S LANDING

Just after we landed, two Indian POWs who had escaped the Japs, arrived, guided by a lad called Stephen Lee. They were suffering from malnutrition and were pitifully clothed. Their joy on release was a spectacle that made us feel very happy. We sent them back to Kuala Belait on the boats that brought us up.

FROM B COY

The undermentioned were the original Officers, Warrant Officers, Sergeants, CQMs and Orderly Room Corporal.

OC	Maj J. Silverstone
2 i/c	Capt John Grant
10 Pl	Lt Paddy Owen, Sgt Jim Dixon
11 Pl	Lt Bayne Geikie, Sgt Nev West
12 Pl	Lt Colin Pitman, Sgt Eric Williams
CSM	WO II Matt Higgins
CQMS	Staff Sgt Eric Easterbrook
Orderly Room Cpl	Cpl Dick Reeves

The Coy consisted of 139 men with an extra 45 men from 3R Pl which were our first and second reinforcements.

Maj Jessel Silverstone left the Bn in the Middle East, being transferred to the Aussies in Greece and was in charge of Line of Communication at which he excelled. He was responsible for destroying all paper work so that it would not fall into enemy hands. Jessel took his batman Frank Rice with him and when things were rather grim he got Frank out of Greece and back to 2/17 Bn. Maj Silverstone was taken POW and returned home after the War.

The Bn, and B Coy in particular, were very proud to have had with them Evelyn Owen — the inventor of the famous Owen Sub-Machine Gun.

Was B Coy the best Coy in the Bn? I was in B Coy, C Coy, E Coy — yes, there was an E Coy — and also attached to Lt A. Mackell, D Coy for the Easter Blue. I cannot see any difference in any Coy within the Bn. They were all SUPER.

Many thanks to those who sent in the following anecdotes and hope they bring back some forgotten events and memories.

INGLEBURN CAMP — 1940
By Athol Roberts

B Coy was called to parade by the CSM, Matt Higgins, and after the usual reports etc. he handed the Coy over to the OC, Maj Jessel Silverstone. The Major then posted his Officers. After all troops were ready for the next order, Jessel asked the Coy if there was anybody who knew about horses and dogs. Immediately, Pts Jack Travena and Smith raised their hands, thinking this will be better than the route march. They were called out by the Major and Travena said he knew horses and Smith likewise with dogs. "Right," said the Major, "run to the Q Store and get a broom and a shovel". They returned with same and the Major said, "There has been a horse and a dog on the parade ground and as you, Trevena, know about horses, you clean up its droppings, and the same for you with the dog's, Smith. At the double now, and clean up and run back to the Coy after you have returned the broom and shovel, so that you can join us on the route march". Who said Jessel did not have a sense of humour?

Did you know that 2/17 Bn was the most forward of any troops in the Desert at Mersa-Brega? B Coy was ordered to go further forward with 11 Pl. Further forward again, No. 6 Sec with Athol Roberts, Jack Britton, Boy "F.F." Farrand, Reg Bennett, Dan Lyneham, Pte Walsh and another went 1 mile further ahead. Still do not know if the Section was to stop the German Army or not.

I remember the Hurricane aircraft that was shot down and fell in the Bn lines and burnt up. After the fire had gone out and everything cooled off, Dan Lynehan and Athol Roberts stripped the Browning machine guns from the plane and dismantled them to finally put together a gun that worked.

Col Crawford, the CO, heard about this gun and came up the line to see it. I cocked the gun and fired several bursts when the CO said, "Corporal, that barrel is slightly bent". "Yes Sir", I replied, "but it does save aiming off a little if needed". The CO must have thought about this gun, because when the ration truck came up that night, lo and behold, there was a new barrel and 1,000 rounds of ammunition with belts for this gun. Apparently the CO got them from the Air Force. What, with a Bren, Spandau, Swartzlose and Breda, we had a fairly good range of machine guns in 6 Sec.

Whilst we were at Tel el Eisa, Pte Syd Andrews, 6'7" tall, and Pte Gunning, 5' tall (if that), asked for new boots. The request was forwarded to the RQMS and the next night the ration truck came up and delivered our food etc. The driver was asked where the boots were. "Oh yes", and threw one pair out of the truck. "Driver," I said, "where are the other pair of boots?" "Inside that pair there", was the reply. And sure enough, Gunning's boots were inside Syd Andrews' size 13 boots. They breed big boys in Queensland — that is where Andrews came from.

Thinking of Andrews brings to mind when we were at Tel el Eisa, we had been out all night on patrol and were naturally a little weary, so those not on sentry duty decided to have a sleep. I was having a nice nap when Tom Brown called out to me, "Hey, Robbo there are some blokes here. One has a lot of red braid and they want to see you". I crawled out of my dugout and, lo and behold, it was Lt Gen Sir Oliver Leese, Comd 30 Corps. I had forgotten that he was to do a tour of inspection.

The General questioned me regarding what was the role of the Pl and, having satisfied him with the answers, he asked if there was anything we needed in the way of supplies. I told him, "Yes Sir, watches and compasses". He told his aide to make a note of same and to take the necessary course of action.

Gen Leese moved on, or rather back, and then Gen Morshead came over to inspect the Pl area. He asked to see a section post. I took him to the section where Pte Andrews belonged. The General looked down into Andrews' fox hole, "Sgt, do you know that is too deep. A man could get buried in that hole". On saying that, he got down into the fox hole and was about 2 feet lower than the top of the hole. "See what I mean, Sgt? I have to jump up to see over the top." I said, "Excuse me sir, but I will get the soldier concerned with this fox hole". I called Pte Andrews to come out of his dugout. "What the bloody hell do you want? I am tired — I have been out on patrol all night". "Enough of that", I answered. "Get out here now". Out he came and he almost collapsed when he saw Gen Morshead. "Get into your fox hole", I said to him, which he did and rested his arms on the top. The General was satisfied. "General", I said, "would you like to see his dugout?" "Yes." On looking at it he declared it was as big as his HQ. The General then left us and I felt that he was an amused man.

While on the mountain, we had a local from the village to do our chores, shopping etc. We called him "Whiskey" — don't know why, but you may guess. I said to him one day, "Whiskey, we want some firewood. "I will get", he said. "Whiskey, you bring wood and I will give you socks." Away he went and returned with a bag full of wood. To get this he had to dig down under the snow. I gave him one sock. He held up two fingers saying, "Etnein" (two feet) — etnein socks. I pointed to the one bag of wood, saying, "Wahad (one) bag — wahad sock". So Whiskey trundled off to get another bag. I often wonder where he is today.

By Bayne Geikie

At midnight, 13/14 April 1941, a bright moonlight night in Tobruk, a fighting patrol of 24 supplied by 11 Pl of B Coy and led by Lt Bayne Geikie with Sgt Bob McElroy as 2 i/c left the perimeter of HQ Coy with the orders to penetrate the enemy lines and bring back a prisoner.

The going was slow since there was some sporadic rifle fire and odd signal wires which were investigated. About 2,000 yds out from the perimeter we sighted an enemy patrol of three coming towards us from the right and went to ground. When the enemy were close enough and the leading Sec opened up with the Bren gun, the enemy patrol scattered and went to ground. Members of the leading Sec, led by Cpl Swede Weldon, Dave Dunning and Rex Burns, rushed the enemy and grabbed one, namely a German Corporal. By the time they got the German onto his feet, Dave Dunning and Rex Burns had stripped him of practically everything except his singlet and underpants. However, Rex Burns could not believe that the Corporal didn't have a watch. He kept going through his clothing asking the German, "Where's your watch?"

Having got a prisoner, the patrol headed back for the perimeter, the prisoner being guarded by Rex Burns, Dave Dunning and Swede Weldon. On the way back, Rex got really cunning and said to the German in his most benign manner, "You haven't got the time on you, have you mate?", to which the German replied, "No, I haven't".

On reaching the perimeter outside HQ Coy, we found the enemy firing had livened up and bursts of tracer bullets were flying in all directions. I decided to split the party to the effect that Swede Weldon and I took the prisoner to the trucks below the escarpment, and Sgt Bob McElroy took the remainder of the Patrol to the trucks, the whereabouts of which we were not sure, due to the excitement of dodging the tracer burst. We found the trucks and headed back to the Bn HQ and the remainder of B Coy. However, half way back we met Capt Curley Wilson leading on foot the remainder of B Coy. He told me the Coy was moving to take up a counter-attack position behind D Coy. The patrol joined B Coy in the march forward to take up a counter-attack position. Curley exchanged places with Swede in the truck and came with me to Bn HQ with the prisoner who we handed over to the CO. As far as I know, this was the first German prisoner taken in Tobruk. When the CO had finished his interrogation of me, Capt Wilson and I joined B Coy behind D Coy. Capt Wilson dispersed the coy and then he and I and my orderly, Jimmy Liddiard, went forward to D Coy to ascertain the situation from Capt John Balfe.

John Balfe was busy taking reports from his forward Pls and in turn reporting to Bn HQ. By the time he was ready to put us in the picture, the German tanks were breaking through the perimeter and we were engaged with enemy shelling, most of which burst between us and B Coy, cutting us off from our Coy.

When the enemy tanks had advanced half way between the perimeter and our post, Capt Balfe ordered us all under ground into one of those concrete posts built by the Italians earlier in the war.

Jimmy Liddiard and I looked after the westerm end of the Post, one on either side of the passage way at the bottom of the steps with fixed bayonets. The German tanks ground their way up to the post, came to a halt and, after a pause, continued east towards 2/13 Bn. This was just before or on first light. I saw the shadows of men jumping over our weapon pit and heard the Germans talking.

When the tanks moved off our Post we manned the weapons pits. Jimmy Liddiard and Bromwich and I were in the easternmost weapon pit. We had our rifles, a Bren gun and an a/tk rifle. When we got into the weapon pit we saw columns of German foot soldiers advancing in the wake of the tanks. Bromwich and I took it in turns to fire the Bren at the Germans who were an easy target since they were enfiladed and went down like packs of cards. We picked off individual Germans with our rifles. Jimmy Liddiard sat on the steps behind us loading the Bren gun magazines for Bromwich and me to fire. It was now pale daylight.

During the activity when I was looking for the source of a large tracer bullet, another tracer bullet hit a cairn of stones behind my head and, looking in the direction from which it came, I found myself looking down a barrel of an a/tk gun 50-60 metres away. I shot the crew of the gun before they had a chance of reloading the gun.

Later we saw German tanks coming from the direction of 2/13 Bn and our hearts sank. We thought we were the only Post holding out and that the Germans were coming to clean us up! However, the tanks headed for the perimeter and then travelled parallel with the wire until they came to John Dinning's Pl Post. We realised then they were in retreat. They stopped at John's Post and tried to take his men prisoner. I sprayed the tanks with Bren gun fire and the Germans who were riding on the tanks scattered in all directions. A burst from the Bren hit in the back the German Major who was conducting the surrender. When he fell the Germans panicked and the tanks retreated out through the gap in the perimeter, their guns blazing at our a/tk guns and dragging behind them what guns they could.

By Ivan Dutton and Joe Wallis — 1941

When we were up Benghazi way, a few chaps from 10 Pl decided to make a recce of the town: Slim Barber, Nev West, Joe Wallis, Ivan Dutton and driver, Darrel Luck. Just after we arrived in the town, the tail board gave way and Slim followed us, bouncing along on his backside unhurt.

On our way back, Nev West sighted some cattle and decided a young bull would help our rations. With the bull on the truck, we headed back to the unit to hang the butchered beef on Bren tripods with ground sheet cover. We found the tripods all set up but Bert Moore and Harry Wells had hung mutton under the ground sheets, so the beef was passed around to be put out of sight. An inspection was made of the area and the Pl was congratulated for having the guns at the ready.

On a patrol out of Tobruk one member kept complaining about his boots hurting and this went on for the duration of the patrol. When they returned, Swede Weldon found he had his boots on the wrong feet. (Confirmed by B. Geikie.)

B Coy was on the airstrip overlooking Tobruk. A truck was seen coming up the road to the NAAFI canteen, and the driver had been sampling the contents of his load. Joe Wallis asked him if he would like a hand to help unload. So a 4-doz case of beer was unloaded and, with the help of Ivan Dutton, it was taken back to the Sec. A 44-gall drum of sand was emptied and the beer placed in the drum, then the sand replaced to cover same.

Soon after the job was done the Canteen Sgt with Capt Wilson made an inspection of the Coy area looking for the beer — none found. Later Capt Wilson came around and asked for a beer. He said, "I know it is here". He was not the only one to taste the contents of the case.

OBOE SIX 1945
By Reg Kennedy

On the morning of the landing at Brunei, after we of 12 Pl had settled in our landing or assault craft, I saw that we had with us a surplus Corporal, equipped and apparently ready to go. When questioned about his identity, he informed me that he was Cpl — (I don't recall his name) from 2/13 Bn. He was an LOB travelling on our ship. He claimed to have participated in every 2/13th action and did not wish to miss this one. We agreed that he could accompany us to our first objective but then he must return to his unit. He wished us luck and then departed.

I am unable to nominate the place where the following incident occurred. However, it was on a hill feature near to where a young soldier named Harold Sharpe of 12 Pl was wounded on the previous day. It was the day after Frank McGrath won his Military Medal. We were being attacked by our own aircraft. Cpl Rowdy (Eddie) Ryan and I were attempting to erect a yellow panel on some low scrub to identify our position to the aircraft. Rowdy suddenly dropped his side of the identification panel, grasped his knee with both hands and hopped around yelling in great delight, "I've got a homer". This he repeated several times, until he realized he had been hit on the leg with nothing more than a clod of dirt. His language and facial expression revealed his disappointment.

Now that all the arguments have been presented and the dust has settled, one could be sure that not one member, not even J.R.B., could make a proper judgement without some degree of bias. However, the great masses would concur that 12 Pl was the best. In respect to this, I rely on the conduct of the aforementioned 2/13 Corporal. He was a relatively senior soldier of vast experience in operational matters. By his choice he had the unique opportunity to assess the qualities and standards of all Pls of the Bn for a period of time, longer than it takes to select most Popes, he travelled with members of the unit.

He was determined to take part in the landing. It is obviously clear that he would want to join the best Pl he could possibly find. In selecting 12 Pl, he established beyond doubt which was the best of the Pls. He also proved himself as a man of impeccable judgement.

RUWEISAT RIDGE — 5TH INDIAN DIVISION JULY 1942
By John Chilcott

I remember the morning we were rushed to back up the 5th Indian Div. We arrived and found our Indian friends had done a good job in holding Jerry off. Sorting out some of the German gear in the back of the truck, I found a good great coat, double breasted, high collar and ankle length — you beaut!!

After digging in the for the night, as Coy Runner I was called by the I Sec bloke to take sketches of our position etc. to BnHQ. He told me to follow the ridge and keep my eye on a particular star. Off I went in my new great coat and arrived safely. After a bit of a natter, I was given directions for my return trip to my Coy, and another star to watch.

There was a fair bit of a hate session going on out to my right and I lost the ridge — and my star. Then I found a minefield — I was lost. I carried on for some time and thought to rid myself of the great coat. After quite some time I came across the flank of one of our Coys who gave me directions. On arrival back after midnight, Snow Vidler (CSM) said, "Chilcott, where the hell have you been?" "Lost". "All right, get your head down, we are moving off early and the OC does not want to see you wearing that German great coat. "It's lost too!"

NEW GUINEA

We had completed our attack up to the knoll above Jivevaneng. We had been counter-attacked a few times but held our positions. Both Harry Wells and I had got hold of a Jap revolver each, also with about 8 rounds each. Things were reasonably quiet and Harry started to leave his rifle back in his dugout and carried his Jap revolver only as he went around the traps checking his men and defences. In the Meantime, I had a chance to try my revolver out. Fire 1 – nothing. Fire 2 – nothing. Fire 3 – nothing. Met up with Harry next morning whilst he was doing his rounds and asked, "Have you tried out that Jap pistol yet?". "No, why?". "Hell", he said and proceeded to try his out with the same result. I sold mine to some Yanks but I don't know what Harry did with his.

After we came off the trail at Jivevaneng, we returned to Heldsbach Plantation for a rest period. As Coy runner, I was sent off to collect the Coy's mail from Bn HQ. As we all know, any parcels for blokes who had left the unit for any reason, were split up by his section, except for anything personal. I had collected all the letters and parcels into the mail bag ready to return to the Coy. One parcel was missing. The owner had left, wounded. This parcel was regular with every mail. I was doing a final check when a wellknown voice cut through the air, "What are you doing, Chilcott?" "Collecting the mail, Major." "Got it all?" "No, Sir? Capt Sheldon's parcel is missing." "You are not getting that, Chilcott." "Why, Sir? All parcels of evacuated personnel are shared." "Not this time." Bert always had a bottle of whiskey sent up in a loaf of bread.!

By Harold McLeod

The following incident occurred when B Coy was making its way up the coast towards Sio Mission. We had a brief respite from pursuing the beaten Jap and, with the lazy sound of shells passing low overhead to blast his short stand about a mile ahead, were told to make the Pl area ready for an inspection by Lt Col Simpson — the "Red Fox". 1 Sec, through attrition due to deaths, wounds, illness, was left with only one possible leader, Gus Leseberg, a good soldier, but one who had his stripes awarded and taken away so regularly by the CO that they never did have time to be sown on. With everything shipshape and everyone standing to, the CO arrived at this Sec and, seeing no Sergeant or Corporal about, enquired of Gus as to who was in charge of the Sec. "I am", Gus replied and this may have been the one and only time that the CO was caught off balance. He actually blanched, before quickly recovering his equilibrium and carrying on with the conventional comments about readiness, disposition, etc.

The incident in retrospect, seems trivial, but to those who were around and were aware of the many scrapes and situations in which Gus was capable of being, it had much humour and irony.

AN UNFORGETTABLE MAN

I do not suppose that medals were ever awarded to Padres but were they to be, then one would surely have gone to Chaplain W.L. "Paddy" Byrne. Not being of his denomination, there were only a few occasions when I met him, the most important of these being when we were cut off by the Jap at Jivevaneng in New Guinea. It was my turn to take over the Bren gun pit siting down the back track which ran straight downhill for some hundred yards before disappearing around a bend in the jungle. I had no sooner taken my position when I saw movement at the bottom of the track and cocked the Bren in anticipation. Fortunately, I held my fire and saw, to my surprise, that it was the Padre strolling up the track. When he was closer I shouted out to him, "For God's sake, Padre, get off the track, it is booby trapped".

The imperturbable Padre did not immediately reply but did so when he was within talking distance and said, "Do not worry, my son, when the Good Lord wants me, He will let me know". With that he turned around and went back down the track. Foolish? Perhaps so; certainly so in my mind until the depth of his trust in the Almighty sank in and I realised that his courage had a deeper foundation than mine.

I was later told that he was at the front of the perimeter, watching the mortar boys in action on one occasion, and politely asked whether he could send off a round (against all rules, of course). The mortar crew readily agreed and showed him how to load and fire, which he did with competancy, saying as the round exploded, "There, split that up amongst you". He was an outstanding character.

EL ALAMEIN BATTLE 1942
HIGHLIGHTS OF "BLACK SUNDAY" 25 OCT 1942
By Bob Anson — Signaller attached to B Coy HQ

B Coy HQ — The battle was now in its 33rd hour. Just after dawn through the smoke, CSM Eric Williams and I can see German tanks to our left front — we count at least 17 with many troop carriers. Heavy shelling commences, and the .88mm flak is bursting behind, over Bn HQ's area. This was the start of day-long shelling, tank assaults and infantry attacks.

Communication with the Sig Offr is "on and off" as lines are chopped. George Henderson and I take turns to maintain the line, and Ross Jamieson and Roy Clark, the runners, work under extremely dangerous exposed conditions. What do I remember? Sgt Eric Williams — he is like the desert flies, everywhere, dropping two sticky bombs alongside us. Eric says, "Hope you don't have to use them!" George replies, "So do I". In the afternoon, as 30 German tanks approach our immediate front, we take another look at the sticky bombs.

At around 1100 hrs, Lt Bob Bennie reaches my shallow shelter where we have the wireless and telephone. Bob had just settled down in a prone position, when the sharpshooter out front wounded him. At this time B Coy had lost all its officers. George Henderson resumes his duel with this sniper — they have been trading shots for some time. The German is holed up in the knocked-out gun pit some 300 yds away.

Moving about under intense fire, the stretcher bearers attend to the wounded, seemingly immune to the shelling, the air bursts, tanks, scout cars and machine gun fire. I am not certain who they were, but I think Martin, Merve and "Sparrow" Nolan. The personal bravery of these men went unrewarded.

At midday, they carry in a badly wounded young German, who has shattered legs. He is left alongside, between George and me. This enemy soldier has two medals on his left tunic pocket. We both widen our shelter and get his body below the ground surface by about 6 inches deep, two sand bags protect his head. Throughout the long afternoon we experience heavy air bursts but, lying on his back, he shows no fear. The only request was water — his needs are great, George and I share our lot with this soldier. At dusk a carrier with our wounded picks him up. I still remember that event in my life, as he clasped my right hand and said, "I thank you".

Lt Hugh Main files us out, to another sector. As we move, we pass a row of the men who were killed, awaiting removal to their last resting place. For me I dare not look into the future, it seems uncertain. Capt Colin Pitman greets us as OC. I am pleased to see him again.

11 PL B COY
By Milton Trudgeon
ON THE ROAD BETWEEN BROOKETOWN AND BRUNEI — 12 JUN 45

I recall the superb spirit of II Pl in crossing the swamp, deployment into a section left, section right, section in reserve and the speed of the advance and attack up the ridge.

The long grass and difficult terrain caused the left section leader to slow down, ask for permission to patrol and again have supporting Vickers Machine Gun fire on the area in front of him. Using my walkie talkie i explained the requests to Captain Rudkin who urged that the speedy advance and attack be maintained.

Although this took up very little of my time, Gordon Broome had advanced quickly, overcome opposition, was standing wounded and asking for support for his section and this I quickly gave him.

Where the ridge flattened and broadened, a fine soldier, Jack Taylor was killed and I often remember him and the two stretcher bearers who rushed to his side. My following verses are about them.

STRETCHER BEARERS

Rush to side of wounded,   Brash to unassuming,
Heedless of any harm,   Men of every type,
Strive to stop the bleeding,   For a fighters life
Stretcher bearers calm.   Stretcher bearers fight.

11 Pl's attack shaped in my mind the first draft of my verses:

AFTER BATTLE

The battle tumult on the ridge   We blindly lift our fallen mate;
to empty echo flees   till last the foeman lies.
and fades away with cordite smoke   Our after-battle prayers and thoughts
among the rubber trees;   from stricken hearts arise —
and milky latex, bullet-tapped   with hearts still hard with hate for foe,
and wood chips, shrapnel-hewn   red-raw for comrade dead,
are weeping on the twisted dead   and troubled much by Jesus Christ,
upon the foxholes strewn.   Who, "Love your neighbour," said.

TRUDGE'S TRAMPS AT BRUNEI BAY AREA
Author unknown

The heat during the following days' advance towards Brunei was terrific and "Bubba" Smith's Bren was very close to the ground. Next day, we were committed to a Pl attack and suffered the sad loss of Pte Jack Taylor, a great chap and a tower of strength to his Sec, and effectionately known as "Squissy". Cpls Broome and Allgood, Ptes Fokes, Neindref and Hyde were wounded. The Pl did a great job and remained steady through a gruelling night. We can look back now and see the humour in some of the happenings. Tom Mix does well in his world of make believe on the screen but "Big Bill" Robby went a-shooting up that ridge in deadly earnest. It is rumoured that 6 Sec took mosquito nets and all into their pits that night when a Jap grenade burst their dreams asunder. "Doc" Walker still can't work out how 2 grenades came back for each one he sent over.

After the air-strike had lifted some of 10 and 12 Pls out of their pits and spattered us with shrapnel, we left our 12 dead sons of heaven and made for Brunei town. We thought we were caster, reserve Pl and all that, but our hopes soon faded and Clifford Bridge with its great pile of bombs and the movement on the high feature (not shown on the map) looked a nasty bit of work. We had to wait for the engineers and crossed and sent a few bursts after what must have been curious Malays. Ned Neindorf says he envied a namesake Ned Kelly his iron vest when 5 Sec were one-out the far side. Who didn't? Malays in canoes on the river, crocs splashing, red lights coming from the town on the water, kept us all alert.

We did it in style at Seria — bungalows, gas, water, washer women, fruit and vegetables. Even the LOBs, "Rabbits" Doyle, "Nick" Nicholls and "Archbishop" Forsyth thought it too good to miss. "Curly" Garven came back from Coy just in time to go out with pains in the pinny. No, wrong again, he went out before that meal of buffalo steak that we were given. The MO's statement, a few days after the feast that a buffalo had been examined and found to be suffering from most of the diseases known to man, sent a few faces green. However, "Bash" Basham is still 15 stone and we are toddling along. "Bluey" Jackson came back from the flame throwers with the blues. Selected apparently because of his fiery locks, he didn't even get a chance to squirt it down a bunker. Wally Hammond left a laundry to join us and we noticed him sniffing his disapproval when the good sorts brought back the washing. Rather strange, as there were looks of decided approval all round — for the washing, of course.

As protective Pl to 20 Bde at Kuala Belait we were widespread and in the out-of-bounds area (to the delight of provosts) for tactical reasons. Hullo "Nails", hullo "Bubba". Who were the boys rushing out half dressed from the shower to grab the two bottles of issue beer brought by the ration truck? They had no ideas of impressing Roly-Poly (the beaut village belle who watched with great interest) but a person of great authority happened along. Did he see potential rivals in these lads of the manly atebrin yellow torsoes?

Most of our time here was filled with sport, cards etc. With talk of a Bde sports coming off, "Flyer" Hill (too fast for many a rugby club) gave the "Harden Hurricane", Sheed Sheedy some of the finer points in the propulsion of the pedal extremities. After watching him fly down the sideline maybe he had something. "Snowy" Gordon, "My Prize" James and "Poker Face" Fokes kept Arthur Ward awake at night and added insult to injury by calling him "Eddie Ward Detective" when everyone knows he is "Eddie Ward Green Grocer".

"Big Robby" with the aid of his petrol-run primus and kit of tools continued to invent things. "Rawhide" Hyde in whose colourful tales of Texas gunmen lightened many a dull moment and hard task, is working on Bill to produce a special light-weight belt-fed Bren for clearing those doggone saloon bars. It's quite a possibility too.

Lt "Duno" or "Debt" McLeod took over from Lt "Trudge" Trudgeon at Belia, the latter going to Labuan to visit a General about a wog. We moved to Seria again, but were soon up-river at Kuala Balait. Many souvenirs of blowpipes, parangs, shields, spears, beads came our way. We caused quite a stir at Bn HQ by asking for a piano to help our concerts. "Duno" pouted the old chest, presented trophies to Dyaks for their efforts and you should have seen the Salutes. They read their routine orders up here and practise them too. "Swoon Crooner" Sheedy, heart throb of the Dyak bobby socks fans, dogged it and refused to go into his song and dance.

EASTER BATTLE — TOBRUK 1941
By Bob Halloway

It was just after midnight when Curly Wilson, OC B Coy, called us together and told of our "Counter Attack" role to support D Coy. We had only arrived in Tobruk the previous day and obviously our knowledge of the terrain was nil. However, we immediately moved forward (B Coy less 12 Pl on patrol duty under Colin Pitman) to close proximity to El Adem Road where our RMO, Slam Sullivan, and Bert Watson, RC Chaplain, had set up the RAP. Slam told us he had been warned by John Balfe to expect a number of bayonet wounds from hand to hand fighting.

Father Bert Watson gave us all General Absolution and once again we set off to a position which we found out later to be about 300 yards behind D Coy HQ. Curly Wilson and Bayne Geikie went forward as normal practice to reconnoitre the forward position leaving Lt Paddy Owen, 10 Pl, behind. Within the hour we were involved in our first enemy action. Curly Wilson and Bayne Geikie were temporarily cut off from our position as we found out later by the infiltration of some 5 or 6 tanks and a number of MG gunners. Paddy Owen was shot and told me to take over his 10 Pl as he was going back for medical attention. It was here that my Regular Army training helped me. As CSM I had to take over the Coy so I told Harry Brady, 2 i/c 10 Pl, to take over in Paddy's place and we moved into the attack led by 10 and 11 Pls under Brady and McElroy respectively and within 10 minutes, Harry Brady was killed, shot through the head by a German explosive bullet. Nev West automatically took over. The boys went berserk and at this stage the initiative of the Australian soldier was never better illustrated.

Despite no idea of our enemy strength, nor where our forward Coy was located in relation to ourselves, we continued to advance. A single Hurricane flew overhead. The pilot saw 4 Messerschmidts coming towards him and he started to turn "tail" then obviously said, "No way!". He turned straight into the face of the enemy and brought one down but had no chance and was shot out of the sky. Next thing the German tanks broke through the forward defence of our lines. The boys were about to use our A/Tk Boyes Rifle against them. My previous Arty training told me we had no chance against them with our available weapons so I ordered them to let the tanks go, "Don't fire and don't give our position away". I knew the RHA would be only too keen to do their job. In the ensuing fighting we caused a number of casualties and captured an arrogant Afrika Korp Lt and some 10 or 12 Inf men whom we sent back under escort to Bn HQ.

It was now close on daylight and we were waiting on full light so we could see where we were going when Colin Pitman arrived and immediately took over. So ended B Coy's involvement in the Easter Battle.

German tanks waiting for artillery fire to end.

FROM C COY
By Bill Shaw

C Coy was formed at Ingleburn under the kindly, yet firm, leadership of Capt Keith Magno and comprised men from all walks of life, although mainly from country areas. Crucial to the development of such raw recruits into the making of soldiers in those early days was the influence of Sgt Maj Ray Rudkin as CSM, under whom a strict discipline was maintained. Many other fine soldiers served with the Coy, and whilst it would not be appropriate to compile a list, two names stand out: Capt George Reid whose patrols in Tobruk became legendary, and Capt John Dinning who led the Coy at Alamein and through New Guinea.

By Cec Greenwood

About the skinniest shrimp of a bloke I ever knew, Sammie Ducrou, had the biggest heart, the most generous nature, and an attitude towards his section mates that could only be described as saintly. On many occasions coming off guard duty in Tobruk he found that the new relief was "crook" in some way, perhaps with a wog. Sam would willingly offer and think nothing of "saddling up" again for another stint of duty. Along with his big heart, it was apparent to all that he was very gullible, and at times was imposed upon.

About our first day in camp in Port Fouad we were busting to get across the harbour to the city of Port Said, but prospects looked dim. Capt Magno took us on a route march, ostensibly in the opposite direction, but by circling around back streets we found ourselves, thanks to the Capt, on a ferry heading for town.

After landing we were instructed to be back at this point in two hours. Came that time, who were missing? — Nigger Rowe and Blondie Wilcox! Arriving just after the ferry had left, they waved us off amid dire threats from the OC. Back at Fouad we returned by a circuitous route to give the impression of a route march, and there on the parade ground to welcome us were N and B. They gave the Capt the snappiest of salutes. How they got back I'm b——ed if I know. . . but you can ask them if you like.

LES NEELY, 13 Pl was a dour, untalkative, slow moving kind of bloke. He had a peculiar ability to drop off to sleep in unusual situations, for instance:

Place: Training stunt, out of camp, in Palestine, 1941. Neely is sent out as sentry, with Lewis gun, to "guard" against "enemy" while others eat lunch. Come time to relieve sentries, "Dutchy" Holland approaches Les, sees he is obviously asleep, creeps up, and steals his Lewis gun. Awakening later, Neely shamefacedly returns to the Pl area and suffers the indignity of having to publicly reclaim his Lewis gun.

Place: Tobruk, dark night, Neely one of a patrol out in no-man's-land. Patrol goes to ground and stays some time, listening and observing. On hand command from the leader, patrol quietly gets up and moves off. Short time later, Sgt counts heads — one missing. Patrol fans out and returns towards its previous position and, after much searching, finds Neely sound asleep, head resting on Bren gun. . . Kick in duds for Les.

INCIDENT AT THE INFANTRY TRAINING BATTALION:

The ITB at Mughazi, Palestine, trained reinforcements for posting to the Bn. In bright moonlight a Sgt instructor prepares his Pl for a night stunt, i.e. advancing in extended line with fixed bayonets up a steep sand dune, and then charging down the other side yelling and screaming to panic the enemy (who were not there).

All goes according to plan up to the top of the dune, but then, at the very bottom of the slope and facing the oncoming fury of the charging, screaming horde, sit two soldiers and four Arabs, with some canvas tent sides in between. Never has an "enemy" been known to move so fast, their disappearance almost instantly. All that's left are the tent sides, obviously intended to be "flogged" to the wogs.

A LOOK AT 15 PLATOON
By Dick "Burglar" Burgess

In the early formation of the Battalion, I firmly believe that the placement of such great men as Hugh Main, Jack Whitaker, and Ken Gibb as Pl Sgts in C Coy, had a distinct bearing, not only in our training but in later times in our operations in the field. With 15 Pl NCOs, what strength we had in Spanky MacFarland, Charlie Cutler and Max Jaggers. They were primarily responsible for our bond of unity which commenced at Ingleburn and was obviously maintained throughout the War.

I wonder how many Inf Coys can boast of having three State Members of Parliament elected in immediate post war years. C Coy had Alan Viney, Stepper Stephens and Charlie Cutler. Stephens and Cutler were, of course, 15 Pl.

That very strong bond, forged in so many areas of war, is still very much in existence.

In a "rest" area after the Salient (where the menu had been rather limited) Pluto Cook, Tommy Smith (driving our English Chev) and self decided that supplementary rations were necessary. Proposed source of supply — the Tobruk food dump. Air raids delayed a start so we visited my brother Jim (2/13 Bn) nearby and prevailed on him to join our little expedition. All went smoothly for a while and many cases of goodies were removed to the perimeter of the fence, as pre-arranged with Tommy. Next things "Hands up or I fire", and two English officers supported by trigger happy Polish guards escorted us to the OIC, from where Pluto, Jim and I were "transported" to the Tobruk gaol. It was a long, long night.

Under open arrest we were returned to our units. Tommy Smith did not know of our apprehension and carried out his part of the mission. The Chev was loaded and returned to base.

At our trial under Lt Col Crawford, our defence was "Sheltering from the air raids", a defence rigorously opposed by the prosecuting English officers who had made the capture in the food dump. Lt Col Crawford, however, showed excellent judgment in extolling the virtues of Pluto and self, and he said that if we claimed we were sheltering from the air raids, he tended to believe us. Verdict: fined 5/- for being in an out-of-bounds area. The looks on the faces of the English officers was indescribable.

The supplementary rations were excellent.

By Bob Pink

At Nuseirat, Palestine, one of the newly arrived reinforcements is condemned to cook-house duties by Sgt Holland. Sgt Robertson had some difficulty in coming to terms with "Dutchy's" uncharacteristic harshness.

"What'd he do Dutchy?" he asked.

"I heard him say Lt —— was a bloody idiot."

"Ah, fair go Dutchy", said Robbo, "he *is* a bloody idiot".

"*I* know he's a bloody idiot", said Dutchy, "*you* know he's a bloody idiot, we *all* know he's a bloody idiot. But these blokes have only just got here. How do *they* know he is?"

"Fair enough, Dutchy", said Sgt Robertson, "fair enough".

Lt "Wimpy" Norton was well known as a gourmet with a keen eye for the odd delicacy. During a four-day stunt at Ravenshoe he was seen to be frequently augmenting his frugal ration with tins of New Zealand whitebait, a favourite of his. Investigation by a secret observer discovered that he had planted "caches" around the route at bivouac points selected when laying out the stunt some weeks before. I can hear his hissing snigger as I write.

Beyond the village of Kumawa along the downhill track, it must have been a disappointment to the CO when he ordered withdrawal back to the village. It was said to be the first time since Benghazi that the unit had yielded ground it had won. Lesser men may have ignored its military soundness and not given the order. But it was late afternoon, the strength of the opposition unknown, and they had both the water and the high ground. The unit went back and dug in. In the morning a Woodpecker MMG was in position under a hut in the village, causing Bn HQ much annoyance. The MG Pl was contacted urgently and given a rough line of fire to eliminate the little rascals. The fire from both directions was intense, and Sgt Bob Reay came through on the field phone to check on the Vickers fire. The CO picked up the phone deep in the HQ hole.

"How are our shots landing, sir?", asked Vic.

"It's at times like these, Sgt", came the reply in pure Fox-Simpson, "that one keeps one's head down."

Later on at Kumawa the good old US Air Force came over to help and Ka-rumped a few drop-shorts close to the C Coy position, sending all members of 14 Pl hastening for cover. Then came the classic Pl Comd's reassurance from Lt "Happy" Graham, prone and gazing skywards, "It's all right chaps, they're ours".

DICKY BENNETT had worked keenly on a booby-trap system on 14 Pl flank. He had left some well-sited grenades with nicely concealed trip wires and was highly satisfied with a job well done. Later on, nature calling, he left the post with his shovel, and after assuming a position of squat wondered casually about a little pop from somewhere on the left. Then he was airborne and running as any bloke would if he found a tripwire under his feet.

Somewhere along the road to Seria in Borneo, a "first" was registered when we passed through a village with smiling and waving residents lining the road as we passed.

By Jack Creber

My introduction to 15 Pl: Transferred from 2 Recovery Section in August and joined C Coy near El Alamein station. Met Capt John Dinning and 15 Pl Offr, John Bray, then Bill Pearce, 7 Sec Cpl. Paired up with "Pithy" MacLennan who promptly put me to work digging a 2-man doover (but without offering to help). While having a smoke, I heard a loud slap followed by a plaintive "Ah! Count". This happened several times and I was wondering what sort of a crowd I'd joined up with. Later on I learned that "Storky" Oxman and "Count" Newell were doover mates. Count was of slight build and short, while Storky was well built and over 6 ft. Apparently Count had drawn a line down the middle of the floor and when Storky dozed off his knees would encroach over the line into Count's half, and the Count, who couldn't get to sleep, took great delight in giving Storky a hard whack to make him retreat to his own side of the doover. They were, really, great mates.

PERSONAL SKETCHES

LAURIE HARVEY — top bloke, top soldier and mate: Situation: Ravenshoe, doing patrol work; no talking, all signals by hand.

Forward scout (me) spots large python near a small bush. For a bit of fun, wait for Laurie but keep pointing upwards. Laurie arrives, still looking up, until about 1 ft from snake. Then looks down, sees snake!! Flies some distance up in the air, comes down swinging machete 50 to the dozen and cuts snake into smithereens. Me — already gone, deeming discretion much the better part of valour.

Moving up from Finschhafen towards Sio, one of the smallest and gamest men in 15 Pl was **JACK SNEDON**. Despite being near 40 and crook with malaria, Jack always insisted on doing his turn to carry the Bren and would keep going until almost dropping with fatigue. I once asked him why he'd joined the AIF, especially the infantry — his reply was that he had a wife and four kids, and so had many more reasons to be there than most of us.

BRIEFS
By Frank Rice

JAKE MacDONALD, in Jivevaneng one morning went on Sick parade (must have been really crook to make such an effort) but when he arrived back at Bn HQ to see the "Doc", the Nips put on an attack. Jake, having previously been in Field Ambulance, lent a hand in the RAP and even held one chap's leg while "Snow" Hughes (RMO) amputated it. Anyway, when Jake finally arrived back at his section, and was asked how he got on, he said he hadn't had time to see "Snow" at all.

By Norm McCarthy

Comforts at Milne Bay left a lot to be desired but fortunately (for us) the Yanks were camped just up the road. Not only did their food dump suffer at the hands of hungry 13 Pl members, but a visit to a Yank concert one night proved even more profitable. Not impressed with the concert, Keith Walsh, Bill Clout and a few more us left early and, on the way out, noticed a big tent full of fold-up stretcher beds. Not being ones to let such a golden opportunity pass by, the boys took one in each hand — thus 13 Pl enjoyed comfortable beds for the rest of our stay in Milne Bay.

By George Gordon

Embarkation day in October 1940 was a long day and, after boarding *Queen Mary* in the evening, all we had had to eat since breakfast in Bathurst was a sandwich. On a prowl through the mighty ship I stumbled on the ship's officers' pantry, and with a loaf of fresh bread, a pound of butter and a leg of ham, set off for home. Easier said than done. The maze of alleyways, corridors and stairs on the "Mary" would defy the greatest of explorers and I became hopelessly lost. What passers-by thought, seeing the booty tucked under my arm goodness knows but, eventually, over an hour later, mainly by good luck, I found our cabin and 14 Pl members tucked into a feed of ham sandwiches.

By "Shorty" Bowker

The Flying Walkie-Talkie: Spread along a ridge during the Brunei operation, 13 Pl came under fire and, having lost contact with 14 Pl, Lt Basil Delves came back to report the situation to Coy HQ. On the way down, the magazine from his rifle was lost and, naturally needing another weapon, asked to borrow my Owen gun. My reply was, "No way! I might want it". However, CSM Athol Roberts chimed in: "Let him have it Shorty, you won't be going anywhere for a while and they'll get it back to you as soon as they can". So away goes my Owen gun. Five minutes later, the Sig Officer, Bill Forster, arrives with a new Walkie-Talkie for 14 Pl, and OC Capt Alan Wright tells the runner (me) to take it up to them. Having been up the track two or three times that morning and seen nothing, the odds seem with me, even without a weapon.

Halfway to 14 Pl and following the sig wire, I turn the corner near the air raid shelter when out steps Honourable Japanese Gentleman diving for his revolver. Being only about six feet away it was him or me, so I let him have the Walkie-Talkie fair between the eyes. Then I take off down the track at a pace which could have given Jesse Owens 10 yards start, plus a classy sidestep to avoid any possible missiles heading in the same direction. Returning later with a party, no sign of the Walkie-Talkie or the Nip. As a consequence of this little contretemps, the war stops for an hour while all W-Ts in the Bn are recalled and the frequency changed.

SERIA TO BADAS (BORNEO)
By Don Stewart and John Hemphill

Call by Sgt Bill Pearce, "Pick up your gear", echoed around the warm air of Seria. "Gear" comprised bully beef, biscuits, tea, canned heat, plus usual WE equipment; also a new officer, Lt J D Andrew. Sadly we lost George Simpson at the Brunei airport "blue".

Orders were to set up an ambush along the single track railway running up-country through thick jungle to the Water Pumping Station at Badas on the Belait River. Across this rail line the Nips had placed fallen trees, rather unpleasant obstacles to negotiate. Attached to the Pl were an "O Pip" (Arty Offr) and a Mortar Sgt.

First night a stray Nip ran into the rear section and was quickly disposed of by Jack Creber and crew. Otherwise the night was quiet, but rain made things very uncomfortable, expecially on piquet, so the first cuppa next morning, brewed by canned heat, was "heaven sent".

Shortly after, a party of 12 to 15 Nips was sighted up the rail track. It was agreed to let the "O Pip" have first crack at them with the result — first shell, left of track; second shell, right of track and third shell, finished them.

Next stop, a timber sawmill which offered cover of a sort and gave us a dry night. In the morning, out of the jungle walked about six Indians who had been POWs and managed to escape their mates' horrible death of having petrol poured over them and burnt alive. These fellows, although starving, would not eat bully beef. We all marvelled at this, but it showed how truly they stuck to their religion.

Next day, "Thunder" Moore's section did a patrol to the Pumping Station before the rest of the Pl moved up in full strength. After arriving at the Pumping Station, Jack Heatley managed to get the diesel train going after the engine heat key was found. This engine then acted as the supply between Badas and Seria.

By Charlie Cutler

Wouldn't It was the *Queen Mary's* news sheet. After a piquet of NCOs was placed on the wet canteen to control drinking, an item of news read:

"They say that the wet canteen piquet CAN produce Birth Certificates".

FOOTBALL MEMORIES:

The Rugby team at Ingleburn and Palestine included three members of 15 Pl, Max Jaggers and Charlie Cutler on the wings, while Harry "Dagwood" Tasker was, to quote Charlie, "the sort of outside centre who made the winger's job easy. He did all the work and left his winger simply to take the ball and ground it over the line".

C Coy generally had a proud record in Battalion (also Brigade) football. As well as the three mentioned, John Broadbent and Jock McLaren of 13 Pl and Bob "Ocker" Hannaford, Roy "Pup" Cooper and John "Cum Cum" Lloyd of 14 Pl represented at Bn or higher level.

CONCERTS

The 20 Bde Tobruk Concert Party, organised in September 1941, included 2/17 performers:

John "Spanky" MacFarland	)	Actors and comedians
Stanley "Stepper" Stephens	)	
Charlie Cutler	:	Baritone singer
George Barry	:	Crooner

The other eight members came from 2/13, Cyril Huggert (compere and singer), Peter Robinson (singer), and John Don (mouth organ virtuoso). 2/15 provided a saxophonist and a violin player who used sig wire for strings. The accordian player was Norm Potter of ASC. The remaining two were a comic singer and a gum leaf player — yes, there was a eucalypt tree somewhere in Tobruk.

After only one practice at the YMCA HQ in Tobruk, the group entertained half 2/17 Bn and some others. Charlie's diary records: "Everything went off very well, and all pleased with our first show". The Concert ran for four nights before different audiences and culminated in a successful performance which was recorded by Chester Willmot for the ABC. It took place in a big cave which had been cleaned out and used by the Italians as an ammo store. Charlie recalls singing "The Legion of the Lost" (which seemed appropriate at the time), also a sketch, along with Stepper and Spanky, entitled "Double Exposure" which appeared to be a highlight, thanks mainly to Spanky's talent.

THE LUCK OF MCKENZIE

In early July 1941, sniping was the "in" thing for both sides in the Tobruk Salient. Bob Dunn and Micky Allsop of C Coy were killed in this duel, and Bruce McKenzie was one who avenged their deaths. In doing so, however he probably qualified as the luckiest Bren gunner in Tobruk.

With Alan "Shirley" Temple spotting for him, Bruce took a pot shot at a German who was silly enough to show his head for a fraction of a second. Before he could duck, a German bullet entered the flash eliminator of Bruce's Bren and burst out through the side when hitting the front of the barrel.

A trifle like that did not deter McKenzie, and he and Alf Spratt continued to take on the Germans until they were relieved by the Italians a few days later.

THE DANGER OF BEING WOUNDED

(A personal experience — by Charlie Cutler)

On the third day of Alamein I had dug a little trench about a foot deep when it began to lightly rain. Into this trench I crouched with gas cape overhead, feeling as safe and comfortable as circumstances permitted.

Then HORROR! Heavy tanks were heard approaching and the vision came of a Tiger tank track running along my little trench with disastrous results to the occupant. So, out I got to reinforce the sides with a couple of sandbags. What good that would do I didn't stop to think. Something like an elephant kicked me in the left knee and I flopped into the dirt a yard or two from my beautiful little trench which, try as I could, I didn't seem able to reach.

Then my troubles began. Pounding across the desert arrived Cec Greenwood and Frank Fields, both of whom I had always considered to be mates of mine. Admittedly bullets were flying thick and fast, but I contested the need to throw me into my little trench with such gay abandon. Frank made up for it a bit by applying a dressing to the wound but I lost track of Cec's whereabouts.

But things were to get worse. Over raced Capt John Dinning, C Coy Comd, who handed me a perfectly good bottle of whisky. Believe it or not but, at the time, I was a near miss teetotaller, but I was also in shock as a result of Fields and Greenwood throwing me so far. So down went a quarter of John's precious whisky.

Then I had to bear with Frank Fields and Roy "Pup" Cooper carrying me back to RAP, enduring as we went, the rude remarks of my less fortunate mates who had not been wounded, and therefore had to fight on.

Capt Slam Sullivan, our greatly admired MO, added to John's whisky a generous dose of morphia and a further topping up of anti-tetanus serum. By this time I not only had a perforated leg but was also magnificently crook in the belly.

Having enthusiastically top-dressed the desert with a mixture of once used whisky, bully beef and biscuits, and not caring whether I lived or died, I made it back by 3-tonner to a British ADS tent where I enjoyed the company of a Free French and a badly wounded German. The Froggie spent most of the night trying to crawl over me to strangle the German whom I had to defend as best I could.

As the night wore on I realised how stupid getting wounded was, and I made a resolution not to do it again and either to stay and fight on or transfer to a less dangerous way of earning a few "bob" a day.

By Hal Pearce:

After growling at the Tobruk tucker, Les "Pembo" Pemberton was appointed Sec cook. The evening meal turned out to be a great improvement, and Sec Leader Eric "Dagwood" Tasker, loud in praise, said: "You'll do me, Pembo, you can be permanent cook". Next morning Pembo was hard to get out of bed, and Eric called him several times: "You're cook, Pembo, get up and get breakfast". To which came Pembo's reply: "You've already had it, Daggy". He'd cooked the whole day's rations the night before. . . collapse of Eric.

A TRIBUTE TO GEORGE REID

George Reid was one of the finest Officers to serve in the Bn. His early Patrol leadership, as Comd of 15 Pl, was outstanding and gave those who served with him a sense of confidence, even invincibility, knowing they followed the best of Patrol leaders. George was, at once, the manliest of men and the gentlest spirit one could ever hope to meet. A firm disciplinarian, he respected the views and made allowances for the weaknesses of his men. His personal courage motivated lesser men to rise above themselves in their desire to emulate him and retain his regard.

George Reid led by deed and by example. He made better men of all who were privileged to serve with him and to enjoy his friendship.

Many a proud, and often bereaved, family received word of their son by personal letter from George. His gentleness brought comfort to those in need and he displayed, until his death in New Guinea, the true attributes of an Officer and gentleman.

By Hal Pearce and Bill "Snake" Shaw:

A popular C Coy character, Ron "R.C." Ford, could always be relied upon to liven up any situation. Part of his repertoire were "phantom broadcasts". Many a time in Tobruk, across the desert would come a frenetic broadcast of the Doncaster or the Epsom Handicap, rising to a climax as Mildura (or some other famous nag) approached the winning post. Again, on a digging party at Tourbal in Syria, "R.C." mounted a high rock and gave a running description preview of 2/17 Bn's return to Sydney. Starting with the Red Fox and including various other identities, this dissertation ended with Reg Mould, his wife, his dog and three sheep to meet him. B Coy, digging defences on the hill some distance away, downed tools and enjoyed the entertainment. It all ended suddenly when the Red Fox appeared round the rock and "R.C." collapsed.

Another time in Tourbal, "R.C." had partaken sufficient Arak to get him into top gear. Although supposed to be on piquet, he came into 8 Sec tent for a cup of coffee when in walked the Orderly Officer. "Where's the piquet?" he asked. "R.C." jumped to his feet, threw a smart salute, and said, "Here, Sir". "Where's your rifle, Ford?" "Down the track, Sir, on fixed lines", came Ron's quick reply.

WHY WAS C COY THE BEST?

Hal Pearce says: "*Of course* it was! Look at the record":—

- Three original members all became Parliamentarians:
  Charlie Cutler, Stepper Stephens and Alan Viney.
- At least ten C Coy personnel were commissioned:
  Ray Rudkin, Hugh Main, Ken Gibb, Charlie Cutler, Spanky McFarland, Cec Greenwood, Ian Moore, Ron Ford, Jim Fletcher, David MacBrown.
- In the sporting field:
  Four members of the 2/17 Bn cricket team, Eric Tasker, Dick Burgess, Bill Pearce, John Thorley.
  Eight of C Coy represented the Bn at Rugby. (See story by Charlie Cutler.)
- In boxing:
  Les Pemberton was ex-Junior Welterweight Champion of NSW.
  Also, Jack Hudson won the featherweight championship on both *Queen Mary* and *Aquitania*.
- In athletics:
  Feb 1943 Bn Sports — C Coy won by 20 points.
  Nov 1944 Bn Sports — C Coy won by 4.5 points from B Coy.
  George Creber — 440 yards Divisional champion.
  Arthur Pullen — 100 yards Battalion champion.

Charlie Cutler says:

"You ask 'Why was C Coy the best?' If it was, then all credit should go to Keith Magno and Claude Brien for their early selection of Officers and Senior NCOs. Although I served with great pride in all three platoons of C Coy, 15 Pl always remained something special. That, in my view, was because of two of the finest men it has ever been my privilege to know, George Reid and Ken Gibb. They created what we turned out to be."

By Alan Wright:

The following is an incident concerning a Jap prisoner during the advance to Sio, either at Sio or just prior to our getting there.

C Coy had been detached inland to provide flank protection and had arrived at the designated area in late afternoon. Coy patrols has been sent out to clear the area and, in due course, had returned to Coy HQ, carrying a Nip soldier on a litter. He had been found lying on the litter inside a native hut and deserted by his fellows. He was brought into Coy HQ at the time Athol Roberts was issuing rations to the platoons. The Nip was suffering from the extreme effects of Beri Beri, was bloated and physically unable to get out of the litter, but was aware and somewhat talkative. Kept saying, "All Japanese gone motor boats" and a few remarks concerning the departure of his fellow soldiers and the apparent hunger of them all.

When he saw Athol issuing sugar to the platoons from the moisture proof rubber bag, he became excited, pointed to the bag and said, "Nippon rice, Nippon rice". "No you silly bastard", said Athol, "not rice — sugar". Again the Jap referred to it as Nippon rice, and pointing. Athol was getting a bit short with him by this and, holding the open bag in front of him said, "Not Nippon rice, Aussie sugar, look!" Whereupon the Nip shoved his hand into the bag, got a fistfull, looked at it and slammed the lot into his mouth.

Bn HQ had directed us to keep the prisoner at Coy HQ until the morning and, as he was completely immobile and unable to be a threat, no special guard was put on him for the night except for the local sentry. However, during the night and, as it was pitch black, the Nip started to cry out and scream and make a dreadful noise. This went on for some time and the response from fellows in the platoons was positive. Calls like, "Shut up, you bastard", to "One more yell and you'll get a bullet", came from everywhere. I began to get a bit fearful for the Nip's safety and hastily secured him with a guard for the night, all of us being unaware of why he was yelling and squealing.

Happily, at first light he was still alive, no one had put a bullet into him during the night. At first light it was revealed to us what the trouble was. When the Nip had shoved the handful of sugar into his mouth, most had gone in but some had spread onto his hands and face. In the moist, humid conditions it had turned to a very sticky mess. During the night he had apparently become itchy in the area of his crutch and had transferred some of the sugary mess down there when scratching himself for relief. Lying on his litter on the ground, it seems the smell of the sugar on him attracted the local ant population who promptly started in to eat it. This in itself would have been irritating enough for him but they carried on when all the stickiness had been eaten, and consumed the flesh underneath also, leaving him raw on face, hands and crutch. No wonder he screamed and yelled all night. There was much sympathy for him in the morning when it became known what had been the matter.

FROM D COY

D Coy was FIRST, LAST and Equal to the BEST.

The first Coy engaged in action was D Coy in the Easter Battle of Tobruk. The last Coy in the front line was D Coy, when the Bn was relieved from Tobruk. D Coy was in the first wave of the assault landing in Borneo, and D Coy was the last Coy in action up-country in Sarawak when the War with Japan finished.

The Coy was fortunate in having John Balfe as original Coy Comd as he set a pattern that the Coy followed throughout the War. There were many very good Offrs and NCOs who served in the Coy as well as some excellent troops.

By John Hedges

The march through Bathurst City was a highlight of our stay. We had a few hours to ourselves and then back to camp. Most of us had taken on a fair quantity of beer.

16 Pl had some trouble getting a go on. Finally, Austin Mackell divided us into two files. Bill Taylor led one and I led the other. The NCO brought up the rear. I think both Bill and I covered a good deal of ground, having difficulty in keeping a straight course.

Our training in Palestine more or less finished with a 4-day exercise near Beersheba. I had taken a bottle of White Horse in my gear and when I suggested offering Austin Mackell a drink, several blokes said, "No, no, he will go crook". However, I have never seen anyone enjoy a drink more. He borrowed my mug and it was about 20 minutes before he finished. I finally said, "For Christ's sake, get it down and give me my mug". Austin returned the drink in Tobruk when he sent Bob Snell and myself half a bottle of Scotch. Unfortunately, there was a parachute troop alarm at the time. Bob and I both thought it was an exercise but were not quite sure, so we consumed the Scotch in a very short time.

Austin Mackell took out our first patrol into Tripolania. He and Tom Cooper went out the day before and spent the time watching a German armoured car. The rest of the patrol followed that evening. We went in a ute to some British Hussars position, from here Austin and Tom picked us up and we moved off with the intention of capturing the armoured car or, at least, Austin did. Austin told Bill Taylor and myself that we would be first into the car and that he would follow. Bill and I did not think much of the idea. A little more than an hour later we saw the car drive off, much to the relief of Bill and myself. I might add that I had volunteered to drive the car, thank Heavens it left.

Finally, to Tobruk, where 16 Pl took over Post 33 together with an attached section from B Coy (Athol Roberts' section).

Reinforcements joined us in July and were well-trained men from the ITB. J.R.B. was the Coy Comd at the ITB and with him were some good NCO's including John Cortis, Stan Geirsh and a few others. Austin Mackell told me that J.R.B. said that he would tell the new arrivals that he was left behind because he was not tough enough. I don't doubt that the "Reo's" got a shock.

SYRIA 1942

At Mt Tourbol camp, it was necessary to go about 400 yards for water, so we usually carried two buckets back to the tent at the one time. One bucket was put aside for drinking and the other for washing.

One night, late, "Gummy" Bill Brennan, a noted arak drinker, who was mostly in the cookhouse, but slept in a 16 Pl tent, was seen to take a mug off a tent pole and drink two or three mugs of water from the washing tin before turning in. Several of us had washed our feet in this water before getting into bed!

Stewart Crowther had a habit, when reading a paper of making remarks to no one in particular. On one occasion, when looking at a photograph of Rommel, announced in a loud voice, "There is the wiley old bastard". At this moment Capt McMaster walked past the tent. He sent for Ken Robertson and Jack Smith and wanted to know why he should be called an "old bastard".

Borneo Campaign very uninteresting, of course a lot of us were getting sick of the War and that did not help much. Bruce Trebeck was OC D Coy and John Clarkson 16 Pl Comd.

The story of D Coy would not be complete without mention of Ted Howard. In May 1940 Ted came in and was posted to 16 Pl 2 Sec. He remained with 2 Sec throughout the War, I don't think he was ever in hospital. I am sure he spent 2 thousand days within the Coy. He was an A/Cpl in Tobruk, reverted to Pte in Palestine, and not promoted again until Borneo. He was on patrol, a few days before the Armistice in Borneo. He got the patrol out of trouble but was himself killed. Ted was English and I would say 17 or 18 years of age in Ingleburn.

HENRY ZOUCH

At the time of the following incident, Henry was a corporal of 18 Pl. He writes of a remarkable feat by one soldier on the second night of the Battle of El Alamein as follows:

"The Battalion advanced without artillery support with D Coy forward left, 18 Pl 9 Sec on the extreme left flank, when I contacted A Coy 2/13 Bn and proceeded to dig in. At this moment, the RAF dropped bombs on our Bn HQ hitting an ammunition truck some 400 yards to our rear, which lit up the whole front.

Approximately 40 yards in front of my section, a number of enemy machine guns opened fire on our Bren Gunners, Bruce Hindson and Horrie Kennedy. This Post was very close and we were losing men because the rocky ground prevented us from digging in. The remaining enemy positions had no field of fire on our position as they ran along facing east. Also, 18 Pl HQ had problems as Lt Al Urquhart was badly wounded by machine gun fire, leaving Sgt Merv McGrath in charge of the platoon.

It was decided that the position in front had to be taken under covering fire of the two Bren Gunners. Whilst waiting for the reserve 7 Sec to join us, out of the blue on my left ran a soldier. In the semi-darkness he looked like an English soldier in Tommy battle dress. He threw a number of grenades into the enemy machine gun post and then jumped in with his sub-machine gun. He worked away from us down the enemy positions, throwing grenades, until I lost sight of him in the darkness some 100 yards away. What happened to him we never heard as we were in the battle for another nine days and nights.

The machine gun post had 10 German soldiers and 8 Spandau machine guns. What a remarkable soldier this man must have been. I wonder if his deeds were ever recorded. No one knew where he came from, but enquiries indicated that he could have been a British commando working independently.

By Charlie Walker

In Tobruk about June 1941 when D Coy was occupying FDLs, Cpl Tom Cooper was given the task of taking out a patrol to locate a minefield so many thousand paces west of our position. The patrol included Ted Folley, Keith Johns, Dave Beale and myself, Ted Folley to be forward scout.

The patrol moved for a considerable time until Ted suddenly called a halt. Tom asked the reason as we were well short of the estimated distance to the minefield. Ted was almost standing on a mine which was part of a field, so he felt around it to ascertain that no booby traps were connected, then carefully lifted it. Tom took a compass bearing on the field and we then returned to our company position. Nobody volunteered to assist Ted in carrying the mine.

By Les McCarthy

I travelled by train to Sydney with another chap from Gloucester and, when we arrived at a large stretch of water, I asked my friend was it the ocean. He said, "No mate, this is the Hawkesbury River".

At Ingleburn I had been detailed to clean our hut out and sweep the parade ground outside. I had just finished when I noticed an officer who was carrying a cane coming towards me. It was our Coy Comd, Capt John Balfe. I saluted him and, after he returned it, we had a discussion about Army life in general. He then said he was on his rounds as Orderly Officer. I asked him was he going in the direction of the Q Store and, when he said, "Yes", I asked would he take the broom back. He was obviously taken aback, but took it anyway. John Balfe became one of my favourite officers.

Before the landing at Lae, Cpl Ross "Swampy" Smith said to me, "This will be your last show, McCarthy, these Nips will get you for sure". I said, "I'll bet you a quid that you will be wounded before me and a further quid that if you do cop it, you will have tripped over a booby trap or something". We both survived the Lae Campaign but, before the Finschhafen landing, the bet was on again. The outcome of this was that, when I was in the 2/1 AGH at Port Moresby, I looked down the ward and saw Swampy limping towards me. I started to laugh at the sight of him, when he stuck his hand out and we shook hands. He said, "You bastard Mac, you forecast this". He told me that he had come out in front of his position, stepped back and heard a fizzing noise. Too late, he had tripped over a booby trap.

By Peter Bryant

The Battalion's stay in the Tel el Eisa area was of long duration and, although not extremely dangerous, involved a very heavy programme of patrolling.

To ease the strain of those manning the front line positions, some amenities were improved to make the infantier's lot a little bit better. Beer ration was increased, other ranks were permitted to buy spirits (scotch being the most popular) and overnight rear leave free of all responsibility in the "B" Echelon area.

It was during one of these periods that Jack Wilson and I were sent back to "B" Echelon to indulge in this small amount of luxury. Duly armed with our bottle of scotch and some bottles of beer, we arrived in the rear area to be faced with a disturbing setback. We lined up in the mess parade to be refused a meal because we did not have the "unexpired portion of the day's rations" with us. Truly a crisis.

However, our predicament was noticed by none other than "Mac" McCarthy (The Wagga Bull) who was the batman to the Battalion's Padre, Father Byrne. Mac himself was a competent cook, and was in the process of preparing a meal for the good Father. This was no ordinary meal — it was a baked dinner being prepared in a converted metal ammunition case. It was no trouble for Mac's expertise to make provision for the two extra hungry mouths. The meal, by everybody's standards, was delicious and, when finished, it was starting to get dark.

With everything cleaned up and all duties done the serious problem of disposing of our scotch and beer arose. Mac came up with the brilliant idea of using the chapel which had an altar carved out of the sand and duly set up with the appropriate candles. The chapel was properly set up to meet any blackout commitments. Mac lit the candles, laid a couple of blankets on the ground in front of the altar and the three of us sat down to a very nice, trouble-free session.

The beauty of the situation was that, when the drinking was finished, we could just roll over and go into a restful worry-free sleep.

We awoke in the morning, tidied up the chapel and prepared ourselves for the return to the frontline post. I am sure the Good Lord would not regard the little party as sacrilege, as it was not meant to be so.

Our heartfelt thanks go to Mac for his hospitality, and Jack and I reckon our 24-hour rest back at "B" Echelon was equally as pleasant as any 6-day leave at Alexandria.

By C E Lemaire

You may recall that small patrols — I think daily — from C and Don Coy positions reported to the CO. The route must have been to the south of Jivenaneng, well clear of the enemy behind the bamboo to the north. Swampy Smith did the job one morning and, whilst speaking to the "Red Fox", cast an envious glance at the half-smoked cigarette discarded by the latter. We had been without tobacco for some time and Swampy, a heavy smoker, was feeling the strain. He edged his way towards the burning bumper, intending, when the CO was not looking, to retrieve it. But the CO was not deceived and, in his precise way, said, "Have you no tobacco, corporal?" When Swampy told him that he hadn't had a draw for days, he was given a packet of Craven A's and instructed to share them with his Section. The corporal returned, full of praise for the CO and expressed the opinion that the "Red Fox" really was human, even compassionate beneath the cold exterior and aloofness.

It was an unhappy day for Don Coy when Mick O'Brien and his section were sent to reconnoitre the bamboo copse to the north of the village. Within seconds of the patrol being spotted by the enemy, three were dead – Mick, "Ocker" Ryan and Col Nash. Gordon Kibby, 2i/c of the Section said on his return that, although the Japs could not be seen behind the bamboo, they distinctly heard the bolt action of rifles. Apparently the targets were almost point blank.

A few days later, Sgt Ted Taylor, a superb soldier, took "Bluey" Hindson to the same area. It was a 2-man reconnaissance patrol but, within a short time, they were back at Pl HQ and Bluey had been shot through the ankle.

AT JIVENANENG

I recall Bob Paynter, 2 i/c of Les McCarthy's Section and one of the rear party, telling of his experiences on rejoining Don Coy in Kumawa. Bob, a laconic sort of bloke and not prone to exaggeration, gave an unforgettable description of what was a torrid four days. He was also a better than average marksman, intrigued by the tactics adopted by the Japs to camouflage their movements. On more than one occasion his target was a bush moving across the open space of the village. With his dead pan humour, he simply said, "I suppose, because the Japs couldn't see me, they reckoned I couldn't see them".

By Jack Rowland

I joined D Coy, 16 Pl towards the end of action at Alamein and was quickly nabbed by Jack Harris for his section because I didn't drink at the time which meant my future quota would be his.

Back in Australia, training at Kairi. After settling in camp on the first day, Gordon Frost and I went to a nearby peanut farm and bought a huge bagful of raw peanuts. The whole Section next day spent most of their time on the latrine.

Our first location in New Guinea was Milne Bay, I think, with plenty of rain. Eventually bedded down in our tent on makeshift supports for our blankets — corrugated iron — rained all night, next morning a stream of water was running through our tent. This pleased Jack Harris no end, so he got his tooth brush out and brushed his teeth, remarking that you don't get running water through your room every day.

BORNEO
(Authors unknown — written in Sept 45)
From 16 Pl

The 14 July was "D" Day for the trip to the interior and fortunately things did not turn out as bad as one would have expected from the tales we had heard of the wilds of Borneo. Taking to the barges, we were off on our 90-mile trip to Marudi with the support of two gunboats. We were ready for the attack at 1430 hrs next day. The Spitfires which proceeded the attack, over-stepped the mark, but caused the Japs to get out very quickly. Meanwhile, the ramps were dropped much too quickly, pushing up a bank of slimy mud for us to cross. 2 and 3 Secs, who had to make the first jump, scrambled through, leaving "Bren-gunner" Banks and "Guts" Gorham, who almost blew his own skull off, hopelessly stuck in the mud. "Cherbourg" Gorham braved the terrors of the jungle and scrounged some timber to construct a "Bailey Bridge" of his own for the rest of us to cross. After a search, we finally found the track to Marudi. The Japs gave us a wide berth leaving the job of taking Marudi a rather simple task.

The next morning, the Pl was detailed for the job of contacting A Coy at Ridan.

The track from here was absolutely the worst on which we had ever ventured. We were forced to proceed in single file and, if you moved off the logs, it was up to the chest in mud. We mastered the situation rather well and were through the worst of it when 2 Sec, our forward force, contacted an enemy ambush. During the ensuing engagement, 1 Sec put in a flank attack. We lost a good mate in the person of Cpl "Hoop" Howard and, with "Doc" O'Donnell and "Texas" Johns wounded, Lt Clarkson ordered a withdrawal. The journey back took 10 hours and would have been doubled had it not been for the assistance rendered by the natives. Coming back into the Coy perimeter we took up positions doing small protective patrols for the next 10 days.

"Curly" Ford was the cause of a stand-to when he opened up with 2 mags of Owen at a snake, finally going in for the kill with a machette. Dogs and pigs often upset 3 Sec's alarm clock (booby trap) causing spasmodic moments of excitement but nothing serious happened during the 8 weeks of our sojourn in this area.

Finally, it was back to the Bn at Seria. Here we sit and here we wait for the ship that will someday take us out of this place and put us on the road to Civvy Street.

From 17 Pl

The qualms that we had had at first about going to Marudi were soon put at rest when eventually we did go on our way up the Baram and landed, only to find that the Japs had shot through, leaving us an easy job at Kuala Ridan. It was when we went up the Bakoeng River on a patrol that we first contacted Lim, the Chinese interpreter, the "Bandit of Bakoeng"! Arriving back at Marudi, we were all pleased to find that all the Japs had disappeared.

Our next adventure was the trip up the Bakoeng — and our Dunkirk — when we heard that 50 or 60 Japs were on their way to greet us. Never was a move so fast. Swampy had rolled a cigarette before telling his section to move to the barge. By the time that he had lit it, everything was gone from the area. Tents were picked up by the poles and they were off.

The night of our farewell from Marudi will live in the memory of us all. We remember the note that came asking for some dehydrated vegetables for the spread. They had everything — water buffalo soup, pork, fowls and all the samso you wanted — or at least needed. Towards the end of the night a little strife came about with the SRD. When the fun really started in earnest, the drink waiter had all the glasses away faster than any barman in Sydney. We really felt important when we left Marudi for Beluru. The whole place lined the wharfs and bade us on our way.

The trip to Beluru and Nakat was an eye-opener but the opportunities for scrounging were far from what we had expected. There were concubines, fifty of them, who were very attractive even for the stalwart bronzed Diggers. Lim was the one who benefitted most from the trip to Nakat. There he got his hands on the supply of rice that the Japs had hoarded. By some means or other he got the rice on the barge. His idea was that, with this supply of rice to back him up, he would be established as "King" of Marudi.

The real personality of Pl HQ was "Shorty" Caffyn, the canteen man par excellence. He was the personality boy with the belles, the only man known to have "put one over" the natives. Then the sentimental drunk, "Wong" Lee the ace earflopper of the platoon.

In 4 Sec we have "Cockroach", the man on the Bren, who will say that black is white if it will win an argument for him. "Oily-tongue" Sam Larkins will be remembered, at least by Swampy Smith and Charlie Lemaire, for he often had them at one another's throat. Our cook, Blue Mullins, cannot go without mention, the ex-shearers' cook, who specialised in those scones which are so familiar to us.

5 Sec's leader, "Guiseppe" Patterson, is noted as a shrewd wallah, but has the distinction of not being caught. Then we have the great lovers, "Bull" Tapp and "Slim" McCullough. We

cannot forget Jim Christopher and his romances around Brunei. It seems that Ah Wong had a very great effect on our Jim — but will it last?

We have the "honour" of having seen more of Borneo than any other platoon of the Battalion. However, maybe that is the reason why we are all the more anxious to be back home. The time in the platoon has been good, as far as these things go, but we are looking forward to when these times will be memories, pleasant, no doubt, but memories.

From 18 Pl

The airstrip was passed and the signs of death caused a check on the holiday spirit. "Cowpoke" Taylor drew first blood — two certainties and one probable. Actually, they were close enough to have a yarn but the Cowpoke is no linguist and, being a rather forceful fellow, severed their connections with the living world.

After a short, but sweet, sojourn in Kuala Belait we embarked for Marudi. Purely a D Coy show and did we lap it up! The actual assault was preceded by a spectacular airstrike made by Spitfires, although nobody ascertained where they actually struck. Fortunately, the Japs took the hint and shot through.

Our patrols to Ridan and "Porky" Graham's outpost, the burial of "Hoop" Howard in those depressing swamps, "Pop" the Iban who we now often picture down at the local wine shop buying his snort of samsu, that evil native concoction which can change a normal man into a "Kordie". "Tom", our Chinese houseboy, whose diplomatic approach for cigarettes was a revelation of tact. There was "Goody" the Eurasian, who made our stay a festive occasion and at every opportunity, filled his home with crafty diggers. "Goody" as mine host can give any of our publicans a mile start and end miles in front. Goody is hospitality with a capital "H".

There were "Lip", the exotic star, that provocative Chinese beauty who captivated the hearts of the cooks, "Ric" Mott and "Goofy" Power, whose departure to Aussie brought "Clicker" Coffey to the fore.

This introduces 7 Sec led by that great military strategist "Punchy" Benham. "Brickie" Duggan, clean-living with a heart of gold and "Reject" Rainey whose brawny torso and swimming ability was the envy of all; "Happy" Thornton, who has that little-girl-back-home complex and tells of racing cars with meteoric speed. The Sec's three "Macs" — Mackenzie, McCrae and MacNamara, a delight to any mother's eye for robust, healthy youth. Then, there were "Wolf" Egan that meandering individual who spreads a grin over the whole world with his perpetual Pepsodent smile; "Pop" Kirton, a worshipper of Baccus, which lead him to frightful indiscretions and produced a peculiar glaze over his keen intelligent eyes; "Peps" the Chinese boy who did the job of a normal house servant.

8 Sec or the Kordies, as they were called, were famed for their ability to present an amazing variety of view points on any available debatable subject but nevertheless, they were a solid team when anything was on. Bert "Sniffy" Smith, whose "I don't agree" caused quite a lot of trouble, led the section. Next came "Babe" Curtin, renowned for his ability never to win an argument — a typical NCO. "The Kid" Penrose was a poor, disillusioned youth whose only ambition was to build his deferred pay to thousands at Randwick. "Kordie" Critchley's peacetime pursuit won't get him past the local wine bar. "Bull" Hindson, honest, sincere and reliable has never been known to have an original thought. "Rabbits" Bean Elesley, was losing pounds and pounds because of his inability to ply his trade of rabbit trapping. "Tas" Huxley would make an impression in Italy and aspires to be a drink waiter which, we all agree, is a commendable ambition. "The Blue Boy" Curtis was a battler and a typical example of a racecourse "urger" or local pub adherent.

9 Sec contained the graft merchants. "Silent" Stuart whose pay still went on; "Slicker" Coffey is a crooner of no mean merit, whose love affairs and drinking sessions were envied by all. "Watto" Watson — long, tired, weary, Watto — worshipped his bed and his ambitions included a position as a billiard room owner with a little SP on the side. "Jerk" Radridge was a very long fellow who sniggered when he laughed and never failed in his methods for a bite. "Allkey Oppe" Alford was the "Take-a-double" man whose paybook balance would be a drinking man's dream.

Pl HQ was led by "Badger", a loot who was a pessimist of undoubted capabilities but deplored the lack of opportunities to prove his worth, God bless him!

Then we were moved to Bakoeng. Our entry by the barge to this area was an unprecedented success, when our backwash sank a canoe containing Swampy Smith and other members of Coy HQ. The sight of numerous bobbing heads in the water and the bow of the canoe poised vertically in the air prior to its final plunge to the bottom was a most humorous spectacle to the beholder and the platoon was liberal with its applause.

At Bakoeng we built our own basket ball court and trained under the rubber trees. Now the Australian soldier is a remarkable person in that he catches on fast. We worked out a system and with Tommy Mason, "Tassie" Huxley and "Mac" to pot the goals, "Happy" and "Punchy" to defend and the old "Bull" Hindson to rush everywhere at once, we reckoned that the weight was right. We returned to Marudi and completely overwhelmed the opposition.

Now, the old platoon broke up and long service men made their way towards Australia. Soon that life would be but a memory and back in civvies, there will be left in us an everlasting comradeship, unbreakable because of our common bond as members of 18 Pl, 2/17 Bn.

By George McCullagh

MIDDLE EAST

We arrived by train at 20 ITB Nuiserat about 2200 hrs. Sgt Dutchy Holland and Sgt Brightwell were the NCOs in charge at the time and can remember being very impressed with the immaculate turnout of their dress — spotless white gaiters, belt and hat band. We were still wearing the khaki bits at the time. Also slightly overawed at the platoon of Ex men who fell in behind us every morning. Eventually joined the Bn at Julis, 5 Sec, 17 Pl, Don Coy.

Met Capt George Reid for the first time, one of the finest gentlemen I have ever met. I can remember him offering to lend money to any of the troops going on leave who were short of cash.

Doug Pattison and I were sent to a machine gun school. I think it was just on Christmas time and we had all our gear stolen one night by the Arabs. This included a heap of parcels as yet unopened, which we had received that afternoon from home. I was left with one shirt, which I happened to be wearing as pyjamas that night, and a tunic which was hanging on one of the wall attachments inside the Indian-type tent. They cleaned out the whole lot of us, even the kit bags we were using as pillows. I had to confront Maj Broadbent at a sort of inquiry as some blokes had a habit of selling surplus gear. He realised we were genuine victims and we were re-kitted. I would still like to know what was in those parcels.

Hector McDonald was our section leader at the time and used to look after the new young blokes.

NEW GUINEA

Lae landing: Rapid advance up coast and on the first night there was rain, the like of which I have never experienced since. A groundsheet was the only protection but actually managed a bit of sleep sitting against a tree.

FINSCHHAFEN

Pretty hairy landing — opposed — I remember tracers coming towards us. We made high ground above beach and the whole lot of us were almost wiped out by the firing of 20mm into the trees just above us. Finschhafen was a much more difficult proposition than Lae. Terrific battle by Don Coy at Jivenaneng after night attack.

Barry Waterhouse was the platoon leader and rather fancied himself as a cook. He use to crush up those hard biscuits and mix them with blackcurrant juice for breakfast — horrible! Didn't make a bad bully beef rissole though.

Merv McGrath was our Pl Sgt at the time and was very fond of grenades — used to hang them around the perimeter attached to stakes with piano wire through the straightened pins. I featured in an incident concerning Merv and his grenades. We were situated on a steep rise overlooking a valley, and I ventured out down the slope to answer a call of nature, carefully avoiding the wire on the way out. However, on the way back I forgot about the bloody thing and walked straight through it. Luckily for me I heard the fizzing sound of the fuse and scuttled back down a couple of yards. I think the steep slope of the ground saved me and the only injury I received was a ringing in the ears for a day or two.

Harking back to Queensland, does anybody remember good old John Hedges who had a bit of a stammer, giving his platoon the order to "whoa" when he couldn't quite get the word "halt" out in time. Everybody enjoyed it, including the officers. Not very military, but very amusing.

Before I leave New Guinea, would it be possible to name the character who named "Easy Street" at Finschhafen? Easy! Blimey! One step up and two back.

BORNEO

By the time we got to Borneo, we young Middle East Reinforcements were "old hands". Most of the 5-Year men had gone, and what with illness and injury, the Battalion renews itself with a bunch of good "reos" who all became part and parcel of the Bn as we ourselves did. I was LOB for the first two days of the campaign and happened to be on the beach when who should arrive by barge but MacArthur and Blamey. MacArthur wet to the knees and old Tom Blamey as dry as a bone (typical MacArthur).

Joined section again — another rapid advance up coast. The coy sent up-river about 80 miles and made camp at a large village called "Marudi". 17 Pl sent out to take up a position down-river on the banks of the Baekong River which was a tributory of the main river. Charlie Lemaire was to earn his M.M. in this area and one of his Sec, Joe Giffin, a big South Coast coal miner, was unfortunately killed.

TOBRUK - THE EASTER BATTLE. By Ron Grant

On the night of April 13, 1941, the Tobruk perimeter was under attack from the German Africa Corps. The German Engineers were clearing a gap through the wire. They established a strong point through the gap forward of post R33. Lieutenant Mackell, Corporal Edmondson, Privates Keogh, Williams, Smith, Foster and myself formed a fighting patrol to storm this enemy strongpost. We made ready with rifle and bayonet and a grenade for each. No automatic weapons were available. Our seven-man patrol fanned out and charged through a hail of enemy fire from six machine guns plus mortars and a small field piece. The gun muzzles flickered at us like powerful searchlights and tracer bullets flew all about us.

Midway we went to ground in a small depression. At about this point, Edmondson was hit in the neck and stomach with bullets, and knocked down. A bright flame erupted about Williams and myself, the air compressed and then expanded, flinging us into the air. My left leg was hit with great force and I thought I had lost it. We had survived an enemy grenade attack. We hurled our grenades, scrambled and ran on. An enemy gunner, lying prone behind his gun, seemed to aim at me and fired to the last before he died by the bayonet as well as his two companions.

Lieutenant Mackell became heavily engaged with an enemy group and was in danger of being overwhelmed. Mackell called out "Jack" and Edmondson, despite his severe wounds, got to his feet and with bayonet cut a path to his officer, undoubtedly saving Mackell's life. Edmondson later died of his wounds in Post R33 and was posthumously awarded the Victoria Cross. The enemy force was about 60 men. A group of about 30 crawled out through the wire.

Editors' Note: The above is a copy of a handwritten record by Ron Grant for the National War Memorial in Canberra. Ron also recorded this text on a cassette held by the Memorial.

The 'Fig Tree' RAP at Tobruk, sited under the only tree in the area. In 1992 it was found still alive.
(AWM 021023)

APPENDIX 9

THE OWEN SUB-MACHINE GUN (OSMG)
EVELYN ERNEST OWEN – INVENTOR
By Ray Rudkin

Evelyn Owen holding his famous gun.

On the formation of the 2/17 Australian Infantry Battalion in May 1940, an early recruit at the age of 25 years was NX22028 Private E.E. Owen, who joined the Battalion to serve with his brothers, Lieutenant Julian M. Owen, known as Paddy, and Corporal Peter W. Owen, both of whom had previous service with 34 Battalion, CMF.

The Owens came from a military background. Their Uncle, Colonel Robert H Owen, CMG, had been a member of the Sudan Contingent from Australia in 1885. Later he joined the Regular Army and served as Chief Staff Officer to the New Zealand Forces in the Boer War of 1899-1902. In the Great War of 1914-18 he commanded 3 Battalion AIF on its embarkation to the Middle East.

Evelyn (Evo) was a student of Wollongong High School and in his youth was intensely interested in explosives and guns. When aged 13 years, an improvised gun backfired and severely wounded him in the stomach. This mishap did not deter him from continuing to experiment with explosives in a backyard shed, reluctantly tolerated by his parents and to a lesser extent by neighbours. In 1939 he built a simple workable Tommy Gun. After many attempts by trial and error to improve the gun's function, he produced in 1939 a prototype for showing to Army Authorities. Emphatically, they were not interested! This weapon he took to Ingleburn Camp and showed to his mates of the 2/17 Battalion. It fired 22" calibre ammunition and he used it to shoot rabbits.

In September 1940, Evelyn was home on final embarkation leave. A neighbour, Mr. Vincent Wardell, who was Manager of Lysaghts Pty Limited of Wollongong, became interested in the gun when on the way home he noticed its barrel protruding from a sugar bag near his front gate, left there by Evelyn to collect later. Vincent's brother, Gerrard, was Lysaghts' Chief Engineer and had served as a Captain in 7 Battalion CMF. With a knowledge of machine guns, Gerrard and a mechanic employed by Lysaghts, Mr Fred Kungler, who had been a gunsmith in Switzerland, were impressed by the simplicity and function of Evelyn's gun. A long story followed of frustration due to delays by Army Authorities countered by the determination of Evelyn and Lysaghts' Management to develop and produce the Owen Gun as an important contribution to the war effort.

The Wardells were known to Mr Essington Lewis, the Director General of Munitions, from previous business dealings and it was arranged through the latter that Evelyn was granted leave to develop and refine his gun in association with Lysaghts. Thereupon Evelyn left Bathurst Camp where the 2/17 Battalion was preparing for embarkation to the Middle East.

To counter weapons used by the Germans in 1940, Great Britain decided to make a sub-machine gun and after rejecting the cheaply produced Lancaster, had adopted the Sten. When the Owen gun came on the scene only three sub-machine guns existed in Australia, a German Bergmann of First World War vintage, held by the Randwick Small Arms School Museum, a confiscated German Schmeisser, held by the NSW Police Headquarters and an American Thompson used for instruction at the Small Arms School.

The first model of Owen's machine gun.

Confronted by obstacles too numerous to mention here, it was not until September 1941 that, in the presence of the Minister for the Army, Mr Spender and Army Officials, the Owen gun underwent a comparative trial with the Thompson, Sten and Bergmann. The Owen outperformed them all when fired in adverse conditions. The others failed badly. This was the first of many successful trials the Owen gun underwent over the War years.

While Lysaghts were having trouble in obtaining ammunition and machine tooling from Ordnance, die casters were at work with a prototype of the new Austen gun, developed from the plans of the Sten and the German Schmeisser guns. In June 1942, the Austen was tested against the Owen with controversial results. In failing an urgent requirement, in July 1942 when the Kokoda Battle was in progress, only 3000 Owen guns had been produced and none had reached the forward troops. Lysaghts claimed that, had not Ordnance unnecessarily delayed their production, they would have by then produced 28,000 guns. Early in 1943 the Australian Military Forces had 30,000 Owens, 20,000 Austens and 20,000 Thompson guns. The following March, on Lysaghts' submission, the intervention of Prime Minister Curtin and his Cabinet was necessary to justifiably countermand a top level Army decision to discontinue production of the Owen in favour of the Austen.

With high morale and good industrial relations, the Lysaghts plants at Port Kembla and Newcastle produced at peek 2,700 Owen guns per month. Total production was 45,479 guns, over 500,000 magazines and 600,000 parts, when the gunshop closed in September 1944.

Australian infantry Battalions in World War II were issued with a limited number of Thompson sub-machine guns in the Middle East; their most practical use was for night fighting in support of the bayonet. Firing .45" calibre ammunition, they were much heavier than the Owen which fired 9 mm bullets. The Thompson was more suited to gang warfare in the streets of Chicago USA and not for desert warfare where it was difficult to prevent fine sand entering the moving parts that caused stoppage.

Conveniently light, with few moving parts, the Owen gun became War Equipment for Infantry Battalions prior to the 2/17 Battalion's entry into the New Guinea Campaign in August 1943 and very soon proved its worth as an effective weapon in Jungle Warfare. Many times the trained soldier's ability to produce quick,effective automatic fire from the hip when suddenly confronted with the enemy, saved his life and possibly those of his comrades.

The Owen gun was withdrawn from the Armed Services in 1966 during the Vietnam War and replaced by the 'F1' which was not popular with the troops. The utility of the infantry soldier's individual weapon has since evolved from either the rifle or the machine carbine to the modern assault rifle. Lysaghts has presented the historic models of the Owen gun to the Australian War Museum in Canberra. Lysaghts presented a final mint production model to the 2/17 Battalion's Museum at Pymble and the Balgownie Heritage Museum. Those that were Army property in New South Wales were 'sea dumped' off Sydney in the 1960's.

Evelyn Owen was the sole beneficiary of Royalties, five shillings per gun. i.e. $22,500; after tax, $8,900. A further $4,000 for the sale of all rights to the Commonwealth made $12,900 in all. An intangible reward was the pride of achievement at a critical time in Australia's defence. Furthermore, fighting soldiers in their thousands were greatly appreciative of Evelyn's part in his unique gift which gave them confidence in their chances of survival. The fame and warm approbation he received was richly deserved. Sadly, Evo died at Wollongong Hospital in 1949 from cardiac arrest when in his 34th year.

APPENDIX 10

PRISONERS OF WAR
By Ray Rudkin

The following soldiers of the 2/17 Bn became Prisoners of War during 1939/45:

NX21419 Pte Blair W (T)	NX25562 Pte Lawrence E W (T)
NX22436 Pte Ford R A F (T)	* NX16597 Pte Laws J E (T)
NX23800 Pte Freeberg N E R (BH)	NX20835 Pte Marstella O E(T)
NX17025 Pte Geddes G (BH)	NX22212 Cpl McKay D W J (T)
NX23802 Pte Higgins M D (T)	NX21869 Pte Woolridge R W(T)
NX60027 Pte Hills J J (T)	NX27975 Sgt McCosker C L (A)
NX21761 Pte Johnson W L (T)	NX46502 Pte Taylor H J (A)
NX17078 Pte Lambourne W R J (T)	NX47829 Pte Williams E F (A)
NX23801 L/Cpl Lavallee P (BH)	NX58816 Pte Worthington N S G (A)

(T) Tobruk, (BH) Bengashi Handicap, (A) Alamein. * Shot while escaping, DOW.

The first prisoners of war of the 2/17 Battalion (BH) were captured by the German Africa Corps during the general withdrawal of the British Eighth Army to Tobruk in April 1941.

When the exodus began, Privates Freeberg, Geddes and L/Cpl Lavallee were detached from their Battalion to guard an ammunition dump and as the retreat began, they jumped aboard the first available vehicle. They were in a convoy of about 40 trucks but on April 8, it

Allied POWs at Klagenfurt, Austria – 1944.
Battalion member L/Cpl P Lavallee is at the rear left.

was ambushed by outflanking German Panzers on a desert track south of Derna. It was 0200 hrs when the fighting began and after an exchange of fire the convoy surrendered. Casualties on both sides were attended by a British hospital unit that was part of the convoy.

Pte Freeberg had shrapnel lodged in his chest and Pte Geddes had an arm amputated. Also captured on this occasion was the Commander of the British Forces in Cyrenaica, General O'Connor, his staff and his predecessor in command, General Neame.

On 14 April 1941 during the Easter Battle of Tobruk, 10 soldiers of 17 Pl, D Coy, (T) were captured when retreating German tanks dominated Post R35 by fire at close range. The defenders were forced to surrender and the tank commander demanded that they climb aboard his tank.

Pte Ford, a member of the Bn's Intelligence Section, was captured on a deep two man night recce patrol in no man's land south of the Tobruk fortress on 22 August 1941. In the darkness he was unable to avoid capture when chased by a mobile patrol which had the advantage of illumination from rocket flares. Fortunately, the Intelligence Officer, Lieutenant Garnsey, who accompanied Pte Ford was able to conceal himself and returned to Bn HQ.

During the Battle of Alamein on 29 October 1942, 4 men were captured (A) when they unsuspectingly walked into an enemy post when delivering meals to forward positions at night.

POWs in the hands of Rommel's forces were evacuated over 700 miles west from Tobruk, staging at Benghazi and Tripoli where they worked mostly on the wharves, then by sea to Italy. Being wounded, Ptes Freeberg and Geddes were flown from Derna to a hospital in Benghazi.

After the surrender of Italy in September 1943, Italian prison guards deserted their posts and the Germans moved to take over all their prison camps. POWs were moved to camps in Austria. During a relaxed period of confinement, Freeberg and Lavallee with thirteen others escaped. However, their 16 days of freedom ended when they were recaptured attempting to cross the border from Italy into Switzerland. Ptes Johnson and Worthington managed to escape via Greece and returned to Australia before their unit returned from the Middle East.

To describe their experiences of privation, loss of freedom, escape attempts, food shortages, the stress of exploding allied naval shells, torpedoes and bombs at sea, the prison camps and eventual repatriation home, are not within the scope of this history. Of all the 2/17 Battalion's POWs, it may be considered fortunate that only Pte J E Laws sadly, did not return home.

Maj Jessel Silverstone, the Bn's first OC of B Coy, left the Bn in March 1941 to command HQ Reception Camp of L of C Units in Greece and became a POW of the Germans.

After the victory in Europe, the last city in Austria to be liberated was Klagenfurt. Stalag XVIIIA was located nearby and on 8 May 1945, the POW days ended for all Bn members.

APPENDIX 11

THE FIRST BAND OF THE 2/17th BATTALION – 1940
By Jack Harris

During early June 1940 some members of the Band were already at Ingleburn but their instruments did not arrive from Ordnance until 26th June.

Early band members were the first Bandmaster Laurie McWhinney, who was to be discharged because of ill health, Drum-Major George Farrar-Pugh, a veteran of the New Zealand Forces in WW1, John Brown later to become Bandmaster, then Bill Maude, "Stumpy" Ryan, George Chamberlain, Jack Allison, "Trotty" Trotman, Terry Yates, Jack Hansen, Ben Jarman, George Ford, Jack Barber, Charlie Bell and Jack Morris. Two members of the RAP, Percy Bingley and Frank Thompson, were included on a temporary basis. Numbers increased early in July by the seconding of bandsmen from units at Sydney Showground.

During WW1 and in the pre-war Militia, bandsmen were usually unit stretcher-bearers, a policy followed by some units of the AIF in WW2. But 2/17 Battalion allocated six bandsmen to each rifle company, two to a platoon, and the remainder to Bn.HQ., and Headquarter Company. Whether this was a decision of the Commanding Officer is not known.

The Mayor of North Sydney made a Presentation of Drums to the Drum Corps on Sunday 11th August and the composition of the band on that occasion and at embarkation aboard the "Queen Mary" on 19/20th October 1940 was as follows:-BAND-MASTER & CORNET - John Brown.

DRUM-MAJOR - George Farrar-Pugh.
SOPRANO CORNET - Jack Stoppelbein.
CORNETS - Tom Coughlan, Bill Bryson, "Trotty" Trotman, Ron Keogh, Cliff Symington, Bill & Joe Maude
FLUGEL HORN - Jack Harris
TENOR HORNS - Howard Lockwood, Charlie Bell, Terry Yates.
BARITONES - Roy Kay, John Laws.
EUPHONIUMS - "Stumpy" Ryan, George Chamberlain.
E & Bb BASSES - Harry Everett, Joe Hills, Jack Hansen, Jack Allison.
TROMBONES - Harry Long, Jack Barber, Jack Morris.
BAND DRUMS - Ben Jarman, George Ford.
DRUM CORPS   BASS DRUM - "Blondie" Wilcox. SIDE DRUMS - Rod Peck, George Pratt, Jim Hunt, Karl Lane, "Darkie" Jacobs.

On Saturday 10th August 1940 at 19.00 hours the Band marched in Liverpool from the Collingwood Hotel to the Town Hall for a Regimental and Farewell Dance. After rendering a few numbers outside the Town Hall the bandsmen moved inside and played the evening's first Waltz. Then a dance band took over, composed mainly of band members as follows:-

PIANO - "Stumpy" Ryan.
TROMBONE & VIOLIN - Harry Long.
DRUMS - George Ford.
GUITAR - Jack Munday (HQ Coy).
TRUMPET - Tom Coughlan.
BASS - Jack Alison.
SAXOPHONE - Les Anderson (D Coy).

It proved to be a very good Dance Band combination and later played at many outside functions during the early history of the band.

Wednesday 14th August 1940 saw the Battalion, led by the Band, march out of Ingleburn Camp on its way to Bathurst. A most extensive programme was carried out by the Band over the following twelve days. The troops were led by the Band through all the major towns along the route as well as many of the smaller towns and villages. The reception by all the people along the way was extremely warm and enthusiastic, particularly that of the children. Some of them took a great delight in throwing apples, oranges and lollies into the big bell of Jack Allison's Bb Bass as he marched along on the right of the first rank. They had probably had some practice when the band of the 2/13th Battalion marched through a couple of days earlier. The march was escorted by a Police Sergeant on a motor-bike and side-car combination.

On 30th August 1940 the Band led the Battalion through Bathurst with other units of 20th Brigade and attached troops, to where the salute was taken by the Governor General of Australia Lord Gowrie VC GCMG CB DSO & Bar. After the final weeks of training at Bathurst it was embarkation time and band instruments were packed away for re-issue a day before arrival and disembarkation at Bombay. Following the journey to Deolali Camp a busy time began for the Band, with involvement in the Changing of the Guard and regular route marches. There was a great deal of interest shown by the local people who perhaps had not previously known the pleasure of a Brass Band. The voyage to the Middle East was completed on the "Rhona". The Band practiced every morning and gave a concert on the after-deck each evening. A full programme awaited the Band at the Kilo 89 camp in Palestine. Each day opened with a march through the Battalion lines at Reveille which brought on a waning of popularity among the troops and caused rude remarks to be passed to bandsmen along with instructions to shove their instruments you know where. Then there were regular Battalion Parades and band practice. On the Parade Ground each afternoon during the inspection of the New Guard, the slow march "Duke of York" was played before the Guard was led past Battalion Headquarters and the Regimental March "Boys of the Old Brigade" was rendered. The C.O. took the salute and after the Changing of the Guard the Band led the Old Guard back to the Battalion Parade Ground. In addition to these military duties at Kilo 89 the Band took its turn with the 2/13th & 2/15th Battalion Bands to play at Brigade Church Parades and on Sunday afternoons it took a programme to the AGH close to Battalion lines.

A proposal for a Band Contest was raised, to be held in Palestine where sixteen battalion bands were based. It was agreed the 2/17th Band should have uniforms that actually fitted in all the right places so Duncan McNab's staff took measurements all round.

However, before the event took place the Battalion was moved from Kilo 89 to the Suez Canal area, with the Band attached to "B" Company at Port Fuad under the command of Major Jessel Silverstone. The Band's duties became similar to those experienced at Kilo 89. On one Sunday, during a sojourn in the Port Said area, the Band led a march to the Anglican Cathedral and participated in the service by playing the selected hymns. In the afternoon a recital was played in the Port Said Gardens, creating a great deal of interest among the City's population. On 10th January 1941 the Battalion returned to Kilo 89 and normal duties were resumed. Troops in the Palestine area paraded at Deir Sunei on 4th February 1941 and were reviewed by the Hon. R.G. Menzies, Prime Minister of Australia.

In mid-February 1941 the Band's instruments were again packed away. A wonderful period of Brass Bandsmanship had ended. Men from all areas of country and city, from Municipal and Town Bands, the Militia and Salvation Army Bands, had been moulded into a wonderful combination, most likely unequalled in the whole of the AIF. Now some of those who had been together since the Ingleburn days, were never to play again as a Band. After a four day exercise in the Beersheba area over 19th/22nd February 1941, the Battalion Commanding Officer, Colonel Crawford, who had always been most supportive of the Battalion Band, addressed the unit on the Parade Ground upon its return to camp, "When you marched back into camp this afternoon" he said, "there was no band to lead you, because our Band is a fighting Band". The Bandsmen had taken their places as infantrymen.

After Tobruk, many of the Bandsmen had been transferred to such units as "The Old & Bold" or invalided out of active service. Tom Coughlan and Harry Long had been seconded to Jim Gerald's Concert Party Band under the directorship of well known dance band leader Jim Davidson. Tom was a brother of Frank Coughlan of Trocadero fame and Tom himself had been with bands at the Trocadero and Palaise Royal. Harry Long was a very talented musician who

The Band of the 2/17 Battalion at Katoomba during the march
from Ingleburn to Bathurst – August 1940.

The Battalion Band leading 15 Platoon of C Coy on a route march
from Seria to Kuala Belait – Brunei.

was Australian Trombone Champion on two occasions after the war. At Hill 69 camp, those of the band remaining were joined by new bandsmen entering the unit. They continued to perform and at times in Syria became amalgamated with members of the 2/13th Battalion Band under the Bandmastership of Cyril Hugget, later to become 2/13 Bn. Adjutant.

After Alamein, at Julis Camp the Band of about fifteen members got together with Jack Morris as Bandmaster. A few of the Ingleburn bandsmen were there to play, including Jack Allison, Ron Keogh, Jack Barber, Jack Hansen and Jack Harris. There were also two men who had been with the Battalion since Ingleburn but never joined the Band. Now they displayed their hidden talents, Terry George on the Euphonium and Merv McGrath on the Tenor Horn. Members of the Band at Ingleburn who were still with the Battalion at the wars end were, Ron Keogh and Jack Harris, and Rod Peck of the Drum Corps.

In their role as infantrymen through various campaigns the bandsmen suffered their share of casualties:-

Joe Hills and John Laws were taken prisoner at Tobruk and John Laws was subsequently shot attempting to escape from a POW camp in Italy.

Charlie Bell KIA on a Salient patrol with Alf Tuckwell.

Terry Yates WIA and lost a foot in Tobruk.

Ron Keogh WIA Alamein.

Jim Hunt WIA Alamein.

Jack Morris WIA Alamein & New Guinea.

Jack Hansen KIA New Guinea

THE SECOND BAND – 1945
By Ian Startup

The second Band of the 2/17th Battalion joined the Unit at Ravenshoe as General Reinforcements on 31 March, 1945. They were drafted from BHQ Singleton NSW and comprised personnel who were trained soldiers with musical/band backgrounds. Assembled in a "pool band" they practised as bandsmen. When the number of players had increased to about 60 - 70 they were split into two groups. One went on draft to a Unit requesting a band and the other remained to keep the "pool" awash.

Upon joining the 2/17th, Lieut H.J.Wasley was appointed Band Officer and the band comprised:-

BANDMASTER - Sgt P.A.Mulholland DRUM MAJOR - Sgt H.C.Hancock
CORNETS - A.J.Broadbridge, Sgt N.H.Curnow, G.H.Fischer , K.B.King, K.A.Palmer.
SOPRANO CORNET - J.C.Curtin FLUGEL HORN - B.N.Clarke
CLARINET - J.D.Anderson. TENOR HORNS - L.W.Evans, A.G.McDonald.
BARITONES - W.G.McGuigan, A.Vickery. EUPHONIUMS - H.W.Turner, H.A.Nelson.
TENOR TROMBONES - A.R.Gregory, L.G.Parry. Eb BASSES - J.H.Allen, G.L.Kingdom.
Bb BASSES - L.J.Luxford, W.R.King. SIDE DRUMS - J.L.Longhurst, I.W.Startup.
TENOR DRUMS - A.Anderson, G.Campesato. BASS DRUM - J.Carrol.

After embarkation at Townsville aboard troopship "David.C.Shanks", three or four recitals a day were played by the band until disembarkation at Morotai. Weapons were then resumed and band instruments put into storage. Band members were allocated to various platoons and sub-units in the Battalion and some to "B" Echelon. Attached to the Tank/Attack Platoon on the approach to Brunei, Bass Drummer Jack Carrol was WIA.

One week after the conclusion of hostilities, the instruments were flown into Brunei and the band was again "open for business". Based at Seria it travelled around for Parades, Recitals and Concerts etc. It was probably the first band ever to perform at Marudi. Following the Battalion breakup, some members returned to civvy street while others went to the BCOF Band in Japan, the Southern Command Band (Vic) and the 29/46 Infantry Battalion Band in Rabaul.

APPENDIX 12

NEW PHOTOGRAPHS AND MAPS

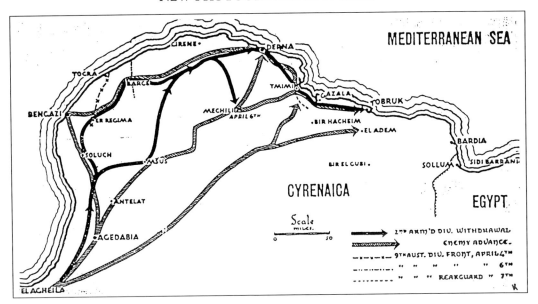

The "Tobruk Derby" – Rommel's advance in Cyrenaica, April 1st-9th, 1941.

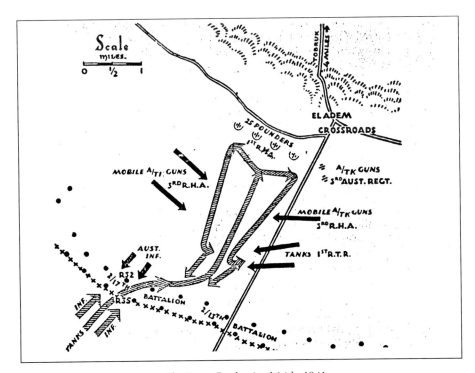

The Easter Battle, April 14th, 1941

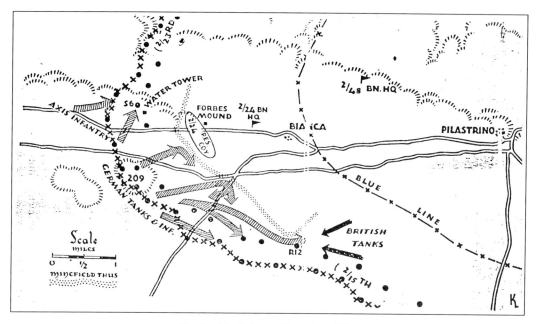

Battle of the Salient – Phases I and II.
The German attack, April 30th-May 1st, 1941

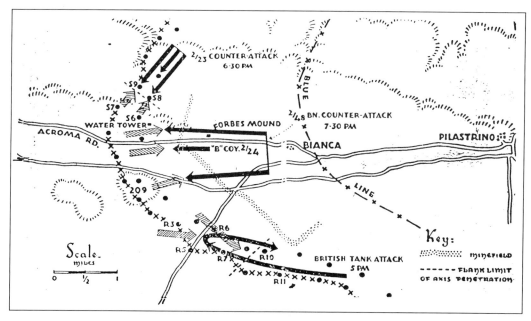

Battle of the Salient – Phase III.
The Garrison's counter-attacks, evening, May 1st, 1941

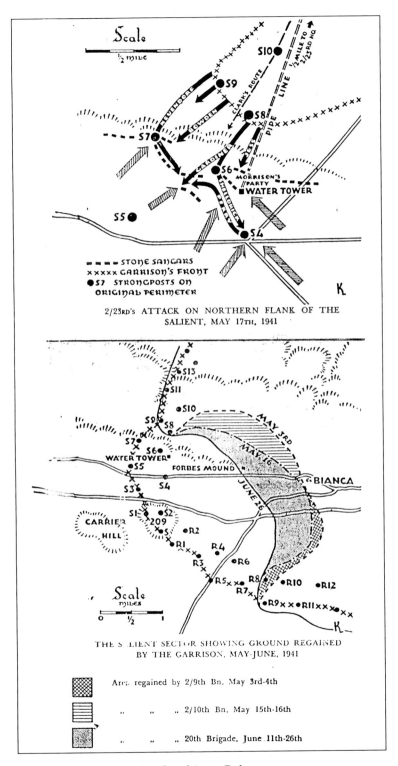

2/23RD's ATTACK ON NORTHERN FLANK OF THE
SALIENT, MAY 17TH, 1941

THE SALIENT SECTOR SHOWING GROUND REGAINED
BY THE GARRISON, MAY-JUNE, 1941

Patrols and Active Defence

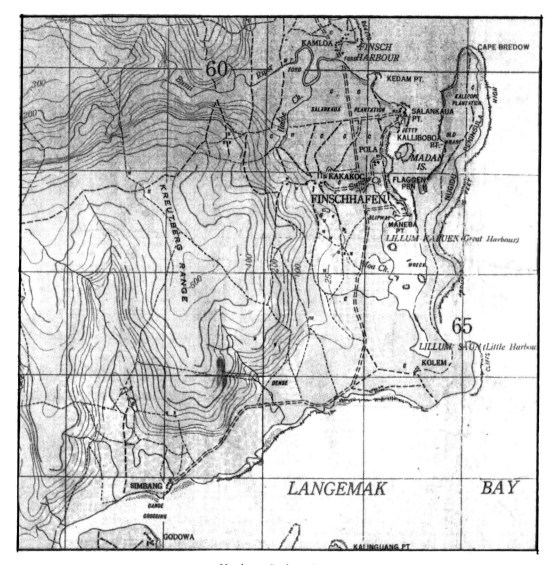

Kamloa to Simbang Route

From Finschhafen Airfield to Kumawa

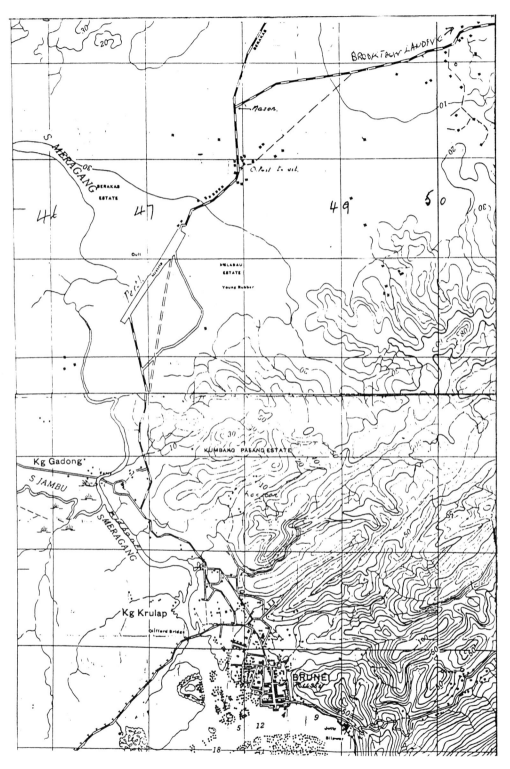

Route Six – Brooketon to Brunei.

APPENDIX 13

SOLDIERS ON LEAVE

Above: On leave in Jerusalem 1942
L-R: Pte J Elrington, Cpl W A Wilcox,
Ptes D N Luck, N J Chapman.

Left: *Men relaxing at the Olympian Café in Beirut*
L-R: *Ptes A W Verrinder, R A Burns,*
R G Insole, F W Peters, D J Berry, G H S Barry.

Top: *Beirut 1941 - L-R: Ptes A R Perry, C J Waller, P Rhoades, E R Marshall, L/Cpl J H S Littlewood.*
Bottom: *On leave Port Said – January 1941- L-R: Lt N B Trebeck, Lt J R Broadbent, Lt F A Mackell, Capt J W Balfe, Lt J H Dinning.*

Left: *Haifa – 1942.*
L-R Standing: *Sgt A J McKean, Cpl J H S Littlewood, Pte R J Cranna.*
Sitting: *Pte W L Carpenter.*

Below: *The Hotel Zion – Haifa Palestine*
L-R: *Lts J B Norris, B Geike, R V Burgess, R S Rudkin, R A Holloway.*

Top: *Kuching 1945.* **L-R Rear:** *Cpl J G Wilkinson, Pte J T Doyle.* **Front:** *Ptes J Smith, C Gleeson, J James.* **Bottom:** *Going on leave - Cairns .* **L-R- Front:** *L G Cook, W Johns, K A Miller, M Harris.* **Centre:** *Capt L C Maclarn, R W Fawell,* **Rear:** *R T Thorn, A F Booth, J S Howard, D J Osborn, Cpl B Bennett, Sgt R J Reay.*

APPENDIX 14

2/17 AUSTRALIAN INFANTRY BATTALION TRAVEL DIARY

1940

1 May	Bn HQ established at the Show Ground, Kensington NSW.
7 May	Bn HQ moved to Ingleburn Camp.
16 May	The first one hundred 2/17 Bn enlistments in camp.
14 Aug	March across the Blue Mountains begins: Ingleburn to Wallacia.
15 Aug	To Penrith.
16 Aug	To Springwood.
17 Aug	To Hazelbrook and Lawson.
18 Aug	To Katoomba.
20 Aug	To Mount Victoria.
21 Aug	To Lithgow.
22 Aug	To Wallerawang.
23 Aug	To Meadow Flat.
24 Aug	To Walang.
25 Aug	To Bathurst Camp.
19 Oct	Entrained at Kelso Station for Darling Harbour - embarked on SS *Queen Mary*.
20 Oct	*Queen Mary* sailed from Sydney Harbour.
25 Oct	*Queen Mary* anchored off Fremantle WA.
27 Oct	*Queen Mary* sailed into the Indian Ocean.
4 Nov	*Queen Mary* anchored off Bombay, India.
6 Nov	Troops disembarked and entrained for Deolali.
7 Nov	Detrained and marched to Deolali Camp.
10 Nov	Entrained at Deolali for Bombay and boarded troopship *Rohna*.
17 Nov	*Rohna* sailed for the Middle East.
23 Nov	*Rohna* anchored off Suez, Egypt.
24 Nov	*Rohna* sailed through the Suez Canal to El Kantara.
25 Nov	Disembarked and entrained for Palestine. Detrained Gaza and marched to Kilo 89 Camp.
15 Dec	Departed Kilo 89 by train for the Port Said Area.
16 Dec	Arrived Port Said Area at sub-unit destinations.

1941

10 Jan	Entrained from Port Said for Palestine.
11 Jan	Detrained at Gaza and marched to Kilo 89 Camp.
27/28 Feb	Entrained at Gaza in two groups, departed for Libya.
1 Mar	Arrived at Mersa Matru, Egypt.
3 Mar	Moved west from Mersa Matru in 20 Bde MT convoy.
5 Mar	Arrived at bivouac 4 miles west of Tobruk, Libya.
6 Mar	Arrived at bivouac near Tocra.
8 Mar	Arrived at bivouac near Agedabia.
9 Mar	Relieved elements of 2/7 Bn (17 Bde 6 Div) NE of Mersa Brega.
22 Mar	Withdrawal by MT to 4 miles south of Ghemines.
23 Mar	Located between Beda Fomm and Benghazi.
24 Mar	Withdrawal by MT to bivouac at Er Regima.
26 Mar	Withdrawal by MT to Benghazi.
27 Mar	Prepared defences above Benghazi.
4 Apr	Withdrawal commenced by MT to Barce.
5 Apr	Prepared defences east of Barce.
6 Apr	Withdrawal commenced by MT to Gazala.
7 Apr	Prepared defences on Gazala escarpment.
8 Apr	Withdrawal by MT to Acroma and prepared defences.
10 Apr	Entered Tobruk Fortress.
11 Apr	Occupied Tobruk Red Line west of El Adem Road.
23/24 Apr	Relieved by 2/15 Bn and became Bde Reserve in the Blue Line.
4/5 May	Relieved 2/13 Bn in the El Adem Sector of the Red Line.

24 May	With 20 Bde became Div Reserve in the Dust Bowl.
4 June	Occupied Bianca in the Salient Sector.
25/26 June	Relieved 2/13 Bn at Forbes Mound right forward Bn of 20 Bde in the Salient Sector.
10/11 July	Relieved by 2/32 Bn, 24 Bde. 20 Bde. became Div Reserve in the Ariente Area.
26/27 July	Relieved 2/9 Bn, 18 Bde, left forward Bn of 20 Bde El Adem Road Sector, Red Line.
7/8 Aug	Relieved by 2/15 Bn and became 20 Bde Reserve in the Blue Line.
18/19 Aug	Relieved 2/13 Bn, right forward Bn of 20 Bde in the Red Line, west of El Adem Road.
3/4 Sep	Relieved by the 3rd Bn, Polish Bde and moved to occupy the Blue Line.
19 Sep	Relieved 2/28 Bn, 26 Bde, East Sector, Bardia Road.
26/27 Sep	Relieved by 2nd Leicester Bn, 16 Bde, 70 Div, part 20 Bde Div Reserve, Ariente Area.
29/30 Sep	Relieved 3rd Bn, Polish Bde in the El Adem Road Sector of the Red Line.
21 Oct	Relieved by the 2nd Bn Leicester Regt, 70 Div.(British).
22/24 Oct	Embarked on HMS *Encounter*, HMS *Kingston* and HMS *Griffin* for Alexandria.
25 Oct	Disembarked, embussed for Amiriya, train to Kantara.
26 Oct	Arrived Kantara, entrained for Palestine.
27 Oct	Detrained Beit Jirja and marched to Hill 69 Camp.
19 Nov	A Coy left by MT for 9th Army HQ, Broumana, Lebanon.

1942

4 Jan	A Coy returned to Hill 69 Camp.
12/13 Jan	Battalion divided, moved by MT and train from Hill 69 to Tripoli in Lebanon.
14 Jan	Bn re-united, moved by MT to Afrine in Syria.
15 Jan	Relieved 2/12 Bn, 18 Bde, in the Turkish Border Area.
14/16 Mch	Relieved by 24 New Zealand Bn and moved by MT and train to Latakia Camp in Syria.
17/21 Apr	Daily staged march from Latakia to Tripoli, Lebanon and moved by MT to Mt Tourbol.
17 Jun	Relieved by 2/48 Bn, 26 Bde, moved to Afrine, Syria, relieved 24 NZ Bn.
1 July	Commenced move south to Egypt by MT and rail.
4 July	MT party left Canal for El Deir near Alexandria.
5 July	First rail party arrived El Deir, having staged at Sidi Bishr.
6 July	Second rail party arrived El Deir, having staged at Sidi Bishr.
9 July	MT moved to defensive position Imayid area.
15 July	MT moved to desert position Map El Hammam 44558861.
17 July	MT moved to El Shammama sector of El Alamein defences.
2/3 Aug	MT moved to Tel El Eisa, relieved coys of 2/23 and 2/48 Bns, 24 Bde on FDLs.
17/18 Sep	Changed with 2/15 Bn in area Point 26 as 20 Bde Reserve with counter attack role.
22/23 Sep	MT move changed over with 2/24 Bn, 24 Bde training area at El Shammama.
22 Oct	MT moved to lying-up position, Battle of El Alamein.
23 Oct	Crossed Start Line west of Tel El Eisa.
24 Oct	Attacked south west to first battlefield FDL.
25 Oct	Attacked west south west to second battlefield FDL.
26 Oct	Attacked north north east to third battlefield FDL.
27 Oct	Attacked north to fourth battlefield FDL - Point 29.
5 Nov	Completed nine days at FDL - defence of Point 29.
6-30 Nov	Moved to rest area north east of Barrel Hill, known as 'Little Italy'.
1 Dec	Moved back to Palestine. First Stage, Wadi Natrun.
2 Dec	Second Stage, Suez Canal.
3 Dec	Third Stage, Asluz.
4 Dec	Fourth Stage, Julis Camp in the Gaza Area.
22 Dec	9 Div Ceremonial Parade on Gaza Airstrip.

1943

20 Jan	MT moved from Julis Camp to Asluz.
21 Jan	MT moved to east bank of the Suez Canal.
22 Jan	MT moved to Tahag Transit Camp.
24 Jan	MT moved to entrain at Quassasin for Suez Camp.
27 Jan	Embarked on HMT *Aquitania* Suez Harbour. At sea.
31 Jan	*Aquitania* arrived at Massawa in the Indian Ocean.
3 Feb	Convoy consists, A*Aquitania*, *Queen Mary*, *Ile de France*.
9 Feb	Convoy refuelled, Addu Atoll in the Maldive Islands.

18 Feb	Convoy arrived Fremantle and left two days later.
27 Feb	Disembarked at Woolloomooloo wharf for Walgrove and Narellan Camps.
1 Mch	All personnel on 'Liddington' Leave.
23 Mch	Bn HQ transferred from Narellan to Walgrove Camp.
31 Mch	Ceremonial parade in Melbourne, interstate members.
2 Apr	9 Div ceremonial parade through the City of Sydney.
17 Apr	Move to Atherton Tablelands in Queensland commenced.
22 Apr	Train move completed at Python Ridge near Kairi.
5 July	MT move to Dead Man's Gully camp near Trinity Beach.
28 July	C Coy embarked on Dutch MS *Van Heurtz* at Cairns.
31 July	Remainder embarked on SS *William Ellery Channing*.
1 Aug	Convoy sailed from Cairns for New Guinea.
4 Aug	Disembarked, then to Stringer Bay Camp, Milne Bay.
20 Aug	Div Exercise 'Coconut', landing on Normanby Island.
21 Aug	Returned from Exercise 'Coconut' to Stringer Beach.
2 Sep	Embarked for Operation 'Postern', west of Lae, New Guinea.
3 Sep	Personnel on LCIs disembarked & re-embarked at Buna.
4 Sep	Landing ' Red Beach', Huon Gulf. Advanced towards Lae.
5 Sep	Advanced towards Lae to east of the Buiem River.
6 Sep	C Coy forward, only coy west of the Buiem River.
7 Sep	All Coys west of the Buiem River.
8 Sep	Extensive protective patrols only.
9 Sep	All coys except B Coy in the area of the Burep River.
11 Sep	B Coy rejoins the Battalion area at the Burep River.
13 Sep	Moved to the east bank, mouth of the Busu River.
14 Sep	Crossed the Busu River to plantation and Yanga Area.
17 Sep	Moved to concentration area west of Busu footbridge.
18 Sep	Crossed to east of the Busu River where bivouacked.
19 Sep	Moved to Bn area at the mouth of the Burep River.
21 Sep	Embarked for the Finschhafen Operation.
22 Sep	Landed on 'Scarlet Beach', north of Finschhafen.
23 Sep	Defended landward approaches to beachhead.
24/30 Sep	Bn less A & D Coys, north of the Bumi River. A Coy at Katika, D Coy at Jivevaneng.
1 Oct	Bn less B Coy, cross Bumi River to relieve other Bde sub-units.
2. Oct	Captured Finschhafen – advanced to Kolem and Simbang.
3 Oct	Moved to Finschhafen airstrip, partly by MT. A & B Coys with support, Bde reserve.
4 Oct	C & D Coys advanced to area Kiasawa. A and B Coys attack north of the Song River.
5 Oct	C & D Coys located Kumawa. A & B Coys north of Song River.
7 Oct	B Coy moved to Jivevaneng, relieved D Coy 2/43 Bn.
8 Oct	A Coy moved to Jivevaneng, 'Kanga Force' HQ.
9 Oct	B Coy captured the 'Knoll', west of Jivevaneng.
11 Oct	C& D Coys relieved by 2/15 Bn, moved to Jivevaneng.
4 Nov	B & C Coys relieved by 2/24 Bn, moved to Heldsbach.
5 Nov	A & D Coys relieved by 2/24 Bn, moved to Heldsbach.
18 Nov	D Coy & A/Tk Pl moved to Song River west of Katika.
2 Dec	Moved to Song River area, relieved 37/52 Bn, 4 Bde.
9 Dec	Moved to protect left flank and rear of 4 Bde in Gusika area.
16 Dec	Occupied vacated 37/52 Bn positions.
17 Dec	Moved to the Lakona area, north of the Sanga River.
21 Dec	Moved to south of Masaweng River as 20 Bde Reserve.
24 Dec	Moved to Hubika area.
27 Dec	Moved to Wandokai area.
28 Dec	Moved to Blucher Point area
31 Dec	Moved to Nanda area.

1944

2 Jan	Moved to Nuzen area.
3 Jan	Moved to Cape King William area.
4 Jan	Bde Advanced Guard, D Coy Van Guard to Mangu River.

5 Jan	B Coy moved forward to Chissi Point.
6 Jan	B Coy Van Guard; Bn reached objective, Kelanoa area.
8 Jan	A Coy Van Guard advanced towards Scharnhorst Point.
9 Jan	B Coy Van Guard advanced to the Buri River,
11 Jan	B Coy Van Guard advanced to the Kapugara River.
13 Jan	A Coy Van Guard advanced to the Goaling River.
15 Jan	B Coy and A/Tk Pl Van Guard advanced to Sio Mission.
20/21 Jan	Relieved by 4 Inf Bn, 8 Bde and sub-units moved back by LCVs to the Saparo River area.
28 Jan	Moved to Kelanoa Harbour area.
31 Jan	Moved by LCMs to the Masaweng River area.
26 Feb	Moved by MT to the Song River area.
2 Mar	Embarked on transport *Clip Fontain* for Milne Bay.
4 Mar	Arrived at Milne Bay.
6 Mar	Departed Milne Bay for Australia.
9 Mar	*Clip Fontain* anchored in Moreton Bay, Qld.
10 Mar	Disembarked and moved by MT to Kalinga Staging Camp.
12 Mar	Bn HQ, Coys HQ, A, and B entrained at South Brisbane for Sydney.
13 Mar	C and D Coys entrained for Sydney.
14 Mar	On arrival at Showground, Bn sent on leave, except rear party.
25 Mar	Bn Rear Party arrived at Ravenshoe Camp, Queensland.
8 July	20 Bde Advanced Guard, moved to Mt Garnet bivouac.
9 July	Bivouacked vicinity the Wild River.
10 July	Bivouacked vicinity the Herbert River.
11 July	Moved to new bivouac area.
13 July	Rehearsed for 9 Div Review on Newman Park Racecourse.
14 July	9 Div Paraded on Newman Park Racecourse.
17 July	Return march began. Bivouacked at the Herbert River.
18 July	Marched to new bivouac at Mt Garnet Map Ref 228798.
19 July	Marched to Ravenshoe Camp.
12 Aug	MT moved to Mont Albion. Field firing with artillery.
17 Aug	MT returned to Ravenshoe Camp.
25 Aug	Bivouacked in the Vine Creek area for Bn exercises
26/31 Aug	Exercised in attack, defence and night training.
1/3 Sep	Bn Advanced Guard exercises.
4 Sep	20 Bde Exercise 'Spitfire'
6 Sep	Bivouacked on the Millstream.
7 Sep	Return marched to Ravenshoe Camp.
15 Sep	Bn night exercise.
18 Sep	MT & rail to Trinity Beach for amphibious training.
27 Sep to	20 Bde coastwise excercise 'Cockatoo', Mowbray River
1 Oct	crossing and returned by MT to Trinity Beach.
5 Oct	Returned by sub-units, MT & train to Ravenshoe.
7 Oct	Return by sub-units, MT & train to Ravenshoe continued.
9 Oct	Moved to camp at Vine Creek School area for Van Guard exercises.
10/11 Oct	Exercise continued then returned to Ravenshoe Camp.
16/19 Oct	Bivouacked in Archer Creek area, engaged in training with A Sqn, 2/9 Aust Armd Regt.
24/28 Oct	20 Bde Exercise 'Kite', offensive operations in open country. Returned to camp by MT.
1 Nov	Moved out for a defence and withdrawal exercise.
2 Nov	Returned to Ravenshoe Camp.
13 Nov	Moved out to astride Palmerston Highway on Div exercise 'Flamingo'.
14/18 Nov	Exercise continued then returned to Ravenshoe Camp.
27 Nov	Moved by MT to Trinity Beach for amphibious training with LSIs.
28/30 Nov	Exercise continued then returned to Ravenshoe Camp.

1945

4/5 Jan	Moved to Toumoulin area, field firing with 58 Bty, 2/6 Fd Regt and B Coy, 2/2 MG Bn.
17 Jan	Moved to bivouac at Wondecla,
19 Jan	Bn moved to Wondecla Racecourse for Divisional Sports.
22 Jan	Returned to Ravenshoe Camp.

16 Feb	Moved out of camp for 'Bn in attack' exercise.
22/23 Feb	Moved out of camp for 'Relief in the line' exercisd. Returned to Ravenshoe Camp.
26 Feb to	Four day Bn exercise with coys tested in open and jungle country
3 Mch	along the Milla Milla Road.
23/24 Mch	Moved by MT to bivouac near Mt Archer for a two Bn attack exercise with the 2/15 Bn and 2/8 Fd Regt.
1/2 May	Moved in two groups by MT to Innisfail and train to stage at Townsville.
6 May	Moved by train, embarked on *David C. Shanks* and sailed for Morotai.
15 May	Arrived at Morotai after calling at Biak.
16 May	Disembarked and moved to Transit Camp.
29 May	Embarked via LSMs on HMAS *Kanimbla*.
4 Jun	*Kanimbla* sailed in convoy for north west Borneo.
10 Jun	Landed at 'Green Beach', near Brooketon, Brunei and advanced along route 6.
11/13 Jun	Advanced along Route 6, and captured Brunei capital.
15/17 Jun	B and C Coys advanced to secure Tutong, including the east bank of the Tutong River.
18/21 Jun	Bn, less A and D Coys, crossed the Tutong River, advanced and captured Seria oilfields.
23/25 Jun	A Coy and D Coys moved from Brunei to Kuala Belait and Seria Golf Course.
30 Jun	C Coy located at Badas for ops in the Bi-Puan area.
6 July	A Coy established at Simbang, later Ridan and Labi.
13 July	C Coy relieved by B3 Pl 2/2 MG Bn, moved to Seria.
14/15 July	D Coy moved in LCMs, escorted by HMAS *Tiger Snake* and one ESB gunboat via the Baram River to Marudi.
4 Aug	D Coy less one pl established at Bakoeng.
13 Aug	Message from 20 Bde, offensive operations to cease.
26 Aug	A Coy less one pl at Belait established at Seria.
15 Sep to	D Coy party moved to Seria from Bakoeng via Belait.
22 Sep	followed by the remainder of the Coy.
1 Oct	Demobilization of Australian Military Forces began.
29 Oct	Bn declared redundant, moved by MT and LST to Labuan, Malaya.
10/19 Dec	2/17 Bn Unit Cadre embarked at Victoria Harbour on the *Pachaug Victory*, sailing via the Celebes Islands and Torres Straits, to Brisbane.
23/27 Dec	Bn Cadre moved by train from Clapham Junction to Sydney and after Christmas leave returned to Ingleburn Military Camp where the Cadre was demobilized.

1946

8 Feb	The 2/17 Australian Infantry Battalion was disbanded.

Top: *His Highness the Sultan of Brunei, arrives with the Sultana for meeting with Commander of 20 Brigade.*
Bottom: *The Sultan and his wife sitting with Brigadier Windeyer and his Staff Officers –*
Captain H H Main the 2/17Bn Liaison Officer is on the right.

INDEX

PERSONNEL & PEOPLE

GENERAL INDEX

PHOTOGRAPHS

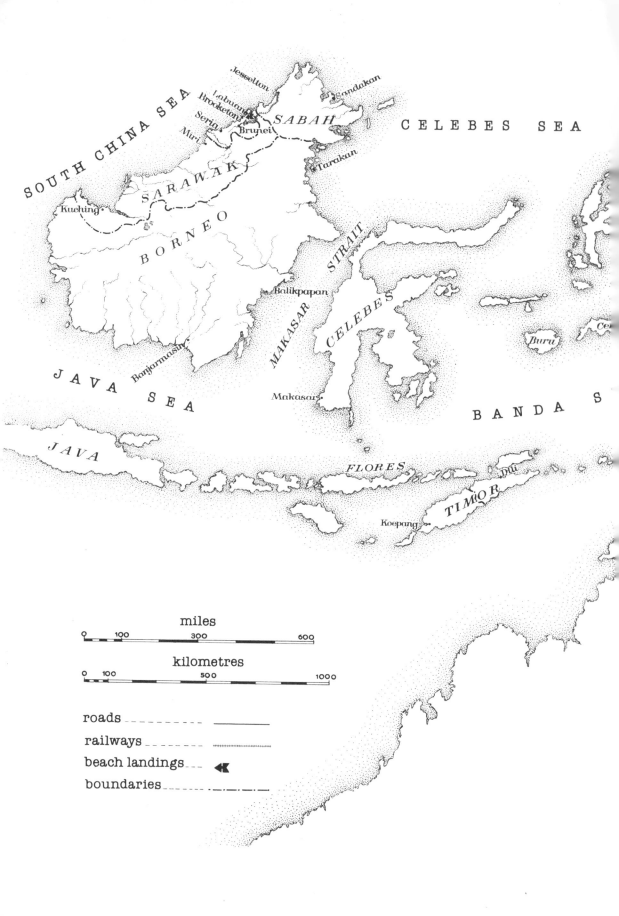